SECOND EDITION

DEVIANT Behavior

JOHN A. HUMPHREY, PhD
Saint Anselm College

FRANK SCHMALLEGER, PhD
Distinguished Professor Emeritus
University of North Carolina at Pembroke

JONES & BARTLETT
LEARNING

World Headquarters
Jones & Bartlett Learning
40 Tall Pine Drive
Sudbury, MA 01776
978-443-5000
info@jblearning.com
www.jblearning.com

Jones & Bartlett Learning
Canada
6339 Ormindale Way
Mississauga, Ontario L5V 1J2
Canada

Jones & Bartlett Learning
International
Barb House, Barb Mews
London W6 7PA
United Kingdom

Jones & Bartlett Learning books and products are available through most bookstores and online booksellers. To contact Jones & Bartlett Learning directly, call 800-832-0034, fax 978-443-8000, or visit our website, www.jblearning.com.

Substantial discounts on bulk quantities of Jones & Bartlett Learning publications are available to corporations, professional associations, and other qualified organizations. For details and specific discount information, contact the special sales department at Jones & Bartlett Learning via the above contact information or send an email to specialsales@jblearning.com.

Production Credits
Publisher, Higher Education: Cathleen Sether
Acquisitions Editor: Sean Connelly
Editorial Assistant: Caitlin Murphy
Associate Production Editor: Lisa Cerrone
Associate Marketing Manager: Lindsay White
Manufacturing and Inventory Control Supervisor: Amy Bacus
Composition: Shawn Girsberger
Cover Design: Kristin E. Parker
Rights and Permissions Supervisor: Christine Myaskovsky
Assistant Photo Researcher: Elise Gilbert
Cover Image: © Martin Barraud/age fotostock
Printing and Binding: Malloy, Inc.
Cover Printing: Malloy, Inc.

Additional photographic credits can be found on page 496, which constitutes a continuation of the copyright page.

Library of Congress Cataloging-in-Publication Data
Humphrey, John A.
Deviant behavior / John Humphrey, Frank Schmalleger.—2nd ed.
p. cm.
Includes bibliographical references and index.
ISBN 978-0-7637-9773-7 (pbk.)
1. Deviant behavior. I. Schmalleger, Frank. II. Title.
HM811.H86 2012
302.5'42—dc22

2011000988

6048

Printed in the United States of America
15 14 13 12 11 10 9 8 7 6 5 4 3 2 1

To my wife, Karen, whose loving inspiration forges the path, and to our son, Gabriel, whose joyful spirit lights the way.

—Jack Humphrey

For Ellen, whose loving and compassionate spirit touches all the lives around her and brings joy to my world.

—Frank Schmalleger

Brief Contents

Contents

Preface

The landscape surrounding the study of deviant behavior is continually changing. New forms of deviance are emerging; older forms are dying out. Some deviance is decriminalized or simply overlooked—no longer thought to be uncommon or to constitute a threat to the social order—and for some new forms of deviant behavior, criminal penalties are imposed or social sanctions are invoked. One thing, however, will always be true: deviant behavior of one form or another will always be with us. There will always be some behaviors that are considered reprehensible, intolerable, and particularly threatening to society.

Because the social nature of deviant behavior evolves across time and space, our understanding of deviance must also change with the times. Today's world order is inextricably tied to the processes of globalization. Globalization—the ability to communicate in nanoseconds worldwide, political and economic interdependence, and borderless cultural exchange—affects daily life across the world. This book recognizes the consequences of globalization for all spheres of social life and expands upon the fact that any contemporary understanding of sociocultural phenomena must include a global perspective. Consequently, the theme of this book is that an appreciation for the interaction between the processes of globalization and particular sociocultural systems, such as that of the United States, is essential to our understanding of deviant behavior in the 21st century.

Deviant Behavior, Second Edition is written for undergraduate students who are interested in the social forces that shape deviance and serve to explain both its stability and change. Our intent in writing this book is to explore the social contexts of deviant behavior, its precipitants, and its consequences. Deviant behaviors—bizarre, unexpected, predatory, or self-destructive acts—are inherently interesting. The paradox of deviance—the personal fascination with behaviors that are often fundamentally abhorrent—is threaded through this text.

Our introductory chapter considers various approaches to the definition of deviant behavior, the forms that it takes, the utility of deviance in society, and the theme of the book. Two chapters on the theoretical understandings of deviant behavior follow. In those chapters, deviant behaviors are considered on two levels of analysis: the individual or micro level, and the societal/subcultural/group or macro level. The micro level of analysis asks why certain individuals engage in particular forms of deviance, while the macro level perspective seeks to explain why rates of behaviors vary across sociocultural groupings.

Each substantive chapter opens with a story that illustrates the form of deviance being considered. The most current information on a wide range of deviant behaviors, from criminal acts to extreme forms of otherwise typical behaviors, is provided. Similarly, the major sociological and social psychological perspectives on deviant behavior are integrated into each chapter. Theoretical formulations of individual involvement in deviant behavior are distinguished from those that account for variations in rates of its occurrence. Finally, a summary at the end of each substantive chapter defines the key variables of each theory that has been discussed, and provides hypotheses that may account for the specific form of deviant behavior being considered.

Substantive chapter topics include criminal homicide, domestic violence, sexual offending, property crime, white-collar and organized crime, cyberdeviance, alcohol abuse, illicit drug use, mental illness, and suicide. In addition, there are chapters on terrorism, extreme forms of everyday behavior (workaholism, internet use, and extreme sports), and positive deviance, which focuses on innovation and creativity.

This book is firmly grounded in traditional sociological and social psychological understandings of deviant behavior. Nonetheless, it presents a challenge to students interested in exploring the emerging shapes of deviant behavior in the 21st century. The study of deviant behavior is undergoing a radical transformation. *Deviant Behavior, Second Edition* encourages students to become engaged in that process.

FOR THE STUDENT

Most of the book's chapters contain web links to professionally written articles available through the Social Science Research Network. Visit the SSRN website at http://papers.ssrn.com/sol3/displayabstractsearch.cfm to access the full text of these articles. SSRN offers a free and unique feature listing email addresses for the authors of posted articles. This allows readers to communicate directly with those who wrote the posted materials.

High-quality, Web-based media materials from sources such as CNN, Time, and National Public Radio are also available in support of this book. These materials are intended to give the reader a sense of how various aspects of deviant behavior are presented to society through media outlets. Visit go.jblearning.com/deviance to access this feature.

Acknowledgments

This book is the result of the unique contributions of valued mentors, trusted colleagues, and the undying support of our families. William J. Farrell's insightful courses at St. Anselm College initially sparked John Humphrey's interest in the study of deviant behavior. Much of the theoretical material for this book is based on an earlier text, *Deviant Behavior: Patterns, Sources, and Control,* that he coauthored with Stuart Palmer. Stuart Palmer's innovative thought and lucid understanding of the human experience is threaded throughout this book.

Meredith Dye's significant contributions to the first edition provide a solid foundation for this revision. From the design of the first edition to its publication, Meredith's understanding of the theoretical underpinnings and substance of deviant behavior was invaluable. Similarly, Julie Capone provided imaginative suggestions, creative editorial assistance, and enthusiastic support for the original project.

Special thanks go to Ann McGurty, whose untiring efforts made the completion of the second edition of this book possible. Many of the challenges inherent in revising a text are unforeseen, yet require a timely and creative response. Ann's keen pedagogical insights, ability to design meaningful illustrations, and attention to detail are reflected throughout this book.

In the end, the second edition of *Deviant Behavior* is indebted to the editorial acumen of Jones & Bartlett's Sean Connelly. Sean's collegial spirit and insightful suggestions for revision inspired this book's unique features. It was a pleasure to work with Sean and his first-rate staff of Megan Turner, Lisa Cerrone, and Elise Gilbert on the development of this book.

Finally, but not least, the efforts of Gordon Armstrong in developing new media possibilities in support of this text, Ellen Szirandi's web-based research, and Janet Bolton's efforts at Milford Publishing Services are very much appreciated.

We would also like to thank the following people for their reviews of the text:

Kristen E. DeVall
University of North Carolina–Wilmington

J.D. Jamieson
Texas State University

Meghan McGhee
Southwestern Oklahoma State University

Beth Pamela Skott
University of Bridgeport

Introduction to the Study of Deviant Behavior

CHAPTER 1

Learning Objectives

After reading this chapter you show know

- How deviant behavior is defined.
- Processes by which social/legal norms are created and violated and the consequences of social/legal norm violation.
- Dimensions of deviant behavior.
- Functions of deviant behavior for society.
- The theme of this book.
- A conceptual framework for the study of deviance.

American society has come a long way since the middle of the 20th century, when strict and widely accepted standards of personal morality inhibited many of the forms of individual expression we take for granted today. Although events like chaperoned dates, blue laws (requiring stores to close on Sundays), and dry counties (in which liquor could not be purchased or served) may seem quaint to most of us today, they were very real for people who lived in this country a mere 50 years ago.

Some parts of the world, however, continue to embrace moral strictures that seem old-fashioned to most Americans today. In Saudi Arabia, for example, the widely feared Commission for the Promotion of Virtue and the Prevention of Vice empowers hundreds of volunteers—usually bearded older men—to act as religious police or morality enforcement squads. These *mutawa*, as they are known, patrol malls, restaurants, parks, and the seashore herding men into mosques at prayer time and ensuring the public separation of unmarried males and females. The *mutawa* can take people into custody for morals violations, including what they consider to be improper clothing. They have been known to disrupt mixed-gender business meetings and are infamous for their involvement in incidents wherein people suspected of "gender mingling" died in custody or in automobile chases.

Unlike the United States, which is a democratic country that practices separation of church and state, Saudi Arabia is an Islamic nation ruled by a king who is closely allied with Muslim clerics and a diffuse religious establishment. Decades of tradition, moreover, have led to an acceptance of moral regulations among most members of Saudi society. Aisha al-Hekmi, an assistant professor at the Saudi University of Tabuk, explains it this way: "The *mutawa* protect our honor, prevent moral decay and westernization of our women. We see all the moral corruption in our neighboring countries," al-Hekmi says, "because they do not have them" (Allam, 2010).

Defining Deviant Behavior

Two viewpoints—the *normative perspective* and the *situational perspective*—have been advanced to define **deviant behavior**. The normative perspective sees deviance as human behavior that violates existing and generally accepted social norms. For example, few people would have any trouble applying the label "deviant" to a man who runs naked down a crowded street. Not only is such behavior typically a violation of widely shared and generally agreed on behavioral standards, but to most people it seems somehow inherently "wrong" and even disgusting. Hence, from the normative perspective, a naked man running down the street not only provides an example of deviant behavior, but it also makes it easy to see the man himself as a "deviant."

The situational perspective shifts the focus away from the individual and to the social situation surrounding the behavior in question. Let's imagine that the naked man running down the street was not alone but instead was among a large party of naked naturalists celebrating a Gaia festival in the midst of a nudist colony fully secured from public view. If such were the case, his behavior might seem to be quite "natural" (pun intended). Not only would such an overt display of physical nudity not have violated the social norms of the colony, it would have reinforced them. Hence, the situational perspective is *relativistic* in that it understands deviance primarily in terms of when and where it occurs.

Some behaviors are defined the same way by both normative and situational perspectives, and activities that are mutually acceptable to both are the most obvious forms of *conformist* or *nondeviant behaviors.* Conversely, when behaviors are negatively defined socially but nonetheless are consistent with the normative structure of society, they may be viewed as *extreme forms of conventional behavior* (e.g., workaholics, overachievers in school, etc.). Finally, certain behaviors do not adhere to the normative structure of society and are almost always situationally condemned. Such behaviors are clearly deviant and often also contravene administrative statutes or criminal law; in the latter case, this would make such behaviors *crimes.* As **Figure 1–1** shows, some forms

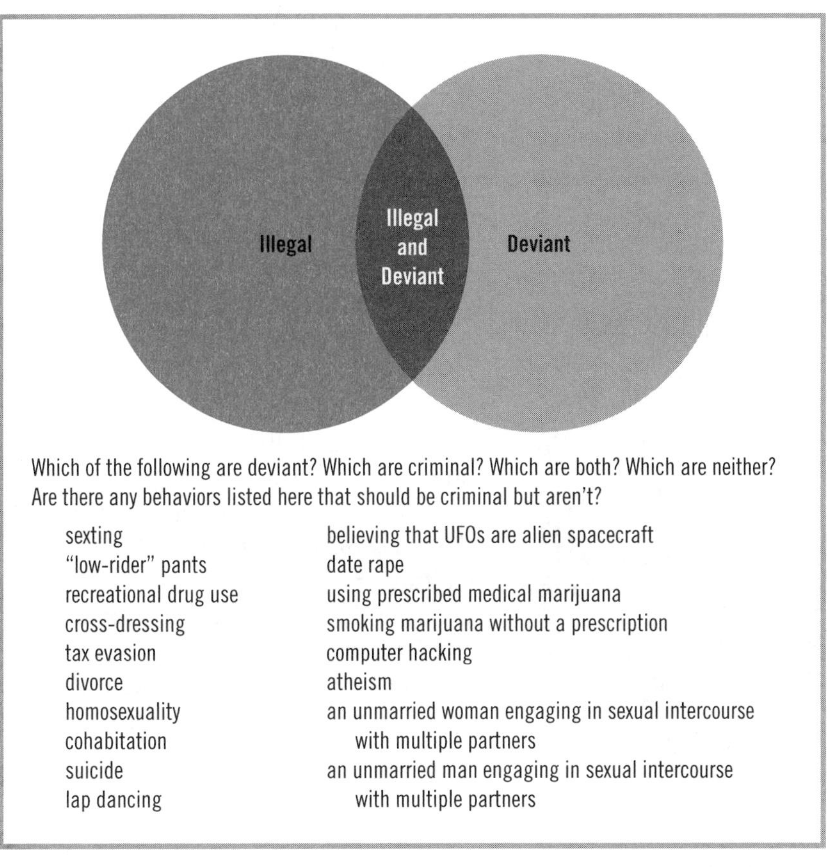

FIGURE 1–1 The overlap between deviance and crime.

of behavior may be against the law but may not be thought of as deviant by a majority of the population (i.e., exceeding the speed limit in certain locales), whereas some behaviors may be deviant but not criminal, and others may be both deviant and criminal. The relationship between crime and deviance is not static, of course, and forms of behavior considered deviant in the past might be legal today, whereas some of today's deviance might be criminalized in the future.

Two sociological concepts—culture and social organization—are particularly useful in determining whether certain behaviors should be classified as deviant. **Culture** refers to "a body of widely shared customs and values which provide general orientations toward life and specific ways of achieving common goals" (Palmer & Humphrey, 1990, p. 2). Culture is fundamental to the social order and relatively stable over time, yet it may provide a dynamic approach to the continually evolving challenges of everyday life. Changes in customs and values may originate among certain segments of the society—for example, adolescents and young adults who are involved in continual changes in style of dress, patterns of speech, and forms of entertainment. Another example is special interest groups that seek to foster the acceptance of particular rights or protections, usually of vulnerable populations or the environment. These cultural changes may become institutionalized and persist through time, or they may be short-lived and disappear from the social landscape. The value of body piercing and tattooing may well dissipate over time, as do styles of dress and verbal expression. Culture provides meaning and stability to everyday life while allowing for innovation, creativity, and the reassessment of traditional customs and values. Culture, then, provides a backdrop for the establishment of acceptable behaviors. Behaviors that fall outside of defined cultural parameters are considered, in varying degrees, deviant (see also Linton, 1955).

Volunteer members of the Saudi Arabian religious police observe a waterfront park. How do they help reduce deviance in Saudi society?

Social organization provides the means for carrying out the complex network of social interactions between individuals, social groups, and institutions. A central purpose of social organization is to ensure that conflict and discord in social interactions do not impede the effective functioning of society. Everyday life is remarkably devoid of mass disruption. For the most part the daily interactions of more than 6.8 billion persons worldwide are carried out in a reasonably predictable and orderly way (http://www.census.gov/). Millions of cars travel at high speeds in close proximity to one another, planes take off and land within minutes of each other, transnational business and commerce is conducted around the clock, and individuals communicate across time and cultures worldwide largely without incident.

Social interaction is organized by a complex set of social norms and roles. **Social norms** are those generally agreed on guides for behavior that provide boundaries for interpersonal relations. **Social roles** are defined by a set of social norms for the behavior of individuals who occupy given statuses within society. For example, a college professor occupies a given status within the academy and in the larger society. Norms for the appropriate behavior of college professors serve as guides to carry out the role of a faculty member.

Social norms may be classified as *expectational* or *behavioral.* **Expectational norms** refer to behaviors that are ideal for individuals who are enacting a particular social role or who are in a given social situation. Expectational norms govern the behavior of persons in positions of high responsibility (e.g., surgeons, airline pilots, heads of state) and persons in extreme life-threatening situations. Acceptable error in the operating room, at the controls of an airliner, or in the Oval Office is extremely

Expectational Norms

Surgeons are understandably held to an extremely high standard of care. Gross surgical malpractice cases, however, are on the rise across the United States. Undamaged limbs are sometimes amputated, healthy organs removed, and holes drilled into the wrong side of a patient's head. Recently, The Joint Commission was empowered to revoke the accreditation of hospitals and other surgical sites if they do not comply with newly established safety regulations. The entire surgical team—surgeons, anesthesiologists, nurses, and technicians—must now take a "time-out" before making an incision in a patient. They must all agree that they have the correct patient on the operating table and that they are actually going to perform the correct surgical procedure. It is mandatory that surgeons "literally sign the incision site, while the patient is awake and cooperating if possible, with a marker that won't wash off in the operating room."

Adapted from http://www.comcast.net/news/print.jsp?fn=/apnes/XML/1500_Health_medical/e2a5d7

The objective approach to deviance assumes that certain behaviors are naturally deviant, in that they go against widespread consensus in society. The affected norms are viewed as absolute.

—Conservapedia.com

limited. Surgeons, for example, are expected to operate on the afflicted part of the patient's body—to always amputate the correct limb and to remove all surgical instruments from the patient's body after an operation. Yet, as we know medical malpractice, pilot error, and political misjudgment does occur, often with dire consequences.

Behavioral norms refer to what persons typically do when occupying a particular social role or in a given social situation. Students are expected to attend class, yet most students miss class on occasion. A minority of students adhere to the expectational norm for class attendance, whereas most students follow more flexible "behavioral" norms. Behavioral norms are significantly influenced by social demographic and situational characteristics. Younger persons are given more flexibility in the ways they dress, speak, and interact in public than are older persons in positions of more responsibility. Behavioral norms establish a range of acceptable behaviors and therefore are far less rigid or exacting than are expectational norms.

SSRN

Mullen, E., & Nadler, J. (2008). Moral spillovers: The effect of moral violations on deviant behavior. Northwestern Law & Econ Research Paper No. 08-03; 3rd Annual Conference on Empirical Legal Studies Papers. http://ssrn.com/abstract=1120444

Strict adherence to expectational norms—always telling the truth and answering questions in a completely honest way—is required when testifying in court or filing an income tax return. However, honest candor is not always expected when your mother asks, "How do you like my new clothes?" In short, expectational and behavioral norms appropriately guide social interactions differently for persons who occupy particular social roles and who are in well-defined social situations (Palmer & Humphrey, 1990).

Situational Perspective and Societal Reaction

Norms governing many behaviors may not be clearly defined, universally accepted, or consistently followed. The situational approach to defining deviant behaviors is particularly useful when there is a lack of consensus about appropriate behavior. Although some behaviors are generally considered inherently deviant—murder, rape, or burglary—the definition of other behaviors depends, in large part, on the social characteristics of the actor, the victim, the social context of the behavior, and the social audience that observes or becomes aware of what occurred. Racial or ethnic slurs, for example, may be viewed as simply the remarks of an ignorant person or may be cause for removal from public office. Graffiti or tagging has alternately been considered an eyesore, malicious damage to public property, or an art form worthy of civic recognition.

The situational approach to understanding deviant behavior contends that behaviors are essentially neutral and take on meaning only when defined by some social entity (Becker, 1963). The situational approach involves a three-step process of (1) defining behaviors, (2) labeling actors, and (3) responding to the label attached to actors. Social behavior may be defined as good or bad, moral or immoral, admired or condemned. Individuals are then labeled as deviant or not depending on their activities, their social characteristics, and the circumstances surrounding their behavior. The intentional ending of the life of another human being may, for example, be criminal homicide, an act of self-defense, a compassionate act intended to end suffering, or legally justifiable, as in the case of the execution of a condemned prisoner or the shooting of a dangerous person by a police officer in the line of duty.

The societal response to any behavior dictates the extent of its deviance. If both the behavior and the actor are labeled as deviant, then the societal reaction or degree of public condemnation of the behavior and the offender indicates the severity of the deviant act. Formal or informal controls may be used to resolve the situation. An enraged wife who runs over her adulterous husband with her Mercedes-Benz may be viewed as justified in her actions (by some other women) or sentenced to 20 years imprisonment (by the criminal justice system) for willful homicide.

An Amish carriage on a street in Bucks County, Pennsylvania. Is the Amish lifestyle deviant? Why or why not?

Issues in the Study of Deviant Behavior

The study of deviant behavior can be approached through a number of important questions. In addition to perceptions of the morality or ethics involved in a deviant act or assessment of the personal repugnance of the individual offender lie several related conceptual issues:

1. How certain behaviors become defined as deviant, and how social and legal norms are created (see Weitzer, 2002)
2. Who violates social norms and why they do so
3. Possible societal reactions to norm violations

4. Consequences of norm violations for the offender and for the larger society
5. What types of social control are used for which kinds of social and legal norm violations and for different types of offenders
6. The impact of the use of formal or informal controls on subsequent social and legal norm violations

Figure 1–2 depicts the complex issues involved in the study of deviant behavior.

Social and legal norms provide the framework for interpersonal relations within social groups. They are essential for group survival over time, ordering interaction, and ensuring that important tasks are accomplished. William Graham Sumner (1906) classifies social norms by the severity of sanction for their violation. He identifies three forms of social norms: *folkways, mores,* and *laws.*

Folkways refer to everyday practices commonly observed within a given culture (e.g., observing holidays by sending cards and gifts at certain times of the year, courteous behavior in public, or responding in customary ways to the greetings of others). Certainly sending Christmas cards in July, pushing others aside to get to the head of the line at the movie theatre, or telling another person about all your problems when asked, "How are you?" are violations of widely accepted folkways. The violation of a folkway may result in the avoidance of the offender, or others may simply consider him or her as strange.

Mores refer to norms that govern more important sociocultural behaviors. Matters of morality and ethics, appropriate dress, and use of offensive language are guided by the mores of a society. When mores are violated, the offender is subject to more stringent social reprisals than are exacted against those who violate folkways. Ostracism, job dismissal, or irreparable damage to one's reputation may follow the violation of mores.

Finally, *laws* are considered the most serious form of social norms. Laws provide a codification of the specific elements of crimes and civil torts and possible sanctions for their violation. Unlike the violation of folkways and mores that invoke informal sanctions, violation of laws may result in a formal response by agents of government.

Typically, the central interests of a group are defined by the recognized leaders of the group or the members who have garnered the most power, influence, or resources. Social constructionists are primarily interested in the processes involved in the formulation of social and legal norms, the imposition of a deviant label on certain violators.

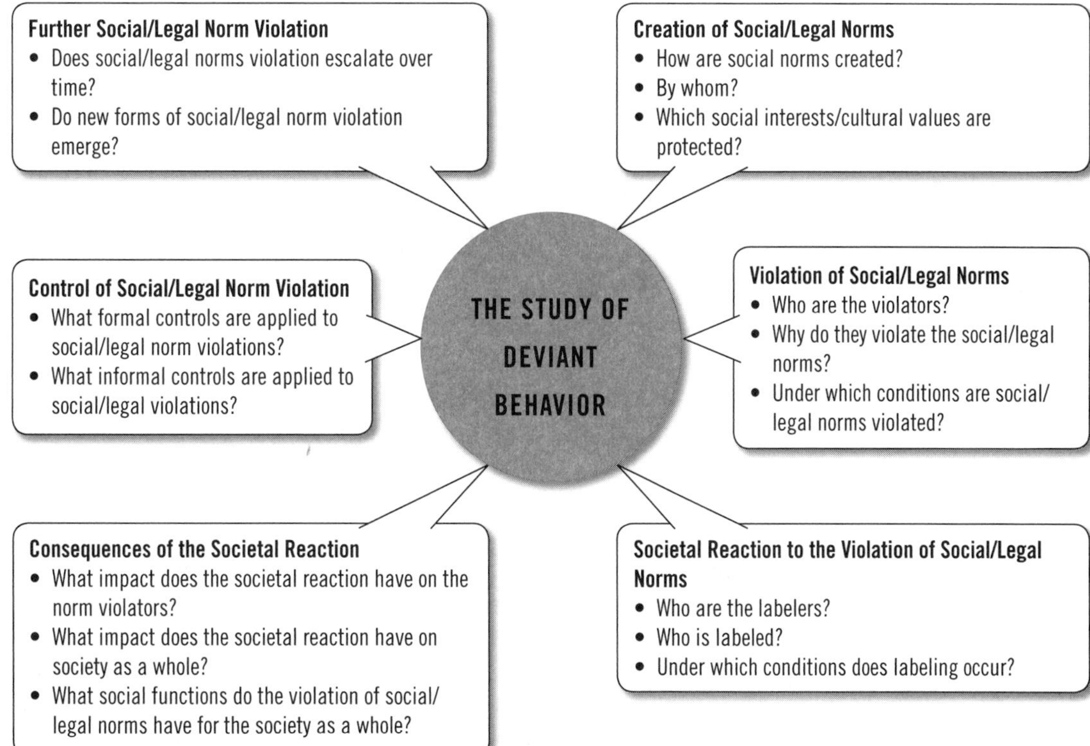

FIGURE 1–2 Issues in the study of deviant behavior.

The violation of important social and legal norms is inevitable. Wide arrays of etiological factors that underlie involvement in deviant behavior have been advanced by theorists who take a positivistic approach to the study of deviant behavior. Positivistic theorists and researchers take an objective view of deviance. That is, certain behaviors are deviant in themselves, and certain social, psychological, or biological factors explain why certain individuals engage in those behaviors. Possible precipitants of rates and individual involvement in deviant behaviors are considered throughout this book. The functional utility of deviant behavior for the survival of a society is also discussed later in this chapter.

The social reaction to the violation and the offenders varies by the severity of offense, the social characteristics of the victim and offender, and their social relationship (Black, 1976). Societal reaction or labeling theorists and researchers focus on the consequences of labeling certain norm violators as deviant and the societal reaction to them (see Schur, 1971; Becker, 1963).

Social control theorists are interested in the ways in which social groups and society as a whole impede the commission of deviant and criminal acts (Hirschi, 1969). Formal and informal control mechanisms are used to control criminal and other deviant behaviors. Formal controls refer to official sanctioning of certain norm violators, typically by agents of the criminal justice system. Offenders may be arrested, adjudicated by the courts, fined, placed under supervision in the community, or incarcerated. The involuntary hospitalization of persons considered to be psychiatrically ill is another means of formal control. Informal social controls typically involve unofficial means of sanctioning deviants within a group. Gossip, ridicule, exclusion from group activities, and ostracism are common forms of informal control.

Attempts to control deviant members of a social group may well exacerbate their offensive behavior. Rather than changing their behavior, the deviants may, for example, escalate their offending, engaging in more severe forms of violence or theft or in newer forms of deviance. This results in the necessity for creating more stringent norms or increasing the penalties for existing social and legal norms. The processes of deviant behavior are thereby set in motion. Redefined norms lead to the inevitability of their violation and renewed societal sanctioning of offenders.

As tolerance of deviant behaviors decreases, societies may evolve into an ever-tightening spiral of more stringent social and legal norms, the propensity to define increasingly more of its members as deviant, and the development of more punitive control strategies. If this downward spiraling process is not reversed, then a repressive system of social control emerges that may well lead to the demise of the society.

Dimensions of Deviance

Deviant behaviors may take on various social dimensions that serve to distinguish them from one another. Most forms of deviance involve behaviors that are carried out in patterned and predictable ways. For example, criminal homicide, armed robbery, and date rape involve offenders and victims and social contexts that transcend individual incidents. That is, typical patterns of interaction between offenders and victims and common social circumstances characterize many forms of deviant behavior. Other forms of deviant behavior are more idiosyncratic or unique to given individuals and therefore do not form repetitive patterns of interaction or are not characterized by common social contexts.

Other dimensions of deviant behaviors are positive or negative, innovative or routine, individual or group behaviors, and episodic or chronic. Many of these dimensions of deviance overlap one another, resulting in the complex, multidimensional nature of deviant behavior. However, to understand how each dimension characterizes the expression of deviance, we consider them along separate continua (Palmer & Humphrey, 1990).

Patterned versus Idiosyncratic

Deviant behaviors, for the most part, form patterns of social interactions. That is, deviant behaviors are carried out in similar ways by individuals who have never met one another, across widely scattered geographically areas. Date rape, for example, involves offenders, victims, and social circumstances in Mississippi that closely resemble those in New York City. The precipitants of many forms of deviant behaviors transcend sociocultural space and individual actors. The sociocultural and subcultural influences on male–female interactions, the distortion of behavioral and verbal cues, and social circumstances marked by social isolation, excessive drinking, and other drug use combine to increase the likelihood of aggressive behaviors. The need of young men to dominate and control their female acquaintances or dates leads to forced sexual behaviors.

Over time, patterns of deviant behavior become institutionalized and are imbedded in the sociocultural fabric. Sociocultural influences shape the motivations for deviant behaviors, the ways they are carried out, and the social contexts in which they occur.

Far less common are the idiosyncratic forms of deviant behavior. Idiosyncratic deviance is unique to particular individuals, typically less socially visible, and may simply be regarded as "odd." Paying a contested property tax bill in pennies delivered to the tax office in 55-gallon drums or using a dead husband's handicapped parking permit are examples of idiosyncratic deviance. Although undeniably deviant, these behaviors are not likely to be repeated or to form institutionalized patterns of behavior.

Positive versus Negative

Deviant behaviors are commonly thought to involve acts that are legally, morally, or ethically prohibited or at the very least are annoying to others. Deviant behavior is thought to have negative consequences for particular individuals and by extension to society at large. A person is the victim of a violent act, of property theft or destruction, of slander or false rumor, or of loud noises and graffiti.

However, deviant behavior need not be thought of in exclusively negative terms. Acts that deviate from normative modes of thinking and acting are necessary for creative problem solving and to bring about social and political change. Scientific advances and creativity in the arts and literature are the consequence of persons deviating in positive ways from conventional practices. Positive deviants are willing to think differently about important problems, offer alternative solutions to them, and inspire others to think differently about the world around them. Mother Theresa provides an apt example of a positive deviant whose extraordinary works affected the lives of millions of persons unknown to her scattered around the world.

SSRN

Jackson, J., Gray, E., & Brunton-Smith, I. Decoding disorder: On public sensitivity to low-level deviance, March 10, 2010. http://ssrn.com/abstract=1567953

Civil rights activists in the South during the 1960s provided the opportunity to vote for a significant number of African Americans across the country, prompted the desegregation of schools and universities, and drew attention to the widespread denial of the Constitutional rights of criminal defendants adjudicated in state courts.

Innovative versus Routine

The innovative process is inherently deviant—a departure from an existing mode of thought or view of the physical or social world. *Innovation* refers to the combining of two or more theoretical concepts or material objects in a new way. By reordering ideas or physical phenomena, discoveries are made and problems are solved. Innovation may come about by years of careful experimentation or in a flash of insight. Artistic and scientific breakthroughs occur in both ways. More typically, creative insights follow the arduous task of painstaking research and thought, but not always.

Innovative forms of deviance may be either positive or negative in their consequences. Scientific discoveries and breakthroughs in the ways we understand the physical world, uniquely perceptive literary and artistic contributions, and philosophical insights are examples of positive forms of innovative deviance. Innovative forms of deviance may also have negative consequences. Cybercrime and terrorism may involve innovative ways of accessing secured computer networks or disrupting the flow of information around the globe.

Routine forms of deviance are far more common than innovative deviance. Routine deviant behaviors typically do not require high levels of cognitive ability or involve concerted effort. Acts of violence, drug and alcohol addition, and most property offenses can be carried out with little effort or extensive planning.

Individual versus Group Deviance

Deviant behaviors may be committed by persons alone, in small groups, or in large crowds. Most forms of deviant behaviors are perpetrated by lone offenders or in the company of a few trusted companions. Acts of violence—murder, rape, armed robbery, and so on—are typically committed by a lone offender. Cybercrime and terrorism, sex offenses, mental illness, suicide, and substance abuse are other examples of individual forms of deviance.

Group deviance may involve the unplanned, spontaneous acts of persons largely unknown to one another who are drawn together for a common purpose. The unruly and often violent outbursts of disappointed soccer fans provide an example of this form of group deviance. Similar kinds of group outrage and acts of destruction may be sparked by minority residents of an inner city after a police shooting of one of their members.

A second form of group deviance depends on an organizational structure and the complicity of a network of persons. Organized criminal activity, corporate malfeasance, and terrorism, both international and domestic, require intricate networks of participants and complex means of communication to be successful. Invisibility and secrecy are hallmarks of organized group deviance. To operate in public view, without public attention, is essential to the persistence of group deviant activities.

Less organized and sophisticated are gang-related forms of group deviance—usually acts of violence directed toward rival gangs. Predatory and retaliatory activities of street gangs are highly visible and typically require little long-range planning. Gang violence is often a spontaneous response to a perceived threat from archrivals.

Episodic versus Chronic Deviance

Deviant behavior may be confined to certain situations and thereby take on an episodic expression. Or, it may be persistent and transcend the immediate social circumstance. Extreme situations may give rise to forms of behavior that individuals would not engage in otherwise. Cannibalism is abhorrent to most people; however, when facing certain starvation, an individual may well eat parts of a deceased occupant of their lifeboat lost at sea. Similarly, binge-drinking partygoers may engage in behaviors that are inconsistent with their sense of morality or ethical principles.

Persistent deviance, however, transcends any situational boundaries. The behavior of a person afflicted with alcoholism or addicted to another drug or gambling is not situation-bound. Rather, the chronic deviant persistently engages in aberrant behavior across a wide range of social situations.

Functions of Deviant Behavior

It is commonly believed that crime and deviant behavior are harmful elements in any society and must be prevented or, at the very least, strictly controlled. Yet, as we shall see later in the text, deviance is viewed as vital to the functioning of any social group.

Emile Durkheim (1938), one of the founders of modern sociology, argued that crime and deviance are not pathological elements of society but are vitally important to its survival. In short, deviant behaviors serve an essential function for societal well-being. Durkheim (1938, p. 67) notes that "crime is normal because a society exempt from it is utterly impossible." To Durkheim, the existence of a particular social entity—an entire society or a constituent community—depends on the formation of strong collective sentiments about the kinds of behaviors that are appropriate for its members. These collective sentiments define behaviors that are good or bad, moral or immoral, legal or illegal. In a sense the collective sentiments about behavior establish distinct boundaries that separate the social collectivity from others and acceptable and unacceptable behaviors among its members. Everyday life is ordered; the work of the community gets done.

The Amish community, for example, has well-defined boundaries between itself and the larger society. The rejection of the conveniences and technological advances of conventional society sets the Amish community apart from its neighbors. Within the Amish community consensually held norms, values, and beliefs clearly demarcate acceptable from unacceptable behavior. Daily interaction among the members of the Amish community is carried out in an orderly and predictable way. Durkheim (1938, p. 70) argues that, "Crime is, then, necessary; it is bound up in the fundamental conditions of all social life, and by that very fact it is useful, because these conditions of which it is a part are themselves indispensable to the normal evolution of morality and the law."

Following the lead of Emile Durkheim, sociologist Kai Erickson (2005) explains how certain behaviors are defined as deviant, the function that deviant behaviors serve in a given community, and the consequences of attempts to control deviant behavior. Erickson (2005, p. 6) argues that "Deviance is not a property *inherent* in any particular kind of behavior; it is a property *conferred* upon that behavior by the people who come into direct or indirect contact with it." As such, "deviance refers to conduct which the people of a group consider so dangerous or embarrassing or irritating that they bring special sanctions to bear against the persons who exhibit it" (Erickson, 2005, p. 6). Deviant behaviors mark the boundaries of a community. Each community occupies a particular "cultural space" and has a distinct "cultural identity." Boundaries emerge then from the "networks of social interactions" that link the daily lives of the members of a community (Erickson, 2005). The boundaries of a community tend to shift over time, and behaviors that were previously considered deviant become commonplace. Yet, the effective functioning of a community depends on the establishment of boundaries that separate conformist from deviant behavior. Deviant behaviors in a sense define the community's identity. Erickson (2005, p. 19) writes: "Every human community has its own set of boundaries, its own unique identity, and so we may presume that every community also has its own characteristic styles of deviant behavior."

If deviant behavior is vital to the functioning of communities, is it then not likely, Erickson (2005, p. 13) asks that "they are organized in such a way as to promote this resource?" The agents of social control—police, courts, correctional and psychiatric institutions—may actually perpetuate the very behaviors they are intended to control. The process of labeling an individual as deviant, long-term segregation from the community, and marginally humane treatment at the hands of their custodians may significantly reduce the chances of a successful conventional life.

Other Functions of Deviant Behavior

IDENTITY. There are several other latent or unintended functions of deviant behavior. First, involvement in various forms of deviance provides a sense of identity, albeit a negative identity, to persons who are unable to gain status or recognition in legitimate ways. Often, teenagers who are not successful in school, excluded from athletic competition, or cannot excel in other areas will be attracted to delinquent gangs. The gang provides a sense of belonging, recognition, and identity. Thus, if conventional means for gaining an identity are not available, then deviant means may be sought.

WARNING OF THE NEED FOR SOCIAL CHANGE. Mass deviance—urban riots, commandeering public buildings, and other acts of civil disobedience—signal the need for social change. Public outrage sparked by unfair social policies, discrimination, or persistent inequality in access to social resources—health, education, and employment—may prompt governmental intervention.

Rapid increases in the use of illicit drugs, the emergence of newer "designer" drugs, or waves of teenage suicidal behavior may well signal the need for societal attention to discontent among the young. Deviant behavior may also provide a means for bringing about social change. Innovative forms of deviance—for example, the use of computer chat rooms as group support for troubled persons—can provide an alternative to more visible and costly psychological care.

SCAPEGOATING AND TENSION RELEASE. The deviants in society provide an ongoing group of persons—some criminal, some eccentric, others simply

Rumspringa: An Amish Custom

The Amish live by a strict set of customs and moral principles. Yet, before an Amish youth commits to the Amish way of life, he or she typically participates in the Amish ritual of *rumspringa,* or period of "running around." *Rumspringa* begins when Amish youths turn 16 and continues until they are married, usually between 19 and 22 years of age. Before *rumspringa* young Amish men and women have not been baptized into the Amish faith and therefore are not technically ruled by their parents or the church. *Rumspringa* then is a time for experimenting with things outside the world of the Amish. Close friendships are formed that continue for a lifetime. A central feature of *rumspringa* is participation in a youth group known as a "gang."

Donald B. Kraybill writes the following:

> About twenty-seven youth groups, called "gangs," ranging in size from 50 to 150 members, crisscross the Lancaster settlement. By the age of 10, an Amish child will be able to name some of the groups—Bluebirds, Canaries, Pine Cones, Drifters, Shotguns, Rocky, and Quakers—and even describe some of their activities. Youth are free to join the gang of their choice. Young people from the same church district or family may join different groups. The gangs become the primary social world for teens before they marry, but the groups vary considerably in their conformity to traditional Amish values.
>
> Some groups are fairly docile, but others engage in boisterous behavior that occasionally makes newspaper headlines. The reputation of the various groups signals how plain or rebellious a young person likely will be. . . . The more rowdy boys "dress around," that is, shed their sectarian garb. Hatless. Wearing styled hair and store-bought jackets, they may "pass" as typical youth in a bar or movie theatre. Young men in some groups will have fancy reflective tape on their buggies and perhaps a hidden radio or CD player inside.
>
> Members of the more rambunctious groups drive cars and sponsor dances, called "band-hops," featuring Amish bands with electric guitars and kegs of beer. Wilder parties often involve the use and abuse of alcohol. And, youth are occasionally arrested for driving cars and buggies under the influence of alcohol.

Source: Adapted from Kraybill, D. B. 2001. The Riddle of the Amish. Baltimore: Johns Hopkins Press, pp. 145–146.

annoying—who can be blamed for many of the ills experienced by persons who have escaped the deviant label. The deviants can be segregated from the mass of society, treated in aggressive and demeaning ways, and stigmatized, often for life, for their deviant behaviors. Once the label of felon, psychotic, or sex offender has been applied, it most often becomes the "master status" of that person (Becker, 1963).

Individuals who are not publicly known as deviant can direct their feelings of frustration, anger, resentment, or simply low self-worth at the deviant. Deviant members of society, then, provide a target for others to vent their pent-up rage and general sense of discontent.

EMPLOYMENT. Societies around the world invest a significant amount of their financial resources and social capital in attempting to control and treat their deviant members. The criminal justice system alone employs hundreds of thousands of persons in federal, state, and local law enforcement agencies, courts, and correctional institutions and community-based programs. In addition, psychiatric institutions, therapeutic communities, and public and private agencies employ a vast number of medical personnel, psychologists, social workers, counselors, and occupational and recreational therapists who attempt to change the lives of deviant members of society. An unimaginable economic burden would be created if suddenly criminal and deviant behaviors were eliminated from society. In short, crime and deviance fuel the economy by providing a livelihood to a vast array of social control agents.

Theme of the Book

This book considers the **processes of globalization**—which include immediate worldwide communication, transnational commerce and trade, and borderless opportunities for political and cultural exchange—as they impact the nature and extent of social deviance in U.S. society and throughout the world. The central theme is that the reciprocal relationship between the processes of globalization and the sociocultural milieu is fundamental to our understanding of deviance in the 21st century.

> . . . globalization is not incidental to our lives today. It is a shift in our very life circumstances. It is the way we now live.
> —Anthony Giddens (2000, p. 31)

This theme derives from the work of two-noted British social theorists—Anthony Giddens (2000) and John Tomlinson (1999)—who argue that a reciprocal relationship exits between globalization and culture. Giddens (2000, p. 28) observes that globalization is "political, technological and cultural, as well as economic." It has an uneven impact on local cultures around the world, strengthening the resolve of some and altering the fabric of others.

> Globalization lies at the heart of modern culture; cultural practices lie at the heart of globalization . . . this is (a) reciprocal relationship.
>
> —John Tomlinson (1999, p. 1)

Tomlinson (1999, p. 2) views globalization as a "complex connectivity—the rapidly developing and ever-densening network of interconnections and interconnectivity that characterize social life." Tomlinson's conceptualization of globalization is consistent with that of McGrew (1992) and others (Castells, 1996, 1997; Lash & Urry, 1994), who stress the reciprocity of global cultural and economic influences. Globalization then involves the reciprocal influences of economic influences and culture. Not only does the global flow of goods and monetary resources reshape culture, but culture in turn modifies the impact of international trade.

Figure 1–3 shows the reciprocal relationships among the processes of globalization and socioculturally defined space—the immediate social context of everyday life. The processes of globalization, characterized by an intricate web of interrelationships and interdependencies, impact the makeup of socioculturally defined space by altering cultural values and meanings attached to everyday behaviors. For example, the value and meaning of time, interpersonal relationships, and material possessions are largely affected by global transmission of Western culture and economic structures. A sense of time urgency, more egalitarian relations between men and women, and the need for material goods to provide pleasure, entertainment, and a sense of self-worth are byproducts of globalization. As the needs and wants of persons in less developed areas of the world begin to parallel those common among persons in the West, a sense of relative deprivation may well follow. Dissatisfaction with one's life circumstances and feelings of frustration about the opportunities to change them may drive some individuals to engage in self-destructive or other destructive forms of deviant behavior.

The relative importance of cultural traditions with the symbols and rituals that provide meaning for life beyond mundane existence is affected. The struggle between materialism and immediate gratification on the one hand and adherence to traditions of altruism and the centrality of common purpose on the other hand is being waged in remote places across the globe. The processes of globalization also influence the normative structure of everyday life. Gender inequality, structural barriers to education and economic opportunities, and the relative ability of the young and the old to influence their life circumstances are emerging issues even in less developed countries.

In brief, the processes of globalization alter the socioculturally defined space in which we live. Cultural and social change, in turn, influence individual behavior. Opportunities to engage in impersonal forms of deviant behaviors may become more attractive. The emergence of

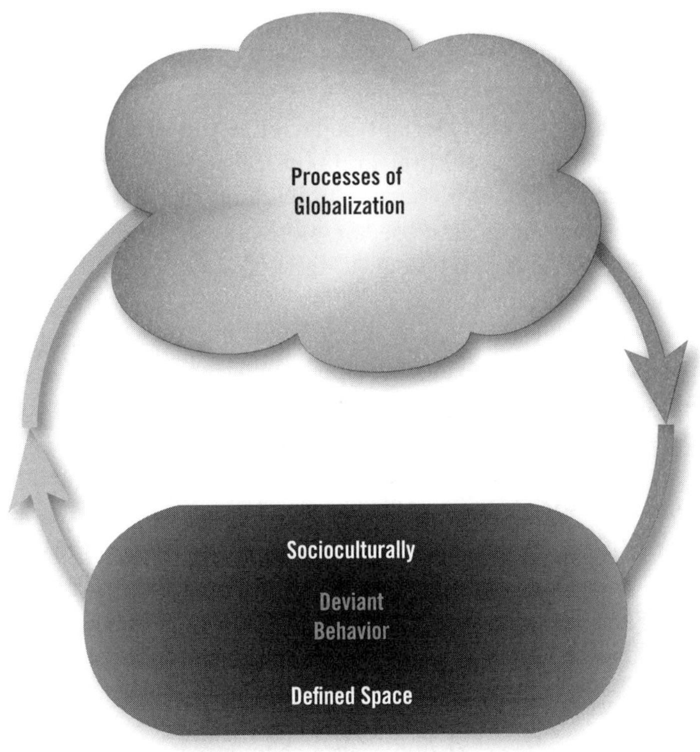

FIGURE 1–3 The theme of this book.

cyberdeviance and transglobal terrorism with their potential to wreak widespread havoc has created the need for innovative strategies for global security, a transnational justice system, and unprecedented cooperation among the nations of the world.

The major sociological and social psychological formulations considered in the following chapters show how culture, social structural arrangements, and interpersonal relationships explain and predict deviant behavior. There is, then, an increasing need for theoretical formulations to take into account the reciprocal relationships among the processes of globalization, socioculturally defined space, and deviant behavior.

Make no mistake, all intellectuals are deviants in the U.S.
—William S. Burroughs, *Yage Letters*

Conceptual Framework for the Study of Deviance

We recognize in this book that deviance is not an isolated individual activity but really a social event. For this reason, we say that deviance is diversely created and variously interpreted—meaning that different people have various interpretations regarding the who, what, when, where, and why of deviant activity.

Figure 1–4 shows that deviant behavior is the result of a coming together of a given social, cultural, and physical setting with a particular person or group of persons possessing individual characteristics, various kinds of prior experiences, and specific motivations. Figure 1-4 is meant to depict the social and psychological dimensions of deviant activity in rudimentary diagrammatic form.

Every act of deviance has a unique set of causes, consequences, and participants. Deviance affects some people more than others, even impacting those who are not direct participants in the act itself. In general, acts of deviance provoke reactions from the individuals they affect. These reactions may involve a few concerned citizens, larger interest groups, and even society as a whole. Concerns about a particular deviant event, or a series of such events, can manifest themselves in the creation of new social policies or laws. As Figure 1-4 shows, reactions to deviance, from the everyday to the precedent-setting, may color the interpretation of future deviant events.

Like other social events, deviance is fundamentally a social construction because members of society interpret its meaning and assign it significance. Just as a given instance of deviant behavior may have many causes, it also carries with it many different kinds of meanings. There may be one meaning for the deviant, another (generally quite different) for observers or victims (if the deviant act is a crime), and still another for agents of social control. For these reasons social scientists apply the concept of social relativity to the study of social deviance. Social relativity means that social events are interpreted differently according to the cultural experiences and personal interests of the initiator, the observer, or the recipient of that behavior. Consequently, deviance has a different meaning to the deviant actor, the sociologist studying it, the police officer who may be investigating it (if it is a crime), and the people experiencing it firsthand. Interpretations of deviant behavior and reactions to it hold consequences for the deviant actor and may lead to new policies or even laws.

The example of saggy pants commonly worn by young males from certain cultural subgroups demonstrates a number of the principles discussed here. Although the origin of saggy pants as a distinctive style of dress is somewhat unclear, it likely stems from the fact that many correctional institutions do not provide inmates with belts, because belts can be used as weapons, to bind others, and in suicide attempts. Combined with the fact that prison clothing is often ill-fitting, such administrative

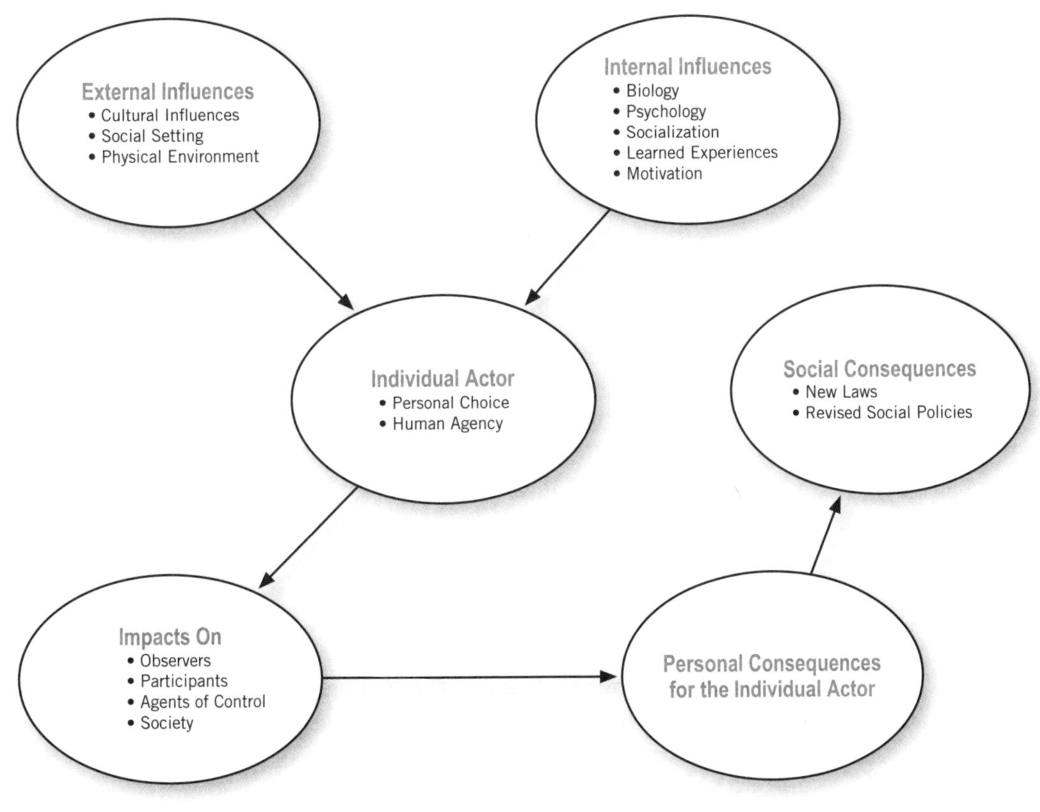

FIGURE 1–4 A conceptual framework for the study of deviant behavior.

policies have led to a common feature among inmate populations—constantly falling pants, with a need for the wearer to repeatedly pull them up. Although the wearing of saggy pants might be acceptable to members of correctional institutions—including inmates, correctional officers, and administrators—wearing them in free society, where different standards of dress traditionally apply, has led to problems. Those who wear them on the "outside" may recognize their prison origin, and such ideologically informed wearers may be expressing allegiance with their imprisoned brothers. Most wearers, however, have probably adopted the style merely because it conforms to fashion trends among the cultural subgroups of which they are members.

Understandably, not everyone has embraced saggy pants as an acceptable fashion statement. In 2010, for example, New York state senator Eric Adams rented two Brooklyn billboards on which he pasted the message "Stop the Sag!" along with a picture of a male model wearing low-slung revealing pants. Adams said he was motivated to rent the billboards after seeing a young man on the subway wearing low-hanging pants. "His behind was showing," said Adams. "All the passengers were looking at him in disgust, but nobody was saying anything" (Saxena, 2010). Some local jurisdictions, including the town of Riviera Beach, Florida, have attempted to criminalize the wearing of sagging pants, saying they constitute a form of indecent exposure. In 2010, even the Fox TV show "American Idol" got involved in the sagging-pants controversy when it aired an audition by 62-year-old rapper Larry Platt, performing the song "Pants on the Ground." The song quickly went viral and received millions of hits after it was posted on YouTube. The question for students of deviance, of course, is how the wearing of sagging pants can be offensive to some but desirable to others—and if either side is "right."

Book Overview

Deviant Behavior explores deviance in the United States and around the world. A wide range of deviant and criminal activities is addressed throughout the book. Each chapter provides an overview of the prevalence and incidence of specific forms of deviant behavior. The substantive chapters follow a similar format: At the outset the issue of definition is addressed; next the prevalence, trends, and patterns of the behavior are presented; and related special topics and particularly deviant subgroups are also discussed. Each chapter concludes with a consideration of the leading theoretical explanations for either the rates or incidence of deviant and criminal behaviors.

Organization

This book is divided into six major parts. Part One: An Overview of Deviant Behavior defines deviance and offers theoretical perspectives to explain deviance. Two chapters are devoted to the explanation of deviance. The first chapter examines individual behavior. Part Two is composed of three chapters and addresses violent forms of deviant behavior including criminal homicide (Chapter 4), assault and battery (Chapter 4), domestic violence (Chapter 5), and suicide (Chapter 6). Parts Three and Four are organized around other categories of deviance, including mental illness (Chapter 7), alcohol abuse (Chapter 8), illicit drug use (Chapter 9), sexual offending

(Chapter 10), property crime (Chapter 11), white-collar and organized crime (Chapter 12), and cyberdeviance (Chapter 13). Additional chapters on positive deviance (Chapter 14) and extreme forms of everyday behavior (Chapter 15) form Part Five. These specialized types of deviance are somewhat unique to the book because they are often overlooked in the study of deviance. This book concludes with Part Six: Terrorism (Chapter 16), which provides an overview of terrorism in the United States and around the world.

Chapter Summary

Deviant behavior may be considered along a continuum. Definitions of deviance involve a complex interplay between

- The actor
- The offended party
- The wider societal audience

Cultural and social organization in a society helps to define what is deviant for that particular society. Social norms—expectational and behavioral—guide social interaction and provide boundaries for acceptable and unacceptable behavior. In this book we use a definition of deviant behavior stating that deviant behavior is an activity that violates the normative structure of society and is socially condemned.

Deviance must be understood on several conceptual levels:

- Creation of social norms, by whom, and which social interests/cultural values are protected
- Violation of social/legal norms and under what conditions
- Labeling of deviance, who is labeled deviant, and under what conditions does labeling occur
- Societal reaction to norm violators
- Formal and informal controls of social/legal norm violation
- Escalation of social/legal norms violation over time and whether new forms of social/legal norms violation emerge

Deviance may be distinguished along several social dimensions:

- Patterned versus idiosyncratic
- Episodic versus routine
- Individual versus group
- Positive versus negative

Although commonly thought of as harmful, deviance serves a number of functions for society:

- Defines boundaries and collective sentiments
- Provides identities for persons unable to gain status or recognition in legitimate ways
- Signals a need for change
- Provides for scapegoating or tension release
- Provides employment of persons to control deviant members of society

Key Concepts

Deviant behavior: Activity that violates the normative structure of society and is socially condemned.

Culture: A body of widely shared customs and values that provides general orientations toward life and specific ways of achieving common goals.

Social organization: The means for carrying out the complex network of social interactions between individuals, social groups, and institutions.

Social norms: Generally agreed on guides for behavior that provide boundaries for interpersonal relations.

Social roles: A set of social norms for the behavior of individuals who occupy given statuses within society.

Expectational norms: Behaviors that are "ideal" for individuals who are enacting a particular social role or who are in a given social situation.

Behavioral norms: What persons "typically" do when occupying a particular social role or in a given social situation.

Processes of globalization: Complex set of processes that involve immediate worldwide communication, transnational commerce and trade, and borderless opportunities for political and cultural exchange.

Critical Thinking Questions

1. Imagine a society without deviant behavior—where everyone continually conforms to the prevailing social norms. Describe the daily lives of the inhabitants of such a society. What are the advantages and disadvantages of total conformity for the society as a whole and for its individual members? Is it possible that a society without deviant behavior would persist through time?

2. Imagine a society without social norms, behavioral expectations, or laws. What would it be like? How would people likely behave?
3. Devise a strategy for the definition of deviant behavior that differs from the normative and situational approaches discussed in this chapter. What forms of deviant behavior might emerge from your definition of deviant behavior? What forms of deviant behavior defined by the normative or situational approach might be omitted?
4. Why are the vast majority of deviant behaviors routine and institutionalized and so few are considered innovative or idiosyncratic?
5. Discuss examples of how the processes of globalization alter local cultural influences on everyday life. How do geographically defined cultures modify the effects of globalization? How does globalization affect forms of deviant behavior in urban areas, small towns, and rural places around the world?

Web Extra

Web-based media materials from high-quality sources such as CNN, Time, and National Public Radio are available in support of this textbook. Visit go.jblearning.com/deviance to access them.

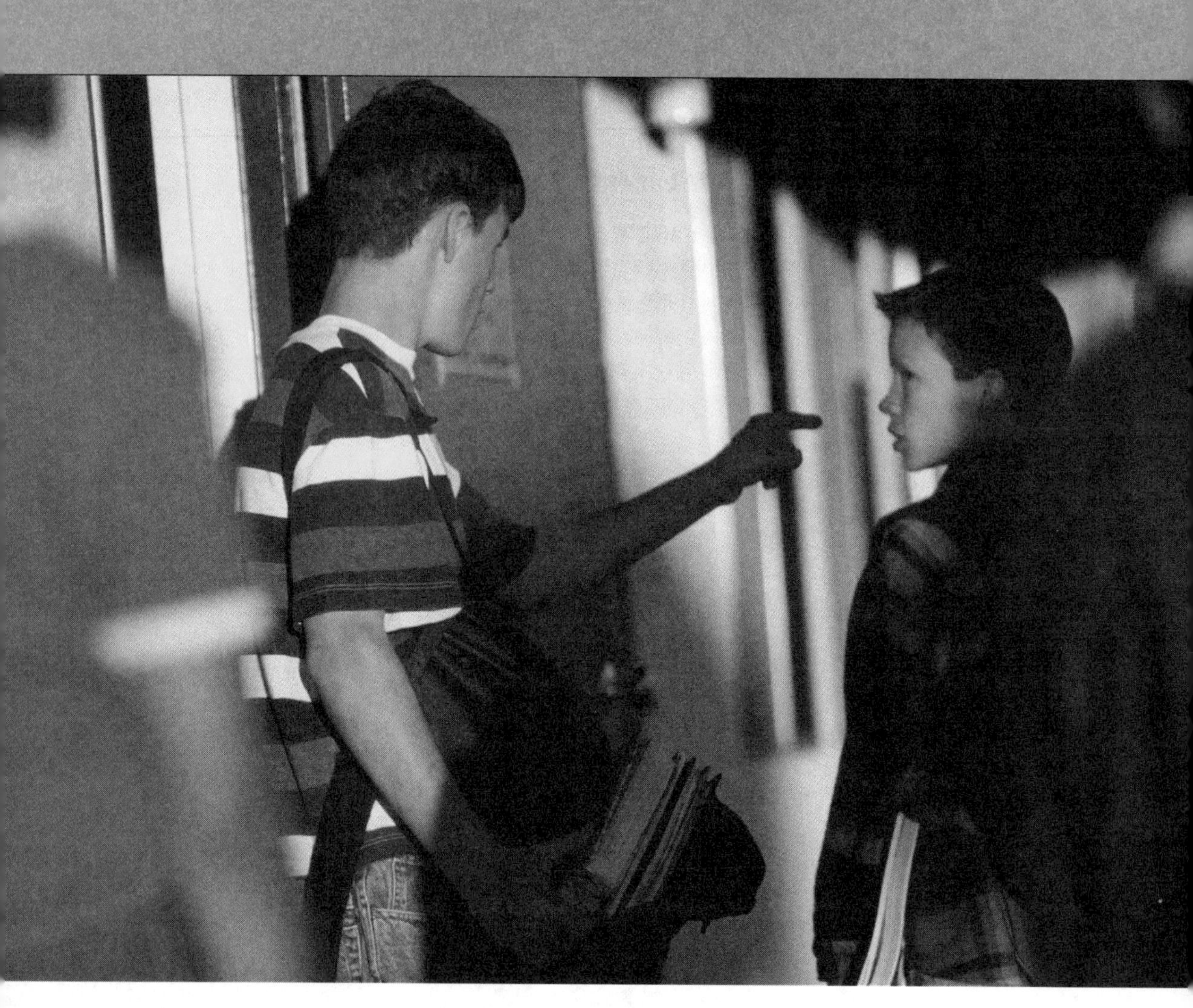

Theories of Individual Forms of Deviant Behavior

CHAPTER 2

Learning Objectives

After reading this chapter you should know

- The contributions made during the Age of Enlightenment to the understanding of deviant behavior.
- The nature of scientific theory.
- The criteria for evaluating a theory.
- The conceptual beginnings, early development, and recent advances of the Neoclassical way of thinking.
- The characteristics of the societal reaction/labeling perspective.
- The nature of control theory.
- The methodological and theoretical advances of the developmental or life-course perspective.

> The deviant is one to whom the label has been successfully applied. . . .
> —Howard Becker (1963, p. 9)

The "Lazy Town" TV show, created in Great Britain and starring the lycra-clad superhero Sportacus and his pink-haired helper Stephanie, has become a worldwide phenomenon and is currently available in 109 countries. Parents and kids generally love the show, which is full of music and inspiring lyrics, including songs like "No One is Lazy in Lazy Town" and "Clean Up." Recently, however, one of the show's characters surprised young viewers by singing the song "Good to be Bad." Lyrics from the song proclaim, "It's good to be bad; It's great to be a crook; It's nice to be a villain like you read about in

> Offenders are but one element in a crime, and perhaps not even the most important.
>
> —Marcus Felson (1998, p. 73)

books!" Parents were worried that impressionable young children might take the words to heart.

Some, however, say that the "good to be bad" theme is one that's already well entrenched in contemporary culture. One area in which being bad is good, they point out, can be found in the double standard surrounding sexual conduct. Whereas women, generally speaking, are expected to be highly selective in their choice of sexual partners, men who claim huge numbers of sexual "conquests" are often highly regarded. Derek A. Kreager and Jeremy Staff, two social psychologists who studied sexuality in American society, reported the following: "According to the sexual double standard, boys and men are rewarded and praised for heterosexual sexual contacts, whereas girls and women are derogated and stigmatized for similar behaviors" (Kreager & Staff, 2009). Putting their findings in social scientific terms, Kreager and Staff explain, "the association between lifetime sexual partnerships and peer status varies significantly by gender, such that greater numbers of sexual partners are *positively* correlated with boys' peer acceptance, but *negatively* correlated with girls' peer acceptance."

A Brief History of Deviance

Attempts to understand socially deviant behavior using explanations derived from the empirical world are relatively recent phenomena. For most of recorded history, spiritual forces were viewed as causing aberrant human social behavior. Most commonly, demonic possession was thought to precipitate deviant behaviors (Huff, 1978). The devil was thought to control or strongly influence the actions of persons, causing them to commit acts of violence, theft, and wanton destruction of property. Denial of sacred precepts and failure to participate in religious ceremonies and observe their practices were thought to result from the influence of the devil. Social control of deviant behavior depended on rooting the devil out of the possessed person. Too often that meant the execution of the deviant person—which, some theologians argued, might save the person's soul but destroy his or her body. Thus, for example, there were 350 crimes punishable by death in England by the middle of the 18th century (Radzinowicz, 1948).

The Age of Enlightenment, alternately known as the Age of Reason, swept Europe during the 17th and 18th centuries. Causes for the occurrence of phenomena in the world, whether physical or social, were being sought in the natural order, in the realm of empirical reality. Metaphysical and spiritual forces were being questioned as the primary and exclusive causes of physical events and human behaviors. Answers to the questions of "why" and "how" things happened, it was argued, are to be found within the phenomena themselves. The causes of physical events—the weather, the potential of the earth to produce edible vegetation, and the workings of the human body—were sought in the interplay of observable physical forces. Likewise, the precipitants of social behavior were to be found in the makeup of human beings and in the social milieu in which they live (Brians, 2000).

The contributions of the neoclassical school during the time of the Enlightenment led to a rethinking about influences on human social behavior and the structure of social life. The search for natural laws to account for phenomena in the physical world led to a desire to discover the laws that governed the social forces that shaped behavior. Faith in the potential of reason and science marked the Enlightenment. Theories that explained and predicted events in the physical world, such as Newton's discovery of gravity and Galileo's observation that the earth revolves around the sun, marked scientific breakthroughs in the 17th and 18th centuries. The **scientific method**—observation, hypothesis development, data collection and analysis, and hypothesis reformulation—drove the quest for knowledge. Scientific theories soon replaced other sources of knowledge—tradition, belief systems, and political and sacred authority. The Age of the Enlightenment was marked by a widespread rejection of State and Church as the sources of knowledge. Scientific explanations sought to supplant all other understanding of the world and the way it operated (Brians, 2000).

This chapter provides an overview of theoretical formulations designed to explain and predict individual forms of deviant behavior. Three theoretical foci guide the discussion of theories of individual forms of social deviance: the **Neoclassical School**, the **societal reaction** or **labeling perspective**, and **social control theory**. Developments within each theoretical focus are traced from their conceptual beginnings, through their early development, and to their more recent advances.

What Is a Theory?

Fundamental assumptions of science are that phenomena in the world are knowable through our senses and are causally related to one another (Goode & Hatt, 1952). To the extent that physical events or behaviors recur in a patterned way, they are viewed as causally related. A central objective of science is to discover the causal relationships among phenomena and, as a result, to predict the probability of the occurrence of a given phenomenon by knowing the nature of its relationship to other phenomena. The tides, for example, are predictable with reasonable accuracy by knowing the variations in the gravitational forces of the earth, sun, and moon.

It is essential to understand what a scientific theory is and how best to assess it. Simply put, a **scientific theory** is a set of interrelated and interdependent propositions designed to predict a given phenomenon. A *proposition* is a statement of the relationship between at least two variables, or phenomena, in the empirical world that are subject to change. For example, age is a variable because it increases over time, and a test score is a variable because it may vary among individuals or it may change for the same individual at different times. Fully developed theories are rarely found in the social sciences. Rather, conceptualizations or descriptions of the possible relationships among social variables are more common. The eminent social theorist, Robert K. Merton (1957, p. 9), observed the following:

> A large part of what is now called sociological theory consists of general orientations toward data, suggesting types of variables which need somehow to be taken into account, rather than clear, verifiable statements of relationships between specific variables.

The theoretical formulations considered in this chapter fall into the category of what Merton (1957, p. 5) calls "theories of the middle range" or conceptualizations of social phenomena. To Merton (1957, pp. 5–6), theories of the middle range are positioned somewhere between "minor working hypotheses" and a "master conceptual scheme," which accounts for a "very large number of empirically observed uniformities of social behavior."

What Is a Theory?
http://psychology.about.com/od/tindex/f/theory.htm

Criteria for Evaluating a Theory

Sociological theorist Ronald Akers (1994, pp. 6–12) set forth criteria essential for the evaluation of a scientific theory in general and theories of crime and deviance in particular. These criteria are logical consistency, scope, parsimony, testability, empirical validity, and usefulness and policy implications. *Logical consistency* refers to the clarity of the concepts or variables used to form the propositions. A theory must also be constructed by logical and consistent ordering propositions. Internal inconsistency of propositions and definition of theoretical concepts are essential elements of a scientific theory.

Scope refers to "range of phenomena" accounted for by the theory. Theories of deviance or crime, for example, that are limited to one form of behavior, say shoplifting, are far less useful than a more encompassing theory of criminal behavior. Related to the scope of a theory is *parsimony*—the ideal in science to discover the simplest theoretical explanation for the broadest set of occurrences. Einstein's theory of relativity $E = MC^2$ is an example of a parsimonious theoretical formulation. Einstein discovered that energy and mass are equivalent and that energy is a function of mass times the velocity of light squared.

The *testability* of a theory is crucial to its usefulness to scientists around the world. Unless a theory lends itself to empirical scrutiny, evidence cannot be gathered to assess the validity of its propositions. A theory must be able to be falsified before it can be accepted even provisionally. A theory may not be testable because the concepts or variables included in the propositions are so ill defined they cannot be empirically measured. Or, the propositions are not logically ordered. Although it is not necessary to measure each concept in a theory, it is critical that the concepts are linked with the measurable concepts in a logical and consistent way.

The *empirical validity* of a theory is the most fundamental assessment criterion. Unless there is scientifically credible evidence that supports a theory, wholly or in part, it may well be abandoned for more promising theoretical formulations. The strength of the evidence in support of a theory and the consistency in the findings of support are key indicators of empirical validity. It is important to understand that causal relationships stated in scientific theories are cast in probabilistic terms. That is, the hypothesis that the greater the *X*, the greater the *Y* means that as *X* increases, the more likely *Y* is to follow, not that *X* will always follow from *Y*.

The *usefulness* and *policy implications* are also important criteria in evaluating a theoretical formulation. Empirically valid theories of criminal and deviant behavior are invaluable in designing and implementing prevention and intervention programs and policies. Key questions that legislators, law enforcers, and public policymakers continually ask are what works and for whom? Rather than approaching the control and prevention of criminal and deviant behavior in a haphazard way, public officials want to know the wisest expenditure of tax dollars. Sound theoretical formulations guide the formation of effective public policy, assist the deviant members of society, and reduce continued victimization (Akers, 1994).

Neoclassical School

Two social philosophers, **Cesare Beccaria** (1963) in Italy and **Jeremy Bentham** (1948) in England, are largely responsible for the development of the Classical School of thought during the time of the Enlightenment in the 18th century. Cesare Beccaria, a shy Italian social philosopher, wrote

Cesare Beccaria, whose writings contributed to development of the Classical School. What principles are embodied in today's Neoclassical School of thought?

a ground-breaking work—*On Crime and Punishment*—setting out the principles that underlie human social behavior. To Beccaria, individuals commonly hold three basic characteristics: *free will, rationality*, and *manipulability*. Beccaria viewed humans as rational beings who possess free will. Their decision to act or refrain from acting involves a conscious, voluntary, and deliberate process. Manipulability refers to the rational pursuit of self-interest. Underlying the decision to act is the principle of hedonism. The **hedonistic principle** holds that persons are motivated to maximize their pleasure and minimize their pain. When deciding to act a certain way, say to commit a deviant act, a person weighs the amount of anticipated pleasure from the action against the amount of pain that may result from committing the act. Simply put, if the pain that attends an act of deviance exceeds the pleasure derived from it, then its commission is less likely.

The English social thinker, Jeremy Bentham (1948), pursued this utilitarian approach to deterrence of crime and deviance. He devised a **hedonistic calculus** that linked the appropriate penalty or pain to each criminal offense. By knowing in advance the penalty for a particular crime, the would-be offender would be deterred. Both Beccaria and Bentham were opposed to the death penalty as a nonutilitarian form of punishment. Inflicting a sufficient amount of pain on the offender, they argued, may effectively deter criminal and deviant behaviors. Given their ability to freely decide to act (free will) and their innate sense of reason, potential offenders would rationally decide to forego acts of deviance.

In the later part of the 20th century, sociologists adopted the principles of human behavior outlined in the 18th century by Cesare Beccaria and Jeremy Bentham. Their approach to crime and deviance came to be known as the Neoclassical School of Thought. The **deterrence doctrine** set forth by **Jack Gibbs** in the mid-1970s is a central component of neoclassical thinking and is based on the principle of hedonism. Gibbs translates hedonism into terms consistent with a cost benefit analysis. The potential costs (or pain) involved in committing a deviant or criminal act must be less than the anticipated benefits (or pleasure), he says, before an individual decides to engage in the behavior. Humans are viewed as rational decision-making individuals who continually assess relative costs and benefits before deciding to act. In short, a rational decision-making process precedes willful engagement in crime and deviance.

A logical derivative of the deterrence doctrine is British criminologists **Derek B. Cornish** and **Ronald V. Clarke's** (1986 and 1987) development of **Rational Choice Theory** and their creation of *Situational Choice Theory*. Both theoretical perspectives focus on an individual's conscious, rational decision making. Again, the costs of acting are weighed against the benefits, and a decision is made. Situational choice theory, however, involves an assessment of the environment in which the criminal or deviant acts are to be played out. The structural features of the situation—lighting, surveillance equipment, police patrol, and citizen watch organizations—influence the probability of deviant behavior. To Cornish and Clarke, *target hardening*, or making physical spaces more defensible and less attractive to perpetrators, deters deviant behaviors. Of course, this may simply lead to **crime displacement,** changing the location of criminal and deviant behavior to a more conducive environment (Cornish & Clark, 1987).

A related conceptualization is **Lawrence Cohen** and **Marcus Felson's** (1979) **Routine Activities Theory.** Routine activities refer to components of an individual's lifestyle that influence the likelihood of his or her becoming a victim of criminal activity. Walking alone late at night, being publicly intoxicated, and displaying large amounts of cash to strangers certainly increase one's vulnerability to crime. Cohen and Felson argue that crime is most likely to occur when three conditions are present: a suitable target, a motivated offender, and the lack of a capable guardian. A suitable target may be a vulnerable person on the street, an isolated convenience store in a rural area, or residence in a high crime neighborhood. Motivated offenders may be present in a variety of settings but only choose to strike when a suitable target is present and a capable guardian is absent. It is the convergence of these three conditions that increases the probability of criminal victimization.

Sociologist **Jack Katz** (1988) provides an insightful analysis of the **seduction of crime**—the exhilaration that accompanies the commission of a criminal or deviant act. Katz observes that most sociologists focus on the sociocultural conditions and social processes that are associated with crime and deviance. The sociological precipitants of crime and deviance are considerably removed from the actual commission of the deviant act. To Katz the central question is this: Why are people who are not inclined to commit a crime one moment determined to do so the next? The answer, Katz argues, lies in the sensual experiences that result from involvement in criminal or deviant behavior. Crime itself is seductive. The very act of committing a crime results in an intensely pleasurable emotional experience. A rush of adrenalin, a sense of euphoria, or a sensual feeling may wash over the offender. In short, the sensual dynamics inherent in criminal and deviant activity motive its participants and serve to perpetuate their involvement.

Societal Reaction/Labeling Perspective

The **Symbolic Interaction Theory** in sociology provides the foundation for the societal reaction or labeling perspective. **Charles Horton Cooley** (1902) and **George Herbert Mead** (1934) are largely responsible for the inception of symbolic interaction perspective within sociology. It was their observation that interpersonal interaction is primarily symbolic. Individuals attach meanings to the gestures, verbal communications, and behaviors of others. One's sense of self is also a product of symbolic social interaction. In Cooley's concept of a *looking-glass self*, he notes that the qualities we assign to ourselves are those we believe others assign to us. We are, in a sense, a reflection of what we believe others think of us. Our sense of self then is a social construction—the result of an interactional process through which the self acquires meaning and self-definition.

George Herbert Mead provides an understanding of the process by which a child develops a unique sense of self. To Mead, humans communicate by means of gestures and symbols. A child begins to give meaning to the gestures and symbolic communications—usually words and pictures—used by others to converse with him or her. In time a child attributes to him- or herself certain characteristics and value to others. Messages of love or disgust, acceptance or rejection, joy or burden may be transmitted to a child. Mead terms this process as *taking the role of the other*, or the ability to view one's self from the perspective of another person. The process of defining and redefining one's self is a lifelong process. Yet the effects of negative labeling in early life may well have long-term adverse effects.

The early work of **Frank Tannenbaum** (1938) underscores the importance of the labeling in perpetuation and escalation of deviant behavior. In 1938, Frank Tannenbaum, a professor of history, recognized that delinquency is a result of a process of "tagging" or labeling first the offensive acts of a juvenile and second the juvenile him- or herself. The process begins with the community as a whole defining the troublesome behaviors as criminal or delinquent offenses. The perpetrators are then seen as violating the law and subject to being processed by the justice system. Tannenbaum viewed the process of arresting, adjudicating, and imposing a sentence by the court as the **dramatization of evil.** Once an individual is "tagged" or labeled as a delinquent, he or she tends to be ostracized by the community. The process of being isolated from conventional society leads to association with others who have also been labeled a delinquent. As a consequence, the likelihood of continued involvement in delinquent activities is markedly increased.

The societal reaction perspective was advanced in the 1950s and 1960s by the work of **Edwin Lemert** (1967) and **Howard Becker** (1963). Lemert provides an analysis of the process of becoming a deviant. He contends that the process involves two stages of development: *primary deviance* and *secondary deviance*. Primary deviance typically refers to minor norm violations—petty theft, use of graffiti, public drunkenness—that may well not evoke an official response by the criminal justice system. The offender usually does not define him- or herself as a criminal or deviant but simply a prankster. However, if an act of primary deviance does result in a public response and an official action is taken—for example, an arrest for shoplifting—then the label of criminal is applied. The process of being arrested, booked, fingerprinted, and adjudicated in court serves to publicly label the offender. Secondary deviance then occurs when the individual's primary deviance becomes publicly known and the person is adjudicated a delinquent or criminal. In response to this negative label, the primary deviant may engage in further deviance "as a means of defense, attack, or adjustment to the overt and covert problems created by the consequent societal reaction to him" (Lemert, 1967, p. 237). In the secondary deviance stage, offending becomes more frequent and typically more serious. The deviant defines him- or herself as "bad"—a rejected person who will retaliate against the society that wronged her or him.

Labeling Theories of Crime. http://www.apsu.edu/oconnort/crim/crimtheory14.htm

In a similar vein, Howard Becker points out that deviance is essentially a social creation. He writes: "*social groups create deviance by making the rules whose infractions constitute deviance*, and by applying those rules to particular people and labeling them as outsiders" [emphasis in original] (Becker, 1963, p. 9). Becker contends that behavior is essentially neutral: In itself it is neither good nor bad. Others must define a person's behavior before it can take on a social value, a judgment of right or wrong, moral or immoral, harmful or benign. Simply put, the process of creating a deviant involves three stages. First, an act must be defined as a deviant act. Second, the actor must be defined as a deviant person. The third stage, however, is critical in the process of becoming a deviant.

In the third stage of the process, the actor must accept the label of deviant and define him- or herself as a deviant. Becker (1963, p. 9) observes, "The deviant is one to whom that label has been successfully applied."

More recently, sociologist **Howard Kaplan** (1980) elaborated on the labeling/societal reaction perspective. Central to Kaplan's formulation is the assumption that behavior is motivated by the desire to achieve and maintain a sense of self-esteem. A person's self-esteem typically derives from his or her ability to recognize highly valued personal characteristics in him- or herself, accept positive evaluations from others, and the ability to avert negative responses from others. However, when a person's self-esteem is undermined, self-derogation—or negative attitudes toward one's self—may ensue.

To Kaplan, **self-derogation**—the process by which a person comes to accept the largely negative judgments of others—is the key concept in the etiology of deviant behavior. An individual who is unable to establish a positive sense of him- or herself is less motivated to conform to the norms of conventional society. That individual may well seek alternate means to gain a sense of self-esteem and may be attracted to deviant groups or lifestyles that provide opportunities for developing unconventional, yet in the view of their fellow deviants, self-enhancing attitudes.

Australian social theorist **John Braithwaite** (1989) adds another dimension to the labeling/societal reaction perspective. His highly innovative theory of **reintegrative shaming** challenges many of the current assumptions about crime deterrence and the rehabilitation of offenders. Reintegrative shaming occurs when the community conveys its disapproval of a deviant person's behavior but maintains respect for the individual. The intention of reintegrative shaming is to send the message to the offender that deviant behavior will not be tolerated; nevertheless, the community values the offender as a person and wants him or her to be reintegrated into conventional society. Braithwaite draws the distinction between reintegrative shaming and stigmatization. **Stigmatization** involves "disintegrative shaming"—the person as well as his or her behavior is labeled as criminal or deviant (Braithwaite, 1989). Ostracized by the community, stigmatized persons are more likely to engage in further criminal or deviant activities. They may seek out deviant subcultures for support and personal recognition, further alienating them from the larger society.

A critical element in reintegrative shaming theory is the deliberate attempt to reassimilate the deviant into the community. By distinguishing between the inherent worth of a person from his or her misdeeds, the

Minor offenders being sentenced to shame in Ohio. Does shaming offenders help to reduce the incidence of repeat offenses?

reintegrative shaming approach to crime deterrence and offender rehabilitation offers an alternative to the retributive response to deviant behavior.

Control Theory

Emile Durkheim's (1951) views on social integration and its effect on deviant behavior provide the backdrop for the development of social control theory. **Social integration** refers to the extent to which individuals accept common cultural values and societal norms to structure their behavior. **Travis Hirschi** (1969) conceptualized integration as a set of **social bonds** between individuals and conventional society. Rather than trying to discover why individuals engage in deviance, Hirschi posed the question why don't people commit delinquent acts?

Hirschi identifies four social bonds: *attachment, commitment, involvement*, and *belief*. Attachment refers to the intensity and variety of interests a person has in common with others in the community. Commitment is reflected in the amount of energy a person expends on community-oriented activities. Involvement is indicated by the person's expenditure of time on projects of common interest. Belief means the acceptance of a common system of values and moral precepts. Hirschi concludes that the stronger the bonds between individuals and conventional social life, the less likely they will engage in deviant behavior.

In more recent years, **Michael Gottfredson** and Travis Hirschi (1990) offered a reformulation of control theory. Their **General Theory of Crime** focuses on **self-control** rather than on bonds to conventional social life. Gottfredson and Hirschi (1990) contend that most crimes are not well planned but are committed to satisfy an immediate need or desire. Low self-control is summarized by Tittle and Paternoster (1993, p. 482) as an

- Orientation toward the present rather than the future (or shortsightedness)
- Attraction to physical rather than mental activities
- Insensitivity to the suffering of others (self-centeredness)
- Intolerance for frustration
- Inclination toward risk-taking and opportunism

Individuals who lack self-control, who are unable to resist the urge for immediate gratification are most prone to involvement in criminal and deviant behaviors. Criminal activity provides a person who has low self-control with several immediate benefits. Gottfredson and Hirschi (1990) note the following:

- There is a long tradition of publicly shaming deviant persons to correct their faults and to deter others in the community.
- Criminal acts provide *easy or simple* gratification of desires.
- Criminal acts are *exciting, risky, or thrilling.*
- Crimes require *little skill or planning.*
- Crimes often result in *pain or discomfort for the victim.*

Sociologist **Charles Tittle** (1995) proposed a control-balance formulation to explain deviant behavior. *Control-balance* refers to the relative amount of control a person has over others in a given situation. The key concept in control-balance theory is the person's control ratio. **Control ratio** refers to the amount of influence individuals have over forces that may control their behavior versus their ability to control those forces. Tittle assumes that individuals strive to maintain a sense of autonomy, a sense of self-determination. No one wants to be told what to do or when and how to do it. Control imbalance often provokes feelings of humiliation, anger, and emotional distress. To correct this control imbalance and the resolve the negative emotions that accompany it, a person may resort to various forms of deviant behavior.

Tittle (1995) identifies five conditions that underlie the occurrence of deviant behavior:

- A predisposition toward being motivated for deviance
- A situational provocation that reminds a person of a control imbalance
- The transformation of predisposition into actual motivation for deviance
- The opportunity for deviant response
- The absence or relative weakness for constraint, so that the mental processes of "control balancing" result in a perceived gain in control

In sum, persons who are motivated to engage in deviant acts need to establish a sense of autonomy, perceive an unbalanced control ratio, and experience a blockage in goal attainment. The immediate situation may trigger recognition of a control imbalance. If suitable opportunities for retaliatory acts are present and constraints against their commission are absent, then an individual may well respond in an antisocial way.

Table 2–1 summarizes the various schools of thought discussed throughout the chapter.

New Theoretical Approaches

The recognition that involvement in deviant behavior varies over time has led to the emergence of life-course perspectives. **Robert Sampson** and **John Laub** (1993) take a **developmental approach** to the understanding of the persistence and desistence of criminal activity across the life span. Their age-graded theory of informal social control proposes that changes in social bonds between an individual and conventional society across the life course account for variations in criminal and deviant behaviors. Two concepts are particularly important to their developmental formulation: trajectories and transitions. *Trajectories* refer to "pathways or lines of development throughout life. These long-term patterns of behavior may include work life, marriage, parenthood, or even criminal behavior" (Sampson & Laub, 1993, p. 100). *Transitions*, however, are "short-term events embedded in trajectories which may include starting a new job, getting married, having a child, or being sentenced to prison" (Sampson & Laub, 1993, p. 100). A related concept is a *turning point*—an abrupt event that redirects the course of a life trajectory.

A life-course trajectory that involves persistent involvement in criminal and deviant activities may be interrupted by transitions that change the nature of the social bonds between the offender and the larger society. Transitions tend to occur at particular ages across the life span.

TABLE 2–1 Theoretical Formulations of Individual Forms of Deviant Behavior

Theoretical Foundations	
Classical school	
1. Beccaria (1764)	*On Crimes and Punishment*
2. Bentham (1789)	*An Introduction to the Principles of Moral and Legislation*
Societal reaction/labeling perspective	
1. Tannenbaum (1938)	*The Dramatization of Evil*
Control theory	
1. Hirsch (1969)	*The Causes of Delinquency*
Early Developments	
Societal reaction	
1. Lemert (1951)	*Primary and Secondary Deviation*
2. Becker (1964)	*The Outsiders*
Recent Advances	
Neoclassical school	
1. Cohen and Felson (1979)	*Routine Activity Theory*
2. Cornish and Clarke (1986)	*Crime as Rational Choice*
3. Katz (1988)	*Seduction of Crime*
Societal reaction/labeling	
1. Kaplan (1980)	*Self-Derogation*
2. Braithwaite (1989)	*Crime, Shame and Reintegration*
Control theory	
1. Gottfredson and Hirschi (1990)	*A General Theory of Crime*
2. Tittle (1995)	*Control Balance Theory*
New Theoretical Approaches	
Life-course formulations	
1. Wolfgang, Figlio, and Sellin (1972)	*Delinquency in a Birth Cohort*
2. Wolfgang, Thronberry, and Figlio (1987)	*From Delinquency to Crime*
3. Sampson and Laub (1993)	*Life Course Analyses*
4. Farrington (1995)	*Delinquent Development Theory*

Marriage, stable employment, and becoming a parent tend to strengthen ties to the community. A turning point in the life of a chronic offender may be a graduation from high school, a significant job promotion, or a civic recognition for a heroic deed. To the extent that transitions and key turning points increase an individual's social bonds, they tend to decrease the probability of continued deviant behavior. Sampson and

Laub (1993, p. 100) conclude that "age-graded changes in social bonds explain changes in crime."

As social bonds are strengthened, so too is one's social capital. *Social capital* refers to the positive relationships between a person and other members of the community and its governmental and social institutions. Being a responsible individual who acts in the best interest of those around him or her results in the accumulation of social capital. Sampson and Laub (1993) point out that as social capital increases, involvement in crime and deviance decreases.

Issues related to the persistence and desistence of offending are considered in a Philadelphia birth-cohort study conducted by Marvin Wolfgang and his colleagues (1972) and British criminologist David Farrington's Cambridge Study in Delinquent Development (1986). In two birth-cohort studies, Marvin Wolfgang and his colleagues at the University of Pennsylvania found that chronic juvenile offenders—those who commit five or more offenses—are developmentally different from single offenders and from nondelinquents. Compared with the nonchronic delinquents, the chronic offenders tend to have lower IQ scores, do less well in school, and are more likely to come from lower socioeconomic backgrounds. In addition, chronic offenders tend to commit their first offense at a younger age. Wolfgang and his colleagues conclude that the earlier the age at onset, the greater the likelihood of chronic offending. A follow-up study showed that the seriousness of offending increased with age but the actual number of crimes committed decreased over time (Wolfgang, Thornberry, & Figlio, 1987).

The findings of David Farrington's developmental study of delinquents also show that antisocial behaviors—dishonesty and aggression—become evident as early as the age of 8 and given a certain social context may well persist into early adulthood. Young offenders from large families where discipline is particularly harsh and inconsistent, social and economic resources are meager, and siblings are also committing delinquent acts are more likely to be set on a trajectory of criminal involvement. Throughout their adolescent years and into adulthood, the persistent offenders tend to spend their time in all-male groups, drink excessively and use illicit drugs, and engage in aggressive and violent behaviors. In short, English delinquent youth are generally "less conforming and less socially restrained" (West & Farrington, 1977).

Farrington (1986) also identified three key transitions that changed the life trajectory of a young offender: employment, marriage, and relocation. Steady employment with possibility of advancement provides an alternative to a relatively meaningless life on the street. Getting married to a person who is not involved in a deviant lifestyle is another important transition in the life of a delinquent. Moving to a low-crime area—the suburbs or a rural place—also tend to reduce the opportunities to continue a deviant career. These three transitions serve to restructure a person's everyday life and interrupt a crime-prone trajectory.

Chapter Summary

Scientific inquiry into human social behavior began to emerge during the time of the Enlightenment and has undergone a slow, uneven, often tumultuous development. The methods of scientific investigation are continually being refined, as are theoretical formulations of a wide range of social and behavioral phenomena. Advances in sociological and social psychological theories of behavior have largely occurred during the 20th century.

I. This chapter considers the
   - A. Foundations of scientific inquiry into deviant behavior
   - B. Essential elements of a viable scientific theory
   - C. Early development and recent theoretical advances designed to explain and predict deviant behavior

II. Sociological explanations of behavior discussed in this chapter include
   - A. Classical and neoclassical schools of crime and deviance
   - B. Societal reaction or labeling perspective
   - C. Social control theory

III. Each theory is designed to explain and predict the participation of individuals in various forms of deviant behavior.

IV. The classical school of crime and deviance, established in the work of Cesare Beccaria and Jeremy Bentham, provides the foundation for the contemporary perspectives of
   - A. Rational choice theory
   - B. Routine activities formulation

V. Societal reaction or the labeling perspective derives from the early work of Charles Horton Cooley and George Herbert Mead. Among the most influential labeling theorists are
   - A. Frank Tannenbaum
   - B. Edwin Lemert

C. Howard Becker
D. Howard Kaplan
E. John Braithwaite

VI. Emile Durkheim's concept of social integration and its consequences gave rise to the development of Travis Hirschi's social bonding theory and his later formulation of self-control theory with Michael Gottfredson.

VII. The developmental approach, or life-course perspective, takes into account the emergence, persistence, and possible desistence of engagement in deviant activities across the life span.

Key Names

Cesare Beccaria
Edwin Lemert
Jeremy Bentham
Howard Becker
Jack Gibbs
Howard Kaplan
Ronald V. Clarke
John Braithwaite
Derek B. Cornish
Travis Hirschi
Lawrence Cohen
Michael Gottfredson
Marcus Felson
Charles Tittle
Jack Katz
Robert Sampson
Charles Horton Cooley
John Laub
George Herbert Mead
Marvin Wolfgang
Frank Tannebaum
David Farrington

Key Concepts

Scientific method: Observation, hypothesis development, data collection and analysis, and hypothesis reformulation used in the quest for knowledge.

Neoclassical School: School of thought developed during the time of the Enlightenment, based on the idea that human beings possess free will and rationally decide to act or refrain from certain activities.

Societal reaction or labeling perspective: Theoretical perspective that focuses on how society reacts to and labels deviance and deviant actors, and how these reactions and labels affect the deviant actor.

Social control theory: A perspective that predicts that weakened or absent social controls lead to deviant behavior.

Scientific theory: A set of interrelated and interdependent propositions designed to predict a given phenomenon.

Hedonistic principle: Belief that persons are motivated to maximize their pleasure and minimize their pain.

Hedonistic calculus: Links the appropriate penalty or pain to each criminal offense.

Deterrence doctrine: A crime control perspective based on weighing the personal costs and benefits associated with committing a deviant or criminal act.

Rational Choice Theory: An individual makes a conscious, rational decision before acting.

Crime displacement: Changing the location of criminal and deviant behavior to a more conducive environment.

Routine Activities Theory: The likelihood of crime increases when there is a suitable target, a motivated offender, and the lack of a capable guardian.

Seduction of crime: The exhilaration that accompanies the commission of a criminal or deviant act.

Symbolic Interaction Theory: Theory that observes interpersonal interaction as primarily symbolic and meaningful.

Dramatization of evil: Process of labeling deviance and deviant actors to describe the arresting, adjudicating, and sentencing of offenders.

Self-derogation: The process by which a person comes to accept the largely negative judgments of others.

Reintegrative shaming: Process by which the community conveys its disapproval of a deviant person's behavior but maintains respect for the individual.

Stigmatization: Disrespectful shaming; the person as well as his or her behavior is labeled as criminal or deviant.

Social integration: The extent to which individuals accept common cultural values and societal norms to structure their behavior.

Social bonds: The integration of an individual with conventional society.

General Theory of Crime: Focuses on self-control rather than on bonds to conventional social life.

Self-control: A person's ability to alter responses and behavior in an effort to resist committing a crime or deviance.

Control ratio: An individual's potential for control over circumstances relative to the potential those circumstances have to control her or him.

Developmental approach (life-course perspective): Attempts to understand the onset, persistence, and desistence of deviant activity across the life span.

Critical Thinking Questions

1. Devise an alternative to the scientific method for the explanation and prediction of deviant behavior. What are the advantages and disadvantages of your innovative method of investigating deviance?
2. What are the limitations of the scientific method of investigation? What kinds of questions are beyond the scope of the scientific method?
3. Are different theoretical formulations needed for different forms of deviant behavior? For example, can violent, property, and victimless deviant acts be explained by the same theoretical model?
4. Are different theoretical models needed to explain the onset of deviant behavior, the persistence, and desistence of that behavior? Which theoretical model(s) do you believe best accounts for the onset, the persistence, and desistence of deviant behavior?

Web Extra

Web-based media materials from high-quality sources such as CNN, Time, and National Public Radio are available in support of this textbook. Visit go.jblearning.com/deviance to access them.

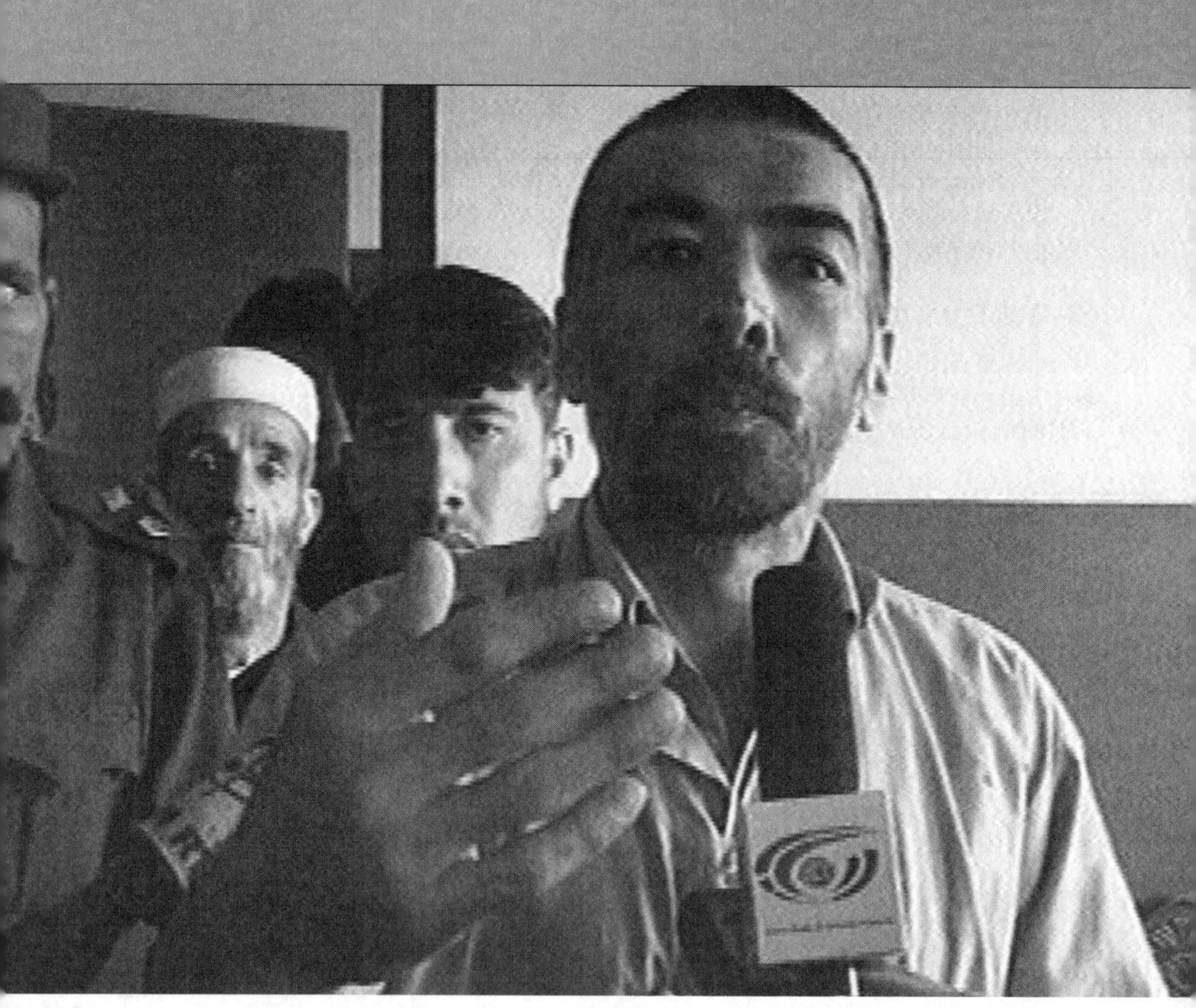

Theories of the Variations in Rates of Deviant Behavior

CHAPTER 3

Learning Objectives

After reading this chapter you should know

- The difference between micro- and macro-level approaches to the study of crime and deviance.
- The contributions of the conflict perspective to the study of crime and deviance.
- The contributions of functionalism to the study of crime and deviance.
- Important elements of the conflict approach to the study of social deviance, principles of the social integration/anomie perspective, social disorganization theory, and differential association/social learning theories.

A few years ago, long after American forces had routed the Taliban in Afghanistan, 41-year-old Abdul Rahman was arrested and accused by police officers in that country of the crime of apostasy—or rejecting Islam. Rahman, a father of two, had been accused by his family of becoming Christian, an offense punishable by death under Shariah law. Shariah law, based on Islamic principles, provides the basis for the legal system in Afghanistan and in a number of other nations in the Middle East.

Abdul Wasi, the Afghan prosecutor in charge of the case, told reporters he had offered to drop the charges against Rahman if he converted back to Islam, but Rahman refused. "He would have been forgiven if he changed back. But he said he was a Christian and would always remain one," Wasi said. "We are Muslims and becoming a Christian is against our laws. He must get the death penalty" (Cooney, 2006).

Shahnawaz Farooqui, a prominent Islamic journalist and scholar based in Pakistan, declared that "[Rahman] will have to be executed." Farooqui explained that "If somebody at one point affirms the truth and then rejects it or denies it, it would jeopardize the whole paradigm of truth. This is such a big offense that the penalty can only be death." The Afghan attorney general agreed, saying that Rahman, who had been found to be in possession of a Bible, should be hanged.

Under pressure from the United States and the United Kingdom, however, Rahman was eventually released and sought asylum in Italy (Associated Press, 2006). Authorities in Afghanistan had apparently decided that he was mentally ill, thereby paving the way for his release and avoiding a confrontation with British and American officials.

Religious bias can work both ways, of course, and in 2010 an overflow crowd turned out for a meeting of the Rutherford County Commission in Murfreesboro, Tennessee, to protest plans by a local Islamic congregation to build a 52,000-square-foot mosque and community center in the area. At the meeting Pastor Allen Jackson of the World Outreach Church told commissioners that "We have a duty to investigate anyone under the banner of Islam" (Fox News, 2010).

Levels of Analysis

Scientific inquiry into the phenomena of deviance tends to focus either on the understanding of the incidence or prevalence of criminal or deviant behavior. Chapter 2 focused on explanations of individual forms of deviance. The central question addressed in Chapter 2 was why certain individuals engage in a given form of deviant behavior while others do not? The present chapter considers a distinctly different sociological question: Why is deviance and criminality more prevalent in some subcultures or social groups than in others? Each question must be addressed at different levels of analysis.

> In the first place crime is normal because a society exempt from it is utterly impossible.
>
> —Emile Durkheim (1938, p. 67)

Micro-level analysis focuses on social processes and personal characteristics—labeling, social bonding, self-control, or derogation—that may account for an individual's involvement in criminal or deviant behavior. **Macro-level analysis** considers the ways in which structural and cultural characteristics of social collectives—societies, subcultures, social groupings—affect the *rates* of crime and acts of social deviance. The rate of crime or deviance typically refers to the number of offenses that occur for every 100,000 persons in a given population. Rates of crime and deviance vary widely around the world and within the United States. Subcultural groups and socioeconomic categories of persons are differentially involved in crime and deviance.

Attempts to explain variations in rates of crime and deviance rely on two macro-level theoretical perspectives: conflict and functionalism. Each of these perspectives and the development of theoretical formulations that derive from them are considered in this chapter.

> The code of the street thus emerges where the influence of the police ends and where personal responsibility for one's safety is felt to begin.
>
> —Elijah Anderson (1999, p. 34)

Conflict Perspective

Conflict can occur on several social levels: international, regional, cultural and subcultural, intergroup and interpersonal. Conflict may itself be deviant, or it may be a precursor to other forms of deviant behaviors. The *conflict perspective* focuses on the ways in which social conflicts affect the prevalence of criminal offending and deviant behavior.

The conflict approach to the understanding of crime and deviance is based in large part on Karl Marx's (1956) analysis of the structure of society. Marx argued that two conflicting classes—the *bourgeoisie* and the *proletariat*—serve to structure society. Because the bourgeoisie are the owners of the means of production in society, they control much of its wealth. The proletariat, or working class, sell their labor to the bourgeoisie but are compensated at a rate far less than its market value. In Marx's terms labor has a *surplus value*—the monetary gain of employers after paying the worker. *Structural inequality* is premised on the concentration of wealth and power in the hands of the bourgeoisie, their exploitation of the proletariat, and their ability to manipulate the legal system to their advantage. Marx argued that a class struggle would erupt, resulting in the overthrow of the bourgeoisie by the proletariat.

Several noted criminologists—Thorsten Sellin (1938), Austin Turk (1969), and Richard Quinney (1977)—adopted a conflict perspective for their theoretical formulations of crime and deviance. To Thorsten Sellin, *conduct norms* define approved and disapproved behaviors within cultural groups. Deviance arises when the conduct norms of one cultural group or subculture clash with another. Conflicts in conduct norms may occur under three conditions:

1. When two cultural groups are in close proximity and the conduct norms of one group conflict with the neighboring group
2. When the laws of a dominant cultural group govern the activities of a subordinate group

3. When members of one cultural group move into an area governed by another cultural group

In each instance the norms that guide the conduct of a cultural group may be considered unacceptable by another and in the extreme may be defined as illegal. Persons who violate the conduct norms of another cultural group may elicit various forms of informal social control—gossip, ridicule, or ostracism—or may be criminally adjudicated (Sellin, 1938).

Austin Turk's conflict model of criminality focuses on the balance of power between authorities in society and persons who are subjected to their control. Social order is maintained to the extent that the members of society accept and support the legitimacy of the authorities. Two sets of norms emerge to reduce the likelihood of conflict in society: norms of domination and norms of deference. The power of the dominant class is endangered when their authority depends on their ability to force their will on others or when authority is premised on an egalitarian relationship with the less powerful in society (Turk, 1969).

Turk specifies the two basic conditions under which social conflict is more likely to occur. First, there are marked differences in important cultural values between those with authority and less powerful members of society. Second, the less powerful members of society are well organized and committed to advancing their cause. As conflict increases, so too does the likelihood that certain behaviors will be defined as criminal. Turk outlines two factors that increase the probability of official criminal sanctioning. First, behavior is more likely to be officially sanctioned when the agents of law enforcement consider it to be a significant criminal offense. Police officers may exercise their discretion not to make an arrest in matters involving minor transgressions, particularly victimless offenses. If the police and the agents of the court—the prosecutors and judges—agree that legal action is necessary to control the criminal behavior and to ensure public safety, then the offender is more likely to be arrested, prosecuted, and officially sanctioned by the courts. Second, the criminal transgressions of the less powerful in society are more likely to be criminalized than those of the more powerful. So-called blue-collar offenses—burglary, robbery, assault, and battery—result more often in official legal sanctioning than do white-collar crimes—embezzlement, insider trading, and price-fixing (Turk, 1969).

Richard Quinney points out that the understanding of crime involves two related processes: (1) legally defining certain behaviors as criminal and (2) imposing the label of criminal on those who engage in such behaviors. It is in the interest of the dominant class in a capitalistic system to control the behavior of the working class. Certain contradictions—poverty, inequality, and unemployment—are inherent in a capitalistic economy. These contradictions give rise to deviant and criminal behaviors among the working classes that justify the institution of repressive means of social control (Quinney, 1977).

The legal order of the state is intended to further the interests of the corporate and business elite, the owners of the means of production. Criminal and deviant behaviors are social constructions fabricated by the dominant economic class to control the working masses. Richard Quinney's theory of the *social reality of crime* focuses on the processes involved in defining certain behaviors as criminal by the political and economic elite, the inevitability of involvement in criminal activities by the disadvantaged in society, and official sanctioning of offenders. In sum, the social construction of crime and deviance is essential to the perpetuation of interests of the dominant classes. By focusing the attention of the justice system on certain kinds of offenses, the criminal activities of the political and corporate elite are typically disregarded or litigated in civil rather than criminal courts.

Alex Thio (1978) sets forth a power theory of deviance. He contends that deviance may be viewed along a range of lower to higher consensus acts. *Consensus* refers to the generally accepted judgment about the seriousness of a deviant act. Thio hypothesizes that the higher the consensus, the less the ambiguity about the potential or actual harm that results from the deviant behavior. Conversely, he argues the lower the consensus, the greater the ambiguity about the seriousness of the deviance.

Thio (1978, pp. 81–86) summarizes his power formulation in three propositions:

1. The more power people have, the more likely they will engage in lower consensus deviance—the "less serious," more profitable, or the more sophisticated type of deviance—with lower probability of being labeled deviant. The more powerful members of society are able to influence the processes involved in criminalizing behaviors and in the enforcement of criminal statutes. As a consequence, the powerful focus political and media attention on certain forms of deviance and divert attention from others.
2. It is more likely that the powerful will engage in lower consensus deviance and the powerless will commit higher consensus deviance. The powerful have opportunities to commit a wide range of economic and fraudulent crimes that are not available to the powerless. Because these offenses are largely "hidden" from public view, they are rarely included in official governmental report on criminal activity. Given vastly greater opportunities to engage in clandestine criminal activity,

Thio contends that the powerful commit disproportionately more crime than the powerless.

3. Deviance by the powerful induces deviance by the powerless that, in turn, contributes to deviance by the powerful. The pervasiveness of the exploitive behavior of the powerful, their flagrant disregard for the welfare of the less fortunate, and their expedient sense of morality prompt acts of rage or low-profit property offenses (typically displaced on available targets). The offenses of the powerless routinely draw attention from the media and elicit a punitive response from the powerful. The wanton acts of the powerless provide the powerful with justification for their self-serving deviance.

More recently, the conflict perspective has been extended to include consideration of family dynamics and issues related to gender. **John Hagan** (1989a) seeks to understand the link between social class and criminal behavior. More specifically, Hagan conceptualizes social class in terms of *power relations*. Social class distinctions imply varying degrees of social power. And power, Hagan argues, must be understood in relational terms. The concept of social class then is understood in the context of the social organization of work. Workers are organized along the lines of their relationship to ownership and authority. The social class of workers is defined by the extent to which they own a business, say, or can exercise authority over other workers. Hagan (1989a, p. 4) notes that "owners

Quinney's Social Reality of Crime

- PROPOSITION 1 Crime is a definition of human conduct that is created by authorized agents in a politically organized society.
- PROPOSITION 2 Criminal definitions describe behaviors that conflict with the interests of the segments of society that have the power to shape political policy.
- PROPOSITION 3 Criminal definitions are applied by the segments of society that have the power to shape the enforcement and administration of criminal law.
- PROPOSITION 4 Behavior patterns are structured in segmentally organized society in relation to criminal definitions, and within this context persons engage in actions that have relative probabilities of being defined as criminal.
- PROPOSITION 5 Conceptions of crime are constructed and diffused in the segments of society by various means of communication.
- PROPOSITION 6 The social reality of crime is constructed by the formulation and application of criminal definitions, the development of behavior patterns related to criminal definitions, and the construction of criminal conceptions.

Source: Quinney, R. (1970). *The Social Reality of Crime.* Copyright © 2001 by Transaction Publishers, New Brunswick, New Jersey. Originally published in 1970 by Little Brown & Company.

of businesses and persons of occupational authority are in a position to commit larger crimes than persons located in employee positions without authority."

Hagan (1989b) extends his power-relations concept of social class to an understanding of gender differences in the rates of juvenile offending. The power relations of the parents outside the home influence the balance of power within the family and impact the socialization experiences of the children. When the power relations of the husband outside the home exceed those of his wife, the family tends to be structured along patriarchal lines. In families with a patriarchal family structure there is more concern with controlling the behavior of female children than that of their male siblings. The wider latitude granted boys within a patriarchal family provides greater opportunities for risk-taking and delinquent behaviors.

However, Hagan (1989b) notes that in more egalitarian families where the power relations of husband and wife outside the home are similar—relatively high or low—male and female children are more likely to be socialized in similar ways. That is, neither girls nor boys within the family are controlled more so than the other. Both genders, therefore, have a similar opportunity to engage in delinquent activities. In short, power-relations differentials outside the home affect the balance of power and control within the family. The balance of power control, in turn, serves to structure familial relations either in a patriarchal or egalitarian manner. The structure of the family influences the extent of power and control exerted over the children. Differential socialization experiences of male and female children explain gender differences in juvenile offending (Hagan, 1989b).

Feminism

The **feminist perspective** on crime and deviance is rooted in the conflict view of the social order. Although there is no single feminist theoretical formulation, common themes contribute to the understanding of crime and deviance. Feminist theorists call attention to the gender bias in theorizing and research on criminal and deviant behavior. Most studies of crime and deviance are limited to analyses of male offenders. An *androcentric approach* to the study of deviant behavior has led to the emergence of the feminist perspective, an alternative theoretical understanding of crime and deviance. **Kathleen Daly** and **Meda Chesney-Lind** (1988), leading feminist theorists, note that two issues concern criminologists interested in gender and crime. First, can theoretical formulations and research findings of studies that are limited to male offending be generalized to the participation of women in crime and deviance? Second, what accounts for the disproportionate involvement of men in most forms of criminal and deviant activity?

Feminist theorists address these issues by focusing attention on an understanding of gender in society and its link to criminal and deviant behavior. The feminist view of gender is inextricably tied to gender stratification and its consequences for women in society. *Patriarchy* is seen as the prevailing social structure, in which men hold a dominant position over women and masculine attributes and behaviors are considered to be markedly preferable to feminine ones. A central theme of feminist theorizing is that male dominance permeates all aspects of social life, both conventional and deviant.

Feminist theorists argue that the influence of social class, race, and age on crime and deviance can only be understood in the context of a patriarchal social structure. Social inequities are inherent in social class positioning, ethnicity, and race, and issues related to age influence criminal and deviant behavior and shape the societal response to it. The disadvantages of social class, race, and age, however, exacerbate gender inequality. Gender inequality is then a central condition that runs through social life. Theories of crime and deviance, feminists argue, must be revamped to include consideration of the complex issues related to gender inequities and their consequences (Danner, 1989).

Functionalist Perspective

The **functional perspective** focuses on the purpose, usefulness, or contribution that a given social phenomenon makes to the social order. Over time, recurrent behaviors form patterns that persist, the functionalists argue, because they serve a useful purpose and contribute to the survival of the society. Whereas **Emile Durkheim** (1938) provided the foundation for functionalism in the later part of the 19th century, **Robert K. Merton** (1968), the eminent Columbia University sociologist, most clearly articulated functional analysis of human social behavior. To Merton, functional analysis is limited to patterned and repetitive sociological phenomena—behavioral patterns, social roles, social norms, and processes. Function refers to "observed consequences [of a given patterned and repetitive action] that makes for the adaptation or adjustment of a given system" (Merton, 1968, p. 51). Forms of deviant behavior are, then, patterned and repetitive actions that serve a function for society. Merton identifies two types of functions: manifest and latent. **Manifest functions** refer to "observed consequences [of a given patterned and repetitive action] that make for the adaptation or adjustment of a given system which are intended and recognized by participants in the system" (Merton, 1968, p. 51). **Latent functions,** however, are "observed consequences [of a given patterned and repetitive action] that make for the adaptation or adjustment of a given system which are neither intended nor recognized by participants in the system" (Merton, 1968, p. 51). Conversely, **dysfunctions** refer to "observed consequences [of a given patterned and repetitive action that lessen the adaptation or adjustment of a given system" (Merton, 1968, p. 51).

Covington, P. (1999). Deviance: Functionalist explanations. *The functionalist explanation of crime.* http://www.sociology.org.uk/pcfcri95.pdf

Negative forms of deviance and criminal behavior are not typically thought to contribute to the survival of society. Rather, there is a deliberate effort to control deviant members of society and to prevent the occurrence of any form of prohibitive behavior. Emile Durkheim (1938) advances a radically different view of deviance. His functional approach rejects the notion that crime and deviance are simply pathological but rather are normal occurrences in society. Crime, in one form or another, is a universal phenomenon. Forms of criminality have changed over time, yet Durkheim (1938, pp. 65–66) notes, "everywhere and always, there have been men who have behaved in such a way as to draw upon themselves, penal repression." Criminal behavior offends vital sentiments held in common by members of a society about the ways in which life should be lived. Violation of the basic norms of social life results in a collective response that reaffirms their importance.

Durkheim further contends that a society without crime is not possible. The establishment of social boundaries between what is considered to be "right and wrong" is vital to the functioning of a society. The *collective conscience* of a society is reaffirmed by the ways in which it responds to deviant acts. Collective sentiments form the basis for the normative structure of society. In the absence of generally agreed on norms to guide behavior, social interaction would become unpredictable. The resulting chaos would make social life impossible. Durkheim (1938, p. 70) concludes that, "Crime is, then, necessary; it is bound up in the fundamental conditions of all social life, and by that very fact it is useful, because these conditions of which it is a part are themselves indispensable to the normal evolution of morality and the law."

Social Integration

Emile Durkheim sought to understand why rates of deviant behavior vary among social groups. In his seminal work, *Suicide* (1951), Durkheim argues that two social forces—integration and regulation—explain rates of suicide. By **social integration** Durkheim meant the extent to which persons were bound into social life or, alternatively, isolated from it. A measure of social integration is the level of adherence to a set of common values. Durkheim hypothesizes that the greater the consensus about important beliefs, symbolic significance, and cultural goals, the greater the social integration of the group. *Social regulation* refers to the extent to which individuals are required to follow the guidelines for their behavior established by the group. The greater the social regulation, the clearer and more certain are the norms that govern social interaction. Social integration and regulation tend to complement one another. As social integration rises, so too does social regulation. Individuals hold common values that provide a foundation for the normative structure of society.

Both social integration and regulation can vary between exceedingly high levels in which the interests of the group supersede those of its individual members to exceedingly low levels in which interests of individuals take precedence over those of the group. Social integration and regulation can also change suddenly, leaving the group members without a sense of meaning and direction.

The extent of social integration and regulation, Durkheim argues, is linked with distinct forms of suicides. Durkheim sets forth three basic types of suicide: altruistic, egoistic, and anomic. *Altruistic suicide* is most common in societies characterized by particularly high levels of social integration. Individuals are enmeshed in the collective. If suicide is considered to advance the interests of the group, then its individual members are willing to sacrifice themselves. Conversely, *egoistic suicide* is more probable under conditions of exceptionally low social integration. Individuals tend to act to enhance their own ends; the effect of their behavior on the welfare of others is rarely considered. Few ties exist between individual members and the larger society. There is no sense of collective well-being. *Anomic suicide* is found when there is rapid change in social integration. Rapid social change creates chaos in the normative structure of society. A state of normlessness exists that leaves individuals without effective guidelines for their behavior. The consequence is often a marked increase in self-destructive behaviors. Conditions of extreme social regulation, Durkheim observed, may also lead to *fatalistic suicide*. Fatalistic suicide occurs when individual behavior is overly regulated by others, making personal autonomy unattainable. The loss of freedom of action, and the opportunity for self-actualization, may well lead to a sense of hopelessness and despair.

Robert K. Merton (1968) seeks to advance Durkheim's understanding of anomie and its consequences. In *Social Structure and Anomie* (1968, p. 132), Merton addresses the question of how "some social structures exert a definite pressure on certain persons in the society to engage in non-conforming rather than conforming conduct." Merton contents that most persons are socialized to want the same cultural goals—status, economic reward, social influence—but do not have the institutionalized means to attain them. As a consequence, **anomie**—a fundamental precursor of deviant behavior—may ensue. Merton's (1968, p. 134) "central hypothesis is that aberrant behavior may be regarded sociologically as a symptom of dissociation between culturally prescribed aspirations and socially structured avenues for realizing these aspirations." Anomie is then defined as the dissociation between cultural goals and available means for attaining them.

Anomie is experienced as **strain**, stress, or tension that requires some form of adaptation. Merton outlines a typology of individual adaptations to the condition of anomie in society. This typology offers a means/goals schema for the understanding of individual adaptations to the experience of anomie.

Conformity is the most typical adaptation to a state of anomie. Most persons in society accept the institutionalized means to culturally approved goals. Educational attainment, pursuit of advancement in one's occupation or profession, and community involvement are accepted means to social status and economic rewards. *Innovation* involves the acceptance of the culturally approved goals but a rejection of the institutionalized means to achieving them. Innovators are persons who devise deviant means to acceptable goals. They may engage in negative forms of deviant behavior—theft, drug dealing, or cybercrime—or innovate in a positive way by creating a work of art or by inventing a labor saving device. *Ritualism* refers to the process of lowering one's expectations for success to a level that is readily attainable. Ritualists do not aspire to increasing career advancement and economic gain. Rather, they seek stable employment that provides good benefits and an adequate retirement plan. They avoid risk-taking ventures, seeking only to live within a highly predictable comfort zone. *Retreatism* characterizes persons who reject both the culturally approved goals and the institutionalized means for achieving them. Retreatists choose to withdraw from conventional society and adopt an alternative lifestyle. Illicit drug use and excessive use of alcohol are common among retreatists. Involvement in cults that foster mentally aberrant and self-destructive behaviors is also characteristic of retreatist lifestyles. Finally, *rebellion* marks the rejection of both the institutionalized means and culturally approved goals and the adoption of new means and new goals. Rebels seek to overturn the existing social order and replace it with a new social structure. This may involve the wholesale repudiation of an entire system of government or the establishment of a rebellious subculture within the larger society (Merton, 1968). **Figure 3–1** summarizes these modes of adaptation.

FIGURE 3–1
Typology of Modes of Individual Adaptation
Source: Modified from Robert K. Merton, 1957, *Social Theory and Social Structure,* New York: Free Press, p.140.

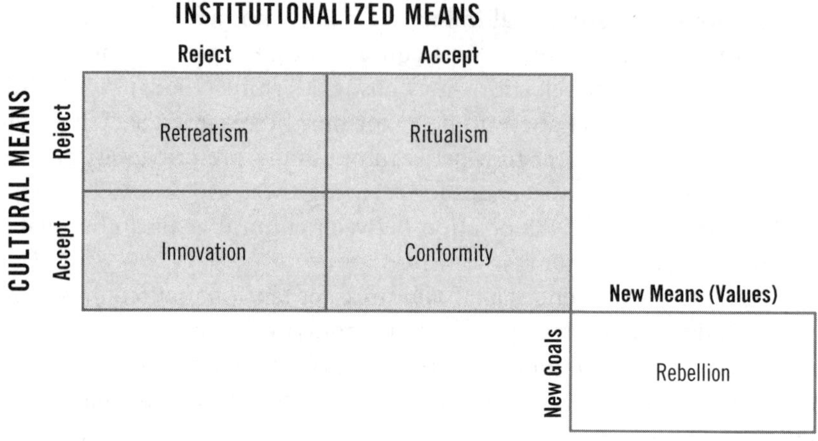

Unlike Robert Merton, **Richard Cloward** and **Lloyd Ohlin** (1960) do not assume an equal access to the means for engaging in delinquent behaviors. Their formulation of differential illegitimate opportunities outlines three subcultures with markedly different patterns of deviance. Each of the three *subcultures*—criminal, conflict or violent, and retreatist—provides its members with different opportunities for criminal activity. *Criminal subcultures* are characterized by opportunities for engaging in crimes of theft, drug dealing, and other forms of profitable illicit activities. Fences are available to convert stolen goods in cash, drug suppliers furnish street dealers with a variety of illicit drugs, and pimps organize the activities of prostitutes. Cloward and Ohlin point out, however, that "would-be offenders" must be accepted into the subculture by proving their criminal skills and ability to work well within the existing organization. *Violent subcultures* develop in areas in which opportunities to profitable criminal activities are not available. Participants in a violent subculture rely on their physical prowess to gain respect and status within the neighborhood. *Retreatist subcultures* are composed of members who do not have opportunities for involvement in a criminal subculture and typically lack the physical ability to gain respect by the use of force or intimidation. Use of mind-altering drugs, involvement in cult rituals, and other forms of oppositional behaviors are characteristic of a retreatist subculture.

More recently, **Robert Agnew** (1992) set forth a strain theory of deviant behavior, based in part on previous conceptions of anomie. To Agnew strain is experienced when aspirations and expectations are not consistently linked with their fulfillment. Typically, the source of strain is negative social interaction, involving blockage by others to the attainment of important needs and goals. Sustained negative social interactions precipitating negative emotions—anger, rage, feelings of worthlessness, and anxiety or depression—may follow. Attempts to alleviate these negative emotions may involve engagement in negative behaviors—verbal or physical aggression or self-injurious behaviors. Strain may also lead to more creative problem-solving strategies. Innovative ways to deal with difficult people may be developed, or alternative paths to goal attainment may be followed (Agnew, 1992).

Chicago School: Social Disorganization

W. I. Thomas and **Florian Znaniecki** (1918) were instrumental in the early formulation of the social disorganization perspective on crime and deviance. Their work on the immigration of polish peasants to Chicago and the subsequent involvement of their children in delinquent behaviors contributed to the development of social disorganization theory. Thomas and Znaniecki observed that the norms for behavior in rural Poland no longer provided adequate guidelines for the everyday life in the city. Competing norms and values created a disorganized existence for Polish adolescents. To Thomas and Znaniecki, **social disorganization** simply meant that the norms for behavior tended to be disregarded by the individual group members. The bonds that existed between the individual and the community in rural Poland were undermined. The Polish community was shattered, no longer able to arrive at a collective solution to their problems.

Clifford Shaw and **Henry McKay** (1969) were instrumental in advancing the social disorganization perspective on crime and deviance. Two questions guided the development of their theoretical formulation. First, why are rates of delinquency markedly higher in some neighborhoods than in others? Second, why do rates of delinquency remain high in certain neighborhoods even when there is a fundamental change in its ethnic and racial makeup? In addressing the first question on the differential rates of delinquency, Shaw and McKay drew on Park, Burgess, and McKenzie's (1928) Concentric Zone Model. These authors observed that five concentric zones characterized Chicago:

- Zone 1, the central business district at the center of the city
- Zone 2, the transitional zone—which housed newly arrived immigrants in deteriorating living conditions, near factories and unused buildings
- Zone 3, the working class area—mostly single family housing units
- Zone 4, residential neighborhoods—in which the middle class lived in single family homes
- Zone 5, the commuter zone—suburban areas that housed the more affluent members of society

Crime and deviance were more commonly found near the center of the city, particularly in zone 2.

Shaw and McKay (1969) found that the transitional zone was characterized by heterogeneity, poverty, and mobility. Heterogeneity refers to a mixture of racial, ethnic, religious, and cultural groups living in the same neighborhood. A sense of community is noticeably absent, persons in the neighborhood are largely strangers, and values and social norms vary considerably across cultural groups. Poverty is pervasive; marginal employment and reliance on welfare is endemic to the area. Mobility of residents is a common occurrence. Individuals and families move from one location to another within the area or move into another part of the city. The continual shifting of the population tends to disrupt everyday life and contributes to the sense of community disorganization and instability. Shaw and McKay argue that it is the interaction of heterogeneity, poverty, and mobility that produces highly disorganized areas. It is within disorganized social environments that crime and deviance thrive.

Shaw and McKay propose a cultural transmission theory to explain the persistence of criminal and deviant patterns of behavior in certain neighborhoods, despite widespread changes in the demographic composition of the residents. Social disorganization is a characteristic of an ecological area—a community or a neighborhood, not necessarily of individuals who reside there. A "differential system of values" within socially disorganized areas may encourage and reward legally prohibited behaviors. Adolescents who move into a socially disorganized neighborhood are exposed to cultural values and social norms that are at odds with conventional society. To Shaw and McKay, **Cultural Transmission Theory** refers to the process by which a differential system of values that supports delinquent behaviors is culturally "passed on" from adolescents currently living in the neighborhood to the more recent arrivals (Shaw & McKay, 1969).

Marvin Wolfgang and **Franco Ferracuti** (1967) sought to explain why violent behaviors tend to be concentrated in certain areas of cities. They observed that most violent behaviors are not well planned but rather are spontaneous acts often prompted by relatively trivial disputes. They advance a subculture of violence thesis to account for disparities in rates of violence and typical forms of violent offending. To Wolfgang and Ferracuti a subculture of violence is characterized by norms and values that support the use of violence to resolve interpersonal conflicts. The willingness to resort to violence is learned, largely unwittingly, by observing everyday interactions in the home or among persons on the street. A violent response in a discordant situation becomes normative—an expectation for behavior. Significant value is place on the ability to act immediately and aggressively to resolve disputes. Failure to do so may well result in widespread ridicule and social isolation.

Walter Miller (1958), an anthropologist, provides insight into the everyday life in a lower class subculture. He observes that six *focal concerns*—trouble, toughness, smartness, excitement, fate, and autonomy—organize the daily life of residents within the inner city. *Trouble* refers to the ongoing difficulties confronted by members of the lower class. Economic insecurity, social rejection, and blockage to needed legal and medical resources compound the problems inherent in the everyday life of the lower class. *Toughness* refers to the emphasis placed on physical prowess and the ability to handle oneself on the street. *Smartness* is translated to mean "street smarts"—the ability to manipulate or to outwit others to one's advantage. *Excitement* in a lower class milieu often involves risk-taking and illicit behaviors. The deadening routine of life on the street is broken by illicit drug use, violence, and theft. *Fate* refers to the belief that most events in life occur randomly, beyond one's ability to influence them. Immediate gratification and a live-for-the-moment mentality guide most decision making. Last, *autonomy* or the desire to act independently from the dictates of others predominates. Freedom of action is highly prized and vigorously pursued. The combined effects of these focal concerns of lower class life markedly increase the likelihood of involvement in criminal and other forms of deviant behavior.

Albert Cohen (1955) provides another explanation of the effects of social class and subcultural participation on delinquent behavior. He argues that two related concepts—status frustration and reaction formation—account for delinquency among lower-class boys. Cohen observes that lower-class boys often are unable to succeed in traditional schools—largely middle-class institutions that expect students to observe definite rules for behavior and decorum. Unable or unwilling to comply with the middle-class values of punctuality, politeness, regard for others' property, and safety, lower-class boys are considered troublemakers, more apt to be disciplined for their behaviors, and excluded from school activities and participation in athletic programs. Unable to gain approval and recognition, lower-class boys experience status frustration. To cope with their status frustration, Cohen argues, they develop a reaction formation to their circumstances. That is, they adopt values that are radically different from those of the middle class. Rather than being on time for school, they are typically late or absent; politeness gives way to loud, unruly behavior; and the property of the school and that of other students is common prey for theft and destruction. In addition, lower-class boys band together in gangs or subcultural groups to provide them with a sense of belonging,

A traditional wrestling match in a dirt field in the Indian city of Nagpur. How might cultural transmission theory apply in the lives of these youths?

approval, recognition, and status denied to them by schools and other middle-class–oriented institutions.

Gresham Sykes and **David Matza** (1957) are less concerned with the social forces that precipitate deviant behavior and more interested in the response of offenders to their own actions. They assume that persons who engage in deviant behaviors suffer a sense of guilt for their behavior. Sykes and Matza want to know how the deviants resolve their feelings of guilt and maintain a positive self-image. They identify five techniques that may be used to justify a deviant act and absolve the offender's guilt. The **techniques of neutralization** are denial of responsibility, denial of injury, denial of the victim, condemnation of the condemners, and appeal to higher loyalties (Sykes & Matza, 1957, pp. 667–669).

Elijah Anderson's *Code of the Street* (1999), an ethnographic account of life on the streets of Philadelphia, provides considerable insight into the dynamics of survival in the inner city. Residents of the inner city are typically not able to rely on the police for protection or the legal system for assistance with resolving disputes. With little faith in law enforcement and the courts, they must rely on an alternative way to ensure their survival. A *Code of the Street* "emerges where the influence of the police ends and where personal responsibility for one's safety is felt to begin" (Anderson, 1999, p. 34).

A key element of the *Code of the Street* is respect. Anderson (1999, p. 33) defines respect as "being treated 'right' or being granted one's 'props' (for proper due) or the deference one deserves." Survival depends on the ability to gain and maintain respect among other residents of the neighbor-

Sykes and Matza's Techniques of Neutralization

- *Denial of responsibility:* Involves the contention that the blame for one's deviant behavior lies with others who have victimized the offender or adverse living conditions.
- *Denial of injury:* Refers to the assertion that the victim was not actually harmed or could well afford any monetary loss that was incurred by committing the offense.
- *Denial of the victim:* Means that any wrong-doing is actually justified on the grounds that the "victim" had been involved in previous injurious acts. Justice has then been served by the act of retribution against the original offender.
- *Condemnation of the condemners:* View that those who would judge the person as deviant are themselves guilty of far worse offenses. Therefore, any attempt to negatively label the person is without merit and should be disregarded.
- *Appeal to higher loyalties:* Means that the deviant rejects the argument of conventional society that he or she is obliged to abide by its laws and moral code. Rather, the offender's loyalties lie with an oppositional subculture or group that often expects the person to engage in criminal or deviant acts.

Source: Sykes, G.M. & Matza, D. (1957). "Techniques of Neutralization: A Theory of Delinquency," *American Sociological Review,* 22: 664–670. American Sociological Association.

Elijah Anderson: On the *Code of the Street*

By the time they are teenagers, most young people have internalized the code of the street, or at least learned to comport themselves in accordance with its rules. . . . the code revolves around the presentation of self. Its basic requirement is the display of a certain predisposition to violence. A person's public bearing must send the unmistakable, if sometimes subtle, message that one is capable of violence, and possibly mayhem, when the situation requires it, that one can take care of oneself. The nature of this communication is determined largely by the demands of the circumstances but can involve facial expressions, gait, and direct talk—all geared mainly to deterring aggression. Physical appearance, including clothes, jewelry, and grooming, also plays an important part in how a person is viewed; to be respected it is vital to have the right look.

Even so, there are no guarantees against challenges, because there are always people around looking for a fight in order to increase their share of respect—or "juice," as it is sometimes called on the street. Moreover, if a person is assaulted, it is essential in the eyes of his "running buddies" as well as his opponents for him to avenge himself. Otherwise he risks being "tried" (challenged) or "rolled on" (physically assaulted) by any number of others. Indeed, if he is not careful, he can lose the respect of his running buddies or "homies" who can be depended on to watch his back in a "jam," the person is vulnerable to being rolled on by still others.

Source: From the *Code of the Street: Decency, Violence, and the Moral Life of the Inner City* by Elijah Anderson.

hood. With respect comes protection from continually being challenged on the street, being provoked into proving one's worth. Those who have not gained respect from others in the neighborhood are subject to unprovoked attacks, both verbal and physical, by anyone who wants to gain personal respect. Respect is a complex, often fragile commodity, difficult to establish and maintain, and once lost is rarely regained.

SSRN

Sharma, R. Peeping into a hacker's mind: Can criminological theories explain hacking? July 12, 2007. http://ssrn.com/abstract=1000446v

Differential Association/Social Learning

The pioneering work of **Edwin Sutherland** (1947), widely regarded as the father of modern criminology, provides a foundation for theories of differential association and social learning. In addition, Sutherland's theory of **differential association** implies that the preexistence of criminal subcultures is essential to the perpetuation of criminal and delinquent behaviors. The central hypothesis of differential association theory is that the greater the interaction with others who advocate the violation of the law, the greater the likelihood that the motives, rationalizations, and techniques for criminal offending will be learned and carried out.

Table 3–1 summarizes the various schools of thought discussed throughout the chapter.

A group of young people "hanging out." How do social learning principles apply to groups like this one?

TABLE 3-1 Theoretical Formulations of Rates of Deviant Behavior

Theoretical Foundations	
Conflict approach	
1. Marx (1844)	*Class Conflict and the Law*
Social integration/anomie	
1. Durkheim (1893)	*The Normal and the Pathological*
2. Durkheim (1897)	*Suicide*
Chicago school: social disorganization	*Cultural and Subcultural Understandings*
1. Thomas and Znaniecki (1918)	*The Concept of Social Disorganization*
2. Shaw and McKay (1942)	*Juvenile Delinquency in Urban Areas*
Differential association/social learning	
1. Sutherland (1947)	*Differential Association*
Early Developments	
Conflict approach	
1. Sellin (1938)	*Culture Conflict and Crime*
2. Turk (1969)	*Crime and the Legal Order*
3. Quinney (1977)	*Class, State, and Crime*
Social integration/anomie	
1. Merton (1938)	*Social Structure and Anomie*
2. Cloward and Ohlin (1961)	*Delinquency and Opportunity*
Chicago school: social disorganization	*Cultural and Subcultural Understandings*
1. Cohen (1955)	*Delinquent Boys*
2. Miller (1958)	*Lower Class Culture*
3. Wolfgang and Farracuti (1967)	*Subculture of Violence*
4. Sykes and Matza (1957)	*Techniques of Neutralization*
Differential association/social learning	
1. Akers (1973)	*Social Learning*
Recent Advances	
Conflict approach	
1. Hagan (1989)	*Power-Control*
2. Daly and Chesney-Lind (1988)	*Feminist Theory*
Social integration/anomie	
1. Agnew (1992)	*A General Strain Theory*
Chicago school: social disorganization	*Cultural and Subcultural Understandings*
1. Anderson (1999)	*Oppositional Culture*
Differential association/social learning	
1. Akers (1998)	*Social Learning and Social Structure*

Sutherland's Nine Propositions of Differential Association

Edwin Sutherland summarizes his theory of differential association in nine propositions:

1. Criminal behavior is learned.
2. Criminal behavior is learned in interaction with other persons in a process of communication.
3. The principal part of the learning of criminal behavior occurs within intimate personal groups.
4. When criminal behavior is learned, the learning includes (a) techniques of committing the crime, which are sometimes very complicated and sometimes very simple; and (b) the specific direction of motives, drives, rationalizations, and attitudes.
5. The specific direction of motives and drives is learned from definitions of the legal codes as favorable or unfavorable.
6. A person becomes delinquent because of an excess of definitions favorable to violation of law over definitions unfavorable to violation of law.
7. Differential associations may vary in frequency, duration, priority, and intensity.
8. The process of learning criminal behavior by association with criminal and anti-criminal patterns involves all the mechanisms that are involved in any other learning.
9. Although criminal behavior is an expression of general needs and values, it is not explained by those general needs and values because noncriminal behavior is an expression of the same needs and values.

Source: From Sutherland, E.H., Cressey, D.R. and Luckenbill, D.F. *Principles of Criminology* 11th edition.

To Sutherland (1947) criminal and deviant behaviors are learned in the same way as other forms of behavior are learned—from close personal association with others. The motive and rationalizations for committing the crime, along with the techniques for its successful execution, are learned from others who encourage criminal offending. The more individuals associate with others who advocate the violation of the law, and the more valued those associations become, the more likely they are to engage in criminal activities. Common need and values, Sutherland observes, do not explain criminal behaviors. The need for status, economic gain, or personal recognition and social influence may either lead to conventional behaviors or to illicit activities. Therefore, they do not provide an adequate explanation of the involvement in crime and delinquency.

Ronald Akers (1998) is largely responsible for the development of a social learning approach to the explanation of deviant behavior. His formulation of social learning considers both the motivation for engaging in deviant acts or conventional behaviors. To Akers, learning deviant or conforming behaviors involves four related processes: *differential association, definitions, differential reinforcement*, and *imitation*. Differential association means interaction with advocates of illicit activities more than with persons who encourage conformist behavior. Definitions refer to the meaning and value given to certain behaviors. Behaviors are not only delimited but are judged to be good or bad, acceptable or unacceptable. Differential reinforcement means that behaviors for which a reward is granted or anticipated will be repeated. The greater the ratio of positive rewards to negative or neutral responses for engagement in a behavior, the more likely it is the behavior will continue. Imitation is the process by which individuals model admired behavior of others. These processes facilitate the learning process that accounts for both deviant and conventional behavior.

A young man gestures to another. What does the theory of differential association say about deviance?

Ronald Akers's Social Learning Approach to Deviance

Sociologist Ronald Akers outlines the processes by which an individual is initiated into criminal or deviant behavior and either continues in or desists from that behavior. He argues as follows:

1. The balance of past and current associations, definitions, and imitation of deviant models and the anticipated balance of reinforcement in particular situations produce or inhibit the initial delinquent or deviant acts.
2. The effects of these variables continue in the repetition of the acts, although imitation becomes less important than it was in the first commission of the act.
3. After initiation, the actual social and nonsocial reinforcers and punishers affect the probability that the acts will be repeated and at what level of frequency.
4. Not only the overt behavior but also the definitions favorable or unfavorable to it are affected by the positive and negative consequences of the initial acts. To the extent that they are more rewarded than alternative behavior, the favorable definitions will be strengthened and the unfavorable definitions will be weakened, and it becomes more likely that the deviant behavior will be repeated under similar circumstances.
5. Progression into more frequent or sustained patterns, rather than cessation or reduction, of criminal and deviant behavior is promoted to the extent that reinforcement, exposure to deviant models, and norm-violating definitions are not offset by negative formal and informal sanctions and norm-abiding definitions.

Source: Akers, R. (1998). *Social learning and social structure* (pp. 53-54). Boston: Northeastern University Press.

Chapter Summary

I. This chapter considers macro-level theories from the conflict and functionalist perspectives.
   A. Conflict theories are premised on the concept of structural inequality. Wealth and power are concentrated in the hands of the bourgeoisie, who use their power to control and exploit the proletariat while manipulating the legal system and other social institutions to their advantage.
   B. Functionalist theories focus on the purpose, usefulness, or contribution that a given social phenomenon makes to the social order.

II. Sociological explanation of behavior discussed in this chapter include
   A. Conflict approach
   B. Social integration
   C. Chicago school of thought: social disorganization, culture, and subcultural understandings
   D. Differential association/social learning

III. Karl Marx provided the foundations for the conflict approach. Other conflict theorists include
   A. Thorsten Sellin
   B. Richard Quinney
   C. Austin Turk
   D. Alex Thio

IV. Advances in the conflict perspective include the power-control theory of John Hagan and the contributions of Kathleen Daly and Meda Chesney-Lind to the feminist understanding of the conflict approach.

V. Emile Durkheim provides a foundation for the functionalist perspective and the theoretical development of the social integration/anomie approach. Notable theorists in the Durkheimian tradition are

A. Robert K. Merton
B. Richard Cloward and Lloyd Ohlin
C. Robert Agnew

VI. The early work of W.I. Thomas and Florian Znaniecki, Clifford Shaw and Henry McKay, and others provide the basis for the perspective sometimes referred to as the Chicago school of thought. The development and more recent advances in the social disorganization theory are indebted to the contributions of

A. Albert Cohen
B. Walter Miller
C. Marvin Wolfgang and Franco Ferracuti
D. Gresham Sykes and David Matza
E. Elijah Anderson

VII. Edwin Sutherland's differential association theory significantly influenced the formulation of social learning theory and the subcultural perspective. Ronald Akers is largely responsible for advancing a social learning approach to the understanding of crime and deviance. The recognition of subcultural variations in the motivation to engage in deviant behaviors and the opportunities to do so run through the theoretical formulations of Albert Cohen, Richard Cloward and Lloyd Ohlin, Marvin Wolfgang and Franco Ferracuti, and more recently the ethnographic work of Elijah Anderson.

Key Names

Karl Marx
W.I. Thomas
Thorsten Sellin
Florian Znaniecki
Austin Turk
Clifford Shaw
Richard Quinney
Henry McKay
Alex Thio
Marvin Wolfgang
John Hagan
Franco Ferracuti
Kathleen Daly
Walter Miller
Meda Chesney-Lind
Albert Cohen
Emile Durkheim
Gresham Sykes
Robert K. Merton
David Matza
Richard Cloward
Elijah Anderson
Lloyd Ohlin
Edwin Sutherland
Robert Agnew
Ronald Akers

Key Concepts

Micro-level analysis: Focuses on social processes and personal characteristics that may account for an individual's involvement in criminal or deviant behavior.

Macro-level analysis: Considers the ways in which structural and cultural characteristics of social collectivities—societies, subcultures, and social groupings—affect crime rates and acts of social deviance.

Feminist perspective: Theoretical perspective on crime and deviance that calls attention to the gender bias in theorizing and research.

Functional perspective: Sociological perspective that focuses on the purpose, usefulness, or contribution that a given social phenomenon makes to the social order.

Manifest functions: Intended consequences of a social action that are recognized by participants in the social system and that benefit a given system.

Latent functions: Consequences of a social action neither intended nor recognized by the participants in the social system but that benefit the system.

Dysfunctions: Consequences of a social action that lessen the adaptation or adjustment of a given social system.

Social integration: The extent to which persons are bound into social life or alternatively isolated from it.

Anomie: Normlessness; the dissociation between cultural goals and available means for attaining goals.

Strain: Stress experienced when aspirations and expectations are not consistently linked with fulfillment.

Social disorganization: Decrease of the influence of existing social rules of behavior on individual members of the group, or the inability of local communities to realize the common values of their residents or solve commonly experienced problems.

Cultural Transmission Theory: Process by which traditions of delinquency are transmitted through successive generations.

Techniques of neutralization: Techniques used to justify a deviant act and absolve the offender's guilt.

Differential association: Term proposed by Edwin Sutherland to describe how individuals socially learn to commit criminal and deviant behavior. Also used by Ronald Akers.

Critical Thinking Questions

1. Rates of deviant behaviors in any given population or subgroup tend to be relatively low. For example, approximately 4 in 100 persons in the general population are involved in a major criminal incident in the United States in a given year. How do theories that explain rates of behavior account for the vast majority of persons who are not involved in criminal or other deviant behaviors?
2. How do social structural arrangements affect social processes that, in turn, account for variations in rates of deviant behaviors?
3. What social and political influences affect the development of theories that explain rates of deviant behaviors? How does the sociopolitical climate shape scientific inquiry into deviant behaviors?
4. What assumptions about society underlie the conflict, functionalist, social disorganization, differential association, and social learning theoretical perspectives?

Web Extra

Web-based media materials from high-quality sources such as CNN, Time, and National Public Radio are available in support of this textbook. Visit go.jblearning.com/deviance to access them.

Homicide

CHAPTER 4

Learning Objectives

After reading this chapter you should know

- The types and definitions of homicide.
- The definitions of assault and battery.
- Trends and patterns in homicide around the world and in the United States.
- Age, gender, and race patterns of homicide.
- Patterns of homicide among special populations.
- The stages of Luckenbill's homicide as a situated transaction.
- The characteristics of victim-precipitated homicide.
- Some of the theories advanced to explain criminal homicide and assault and battery.

In 2010 Stephen Griffiths, a 40-year-old criminology graduate student at Bradford University in northern England, was arrested and charged with the murder of three women (Hui, 2010). At his arraignment Griffiths was asked to give his name, and he responded by identifying himself as "the crossbow killer." Authorities say that Griffiths used a crossbow to kill one of his victims, shooting her in the face with an arrow.

> Is it hard for the reader to believe that suicides are sometimes committed to forestall the committing of murder? There is no doubt of it. Nor is there any doubt that murder is sometimes committed to avert suicide.
>
> —Karl Menninger (www.bartleby.com/63/14/2014.html)

Griffiths, who was unable to make bail, had been researching modern forensics techniques and comparing them with those used by the police over 100 years ago. He was reputed to have a special interest in studying Jack the Ripper. News reports said that in his personal postings on MySpace, Griffiths had described himself as "the misanthrope who brought hate into heaven" (Metro, 2010).

Definition of Criminal Homicide

In this chapter we consider two forms of interpersonal violence: criminal homicide and assault and battery. These two acts of violence are known legally as crimes against the person, ranging from the intentional killing of another human being to the intent to do bodily harm.

In general, **criminal homicide** is the intentional killing of one human being by another without justification or excuse. **Justifiable homicides** include a court-ordered execution of a convicted offender or the killing of an enemy by a member of the military in the line of duty. **Excusable homicides** typically involve the accidental or non-negligent killing of another human being. There is neither intention to kill nor evidence of wrongful or flagrant carelessness on the part of the person who caused the death (Schmalleger, 2002).

Those homicides that are not justifiable or excusable involve the intention of the perpetrator to place another human being in danger of bodily harm or death. Criminal homicide is legally separated into two forms: **murder** and **manslaughter.** Both murder and manslaughter are further divided into first and second degrees of seriousness. Two considerations serve to distinguish the levels of seriousness: premeditation and provocation. **Premeditation** refers to the "act of deliberating or meditating upon, or planning, a course of action" (Schmalleger, 2002, p. 262). Two closely related legal concepts are malice and malice aforethought. **Malice** legally means the "intentional doing of a wrongful act without just cause of legal excuse" (Schmalleger, 2002, p. 262). **Malice aforethought** means "an unjustifiable, inexcusable, and unmitigated person-endangering-state-of-mind" (Schmalleger, 2002, p. 263). Both premeditation and malice aforethought imply a time lapse between the formation of the idea to kill in the mind of the offender and the actual carrying out of the murder. During the time lapse the perpetrator is able to make plans, secure a weapon or strategy for killing the intended victim, and deliberate on the final decision to carry out the killing. Typically, homicides that involve poisoning, lying in wait, and torture are considered first-degree cases.

> A key element in the "Code of the Street" is respect—"being treated 'right' or being granted one's 'props' (or proper due) or the deference one deserves."
>
> —Elijah Anderson (1994, p. 33)

The provocation of the victim is an important consideration when determining the degree of criminal liability in a murder case. **Provocation** of the victim may either be verbal, physical, or both and implies the active involvement of the victim in the lethal encounter. The victim may well have been the first one to use physical force against his or her killer (see Wolfgang's *Victim-Precipitated Homicide* considered later in this chapter). Or the victim may have verbally taunted the offender, thereby contributing to the fatal attack. Murder in the second degree is, in part, distinguished from murder in the first degree by the extent of the victim's provocation.

Similarly, manslaughter involves less premeditation or malice aforethought on the part of the offender and greater victim provocation than either murder in the first or second degree. Again, manslaughter is divided into first and second degree. In some jurisdictions the degrees of manslaughter are known as voluntary or involuntary manslaughter and non-negligent or negligent manslaughter. The most serious form of manslaughter involves some degree of intention on the part of the offender to harm the victim. The assault, however, is typically carried out in a spontaneous act of violence, with little time for deliberation. Street fights or barroom brawls are typical examples of first-degree manslaughter. In many instances the eventual offender could easily have been the victim. Fatal encounters that erupt in the passion of the moment and involve considerable provocation—by the victim and/or offender—are legally processed as first-degree manslaughter cases.

Second-degree manslaughters, however, do not involve the intention to kill or to harm the victim but result from the negligent actions of the offender. A person who is intoxicated or who is operating a motor vehicle illegally (e.g., speeding, carelessly or recklessly) and who causes the death of another may be held liable for second-degree manslaughter. Intentionality and provocation are not at issue in cases of second-degree manslaughter. Rather, the central consideration is the negligent or illicit behavior of the offender.

Definitions of Assault and Battery

Much confusion exists with regard to the meanings of the crimes of assault and battery. Although the two crimes are related, each must be understood as distinct offenses. **Assault** may take either of two forms: (1) an attempt to commit bodily injury to another human being or (2) putting another in fear of imminent bodily injury. The crime of assault implies the present ability to carry out the assault—that is, the assailant must be in the presence of the intended victim. For example, an assault cannot be committed on the telephone or by threatening someone by e-mail. In addition, the assailant must be physically able to carry out the intended injury. The harm to the victim, however, does not need to involve a serious injury. The crime of assault may occur simply by attempting to touch someone in an offensive way (Schmalleger, 2002, p. 291).

Battery refers to the actual offensive touching or unwanted physical contact between the assailant and victim. The contact does not need to result in a physical injury to be considered a battery; simply the lack of consent of the victim to be touched is sufficient. Often, the crimes of assault and battery are linked to refer to an offense that involves the actual physical injury of the victim. The most serious form of assault and battery is aggravated assault. **Aggravated assault** refers to "an assault which is committed with the intention of committing an additional crime, such as assault with intent to commit a felony; assault with intent to commit murder; assault with intent to commit rape, sodomy, mayhem, robbery, or grand larceny; and assault with intent to commit any other felony" (Schmalleger, 1999, p. 293). Dangerous weapons, (e.g., firearms, knives, clubs) or objects that can be used as dangerous weapons, (e.g., rocks or bricks, ropes, belts, or clothing apparel) are typically involved in an aggravated assault. An abbreviation commonly used by law enforcement officers when booking an alleged offender for aggravated assault is **ABWDWWITKRSBI:** **A**ssault and **B**attery **W**ith a **D**eadly **W**eapon **W**ith **I**ntent to **K**ill **R**esulting in **S**erious **B**odily **I**njury. This reflects the essential elements of the crime of aggravated assault and serves to distinguish it from the lesser forms of assault and battery.

Homicide Around the World

Given the publicity that surrounds violence in U.S. society, it is often thought that the United States has the highest murder rate in the world. However, most recent data show that homicide rates in 42 of 121 nations with known homicide rates exceed that of the United States. Colombia's homicide rate (62.7) is the highest in the world, followed by Lesotho (50.7), South Africa (47.5), Jamaica (34.4), Venezuela (33.2), El Salvador (31.5), Guatemala (25.5), and Russia (19.9). The U.S. rate (5.6) is similar to Lebanon's rate (5.7) but less than one-tenth that of Colombia. The lowest rates of homicide across the globe are found in the Sudan (0.3), Egypt (0.4), and Japan (0.5), which is tied with Singapore, Botswana, and Morocco. European countries with rates less than 1.0 include Greece, Denmark, Austria, and Ireland (Photius.com/rankings/murder_rate_of_countries_2000-2004.html).

The United States, however, does have the highest rate of gun-related homicides in the world. In a recent study of gun-related deaths, suicides, and accidents, the Centers for Disease Control and Prevention reports that of the 36 richest nations, the gun-related homicide rate in the United States (14.24) is five to six times higher than in Europe or Australia and New Zealand and 95 times higher than in Asia (Carter, 1998). Put another way, in a recent year 45% of the gun-related deaths in the 36 richest nations in the world occurred in the United States. Other nations with high firearm homicides are Brazil (12.9), Mexico (12.7), and Estonia (12.3). Nations in the Far East and British Isles with the lowest rates include Japan (0.05), South Korea (0.12), Hong Kong (0.14), Mauritius (0.19), Singapore (0.21), England and Wales (0.41), and Scotland (0.54) (Krug, Powell, & Dahlberg, 1998).

SSRN

Mikhail, J. Is the prohibition of homicide universal? Evidence from comparative criminal law. Symposium, *Brooklyn Law Review.* Forthcoming; Georgetown Public Law Research Paper No. 10-21. http://ssrn.com/abstract=1573194

Patterns and Trends in U.S. Criminal Homicide

Figure 4–1 shows that over the past half century the homicide rate in the United States has varied widely, from rates below 5 per 100,000 persons in the general population in the 1950s to rates of about 10 in the beginning of the 1980s and at the end of that decade, and again in the early 1990s. More

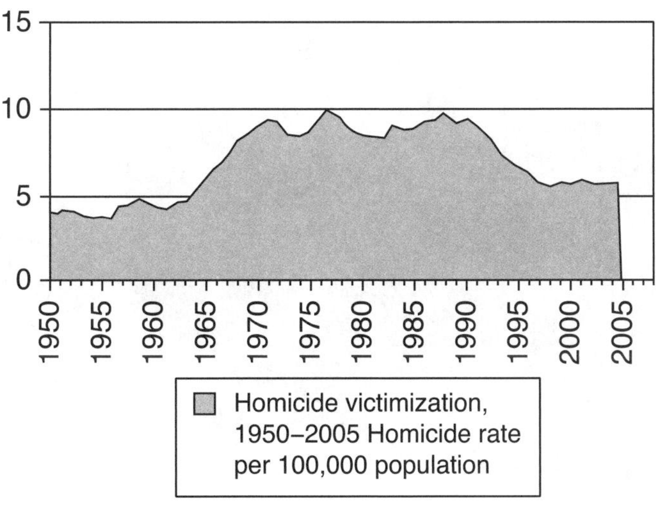

FIGURE 4–1 Homicide victimization in the United States, 1950–2008.

Source: Modified from Bureau of Justice Statistics-Homicide Trends in the United States, and FBI's Uniform Crime Report.

recently, there has been a decline in the homicide rate in the United States. The homicide rates at the turn of the century are similar to homicide rates in the 1960s. The sharp fall in homicide rates that began in the mid-1990s extended through the end of the 20th century. However, at the beginning of the new millennium the homicide rate has remained relatively constant (Fox & Zawitz, 2010).

Homicide rates vary around the country (**Figure 4–2**), from the highest rates (8.8) in Louisiana and Maryland to the lowest rates (below 1) in New Hampshire and North Dakota. Three regions in the United States—New England and states in the West South Central and Mountain regions—have consistently lower rates of homicide. The Pacific and West South Central regions have homicide rates that are above the national average. The Middle Atlantic, East North Central, East South Central, and South Atlantic regions largely follow the national trend (Fox & Zawitz, 2010).

Homicide Rates by Location and Population

Homicide rates also vary among urban, suburban, small cities, and rural areas (**Figure 4–3**). Homicide is disproportionately committed in large

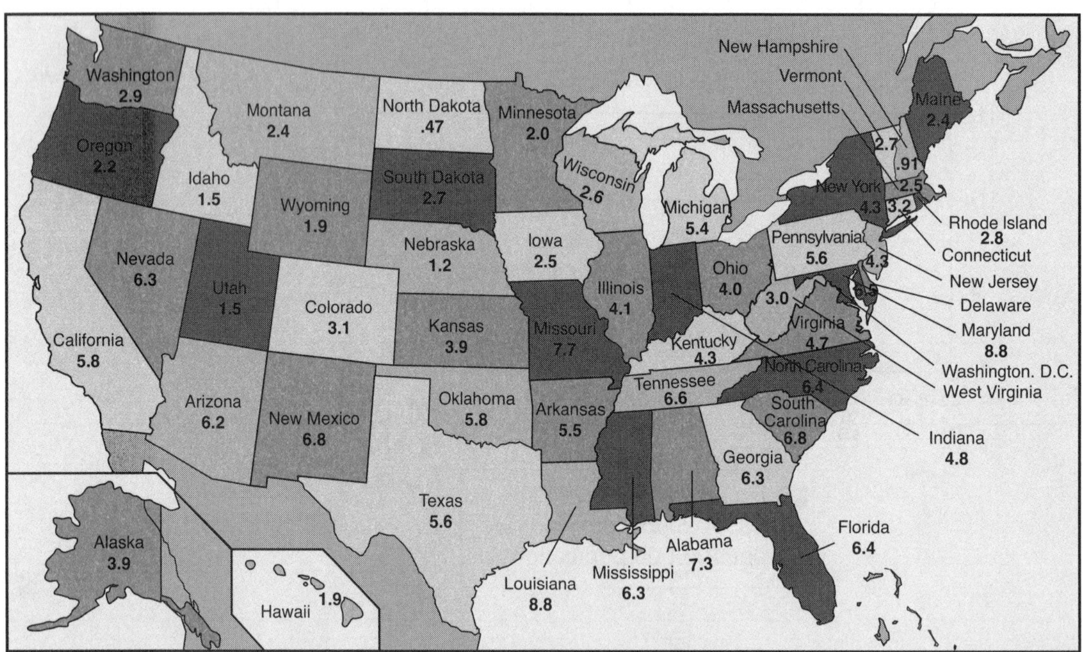

FIGURE 4–2 Homicide rates in the United States by state, 2008.

Source: Data from FBI's Uniform Crime Report.

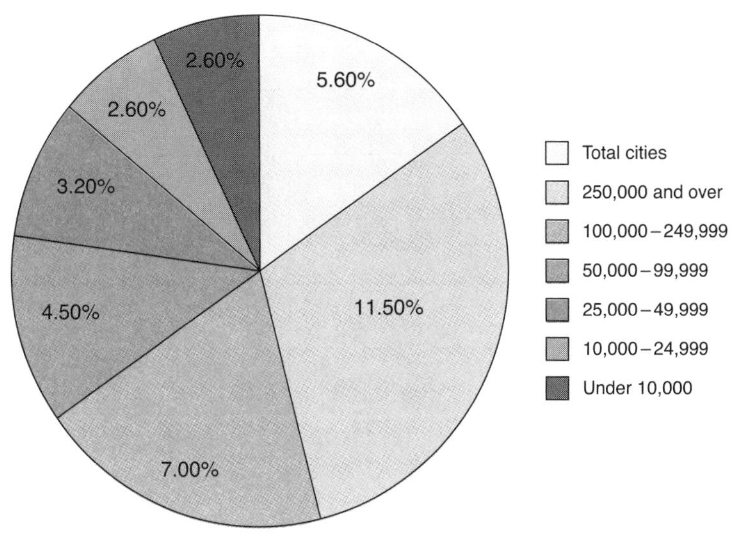

FIGURE 4–3 Homicide by size of place, 2008.
Source: Modified from the FBI's Uniform Crime Report.

urban areas. Rural areas, small cities, and suburban areas have rates well below half of those found in urban areas. Cities of 100,000 residents or more account for one-half of all the homicides committed in the United States; almost one-quarter of the homicides occurred in cities with a million residents or more. Therefore, when homicide rates decline in larger urban places, the rate for the country as a whole falls sharply (Fox & Zawitz, 2010).

Structural Characteristics of Criminal Homicide

Homicide is structured by the age, gender, and race of the offender and the victim. That is, the probability of killing someone or being killed is influenced by these basic structural characteristics of the individual. We consider the patterns of homicide by age, gender, and race separately and then discuss their combined effects (Fox & Zawitz, 2010).

Age and Gender

For both males and females, homicide victimization (**Figure 4–4**) and offending (**Figure 4–5**) is most likely to occur between the ages of 20 and 34 and second most likely to occur between the ages of 35 and 49. Persons at the extremes of the age spectrum—those aged 65 years or older and 12 or younger—are the least likely to murder or to be murdered (Fox & Zawitz, 2010; Uniform Crime Report, 2008).

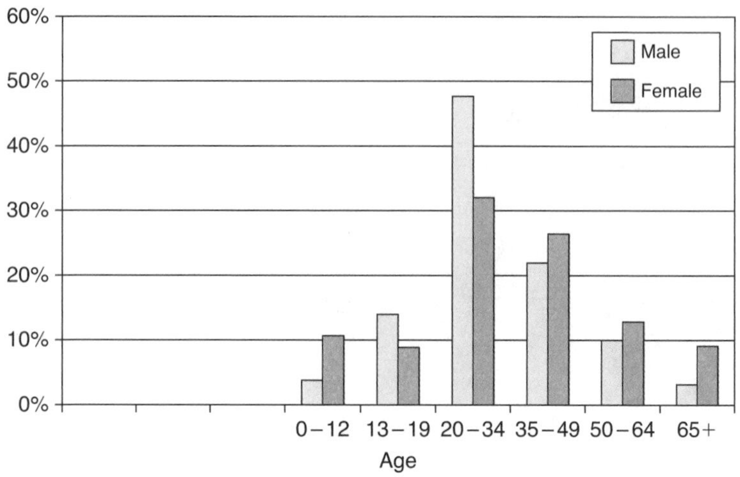

FIGURE 4–4 Homicide victimization by gender and age as a percent of total homicides, 2008.
Source: Modified from the FBI's Uniform Crime Report.

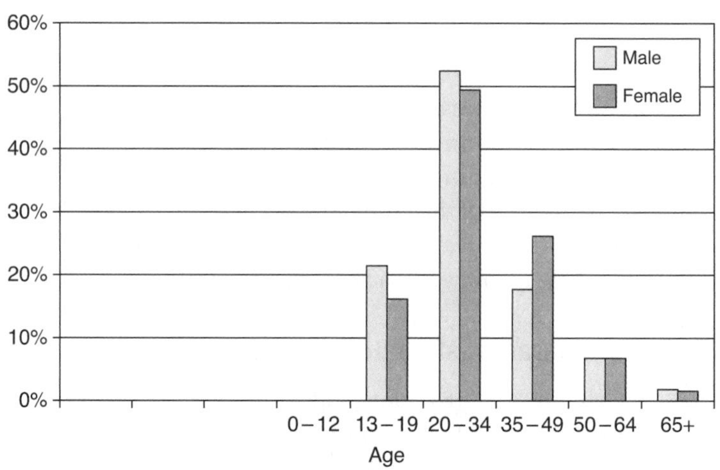

FIGURE 4–5 Homicide offending by gender and age as a percent of all homicide arrests, 2008.
Source: Modified from the FBI's Uniform Crime Report.

Males are far more likely to commit homicide or to be a victim of homicide than females. Males typically commit about 9 in every 10 homicides in the United States and account for about 3 in every 4 of its victims (**Figure 4–6**). The most recent data show that males are nine times more likely to commit murder and four times more likely to be murdered than females.

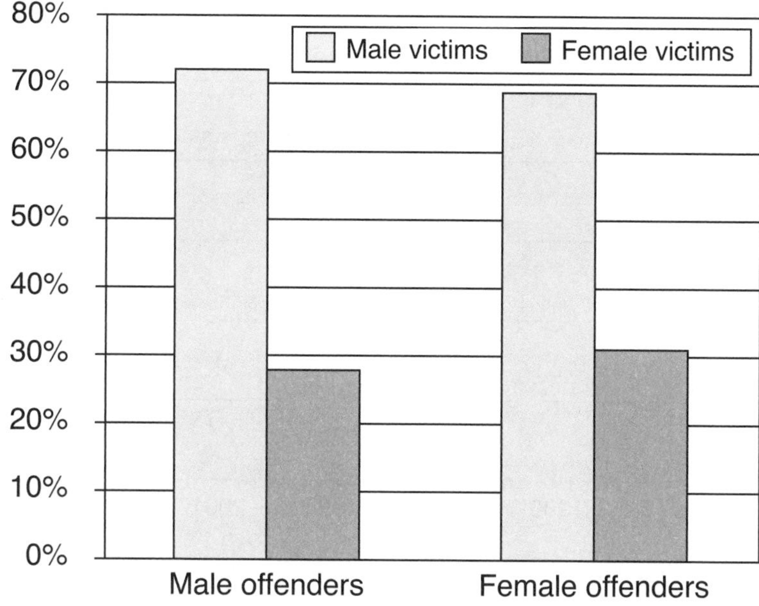

FIGURE 4–6 Gender of homicide offender by gender of homicide victims, 2008.
Source: Modified from the FBI's Uniform Crime Report.

The predominant gender pattern in homicides is male-on-male homicide, while female-on-female murder is least likely to occur. About 2 in every 3 homicides involve a male offender and a male victim. Slightly more than 1 in 5 involves a male offender and a female victim, and 1 in 10 involves a female offender and male victim. Only 2.4 times in every 100 homicides will a female kill another female. Compared to men, women are more likely to be killed by an intimate partner or in a sex-related offense (Fox & Zawitz, 2010).

Race

Although Black involvement in homicide exceeds that for Whites, they tend to follow similar trends over time. It is the case, however, that Blacks in the United States are seven times more likely to commit murder and six times more likely to be murdered than are Whites (**Figure 4–7**). Criminal homicide is predominately intraracial. Black offenders are responsible for 94% of the homicidal deaths of Black victims, and White offenders are responsible for 86% of White homicide victims (**Figure 4–8**). Interracial homicide is most likely to involve strangers (25%), about three times more likely than the murder of a friend or acquaintance (Fox & Zawitz, 2010).

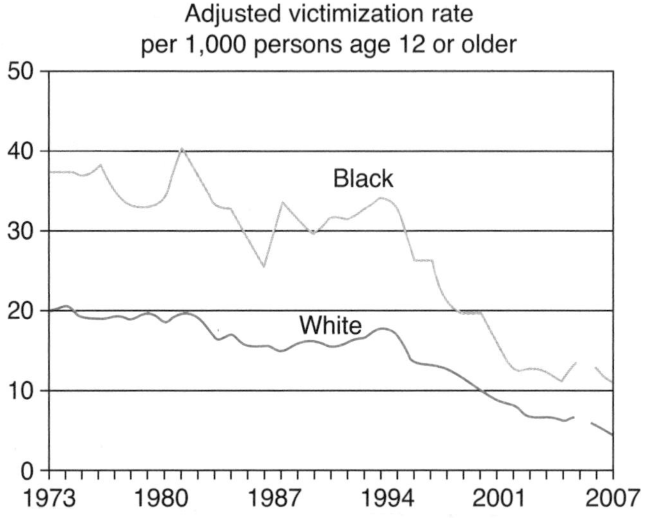

FIGURE 4–7 Violent crime rates by race of victim, 1973–2007.

Source: Reproduced from the Bureau of Justice Statistics.

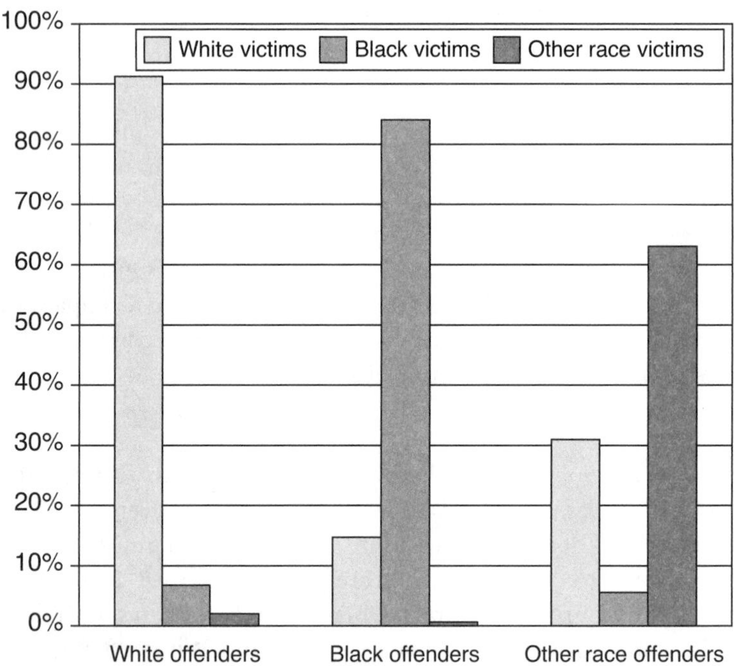

FIGURE 4–8 Homicide victimization by race, 2008.

Source: Modified from the FBI's Uniform Crime Report.

A police officer talks with a supervisor at the site of a homicide. Why is the American homicide rate so high relative to many other countries?

A drug-related killing in Mexico. Is it likely that Mexican drug violence will spread to the United States?

Victim–Offender Relationship

Most homicide offenders and victims are known to each other. The offenders and victims are strangers in only 12.3% of the homicides in the United States. Friends and acquaintances are involved in murder 30.5% of the time, more so than all other relationships combined, except those that cannot be determined (44.2%). Since the turn of the century, the unknown relationship homicides have risen sharply (Uniform Crime Report, 2008).

Elderly

The elderly are far less likely to be involved in criminal activity either as an offender or victim than are younger persons. About 1 in 20 homicides claims the life of an elderly person. The homicide victimization rate for persons over 65 is 2 per 100,000 persons in this age category, whereas the rate of offending is less than 1 per 100,000.

As with younger persons, the risks of homicide victimization vary widely by gender and race. The rate of homicide victimization is twice as high for older males (4 per 100,000) than it is for older females (2 per 100,000). Elderly Black homicide victimization rates (12 per 100,000) are six times higher than that of older Whites and four times higher than other racial groups combined (Klaus, 2000).

Children and Adolescents

Since the mid-1970s the homicide rate of children under the age of 5 has remained remarkably stable for Whites but has declined markedly for Blacks and less so for other racial groups (Fox & Zawitz, 2010). About 1,600 children and adolescents are murdered in the United States each year. With a rate of 3.0 per 100,000 for persons under the age of 18, the

United States ranks first among developed nations in child and adolescent homicide (Snyder & Sickmund, 2006). Excluding the victimization of infants, children and adolescents are twice as likely to be murdered in the United States than in the developed nation with the next highest child homicide rate and five times more likely to be murdered than in the other 25 developed countries combined. Over the later third of the 20th century, all causes of death of children have declined, except homicide (World Health Organization, 1995).

Homicide at a Glance

Global Patterns and Trends

Countries with the highest murder rates (victims per 100,000 persons per year) are as follows:

- South Africa 125.9
- Colombia 114.5
- Guatemala 43.9
- Thailand 41.4
- Paraguay 19.3
- Mexico 17.7
- Belarus 13.4
- Lithuania 12.2
- Zimbabwe 11.9
- Estonia 11.9
- Latvia 11.2
- Barbados 10.4
- Ukraine 9.2
- United States 9.1

Countries with the lowest murder rates are as follows:

- Sudan 0.3
- Egypt 0.4
- Japan 0.5 (tied with Singapore, Botswana, Morocco, and Madagascar)
- Hong Kong 0.6 (tied with the United Arab Emirates and Oman)

U.S. Patterns and Trends

- Homicide and assault and battery victimization and offending rates are highest in larger cities with populations above 500,000. Rural areas have the lowest rates of violent crime.
- Minorites—African Americans, Native Americans, and Hispanics—are disproportionately represented among victims and offenders of homicide and assault and battery. For example, African Americans are seven times more likely than Whites to be murdered and eight times more likely than Whites to commit homicide.
- Homicide and assault and battery typically involve male offenders and male victims.
- Violent crime victimization and offending varies across the age spectrum. The rates increase through the teenage years, crest in the early twenties, and steadily decrease through the remaining years. With few exceptions, this pattern exists for all race, gender, and ethnic groups.

Sources: Reproduced from the Bureau of Justice Statistics and Nationline, "Overall Homicide Rate per 100,000 pop.," http://www.nationmaster.com/graph/cri_gun_vio_hom_ove_hom_rat_per_100_pop-rate-per-100-000-pop. (Accessed March 1, 2011).

Homicide ranked as the fourth leading cause of death for children between 1 and 11 years old and the third leading cause of death for adolescents between 12 and 17 years old (Snyder & Sickmund, 2006, p. 20). About 1 in 10 homicide victims in the United States is 18 years of age or younger, about one-third are females, and 47% are Black. A firearm is used more than half the time, making it the most usual weapon involved in adolescent homicide. Victims most often know their perpetrators: somewhat less than 4 in 10 are family members, 47% are acquaintances, and 15% are strangers (Finkelhor, 1997; Finkelhor & Ormrod, 2001a).

EARLY CHILDHOOD. There are distinct differences in homicide victim–offender relations found in early childhood, in the middle years, and in adolescence. The rate of early childhood homicide victimization is 2.6 per 100,000. Boys are somewhat more likely to be killed than are girls (54% vs. 46%), but males are considerably more likely than females to be offenders (58% vs. 42%). However, when the victim is an infant in the first 6 days of life, two-thirds of the time the homicide offender is the mother.

Family members kill young children more than 7 in 10 times, usually by battering them with their hands or feet or strangling or suffocating them. Children under the age of 1 are particularly vulnerable to suffocation (Finkelhor, 1997; Finkelhor & Ormrod, 2001a).

MIDDLE CHILDHOOD. Rates of homicide victimization in the middle childhood years (6 to 11) are the lowest of any age group in the United States (0.6 compared with 2.2 for persons 65 and over). Family members commit about 6 in 10 of these murders, half the time with a gun. Half the offenders are over the age of 30, and one in eight are unknown to the victim. A variety of circumstances surrounds the murder of children in the middle years, including acts of pedophilia, gang murders, negligent homicide by persons playing with guns, and felony murders (Finkelhor, 1997; Finkelhor & Ormrod, 2001a; Snyder & Sickmund, 2006).

ADOLESCENT YEARS. In the adolescent years homicide increases dramatically and is markedly different from the victimization of younger persons. Homicide in the teen years is 10% higher than for persons at any other age. Patterns of victimization among teens tend to resemble those of adults. About 8 in 10 of the victims and 95% of the offenders are male, 86% of the homicides are committed with a firearm, but only 1 in 11 involves a family member as the offender. Other teens or young adults are responsible for killing two of every three adolescents in the United States (Finkelhor, 1997; Finkelhor & Ormrod, 2001a; Snyder & Sickmund, 2006).

JUVENILE OFFENDERS. Juveniles are more likely to commit homicide with other persons than are older offenders. In a given year about 1,300 homicides are attributed to juvenile offenders in the United States; somewhat more than half the time juveniles were the sole offender and about 4 in 10 times they acted with an adult (Snyder & Sickmund, 2006).

About 82% of juveniles who commit homicide are male, 46% are Black, and more than 8 in 10 are between 15 and 17 years of age. Marked gender and age differences in the choice of victims are also found. Male juvenile homicide offenders are most apt to kill an acquaintance or a stranger and least likely to kill a family member. Female juvenile homicide offenders, however, are most likely to kill within the family and least likely to victimize a stranger (Snyder & Sickmund, 2006).

Most juvenile homicide offending is intraracial. Overall, more than 8 in 10 of the juvenile homicides involve offenders and victims of the same race or ethnic group. About 9 in 10 times young White offenders victimize another White, and 76% of the time a Black offender will choose a Black victim (Snyder & Sickmund, 2006).

ASSAULT AND BATTERY OF CHILDREN. Analyses of the National Crime Victimization Survey and other data on the criminal victimization of children by David Finkelhor, Director of the Crimes Against Children Research Center at the University of New Hampshire, and his colleagues (Finkelhor & Ormrod, 2001b) reveal several striking findings. With the exception of criminal homicide, juveniles (aged 12 to 17) are more than twice as likely to be victimized by crime than are adults.

Homicide as a Situated Transaction

In many cases a conflict between two persons begins with verbal taunts, accusations, or threats and escalates into battery, serious injury, or death. David Luckenbill (1977) views this process as a *situated transaction* in which either person may ultimately become the victim or the offender. Luckenbill describes a six-stage process that ends in homicidal death. In the first stage, the eventual offender perceives the victim's actions or verbal communication to be offensive or to compromise his or her sense of respect from important others. In the offender's view the behavior of the victim is intended to provoke an immediate reaction. In stage two, the offender relies on bystanders to confirm his or her judgment about the derogatory behavior of the victim. The offender then responds in stage three with a demand that the victim stop the provoking behavior and makes it clear that action will be taken if the antagonistic behavior does not stop. In stage

Wrong Place, Wrong Time

John Rich, M.D., the author of *Wrong Place, Wrong Time* and an innovator in violence prevention among the young, asked Jimmy, an adolescent victim whom he was mentoring, why violence is so commonplace among people he knows. The young man replied as follows:

> It's like this: Everybody's trying to ill these days . . . . everybody is trying to make a rep for themselves, you know what I am saying? That's what I did, running around busting mad caps—shooting guns.
>
> When I go around my neighborhood, I'm known by everybody. Everybody knows me. People don't like to be nobodies these days, they like to be somebody or try to be somebody.

Another of Dr. Rich's mentees explained Jimmy's answer:

> Think about it: those who can't be famous settle on being infamous. If you can't respect me, then fear me. So if they don't acknowledge his humanity and he ain't allowed to exist among the respect community, then he'll be a part of the fear community (pp. 48 and 60).

In the end, Dr. Rich concluded the following:

> . . . being known kept their enemies at bay. Being respected was a form of self-defense.
>
> . . . since Jimmy used violence to gain street credibility and become *somebody*, the person who wounds or kills Jimmy will gain street cred. Thus the continuity of violence, havoc, death in the streets of the inner cities (p. 65).

Source: John A. Rich, *Wrong Place, Wrong Time: Trauma and Violence in the Lives of Young Black Men.* Baltimore, MD: Johns Hopkins University Press, 2009.

four the offender continues to convey to the victim the possible dire consequences of the victim's taunting. Preparation for combat occurs in stage five when the offender or victim produces a weapon or finds one at the scene. The situated transaction now escalates into a violent confrontation, which results in the death of the victim. The homicidal process ends in stage six when the offender either leaves the scene or is detained by witnesses.

SSRN

Fontaine, R. G. (2009). The wrongfulness of wrongly interpreting wrongfulness: Provocation interpretational bias and heat of passion homicide. *New Criminal Law Review, 12*(1), p. 69. http://ssrn.com/abstract=1087820

To Luckenbill, homicide involves a dynamic series of interactions between the victim and the offender. The victim is an active participant in the commission of a homicide. Interpersonal conflicts are common occurrences; homicide and assault and battery are by contrast far less usual. It is important, therefore, to understand the dynamic interplay between persons who engage in conflict-ridden interactions and how the process by which verbal taunting and physical gesturing culminates in homicidal death. Cultural and ecological considerations also help us to understand the dynamics of homicide. In Luckenbill's study, he found that witnesses were present in 70% of the homicides, in 36% of the cases the offender was armed before the altercation with the victim, and 42%

of the homicides occurred in public places (bars and taverns, streets, and informal gathering places).

SSRN

Stubbs, J., & Tolmie, J. (2005). Defending battered women on charges of homicide: The structural and systemic versus the personal and particular. In W. Chan, D. E. Chunn, & R. Menzies (Eds.), *Women, mental disorder and the law.* London: Glasshouse Press, pp. 191–210. http://ssrn.com/abstract=984164

Victim-Precipitated Homicide

Marvin Wolfgang (1958) introduced the concept of victim-precipitated homicide while studying patterns of criminal homicide in Philadelphia. **Victim-precipitated homicide** means that the victim was the first one to use physical force against the person who ultimately became the homicide offender. Wolfgang determined that victim-precipitated homicide occurs in 26% of all cases of criminal homicide. If verbal aggression were included in the definition of victim-precipitated homicide, it is likely that the victim would have provoked more than half of all intentional and unjustifiable killings.

SSRN

Stubbs, J., & Tolmie, J. (2008). Battered women charged with homicide: Advancing the interests of indigenous women. *Australian & New Zealand Journal of Criminology, 41*(1), pp. 138–161. http://ssrn.com/abstract=1330723

Theories of Criminal Homicide, Assault, and Battery

As with suicide, theories applicable to the understanding of criminal homicide, assault, and battery can be considered on two levels of analysis: macro, or the societal or group level, and micro, or the individual level. When we seek to explain and predict rates of criminal homicide and assault and battery, we use macro-level theories of analysis. However, when we are interested in understanding individual behavior, we use micro-level theories of analysis. **Table 14–1** shows the theories, social predictors, and hypotheses of homicide and assault and battery.

An assault in progress. Which of the various theories of assault found in this chapter best explains street-level violence?

TABLE 4-1 Explanations of Homicide, Assault, and Battery Rates

Theories and Theorists	Sociological Predictors	Hypotheses
Integration		
Henry and Short	Prestige	Homicide, assault, and battery increase as the status (prestige) of individuals diminishes.
	External restraints	Homicide, assault, and battery increase as the strength of external restraints increases.
	Relational system	Homicide, assault, and battery increase as the strength of the relational system increases.
Merton	Anomie	The greater the level of anomie, the greater the possibility of homicide, assault, and battery.
Social Disorganization		
Wilson	Concentration of poverty	Neighborhoods characterized by concentrations of poverty experience higher homicide, assault, and battery rates.
Opportunity and Subculture		
Cloward and Ohlin	Opportunity	Individuals who cannot gain access to legitimate opportunity for success seek entrance to illegitimate structures for violence.
		Participation in violent opportunity structures increases the probability that the individual will commit homicide, assault, and battery.
Wolfgang and Ferracuti	Subcultures for violence	Where deprivation of economic goods is great, subcultures of violence develop.
		Participation in subcultures of violence increases the acceptance of subcultural customs and values for violence as a response to frustrating conditions.
		Acceptance of such values increases the likelihood for committing homicide, assault, and battery.
Miller	Focal concerns of the lower class: Toughness	The greater the acceptance of the focal concerns, the greater the probability of violent behavior.
		Smartness Excitement Fate Autonomy
Sutherland	Differential association	Individuals who are exposed to definitions favorable toward homicide and assault and battery are more likely to commit these offenses.

/ continues

TABLE 4–1 Explanations of Homicide, Assault, and Battery Rates / continued

Theories and Theorists	Sociological Predictors	Hypotheses
Social Bonding and Control		
Hirschi	Attachment	The weaker the attachment to conventional society, the more likely the individual will commit homicide, assault, and battery.
	Commitment	The weaker the commitment to conventional society, the more likely the individual will commit homicide, assault, and battery.
	Involvement	The greater the involvement in conventional activities, the less likely the individual will commit homicide, assault, and battery.
	Belief	The stronger the belief in conventional values and norms, the less likely the person will commit homicide, assault, and battery.
Gottfredson and Hirschi	Self-control	Individuals with high self-control will be less likely to engage in homicide, assault, and battery.
Agnew	Strain/stress	The greater the strain, the greater the negative emotional reaction.
		The greater the negative emotional reaction, the more likely an individual will commit homicide, assault, and battery.
Routine Activity		
Cohen and Felson	Suitable targets Motivated offender Guardians	Homicide, assault, and battery are likely to occur when there is a suitable target, a motivated offender, and a lack of capable guardians.
Frustration-Aggression		
Dollard and colleagues	Frustration Aggression	High levels of frustration increase levels of aggression.
		Increased levels of aggression are likely to result in homicide, assault, and battery.
Palmer	Unreciprocity	Unreciprocity increases levels of frustration.
		Increased levels of frustration result in high levels of aggression.
		This increased aggression is likely to result in homicide, assault, and battery.

Social Integration

Emile Durkheim's *Suicide* (1951) provides the foundation for Andrew Henry and James Short's (1954) theory of homicide and suicide. Three key variables—status, strength of the relational system, and external restraint—

serve to explain and predict homicide and, by extension, assault and battery. Status refers to the influences one has over decisions made by members of a given social group or collectivity. The strength of the relational system is measured by the involvement in networks of social relationships. External restraint refers to the extent to which a person is required to conform to the demands and expectations of others.

Henry and Short hypothesize that as status decreases, the strength of the relational system increases along with external restraints on behavior. Lower status persons are more involved with others, either with neighbors in crowded residential areas or with fellow employees in production and assembly line work, or in other group work settings. As the proximity of others increases, so too does the likelihood of interpersonal conflict and group discord. Lower status also denotes relative powerlessness. That is, lower status persons are often told what to do and when and how to do it; rarely are they able to demand that others carry out their wishes. The inability to influence much of their lives is exceedingly frustrating for lower class persons. Simply put, two social conditions follow from being positioned in the lower strata. First, as status decreases, the probability of interpersonal conflict increases. Second, as status decreases, external restraints increase, resulting in elevated levels of frustration. Henry and Short hypothesize that both of these social conditions increase the probability of criminal homicide and, arguably, related forms of interpersonal violence.

Robert K. Merton (1968) also draws on Durkheim's formulation of integration, with particular focus on his concept of anomie or normlessness. To Merton, anomie is a social condition that is obtained when institutionalized means do not lead to the attainment of culturally approved goals. For example, when completing an educational program does not result in getting a job or when full-time employment does not provide sufficient income to pay one's bills, a condition of anomie is said to exist. As explored in Chapter 3, Merton identified five adaptations to the condition of anomie: conformity, innovation, ritualism, retreatism, and rebellion. Two adaptations—innovation and rebellion—are particularly applicable to criminal homicide and assaultive behavior. *Innovation* refers to the acceptance of culturally approved goals (e.g., money, status, power) but the rejection of the institutionalized means for attaining them. Innovators may use forms of coercion to gain status within a group; physical force may be used to establish power and dominance over others. Money and material possessions may be taken from others by force.

To Merton, *rebellion* occurs when both the institutionalized means and culturally approved goals are rejected and replaced by alternative means and goals. In a sense rebellion involves overturning the existing social structure and developing a new order. This new order makes possible the violent acquisition of an infamous, threatening social status. Examples of rebellion fall along a continuum from large-scale political revolutions to the actions of Neo-Nazi and other White supremacist and hate groups.

Social Disorganization

William Wilson (1987) and others advanced a social disorganization formulation to account for violent behavior, particularly among African Americans in the inner city. To Wilson, the concentration of poverty is key to the understanding of social disorganization within certain sectors of large urban areas. Poverty is endemic among urban African Americans; 38% of extremely poor African Americans live in the worst inner city neighborhoods, compared with 7% of extremely poor Whites in the United States (Sampson & Wilson, 1995). These neighborhoods are physically dilapidated areas characterized by high unemployment with few opportunities for job training or employment prospects. A sense of fatalism hangs in the air, and living for the moment is common and intensified. Minor misunderstandings or perceived affronts may quickly escalate into violent altercations. Unable to obtain desired material goods (e.g., clothes, jewelry, etc.) legitimately, they are simply taken by force if necessary.

Elijah Anderson's (1999) investigation of life on the streets in Philadelphia provides considerable insight into daily interactions within the inner city. In his *Code of the Street* (Anderson, 1999), Anderson describes in detail the interplay between the social conditions that characterize interactions among the residents of a largely African American neighborhood and the negotiations that are made between the residents and the larger Philadelphia society. Key to the understanding of the *Code of the Street* is the issue of respect. Anderson defines respect as being treated "right" or being granted one's "props" (for proper due) or the deference one deserves (Anderson, 1999, p. 33). Within the street culture, respect is a critical component of social capital, an insulator against being bothered by others or provoked into altercations. The absence of respect from others means that one is always subject to being victimized, being verbally or physically harmed, or having goods stolen or destroyed. Subtle forms of being shown disrespect, or being dissed—for example, prolonged eye contact—increase the risk of further disgrace. Respect is a fragile commodity, difficult to gain and to keep. It must be carefully negotiated and guarded.

The interactional dynamics that surround the quest for respect often lead to violent street encounters. Physical prowess is admired and a basis for respect. Challenges from others are common, and physical violence is often required to maintain respect. Any sign of weakness or unwillingness to confront assailants results in the loss of respect. When respect is

The Code of the Streets

At the heart of the code is the issue of respect—loosely defined as being treated "right," or granted the deference one deserves.

In street culture, especially among young people, respect is viewed as almost an external entity that is hard-won but easily lost, and must constantly be guarded. The rules of the code in fact provide a framework for negotiating respect. The person whose very appearance—including his clothing, demeanor, and way of moving—deters transgressions feels that he possesses, and may be considered by others to possess, a measure of respect. With the right amount of respect, for instance he can avoid "being bothered" in public. If he is bothered, not only may he be in physical danger but he has been disgraced or "dissed" (disrespected). Many of the forms that dissing can take might seem petty to middle-class people (maintaining eye contact too long, for example), but to those invested in the street code these actions become serious indications of the other person's intentions. Consequently, such people become very sensitive to advances and slights, which could well serve as warnings of imminent physical confrontation.

Source: From *The Code of the Street: Decency, Violence, and the Moral Life of the Inner City* by Elijah Anderson.

diminished or lost, its restoration is extremely difficult, and often impossible. With few economic resources or marketable skills, the person is relegated to a life among others who view him or her as easy prey.

Routine Activities

Lawrence Cohen and Marcus Felson (1979) contend that three conditions serve to greatly increase the probability of criminal activity. First, there must be a motivated offender to carry out the crime (e.g., criminal homicide and assault and battery). Second, there must be a suitable target or victim. Third there must be an absence of a guardian for the potential victim. These three conditions must converge in time and space for criminal activity to occur. As we have seen, social conditions in inner city neighborhoods provide opportunities for criminal behavior not found in other sectors of the city. In addition, risk-taking behaviors—walking alone late at night in unfamiliar places, drinking to excess in night clubs or bars, flashing large amounts of money, or engaging in provoking and aggressive behavior—understandably place a person at greater risk for violent victimization.

Strain

Robert Agnew (1992) set forth a strain theory of deviant and criminal behavior of particular relevance to criminal homicide and assaultive behavior. To Agnew, strain is largely generated by negative interpersonal relations. Sustained interaction with others who thwart a person's ability to attain legitimate goals (e.g., educational, occupational, affiliation, and respect) is stressful and typically results in negative emotions. These negative emotions—anger, resentment, jealousy, anxiety, or depression—require the person to develop a coping strategy to alleviate the resultant tension. Conditions in the surrounding social environment may exacerbate the interpersonal tension and serve to reduce the chances of adapting positively to experiences of strain. In the absence of viable outlets for tension reduction or healthy alternatives to destructive behaviors, interpersonal violence becomes more probable.

Frustration–Aggression

In 1939 John Dollard and his colleagues introduced their frustration–aggression hypothesis. The frustration–aggression hypothesis states that frustration always leads to aggression. Frustration occurs when an individual is blocked from the attainment of important needs and goals. If others make it impossible or significantly impede an individual from getting what he or she needs or wants, then frustration is acutely felt. To Dollard and his colleagues, some form of aggression always follows. Aggression may be turned inwardy—directed toward the self in the form of suicidal behavior, mutilation, depression, or addiction. Aggression may also be turned outwardly—directed toward others in the form of homicidal or assaultive behavior, either physical or sexual or both.

Disadvantaged individuals and groups experience a wide range of frustrations in their everyday lives. Frustrations are endemic to life in the lower socioeconomic strata of society. Acute frustrations begin in childhood with limited access to medical and dental resources, inferior clothing and school supplies, and caretakers who themselves are burdened by economic and social deprivation and who are not able to spend the time each child needs to advance in school. The cycle of poverty continues from one generation to the next; so too do the attendant frustrations and ensuing expressions of aggression. Verbal aggression often leads to explosive violence. The possibility of injury or death is always present.

Unreciprocity

Stuart Palmer (1972) reformulates the frustration-aggression hypothesis into the reciprocity and unreciprocity in role relationships. Palmer argues that unreciprocity in role relationships explains and predicts homicide and assaultive behaviors. Unreciprocity is experienced when others in complementary roles—wives and husbands, employers and employees, parents and children—inhibit or render impossible the carrying out of our roles. Unreciprocity is frustrating for an individual and, if experienced over an extended period of time, may well lead to violent behavior.

Social Control

Travis Hirschi (1969) poses the following question: Why don't individuals engage in criminal or delinquent behavior? To Hirschi, it is as important to understand individuals' reluctance to commit crimes as it is to understand why they willingly do so. He contends that the greater the integration of the individuals into conventional society, the less likely they are to commit acts of violence toward others. Four bonds that tie an individual to conventional society are used to measure integration: attachment, commitment, involvement, and belief. Attachment refers to the willingness of individuals to conform their conduct to the norms of the larger society. Evidence of commitment is found in the investment of time and energy in conventional activities—school, work, family, and civic projects. Involvement is indicated by the intensity in which a person engages in conventional activities. Belief refers to conviction that there is a common value system and one is morally bound to live in accordance with it.

More recently, Michael Gottfredson and Travis Hirschi (1990) proposed a general theory of crime. Central to the general theory—intended to account for all forms of crime—is the concept of self-control. The lack of self-control is manifest in various related ways. Gottfredson and Hirschi observe that "people who lack self-control will tend to be impulsive, insensitive, physical (as opposed to mental), risk-taking, shortsighted, and nonverbal, and they tend therefore to engage in criminality and analogous risk-taking behavior" (Gottfredson & Hirschi, 1990, p. 89). The overriding benefit of crime, to Gottfredson and Hirschi (1990, p. 89), "is not pleasure but relief from momentary irritation." Individuals who routinely engage in behaviors that demonstrate their lack of self-control are, understandably, at greater risk for involvement in spontaneous, often explosively violent, attacks on others.

Subcultural Considerations

Various subcultural formulations of crime and deviance inform our understanding of homicidal and assaultive behaviors. Richard Cloward and Lloyd Ohlin (1960) consider both subcultural and opportunity factors in attempting to account for variations in forms of crime and violence. Three subcultures identified by Cloward and Ohlin—criminal, violent, and retreatist—serve to structure opportunities for criminal activity. The opportunity to engage in crimes-for-profit—drug dealing, burglary, auto theft, gambling, and so on—depends on integration into a criminal subculture. Sources of drugs, fences for stolen goods, car "chop shops," or dealers in "hot" cars, must be available to the would-be criminal. Violent subcultures arise in places where for-profit criminal activities are less available. Physical force is commonly used to gain respect, status, or a "rep" from others. Physical aggression is also a means to acquire money and goods from others. Retreatist subcultures attract members who do not have opportunities or motivation to engage in a criminal subculture or the physical prowess to use violence to meet their needs. Retreatists tend to withdraw into a lifestyle dominated by substance abuse, psychiatric impairment, demonic rituals, or cult behavior.

As expected, homicidal and assaultive behaviors are most common within violent subcultures. However, criminal subcultures are also marked by considerable interpersonal conflict surrounding the myriad of illicit activities carried out on a daily basis. Disputes over drug sales and markets, theft of stolen goods, and threats of physical harm made to family members or friends must be settled within the neighborhood and among the combatants.

Marvin Wolfgang and Franco Ferracuti (1967) contend that acts of homicide and assaultive behaviors become far more likely with a subculture of violence. To Wolfgang and Ferracuti, subcultures of violence are marked by a constellation of norms and values that support the use of violence to settle interpersonal disputes. The willingness to resort to violence to resolve conflict is a learned response, observed at home and played out on the street. Wolfgang and Ferracuti (1967, pp. 188–189) describe a subculture of violence as follows:

> Quick resort to physical combat as a measure of daring, courage, or defense of status appears to be a cultural expression, especially for lower socioeconomic class males of both races. When such a culture norm response is elicited from an individual engaged is social interplay with others who harbor the same response mechanism, physical assaults, altercations, and violent domestic quarrels that result in homicide are common.

In a similar vein, Walter Miller's (1958) conceptualization of the focal concerns of the lower socioeconomic classes helps us further understand the dynamics of everyday life that may result in violent altercations and, at times, death. Miller identified six focal concerns of lower class life: trouble, toughness, smartness, excitement, fate, and autonomy. Briefly, trouble refers to the frustrations—financial, social, and legal—faced on an ongoing basis that combine to make life for the economically deprived exceedingly stressful. Toughness—the value of physical prowess and fearlessness—is highly prized. Smartness means the ability to "con" or outwit others or the possession of "street smarts" or knowledge of survival strategies for life largely unprotected by the police. With few resources, excitement for lower class persons tends to revolve around largely illicit and risk-taking activities such as drug use, fighting, sexual encounters, and gambling. Fate refers to the belief that life events are beyond one's control. Things just happen and there is nothing that can be done about it. A "live-for-the-moment" mentality predominates. Although life is subject to uncontrollable forces, there is nonetheless a concern with autonomy or the freedom from restrictions. There is great value placed on being able to act independently of the wishes of others—to be one's own person. These six focal concerns combine to increase the likelihood of violent encounters within the lower socioeconomic strata of society.

Chapter Summary

I. Criminal homicide is the intentional killing of one human being by another without justification or excuse.
   A. There are two types of criminal homicide:
      1. Murder (first and second degree)
      2. Manslaughter (first and second degree)
   B. Two considerations serve to distinguish between each type and the seriousness of each degree:
      1. Premeditation
      2. Provocation

II. Manslaughter involves less premeditation on the part of the offender and greater victim provocation than murder. Second-degree manslaughter does not involve the intention to kill but results from the negligent actions of the offender.

III. Homicides where there is neither intention to kill nor evidence of wrongful or flagrant carelessness are considered justifiable homicides and excusable homicides.

IV. Assault is (1) an attempt to commit bodily injury to another human being or (2) putting another in fear of imminent bodily injury. The crime of assault implies the present ability to carry out the assault.

V. Battery refers to the actual offensive touching or unwanted physical contact between the assailant and the victim.

VI. The most serious form of assault and battery is aggravated assault, or an assault committed with the intention of committing an additional crime.

VII. ABWDWWITKRSBI—Assault and Battery With a Deadly Weapon With Intent To Kill Resulting in Serious Bodily Injury—is an abbreviation used by law enforcement officers to distinguish between aggravated assault and assaults of a lesser nature.

VIII. Although the United States is not the most murderous nation, it does lead the world in gun-related homicides.

IX. At the beginning of the new millennium an increase in the homicide rate, particularly in urban areas, was evident.

X. Homicides vary from urban, suburban, small cities, and rural areas. Homicide is disproportionately committed in large urban areas. As a result, when homicide declines in larger urban places, the rate for the country as a whole falls sharply.

XI. Persons aged 20 to 34 are most likely to commit homicide or to be a victim of homicide.

XII. Males are far more likely to commit homicide or to be a victim of homicide than are females.

XIII. Homicide is essentially an intraracial event, disproportionately involving Black Americans as both victims and offenders.

XIV. The elderly are far less likely to be involved in criminal activity either as an offender or victim than are younger persons. However, the elderly are considerably more likely to be killed during the commission of another felony (e.g., robbery, burglary, or larceny) than are younger homicide victims. Persons over age 65 are twice as likely to be murdered by their relatives or intimates than are younger persons.

XV. Overall, women are far less likely to be the victim of a homicide than men but are more likely to be victimized by an intimate partner than are men.

XVI. Luckenbill's situated transaction is a conflict between two persons involving the escalation of verbal taunts, accusations, or threats to battery and serious injury or death. He describes six stages:

A. The first stage involves offensive actions or verbal communication and the threat to lose respect from others.
B. In the second stage bystanders confirm the derogatory behavior.
C. Stage three involves the demand of the offender to stop the provoking behavior.
D. The offender conveys to the victim the dire consequences of the victim's taunting in stage four.
E. A weapon is produced in stage five and the violent transaction takes place.
F. The process ends with stage six when the offender leaves the scene or is detained by witnesses.

XVII. Victim-precipitated homicide, introduced by Marvin Wolfgang, means that the victim was the first one to use physical force against the person who ultimately became the homicide offender.

Key Concepts

Criminal homicide: The intentional killing of one human being by another without justification or excuse.

Justifiable homicide: Court-ordered executions of convicted offenders or the killing of an enemy by a member of the military in the line of duty.

Excusable homicide: The accidental or non-negligent killing of another human being.

Murder: A form of homicide that involves premeditation and malice aforethought on the part of the offender.

Manslaughter: A form of homicide that involves less premeditation or malice aforethought on the part of the offender and greater victim provocation than other forms of homicide.

Premeditation: The act of deliberating or meditating upon, or planning, a course of action.

Malice: The intentional doing of a wrongful act without just cause or legal excuse.

Malice aforethought: An unjustifiable, inexcusable, and unmitigated person-endangering state of mind.

Provocation: The active involvement of the victim, either verbal or physical, in the lethal encounter.

Assault: An attempt to commit bodily injury to another human being; putting another in fear of imminent bodily injury.

Battery: The actual offensive touching or unwanted physical contact between the assailant and victim.

Aggravated assault: An assault that is committed with the intention of committing an additional crime.

Victim-precipitated homicide: Concept introduced by Marvin Wolfgang to describe homicides where the victim was the first one to use physical force against the person who ultimately became the homicide offender.

Critical Thinking Questions

1. Rates of homicide and aggravated assault vary widely among subcultural groupings. Which sociocultural factors might account for a high rate of violence in one subculture and a low rate in another? Discuss two theories that might account for the differences in rates between the two subcultural groups.
2. Choose two explanations for gender differences in violent offending and victimization. What are the advantages and limitations of the theoretical explanations that you have chosen?
3. Identify two sociocultural changes that might bring about a reduction in the violent victimization of children. How might these sociocultural changes affect the incidence and rate of childhood physical and sexual victimization?
4. Marked variations in violent offending and victimization occur across the life span. How does life-course analysis account for age-related differences in violent offending and victimization?

Web Extra

Web-based media materials from high-quality sources such as CNN, Time, and National Public Radio are available in support of this textbook. Visit go.jblearning.com/deviance to access them.

Check out these websites for additional information on homicide:

http://homicideworkinggroup.cos.ucf.edu/

http://www.ojp.usdoj.gov/bjs

http://www.fbi.gov

http://www.ojp.usdoj.gov/nij

http://www.ncjrs.org

STOP
DOMESTIC
VIOLENCE

Domestic Violence

CHAPTER 5

Learning Objectives

After reading this chapter you should know

- Legal understandings of domestic violence.
- Social understandings of terms related to domestic violence.
- The prevalence of domestic violence.
- The consequences of domestic violence for victims, perpetrators, and others.
- Risk factors for domestic violence.
- The nature and extent of use of corporal punishment in American families.
- Various theories that might help explain domestic violence.

In late 2009, 20-year-old Noor Almaleki was run over by her father in a Peoria, Arizona, parking lot. She died a few days later, apparently the victim of an "honor killing," meant to preserve her family's honor. Noor's "crime" was moving in with an American man and rejecting the husband whom she had married in Iraq, an offense that brought shame on her family when seen from the point of view of traditional Iraqi values. Maricopa County prosecutor Stephanie Low told reporters that by the father's "own admission, this was an intentional act, and the reason was that his daughter had brought shame on him and his family" (Dorell, 2009). Almaleki's father, Faleh Almaleki, was charged with murder.

The Almaleki killing was the seventh honor killing in the United States by Muslim immigrants during the past 2 years, raising concern over traditional tribal values and forms of behavior transplanted from one society to another. Similar killings have taken place in other Western societies. In 2007, for example, 52-year-old Mahmod Mahmod and his 51-year-old brother, Ari Mahmod, pleaded guilty to planning the killing of the older brother's daughter, 20-year-old Banaz Mahmod (Dodds, 2007). Banaz was strangled with a shoelace and her body stuffed into a suitcase and buried in a backyard garden after she was accused of shaming her family by leaving an abusive arranged marriage. Her family, Kurdish Iraqis, had emigrated to England in 1998 when Banaz was only 11 years old. Statistics in Britain show that 25 women have been killed by Muslim relatives over the past 10 years for perceived honor offenses.

Some Muslim leaders point out that Islam does not mandate honor killings and that such crimes predate the Muslim religion. Not everyone agrees. Phyllis Chesler, author of *Woman's Inhumanity to Woman*, points out that "the religion has failed to address this as a problem and failed to seriously work to abolish it as un-Islamic" (Dorell, 2009).

"You look at these scattered houses, and you are impressed by their beauty. I look at them, and the only thought which comes to me is a feeling of their isolation, and of the impunity with which crime may be committed there. . . . Think of the deeds of hellish cruelty, the hidden wickedness which may go on, year in, year out, in such places, and none the wiser."
—Sir Arthur Conan Doyle (1984) (Sherlock Holmes to Dr. John Watson)

Domestic violence refers to the intentional physical or psychological injury of a family member by another. Family members may be either a victim, an offender, or, in some instances, both. Acts of domestic violence range from assault involving the use of a lethal weapon to witnessing family aggression. Domestic violence ranges from life-threatening offenses to simply an awareness of physical or psychological abuse. Victims of domestic violence around the globe, however, are disproportionately women and children. More powerful members of the family—usually by virtue of their status outside the home, physical dominance, or violent demeanor—habitually victimize the vulnerable members of the household with impunity.

Until recent years violent behavior within the home was largely hidden from public scrutiny. Significant advances have been made in public awareness of the pervasiveness of domestic violence and its debilitating effects; in the passage of domestic violence legislation at the federal, state, and local levels; in the commitment of advocacy groups for women and children; and in innovative law enforcement strategies for protecting the victims of violence and controlling their offenders.

In this chapter we consider the wide spectrum of domestic violence, patterns of its occurrence, and consequences for its victims. Familial conditions that give rise to domestic violence and serve to ensure its perpetuation are also considered. Finally, we discuss theoretical formulations that explain the rates or the incidence of various forms of domestic violence.

"The closer the social relationship, the more intense the conflict."
—Lewis Coser (1967)

Legal Definitions

Domestic violence encompasses several forms of abusive behavior: physical, sexual, emotional, or psychological. In the main, domestic violence involves coercion through the use of intimidating, threatening, harmful, or harassing behavior. The Violent Crime Control and Law Enforcement Act (1994) defines domestic violence as "felony or misdemeanor crimes of violence committed by a current or former spouse of the victim, by a person with whom the victim shares a child in common, by a person who is cohabiting with the victim as a spouse, by a person similarly situated to a spouse of the victim under the domestic or family violence laws of the jurisdiction."

SSRN
Bettinger-Lopez, C. (2008). Human rights at home: Domestic violence as a human rights violation. *Columbia Human Rights Law Review, 40,* 19–77. http://ssrn.com/abstract=1310316

Social Definitions

Beyond the legal definitions of the various forms of domestic violence, there are social definitions of assaultive behavior in the home. Social definitions refer to the meanings and interpretations that individuals attach to their own behavior and to the behavior of persons with whom they interact. We interpret our own behavior: We act for reasons that make sense to us. Similarly, we interpret the motivations of others, for example, as kind or mean, helpful or harmful, appropriate or inappropriate.

Crucial to social understandings of domestic violence are those factors that influence the meanings and interpretations attached to the offender's behavior. Women may interpret the violent behavior of their husbands or intimate partners as justifiable or excusable—"I deserved it" or "He was drinking and didn't know what he was doing." Or, they may interpret the violent partner's behavior as vicious and criminal or the result of a serious mental disorder. Victims of spousal assault construct a "definition of the situation" that takes into account their economic resources and social supports, religious beliefs, and access to legal assistance and protective programs. Women who are economically dependent, who believe divorce is religiously prohibited, who do not gain emotional support from others, or who do not have access to police or legal assistance or protective shelters are less likely to see alternatives to their abusive situation. They tend to define their situation as hopeless and themselves as helpless to change it.

SSRN

Tuerkheimer, D. (2006). Crawford's triangle: Domestic violence and the right of confrontation. *North Carolina Law Review, 85*(1). http://ssrn.com/abstract=892620

Learned helplessness characterizes women who find themselves in this situation. Learned helplessness refers to the inability to predict the outcomes of one's actions (Meuer, Seymour, & Wallace, 2002). Because battered women find it difficult to know what their abusive partners may do in response to their behavior, they tend to limit themselves to acting in safe ways—asking permission before deciding to do the most mundane things. Learned helplessness results from the development of a "survival" strategy for the battered women (Walker, 1979). Battered women's lives tend to focus on devising ways to adapt to their abusive relationship. If an abused woman defines herself as "helpless" and her situation as intractable, then she is less likely to define her abuser as criminal and more likely to be repeatedly victimized.

Extent and Nature of Domestic Violence

Intimate Partner Violence

Figure 5-1 shows that intimate partner victimization has been on the decline over the past several decades. Intimate partner violence occurs

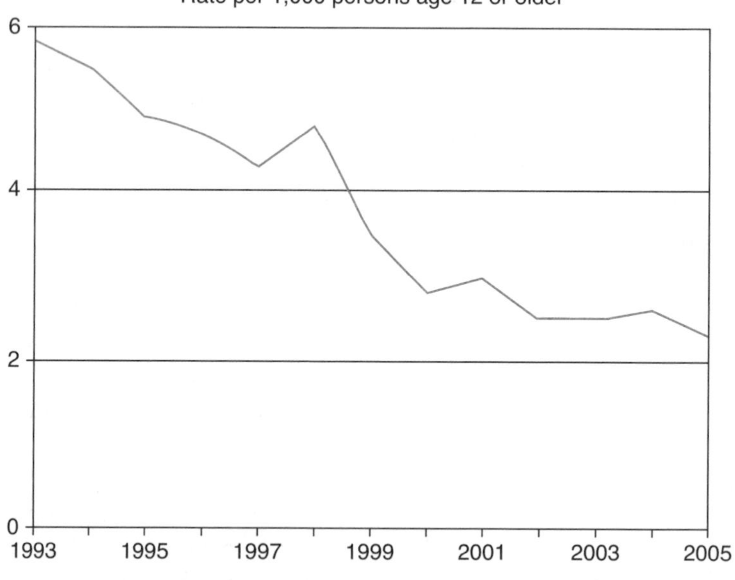

FIGURE 5–1 Nonfatal intimate partner victimization rate, 1993–2005.

Source: Shannan Catalano, Ph.D., Intimate Partner Violence in the U.S. Bureau of Justice Statistics, Office of Justice Programs, 2007. Posted at: http://bjs.ojp.usdoj.gov/content/intimate/ipv.cfm

between two people involved in a close relationship and includes current or former spouses and dating partners (cdc.gov/violenceprevention). The Centers for Disease Control and Prevention recognizes four types of intimate partner violence: *physical violence,* hurting or attempting to hurt a person by physical force; *sexual violence,* a forced sexual act without consent; and *threats,* emotional abuse, such as threatening a person, their possessions, or loved ones, or undermining a person's self-worth. Annually women suffer about 4.8 million intimate partner physical assaults and rapes. Approximately 2.9 million men are victims of physical assault each year. Females account for 78% of the more than 1,500 deaths that result from intimate partner violence (cdc.gov/violenceprevention).

Domestic violence occurs in all racial and ethnic groups and across all socioeconomic classes (Hotaling & Sugarman, 1990). Intimate partner violence occurs in one in three of marriages in the United States (Bachman & Saltzman, 1995). Murray Straus and Richard Gelles (1995) estimate that more than one in seven U.S. men batter their wives, and one in three of these violent attacks involve punching, beating up, or are carried out with a knife or gun. American women are victimized by their intimate partners or former partners six times more frequently than by a stranger and are more likely to be injured by their intimate partner (Bachman & Saltzman, 1995).

Domestic violence is exceedingly costly for victims and for society as a whole. Victims of intimate partner violence suffer about 2 million injuries each year; more than one in four require medical attention. Losses of more than $5.8 billion result from intimate partner rape, physical assault, and stalking each year. Medical expenses and mental health services account for about $4.1 billion, with the remaining loss of $1.7 billion due to losses of productivity and lifetime earnings. It is estimated that about 8 million days of paid labor are lost due to intimate partner violence, or the equivalent of 32,000 full-time jobs (U.S. Department of Health and Social Services, 2003).

Child Maltreatment

Each state is required to provide both criminal and civil definitions of the forms of **child maltreatment.** Although there are variations in the legal definitions across states, there is general consensus about the elements of each of the three forms of child maltreatment, which are child abuse and neglect, sexual abuse, and emotional abuse (including psychological/verbal abuse/mental injury).

Child abuse and neglect is defined as (1) any act or failure to act on the part of a parent or caretaker that results in death, serious physical or emotional harm, sexual abuse or exploitation, and/or (2) an act or failure to act that presents an imminent risk of serious harm.

Sexual abuse is defined as (1) the employment, use, persuasion, inducement, or coercion of any child to engage in, or assist any other person to engage in, any sexually explicit conduct or simulation of such conduct for the purpose of producing a visual depiction of such conduct or (2) the rape, and in cases of caretaker or interfamilial relationships, statutory rape, molestation, prostitution, or other form of sexual exploitation of children or incest with children.

Emotional abuse refers to acts of omission by the parents or other caregivers that have caused or could cause serious behavioral, cognitive, emotional, or mental disorders. Examples include traumatizing forms of punishment (e.g., being put under the hood of a running car) (Child Abuse Prevention and Treatment Act [CAPTA], 2003, p. 44).

U.S. state and local child protective services receive over 3 million complaints of child abuse or neglect each year. Child maltreatment accounts for around 770,000 of the complaints, resulting in a child maltreatment rate of 10.2 per 1,000 children across the United States. Seven in 10 children are victims of child neglect, 16% are physically abused, 9% are sexually abused, and 7% are abused emotionally (cdc.gov/violenceprevention). David Finkelhor and his colleagues at the Center for Crimes Against Children estimate that one in five U.S. children are victims of some form of child maltreatment during childhood. Of these children, 1% are sexually assaulted, 45% suffer child neglect, 9% are physically abused, and 12% are victims of emotional abuse (Finkelhor et al., 2008).

AGE, GENDER, AND RACE OF THE VICTIMS. Child maltreatment victimization rates are highest for infants through the age of 3 and lowest for teenagers between 16 and 17 years of age. Overall, the victimization of girls (10.8 per 1,000) is greater than for boys (9.7 per 1,000). Child maltreatment rates are highest for African Americans (16.6 per 1,000), followed by Native Americans/Alaska Natives (13.9) and multiracial children (13.8) (cdc.gov/violenceprevention).

An estimated 1,740 children from infancy to age 17 die each year as a result of abuse or neglect, for a rate of 2.3 per 1,000 children. Eight in 10 victims are under the age of 4, 10% are between 4 and 7 years of age, and the remaining 10% are between the ages of 8 and 17 (cdc.gov/violenceprevention).

AGE, GENDER, AND OFFENDER–VICTIM RELATIONSHIP. Parents, typically under the age of 39, are more apt to maltreat their children than other relatives

"I'm in Fear of My Life Right Now"

Sonye Herrera hid in the bathroom. She locked the door. Her heart was pounding. Her father was in another rage, storming around the house. How long before he found her?

Finally, Sonye had decided that she could stand it no more. She had vowed to take him on herself—get him arrested, send him to prison. But she overlooked one immutable reality: She was 15 years old, a child by law and in fact.

Now alone in the bathroom with a cordless phone, she dialed 911. Her father had been drinking. This time he had hit Sonye. Her mother tried to fend him off. But he was talking crazily, and Sonye was on crutches with a sprained ankle, unable to run.

"I'm in fear of my life right now," she told a 911 operator, her voice breaking as she gave her address.

Five minutes ticked by.

Ten minutes.

Twenty minutes.

Still the police did not come.

"What is your name?" the operator asked.

"I'm Sonye Herrera."

"Excuse me?"

"Sonye. Please, I don't have time."

"How old are you?"

"I'm 15, I don't have time. . . . I don't have time. Just come here."

"Are there any weapons in your home at all?"

"No."

"No weapons?"

"Spell your name for me."

"S-O-N-Y-E. Please I don't have time to be doing this. Can't you send the cops over here?"

Twenty-eight minutes later, Sonye's mother ran from the house screaming: "Someone help me! Call the cops! He shot my daughter! Help me! Help me!" A few minutes later, Sonye's father shot her mother in the head and then killed himself. Sonye and her mother were buried together.

Source: Adapted from "A Child's Unheeded Cry for Help: Teen Decided to Take on Abusive Father Herself" by staff writer Donna St. George. *The Washington Post.* June 8, 2001.

or caretakers. Women make up the majority—about 6 in 10—of the perpetrators of child maltreatment, particularly of younger children. Women perpetrators acting alone account for almost 6 in 10 of the medical neglect cases of child maltreatment, over half of child neglect, and more than one-third of physical abuse cases. Male offenders, however, account for the majority of sexual abuse of children (U.S. Department of Health and Human Services, 2000, 2008).

Elder Abuse

Considerably less is known about the extent and nature of elder abuse in the United States. The most recent findings from the National Elder Abuse Incidence Study (1998), however, show the following:

1. Approximately 450,000 persons over the age of 60 are victims of domestic abuse or neglect.
2. An additional 101,000 persons over the age of 60 experience self-neglect.
3. Elderly women are disproportionately victimized. Women make-up more than two of every three victims of elder abuse.
4. About 9 in 10 times the perpetrator of elder abuse is a member of the victim's family, and 2 in 3 three times the abuser is a spouse or an adult child.
5. Elderly persons who neglect themselves are most often frail, depressed, and confused.

Consequences of Domestic Violence

Consequences for Intimate Partners

Spousal assault and other forms of intimate partner violence have both immediate and often long-term negative effects on the victim and children in the home. Partner violence is traumatic for the victim, creating an atmosphere of fear and a sense of helplessness. The initial painful realization that a loved one is capable of a sudden and explosive act of violence is often followed by the victim's experience of anxiety and/or depression, diminished self-worth, substance abuse, and suicidal thoughts (Dutton, 1993; Gelles & Harrop, 1989; Orava, 1996).

The effects of intimate partner violence, however, vary by gender. Women are more likely than men to suffer negative social and psychological effects after their victimization. Murray Straus and Richard Gelles' (1995) second National Survey of Family Violence shows that overall women experience twice the number of negative effects of intimate partner violence than do men. Compared with their male counterparts, more women who are severely abused by their partners spend days in bed because of illness (23% vs. 15%), experience psychosomatic symptoms (44% vs. 26%), indicate elevated stress levels (61% vs. 34%), or feel extremely depressed (58% vs. 30%) (Stets & Straus, 1990; Straus & Gelles, 1995).

There is a dynamic interplay among the consequence of intimate partner violence. Jean Giles-Sims (1998) observes that women who have

AT A GLANCE

Domestic Violence

- More than 90% of domestic violence victims are women, whereas as many as 95% of domestic violence perpetrators are male.
- More than one in four women around the world suffer violence from an intimate partner. One of every four U.S. women report they have been physically abused by a husband or boyfriend at some point in their lives. Thirty percent of Americans say they know a woman who has been physically abused by her husband or boyfriend in the past year.
- Although women are less likely than men to be victims of violent crimes overall, women are five to eight times more likely than men to be victimized by an intimate partner.
- Domestic violence is the leading cause of injury to women between ages 15 and 44 in the United States, more than car accidents, muggings, and rapes combined.

Children Who Witness Domestic Violence

- An estimated 3.3 million children are exposed to domestic violence.
- Boys who witness family violence are more likely to batter their female partners as adults than are boys raised in nonviolent homes. Girls who witness their mothers' abuse have a higher rate of being battered as adults.

Child Abuse

- There are 772,000 substantiated cases of child maltreatment each year, resulting in a child maltreatment rate of 10.2 per 1,000 children.
- Seven in 10 children were victims of child neglect, 16% were physically abused, 9% were sexually abused, and 7% were emotionally abused.
- In 8 of 10 reported cases of child abuse, the alleged perpetrator is the child's parent.

Sources: UNICEF, Bureau of Justice Statistics, U.S. Department of Health and Human Services, U.S. Department of Justice, Lieberman Research INC., New Hampshire Coalition Against Domestic and Sexual Violence (www.NHCADSV.org), National Crime Victimization Survey, National Violence Against Women Survey, Crimes Against Children Research Center, Centers for Disease Control and Prevention.

a sense of powerlessness, hopelessness, and diminished self-esteem tend to suffer from depression and are unable to leave an abusive relationship. Women whose sense of self has been undermined may well turn to alcohol or other drugs as a temporary respite from their domestic situation. And the sense that they are hopelessly trapped in a violent relationship may precipitate suicidal behaviors.

Consequences for Children

Children who are the victims of maltreatment or who are physically or sexually abused in their homes are more likely to engage in antisocial behavior, criminal activity, and domestic violence later in life. Abused or neglected children are 53% more likely to be arrested as a juvenile, 38% more likely to be arrested as an adult, and 38% more likely to commit a violent crime (Widom, 1992). Maltreated children are also significantly more likely to become abusive husbands and fathers (Daro & Cohn, 2000; Edelson, 2000; Tolan, 2000).

Exposure to parental violence, either as a direct witness or by inference from the threats, screams, and sounds of assaultive behavior, also has pronounced negative effects on children and adolescents (**Table 5–1**). Janis Wolak and David Finkelhor (1998) identify behavioral, physical, emotional, and cognitive symptoms of exposure to partner violence. These symptoms may be a direct or an indirect consequence of parental violence (Jaffe et al., 1990). Direct consequences include physical danger to the child, emotional and behavior problems (e.g., posttraumatic stress disorder), fearfulness, isolation, running away from home, and learning to use aggressive behavioral strategies to control situations. Indirect consequences refer to the effects of partner violence on the health and behavior of the child's parents over time. Typical of the indirect consequences are stress-related health disorders of the mother, the father's overt expression of anger and irritability, and the child's being subjected to severe and arbitrary punishment by distraught parents. In addition, exposure to parental violence is associated with suicide attempts by the child, experimentation with alcohol and drugs, teenage prostitution, and engagement in sexually assaultive behavior (Wolfe et al., 1995).

SSRN

Raeder, M. (2005). Remember the ladies and the children too: Crawford's impact on domestic violence and child abuse cases. *Brooklyn Law Review, 71,* 311. http://ssrn.com/abstract=875445

Risk Factors for Domestic Violence

Key risk factors for becoming a victim of domestic violence have been identified. For both women and men, being a victim of maltreatment in

TABLE 5–1 **Symptoms of Children Exposed to Partner Violence**

Behavioral	Physical	Emotional	Cognitive
Aggression	Failure to thrive	Anxiety	Poor academic performance
Tantrums	Sleeplessness	Depression	Language lag
Acting out	Regressive behaviors	Withdrawal	
Immaturity	Eating disorders	Low self-esteem	
Truancy	Poor motor skills	Anger	
Delinquency	Psychosomatic symptoms		
	Rejection by peers		

Source: Wolak, J. and Finkelhor, D. "Children Exposed to Partner Violence." In Jasinski, J. and Williams, L. (Eds.), Partner Violence: A Comprehensive Review of 20 Years of Research. Copyright © 1998 SAGE Publications, Inc.

childhood significantly increases the risk of being a victim of domestic violence. And for both women and men, the risk of victimization is significantly greater when there is a disparity in their relative status. That is, when a woman makes more money than her partner, she is at greater risk for victimization. Similarly, when a man's race or ethnicity differs from his partner, he has an elevated risk of being victimized by his spouse. Gerald Hotaling and David Sugarman (1986) identify eight risk markers for husbands who victimize their wives:

1. Sexual aggression toward the wife/partner
2. Violence toward the children
3. Witnessing parental violence as a child or teen
4. Working-class status
5. Excessive alcohol usage
6. Low income
7. Low assertiveness
8. Low educational level

Similarly, for women, the risk of intimate partner violence is significantly greater when cohabiting versus married, African American versus White, living with a verbally abusive partner or a partner who controls access to family, friends, or economic resources. Angela Browne's (1987) groundbreaking study of battered women who kill their abusers shows they differ from other women victims in the following ways:

- Frequent intoxication by their victims
- Drug use by their victims
- Frequent abuse
- Serious injury at the hands of her victim
- Rape or sexual victimization by the victim
- Threats by the victim to kill her
- Suicide threats by her

Domestic violence is experienced across socioeconomic classes. Children and adolescents who witness parental abuse commonly suffer adverse emotional and behavioral consequences.

SSRN

Weissman, D. M. The personal is political—and economic: Rethinking domestic violence. *Brigham Young University Law Review*, Forthcoming; UNC Legal Studies Research Paper No. 937110. http://ssrn.com/abstract=937110

Why Do They Stay?

The obvious question is why women stay in abusive relationships. Richard Gelles (1987) argues that there are three factors that influence the decision of a woman to remain in an abusive relationship. First, women tend to stay

Women Lift the Veil on Abuse

When she heard about the slaying last summer, Naila knew it was time to escape.

Another young Pakistani bride, Shahpara Sayeed, had been set afire in the Uptown neighborhood, allegedly by her husband of 2½ years. Police said he poured gasoline in a taxi and lit a match on North Glenwood Avenue in broad daylight.

After Naila's brother-in-law saw news of the slaying on television, he taunted her.

"I'll burn you," Naila said he told her. "I'll do the same to you as Shahpara Sayeed."

According to the World Health Organization, domestic violence occurs among all races, classes, and ethnic groups across the globe with striking similarity. Yet immigrant women in the United States may be at increased risk because of their social isolation and cultural barriers to seeking help. Separated from the support of family and friends at home and reluctant to seek legal aid within the United States, many immigrant women are particularly vulnerable to domestic violence.

Source: Adapted from "Women Lift the Veil On Abuse" by Teresa Puente and Noreen Ahmed-Ullah, Chicago Tribune staff reporters. Originally published in the *Chicago Tribune*, June 3, 2001. www.vachss.com/help_text/archive/women_lift.html

in abusive relationships in which they are assaulted less frequently and less severely. As expected, women who are repeatedly and severely victimized tend to leave the relationship. Second, the more a woman was physically abused as a child, the more likely she is to stay with an abusive husband. Abused children appear to view violent behavior as normal and learn to tolerate it. Third, women who stay with an abusive partner tend to be less educated and either unemployed or holding low-paying jobs. Women with few resources are more likely to endure an abusive relationship and less likely to seek assistance from others.

Women face many obstacles when deciding whether to stay in an abusive relationship (Meuer, Seymour, & Wallace, 2002). **Table 5–2** presents 13 of these obstacles.

Cycle of Violence

To Lenore Walker (2000) the concept of a "**cycle of violence**" describes the process that characterizes intimate partner violence. She outlines three phases in the cycle of violence, each varying in intensity and duration. *Phase One* is marked by a buildup of tension and hostility in the relationship. The eventual abuser becomes increasingly negative toward his partner; the victim tends to withdraw from him to avoid a confrontation. The abuser may perceive the victim's avoidance as a threat to leave him, which triggers increased oppressiveness, jealousy, and possessiveness. In *Phase Two* the actual battering occurs. The violent episode may only take a few minutes but is followed by an extended period of adaptation to the shock-

TABLE 5-2 Why Women Stay: Obstacles to Leaving an Abusive Relationship

1. Economic dependence on the abuser.
2. Fear for her safety and the safety of her children and/or other members of the family.
3. Isolation from a support system.
4. Low self-esteem, resulting from the degradation of the abuse.
5. Beliefs about family—all problems should be resolved within the family, no one else needs to know.
6. Beliefs about marriage—marriage is sacred and forever.
7. Belief she is the only person who can stop the abuser—reinforced by the abuser's plea that the victim is the only one who understands him.
8. Belief that he will find her if she tries to leave.
9. Lack of options and resources.
10. Fear of being seriously hurt or killed if she attempts to leave.
11. Threats against others if the victim leaves.
12. Health concerns—the victim physically unable to leave.
13. Society's ageist response to elder victims—complaints of abuse by elderly tend to be dismissed.

Source: Jones & Bartlett Learning gratefully acknowledges the U.S. Department of Justice, Office of Justice Programs, Office for Victims of Crime (OVC), for allowing us to reproduce, in part, the 2002 National Victim Assistance Academy Textbook , Chapter 9, "Domestic Violence." This chapter was prepared by Tess Meuer, Anne Seymour, and Harvey Wallace, under OVC grant # 95-MU-GX-K002 (S 7) to the Victims' Assistance Legal Organization, Inc. (VALOR). The opinions, findings, and conclusions or recommendations expressed in the textbook are those of the authors and do not necessarily represent the official position or policies of the U.S. Department of Justice.

ing behavior of the batterer. The emotional fallout for the victim—feelings of helplessness, depression, and malaise—is usually evident between 24 and 48 hours after the assault. *Phase Three* is considered the "honeymoon phase" in which the abusive partner attempts to convince his victim of his sorrow for his actions and pleads for forgiveness. He makes extraordinary efforts to be kind and solicitous toward his abused partner. He may elicit the help of friends or family members to aid in his attempt to convince the victim that he can be trusted and deserves her love and understanding. Nonetheless, he does believe that the battering has served a purpose and that he may not have to engage in further violence toward his partner.

Corporal Punishment

The use of corporal punishment is pervasive in U.S. families. Approximately one-third of infants and 94% of toddlers are spanked, a practice that for about one-third of them continues into the early teen years (Straus & Donnelly, 2006). For example, four in ten 14-year-olds and one in four 17-year-olds experience corporal punishment (Straus & Donnelly, 2009). Corporal punishment is, for the most part, intended to correct the unruly behavior of children. Until recently pediatricians and social scientists have overlooked the adverse consequences of the use of corporal punishment.

SSRN

Fuller, J. M. (2009). The science and statistics behind spanking suggest that laws allowing corporal punishment are in the best interests of the child. *Akron Law Review, 42*(243). http://ssrn.com/abstract=1357669

Murray A. Straus, founder of the Family Research Laboratory at the University of New Hampshire, began investigating the use of corporal punishment and its various effects on children and adolescents. His findings and those of other researchers have provided considerable evidence that the use of corporal punishment has deleterious effects on subsequent behavior of children and adolescents and on their emotional well-being and cognitive development. Conversely, not spanking a child has beneficial consequences for a child. Straus and Donnelly (2009, p. 4) define **corporal punishment** as "the use of physical force with the intention of causing a child to experience pain, but not injury, for the purpose of correction or control of the child's behavior." Straus, Sugarman, and Giles (1997) report that children who are spanked are significantly more likely to continue their antisocial behavior (e.g., lying, trouble at school, deliberate misbehavior) 2 years later. Furthermore, the more the child is spanked, the greater the frequency of antisocial behavior in the future. These findings hold even when taking into account the child's gender, race or ethnicity, level of antisocial behavior before the use of corporal punishment, the socioeconomic status of the family, the emotional support of the parents, and the cognitive stimulation provided in the home. In short, it does not matter if the child is male or female, White or non-White, particularly unruly before the use of corporal punishment or not, from a well-to-do or poor home, or was given emotional support or cognitive stimulation at home, corporal punishment increases the risk a child's emotional disorder and antisocial behavior.

Parents argue while a child listens. What symptoms are typically displayed by children involved with caregivers in abusive relationships?

Ten Myths About Corporal Punishment

1. Spanking works better.
2. Spanking is needed as a last resort.
3. Spanking is harmless.
4. One or two times won't cause any damage.
5. Parents can't stop without training.
6. If you don't spank, your child will be spoiled or run wild.
7. Parents spank rarely or for only serious problems.
8. By the time a child is a teenager, parents have stopped.
9. If parents don't spank, they will verbally abuse their child.
10. It is unrealistic to expect parents never to spank.

Source: Straus, M., and D. Donnelly. 2001. *Beating the Devil Out of Them: Corporal Punishment in American Families and its Effects on Children.* New Brunswick, NJ: Transaction Publishers.

Corporal punishment is also linked to fighting in school. Evidence is available that kindergarten children who are spanked are twice as likely to physically attack another child at school within 6 months. Children who are administered severe forms of corporal punishment—more than a slap or a tug on an arm—are four times more likely to assault another kindergarten student. An additional recent study shows that the more children are subjected to corporal punishment, the more likely they are to engage in fighting in school 5 years later. The link between corporal punishment and antisocial behavior is evident for both boys and girls at all ages and races (Gunroe & Mariner, 1997; Straus, 2000b).

SSRN

Shmueli, B. (2007). What has feminism got to do with children's rights? A case study of a ban on corporal punishment. *Wisconsin Women's Law Journal, 22,* 177–233. http://ssrn.com/abstract=1514368

Children who are slapped by a parent have a greater probability of assaulting a parent a year and a half later. Child-to-parent assault is more likely even when taking into account the race, the family's socioeconomic status, the child's physical size, attitude toward aggression, and attachment to the parent (Brezina, 1999). Corporal punishment of boys is also linked to their use of violence in a dating relationship. The use of physical force on a girlfriend is far more common among boys who have been hit by a parent (Simons et al., 1998).

A national study of 960 U.S. children shows that corporal punishment tends to restrict cognitive development of children. Cognitive ability in the early stages of development (children aged 1 to 4) is measured by body part recognition, memory for locations, and motor and social development. The effect of several variables—mother's education; mother's age at the time the child was born; the child's age, gender, and birth weight; father's presence in the home; mother's supportiveness and cognitive stimulation; ethnicity; number of children in the home—is controlled

Corporal Punishment in Childhood

The more corporal punishment a child experiences, the more likely he or she is to

- *In childhood*
  - Hit other children.
  - Act out aggressively in other ways, such as hitting parents.
  - Experience less rapid cognitive development.
- *In adulthood*
  - Be depressed or suicidal.
  - Physically abuse children or spouse.
  - Engage in other violent crimes.
  - Have a drinking problem.
  - Be attracted to masochistic sex.
  - Not achieve a high occupation or income.

Source: Straus, M., and D. Donnelly. 2001. *Beating the Devil Out of Them: Corporal Punishment in American Families and its Effects on Children.* New Brunswick, NJ: Transaction Publishers.

in an attempt to isolate the impact of corporal punishment on cognitive development. The results show that cognitive development of children is impeded by the use of corporal punishment (Straus & Paschall, 1998).

Using data from a national sample of 6,002 U.S. families, Straus and Kantor (1994) investigate the possible link between corporal punishment of teenagers and adverse behavioral and psychological effects later in life. They hypothesize that the more teenagers experience corporal punishment, the more likely they are to be depressed, have suicidal thoughts, abuse alcohol, and assault their wives or children later on.

Theories of Domestic Violence

Exchange/Social Control Model

Richard Gelles (1994) has integrated exchange and social control formulations to account for violence in the family. Exchange theory (**Table 5–3**) posits that human social behavior is motivated by the desire to maximize rewards and minimize punishment or costs associated with certain actions. If others provide benefits to an individual for behaving in a certain way, then he or she will tend to continue that behavior. The continuation of the social interaction, then, depends on the extent of reciprocity involved. However, if there is an absence of reciprocity between the interacting parties, then interpersonal conflict and violence may well ensue.

TABLE 5–3 Explanations of Domestic Violence Rates

Theories and Theorists	Sociological Predictors	Hypotheses
Power Dominance Theory		
Straus	Power Imbalance Stress Conflict	Broad social-structural conditions produce stress and conflict in family systems. When stress is coupled with violent childhood experiences, domestic violence is more probable.
Feminist Theory *Gender/Inequality Theory*		
Yllö Dobash and Dobash	Patriarchy	Patriarchy teaches men how and when to use violent techniques. Men maintain power and control through violence against women.
Subculture Theory		
Wolfgang and Ferracuti	Subcultures of violence	Participation in subcultures of violence increases the acceptance of subcultural customs and values for violence as a response to frustrating conditions. Acceptance of such values increases the likelihood of committing domestic violence.

Individual Level Explanations of Domestic Violence

Theories and Theorists	Sociological Predictors	Hypotheses
Social Learning Theory		
Akers	Differential reinforcement	Individuals who hold attitudes that disapprove of domestic violence are less likely to commit domestic violence. The greater the costs for domestic violence, the less likely the individual is to commit domestic violence.
Glaser	Differential identification	Individuals are more likely to commit domestic violence if they identify with another person who views domestic violence as acceptable.
Routine Activities Theory		
Cohen and Felson	Motivated offender Suitable target Absence of guardian	Domestic violence is likely to occur when there is a suitable target, a motivated offender, and a lack of a capable guardian.

/ continues

TABLE 5–3 Explanations of Domestic Violence Rates / continued

Individual Level Explanations of Domestic Violence		
Theories and Theorists	**Sociological Predictors**	**Hypotheses**
Control/Exchange Theory		
Gelles	Inequality Privacy Social control	Family members are more likely to use violence in the home when they expect that the costs of being violent are less than the rewards. The absence of effective social controls over family relations decreases the costs of one family member being violent toward another. Certain social and family structures serve to reduce social control in family relations and therefore reduce the costs and/or increase the rewards of being violent.
General Strain Theory		
Agnew	Strain/stress	The greater the strain experienced by an individual, the greater the experience of negative emotions. The greater the negative emotional experience, the more likely an individual will commit domestic violence.
Self-control Theory		
Gottfredson and Hirschi	Self-control	The greater the individual's self-control, the lower the probability of engaging in domestic violence.
Frustration–Aggression Theory		
Dollard and colleagues	Frustration Aggression	High levels of frustration increase levels of aggression. Increased levels of aggression are likely to result in domestic violence.
Unreciprocity		
Palmer	Unreciprocity	Unreciprocity increases levels of frustration. Increased levels of frustration are likely to result in higher levels of domestic violence.

Gelles (1994, p. 274) notes that "A central (and perhaps a greatly oversimplified) proposition of an exchange/social control theory of family violence is that *people hit and abuse other family members because they can*." If the perceived benefits for assaulting a family member—exertion of control and dominance and the immediate release of tension—outweigh the potential costs—public disgrace, arrest or abandonment—then domestic violence is more probable. In addition, the social control formulation proposes family violence is more likely when there is an "absence of social controls which would bind people to the social order and negatively sanction family members for acts of violence" (Gelles, 1994, p. 275).

Gelles (1994) summarizes his exchange/social control formulation in the following three propositions:

1. Family members are more likely to use violence in the home when they expect the costs of being violent are less than the rewards.
2. The absence of effective social controls over family relations decreases the costs of one family member being violent toward another.
3. Certain social and family structures serve to reduce social control in family relations and therefore reduce the costs and/or increase the rewards of being violent.

Gelles (1994) also argues that three social conditions increase the likelihood of violence within the home: privacy, inequality, and the cultural link between violence and being a "real man."

PRIVACY. What occurs within the confines of the U.S. home is largely a private matter. Wide discretion in the forms that interaction between family members may take is socially and legally permissible. Wives and husbands, children, and grandparents may act toward one another in the privacy of their homes in ways that are inappropriate in a public setting and legally sanctioned if directed toward someone outside the family.

Domestic privacy, then, limits the extent of social control over family interaction. Both formal and informal means of control are used less frequently and with less severe sanctions in matters involving domestic violence. Except in rare instances, neighbors are reluctant to interfere in family altercations; law enforcement agencies are restricted by specific guidelines for dealing with calls involving domestic violence. As a consequence, there is an absence of social controls over intrafamilial matters that increase the opportunity for assaultive behavior in the home.

INEQUALITY. Families are typically characterized by inequality among their members. Status differences between spouses flow from the economic resources of husbands and wives—husbands often have a higher paying job with more social prestige than their wives. Wide status differences are evident between parents and their offspring—children are most often physically weaker, economically dependent, and without ready access to guardians outside the home. These inequities serve to structure offender–victim relations in domestic violence. The victimization of women and children is not only more frequent, but the physical and psychological consequences are more severe. Women, and by extension their children, often lack the economic resources to seek legal assistance or to leave the hostile situation. They may also be so intimidated by the threat of more severe beatings that they are reluctant to take advantage of publicly supported programs for battered women and children. As a result, men can act violently toward their wives and children with impunity.

VIOLENT BEHAVIOR AND THE "REAL MAN." The U.S. culture provides considerable support for the belief that "real men" are also violent men. Men are culturally expected to be decisive, act aggressively, and appreciate competitive and violent sports. This is particularly true for men who live in "subcultures of violence," where violence is seen as a viable means to settle disputes (see Wolfgang & Ferracuti, 1967). In the home men are considered the "head of the household" and as such they control important decisions; they expect to be treated with deference and respect. When these cultural expectations are not met, wives and children may well be dealt with in a violent manner. The link between manliness and the willingness to use violence to establish dominance and control underlies much of domestic violence (Gelles, 1994).

Power and Dominance

Murray A. Straus and his colleagues (1995) in the Family Violence Research Program at the University of New Hampshire have developed a balance of power/gender inequality formulation of domestic violence. In families characterized by an asymmetrical power structure—where typically the husband's wishes take precedence over those of his wife—the probability of domestic violence is increased. The dominance of men within the family is played out in the larger context of the social conditions that affect family interactions.

The experience of stress in everyday life impacts life within the family. Stress and conflict experienced in the workplace or school, in the neighborhood or community, or in the larger society may well affect the behavior of family members toward one another. The consequences of socioeconomic inequity add further to the stress generated by daily interactions outside the family. The lack of job opportunity or stability is a primary source of stress within the family. Marital conflict often is precipitated by financial problems with few prospects for economic recovery or stability.

Yet, Straus and his colleagues (1995) argue that stress experienced by family members does not adequately account for domestic violence. When husbands and wives have also been violently victimized or witnessed violence in their family of origin, or when the family is immersed in a "subculture of violence" that legitimates the use of violence, the chances that familial stress will erupt in a violent altercation are greatly increased.

Power theory takes into account a myriad of social conditions that generate stress for family members. It also recognizes the stressful consequences of gender inequality and sexism for husband–wife interaction. However, power imbalance theory is not limited to issues related to gender inequality in attempting to account for domestic violence.

Feminist Theory

Feminist theorists focus their attention on the patriarchal structure of society to explain the violence of men toward their female intimate partners (Dobash & Dobash, 1988; Yllö, 1984; Yllö & Bograd, 1988). Male dominance is the key to understanding the victimization of wives and paramours. Men, it is argued, set expectations for the behavior of their intimate partners. When these women fail to live up to these expectations, men resort to violence to establish their position of dominance in the relationship. The Dobashs (1988), a husband and wife team of feminist researchers from Wales, argue that men learn to use physical force largely by participating in a violent male subculture.

Kersti Yllö (1984, 1988) argues that issues related to gender and power are critical to understanding domestic violence. Male dominance within the family is viewed as a reflection of the power structure of the larger society. Simply put, men resort to violence to exert coercive control over women. Feminist theorists argue that men batter women because they gain considerably from doing so. Not only does violence result in the domination of a woman at the time it is carried out, but it also establishes gender differences in the social relationship.

Subculture of Violence

Marvin Wolfgang and Franco Ferracuti's (1967) subculture of violence formulation helps us understand the context in which domestic violence may occur. Families in neighborhoods that are characterized by norms and values that support the use of violence to settle interpersonal disputes are more likely to resort to violence to resolve family conflicts. The family then models the behavior that is prevalent within its surrounding subculture. Children witness violent outbursts in the home and are often the targets of parental assault. Violent behavior becomes a learned response—an appropriate, expected, and effective way to get what you want immediately or to control the behavior of other people.

Routine Activities

The tenets of Lawrence Cohen and Marcus Felson's (1979) routine activities approach to understanding criminality are particularly applicable to violence within the family. Cohen and Felson argue that criminal activity requires (1) a motivated offender to carry out the offense, (2) a suitable target or victim, and (3) an absence of a guardian for the potential victim. When these three conditions converge in time and space, criminal offending becomes more probable.

As Richard Gelles (1994) points out, family violence differs from other forms of assaultive behavior. Men who have accepted the cultural view that real men use violence to maintain dominance over their wives and children carry out intrafamily violence in the privacy of the home, often characterized by an inequitable spousal relationship. Men who believe that the use of violence against wives and children is a mark of their manliness are certainly *motivated offenders*. Wide disparities in economic and other resources of wives and by extension their children—characteristic of inequitable relations between husband and wives—provide *suitable targets* for family violence. And the privacy of the home virtually ensures the *lack of a guardian* for the intended victim.

Strain

Strain theory, set forth by Robert Agnew (1992), focuses on negative interpersonal relations as a primary source of stress for the individual. Sustained family conflict has been found to generate particularly devastating negative emotions (e.g., jealousy, rage, resentment, and depression). Healthy coping strategies are required if an individual is to reduce the resultant tension. Prior experiences with family violence, either as a witness or a victim, and integration into a subculture of violence may impede the development of effective coping strategies and increase the likelihood of domestic violence. The use of violence tends to worsen the strained relations within the family, resulting in the perpetuation of negative emotional states for both the victim and offender. In brief, the cycle of negative familial relations leads to negative emotions that may erupt in acts of violence toward family members. However, violence within the family further strains the fragile relations among the family members and sets in motion a new wave of negative emotions with which to cope.

Frustration–Aggression

The frustration–aggression hypothesis of John Dollard and his colleagues (1939) states that the experience of frustration always leads to aggression. Frustration may be seen as a blockage to goal attainment. Certainly, the behavior of family members often involves impediments to one another's goals—husbands have expectations for their wives and wives for their husbands that may not be met, parents expect their children to behave in ways that are disregarded, and children's demands may well be in conflict with their parents' willingness or ability to grant. In short, family life is fraught with frustrating experiences. The aggression that follows may be verbal—shouting, threatening, and at times abusive. But, it may soon escalate into pushing, shoving, slapping, or more severe forms of physical aggression. The inability to control the situation by violence or the threat of violence is itself frustrating, leading to the recurrence of assaultive behavior.

Unreciprocity

Stuart Palmer (1972) has recast the frustration–aggression hypothesis in role terms. He argues that unreciprocity in role relationships accounts for aggressive and violent behavior. Unreciprocity is experienced when others in complementary roles (e.g., wives and husbands, parents and children), interfere with the roles' performance. Husbands may attempt to control their wives' behavior or access to economic resources, thereby impeding their opportunities to socialize outside the family or to be able to adequately care for the children. Wives may make inordinate demands on the husband's time or economic resources. Unreciprocity in familial relations is marked by controlling and domineering behavior or manipulative or relentlessly demanding behavior. If unreciprocity in the relations among family members persists, then some form of aggression is highly likely. As aggressive behaviors escalate, physical violence may well follow.

Self-Control

In their General Theory of Crime, Michael Gottfredson and Travis Hirschi (1990) argue that the lack of self-control predicts involvement in all forms of criminal activity. Persons who lack self control tend to be "impulsive, insensitive, physical (as opposed to mental), risk-taking, shortsighted, and nonverbal, and they tend therefore to engage in criminality and analogous risk-taking behavior" (Gottfredson & Hirschi, 1990, p. 90). To Gottfredson and Hirschi (1990, p. 90), criminal offending provides "relief from momentary irritation." Often, husband and wives assault one another simply to end an explosive encounter—an argument that neither side is willing to negotiate—or to assert control over the other person or the present situation. When self-control is weak, conflict between spouses or parents and their children may erupt into acts of aggression and violence.

Social Learning Theory

Ronald Akers's (1994) social learning formulation considers factors that generate deviant or conforming behavior. To Akers, learning deviant or conforming behaviors involves four related processes: differential association, definitions, differential reinforcement, and imitation. *Differential association* means interaction with persons who favor the violation of the law far more so than with persons who advocate conformist behavior. The more time an individual spends with others who condone the use of violence in the home—"to keep wives and children under control"—the more likely that person is to engage in wife battering and child abuse. *Definitions* refer to the meaning that is assigned to certain behaviors. Akers (1994, p. 97) notes that they are "the orientations, rationalizations, definitions of the situation, and other evaluative and moral attitudes that define the commission of an act as right or wrong, good or bad, desirable or undesirable, justified or unjustified." When spousal assault and severe corporal punishment are defined as normative, necessary, and justifiable, they will be routinely carried out in the home. *Differential reinforcement* of a given behavior is a consequence of the rewards received or anticipated. Behaviors that are positively rewarded tend to be repeated. Domestic violence may be positively rewarded by the compliance of the victim with the wishes of the perpetrator. Wives may acquiesce to the demands of their husbands; children may carry out the wishes of their parents or forego expecting their parents to condone their behavior. When acts of violence against family members result in a desirable outcome for the offender, they are reinforced and most often repeated. *Imitation* means simply that individuals model or copy the behavior of others. Children who have witnessed violence between their parents or who have been the victims of abuse at the hands of their caretakers may learn that these behaviors are effective means for controlling others and for immediate gratification. Because it seemed to work for their parents, it becomes a viable strategy for dealing with their own wives and children.

Differential identification, introduced by Daniel Glaser (1956), is closely related to the concept of differential reinforcement. He points out that a deviant may well identify with another who is likely to condone her or his behavior. The concept of differential identification helps us to understand why not all children who are exposed to violent behavior in the home batter their wives or abuse their children. If children or adolescents do not identify with a violent parent, then they are less apt to see violence as an acceptable strategy for controlling members of their family. Their lack of identification with an abusive parent may result in abhorrence for violence either within the home or outside of it. Differential identification is then another element in the complex process of learning patterns of behavior.

Chapter Summary

Domestic violence is coercive behavior through the use of intimidating, threatening, harmful, or harassing behavior. Domestic violence includes physical abuse, sexual abuse, and emotional or psychological abuse. Crucial to social understandings of domestic violence are those factors that influence the meanings and interpretations attached to the offender's behavior.

Domestic violence occurs in all racial and ethnic groups and across socioeconomic classes. Women are more likely to be victimized by their intimate partners than are men. Approximately 772,000 U.S. children are victims of child maltreatment each year. Most of these children are victims of neglect, followed by physical abuse, sexual abuse, and either medical neglect or psychological abuse.

Being a victim of child maltreatment significantly increases the risk of being a victim of domestic violence. Also, the risk of victimization is significantly greater when there is a disparity in the relative status between victim and offender. In addition, intimate partner violence is significantly greater for those who are cohabitating versus married, African American versus White, living with a verbally abusive partner, or one who controls access to family, friends, or economic resources.

Children who are the victims of maltreatment or who have been physically or sexually abused in their homes are more likely to engage in antisocial behavior, criminal activity, and domestic violence later in life. There is considerable evidence that homes marked by violence between spouses are also places in which children are abused or neglected.

Considerable evidence exists to support the idea that corporal punishment has deleterious effects on subsequent behavior of children and adolescents and on their emotional well-being and cognitive development. Conversely, not using corporal punishment has beneficial consequences for a child.

Key Concepts

Domestic violence: The involvement of any family member in the intentional physical injury of another; coercion through the use of intimidating, threatening, harmful, or harassing behavior.

Learned helplessness: The inability to predict how an abuser will react to one's actions; a process that results in devising ways to adapt to an abusive relationship.

Child maltreatment: Child abuse and neglect, sexual abuse, and emotional abuse.

Child abuse and neglect: Any act or failure to act on the part of a parent or caretaker that results in death, serious physical or emotional harm, sexual abuse or exploitation; an act or failure to act that presents an imminent risk of serious harm.

Sexual abuse: The employment, use, persuasion, inducement, or coercion of any child to engage in any sexual behavior, including rape, statutory rape, incest, molestation, prostitution, or other form of sexual exploitation of children.

Emotional abuse: Acts of omission to acts by the parents or other caregivers that have caused or could cause serious behavioral, cognitive, emotional, or mental disorders.

Cycle of violence: The term coined by Lenoir Walker to describe the process that characterizes intimate partner violence.

Corporal punishment: The use of physical force with the intention of causing a child to experience pain, but not injury, for the purpose of correction or control of the child's behavior.

Critical Thinking Questions

1. What is the link between involvement in domestic violence either as an offender or a victim and the likelihood of engaging in violent behavior outside the home?
2. What are the sociocultural roots of domestic violence, including child and elder victimization? What are the intrafamilial conditions that exacerbate an adverse sociocultural milieu?
3. Jim is 10 years old, and he and his 6-year-old sister, Sally, have witnessed their father beating their mother on many occasions. They, too, have suffered physical injury repeatedly at the hands of their father. It is now 12 years later and Jim and Sally are each employed as unskilled

laborers and will be married in the same year. In the next 4 years Jim and Sally will each have three children. Describe the domestic life for Jim and Sally. What factors increase or decrease the likelihood of domestic violence?

4. Discuss the sociopolitical conditions that serve to perpetuate the forms of violent behaviors that occur in the home. What factors serve to significantly reduce the occurrence of domestic violence?

Web Extra

Web-based media materials from high-quality sources such as CNN, Time, and National Public Radio are available in support of this textbook. Visit go.jblearning.com/deviance to access them.

Check out these websites for additional information on domestic violence:

http://www.ncadv.org

http://www.unh.edu/frl

http://www.unh.edu/ccrc

Irreversible illness ? Unbearable suffering ?
Die with Dignity
Join FinalExitNetwork.org

Suicide and Life-Threatening Behaviors

CHAPTER 6

Learning Objectives

After reading this chapter you should know

- The medical, legal, and cultural definition of suicide.
- Patterns and trends of suicide around the world and in the United States.
- Precipitating factors, risk factors, and protective factors of suicide.
- How suicides impact young people in the United States.
- What global trends and patterns of suicide reveal.
- Some of the characteristics of those who attempt suicide.
- How psychiatric illnesses are related to suicide and suicide attempts.
- Some of the risk factors useful in identifying possible suicidal behavior.
- How the suicide process develops.
- Special topics including homicide followed by suicide, suicide by cop, and assisted suicide.
- Some of the theories offered to explain suicide.

In mid-2010 a billboard that some found shocking was erected in San Francisco near the intersection of Howard Street and South Van Ness Avenue. Its message, spelled out in large letters, was simple: "My Life, My Death, My Choice." At the bottom of the billboard the name of the sponsor appeared, FinalExitNetwork.org (Gulezian, 2010). The Network (also known as FEN), which states it does not encourage anyone to end their life, officially supports assisted suicide when medical circumstances warrant a person's making such a decision. FEN has plans to erect similar signs in Florida and New Jersey, but the San Francisco sign sparked outrage among some religious fundamentalists as well as those concerned that its proximity to the San Francisco-Oakland Bay Bridge and the Golden Gate Bridge—sites notorious for suicides—might tempt more people to leap off the spans. The Golden Gate Bridge has had more suicides than any other bridge in the world—more than 1,200 (Guthmann, 2005).

Not only is assisted suicide a controversial topic, but FEN has itself been at the center of an ongoing debate. In 2010 four FEN members were indicted by a Forsyth County, Georgia, grand jury and charged with helping a cancer victim end his life in a Georgia home. Assisting someone to commit suicide is a felony in Georgia, and if convicted of the charges, members of the group could spend up to 5 years in prison.

Although many Americans remain uneasy with the idea of suicide, Jerry Dincin, vice president of FEN, says a battle over the right to die with dignity is underway and assisted suicide could easily become "the human right of the 21st century" (Bowers, 2009).

Suicide and other acts of self-destruction represent a complex set of behaviors, some intentional and deliberate, others ambivalent and reckless. Wide cultural differences exist in the meanings attached to suicidal behavior and its appropriateness as a form of death. The decision to end one's own life may be viewed as morally reprehensible and religiously prohibited, permitted under well-defined circumstances, or an expected form of death for some members of society.

Suicidal behavior tends to be structured by age, gender, and race, as are other forms of violent behavior. In this chapter we consider the diversity of suicide and self-destructive behavior across the globe, the differential involvement of various segments of society, and theoretical understandings of the influence of social structural arrangements, cultural meanings, and values given to suicidal behavior and its various precipitants.

Medical and Legal Definitions of Suicide

Suicide is typically defined as the willful, deliberate, and voluntary termination of one's life. Medical examiners, coroners, and public health officials in the United States rely on the definition of suicide provided by Centers for Disease Control and Prevention (CDC) in Atlanta. The CDC defines suicide as a "fatal self-inflicted destructive act with explicit or inferred intent to die" (www.cdc.gov).

The World Health Organization (WHO) provides a broad, yet succinct, definition of suicide. The WHO defines suicide as "a suicidal act with a fatal outcome"; a suicidal act is considered to be a "self-injury with varying degrees of lethal intent." These medical–legal definitions of suicide provide considerable latitude in their interpretation (www.who.org).

The intention to end one's life is an essential element in the determination of suicide. Suicidal intention may be either *explicit*—as in the case of suicide notes and powder burns on the hand of the victim—or *implicit*—inferences drawn from autopsy results or toxicological tests, reports of the victim's emotional state before death, expressions of the desire to die, and making plans to carry out a suicide (Jamison, 1999).

According to the guidelines set forth by the CDC, self-inflicted death may be determined by pathological (autopsy), toxicological, investigatory, and psychological evidence and by statements of the decedent or witnesses. Intent to kill oneself is evident if "at the time of injury, the decedent intended to kill himself/herself or wished to die and that the decedent understood the probable consequences of his/her actions" (www.cdc.gov).

In many cases circumstantial evidence provides the only clue about the cause of death. Therefore, the final determination by the medical examiner or coroner may well be influenced by political expediency, family intervention, or lack of medical certainty on the part of the medical examiner or coroner. Accidental deaths or involvement in reckless and high-risk behaviors that result in one's death is not included among deaths by suicide (www.cdc.gov).

Forensically trained medical examiners, for the most part, are found in large urban areas and in medical school settings. It is still the case in the United States that decisions about the cause of death are made by medical doctors without forensic training or by coroners without medical training. The misclassification of the cause of death, particularly in the case of suicide, may be problematic. Deaths due to drug overdose, drowning, falls, and one-car accidents are particularly difficult to classify. Estimates of misclassification range from 50% in earlier studies to 10% more recently (Jamison, 1999).

In short, although the medical–legal definition of suicide is accepted across the United States, the availability of forensic pathologists who serve as medical examiners is limited. This shortage of forensically qualified medical doctors is far more pronounced outside the United States.

There is but one truly serious philosophical problem, and that is suicide. Judging whether life is or is not worth living amounts to answering the fundamental question of philosophy.

—Albert Camus (www.websyntax.com/camus/quotes/bysubject.asp)

Mostly, I have been impressed by how little value our society puts on saving the lives of those who are in such despair as to want to end them. It is a social illusion that suicide is rare. It is not.

—Kay Jamison (1999, p. 310)

SSRN

McGee, R. W. (1997). Suicide is a property right; Assisted suicide is a contract right. *Commentaries on Law & Public Policy.* http://ssrn.com/abstract=845813

SSRN

Rubin, E. L. (2010). Assisted suicide, morality and law: Why prohibiting assisted suicide violates the establishment clause. Vanderbilt Public Law Research Paper No. 10-02. *Vanderbilt Law Review.* http://ssrn.com/abstract=1546648

Suicide Around the World

The suicide rate is calculated as the number of deaths caused by suicide per 100,000 persons in the general population. Keeping in mind the caution with regard to the under-reporting of suicide across the world and within the United States, suicide rates are known to vary widely. Approximately 1 million people kill themselves each year around the world. That is, for every 100,000 persons in the world, 16 will take their own lives, or 1 person every 40 seconds. Over the past 45 years, suicide across the world has increased by 60%, making it one of the three leading causes of death in the world for those aged 15 through 44 (www.iasp.info; WHO, 2009).

Except for The People's Republic of China, suicide rates for males exceed those for females. Chinese women kill themselves at a rate (14.8) slightly above the world rate, whereas the male suicide rate (13.0) is below the world rate. However, in all other countries for which the WHO has collected recent data on suicides, national male rates of suicide are typically two to five times higher than those for females. Exceedingly high rates of male suicide are found in Belarus (63.3), Lithuania (53.9), the Russian Federation (53.9), Sri Lanka (44.6), Hungary (42.3), and the Ukraine (40.9). The highest rates of female suicide are found in The People's Republic of China (14.8), Sri Lanka (16.8), Hungary (15.6), Republic of Korea (14.1), and Japan (13.7) (www.who.int/mental_health/prevention/suiciderates/en/print/html). Countries with the lowest rates of male suicides are Egypt (0.1), the Syrian Arab Republic (0.2), and Jamaica (0.3). Interestingly, Egypt and the Syrian Arab Republic each report a suicide rate for women of zero. Other countries for which the suicide rate for women is zero are Antigua and Barbuda, Honduras, Saint Kitts and Nevis, Saint Vincent and The Grenadines, and Seychelles (www.who.int/mental_health/prevention/suicide rates/en/print/html).

Rate of Suicide in the United States

Figure 6–1 shows that although the suicide rate for males is declining, it is consistently higher than the suicide rate for females. The overall rate of suicide among females across the country remains fairly stable over time.

Suicide is the 11th leading cause of death in the United States (**Figure 6–2**). In recent years more than 34,000 deaths each year are attributed to suicide, for a rate of 11 per 100,000 persons. However, rates of suicide vary widely across the United States. Suicide rates are highest in Alaska (21.8), New Mexico (20.4), Wyoming (19.3), and Colorado (16.7). Suicide rates are lowest in Connecticut (7.7), Massachusetts (8.0), Rhode Island (9.1), Maryland (9.2), and Hawaii (www.cdc.gov).

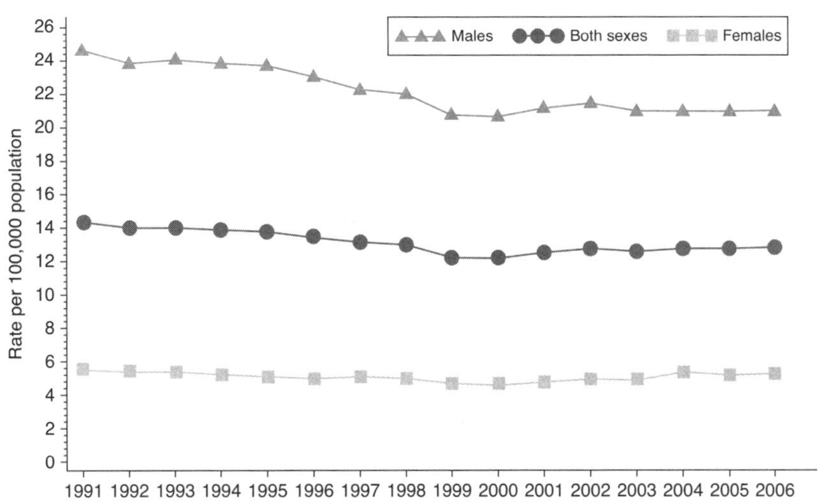

FIGURE 6–1 Trends in suicide rates among persons ages 10 and older, by gender, United States, 1991–2006.

Source: Reproduced from Centers for Disease Control and Prevention

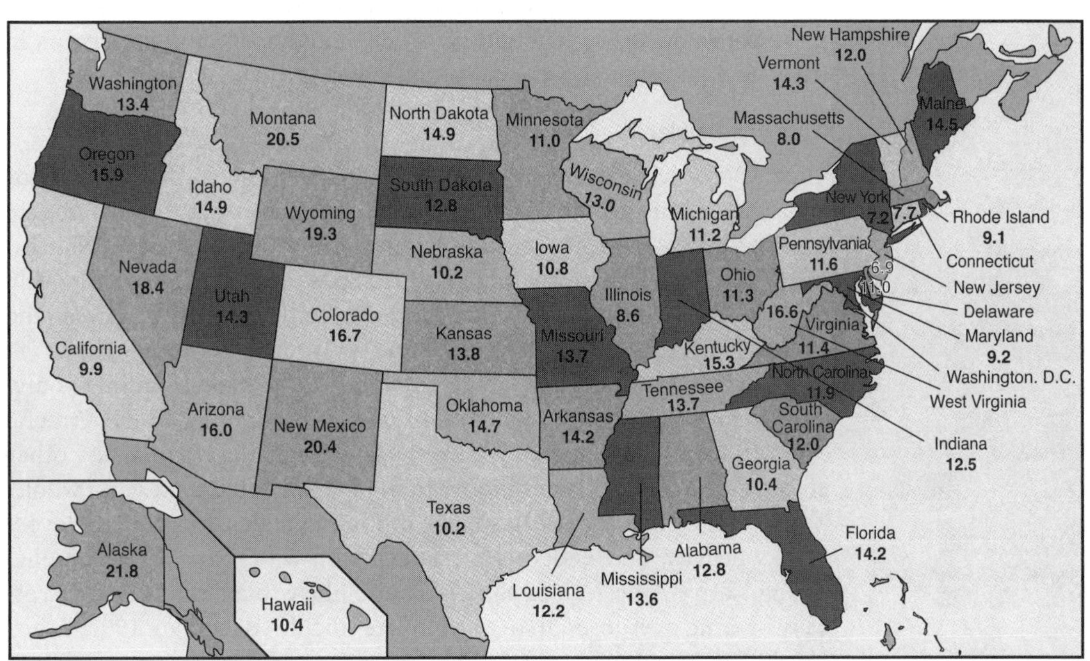

FIGURE 6–2 Suicide rates per 100,000 in the United States, 2007.

Source: Data from Centers for Disease Control and Prevention

Age and Gender

Figure 6–3 shows that for males the rate of suicide is consistently higher among those over the age of 65, followed by men between 25 and 64, and is least likely among those less than 25 years of age.

There are 9.1 completed suicides in the United States every day, or 1 every 16 minutes (www.cdc.gov). Suicide is the 7th leading cause of death for males and the 16th leading cause of death for females. Males account for 8 of every 10 suicides in the United States. That is, males are 3.6 times more likely to kill themselves than are females, but females attempt suicide three times more often than males (www.cdc.gov/violenceprevention).

Figure 6–4 shows that for females the highest rates of suicide are found among those between the ages of 25 and 64, followed by older women—those 65 years of age and over, and is lowest among those under the age of 24. For women, suicides tend to rise rapidly between the ages of 40 and 54 (www.cdc.gov). Suicidal behavior is more common among single, separated, divorced, or widowed women. Loss of family ties or crises in interpersonal relations are among the leading precipitants of suicide attempts in women. Mood disorders, including depression, dysthymia (a major depression disorder), and seasonal affective disorder, are more common in women and have been cited as underlying factors in their suicidal behavior (www.afsp.org/index-1.htm).

Race and Gender

The rate of suicide among Native Americans is reportedly higher than for any other ethnic group. The most recent data show that the suicide rate among Native Americans (including Native Americans and Alaska Natives) is 1.5 times higher than that for the United States as a whole. Approximately 64% of all Native American suicides are committed by males between the ages of 15 and 24 (www.cdc.gov).

The Native American suicide rate tends to be highest among young adults and declines with age. The suicide rate of young Native Americans (15 to 24 years of age) is three to four times higher than any other ethnic group and 1.5 times higher than for the United States as a whole. The typical Native American suicide is a young male who is unemployed, drinks heavily, and ends his life either with a firearm or by hanging. Young Native American females are more likely to attempt suicide, typically by drug overdoses, than to complete suicide (Bachman, 1992; Echo-Hawk, 1997; www.cdc.gov).

Ronet Bachman (1992, p. 120), in her in-depth investigation of violent death among Native Americans, finds that "economic deprivation

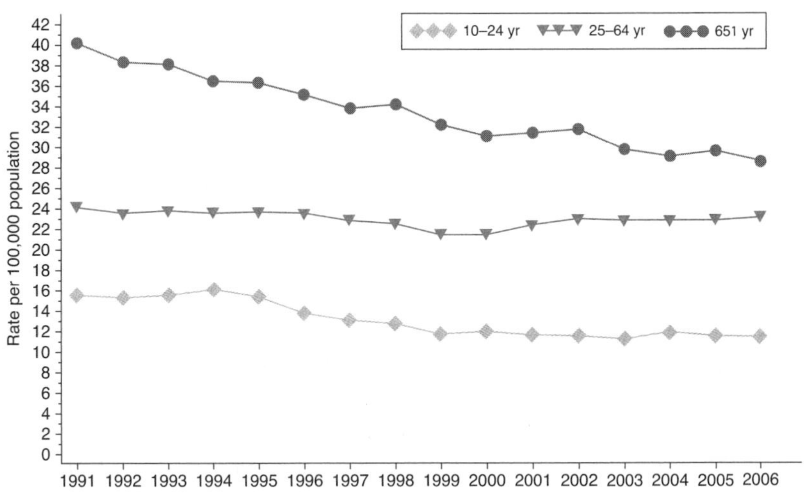

FIGURE 6–3 Trends in suicide rates among males, by age group, United States, 1991–2006.

Source: Reproduced from Centers for Disease Control and Prevention.

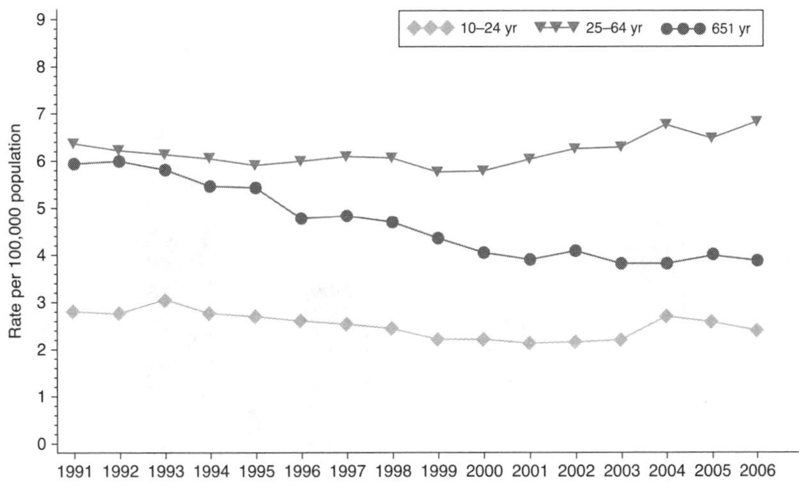

FIGURE 6–4 Trends in suicide rates among females, by age group, United States, 1991–2006.

Source: Reproduced from Centers for Disease Control and Prevention.

has a significant and positive impact on suicide within reservation communities." Suicide rates on the reservation increase with unemployment, dropout, and poverty rates. Bachman also observes that the suicide rate is highly correlated with the homicide rate.

It is apparent that suicide is related to the structural circumstances within communities, such as unemployment and poverty. When communities provide little opportunity for economic self-sufficiency, frustrations appear to manifest in acts of violence. These acts tend to be nondiscriminatory and are directed both toward the self in acts of suicide or toward others in acts of assault that are often lethal (Bachman, 1992).

The suicide rate is much higher among White Americans (12.9) than Hispanic Americans (5.4) and African Americans (4.9) (**Figure 6–5**) and among older persons than younger persons (www.cdc.gov). White males commit more than 7 in 10 of all suicides in the United States. An additional 18% are White females. Whites then account for about 9 in every 10 suicides in the United States.

Elderly Suicides

Among White Americans, the risk of suicide tends to increase with age (**Figure 6–6**). Persons over the age of 65 are significantly more apt to end

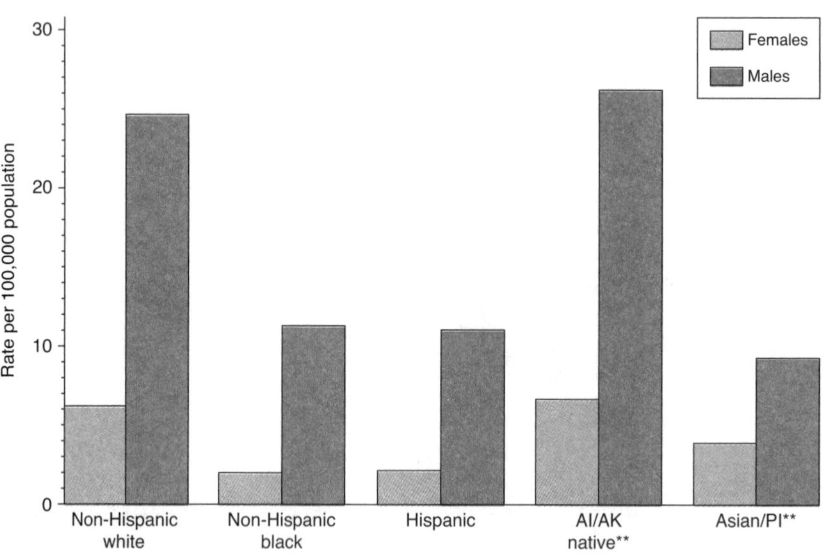

FIGURE 6–5 Suicide rates among persons ages 10 and older, by race/ethnicity and gender.
Source: Reproduced from Centers for Disease Control and Prevention.

their own lives than younger persons. Men disproportionately account for elderly suicides, more so than other age groups. Older men are at greatest risk to end their own life. Among elderly men, the divorced or widowed are 2.7 times more likely to kill themselves than are those who are married and 1.4 times more likely than the never-married. Similarly, elderly women who are divorced or widowed are 1.8 times more likely to commit suicide than are elderly married women and 1.4 times more likely than their never-married counterparts (www.cdc.gov).

Although separation, divorce, or widowhood elevate the risk of suicide in general, other risk factors set the elderly apart from the young. Physical illness, depression, and social isolation are more pronounced among the elderly. The elderly are also more apt to have sought medical attention just before their suicide. Whereas the elderly make fewer suicide attempts, they tend to use more lethal methods (Pearson, Conwell, Lindesay, Takahashi, & Caine, 1997; www.cdc.gov).

A global epidemic of elderly suicide is underway. The WHO reports that Hungary has one of the highest rates of elderly suicides worldwide (168.9 for men and 60 for women). Rural China also has an exceedingly high rate of elderly suicide (142.6 for men and 100.8 for women). By contrast, the U.S. rates for elderly (over 75 years) men and women in the United States are 50.7 and 5.6, respectively; Canadian rates for elderly men and women are 26.6 and 3.7, respectively (www.who.org).

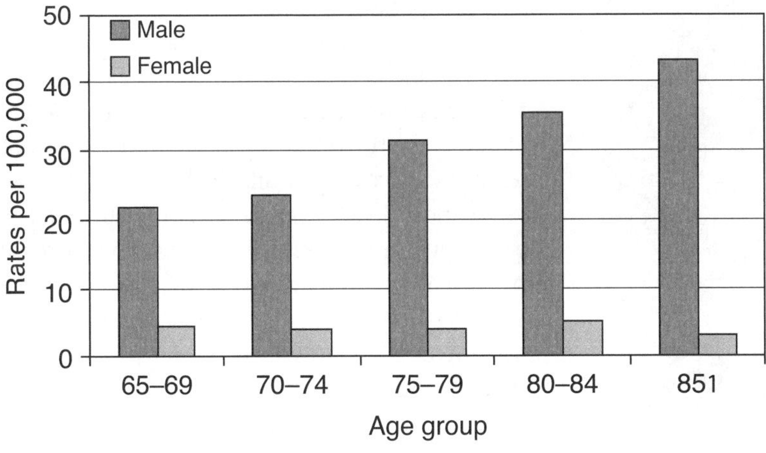

FIGURE 6–6 Suicide rates for persons ages 65 and older.

Source: Reproduced from Centers for Disease Control and Prevention.

Elderly Suicides

- Although the elderly are about 12.5% of the population, they account for about 15.7% of all suicides.
- The elderly suicide rate is about 50% higher than for all other age groups combined.
- Older White males have the highest rate of suicide, about 31.1 per 100,000, or almost three times the rate for the U.S. population as a whole.
- Older persons attempt suicide less frequently than do younger persons, but they complete the suicidal act. For persons over the age of 65, there is one completed suicide for every four attempts.
- Older men account for 85% of elderly suicides, 7.3 times more than for elderly women suicides.
- Beyond undiagnosed or untreated depression, common risk factors for elderly suicide include
  - Recent death of a loved one
  - Physical illness, uncontrolled pain, or the fear of a prolonged illness
  - Perceived poor health
  - Social isolation and loneliness
  - Major changes in social roles (e.g., retirement)

Source: Reproduced from Centers for Disease Control and Prevention.

A teenager contemplates suicide. What kinds of life stressors might lead to suicidal thoughts among young people?

Youth

Suicide is uncommon among children and early adolescents (**Figure 6–7**). The suicide rate among that group has declined somewhat in recent years. The suicide rate among later adolescents (15–19 years) is declining more noticeably. However, for persons between the ages of 15 and 24, suicide is the third leading cause of death. More teenagers and young adults die from suicide than from cancer, heart disease, AIDS, birth defects, stroke, pneumonia and influenza, and chronic lung disease combined (www.cdc.gov).

The stresses of life often overwhelm college and university students. Conflicting demands on their time and energy increasingly lead to self-medication—drug and alcohol abuse—and other self-destructive behaviors. Suicide is the second leading cause of death among undergraduates.

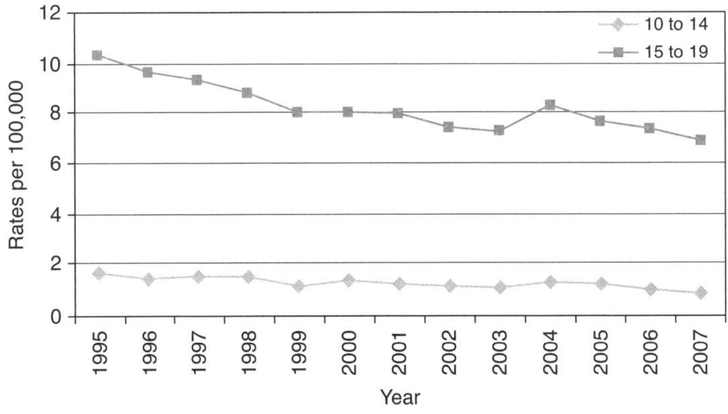

FIGURE 6–7 Suicide rates for persons aged 10–14 and 15–19; 1995–2007.
Source: Reproduced from Centers for Disease Control and Prevention.

Higher youth suicide rates are evident across the globe. The highest rates of youth suicide—more than 30 per 100,000—are found in Finland, Latvia, Lithuania, New Zealand, the Russian Federation, and Slovenia. Japan and countries in Western Europe tend to have youth suicide rates below 15 per 100,000. Overall, the suicide rate for young men (15–24 years) consistently exceeds that for their female peers, except in Sweden where females are as equally likely to commit suicide as males (www.who.org).

Youth Suicides in the United States

- Suicide ranks as the third leading cause of death for young people (15–24 years); only accidents and homicide occur more frequently.
- About 11 persons between the ages of 15 and 24 commit suicide each day, or one every 2 hours and 7 minutes.
- Over the past 60 years the suicide rate for young men (15–24 years) rose by 400% and doubled for young women.
- Males between 15 and 19 years of age are 4.7 times more likely to commit suicide than are their female peers, and males between the ages of 20 and 24 are 5.3 times more likely to kill themselves.
- For every complete suicide among the young, there are an estimated 100 to 200 attempted suicides.
- Suicide is the second leading cause of death for college students.
- An estimated 1,000 college students commit suicide each year.
- One in 12 college students has made a suicide plan.
- College students with a mental health problem are at highest risk for suicide. Males, Asians and Hispanics, and students under the age of 21 are at particularly high risk for suicide.

Sources: Reproduced from Centers for Disease Control and Prevention.

Precipitants of Suicide

Several factors are known to increase the risk of suicidal behavior. These factors may be considered on three levels: social structural positioning (e.g., age, race, gender, and marital status), life circumstances (e.g., stress, social losses, and relationship crises), and individual (e.g., mental or physical illness, alcohol and drug abuse, perceptions of helplessness and hopelessness).

Life Circumstances

For many of us everyday life may be turbulent at times, a wild and unpredictable series of tragic events that leave us with the sense that life is hopeless and we are helpless to do anything about it. If this sense of hopelessness and helplessness persists, it begins to significantly compromise our problem-solving ability. Farber (1968) observed that when hope is

Suicide: Global Trends and Patterns

- In the past 45 years, the world suicide rate has increased about 60%. Worldwide suicide is the 13th leading cause of death and among the three leading causes of death among those aged 15 to 44 years.
- Approximately 1 million people die from suicide each year, a global rate of 16 per 100,000 persons, or one suicide every 40 seconds.
- Females worldwide experience a lower suicide rate than males, with the exception of the People's Republic of China.

Suicide: U.S. Trends and Patterns

- More than 34,000 persons commit suicide each year in the United States.
- About one-half million persons who attempt suicide are treated in emergency rooms each year.
- About 1.5 times more people die from suicide than from homicide.
- Overall, suicide is the 11th leading cause of death for all Americans and is the 3rd leading cause of death for young people aged 15 to 24.
- For each completed suicide there are an estimated 16 attempted suicides. More than 5 million living Americans have attempted to kill themselves.
- Nearly 3.6 times as many teen boys commit suicide as girls, but girls are more likely to attempt suicide.
- Firearms are the most common method used by male suicide victims. However, poisoning is more commonly used by female suicide victims.

Sources: The WHO (http://www.who.mt.mental_health/pages/suicide.html); Statistics on Suicide (http://www.rochford.org/suicide/resource/stats/); U.S. Public Health Service, The Surgeon General's Call to Action to Prevent Suicide. Washington, DC: 1999; Centers for Disease Control and Prevention, Suicide and Attempted Suicide, MMWR 2004:53:471–498; http://www.afsp.org; http://www.nimh.nih.gov; http://www.suicidology.org; www.cdc.gov.

lost, our sense of competence is also lost. Competency means that we have control over what happens to us, that we can influence the circumstances of life that most matter to us. When this is lost and a strong sense of hopelessness and helplessness take hold, persistent thoughts of suicide may follow. A plan to put those thoughts into action may seem to be needed.

Jack Gibbs (1968, p. 17) asserts that the fundamental etiological factor in suicide is the "disruption in social relations." Disruption in social relations refers to an interruption in a regular pattern of social interaction. Gibbs (1968, p. 17) sets forth two propositions on the link between disruptions in social relations and suicide: "(1) The greater the incidence of disrupted social relations in a population, the higher the suicide rate of that population; and (2) all suicide victims have experienced a set of disrupted social relations that is not found in the history of non-victims." Disruption in social relations typically refers to the loss of an important social role (spouse, parent, job or occupation, close friend, etc). Social losses, particularly of persons close to us through death, abandonment, or rejection, may well precipitate our sense of hopelessness and helplessness. When loss is final, when there is no chance for recovery of the lost person, job, reputation, or status in the community, suicide may appear to provide the ultimate solution.

Attempted Suicide

Attempted suicide is far more common than completed suicide. Although there are no official national data on attempted suicide, it is estimated that more than three-quarters of a million suicides are attempted in the United States each year (National Institute of Mental Health, 2003). For every completed suicide there are estimated to be 18 to 20 attempted suicides (Mosiciki, 1996). Five million Americans are now alive who have attempted to kill themselves (American Association of Suicidology, www.suicidology.org).

Women, particularly younger women, are between two and three times more likely to attempt suicide than men. In the United States, females account for about 9 in every 10 adolescent suicide attempts. Overall, the ratio of female-to-male suicide attempts is between two and three to one (Stephens, 1987).

Suicide has been called a "cry for help" (Farberow & Schniedman, 1961). This is especially the case for suicide attempters who for the most part are trying to call attention to a problematic life situation and to elicit others in changing it. An attempt to manipulate one's life circumstances, rather than to cause one's death, influences the lethality of means and the location of the attempt. Less lethal means are typically used in a suicide attempt (e.g., drug overdose, wrist slashing, or gas poisoning) (Peck, 1985–1986). The timing of the attempt and the place it occurs are chosen to maximize the chances of a rescue.

Suicide attempters are typically more ambivalent about living or dying than are persons who complete suicide. Their uncertainty is reflected in the high incidence of warnings, often vague and mostly ignored. Suicide attempts also use less lethal means to kill themselves than do suicide completers. Typically, suicide attempters will overdose on sleeping pills, cut their wrists, or try to asphyxiate themselves (Peck, 1984, 1985–1986).

Ronald Maris's (1981) comparison of suicide completers, nonfatal suicide attempters, and natural deaths shows that suicide attempters tend to be young depressed females who use less lethal methods (e.g., poisoning and cutting) but are prone to make multiple attempts. Rigidity of thought, reliance on others for emotional support, feelings of helplessness, and the inability to see alternatives to life circumstance or solutions to current problems are common among suicide attempters (Clifton & Lee, 1995).

Psychiatric Illness and Suicide

To Kay Jamison, M.D. (1999), healthy people do not kill themselves. Persons with one or more psychiatric symptoms account for an estimated 90% to 95% of all suicides. About 1 in 10 schizophrenics die at their own hand. About 3 in 10 persons suffering from a psychotic disorder will attempt suicide in their lifetimes; more than 42% of those suffering from schizoaffective disorder or a major depressive disorder will attempt suicide in their lifetime (Radomsky, Haas, Mann, & Sweeney, 1999).

Jamison (1999, p. 104) contends that "Psychiatric illness, depression and particularly depression combined with alcohol and drugs are the major causes of suicide." She further observes that an estimated 30% to 70% of people who kill themselves are victims of mood disorders; the rate is even higher when depression coexists with alcohol or drug abuse. Simply put, *depression + drugs = suicide* (Jamison, 1999).

Certain forms of psychiatric illness elevate the risk of suicide. Suicide attempters are 38 times more likely to kill themselves, those suffering from mood disorders (depression) 20 times more likely, manic-depressives 15 times more likely, and schizophrenics more than 8 times more likely (Harris & Barraclough, 1997). Jamison (1999, pp. 102–103) notes the following:

> Two things seem to be true: First, although there are exceptions, almost everyone who has a physical illness and subsequently commits suicide also has a psychiatric illness. Second, most of the medical conditions that do show a significant increase in the rate of suicide—temporal lobe epilepsy, Huntington's disease, multiple sclerosis, spinal cord injury, HIV/AIDS, head and neck cancer—originate or strongly influence the brain and the rest of the nervous system. These medical disorders can cause extreme mood swings, and in some instances dementia.

Maris (1981) also finds that suicide victims in Chicago are more likely to have a history of mental disorder than persons who die of natural causes. He reports that 40% of suicide victims and 50% of suicide attempters have been hospitalized for psychiatric illness in their lifetime compared with 3% of persons who die of natural causes.

Risks for Suicide

Although risk factors do vary by age, gender, and ethnicity, certain individual attributes and behaviors are known to elevate the probability of suicide. Among these risk factors are the co-occurrence of mental disorders (e.g., depression and alcohol abuse, impulsivity and aggression, the use of highly lethal means in attempting suicide) (Brent et al., 1994; Cornelius et al., 1995; Henriksson et al., 1993).

To Jamison (1999), the symptoms of impending suicide attempts are well established. These symptoms are outlined in the box on the next page. She points out that the symptoms of suicide vary in severity and in duration. Rarely do individuals manifest all symptoms, but several may be experienced at a given time. If, for example, a person has feelings of guilt, hopelessness, helplessness, and worthlessness; is experiencing fatigue or loss of interest in ordinary activities; is abusing drugs and/or alcohol; and these symptoms last more than 2 weeks, then the risk of suicidal behavior is greatly increased.

In addition, Christine Sadowski of the Mayo Clinic notes that warning signs of suicide should be taken seriously. It is not true that people who threaten suicide do not carry it out. Such suicidal threats include saying, for example, "I wish I had never been born" or "Everyone would be better off if I were dead"; **withdrawal,** the unwillingness to communicate or desire to be left alone; **mood swings**; rapid changes in personality; **self-destructive behavior,** including risk-taking behaviors and pronounced drug or alcohol use; and **experience of a life crisis or trauma,** usually involving the loss of an important status or social role (see www.mayohealth.org/mayo/9709/htm/suicide.htm).

Clues to Suicide

Suicidal persons typically provide clues of their intention to kill themselves. These clues may be subtle behavioral changes (e.g., putting one's affairs in order or off-handed remarks like, "No one would care if I was not here anymore"). Most often, suicide is not an impulsive act but is carefully planned. Clues are given but are often missed by those close to the victim (Leenarrs, 1999). Edwin Schneidman (1996) finds that 90% of persons who commit suicide give verbal or behavioral clues within a week of their deaths.

About 75% of suicide victims visit a doctor in the last 4 months of their lives. Suicidal persons often present to a physician with feelings of helplessness and hopelessness, yet these feelings tend to be overlooked. Shneidman (1996, p. 353) also notes that "All verbal indications should be taken seriously." Actual suicide attempts are most common among completed suicide. About 8 in 10 suicide victims have previously attempted suicide. Although suicide attempts may appear to be "attention-getting" ploys, they are more often attempts to change an intolerable life situation. If the attempt does not result in a change in the conditions of one's life, then repeated and typically more serious attempts may be made.

Suicidal Symptoms

- Disruptive sleeping or eating patterns
- Ruminative feelings of guilt, hopelessness, helplessness, or worthlessness
- Persistent sad or depressed mood, especially for no obvious reason
- A noticeable loss of pleasure in activities and little enjoyment in things that used to bring much enjoyment
- Fatigue or loss of interest in ordinary activities, including sex
- Difficulty concentrating and indecisiveness
- Irritability, with increased crying, anxiety, and/or panic attacks
- Increased use or abuse of drugs and/or alcohol
- Persistent physical symptoms or pains that do not respond to treatment
- Rapid loss or gain in weight
- Preoccupation with death; thought or talk of self-destruction or suicide
- Increased visits or calls to friends or relatives
- Putting one's affairs in order and giving things away
- Suddenly happier and calmer

Source: Modified from Jamison, K., 1999, Night Falls Fast, New York: Alfred Knopf.

Suicide Process

Jerry Jacobs (1967) contends that persons who end their own lives must in some way resolve the social prohibitions of suicide. He describes the process through which rationalizations for accepting suicide are built:

1. A person experiences a series of overwhelming and seemingly unsolvable problems.
2. These problems are viewed as part of a never-ending and progressively worsening pattern of personal tragedies.
3. Death is seen as the only way to free one's self from the continual misery.
4. Because supportive others are unable to be found, the person becomes increasingly more socially isolated.
5. Ways are sought to overcome their perceived sense that society condemns suicide as immoral.
6. Social isolation facilitates the withdrawal from any social prohibitions against suicide.
7. The decision to commit suicide is rationalized as not a denunciation that life is sacred but its affirmation despite the desire to end the misery of one's life.
8. The suicide victim tends to view life's problems as not of their making and can only be resolved by self-inflicted death.
9. Once suicide becomes inevitable, the person no longer feels responsible or guilty for the decision to end his or her own life.
10. To ensure they will not be condemned in the afterlife, they ask God for forgiveness or request in a note that their survivors pray for them.

Contagion of Suicide

A phenomenon known as the contagion of suicide, or suicide clustering, which occurs mostly among youth, is well publicized. The contagious nature of suicidal behavior has been known for centuries. Suicide epidemics are documented in Ancient Greece and among the Romans 600 years before Christ. More recently reports of suicide clustering, for the most part, involve teenage and young adult victims. Analyses of suicide clusters among adolescents find that imitation is a key factor; however, suicide victims tend to have a history of suicide attempts, threats, and other self-destructive behaviors. The suicide of persons admired by the victim may legitimize the suicide of an adolescent. Or, the desire for revenge or instant recognition may prompt an adolescent to end his or her own life (Jamison, 1999).

SSRN

Wei, M. (2008). University policy and procedural responses to students at risk of suicide. *Journal of College and University Law*. http://ssrn.com/abstract=1031405

Special Topics

Suicide Notes

Edwin Schneidman (1996), a pioneer in the analysis of suicide notes, observes that they are usually written at the time of the suicide, just before killing oneself. Suicide notes must be understood, therefore, in the context of the suicidal act, filled with the emotions that attend the taking of one's own life. What can be learned from notes left by suicide victims?

Suicide notes are used in an attempt to discover the underlying dynamics of suicide or to gain particular insight into the suicidal mind. Feelings of love and hate, fear and rejection, shame and humiliation are commonly expressed in suicide notes (Schneidman, Farberow, & Litman, 1994). Suicide notes are then valuable sources of information about the thinking and feeling of the victim at the time of the suicide; the stress of ending one's own life necessarily limits the complexity of the note; and in the context of the victim's life history, suicide notes provide insights into the events that led to the ending of one's own life (Schneidman, Farberow, & Litman, 1994).

Homicide Followed by Suicide

Suicide committed by a person who has just killed someone else is a rare event. Yet there is considerable variation across cultures and at different times in history. For example, suicide followed homicide 42% of the time in Denmark; 33% in England; 22% in Australia; 11% in Israel; 10% in Edmonton, Winnipeg, and Calgary; and 4% in the United States (Landau, 1975; Silverman & Mukherjee, 1987; West, 1966). Stack (1997, p. 436) hypothesizes that the variation in **homicide–suicide** may be due to "the extent to which cultures foster self-blame and the extent to which murderers experience guilt after a homicide."

D. J. West's (1966) classic study of homicide followed by suicide in England compares 148 homicide–suicide cases with 148 homicides. He reports that homicides are quite similar to the general population in terms of occupation status, whereas the homicide offenders alone are most often drawn from the lower occupational groupings. In addition, West finds that the suicide offenders are more likely to kill family members, to kill multiple victims (particularly their children), to be young females (41%), and to be less likely to have a criminal record than the homicide-only offenders. In the United States Wolfgang finds that White homicide offenders are more likely to kill themselves than are Black offenders. About one in four of the homicide offenders in Wolfgang's study are White, whereas half of the homicide–suicide cases involve

White offenders. One-third of the suicide offenders have an arrest record, compared with two-thirds of the homicide-only offenders. Unlike West's study in England, Wolfgang (1958) finds that the homicide-only offenders (92%) are overwhelmingly male.

In sum, homicide offenders who kill themselves soon after the murder are far more likely to be emotionally tied to their victims than are offenders who do not commit suicide. West (1966, p. 46) observes the following:

> As far as they go, the statistics available in these three communities all fit the hypothesis that murderers who kill themselves, compared with murderers in general, form a less socially deviant group, and that their relationships to their victims are more often close and intimate.

Steven Stack (1997) outlined seven patterns that characterize homicide–suicides: frustrated personal relationship, ambivalence, jealousy and morbid jealousy, separation, depression, helplessness, and guilt. **Frustrated personal relationships** refer to the chaotic nature of the personal relationship found between the victim and offender in homicide–suicide cases. The relationship is fraught with abuse, separations, and chronic upheaval (Rosenbaum, 1990). *Ambivalence* is an integral part of the chaotic relationship that existed before the homicide–suicide. An emotionally charged love–hate relationship is evident along with strong dependency on the person who is both adored and despised. *Jealousy and morbid jealousy* refer to the fear that one's romantic partner is unfaithful. Within the context of an otherwise discordant relationship, the added stress of infidelity significantly increases the risk of a homicide–suicide (West, 1966). *Separation* is a key precipitating event in a homicide–suicide. *Depression* typically follows separation and is closely linked to suicide. *Helplessness* is a consequence of the combination of a rage sparked by the irreversible loss of a person on whom the offender is dependent. Caught in the conflict of emotions, the offender chooses to end the life of one's partner and oneself. *Guilt* floods in immediately after the homicide of a partner. The murder of someone loved deeply, albeit chaotically, renders life unbearable. Self-inflicted death becomes the only way to end the offender's overwhelming sense of guilt.

Stack (1997) provides analyses of 16,245 homicide cases in Chicago between 1965 and 1990, involving 265 homicides followed by the offender's suicide. In cases of homicide–suicide both the offender and victim are somewhat older than in the cases of homicide-only. The mean age of the homicide–suicide offenders is 39.7 compared with 28.7 for the homicide-only cases. The mean age of the homicide–suicide victims is 35 compared with 32 for the homicide-only cases. The victim in homicide–suicides is disproportionately female (78.5% vs. 18% for the homicide-only cases); male (97% vs. 86%), and White (36% vs. 15.5%). By contrast, homicide–suicide offenders are only somewhat more likely to be White (32% vs. 28.7%). In addition, the victims in homicide–suicide cases are far more likely to be spouses (45% vs. 9%), girlfriend/boyfriend (11.7% vs. 3%), an ex-lover (8% vs. 0.9%), or a child (7.6% vs. 2%).

Stack (1997) hypothesizes that when an offender kills someone emotionally close to him or her, guilt or self-blame is most likely. His findings show that the odds of a homicide–suicide are 12.68 times greater in cases of ex-spouse/lover, 6.11 times greater for current boyfriend/girlfriend, and 1.88 times greater for friends compared with nonintimate homicides. When a child is the victim, the odds are 10.28 times greater that the offender will commit suicide compared with nonintimate homicides.

Assisted Suicide

In October 1997, Oregon became the first state to legalize physician-**assisted suicide**. The **Death with Dignity** (Oregon Revised Statutes, 1997) statute established certain criteria that must be met before a physician can assist in the termination of life:

- The person must be terminally ill.
- The person must have 6 months or less to live.
- The person must make two oral requests for assistance in dying.
- The person must make one written request for assistance.
- The person must convince two physicians that she or he is sincere, is not acting on a whim, and that the decision is voluntary.
- The person must not have been influenced by depression.
- The person must be informed of "the feasible alternatives, including but not limited to, comfort care, hospice care and pain control."
- The person must wait for 15 days.

In November 2008, Washington joined Oregon in legalizing physician-assisted suicide. In the state of Washington, persons who wish to undergo an assisted suicide must make two requests—one orally and one in writing—2 weeks apart. The person must be of sound mind, not the victim of depression, and the requests must be approved by two doctors. A doctor, however, is not permitted to administer the lethal drug.

Wide cultural differences are evident in the practice of physician-assisted suicide. In Switzerland, physician-assisted suicide has been legally condoned for more than 60 years. Both physician and laypersons are permitted to assist in a suicide. Known as EXIT practices, Swiss law requires a person to be a Swiss resident, 18 years of age, mentally competent, and with "intolerable health problems" to be eligible for an assisted suicide. In addition, the application must be made in person, and there must be no evidence of coercion or influence by a third party. A single physician can make the decision to grant permission for an assisted suicide. But in difficult cases, a team composed of a lawyer, a psychiatrist, and a physician must grant permission (Schaer, 1996).

Physician-assisted suicide is also permitted in the Netherlands. A recent study of 114 cases of physician-assisted suicide and 535 cases of euthanasia in the Netherlands shows that more problems occur during the completion of a physician-assisted suicide than with the completion of euthanasia. In 18% of the cases the physician-assisted suicide patients are unable to take the medication—the physician must administer the fatal dose (Dutch Study, 2000).

Forms of assisted suicide are practiced in Australia, Japan, and Holland. In Australia physician-assisted suicide per se is not permitted, and active euthanasia is condoned under controlled conditions. In Japan mercy killings are permitted under four conditions: (1) the patient is suffering from unbearable pain, (2) death is inevitable and imminent, (3) all possible measures have been taken to eliminate the pain with no other

Right-to-die advocate Dr. Jack Kevorkian is shown with his "suicide machine" in Michigan, in 1991. Kevorkian served 8 years in prison after being convicted of second degree murder for helping an incurably ill man kill himself. He was paroled in 2007 and continues to advocate doctor-assisted suicide. What's your position on the subject?

I will not give a lethal drug to anyone if I am asked, nor will I advise such a plan.
—The Hippocratic Oath

treatment left open, and (4) the patient has clearly expressed his or her will to approve the shortening of his or her life. Holland legally prohibits euthanasia; however, as of 1993 physicians cannot be prosecuted for its practice. Physicians can therefore assist in the suicide of a patient if (1) the patient is in intolerable pain (including emotional pain), (2) the patient has repeatedly and lucidly asked to die, (3) two doctors agree on the procedure, (4) relatives are consulted, and (5) the death is reported (Knickerbocker, 1998; www.euthanasia.com).

Suicide by Cop

Suicide by cop refers to an event in which an individual's behavior constitutes an imminent danger of serious injury or death and is intended to cause a law enforcement officer to use fatal force to defend him- or herself. Goals of the victims of "suicide by cop" are either instrumental or expressive. A goal is instrumental when victims: "(1) attempt to escape or avoid the consequences of criminal or shameful actions; (2) using a forced confrontation with police to reconcile a failed relationship; (3) hoping to avoid the exclusion clauses of life insurance policies; (4) rationalizing that

Adherence to the principles of the practice of medicine set forth in the Hippocratic Oath is ignored by most doctors in the United States. Yet, the issue of whether or not a terminally ill patient has the right to die and should be assisted in doing so by a medical doctor is largely unsettled across the country. Two states, Oregon and Washington, have passed laws that permit a medical doctor to assist terminally ill persons in choosing to end their own lives. The statutes, referred to as "Death with Dignity" laws, specify the persons who are eligible for a physician-assisted suicide and the process the person and the medical doctor must follow before the suicide is carried out.

Before the U.S. Supreme Court ruled in 2006 that it was the state's decision to allow physician-assisted suicide or not, Jack "Doctor Death" Kevorkian said he, with the aid of his "suicide machine," administered lethal medications to about 130 persons. As a result of his participation in the suicide of a 52-year-old man with amyotrophic lateral sclerosis (more commonly known as Lou Gehrig's disease), Dr. Kevorkian was incarcerated for 7 years in Michigan. In the flagrant disregard of Michigan law, he videotaped the suicide, which was later featured on *60 Minutes*.

Should the right to end one's life be legally protected? And, should physicians and possibly others be protected from criminal prosecution if they assist a person who wants to die?

Source: Based upon information from Kate Pickert, "A Brief History of Assisted Suicide," Time, March 3, 2009.

Suicide by Cop

A well-mannered 19-year-old college student addressed a note to police before he got himself shot to death. Earlier that day he bought goodbye cards for family and friends and a toy gun. Later, when stopped by police for speeding and erratic driving, he pulled his toy gun and advanced toward officers. After ignoring repeated commands, the officers fired their weapons, shooting him three times. Police then learned that he was carrying a toy gun and that he had planned his death. In the goodbye cards, family, friends, and police learned of his depression over a $6,000 gambling debt.

Sources: Eltman, F. 1997. "Student Commits Suicide-by-Cop." The Detroit News, November 18. Stincelli, R. "Suicide-by-Cop" Web posted at www.suicidebycop.com.

while it may be morally wrong to commit suicide, being killed resolves the spiritual problem of suicide; or (5) seeking what they believe to be a very effective and lethal means of accomplishing death" (Mohandie & Meloy, 2000, pp. 384–385). Victims who focus on expressive goals "are communicating (1) hopelessness, depression, and desperation; (2) a statement about their ultimate identification as victims; (3) their need to save face by dying or being forcibly overwhelmed rather than surrendering; (4) their intense power needs; (5) rage and revenge; (6) their need to draw attention to an important personal issue" (Mohandie & Meloy, 2000, p. 385).

In a recent study of police shooting across North America, Mohandie, Meloy, and Collins (2009) report that 36% of police shooting involve a suicide-by-cop incident. These researchers note that "there is a high degree of desperation, hopelessness, impulsivity, self-destructiveness, and acting out among subjects encountered by the police in such events" (Mohandie, Meloy, & Collins, 2009, p. 461)

SSRN

Shafiq, M. N., & Abdulkader, S. (2008). Education, income and support for suicide bombings: Evidence from six Muslim countries.http://ssrn.com/abstract=1163046

Theories of Suicide

Theories of suicidal behavior may be divided into those that explain and predict either rates of suicide or the self-destructive behavior of individuals. At times, theoretical formulations primarily intended to account for rates of suicide have been used in studies of individual behavior. However, this chapter considers the various theories at either the macro (societal or social collectivity) or micro (individual) level of analysis.

Explanations of Suicide Rates

Table 6–1 lists the theories, sociological predictors, and hypotheses that explain suicide rates.

TABLE 6–1 Explanations of Suicide Rates

Theories and Theorists	Sociological Predictors	Hypotheses
Integration		
Durkheim	Integration	The greater the social integration, the lower the suicide rate.
	Anomie	The greater the level of anomie, the higher the suicide rate.
Gibbs and Martin	Status integration	The greater the degree of status integration, i.e. role conflict, the lower the suicide rate.
	Role conflict	
Henry and Short	Prestige	As prestige of individuals becomes greater, the suicide rate increases.
	External restraints	As the external restraint placed on behavior decreases, the suicide rate increases.
	Relational system	As the strength of the relational system decreases, the suicide rate increases.
Merton	Anomie	The greater the level of anomie, the greater the possibility of retreatism and suicide.
	Retreatism	
Conflict		
Thio	Power and status groups	Higher status, more powerful individuals are more likely to voluntarily commit suicide, whereas lower status individuals are more likely to be coerced into committing suicide.

SOCIAL INTEGRATION. Attempts to explain and predict rates of suicide are greatly indebted to the pioneering work of Emile Durkheim (1951) in the latter part of the 19th century. Durkheim, a founding father of sociology, conducted one of the first theoretically based empirical studies of suicide. In his book *Suicide*, Durkheim advances the theory that the degree of integration of a society or social grouping explains its rates of suicide. Integration refers to the understanding and acceptance of values considered essential to social life. Societies and social collectivities may be characterized by high levels of social integration, that is, widespread adherence to common values, low integration or few, if any, values held in common, or changes in the degree of value acceptance.

Based on the extent and nature of social integration, Durkheim argues that there are three basic types of suicide: altruistic, egoistic, and anomic. *Altruistic suicide* occurs in societies or social collectivities characterized by excessively high levels of social integration. Individuality is lost to the collective interests. A person lives for the good of his or her society and is willing to sacrifice everything, even life itself, for the welfare of others. For example, Kamikaze pilots in World War II were willing to dive bomb their planes into enemy ships to assist the Japanese war effort. *Egoistic suicide*, on the other hand, occurs when a society is characterized by little social integration. Members of society are essentially disconnected from one another, social ties are weak or broken, and individualistic behavior predominates. In the absence of involvement with others, life may lose meaning and suicide may ensue. *Anomic suicide* occurs when there is rapid change in the social integration. This sudden change may be the result of economic chaos, either positive or negative, widespread social mobility, or unpredicted upheavals in life circumstances. Individuals are thrown into disarray; norms or guides for their behavior either nonexistent or are no longer applicable. Persons who suddenly find themselves bankrupt, unemployed, abandoned, or friendless experience what Durkheim terms *anomie* or a state of normlessness. Integration into social life is suddenly disrupted. Individuals are left without viable guides for their behavior.

Durkheim adds a fourth form of suicide, fatalistic, to his typology. *Fatalistic suicide* refers to the condition of overregulation of individual behavior. When individual behavior is tightly controlled by others and personal autonomy is rendered impossible, a sense of powerlessness may ensue. Under conditions of inordinate regulation of behavior, fatalistic suicide may result.

Sociologists Jack Gibbs and Walter Martin (1964) propose an innovative conceptualization of social integration. They contend that status integration and the related concept of role conflict are key factors in understanding the link between social integration and suicide. Status integration refers to the frequency that a set of statuses is found in a population (e.g., male engineer, female nurse, etc.). Unusual configurations of statuses are a measure of the lack of status integration (e.g., female airline pilots or male preschool teachers). The absence of status integration leads to role conflict or clash of expectations of one role with another (e.g., being a mother and a medical doctor). The more unusual the configurations of one's status, the greater the experience of role conflict and the more likely suicide becomes.

Drawing on the work of Durkheim, anthropologist Andrew Henry and sociologist James Short (1954) contend that rates of suicide are predicted by three key variables: prestige, strength or the relational system, and the level of external restraint. Prestige typically refers to the status within any social grouping. Status denotes influence over group decisions or extent of deference granted to persons of higher social ranking. The strength of the relational system means the extent to which persons are involved in networks of social relationships with others. External restraint refers to the extent to which a person is required to conform to the demands and expectations of others.

To Henry and Short, the interplay of these three variables serves to explain and predict rates of suicidal behavior. As status increases, the strength of the relational system tends to decrease. That is, persons of higher status are less likely to interact with a wide range of other people, limiting their social contacts to a carefully chosen few. Also, as status increases, the need to comply with the demands and expectations of others decreases. The less the involvement with others and the more removed from their restraints, the less other persons are to be blamed when frustration is experienced. Put another way, persons who are low in status, highly involved in the lives of others, and must meet the demands and expectations of many others have several external targets to blame for life's frustrations. In the absence of these external causes for problematic events or circumstances, the self must bear the burden of frustration. In the extreme, suicide becomes more probable.

Robert K. Merton (1957), a founding structural-functional theorist in sociology, attempts to define more specifically what Durkheim meant by anomie. To Merton, anomie refers to the disjunction between culturally approved goals and the institutionalized means for attaining them. It is assumed that persons within a given culture are socialized to strive for the same goals—status, economic well-being, leisure, and so on—but for many the means to reach these goals—advanced education, occupational prestige, social opportunities, and economic fortune—may not be available or may not lead to the culture's most prized goals. This may lead to what Merton terms *retreatism,* or the rejection of the culturally approved goals and the institutionalized means for pursuing them. Retreatism may take the form of alcohol or drug addiction, depression and mental disorder, an alternative lifestyle (e.g., joining a cult or becoming a marginally employed drifter), or in the extreme suicidal behaviors.

SOCIAL CONFLICT. Social conflict theorists argue that the status arrangements and resultant power in society tend to precipitate varying forms of suicide.

As status increases or decreases, so too does a person's relative power and influence. Sociologist Alex Thio (1983) contends that suicide among the more powerful members of society is a voluntary act, whereas among the less powerful it is coerced. With increased power comes higher expectations for a life of ease and comfort; tolerance for adversity is lowered. The prospect of a life of hardship—economic, social, or physical—is unthinkable. Suicide may provide the only solution to impending misery. Among the powerless, however, suicide is more a consequence of the experience of everyday deprivation and uncertainty. Access to needed resources—medical, educational, job opportunities—is limited by the power structure of society. The powerless largely depend on available employers close at hand. Lives are played out in the factories, fields, and mines of their employers. Alternatives are few and rarely sought. Life's circumstances may combine to coerce the decision to kill one's self.

Explanations of Individual Suicidal Behavior

Various explanations of the suicidal behavior of the individual have been advanced (**Table 6–2**). Some are drawn from Durkheim's integration-regulation formulation and others from social strain, social learning, rational choice, and phenomenological approaches.

SOCIAL BONDING AND CONTROL. Travis Hirschi's (1969) sociological theory of deviant behavior draws on Durkheim's (1951) formulation of social integration. Hirschi argues that integration can be conceptualized as a set of four bonds between the individual and the larger society: attachment, commitment, involvement, and belief. Attachment refers to the extent to which individuals internalize the norms of society and are affected by others' reactions to their behavior. Commitment means the individual places great importance on engaging in conventional behavior and advocating highly prized cultural values. Involvement refers to the amount of time and effort an individual spends on conventional activities intended to contribute positively to others as opposed to involvement in idiosyncratic, self-serving behaviors. Belief connotes the person's deeply held conviction that their culture's values are essential for the functioning of society and must be strongly supported. When the individual's bonds to society are weakened or nonexistent, external controls of their behavior are largely absent. This lack of control over behavior leaves the individuals without normative guides and supports. Engagement in self-destruction may well follow.

SOCIAL STRAIN. Robert Agnew (1992) also draws on the work of Durkheim (1951) and Merton (1957) in formulating his strain theory of deviant

TABLE 6–2 **Explanations of Individual Behavior**

Theories and Theorists	Sociological Predictors	Hypotheses
Social Bonding and Control		
Hirschi	Attachment	The weaker the attachment to conventional society, the more likely the individual will commit suicide.
	Commitment	The weaker the commitment to conventional society, the more likely the individual will commit suicide.
	Involvement	The greater the involvement in conventional activities, the less likely the individual will commit suicide.
	Belief	The stronger the belief in conventional values and norms, the less likely the person will commit suicide.
Strain		
Agnew	Strain/stress	The greater the strain, the greater the negative emotional reaction.
		The greater the negative emotional reaction, the more likely an individual will commit suicide.
Social Learning		
Akers	Definitions of behavior	Individuals who hold attitudes that disapprove of suicide are less likely to commit suicide.
	Differential reinforcement	The greater the punishment for suicide, the less likely an individual is to commit suicide.
Rational Choice		
Clarke and Cornish	Cost-to-benefit analysis	The greater the cost or benefit associated with suicide, the more likely an individual is to commit suicide.
Imitation		
Phillips	Imitation	If an individual observes a suicide, then he or she is more likely to commit suicide.
Phenomenological		
Douglas	Meaning	If a person views suicide as a form of revenge, then he or she is more likely to commit suicide.
		If a person views suicide as a way of gaining sympathy from others, then he or she is more likely to commit suicide.

behavior. To Agnew, strain refers to the discrepancy between an individual's aspirations and expectations and their goal attainment. Strain results when our relations with other people are so disruptive that we are unable to achieve important goals (e.g., going to school, work, caring for our children, etc.). Strain causes negative emotions—fear, anger, anxiety, and depression—that must be dealt with by the individual. When coping strategies are no longer effective, self-destructive behaviors may emerge.

SOCIAL LEARNING. Social learning theory may also be used to account for an individual's suicidal behavior. Ronald Akers (1985), a pioneering sociological theorist, argues that most deviant behavior can be explained by social learning. He notes that whether a person engages in suicidal or other forms of deviance depends, in large part, on the meanings attached to behavior and the rewards anticipated from engaging in it. Individuals tend to repeat behaviors that provide desired rewards and benefits—behaviors that are reinforced by others. All behaviors are not equally rewarded or result in benefit to the individual. To Akers, differential reinforcement—the rewards and benefits that attend certain behavior but not others—explains why individuals engage in certain forms of deviant behavior and others do not. By assigning positive value to suicidal behavior, others may reinforce an individual's involvement acts of self-destruction. To the extent to which suicidal acts are differentially reinforced—rewarded more so than nonsuicidal behaviors—they are more often repeated.

RATIONAL CHOICE. Rational choice formulations of deviant and criminal behavior are founded on the central tenets of the Classical School of Criminology established in the mid-18th century. Social philosophers Cesar Beccaria (1963 [1764]) and Jeremy Bentham (1948 [1780]) were among the first to advance the hedonistic principle as an explanation for human social behavior. They argue that individuals are fundamentally rational beings, endowed with free will, who consciously and deliberately decide to engage in certain behaviors and not others. When deciding what course of action to take, individuals evoke the hedonistic principle. Simply put, the hedonistic principle posits that individuals seek to maximize their pleasure and minimize their pain when deciding on a certain behavior. The relative benefits versus costs of engaging in a behavior are rationally assessed and a choice is then made. Suicide is the outcome of the process of weighing the alternatives of choosing to live or to die at one's own hand.

David Phillips (1974) and Jack Douglas (1967) set forth two further innovative conceptualizations of individual suicidal behavior. Phillips' groundbreaking work on the link between imitation and suicide informs much of the subsequent research in the United States, Germany, and

Japan (Ishii, 1991; Jonas, 1992; Stack, 1996). The *imitation* approach to the understanding of an individual's decision to commit suicide is simply that suicides that receive much media attention, either in print or television coverage, thus tend to precipitate increased suicidal behavior. The more the media attention, the more probable are "copycat" suicides. Related to the phenomenon of imitation is the concept of differential identification. *Differential identification* refers to the varying effects the characteristics of the suicide victim have on the imitation process. That is, widespread media attention to a suicide of a well-known person (e.g., a political leader or entertainment celebrity) may result in more imitation or copycat suicides than the suicide of an unrecognized person (Wasserman, 1984). Phillips argues that suicides of highly visible persons are more likely to prompt imitation suicides.

Finally, sociologist Jack Douglas provides an alternative way of understanding a person's suicidal behavior. Taking the *phenomenological approach* to the explanation of suicide, Douglas focuses on the meanings that an individual attaches to his or her behavior. The meanings attached to behavior serve to guide individual action. To understand suicidal behavior, Douglas contends, it is necessary to reconstruct the personal meanings of suicide that lead to self-inflicted death. Douglas (1967, pp. 284–319) offers four broad categories for the meanings of self-inflicted death:

- As a means of transforming the soul from this world to the other world
- As a transformation of the substantial self in this world or in the other world
- As a means of achieving fellow-feeling (sympathy)
- As a means of getting revenge

The phenomenological approach seeks to understand the decision to end one's life from the vantage point of the victim. It informs us about the processes involved in finding meaning and value in the act of suicide. Suicide is viewed as beneficial to the victim: It must take on a positive meaning to be carried out.

Chapter Summary

In this chapter we considered the global nature of suicide, its cultural and structural variations, and theoretical understandings of suicidal behaviors. We also reviewed special topics on suicide: minority, including Native

American, involvement, the rise in self-destructive acts among the young and the elderly, physician-assisted suicide, and suicide by cop. We learned the following:

- Suicide is one of the three leading causes of death in the world for people 15 to 44 years of age.
- Males typically have higher suicide rates than females.
- Whites have higher suicide rates than other racial or ethnic groups.
- Suicide rates are rising fastest among the young.
- Similar rises are seen among Native American populations.
- Suicide rates are highest in the western United States.
- The south, however, leads the nation in the use of firearms for suicide.
- More people attempt a suicide each year than actually complete a suicide.
- Suicide is more common among the single, the divorced, and the widowed.
- The risk of suicide tends to increase with age. Older men have an elevated risk of suicide. Elder suicide is not uniformly experienced around the globe.
- Social structural positioning, life circumstances, previous suicide attempts, and psychiatric illness are precipitating factors for suicide.
- The warning signs for suicide have been well established. Suicide threats, withdrawal from others, mood swings, self-destructive behavior, and the experience of life crisis or trauma are common warning signs of suicide.
- Suicide notes are valuable sources of information about the thinking and feeling of the victim at the time of the suicide. Common themes found in suicide notes include hate, love, shame and disgrace, fear (particularly of insanity), and traumatic rejection and self-abnegation.
- Homicide followed by suicide is a rare event that varies considerably across cultures. Seven patterns that characterize these suicides include frustrated personal relationships, ambivalence, jealousy and morbid jealousy, separation, depression, helplessness, and guilt. Homicide–suicide offenders are more likely to be emotionally tied to their victims than are offenders who do not commit suicide.

- Oregon and Washington are the only states in the United States to legalize physician-assisted suicide. Physician-assisted suicide is permitted in such countries as The Netherlands, Australia, Japan, and Holland.
- Suicide by cop refers to an event in which an individual's behavior constitutes an imminent danger of serious injury or death and is intended to cause a law enforcement officer to use fatal force to defend him- or herself.

Key Concepts

Suicide: The willful, deliberate, and voluntary termination of one's life.

Withdrawal: The unwillingness to communicate or desire to be left alone.

Mood swings: Rapid changes in personality.

Self-destructive behavior: Risk-taking behaviors and pronounced drug or alcohol use.

Experience of a life crisis or trauma: The loss of an important status or social role.

Homicide–suicide: Suicide committed by a person who has just killed someone else.

Frustrated personal relationships: The chaotic nature of the personal relationship found between the victim and offender in homicide–suicide cases.

Assisted suicide: Suicide act by which a physician can assist in the termination of life.

Death with Dignity Act: Oregon statute that established certain criteria that must be met before a physician can assist in the termination of life.

Suicide by cop: An event in which an individual's behavior constitutes an imminent danger of serious injury or death and is intended to cause a law enforcement officer to use fatal force to defend him- or herself.

Critical Thinking Questions

1. The medical–legal definition of suicide is complex and often subject to individual interpretation. Describe in detail three cases in which an "actual" suicidal death could be misclassified. How might the medical–legal errors be averted in the determination of causes of suicidal death?
2. Except for China, what accounts for the otherwise universal higher male than female rate of suicide? Why is the male–female suicide ratio different in China?

3. Why is there such a marked gender difference in involvement in homicide followed by suicide? What kinds of social processes precede a male-perpetrated "homicide followed by suicide" and a female-perpetrated "homicide followed by suicide" event?
4. Is the taking of one's own life ever justified? Discuss at least three key reasons for your decision to either reject suicidal death as unjustified under any conditions or provide three reasons and circumstances in which suicide is justifiable.

Web Extra

Web-based media materials from high-quality sources such as CNN, Time, and National Public Radio are available in support of this textbook. Visit go.jblearning.com/deviance to access them.

Check out these websites for additional information on suicide:

http://www.nimh.nih.gov

http://www.cdc.gov

http://www.AFSP.org

http://www.suicidology.org

Mental Illness

CHAPTER 7

Learning Objectives

After reading this chapter you should know

- The nature of mental illness.
- The cultural, social, and medical definitions of mental illness.
- The forms and prevalence of mental illness, including the sociodemographic variations in prevalence.
- The prevalence of mental disorders in the United States.
- The medical and sociocultural explanations for mental illness.

One side effect of the war in Iraq came to the forefront in 2010: an epidemic of mental illness among Iraqi civilians. For many, it is an illness fostered by traumatic experiences, including bombings, shootings, terrorist attacks, and assassinations, and by the general social disorganization that war always brings. Only 100 or so psychiatrists remain in the country, which has a population of 30 million, causing an unimaginable burden of cases involving depression, extreme anxiety, and other forms of mental illness according to the Huffington Post Investigative Fund (Liptak, 2010).

The story of 38-year-old Dhia Hardan is typical (Fadel, 2010). Hardan, who suffers from manic depression, repeatedly visits a mental hospital for short stays to play music for patients and to be medicated. When he leaves the hospital he fears that he will be killed by members of the Taliban who blend in seamlessly with the local population. The Taliban prohibits listening to or playing music, and Hardan knows that he could be especially targeted as a misfit because the mentally ill are highly stigmatized in Iraq. "I feel the whole universe is shrouded in darkness, without hope, without life," Hardan says. "I even hate to walk out the door." Yet, in some ways Hardan is lucky. About 80% of patients are abandoned by their families and end up homeless.

Amir Hussain, one of the few psychiatrists still practicing at Iraq's two remaining psychiatric hospitals, says that the stories of suffering and barbarism that patients tell are astounding. But, he says, "We are so used to hearing it . . . I think our emotions are frozen" (Goode, 2008). One of the main problems facing caregivers, says Hussain, is that patients have no time to recover before experiencing new trauma. "There is [always] new stress, grief after grief, losses after losses, violence after violence," he says.

Nature of Mental Illness

Considerable controversy surrounds the definitions of mental illness, its etiology, and treatment. Competing biological, psychological, and sociological definitions and explanations of mental illness are found around the world. Cultural variations in the forms and prevalence of mental illness must be understood. This chapter considers the intricate sociocultural dimensions of mental disorders across the globe as well as theoretical formulations of the incidence and prevalence of mental illness.

Behaviors labeled as mental illness have evolved over the centuries. Nearly all forms of disruptive or disapproved behavior were once believed to stem from demonic possessions. Immorality and a wanton lifestyle were considered the underlying cause of mental disorders. In the 18th century "lunatics" or "the insane" were beaten, publicly displayed, or put away in asylums. Public viewing of caged and chained lunatics was held on Sundays in many of these asylums. It was believed that nothing could be done for the insane; they were irreparably damaged and permanently impaired (Mumford, 1983).

> . . . the best [psychiatric] diagnoses are provisional and somewhat fictional.
>
> —Barry Nurcombe, director of child and adolescent psychiatry at Vanderbilt University (http://www.mentalhealthfacts/quotes.htm)

With the advent of psychotherapeutic drugs in the mid-20th century, physicians and others associated with institutions for the mentally ill began treating their patients more humanely. The medical model emerged as the dominant explanation and treatment strategy for those afflicted with a mental disease. Organic causes were sought for the mental illness. Highly effective drug therapies replaced confinement, which was often under brutal conditions. For the first time, a decline occurred in the number of patients housed in mental hospitals, and this resulted in the ability to successfully treat them in a community setting (Mumford, 1983).

Definition of Mental Illness

Multiple, often conflicting, definitions of mental illness are offered. Legal and medical professionals as well as laypersons interpret and define mental illness according to different values, goals, and interest group affiliations. As with other forms of deviance, the definition of mental illness is influenced by the social and cultural context in which it occurs and also by the value judgments of mental health practitioners. Consequently, the meanings attached to mental illness continually change, new forms are recognized, and other forms redefined or eliminated over time.

Over the years it [the National Committee for Mental Hygiene] has championed for the promotion of "mental health" despite the fact that nobody knows what it is or how to do it.

—E. Fuller Torrey, psychiatrist

SSRN

Jones, J.T.R. (2008). *Severe mental illness in the academy: A secret revealed. Louisville bar briefs* (pp. 10–11). University of Louisville School of Law Legal Studies Research Paper Series No. 2008-30. http://ssrn.com/abstract=1091328

Cultural Definitions

Societies share "particular historical traditions, challenges, opportunities and stresses that provide a common experience. These experiences create a distinctive context that influences how basic psychological processes are expressed within a given culture" (National Institute of Mental Health [NIMH], 1999a). **Culture**—the values and norms of a society—affects conceptions of behavior and the definition of mental illness. Normative behaviors in one culture may be viewed as symptomatic of a mental disorder in another (Lemelson & Winters, 2001). **Cultural relativism** refers to cross-cultural variation in the social construction of reality. Manifestations of mental disorder are socially and culturally constructed. For example, in the United States and other developed countries, persons who hallucinate are considered to be mentally ill. In other cultures, however, individuals who experience visions or hear voices are honored.

In rural Laos, unprovoked assaultive or destructive behavior, social isolation, self-endangerment due to neglect or self-destructive acts, nonviolent but disruptive or inappropriate behavior, and inability to do productive work characterized natives who were called insane. But hallucinations are rarely used by Laotians to identify insanity (Mumford, 1983, p. 416).

The Dobu of the South Pacific provide another example of cultural relativism. With a limited food supply, the Dobu are a highly paranoid and suspicious people who typically distrust their fellow tribesmen. Dobu who are not distrustful and constantly vigilant are considered mentally ill (Palmer & Humphrey, 1990).

Some mental disorders and responses to mental disorders are *culture bound*, that is, unique to the culture in which they are found. In Japan, cultural-bound neuroses stem from an "overwhelming sense of obligation and dependence. Shinkeishitsu (nervous temperament), for example, involves hypersensitivity, perfectionism, social withdrawal or total discomfort in unfamiliar surroundings" (Increasing Signs of Stress, 1983, p. 67). **Table 7–1** provides a description of several other **culture-bound disorders**.

Treatment methods reflect cultural differences as well. Because the Japanese culture places value on work and service to others, many of the treatment methods are aimed at getting patients back to work. Morita explains one such therapy.

For a week patients are confined to bed, with no visitors, no TV, and no reading material. Forced to wallow in their own thoughts, they come

TABLE 7–1 **Culture-Bound Syndromes**

Syndrome	Culture	Symptoms
Amok	Malaysia, Laos, Papua New Guinea, Puerto Rico, Navajos	Brooding, followed by violent behavior, persecutory ideas, amnesia, exhaustion. More often seen in men than women.
Ataque de nervios	Latin America	Uncontrollable shouting, crying, trembling, heat in the chest rising to the head, verbal or physical aggression, seizures, fainting.
Ghost sickness	Native Americans	Nightmares, weakness, feelings of danger, loss of appetite, fainting, dizziness, hallucinations, loss of consciousness, sense of suffocation.
Koro	Malaysia, China, Thailand	Sudden and intense anxiety that the penis (in males) or the vulva and nipples (in females) recede into body and cause death.
Latah	East Asia	Hypersensitivity to sudden fright, trancelike behavior most often seen in middle-aged women.
Susto	Mexico, Central America	Appetite disturbances, sleep disturbances, sadness, loss of motivation, low self-worth, after a frightening event. Sufferers believe their soul has left their body.
Taijin kyofusho	Japan	Intense fear that one's body displeases, embarrasses, or is offensive to others.

Source: Carson, R.C., Butcher, J.N. *Abnormal Psychology and Modern Life*, 9th ed., ©1992. Printed and Electronically reproduced by permission of Pearson Education, Inc., Upper Saddle River, New Jersey.

Psychiatric Care in Asia

In Asia, spirituality is considered vital to a person's mental health and general well-being. The word *spirituality*, often used interchangeably with religious involvement, refers to the process of discovering meaning in one's life.

Haroon Rashid Chaudhry, professor of psychiatry at Fatima Jinnah Medical College in Lahore, Pakistan, notes that spirituality and religion "are part of a very powerful medium to help in the healing process. Spiritual people know the meaning and goal of their life . . . they can easily cope with stress and have the ability to adjust in every situation."

The Spirituality and Psychiatry Special Interest Group (2006) of the Royal College of Psychiatrists cite the following outcomes of spirituality:

- Being self-reflective and honest.
- Being able to remain focused in the present, remaining alert, unhurried and attentive.
- Being able to rest, relax, and create a still, peaceful, state of mind.
- Being able to develop greater empathy for others.
- Being able to find courage to witness and endure distress while sustaining an attitude of hope.
- Being able to develop improved discernment; for example, when to speak or act and when to remain silent.
- Being able to grieve and let go.

In the East, then, spirituality is recognized as a way to enhance one's mental health and as a means to more effectively treat mental disorders.

Sources: Chaudhry, H.R. (2008). Psychiatric care in Asia: Spirituality and religious connotations. *International Review of Psychiatry, 20*(5), 477–483; The Spirituality and Psychiatry Special Interest Group. (2006). *Spirituality and mental health.* Cited in Chaudhry, H.R. (2008). Psychiatric care in Asia: Spirituality and religious connotations. *International Review of Psychiatry, 20*(5), 477–483.

to see that action is better than endless self-obsession. Patients then work outdoors for 2 weeks, going from light to heavy labor. They also attend indoctrination lectures. No talk about the self is allowed (Increasing Signs of Stress, 1983).

Another Japanese therapy, Naikan (introspection), is a directed meditation program where the therapist urges those in treatment to focus on their ingratitude toward the sacrifices of important persons in their life. The therapist then instructs that the only escape from mental anguish is to plunge oneself into acts of service (Increasing Signs of Stress, 1983).

Social Definitions

Sociologists offer many definitions of mental disorder and theoretical explanations for its occurrence. Although conflicting conceptualizations are evident, it is generally conceded that key to the understanding of mental illness is social perception. The definition of mental illness is essentially based on (1) value judgments made by mental health professionals, (2) normative expectations and reactions of society, and (3) differing beliefs about the causes of mental illness (Clinard & Meier, 1998; Mechanic, 1968).

VALUE JUDGMENTS. Psychiatrists and mental health professionals—clinical psychologists, psychiatric social workers, and counselors—variously define mental illness. In the *Diagnostic and Statistical Manual of Mental Disorders* (DSM-IV) (2000), the American Psychiatric Association provides a set of criteria for the diagnoses of mental illness. However, the judgments of practitioners are often guided by their individual values and beliefs. As a result, assessments of behavior vary; similar symptoms may receive different diagnoses by different practitioners. Diagnostic decisions are often influenced by prior experience with the symptoms or an idealized view as to what constitutes normal behavior (Clinard & Meier, 1998). The individual's emotional state, physical illnesses, stressful life events, and social and occupational functioning may also be taken into account when evaluating his or her mental health (Atkinson et al., 1996).

NORMATIVE EXPECTATIONS, SOCIETAL REACTIONS, AND LABELING. Sociologists tend to define mental illness as a departure from normative guidelines or expectations for behavior. *Normative violations*—behaviors that are disruptive, offensive, or highly unusual—may evoke a societal reaction. These behaviors and the individuals who express these behaviors may then be labeled as mentally ill and responded to as such. Societal reactions and labeling produce new social roles for those considered mentally ill.

Political Dissenters and Forced Psychiatric Hospitalization

It is disturbing to hear that political dissenters and protesters are being confined in psychiatric hospitals and declared mentally ill by government officials or others in powerful positions. However, it is not uncommon. Evidence of this was once seen in the former Soviet Union and more recently in rural China. Huang Shurong, a 42-year-old Chinese woman, spent 210 days of the past 3 years involuntarily committed to several psychiatric hospitals in rural China. Government officials forced her into the hospitals after she protested a local land dispute. During her confinement she was subjected to drug and electroshock therapy, although her friends, family, and even some psychiatrists insisted she was not mentally ill. She was finally discharged when doctors could no longer justify keeping her hospitalized. Ms. Huang is not the only political dissenter forcefully hospitalized. While confined, Ms. Huang roomed with five other political dissenters.

Source: Based on an article by Rosenthal, E. 2002. "In Rural China, Mental Hospitals Await Those Who Rock the Boat." New York Times, February 16, 2002. Web posted at http://www.nytimes.com/2002/02/16/international/asia/16CHIN.html?ex=1014879719&ei=1&en=89flecc9c9cf65c7

A depressed young woman. Why do some people believe that mental illness is subject to the personal control of the afflicted?

Over time, the stigmatized person may fully adopt the mentally ill role. Norms and the violation of norms, along with societal reactions and the subsequent processes of societal labeling, are therefore crucial processes in defining mentally ill behavior.

BELIEFS ABOUT MENTAL ILLNESS. The work of David Mechanic (1968) and others (Schnittker et al., 2000) focuses on how mental illness is differentially perceived across cultures and forms of social organization. Mental illness is either viewed as a behavior that can be controlled by the afflicted person or viewed as beyond the will of the individual to control. These conflicting views on mental illness often shape how groups define and treat mentally ill behavior. However contradictory, both views are usually accepted as definitions of and explanations for mental illness.

Medical Definition

Most psychiatrists, psychologists, and other medical professionals refer to mental illness as a disease resulting from some genetic abnormality or inherited vulnerability. According to the **medical model**, mental disorders are comparable with physical disorders, requiring medical diagnoses and treatment. In the ***Diagnostic and Statistical Manual of Mental Disorders*, 4th edition (DSM-IV-TR)** (2000), the American Psychiatric Association provides standard criteria for the diagnosis and treatment of specific mental disorders. The box on this page presents 15 categories of mental disorders listed in the manual. Each main category includes numerous subcategories. Over 450 specific mental disorders are included in the latest revision of the DSM-IV.

Mental disorders are classified as either **organic disorders** (Alzheimer's disease, senile psychosis, and paresis), which originate from physiological difficulties and organic causes, or **functional disorders,** which include several related disorders whose underlying causes are less well known. Sociological explorations of mental illness tend to focus on the functional disorders. These disorders take many forms but are traditionally known as **psychoses** and **neuroses**. Psychoses are the most debilitating disorders and often require long-term treatment. Neuroses are minor disorders, typically characterized by anxiety, depression, and maladaptive behavior. These disorders rarely require hospitalization. Some of the most common and well-known functional disorders are outlined below (see DSM-IV).

DEPRESSION. **Unipolar (major) depression** is classified as a serious mood disorder and is distinguished from normal depressive moods. Feeling down or blue as everyday stresses, losses, or life changes occur is usually

Main Diagnostic Categories (DSM-IV)

1. Disorders usually first diagnosed in infancy, childhood, or adolescence
2. Delirium, dementia, amnesic, and other cognitive disorders; mental disorders due to a general medical condition
3. Substance abuse disorders
4. Schizophrenic disorders
5. Mood disorders
6. Anxiety disorders
7. Somatoform disorders
8. Dissociative disorders
9. Sexual and gender identity disorders
10. Factitious disorders
11. Eating disorders
12. Sleep disorders
13. Impulse-control disorders
14. Personality disorders
15. Adjustment and other disorders

Source: Adapted from DSM-IV.

temporary and fades away within a few weeks. The American Psychiatric Association considers depression abnormal only when it is out of proportion to the event and continues past the point at which most people begin to recover (Atkinson et al., 1996, p. 524). In addition to emotional symptoms, such as a depressed mood, a depressive disorder is marked by cognitive, motivational, and physical symptoms. Some of these symptoms include dissatisfaction and anxiety; changes in appetite, sleep, and psychomotor functions; loss of interest and energy; feelings of guilt; thoughts of death; and diminished concentration.

BIPOLAR DISORDER. **Bipolar disorder**, also known as **manic-depressive disorder**, differs from unipolar depression in that the former involves pronounced mood swings from depression to uncontrolled mania, whereas persons with unipolar disorder experience depression only. Manic behavior is recognized by elevated mood, increased psychomotor activity, and racing thought processes. Persons in the manic phase of their bipolar disorder experience a sense of omnipotence, coupled with a pronounced lack of judgment about the consequences of their actions. They do not believe they need to sleep or eat but believe they can continue to function for extended periods of time at an increasingly accelerated pace. **Table 7–2** shows the differing patterns in manic and depressive behavior found in bipolar disorder.

TABLE 7–2 **Differing Patterns in Manic and Depressive Behavior**

	Manic	Depressive
Emotional characteristics	Elated, euphoric Very sociable Impatient at any hindrance	Gloomy, hopeless Socially withdrawn Irritable
Cognitive characteristics	Racing thoughts Flight of ideas Desire for action Impulsive behavior Positive self-image Delusions of grandeur	Slowness of thought processes Obsessive worrying Inability to make decisions Negative self-image, self-blame Delusions of guilt and disease
Motor characteristics	Talkative Hyperactive Does not become tired Needs less sleep Increased sex drive Fluctuating appetite	Decreased motor activity Tired Difficulty sleeping Decreased sex drive Decreased appetite

Source: Sarason, Irwin G.; Sarason, Barbara R., Abnormal Psychology: The Problem of Maladaptive Behavior, 8th ed., ©1996. Printed and Electronically reproduced by permission of Pearson Education, Inc., Upper Saddle River, New Jersey.

PERSONALITY DISORDERS. Personality disorders are characterized by "longstanding patterns of maladaptive behavior that constitute immature and inappropriate ways of coping with stress or solving problems" (Atkinson et al., 1996, p. 513). An individual diagnosed with these types of disorders may express manipulative behavior, disorganized and unstable mood or behavior, and thought disturbances. Personality disorders are usually recognizable during childhood, and many have a lifetime or near-lifetime duration. Symptoms of these disorders may not become evident, however, until the individual encounters an extremely stressful situation. Personality disorders often co-occur with other mental disorders, most commonly mood disorders.

Antisocial, narcissistic, histrionic, schizotypal, dependent, and borderline are a few of the different types of personality disorders. Many personality disorders share common features that are easy to confuse with one another. In general, though, personality disorders are distinguished from one another by odd and eccentric behavior; dramatic, emotional, or erratic behavior; and anxious or fearful behavior.

SCHIZOPHRENIA. Schizophrenia and related schizophrenic disorders are the most chronic, severe, and disabling of the mental disorders. The psychotic behavior associated with schizophrenia involves alterations in thought, perception, and consciousness; these alterations are often referred to as hallucinations or delusions. Individuals with schizophrenia may hear voices that are not there, exhibit disorganized speech and behavior, or seem to lose touch with reality. The symptoms of schizophrenic disorders take either positive or negative forms. A positive symptom reflects an excess of normal functions such as suspiciousness and delusional behavior. Negative symptoms involve a loss or decrease in normal functioning, including flat affect or lack of emotion, loss of motivation or initiative, loss of energy, and the inability to experience pleasure.

ANXIETY DISORDERS. Anxiety disorders include panic disorder, obsessive-compulsive disorder, posttraumatic stress disorder, generalized anxiety disorder, and phobias. In each of these disorders, "an anxiety disorder may be said to exist if the anxiety experienced is disproportionate to the circumstance, is difficult for the individual to control, or interferes with normal functioning" (U.S. Department of Health and Human Services, 1999a). Anxiety disorders may stem from very specific situations or objects, as in the case of phobias, or more diffuse, nonspecific circumstances. The latter are characterized by chronic and excessive worrying, restlessness, and tension. Some additional signs of anxiety include feeling of fear or dread,

AT A GLANCE

Global Patterns

- Mental disorders account for 4 of the 10 leading causes of disability worldwide.
- One in every four persons will suffer from some form of mental disorder in their lifetime.
- More than 450,000,000 people globally suffer from a mental disorder: 154 million from depression, 91 million from alcohol abuse disorder, 25 million from schizophrenia, and 15 million from a drug abuse disorder.
- Reports show that psychiatric and neurological conditions could increase their share of the total global disease burden by almost half, from 10.5% to almost 15% by 2020.

United States

- An estimated 26.2% of Americans aged 18 and older—about one in four adults (57.7 million people)—suffer from a diagnosable mental disorder.
- About one in six of the U.S. population (17%) suffers from a serious mental illness.
- Some 45% of persons who suffer from mental illness also have two or more co-occurring mental disorders.
- Depression is the leading cause of disability for persons between 15 and 44 years of age. Depression affects about 14.8 million persons over the age of 18 (6.7% of the adult population) in the United States.
- About 40 million U.S. adults over the age of 18 have some form of anxiety disorder. Anxiety often co-occurs with depression and/or substance abuse.
- Schizophrenia is considered the most chronic of the mental disorders, affecting about 1.1% of the U.S. population aged 18 and older. Both men and women are equally likely to suffer from schizophrenia.
- Over 20% of children and adolescents in the United States are estimated to have mental disorders.
- Anxiety disorders affect as many as 13% of young people and are the most common mental health problems that occur in children ages 9 to 17 years old.
- In the United States, 1 in 10 children and adolescents suffers from mental illness severe enough to cause some level of impairment.

Sources: Murray, C. and A. Lopez (eds.) 1996. The Global Burden of Disease. Cambridge, MA: Harvard University School of Public Health on behalf of the World Health Organization and the World Bank, Harvard University Press; NIMH. 2001a. The Impact of Mental Illness on Society. Web posted at http://www.nimh.nih.gov/publicat/burden.cfm; Satcher, D. 1999a. Mental Health: A Report of the Surgeon General. Department of Health and Human Services; NIMH. 2001b. The Numbers Count: Mental Disorders in America. Web posted at http://www.nimh.nih.gov/publicat/numbers.cfm; Satcher, D. 1999b. Mental Health: Culture, Race and Ethnicity. A supplement to Mental Health: A Report of the Surgeon General. Department of Health and Human Services; NIMH. 2001c. Women hold up half the sky: Women and mental health research. Web posted at http://www.nimh.nih.gov/publicat/womensoms.cfm; http://www.nimh.nih.gov/health/publications/the-numbers-count-mental-disorders-in-america/index.shtml; Let's Talk Facts about Mental Health of the Elderly. 1997. Washington, DC: American Psychiatric Association. Web posted at http://www.psych.org/public_info/elderly.cfm; NIMH. 1999b. Brief Notes on the Mental Health of Children and Adolescents.

rapid heart rate, lightheadedness or dizziness, perspiration, cold hands/feet, and shortness of breath. These symptoms may be related to separation, animals, social fears, or nature fears. For example, individuals may fear being in crowds or being alone, or they may be afraid of snakes or heights.

Epidemiology of Mental Illness

Although the manifestations of mental illness vary from culture to culture, most societies possess some concept of mental disorder. A wide range of

Globalization and Mental Illness

Over the past thirty years, we Americans have been industriously exporting our ideas about mental illness. Our definitions and treatments have become the international standards. Although this has often been done with the best of intentions, we've failed to foresee the full impact of these efforts. It turns out that how a people in a culture think about mental illnesses—how they categorize and prioritize the symptoms, attempt to heal them, and set expectations for their course and outcome—influences the diseases themselves. In teaching the rest of the world to think like us, we have been, for better and worse, homogenizing the way the world goes mad.

But with the increasing speed of globalization, something has changed. The remarkable diversity once seen among different cultures' conceptions of madness is rapidly disappearing. A few mental illnesses identified and popularized in the United States—depression, post-traumatic stress disorder, and anorexia among them—now appear to be spreading across cultural boundaries and around the world with the speed of contagious diseases. Indigenous forms of mental illness and healing are being bulldozed by disease categories and treatments made in the USA.

There is no doubt that the Western mental health profession has had a remarkable global influence over the meaning and treatment of mental illness. Mental health professionals trained in the West, and in the United States in particular, create the official categories of mental diseases. The American Psychiatric Association's *Diagnostic and Statistical Manual of Mental Disorders*, the *DSM* (the "bible" of the profession, as it is sometimes called), has become the worldwide standard. In addition American researchers and organizations run the premier scholarly journals and host top conferences in the fields of psychology and psychiatry. Western universities train the world's most influential clinicians and academics. Western drug companies dole out the funds for research and spend billions marketing medications for mental illnesses. Western-trained traumatologists rush in wherever war or natural disasters strike to deliver "psychological first aid," bringing with them their assumptions about how the mind becomes broken and how it is best healed.

Source: Excerpted from Ethan Watters, *Crazy Like Us*, New York: Simon & Schuster, 2010; and National Public Radio's Talk of the Nation, January 12, 2010 posted at: http://www.npr.org/templates/story/story.php?storyId=122490928

epidemiological studies shows "severe psychoses seem to be recognized and to occur, everywhere" (Murphy, 1976, p. 1019). Cross-cultural studies of schizophrenia conducted by the World Health Organization (1991) show similar types of symptoms and prevalence in the following culturally diverse countries: Colombia, the former Czechoslovakia, Denmark, England, India, Nigeria, the former Soviet Union, Taiwan, and the United States. Cultural differences are found in symptom expression, tolerance, and course of the illness. The reluctance to diagnose a person as depressed and variations in tolerance for mentally ill behavior account for much of the differences in prevalence of mental illness around the world (Murphy, 1976). Cultures that share common concepts of mental illness often share similar rates of mental illness (U.S. Department of Health and Human Services, 1999b).

SSRN

Bard, J. S. (2005). Re-arranging deck chairs on the Titanic: Why the incarceration of individuals with serious mental illness violates public health, ethical, and constitutional principles and therefore cannot be made right by piecemeal changes to the insanity defense. *Houston Journal of Health Law and Policy, 5*(1). http://ssrn.com/abstract=663882

Prevalence of Mental Disorders in the United States

Approximately one in four adults in the United States over the age of 18 has a diagnosable mental disorder. About 6% of adults have a serious mental illness and experience some significant functional impairment. Depression is the most disabling mental disorder suffered by person between the ages of 15 and 44 in the United States. Anxiety disorders, however, are the most prevalent form of mental illness, affecting more than 40 million American adults. **Table 7–3** shows the prevalence of the more common forms of mental disorders among adults in the United States.

TABLE 7–3 **Prevalence of Common Mental Disorders in the United States**

Disorder	Percent of U.S. Adults, aged 18 and over
Mood disorders	9.5
Anxiety disorders	18.1
Panic disorder	2.7
Posttraumatic stress disorder	3.5
Obsessive-compulsive disorder	1.0
Major depressive disorders	6.7
Bipolar	2.6
Schizophrenia	1.1

Source: National Institute of Mental Health. The Numbers Count: Mental Disorders in America. Bethesda, MD: National Institute of Mental Health posted at: http://www.nimh.nih.gov/health/publications/the-numbers-count-mental-disorders-in-america/index.shtml

Costs of Mental Illness

Mental illness ranks among the five most costly medical conditions in the United States. **Figure 7–1** shows that the annual expenditure for the treatment of mental illness ($57.5 billion) is the same as for cancer and more than for asthma ($51.3 billion). Only heart conditions and trauma-related disorders cost more to treat than mental disorders. The percent increase in the cost for the treatment of mental illness has exceeded that for each of the four other costliest medical conditions. In addition, only asthma suffers (48.5 million) outnumber persons afflicted with mental disorders (36.2 million), followed by persons with trauma-related disorders (34.9 million), heart conditions (19.7 million), and cancer (11.1 million).

In a national study of the cost of mental illness, Harvard professor of health care policy Ronald Kessler and his colleagues found that American's suffering from serious mental illness lose $193.2 billion in earnings each year. The average salary of the seriously mentally ill is $22,545 compared with $38,852 for persons who are not mentally ill. The researchers note that 75% of the lost earnings are the result of income reduction among working mentally ill persons and 25% is attributed to the inability of the seriously mental ill to be able to work at all (Kessler et al., 2008).

Dr. Thomas R. Insel of the NIMH (2008) extends the cost of mental illness by adding the direct costs of health care for the mentally ill ($100.1 billion [Mark et al., 2007]) and disability benefits ($24.3 billion) to the loss of earnings ($193.2 billion). He estimates the total cost of mental illness is $317.6 billion annually.

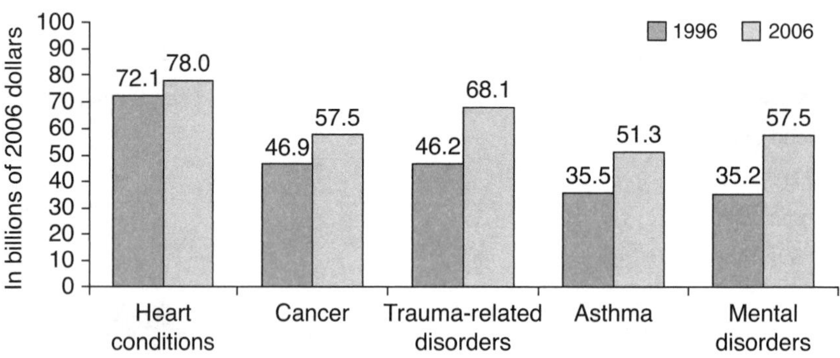

FIGURE 7–1 Expenditures for the five most costly medical conditions, 1996 and 2006.
Source: Soni, Anita. The Five Most Costly Conditions, 1996 and 2006: Estimates for the U.S. Civilian Noninstitutionalized Population. Statistical Brief #248. July 2009. Agency for Healthcare Research and Quality, Rockville, MD. http://www.meps.ahrq.gov/mepsweb/data_files/publications/st248/stat248.pdf

Sociodemographic Variations in Prevalence

GENDER. According to most research, men and women in the general population are *equally likely* to have some form of mental disorder. Differences are found, however, in patterns or varying forms of mental illness (Tansella, 1998). Studies such as those of the World Health Organization show "men have more problems related to alcohol, drug abuse and antisocial behavior, while women suffer more from anxiety, depression and eating disorders" (Tansella, 1998, p. 26). Anxiety, depression, and some personality disorders are twice as prevalent among females as males. A recent survey shows that women are at greater risk than men for developing posttraumatic stress disorder after a traumatic life event (NIMH, 2001c). Of the depressive disorders, women are twice as likely to experience unipolar depression, whereas both genders are equally likely to experience bipolar depression (NIMH, 2001c). Men and women also experience schizophrenic disorders with equal frequency (Robins & Regier, 1991).

AGE. The overall prevalence of mental disorders in the United States is approximately 15% to 25% for every age group (U.S. Department of Health and Human Services, 1999a). However, mental disorders are more common among adults aged 18 to 54. It is well documented that young adults experience some of the highest rates of mental illness. Depressive disorders and schizophrenia are usually diagnosed in the early to mid-20s. Cross-national cohort studies show an increase of major depression among younger individuals (Cross National Collaborative Group, 1992).

Children and adolescents are affected by many of the same mental disorders as adults. Studies in the United States and other countries find that 1 in 10 children has a mental disorder (NIMH, 1999b). Of this age group, 13% are affected by an anxiety disorder (Shaffer et al., 1996). In addition, disruptive disorders such as attention deficit disorder and conduct disorder affect approximately 10% of children and adolescents aged 9 to 17. Schizophrenic disorders are thought to be extremely rare in children (U.S. Department of Health and Human Services, 1999a).

RACE. Racial differences for overall rates of mental illness are not clear. Ethnic groups often experience culture-bound syndromes, which account for some variation in the prevalence of mental disorders. Culture-bound syndromes seen in Hispanic Americans include *susto* (fright), *nervios* (nerves), *mal de ojo* (evil eye), and *ataque do nervios* (nervous/panic attacks). Symptoms of an *ataque do nervios* may include screaming uncontrollably, crying, trembling, verbal or physical aggression, dissociative experiences, seizure-like or fainting episodes, and suicidal attempts (U.S. Department of Health and Human Services, 1999b).

Racial groups who live in similar communities and share similar lifestyles appear to have similar rates of mental illnesses. Certain segments of minority populations including Native Americans, Latino and Hispanic Americans, and African Americans are "over-represented in high-need populations that are particularly at risk for mental illness" (U.S. Department of Health and Human Services, 1999b). These include refugees, the homeless, the incarcerated, those on welfare or in foster homes, and those exposed to violence, alcohol, or substance abuse.

Racial differences are found, however, when assessing the prevalence of specific disorders. Members of these high-need populations have higher rates of both lifetime histories and active disorders than do other groups. Somatization (i.e., hypochondria) is more common among African Americans than among White Americans. African Americans are more likely to have phobias and schizophrenia but less likely to have depressive disorders (Clinard & Meier, 1998). Findings on Native American populations indicate that rates of mental illnesses, including disruptive behavior, substance abuse disorders, and comorbid disorders, run extremely high compared with Whites (Beals et al., 1997). Differences in specific disorders are also found among Hispanic Americans. The Surgeon General's report on mental health, race, and ethnicity (U.S. Department of Health and Human Services, 1999b) outlines these differences:

- Adult Mexican immigrants have lower rates of mental disorders than Mexican Americans born in the United States, and adult Puerto Ricans living on the island tend to have lower rates of depression than Puerto Ricans living on the mainland.
- Studies have found that Latino youth experience proportionately more anxiety-related and delinquency problem behaviors, depression, and drug use than do White youth.
- Regarding older Hispanic Americans, one study found over 26% of its sample were depressed, but depression was related to physical health; only 5.5% of those without physical health problems said they were depressed.

MARITAL STATUS. A number of studies find that being married is associated with good mental health and low incidence of mental illness. The divorced or separated, the widowed, or the never married often exhibit the poorest mental health. With regard to gender, the effects of marriage on mental health are not consistent. In some studies it is hypothesized that the positive effects of marriage are mainly limited to men (Bernard, 1982). Other studies conclude that the marriage relationship is stronger for women (Gove et al., 1972). The Midtown Manhattan Study (Srole & Fischer, 1978) finds that married men experience the lowest rates of mental illness, followed by single men, and last divorced men. Women exhibit a different pattern. Single women show the lowest rates of mental illness, followed by the married. The highest rates are again found among the divorced.

SOCIAL STATUS. Studies of the effect of social status (i.e., class, socioeconomic status, and educational level) on mental illness show that severe psychiatric disorders are disproportionately concentrated in the lowest social classes (Dohrenwend et al., 1992; Dohrenwend & Dohrenwend, 1975; Hollingshead & Redlich, 1958; Kessler & Cleary, 1980; Miech et al., 1999; Nordenmark & Strandh, 1999; Weich & Lewis, 1998; Wheaton, 1980). In contrast, members of the upper socioeconomic strata are more likely to experience minor disorders such as neuroses. One explanation is that people with mental illness are less likely to be consistently employed. Their mental illness impairs social mobility and status attainment. Consequently, those with mental illness tend to drift downward because of unemployment and financial strain (Dohrenwend et al., 1992). Persons in the lower socioeconomic strata also are subjected to more severe life stresses than those with more social resources. Poverty, low income, and a low standard of living are accompanied by few resources for coping with such stressors.

The accumulation of social stressors may well trigger the onset of a mental disorder (Dohrenwend et al., 1992). Labeling and attribution theorists contend that persons in the upper socioeconomic group typically react to the aberrant behavior of members of the lower social classes as indicative of mental illness. Commonly held beliefs about the causes of mental illness within the lower classes influence their prevalence of mental disorders. For example, lower-class persons may attribute their social status, health, and life chances to fate, bad luck, and other forces beyond their control (Wheaton, 1980).

Special Topics in Research

Sociological research on mental illness tends to focus on sociodemographic variations in the prevalence of mental disorders, the social processes that may precipitate mental illnesses, and the everyday experiences of the mentally ill. Sociologists examine value judgments, normative expectations, and cultural beliefs associated with mental illness.

SSRN

Cormier, J. W. (2010). Providing those with mental illness full and fair treatment: Legislative considerations in the post-Clark Era. *American Criminal Law Review, 47*(1), 2010. http://ssrn.com/abstract=1601642

Family Experience, Inherited Vulnerabilities, and Stressful Life Events

It is commonly accepted that at least some forms of mental illness are a result of inherited vulnerabilities. Schizophrenia and manic-depressive disorder are two diagnoses thought to be associated with genetic components.

Brain scans, genetic markers, and studies of drug effectiveness provide evidence that genetic factors predispose some individuals to mental illness.

Inherited vulnerabilities and genetic predispositions to mental illness operate in conjunction with stressful life events (Matsumoto, 1997). Family experiences, including marital discord, divorce, role conflicts, and childhood trauma, become major sources of stress for individuals and are associated with the prevalence of mental illness (Paykel, 1974). Parent–child relationships characterized by conflict and stress also relate to the development of mental illness. Debilitating conditions in their family of origin may contribute to one's mental illness later in life. For example, parents who themselves are mentally ill or who practice domineering, rejecting, and overprotecting styles of parenting may well increase the vulnerability of their children to mental illness. Theodore Lidz and his colleagues (1965, p. 362) propose three such conditions that may affect the development of children in this way:

1. A deficiency in parental nurturing of the child, which leads the child to have severe difficulty in achieving autonomy in the sense of adequate independence and ability to take responsibility.
2. Defective socialization of the child by the family as a social institution. The integrated development of the child, the learning of appropriate age and gender roles, and the achievement of an integrated ego structure are consequently blocked.
3. Defective transmission by the family of basic communicative and other instrumental cultural techniques to the child.

Depressive and anxiety disorders as well as schizophrenia are disproportionately found among individuals who experience these types of stressors within parent–child relationships.

Stress may also result from adverse life circumstances and events. Dohrenwend and Dohrenwend (1975) find that persons—most notably of lower social status—who experience economic deprivations and chronic job disruptions are more vulnerable to mental disorders. Stress, however, does not by itself produce mental illness. People experience and withstand considerable stress yet do not become mentally ill. In many cases mental illness results from maladaptive perceptions and responses to stressful life events.

Social Causation Versus Social Selection

The **social causation tradition** focuses on the role of social stressors in the etiology of mental illness. Social causation theorists argue that the stress of poverty, unemployment, and low socioeconomic status actually produces mental illness. The **social selection tradition** examines social stressors that result as a consequence of mental disorder. Advocates of the social selection approach contend that the stress inherent in being mentally ill itself precipitates downward mobility and diminished economic opportunities (Dohrenwend et al., 1992; Miech et al., 1999). This perspective views mental illness as impairment to status attainment. Those who have mental disorders find it difficult or almost impossible to complete their education or even to find and maintain employment. In the face of diminished resources, their ability to cope with the problems inherent in their mental illness is severely compromised.

Both traditions are generally accepted as plausible causes and consequences of mental illness. Neither has been sufficiently refuted in the literature. Most studies find that the relationship between stress and mental illness is bidirectional. That is, stress may lead to mental illness that may produce a more stressful life situation (Acharya, 2001). **Figure 7–2** illustrates the tenets of each approach.

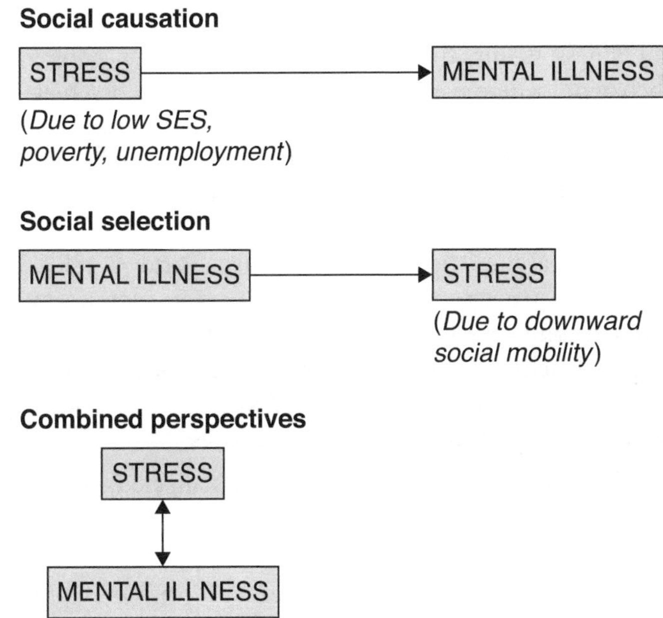

FIGURE 7–2 Social causation and social selection traditions—The role of stress as a cause and a consequence of mental illness.

Source: Adapted from B. Dohrenwend et al. 1992. "Socioeconomic Status and Psychiatric Disorders: The Causation-Selection Issue." Science. 255: 946–952.

Labeling, Societal Reaction, and Social Roles

The process involved in the societal labeling of mental illness produces unintended consequences. Central to the labeling approach is Robert Merton's (1957) concept of a self-fulfilling prophesy. That is, the process of labeling a person as mentally ill results in the very behavior that portends mental illness. The person is viewed as being what he or she is labeled. When a negative label is assigned to an individual, their behaviors are interpreted as being consistent with that label. Otherwise "normal" behaviors—an expectant mother singing to her unborn child on a bus—may be viewed as evidence of a mental disorder.

MYTH OF MENTAL ILLNESS. Psychiatrist Thomas Szasz (1974) views mental illness not as a real, biological illness but as a myth. Accordingly, he opposes the classification of thoughts, feelings, and behaviors as diseases. Although Szasz acknowledges that mental illness does exist, he holds that society labels individuals as mentally ill because their behavior is morally or otherwise unacceptable to the group. Mental illness therefore does not lie within the individual. Rather, it is a societal response to such behavior.

In the *Myth of Mental Illness* (1974), Szasz describes societal responses to mental illness within the framework of a "game-playing model of human behavior" where players—the mentally ill and psychiatrists—act out certain behaviors socially defined by their roles. He describes the roles as impersonations that may be calculated and deliberate. Individuals may act mentally ill in an effort to elicit help from others or to escape sanctions for criminal actions.

Szasz (1974) argues that psychiatrists also perform roles. Psychiatrists socially construct a view of mental illness in such a way that the public rarely disputes the legitimacy of psychiatric diagnoses. The act of diagnosing or labeling behavior as mentally ill is one way that medical professionals exert control over such behaviors. Szasz (1974, p. 37) offers five reasons for why psychiatrists make diagnoses:

1. Scientific—To identify the organs or tissues affected and perhaps the cause of the illness
2. Professional—To enlarge the scope, and thus the power and prestige, of a state-protected medical monopoly and the income of its practitioners
3. Legal—To justify state-sanctioned coercive interventions outside of the criminal justice system
4. Political-economic—To justify enacting and enforcing measures aimed at promoting public health and providing funds for research and treatment on projects classified as medical

5. Personal—To enlist the support of public opinion, the media, and the legal system for bestowing special privileges (and impose special hardships) on persons diagnosed as (mentally) ill

Accordingly, psychiatrists are given authority to label mental illness. This authority leads to the depriving of freedoms for some and the relieving of individual responsibility for others.

MENTALLY ILL ROLE. Thomas Scheff's (1966) examination of mental illness also focuses on the process of societal labeling and the role-playing model. He begins his analysis with a definition of mental illness, which is derived from the labeling perspective. Mental illness, or the symptoms of mental illness, is seen as residual rule-breaking or *residual deviance*—any nonconforming, disruptive behavior that is not otherwise defined as criminal. As a consequence of their behavior, rule-breakers are labeled as mentally ill. **Table 7–4** summarizes the leading explanations for rates of mental illness.

Unlike Szasz, Scheff is interested in how individuals come to play the mentally ill social role. Scheff proposes that stereotypes, learned at an

TABLE 7–4 **Explanations for Rates of Mental Illness**

Theory	Sociological Predictors	Hypotheses
Integration		
Durkheim	Social integration	The greater the social integration, the lower the rate of mental illness.
Social Disorganization and Anomie		
Merton	Anomie	The more anomic social life is, the greater the likelihood that mental illness will occur.
Conflict		
Thio	Power status	High-status, more powerful individuals are more likely to experience neurotic forms of mental illness, whereas low-status, less powerful individuals become psychotic.
Sellin	Culture conflict	If a society is characterized by culture conflict, then there is a greater likelihood that mental illness will occur.

/ continues

TABLE 7–4 Explanations for Rates of Mental Illness / continued

Explanations of Individual Levels of Mental Illness

Theorist	Sociological Predictors	Hypotheses
Strain		
Agnew	Strain	If an individual cannot escape or adapt to strain, then he or she may become angry and frustrated. This frustration may lead to mental illness.
Labeling and Societal Reaction		
Scheff	Societal reaction labeling	If an individual engages in nonconforming behavior that is not considered criminal, then he or she may be labeled mentally ill. If an individual is labeled mentally ill, then he or she may eventually assume that exact role.
Szasz	Societal reaction labeling	If an individual's behavior is immoral or unacceptable to the group, then he or she may be labeled mentally ill.

early age, and other cultural expectations of the mentally ill help labeled persons play the role of a mentally ill person. He offers three propositions pertaining to the acceptance of this role. First, "labeled deviants may be rewarded for playing the stereotyped deviant role" (Scheff, 1966, p. 84). Second, "labeled deviants are punished when they attempt to return to conventional roles" (Scheff, 1966, p. 87). Last, "in the crisis occurring when a residual rule-breaker is publicly labeled, the deviant is highly suggestible, and may accept the proffered role of the insane as the only alternative" (Scheff, 1966, p. 88). In summary, those labeled as mentally ill usually accept the role as their own, either because of rewards and punishments or because they believe there is no alternative role available to them.

BEING SANE IN INSANE PLACES. D. L. Rosenhan (1973) and Erving Goffman (1961) provide analyses of the role of institutionalized mental patients and of how they are treated by the hospital staff. Hospitalized mental patients must match their behavior to the role expectations of the staff. Behavior that is inconsistent with these expectations is viewed as evidence of psychiatric illness.

Rosenhan's (1973) experiment questions traditional psychiatric diagnoses and how "diagnosis betrays little about the patient but much about the environment in which an observer finds him" (p. 251). His experiment involves eight professionals, all of sound mind, who pose as mental patients. Their objective is to determine if hospital staff can distinguish between those who are sane and those who are not.

Each pseudo-patient gains entrance into the psychiatric ward complaining of hearing voices. Accurate information is offered as to their life history, relationships with family, and work and school experiences. Upon secret admission, each pseudo-patient stops displaying any symptoms of abnormality and behaves as he or she might in any other setting. Without knowing what to expect, the pseudo-patients assume their experiment will be recognized and they will be discharged from the hospital. Everyday behaviors such as writing in a notebook, however, are documented as evidence of psychological disturbance. Despite being perfectly sane, none of the pseudo-patients is immediately released from the mental hospital.

Goffman provides an insightful analysis of life within a mental hospital and the moral career of mental patients. He observes that the role as mental patient begins with a set of mortifying experiences (i.e., restricted free movement, communal living, and diffused authority of hospital staff). Patients define their roles by these experiences and are socialized to accept the role of a mentally ill person. Doing so ensures rewards rather than punishments and eventual discharge from the hospital. Patients who are easily managed, who submit to hospital routines, and who follow staff directives are labeled by the hospital staff as mentally healthy; patients who are not submissive and compliant are viewed as mentally ill.

Theoretical Explanations of Mental Illness

As shown in the previous sections of this chapter, medical explanations for mental illness are commonly accepted. Mental disorders are thought to result from physical processes within the body, most often chemical imbalances or brain dysfunctions. Individuals may possess hereditary vulnerability to mental disorders. More often, biological and genetic factors are compounded by stress and other environmental factors to produce mental illness in certain individuals. Stressful life events may trigger the onset of a psychotic episode, acute anxiety, or sudden depression. Psychiatrists, psychologists, and other mental health professionals consistently adopt the medical model for the diagnoses, treatment, and understanding of mental illnesses.

Sociocultural explanations also contribute to the explanation of mental illness. The societal reaction or labeling perspective provides insight into how mental illness is defined and used to socially control

Being Sane in Insane Places

"If sanity and insanity exist, how shall we know them" is a question considered by D. L. Rosenhan (1973) in his classic study "On Being Sane in Insane Places." To answer this question, Rosenhan selected eight mentally healthy people to pose as "pseudo mental patients" and gain admission to a psychiatric hospital for treatment. The eight pseudo mental patients were a graduate student, three psychologists, a pediatrician, a psychiatrist, a painter, and a housewife. The psychiatric hospitals were located on the East and West coasts of the United States. Soon after admission to the various mental hospitals, the psychiatric symptoms presented at admission were no longer exhibited by the pseudo mental patients. Rosenhan's investigation of psychiatric labeling concludes as follows:

> A psychiatric label has a life and influence of its own. Once the impression has been formed that the patient is schizophrenic, the expectation is that he will continue to be schizophrenic. When a sufficient amount of time has passed, during which the patient has done nothing bizarre, he is considered to be in remission and available for discharge. But the label endures beyond discharge, with the unconfirmed expectation that he will behave as a schizophrenic again. Such labels conferred by mental health professionals, are as influential on the patient as they are on his relatives and friends, and it should not surprise anyone that the diagnosis acts on all them as a self-fulfilling prophesy. Eventually the patient accepts the diagnosis, with all its surplus meanings and expectations, and behaves accordingly.
>
> The inferences to be made from these matters are quite simple. The sane are not sane all of the time. We lose our tempers "for no good reason." We are occasionally depressed or anxious, again for no good reason. And we may find it difficult to get along with one or another person—again for no good reason that we can specify. Similarly the insane are not always insane. . . . [The] bizarre behaviors upon which their diagnoses were allegedly predicted constituted only a small fraction of their total behavior. If it makes no sense to label ourselves as permanently depressed on the basis of an occasional depression, then it takes better evidence than is presently available to label all patients insane or schizophrenic on the basis of bizarre behaviors or cognitions.

Source: Rosenhan, D. L. (1973). On being sane in insane places. *Science, 179,* 250–258.

deviant individuals or those who are labeled as mentally ill. Szasz (1974) and Scheff (1966) offer two theories of mental illness from this perspective. Additional sociological theories, including integration, strain, and conflict theories, can be applied to the study of mental illness. In addition to explaining why individuals experience mental illness, these theories help explain rates of mental illness in societies.

Integration Theories

Emile Durkheim's (1951) theory implies that extremely high or low levels of societal integration can give rise to anxiety and mental disorders. In cases of low integration, members of society are detached from the group. Rates of mental disorders and levels of anxiety are high due to uncertainty in life and low social support. In cases of high integration, society members are extremely emerged in the group. Rates of mental illness and anxiety may be lower due to greater social supports and predictability. Stress, depression, and repressed aggression may also be experienced, however, because individuality is discouraged and emphasis is placed on group cohesion. Suicide rates in these types of societies are often high.

Social Disorganization and Anomie

Robert Merton's (1957) theory of social disorganization and anomie focuses on the stress that results from the inability to reach culturally defined goals, a condition he terms "anomie." Societies who experience these anomic conditions react in various ways to the stress and are often characterized by high rates of mental illness.

Robert Agnew (1992) furthers this idea by examining individual adaptation to anomic conditions. For some, he contends, opportunities to reach culturally defined goals are blocked by anomic conditions, the loss of something positive, or the presence of negative events. These blocked opportunities are in themselves a source of stress. Individual maladaptation to such stress may lead to mental illness.

SSRN

Jones, J. T.R. (January 2008). Mental illness, stigma, and the person in the office next door. *The Courier-Journal.* http://ssrn.com/abstract=1087126

Conflict

Culture conflict theories such as that of Thorsten Sellin (1938) suggest that deviance results from the clash of norms and values between different cultures over what is acceptable behavior. Societies characterized by culture conflict may also foster mental illness. Individuals caught between two cultures experience uncertainty over appropriate behavior. Uncertainty alone may produce stress. But in the case of an individual who exhibits inappropriate behavior, he or she may be labeled as peculiar or, in some cases, mentally ill. According to Sellin, culture conflict arises between cultures and within cultures, for example, middle-class versus lower-class norms.

Alex Thio (1978) proposes a power conflict theory of mental illness. In his view, powerful members of society exploit the less powerful members in their quest for power. This quest for power leads to neurotic behavior disorders. To draw attention away from these disorders and toward the reactions of the powerless to exploitation (e.g., aggression), the powerful label the powerless as psychotic. The powerless lack treatment for their psychoses and do not possess the authority to dispute the label. As a result, the psychoses of the powerless are perpetuated and viewed as culturally more severe than neuroses.

Chapter Summary

Although the nature and definitions of mental disorders vary from country to country and over time, some form of mental illness is seen across the globe. Disorders are most common among the young, the lower socioeconomic classes, the divorced or separated, and certain high-risk populations.

The medical model of mental illness dominates what is known and accepted about mental disorders. Psychiatrists and mental health professionals diagnose and treat mental disorders according to set criteria in the DSM-IV. Organic and functional disorders along with psychoses and neuroses are defined. Numerous specific disorders are also included. Some of the most common and well-known disorders include

- Depression
- Bipolar disorder
- Anxiety disorders
- Personality disorders
- Schizophrenia

Approximately one in four American adults over age 18 has a diagnosable mental disorder. About 6% of adults have a serious mental illness and experience some significant functional impairment. Depression and anxiety are the most common forms of mental illness. Each affects 19 million adults per year. Schizophrenia affects relatively few people, but it is considered one of the most chronic and severe mental disorders known today.

Mental illness is socially and culturally defined with regard to the norms, values, and beliefs of a given society. As a result, some disorders are culturally bound, whereas others are seen in almost every culture.

Key Concepts

Culture: The norms, values, and beliefs of a given society or group.

Cultural relativism: Cross-cultural variation in the social construction of reality.

Culture-bound disorders: Mental disorders that are unique to the culture in which they are found.

Medical model: Mental disorders are attributed to some genetic abnormality or other inherited vulnerability.

***Diagnostic and Statistical Manual of Mental Disorders*, 4th edition (DSM-IV-TR):** Publication of the American Psychiatric Association used to diagnose mental disorders according to standardized criteria.

Organic disorders: Mental disorders that originate from physiological or organic causes.

Functional disorders: Group of related disorders whose causes are less well known.

Psychoses: The more severe forms of mental disorders; often require long-term treatment.

Neuroses: The less severe disorders such as depression and anxiety; often referred to as minor disorders.

Unipolar (major) depression: Serious mood disorder classified in the DSM-IV; characterized by emotional, cognitive, motivational, and physical symptoms.

Bipolar (manic-depressive) disorder: Serious mood disorder classified in the DSM-IV; characterized by episodes of manic and depressive behavior.

Personality disorders: Maladaptive, immature, and inappropriate ways of coping with stress or solving problems, manipulative behavior, disorganized and unstable mood or behavior, and thought disturbances.

Schizophrenia: Severe and chronic mental disorder classified in the DSM-IV; characterized by alterations in thought, perception, and consciousness, for example, hallucinations or delusions.

Anxiety disorders: Anxiety that is disproportionate to the circumstance, that is difficult for the individual to control, or that interferes with normal functioning.

Social causation tradition: Idea asserting the role of social stressors in the etiology of mental illness.

Social selection tradition: Idea asserting that social stressors are a consequence of mental disorders.

Critical Thinking Questions

1. The manifestations of mental disorder vary widely around the world, yet there are a limited number of medically recognized psychiatric diagnoses. What might account for this seemly incongruous finding?
2. Consider the efficacy of the "myth of mental illness." Is mental illness a social construction fabricated by psychiatric professions, or are psychiatric diagnoses as legitimate as any other medical diagnoses?
3. What sociocultural conditions and social processes are most likely to generate high rates of psychotic versus less debilitating forms of mental disorder?
4. Depression is the most prevalent form of mental illness found around the world. What accounts for the prevalence of depression across widely disparate cultures? Why do women suffer from depression more so than men worldwide?

Web Extra

Web-based media materials from high-quality sources such as CNN, Time, and National Public Radio are available in support of this textbook. Visit go.jblearning.com/deviance to access them.

Check out these websites for additional information on mental illness:

http://www.nimh.nih.gov

http://www.samhsa.gov

http://www.apa.org

PACE

Alcohol Abuse

CHAPTER 8

Learning Objectives

After reading this chapter you should know

- Definitional issues related to alcohol abuse.
- The nature and prevalence of alcohol abuse worldwide and in the United States.
- Differences in alcohol abuse among various gender, age, race/ethnic, and special populations.
- The influence of culture on alcohol abuse.
- The effect of religious practices and spirituality on alcohol abuse.
- The disease concept of alcohol dependence.

About 2 A.M. on a June morning in 2010 outside the Weiland Brewery Restaurant in the 400 block of East 1st Street in Los Angeles, California, residents and patrons leaving the bar reported hearing a gunshot. Reports quickly surfaced that at least one shot had been fired by one of three drunken LAPD officers who pulled a handgun and discharged the weapon in the direction of a street lamp outside the brewery (Blankstein & Rubin, 2010). Although the officers were not immediately identified, a preliminary investigation by the police department showed that the officer who was said to have fired the shot had been significantly impaired after a night of heavy drinking with friends.

Surprisingly, studies have found that alcohol abuse among police officers in the United States is about double that of the rest of the population. "While the social use of alcohol may be accepted in most professions," says Paul M. Weber, president of the Los Angeles Police Protective League, "excessive drinking by police officers can impair their ability to function properly at work and may result in disciplinary issues" (Blankstein & Rubin, 2010)

Excessive drinking, particularly among the young, is a global phenomenon. The processes of globalization may accelerate excessive drinking practices (Stares, 1996). This chapter considers definitional issues related to alcohol and illicit drug consumption and the extent and social structural patterns of use across the world and in the United States. Substance use among special populations, including Native Americans, college students, and the elderly, is also considered. Attention is given to the impact of culture, religion, and spirituality on drinking practices and illegal drug use. Finally, theoretical explanations of rates of substance abuse and individual precipitants are provided.

Definitions

Since Swedish physician Magnus Huss introduced the concept of **alcoholism** in 1849, its definition has undergone several changes. To Dr. Huss, alcoholism simply meant a disease caused by excessive alcohol consumption (Keller & Doria, 1991). Scientific advances, cultural and religious perspectives, and legal considerations have contributed to numerous reinterpretations of alcoholism. The National Council on Alcoholism and Drug Dependence and the American Society of Addiction Medicine define alcoholism as a primary, chronic disease with genetic, psychosocial, and environmental factors influencing its development and manifestations (Flavin & Morse, 1991, pp. 266–271). The disease is often progressive and fatal. It is characterized by continuous or periodic impaired control over drinking, preoccupation with the drug alcohol, use of alcohol despite adverse consequences, and distortions in thinking, most notably denial.

What was once called the "American Disease" is fast becoming a global habit.
—Paul B. Stares (1996)

This definition of alcoholism is consistent with the diagnosis of substance dependence provided in the American Psychiatric Association's *Diagnostic and Statistical Manual of Mental Disorders* (DSM-TR) (2000) and the *International Classification of Diseases*, 10th edition. The DSM-IV sets forth the criteria for substance dependence. At least one or more of the following criteria must occur during a 12-month period:

- Recurrent substance use resulting in a failure to fulfill major role obligations at work, school, or home (such as repeated absences or poor work performance related to substance use; substance-related absences, suspensions, or expulsions from school; or neglect of children or household).

- Recurrent substance use in situations in which it is physically hazardous (such as driving an automobile or operating a machine when impaired by substance use).
- Recurrent substance-related legal problems (such as arrests for substance-related disorderly conduct).
- Continued substance use despite having persistent or recurring social or interpersonal problems caused or exacerbated by the effects of the substance (e.g., arguments with spouse about consequences of intoxication and physical fights).

Underage drinking has reached epidemic proportions in America.

—Joseph A. Califano, Jr., National Center on Addiction and Substance Abuse Chairman and President (2002)

The National Institute on Alcohol Abuse and Alcoholism (www.niaaa.nih.gov) notes that **alcohol dependence syndrome** is marked by the following:

- **Craving**: A strong need or compulsion to drink.
- **Loss of control**: The frequent inability to stop drinking once a person has begun.
- **Physical dependence**: The occurrence of withdrawal symptoms, such as nausea, sweating, shakiness, and anxiety, when alcohol is stopped after a period of heavy drinking. These symptoms are usually relieved by drinking alcohol or by taking another sedative drug.
- **Tolerance**: The need for increasing amounts of alcohol to get "high."

Alcohol Use Around the World

There are wide variations in the use of alcohol around the world. Each year the average per capita consumption of alcohol is 1.6 gallons. The World Health Organization (WHO) provides data on the per capita consumption of alcohol for persons over the age of 15 in 153 countries. The countries with the highest annual per capita consumption (in liters) are Uganda (19.47), Luxembourg (17.54), Czech Republic (16.21), Ireland (14.45), Republic of Moldova (13.88), France (13.54), and Réunion (13.39). The countries with the lowest annual per capita consumption are Iran, Kuwait, Libyan Arab Jamahiriya, Saudi Arabia, Somalia, and Bangladesh (0.00), Mauritania (0.01), Pakistan (0.02), Algeria (0.03), Nepal, Comoros, and Yemen (0.08), Indonesia, and Egypt (0.10). By contrast, the United States (8.51) ranks 41st on the list, behind other English-speaking countries: Bermuda (9.21), New Zealand (9.79), and the United Kingdom (10.39) and just ahead of Canada (8.47) (WHO, 2004). Overall, Europeans consume the most alcohol (3.1 gallons per capita), followed by North American (2.5 gallons) and eastern Mediterraneans (2.0 gallons).

The WHO (2010) reports more than 76 million people suffer from alcohol use disorders, including alcohol dependence and abuse. The dire consequences of alcohol abuse worldwide are measured in various ways.

Alcoholism as a Disease

E. M. Jellinek, a pioneer in alcoholism research, takes the view that excessive drinking may involve an underlying disease process. His typology of alcoholism includes four distinct categories, two of which are disease related. The disease-related forms are gamma alcoholism and delta alcoholism. Gamma alcoholism involves physiological processes resulting in increased alcohol tolerance and progressive loss of control over its use. Delta alcoholism also involves metabolic and other biochemical changes but is characterized by the *inability to abstain* from alcohol rather than the *loss of control* over its use.

Two nondisease forms of alcoholism are termed alpha and beta. Alpha alcoholism is characterized by excessive drinking that results in a psychological rather than a physical dependence. Alpha alcoholics do not typically suffer from physical illnesses associated with their drinking. Beta alcoholism, however, does involve physical deterioration but is not marked by either physical or psychological dependency.

Jellinek identifies a four-phase process in the development of the disease of alcoholism:

- *Phase I* is the prealcoholic stage in which drinking becomes progressively more excessive. Increasingly larger amounts of alcohol are needed to achieve a state of well-being.
- *Phase II* is the early alcoholic stage marked by defensive attitudes toward drinking, such as denial of a drinking problem or rationalization for increasing consumption. Physical symptoms—blackouts, shakes, loss of memory—are also evident in the early alcoholic stage.
- *Phase III* is known as the crucial phase in the development of alcoholism. In this stage there is a loss of control over drinking and a physical need for alcohol. Drinking is no longer a matter of personal choice but becomes a necessary part of daily life.
- *Phase IV* is the chronic stage in the development of the disease. In all respects this is the terminal phase of alcoholism. The alcoholic goes on drinking sprees that last for days at a time; physical deterioration, including malnutrition, cirrhosis, and neurological damage, is pronounced. If left untreated, the alcoholism may result in a complexity of medical problems that often result in premature death.

Source: Based on information from Jellinek, E. M. (1960). The Disease Concept of Alcoholism. New Haven, CT: College and University Press.

For example, 1.8 million deaths each year across the globe are alcohol related. Another measure is "disability-adjusted years," or the number of years lost due to premature deaths or years living in a disabled condition. It is estimated that more than 58 million alcohol-related disability-adjusted years are lost each year worldwide.

Figure 8–1 shows the distribution of disability-adjusted years worldwide. Eastern Europe and Russia and Kazakhstan have the highest number of alcohol-related disability-adjusted years, followed by South and Central America and China and Mongolia.

Substance Use in the United States

Findings from the most recent National Survey on Drug Use and Health provide a profile of substance use among persons 12 years of age and older in the United States. Considering alcohol use, the survey (Substance Abuse and Mental Health Services Administration [SAMHSA], 2010) shows the following:

- About half of Americans (51.6%) had at least one drink in the previous month.
- Among persons 12 years or older, drinking among males (57.7%) exceeds that of females (45.9%).
- Somewhat more than one in five (23.3%) report binge drinking (five or more drinks during a single occasion) in the previous month.

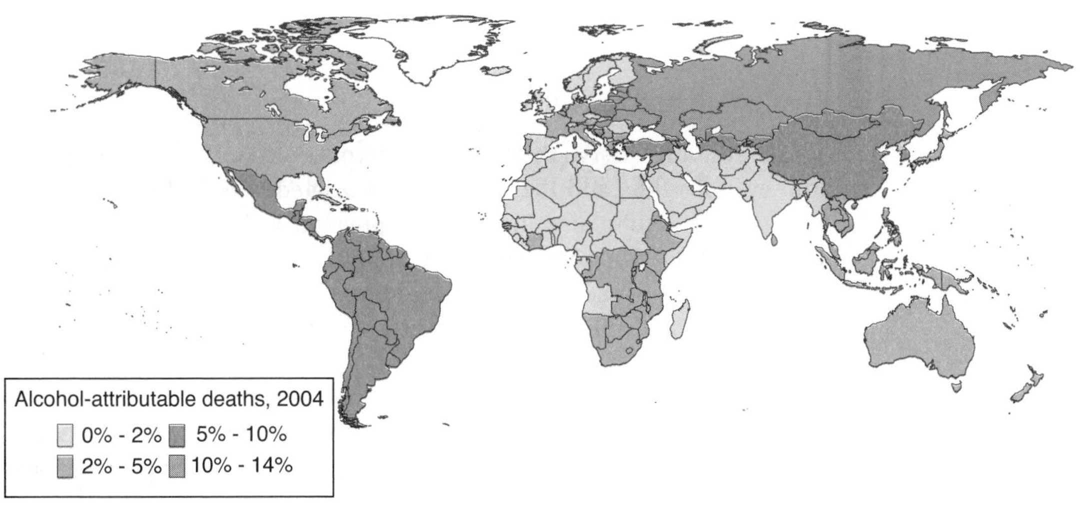

FIGURE 8–1 Burden of disease attributable to alcohol.

Source: World Health Organization, Global Status Report on Alcohol and Health, Geneva, Switzerland: WHO Press, 2011.

- About 7% admit to heavy drinking (five or more drinks during a single occasion on 5 or more days in the previous month).
- The Northeast region of the United States leads the nation in percentage of its population who drink (56.8%) and the South has the lowest percent of drinkers (47.3%). More than half the residents in the Midwest (54.2%) and West (51.8%) also drink alcohol at least occasionally.
- More than half of the residents of metropolitan areas drink at least occasionally, compared with about one in four residents of nonmetropolitan areas.
- Sixty-one percent of college-educated persons drink, about 4 in 10 binge drink, and 16.3% drink heavily compared with persons 18 to 22 years of age who were not full-time college students who drink (54.2%), binge drink (38.1%), and drink heavily (13%).
- Excessive alcohol use—binge and heavy drinking—markedly decreases with age.

SSRN

Pruitt, L. R. (2009). The forgotten fifth: Rural youth and substance abuse (October 6, 2008). *Stanford Law & Policy Review, 20,* 259. UC Davis Legal Studies Research Paper No. 150, http://ssrn.com/abstract=1279669

Figure 8–2 shows that alcohol consumption increases through age 25 and then begins to decline. The reduction in alcohol use across the life span is evident for both genders and all races and ethnic groups. For example, binge and heavy drinkers are most often found among persons between 18 and 29 years old and least common among persons over the age of 60. For example, 41% of persons between 18 and 25 engage in binge drinking and 14.5% are heavy drinkers compared with 8.2% of persons over 65 who binge drink and 2.2% who are heavy drinkers (SAMHSA, 2010).

Culture and Alcohol Use

Wide variations exist in the cultural patterns of alcohol use, its integration into everyday life, and the meanings associated with it. Culture shapes all aspects of alcohol use, including its physical and social consequences. D. B. Heath (1982) notes that sociocultural factors are as critical to the understanding of the influence of alcohol on behavior as psychological considerations. Culture, in short, exerts a powerful influence over the use of alcohol across the globe.

In cultures where drinking is an integral part of everyday life, alcohol dependency is low. R. H. and E. M. Blum (1969, pp. 188–227) observe, "In those cultures where drinking is integrated into religious rites and customs, where the place and manner of consumption are regulated by tradition and where, moreover, self-control, sociability, and 'knowing how to hold one's liquor' are matters of manly pride, alcohol problems

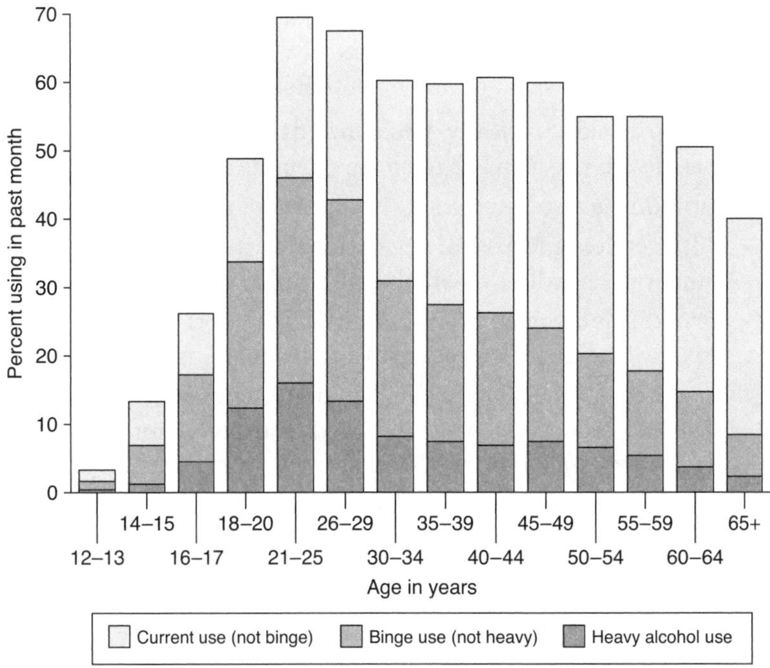

FIGURE 8–2 Current binge and heavy alcohol use among persons aged 12 and older, by age, 2008.
Source: Results from the 2009 National Survey on Drug Use and Health. Office of Applied Studies (OAS), Substance Abuse and Mental Health Services Administration (SAMHSA), U.S. Department of Health and Human Services, www.oas.samsha.gov

are at a minimum, provided no other variables are overriding." Two cultures, Italian and Jewish, illustrate the importance of the integration of drinking practices into everyday life. To anthropologist Donald Heath (1995), the low rates of alcoholism among Italians and Jews are a consequence of effective cultural socialization. Children are introduced to alcohol as part of their regular family life and learn to drink moderate amounts while still young. In both countries, alcohol is commonly drunk with meals and is considered a natural and normal food. Most people agree that alcohol in moderation, for those who choose to drink, is necessary and that abuse is unacceptable and results in immediate sanctions.

In their classic study of Jewish drinking practices, sociologists Bruce Berg and Barry Glassner (1980) identified four cultural processes that reduce problematic alcohol use. First, alcohol abuse is linked with being a non-Jew. Second, early in life children learn that drinking in moderation is part of religious and family customs and carries symbolic importance to a Jew. Third, Jews who drink moderately tend to associate with other Jews who do the same. Fourth, Jews learn techniques to avoid being pressured into drinking excessively.

Findings from several cross-cultural studies provide remarkably consistent conclusions about the use of alcohol. N. E. Zinberg (1981) identifies five cultural conditions that promote nonproblematic drinking practices:

- Group drinking is clearly differentiated from drunkenness and associated with ritualistic or religious celebrations.
- Drinking is associated with eating, preferably ritualistic feasting.
- Both genders and several generations are included in the drinking situation, regardless of whether all drink.
- Drinking is divorced from the individual's effort to escape personal anxiety or difficult (intolerable) social situations.
- Inappropriate behavior when drinking (aggression, violence, overt sexuality) is absolutely disapproved, and protection against such behavior is offered by the "sober" or less intoxicated.

SSRN

Angelucci, M. (March 2007). Love on the rocks: Alcohol abuse and domestic violence in rural Mexico. IZA Discussion Paper No. 2706. http://ssrn.com/abstract=981690

Figure 8–3 shows marked racial/ethnic differences in alcohol use and binge and heavy alcohol drinking. Whites are most likely to drink

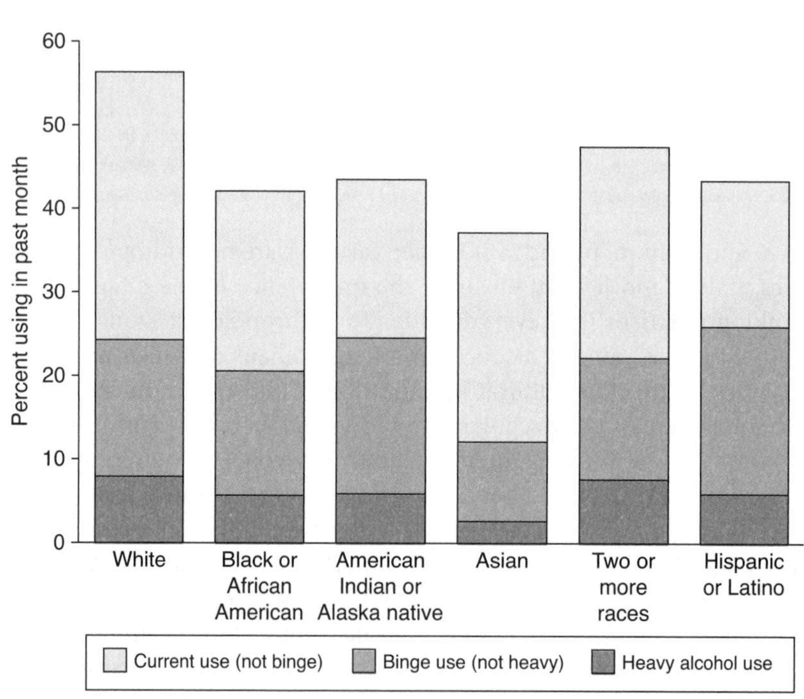

FIGURE 8–3 Current binge, and heavy alcohol use among persons ages 12 or older, by race/ethnicity, 2008.

Source: Results from the 2009 National Survey on Drug Use and Health. Office of Applied Studies (OAS), Substance Abuse and Mental Health Services Administration (SAMHSA), U.S. Department of Health and Human Services, www.oas.samsha.gov

Sex and Substance Abuse

Recently, the National Center on Addiction and Substance Abuse at Columbia University conducted a study of the possible link between sexual activity and substance abuse among teenagers. Although sexual activity does not cause substance abuse, nor does substance abuse cause sexual activity, the study finds a strong link between the two forms of behavior. The following are among the key findings:

- Compared with teens with no sexually active friends, teens who report half or more of their friends are sexually active are
  - More than six and one-half times likelier to drink
  - 31 times likelier to get drunk
  - 22.5 times likelier to have tried marijuana
  - More than five and one-half times likelier to smoke
- Teens who spend 25 or more hours a week with a boyfriend or girlfriend (compared with teens who spend less than 10 hours a week with a boyfriend or girlfriend) are
  - Two and one-half times likelier to drink
  - Five times likelier to get drunk
  - 4.5 times likelier to have tried marijuana
  - More than 2.5 times likelier to smoke
- Girls with boyfriends 2 or more years older (compared with girls whose boyfriends are less than 2 years older or who do not have a boyfriend) are
  - More than twice as likely to drink
  - Almost six times likelier to get drunk
  - Six times likelier to have tried marijuana
  - Four and one-half times likelier to smoke

Source: Adapted from The National Center on Addiction and Substance Abuse (CASA) at Columbia University. 2004. National Survey of American Attitudes on Substance Abuse IX: Teen Dating Practices and Sexual Activity New York: Author. Web posted at: www.casacolumbia.org/Absolutenm/Articlefiles/380-August_2004_CH_Teen_Survey.pdf

and to be heavy drinkers, followed by persons of two or more races. Hispanics and Native Americans are most likely to engage in binge drinking. Asians are the least likely to use alcohol, binge drink, or engage in heavy drinking (SAMSA, 2010).

SSRN

Bhuyan, S., & Reggimenti, M. (2000), Demand for alcohol by college students: An empirical evaluation, http://ssrn.com/abstract=232413

Religion, Spirituality, and Substance Use

The possible effect of religion and spirituality on the use of various substances is the focus of a recent report issued by the National Center on Addiction and Substance Abuse at Columbia University. Religion is defined as "a set of particular beliefs about God or a higher power shared by a group of individuals, and the practices, rituals, and forms of governance that define how those beliefs are expressed" (National Center on Addiction

AT A GLANCE

Global Patterns and Trends

- The age of initiation into alcohol/drug use is declining across the globe.
- There has been an increase of alcohol use among women. Women are also at higher risk for alcohol-related harm than men.

U.S. Patterns and Trends

- About half of the U.S. population 12 years of age and older use alcohol; 23.3% participated in binge drinking, and 6.8% were considered heavy drinkers.
- Twenty-nine percent of underage persons (aged 12 to 20) report drinking alcohol.
- Binge drinking is concentrated in the age range from 18 to 25.
- College students are more likely than their peers not in college to drink, binge drink, and drink to excess.
- Approximately 12% of adult Americans meet the diagnostic criteria for alcohol dependence at some time in their life.
- Persons who are alcohol dependent are four times more likely to have started drinking before the age of 15.

Sources: The National Center on Addiction and Substance Abuse. 2002. "Teen Tipplers: America's Underage Drinking Epidemic," New York: Columbia University; Mayor, S. 2001. "Alcohol and Drug Misuse Sweeping the World, says WHO," British Medical Journal, 322: 7284; Settertobulte, W., B. B. Jensen, and K. Hurrelmann. 2001. "Drinking Among Young Europeans," World Health Organization-Regional Office for Europe; United Nations World Drug Report 2000. 2000. Oxford: Oxford University Press; Substance Abuse and Mental Health Services Administration (SAMHSA). 2010. National Survey on Drug Use and Health. Rockville, MD: U.S. Department of Health and Human Services.

and Substance Abuse, 2001, p. 5). Spirituality refers more to a personal expression of belief and is defined as "a deeply personal and individualized response to God, a higher power, or an animating force in the world" (National Center on Addiction and Substance Abuse, 2001, p. 5). It is possible, therefore, to be spiritual without having an affiliation with a particular church or religious organization.

Analyses of national data collected in three separate studies show the following:

- Adults who deny that religious beliefs are important to them are one and one-half times more likely to drink, three times more likely to binge drink, four times more likely to use illicit drugs, and six times more likely to use marijuana than adults who report that religious beliefs are important to them.
- Adults who do not participate in religious services are two times more likely to drink, five times more likely to use illicit drugs, seven times more likely to binge drink, and eight times more likely to use

marijuana than adults who participate in religious services at least once a week.

- Teenagers who deny that religious beliefs are important to them are three times more likely to drink and binge drink, four times more likely to use marijuana, and seven times more likely to use illicit drugs than teenagers who report that religious beliefs are important to them.
- Teenagers who do not participate in religious services are two times more likely to drink, three times more likely to use marijuana and binge drink, and four times more likely to use illicit drugs than teenagers who participate in religious services at least once a week.
- Substance-dependent persons are more likely to become drug free if they participate in a spiritually based program such as Alcoholics Anonymous or Narcotics Anonymous (www.casacolumbia.org).

More than six decades ago Bill Wilson and Dr. Bob Smith cofounded **Alcoholics Anonymous** (Alcoholics Anonymous, 2001). Arguably, Alcoholics Anonymous is the most successful recovery program for alcoholics worldwide. Alcoholics Anonymous is a spiritually based rehabilitation strategy that combines group support, individual mentoring, and personal awareness and commitment. A fundamental precept of Alcoholics Anonymous is the alcoholic's recognition that he or she is, in fact, an alcoholic. Alcoholics in the program must also accept that they are powerless over their alcoholism and that they desire to stop drinking. Fearless and uncompromising self-examination is coupled with a willingness to compensate those whom they have injured. By active participation in this program, recovering alcoholics are guided through their recovery—"one day at a time."

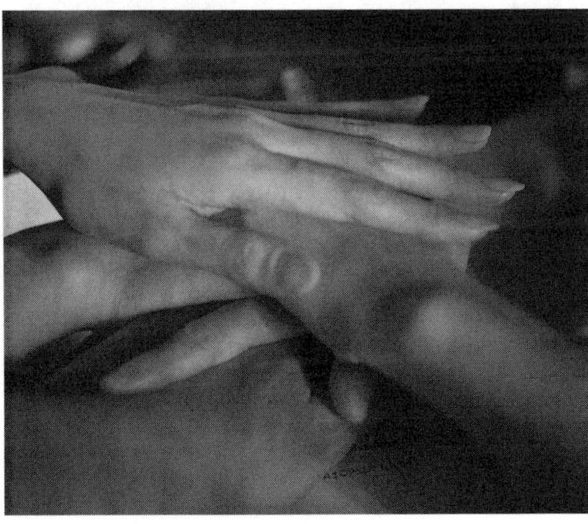

Spirituality in practice. Why are spiritually-based substance abuse rehabilitation programs more effective than many other kinds of strategies?

Twelve Steps of Alcoholics Anonymous

Step One: Admitted we were powerless over alcohol—that our lives had become unmanageable.

Step Two: Came to believe that a Power greater than ourselves could restore us to sanity.

Step Three: Made a decision to turn our will and our lives over to the care of God "as we understood Him."

Step Four: Made a searching and fearless moral inventory of ourselves.

Step Five: Admitted to God, to ourselves, and to another human being the exact nature of our wrongs.

Step Six: Were entirely ready to have God remove all these defects of character.

Step Seven: Humbly asked Him to remove our shortcomings.

Step Eight: Made a list of all persons we had harmed and became willing to make amends to them all.

Step Nine: Made direct amends to such people wherever possible, except when to do so would injure them or others.

Step Ten: Continued to take personal inventory and when wrong promptly admitted it.

Step Eleven: Sought through prayer and meditation to improve our conscious contact with God "as we understood Him," praying only for knowledge of His will for us and the power to carry that out.

Step Twelve: Having had a spiritual awakening as the result of these steps, we tried to carry this message to alcoholics and to practice these principles in all our efforts.

Source: The Twelve Steps are reprinted with permission of Alcoholics Anonymous World Services, Inc. ("AAWS") Permission to reprint the Twelve Steps does not mean that AAWS has reviewed or approved the contents of this publication, or that AAWS necessarily agrees with the views expressed herein. A.A. is a program of recovery from alcoholism only - use of the Twelve Steps in connection with programs and activities which are patterned after A.A., but which address other problems, or in any other non-A.A. context, does not imply otherwise.

Onset of Alcohol Use

Figure 8–4 shows that family drinking history markedly affects the onset of alcohol use. Teenagers from families with a history of alcoholism are more likely to begin to use alcohol earlier than those from nonalcoholic families. In addition, persons from alcoholic families are more likely to develop a dependency on alcohol at some point in their lifetime (http://pubs.niaaa.nih.gov/publications/arh321/3-15.htm).

Figure 8–5 shows that the onset of alcohol dependence is typically between the ages of 18 and 24 and declines with age. Patterns of alcohol dependence tend to follow rates of consumption and binge drinking. **Table 8–1** outlines some of the explanations that have been offered to explain varying rates of alcohol abuse.

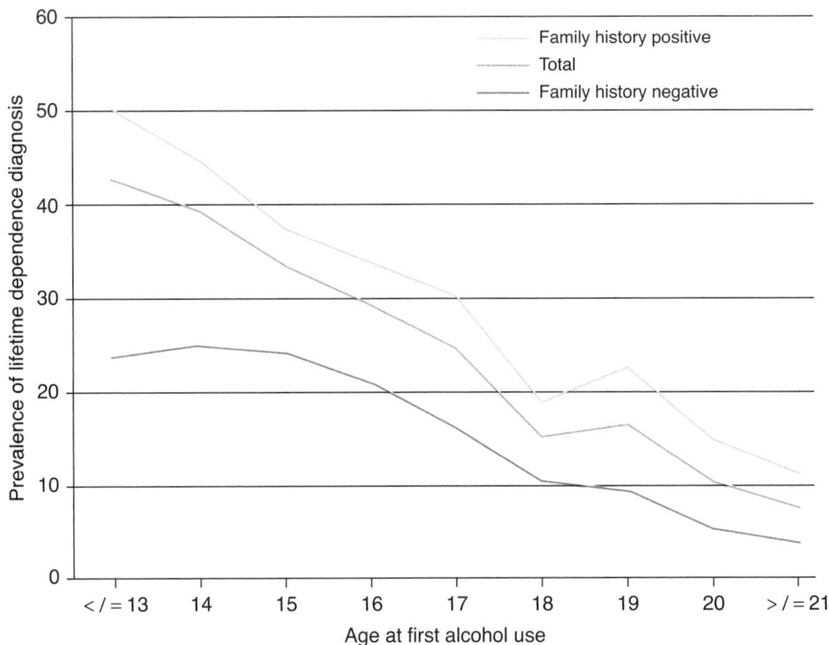

FIGURE 8–4 Family history of alcoholism and age of first alcohol use.

Source: 2001–2002 National Epidemiologic Survey on Alcohol and Related Conditions. National Institute of Health.

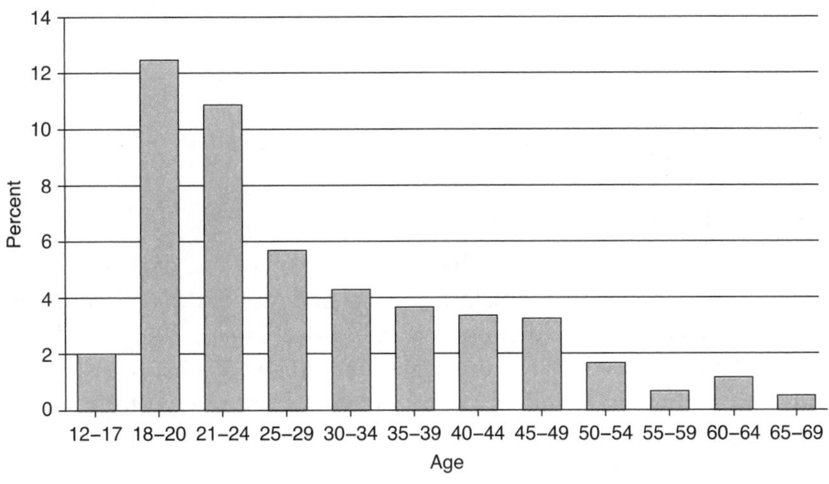

FIGURE 8–5 Alcohol dependence by age, 2003.

Source: Results from the 2009 National Survey on Drug Use and Health. Office of Applied Studies (OAS), Substance Abuse and Mental Health Services Administration (SAMHSA), U.S. Department of Health and Human Services, www.oas.samsha.gov

TABLE 8–1 **Explanations of Rates of Alcohol Abuse**

Theory and Theorists	Sociological Predictors	Hypotheses
Social Integration		
Merton	Anomie	The greater the disjunction between institutionalized means and culturally approved goals, the higher the rate of alcohol abuse.
	Retreatism	The greater the rejection of institutionalized means and culturally approved goals, the greater the retreatist behavior in society. The greater the retreatist behavior in society, the higher the rate of alcohol abuse.
Subcultural Opportunities		
Cloward and Ohlin	Retreatism Subcultures	The fewer the subcultural opportunities—either legitimate or illegitimate—for success, the more likely retreatist subcultures emerge. The more retreatist subcultures in a given society, the higher the rate of alcohol abuse.
Bales	Cultural tension	As tension and stress increase in a given culture, and as effective means of tension reduction decrease, the higher the rate of alcohol abuse.
Cultural Integration		
Blum and Blum	Cultural integration	The more drinking is integrated into the customs of daily life, the lower the rate of alcohol abuse.

Special Populations

College Students

Drinking on college campuses has long been pervasive, often excessive, and more recently linked to risky behaviors and dire health consequences (National Center on Addiction and Substance Abuse, 2007; Wechsler, 1995). About 83% of college undergraduates drink at least occasionally, 40% binge drink (five drinks in a row for men and four in a row for women), and 48.2% drink with the intention of getting drunk (Wechsler, 2002). Undergraduate males (50.1%) are more likely to engage in binge drinking (five or more drinks in a row on any one drinking occasion) than are their female counterparts (34.4%). However, if binge drinking is adjusted to four drinks in a row for women, there is little gender difference. Using the criteria set forth in the DSM-IV, it is estimated that 1.8 million full-time college students (22.9%) are alcohol and/or drug abusers or dependent, compared with 8.5% of the general population who meet the DSM-IV criteria (National Center on Addiction and Substance Abuse, 2007). Compared with their peers who are not students, undergraduates are more likely to engage in binge drinking. Binge drinking is associated with the significantly greater risks of health problems, car accidents, personal injury, aggressive behavior, and sexual assault and victimization (National Center on Addiction and Substance Abuse, 2007; Wechsler, 1995).

The onset of drinking and other drug use typically occurs in adolescence (Gledhill-Hoyt et al., 2000). For almost 7 in 10 marijuana smokers, initiation into its use began while in high school. However, one in three regular users of marijuana began using the drug after the age of 18, usually as a college student. Occasional drinking behaviors tend to begin before entrance into college and continue during the undergraduate years. Less than one in three college students (about 28%) began drinking or engaged in binge drinking after the age of 18.

The use of multiple substances is common among undergraduate students. Typically, binge drinking accompanies marijuana smoking or the use of other drugs. About 9 of every 10 college students who smoke marijuana also binge drink or use other illicit drugs. Similarly, 87% of undergraduates who use illicit drugs other than marijuana also binge drink or use multiple illicit drugs (Gledhill-Hoyt et al., 2000). Put another way, the more frequently an undergraduate binge drinks, the more likely the student will also smoke marijuana, use cocaine, or other illicit drugs (Jones et al., 2001).

The physiological and mind-altering effects of alcohol and most psychotropic drugs are affected by several factors, including an individual's physical health, level of fatigue, emotional state, and social circumstances surrounding the use of the drug (Hanson & Venturelli, 2001). Distinct differences in the ways men and women metabolize alcohol are also well known. Women become intoxicated more quickly than men, and they remain intoxicated for a longer time. Women also become dependent on alcohol more readily than men (Alexander & La Rosa, 1994). One of the most common methods of determining the effects of alcohol on an individual's ability to function dependably considers three factors: gender, body weight, and amount of alcohol consumed. An individual's blood alcohol concentration is a function of these three variables taken together.

Native Americans

There is considerable evidence that Native Americans as a whole have a disproportionately high rate of alcohol dependency. A recent national study of alcohol and illicit drug use found that about 18% of Native American and Alaska Natives were in need of substance abuse treatment in the previous year—almost twice that for the United States as a whole (9.6%). Binge drinking is particularly high among Native American and Alaska Native adults (30.6%) and far exceeds that for all other adults (24.5%).

Nonetheless, there is wide variation in alcohol abuse among the 300 Native American tribes with more than 2 million members. Estimates range from 30% to 84% of tribal members who drink alcohol, compared with about 67% in the general population. Overall, problematic drinking is about twice as common among Native American men than among women. Alcohol abuse is implicated in more than one in four deaths of Native American men compared with about one in seven deaths of tribal women (Moran & Moran, 1995).

Distinct patterns of drinking behaviors can be found among Native Americans both young and old. Typically, all available alcohol—usually considerable quantities—is consumed in a relatively brief period of time. What there is to drink is shared among the members of the group in a "binge drinking" fashion (May, 1996).

Two types of Native American drinkers have been identified. "Anxiety drinkers" become intoxicated on a regular basis and manifest a range of alcohol-related medical and interpersonal problems. High unemployment rates are evident among the anxiety drinkers, and they typically succumb to a premature death caused by their excessive drinking. "Recreational drinkers" are more occasional users of alcohol than the anxiety drinkers, but when they do drink they do so with the intention of becoming intoxicated. Car accidents, fighting, driving under the influence, and other forms of disorderly conduct are common among recreational drinkers. It is estimated that recreational drinkers account for about two of every three Native Americans who abuse alcohol (May, 1996).

Various explanations are offered to account for high rates of alcohol abuse among Native Americans. The anomic conditions of tribal life characterized by widespread blockage to educational and occupational opportunities found in the larger society are thought to precipitate excessive drinking and other drug use (Jessor et al., 1968). Social disorganization—the disintegration of cultural traditions and upheavals within the family—is also viewed as generating conditions conducive to substance abuse (Bachman, 1991). Related to a disorganized social milieu is the sense that cultural identity has been lost, and along with it a feeling of self-worth and social determination (Bachman, 1992).

Criminologist Malcolm D. Holmes and Native American researcher Judith A. Antell (2001) offer an alternative view of Native American drinking patterns. They contend that Native Americans and Whites devise differing "symbolic-moral universes" to explain deviant behavior. These social constructions provide two conflicting frameworks for understanding the etiology of Native American drinking behaviors and effective methods of altering them. The symbolic-moral universe of Native Americans focuses on their collective experience of exploitation and cultural decimation at the hands of White intruders. The consequences of White expansion into Native American habitats and their disregard for promises made and for the integrity of tribal cultures are now experienced as widespread economic deprivation and despair. To combat their destructive drinking practices, Native Americans advocate the reestablishment of their tribal identity and cultural heritage. At the same time they argue that educational and economic opportunities must be made available to Native Americans. In addition, cultural identification is viewed as consistent with economic progress and serves to ameliorate the problematic substance use of Native Americans.

Elderly

Alcohol consumption tends to decline with increasing age. Among the elderly about 52% of men and 68% of women abstain from the use of alcohol. However, about 3 in 10 of the 10 million alcoholics in the United States are over the age of 60 (Gupta, 1993). Estimates of alcoholism among the elderly range from 2% to 10% of the general population (Egbert, 1993). The onset of alcoholism occurs in later life about one-third of the time, whereas two-thirds of the older alcoholics developed their dependence earlier in life (Rigler, 2000). Experiences of later life—loss of health, death of friends and family members, depression—may trigger late-onset alcoholism. Women and minorities are more apt to develop an alcohol dependency later in life (Gomberg, 1995; Mulford & Fitzgerald, 1992).

Explanations of Alcohol Abuse

Although numerous theories have been offered to explain alcohol and drug dependence, particular attention is given here to sociological and social psychological formulations. Much attention has been given in recent years to the biological roots of the excessive use of alcohol and other drugs. However, issues related to the processing of alcohol in the human body and the biochemical underpinnings of addiction are beyond the scope of this book.

Rates of Alcohol Abuse

CULTURE AND SUBCULTURE. Sociologist Robert Bales (1946) focuses on the cultural basis for excessive drinking behavior. He argues that cultures may generate various levels of stress and tension, typically accompanied by related negative emotions of anger, resentment, and depression. The use of intoxicants is also culturally defined as either an appropriate or inappropriate way to relieve stress. If the use of alcohol is condemned in a given culture, then alternative means of tension reduction may be provided. To the extent that a culture positively sanctions the use of alcohol or other drugs to alleviate stress and fails to provide other effective methods of stress reduction, that culture will experience high rates of alcohol and other drug dependence.

Richard Cloward and Lloyd Ohlin (1960) argue that subcultural opportunity structures may account for distinct patterns of deviant behaviors. Cloward and Ohlin consider three distinct subcultures: criminal, violent, and retreatist. The retreatist subculture has particular relevance for the understanding of variations in rates of alcohol and drug dependence. When opportunities to engage in lucrative criminal behaviors are blocked and violent means to status and recognition are not available, retreatist subcultures may emerge. Individuals who have otherwise blocked alternative deviant opportunities may gravitate to subcultures that have ready access to illicit drugs and alcohol. Retreatist subculture provides the opportunity and social supports necessary for the progressive use of intoxicants.

SOCIAL INTEGRATION. Robert Merton (1968), a colleague of Richard Cloward and Lloyd Ohlin, offers a related formulation. Retreatism is one of Merton's five responses to anomie, a disjunction between institutionalized means and culturally approved goals in society. When the institutionalized means do not lead to culturally approved goals, there may be a widespread rejection of both means and goals. To avoid the stress and tension that follows from anomic social conditions, one may retreat into the solace provided by drug and alcohol abuse.

CULTURAL INTEGRATION. To the extent that drinking is integrated into everyday life, alcohol use is regulated by social norms and cultural traditions. Drinking is positively sanctioned, expected behavior for all members of the family. Drinking commonly accompanies a meal or is part of a religious ritual. Excessive drinking is abhorrent, a violation of the culture's time-honored values and traditions. Persons who violate norms and customs that surround the use of alcohol may be severely sanctioned or ostracized from their family and close friends (Blum & Blum, 1969).

SSRN

Duarte, R., Escario, J. J., & Molina, J. A. (January 2007). Peer effects, unobserved factors and risk behaviours: An analysis of alcohol abuse and truancy among adolescents. IZA Discussion Paper No. 2589, http://ssrn.com/abstract=964975

Individual Alcohol Abuse

Table 8–2 outlines some possible explanations for the use of alcohol by individuals. The remaining sections of this chapter examine those explanations in some detail.

SELF-DEROGATION. Howard Kaplan's (1995) formulation of self-derogation provides a social psychological perspective on the etiology of substance abuse. Kaplan argues that the desire for self-esteem is a primary motivation for individual behavior. Self-esteem or a positive attitude toward one's self is contingent on the following: personal characteristics or abilities that are highly valued by the individual, positive response by significant others, and the ability to deflect negative responses and accept positive responses from others as valid. If these conditions for the development of self-esteem cannot be met, then the processes of self-derogation may ensue.

Self-derogation or negative attitudes toward one's self tend to undermine the individual's motivation to conform to the norms of conventional

TABLE 8–2 **Explanations of Individual Alcohol Abuse**

Theory and Theorists	Sociological Predictors	Hypotheses
Social Strain		
Agnew	Stress/tension	As stress and tension increases, negative emotions increase. As negative emotions increase, the likelihood of alcohol dependence increases.
Self-Derogation		
Kaplan	Self-derogation	The greater the self-derogation, the greater the likelihood of alcohol dependence.
Social Learning		
Akers	Differential association, definitions, differential reinforcement, and imitation	The greater the primary association with persons who define substance abuse as justifiable and pleasurable, the more likely those definitions will be reinforced and substance abuse behaviors imitated. The more involvement in the substance abuse learning process, the more likely it is that alcohol dependence will occur.

society and increase motivation to engage in forms of deviant behavior that may provide an escape from their experiences of social devaluation. Commonly, a devalued person will reject the norms of those groups that are the source of his or her negative self-attitudes and seek membership in less conventional groups. Deviant group membership provides a respite from attacks on one's self-esteem and thereby provides opportunities for alternative forms of self-enhancing behaviors. In the short term, drinking to excess or the use of mind-altering drugs may provide the user with a way to counter the processes of self-derogation and establish a sense of well-being.

SOCIAL STRAIN. Sociologist Robert Agnew's (1992) formulation of social strain points out that negative social relations typically give rise to particularly stressful emotional states. Persons entangled in adverse interpersonal relationships commonly feel anxiety, depression, anger, and futility. Mood-altering substances, alcohol, and a variety of drugs may be used to relieve acute emotional distress. Often, the effects of alcohol and other drugs, both licit and illicit, exacerbate the situation. As interpersonal relations further deteriorate, the use of intoxicants may well increase.

SOCIAL LEARNING. Central to Ronald Akers's (1985) social learning formulation are four interrelated concepts: *differential association, definitions, differential reinforcement*, and *imitation*. These concepts provide a framework for the process of learning to engage in deviant forms of substance use. The concept of differential association, drawn from Edwin Sutherland's (1947) theory by the same name, refers to the extent of interaction with members of groups that advocate deviant substance use. Definitions of substance use as justifiable, desirable, and pleasurable are learned in the context of primary group interaction. Differential reinforcement refers to the anticipation that the rewards of alcohol abuse markedly exceed any possible negative sanctions. Excessive drinking is differentially reinforced when the expected pleasure overshadows any adverse social or legal response. Imitation is simply modeling one's behavior after that of others.

Chapter Summary

Wide variations in excessive drinking practices are found around the world and in the United States. Alcohol abuse is particularly prevalent among the young worldwide.

Definitional issues related to substance dependence are considered:

- Tolerance refers to either the need for increased amounts of the substance in order to achieve intoxication (or the desired effect) or a marked diminished effect with continued use of the same amount.
- Substance dependence occurs when at least three of the following criteria are met during a 12-month period:
  - Substance is often taken in larger amounts or over a longer period than intended.
  - Persistent desire or unsuccessful efforts are made to cut down or control substance use.
  - A great deal of time is spent in activities necessary to obtain the substance, use the substance, or recover from its effects.
  - Important social, occupational, or recreational activities are given up or reduced because of substance abuse.
  - Continued substance use occurs despite knowledge of having a persistent or recurrent psychological or physical problem that is caused or exacerbated by the use of the substance.

When drinking practices are integrated into everyday life, alcohol dependency tends to be low. Notable examples are Italian, French, and Jewish cultures. When drinking practices are not integrated into everyday life, alcohol dependency tends to be high. Notable examples are the Irish, Native American, and youth cultures.

The disease concept of alcohol dependence dominates research on the etiology and treatment of substance abuse.

Key Concepts

Alcoholism: A primary, chronic disease with genetic, psychosocial, and environmental factors that influence its development and manifestations; often progressive and fatal.

Alcohol dependence syndrome: As noted by the National Institute on Alcoholism and Alcohol Abuse, a syndrome characterized by craving, loss of control, physical dependence, and tolerance as each relates to the use of alcohol.

Craving: A strong need or compulsion to drink.

Loss of control: The frequent inability to stop drinking once a person has begun.

Physical dependence: The occurrence of withdrawal symptoms such as nausea, sweating, and anxiety when a drug is no longer used.

Tolerance: Either a need for increased amounts of the substance to achieve the desired effect, or marked diminished effect with continued use of the same amount.

Alcoholics Anonymous: Founded by Bill Wilson and Dr. Bob Smith as a spiritually based recovery program and support group for alcoholics.

Critical Thinking Questions

1. The use of alcohol is common around the world. However, consumption levels vary markedly as do rates of alcoholism. What accounts for the apparent disconnect between the amount of alcohol consumed in a given culture and its rate of alcoholism?
2. Is the process of becoming addicted to alcohol linked in any way to the process by which an individual seeks to recover from that addiction? Put another way, are the same social circumstances and motivations that brought about the person's addiction involved in the recovery process?
3. Compare the socialization process that tends to increase or decrease the likelihood of becoming addicted to alcohol. What accounts for persons whose family members or close friends are substance abusers and they are not?

Web Extra

Web-based media materials from high-quality sources such as CNN, Time, and National Public Radio are available in support of this textbook. Visit go.jblearning.com/deviance to access them.

Check out these websites for additional information on alcohol abuse:

http://www.niaaa.nih.gov

http://www.samhsa.gov

http://www.casacolumbia.org

http://www.niaa.org

Illicit Drug Use

CHAPTER 9

Learning Objectives

After reading this chapter you should know

- Definitional issues related to illicit drug use.
- The nature and prevalence of illicit drug abuse worldwide.
- The nature and prevalence of illicit drug abuse in the United States.
- Explanations of rates of and individual involvement in illicit drug use.

On June 23, 2010, suspected drug kingpin Christopher "Dudus" Coke was arrested by police outside Kingston, Jamaica, and extradited to the United States one day later.

Less than a year earlier, Coke had been charged by the New York U.S. Attorney's office with leading an international criminal gang known as the Shower Posse, whose activities included drug distribution and illegal trafficking in firearms. The name "Shower Posse" is said to have come from the tendency among gang members to spray their enemies with a continuing hail of bullets (Fox News, 2010).

The arrest of the 41-year-old Coke came more than a month after officials began a search for him in the slums of West Kingston, known as Tivoli Gardens. In that area Coke gained something akin to sainthood among local residents through his community support efforts, including handing out money to the poor for food and clothing and building medical centers throughout the area (CNN International, 2010). Desmond Richards, editor of a local Jamaican newspaper, told the *Miami Herald* that "you could describe [the Shower Posse's activities] as a welfare system. They provide resources and operate what you could call a second-tier justice system."

Although reputed to be ruthless with his drug-selling competitors, Coke's folk-hero status inspired members of the local community to mount armed resistance to police officers searching for him. Seventy-six people died in the violence that ensued, including a number of police officers. Four police stations came under heavy attack, apparently by Coke's supporters who had rallied to his defense from around Jamaica.

"So long as large sums of money are involved—and they are bound to be if drugs are illegal—it is literally impossible to stop the traffic, or even to make a serious reduction in its scope."
—Milton Friedman, Recipient of the Nobel Prize for Economics (Friedman & Friedman, 1984)

After Coke's arrest, Michael Braun, a former DEA official, told reporters that Coke "is the head of an organization, a cartel, or a syndicate that has a global impact and also has a direct impact on the United States." Coke's U.S. associates were said to be running a large drug and gun-smuggling operation in parts of New York City, including Queens and the Bronx (Weiss, 2010).

Illicit drug use, like excessive alcohol consumption, is a global phenomenon. It is estimated that the annual worldwide expenditure on illicit drugs exceeds $321 billion. That is, more money is spent on illicit drugs each year than the gross domestic product (GDP) of 88% of the countries worldwide (United Nations, 2005). The annual wholesale value of illicit drugs marketed across the globe ($94 billion) far exceeds the wholesale market value, for example, of wine ($17.3 billion), wheat ($16 billion), and coffee ($5.7 billion) (United Nations, 2005).

This chapter considers definitional issues related illicit drug use and the extent and social structural patterns of use across the world and in the United States. In addition, theoretical explanations of rates of substance abuse and individual precipitants are provided.

Definitions

Several related terms must be understood before discussing the use of illicit drugs. First, the concept of a **drug** must be considered. A physical substance may be classified as a drug if it causes recognizable physical or psychological effects (Stephens, 1987). It is often assumed that a physical substance classified as a drug consistently produces recognizable physiological effects and that those effects are predictable from one user to the next. Sociologist Eric Goode (2005), however, points out that the classification of a substance as a drug, its legal status, and its physical or psychological effects are largely matters of social and cultural definition.

The legal status of a drug is contingent on the social perception that its use may impede an individual's ability to perform essential roles—caregiver, student, employee—or its use may prompt wanton and threatening behavior (Tittle & Paternoster, 2000). In the absence of any therapeutic value, a substance may be rendered illegal; its use and distribution are then considered criminal offenses. Physiological and mind-altering effects of a drug are also affected by the sociocultural context of its use. Expected effects of a drug and the effects that are actually experienced are largely learned from other drug users and become socially defined and interpreted (Becker, 1963; Goode, 2005) (**Table 9–1**).

The second term is **addiction**, which refers to a physiological dependence on a substance. When the substance is not available, the addicted person experiences pronounced distress, known as a withdrawal or abstinence syndrome. Addiction may also involve psychological dependence, a strong emotional need for the substance in the absence of a physical dependence on it (Abadinsky, 1989; Granfield & Cloud, 1996; Tittle & Paternoster, 2000).

Sociologist Ronald Akers (1991) argues that addiction involves two processes: dependence and **tolerance**. Dependence results from the physical effects of the substance that are sustained only with its continual use. The sudden cessation of the use of certain drugs, notably heroin, morphine, or methamphetamines, may cause severe physical and psychological discomfort. A long-time drug user who stops using drugs may become extremely agitated, nervous, depressed, or unable to sleep or eat. Physical symptoms typically accompany a general feeling of emotional distress. The former drug user may develop stomach ailments, an elevation in temperature, and other symptoms that commonly accompany severe influenza. Dependence on certain drugs is, in part, related to the desire to avoid **withdrawal** symptoms that follow an interruption in drug use (Lindesmith, 1947, 1968).

Over time a drug user may develop a tolerance to a particular drug. That is, the drug user must increase the amount of drug consumed to achieve the desired effect. The physiological advantages that accompany the use of the drug are lost unless taken in sufficient quantities. The inability to stave off the ill effects of withdrawal is another drawback of drug tolerance. The drug user must maintain a certain level of intake to ensure that the symptoms of withdrawal do not occur. In short, drug tolerance sets up a vicious cycle of the increasing need for a drug—a need that may well exceed the user's physical ability to sustain (Tittle & Paternoster, 2000).

TABLE 9–1 **Commonly Abused Drugs** / continued

Substance: Category and Name	**Commercial and Street Names**	**DEA Schedule*/ How Administered†**	**Intoxication Effects and Potential Health Consequences**
Cannabinoids			
Hashish	Boom, chronic, gangster, hash, hash oil, hemp	I / Swallowed, smoked	Euphoria, slowed thinking and reaction time, confusion, impaired balance and coordination
Marijuana	Blunt, dope, ganja, grass, herb, joint, Mary Jane, pot, reefer, sinsemilla, skunk, weed	I / Swallowed, smoked	Cough, frequent respiratory infections; impaired memory and learning; increased heart rate, anxiety; panic attacks; tolerance, addiction
Depressants			
Barbiturates	Amytal, Nembutal, Seconal, Phenobarbital; barbs, reds, red birds, phennies, tooies, yellows, yellow jackets	II, III, V / Injected, swallowed	Reduced anxiety; feeling of well-being; lowered inhibitions; slowed pulse and breathing; lowered blood pressure; poor concentration Fatigue; confusion; impaired coordination, memory, judgment; addiction; respiratory depression and arrest, death *For barbiturates:* sedation, drowsiness Depression, unusual excitement, fever, irritability, poor judgment, slurred speech, dizziness, life-threatening withdrawal. *For benzodiazepines*: sedation, drowsiness Dizziness *For flunitrazepam:* visual and gastrointestinal disturbances, urinary retention, memory loss for the time under the drug's effects *For GHB:* drowsiness, nausea Vomiting, headache, loss of consciousness, loss of reflexes, seizures, coma, death *For methaqualone:* euphoria Depression, poor reflexes, slurred speech, coma
Benzodiazepines (other than flunitrazepam)	Ativan, Halcion, Librium, Valium, Xanax; candy, downers, sleeping pills, tranks	IV / Swallowed, injected	
Flunitrazepam‡ (club drug)	Rohypnol; forget-me pill, Mexican Valium, R2, Roche, roofies, roofinol, rope, rophies	IV / Swallowed, snorted	
GHB‡ (club drug)	Gamma-hydroxybutyrate; G, Georgia home boy, grievous bodily harm, liquid ecstasy	I / Swallowed	
Methaqualone	Quaalude, Sopor, Parest; ludes, mandrex, quad, quay	I / Injected, swallowed	

/ continues

TABLE 9–1 **Commonly Abused Drugs** / continued

Substance: Category and Name	**Commercial and Street Names**	**DEA Schedule[*] / How Administered[†]**	**Intoxication Effects and Potential Health Consequences**
Dissociative Anesthetics			
Ketamine (club drug)	Ketalar SV; cat Valiums, K, Special K, vitamin K	III / Injected, snorted, smoked	Increased heart rate and blood pressure, impaired motor function/memory loss; numbness; nausea/vomiting *Also, for ketamine*—at high doses, delirium, depression, respiratory depression and arrest
PCP and analogs	Phencyclidine; angel dust, boat, hog, love boat, peace pill	I,II / Injected, swallowed, smoked	*For PCP and analogs*—possible decrease in blood pressure and heart rate, panic, aggression, violence Loss of appetite, depression
Hallucinogens			
LSD (club drug)	Lysergic acid diethylamide; acid, blotter, boomers, cubes, microdot, yellow sunshines	I / Swallowed, absorbed through mouth tissues	Altered states of perception and feeling; nausea Persisting perception disorder (flashbacks) *Also, for LSD and mescaline:* increased body temperature, heart rate, blood pressure; loss of appetite, sleeplessness, numbness, weakness, tremors *For LSD:* persistent mental disorders
Mescaline	Buttons, cactus, mesc, peyote	I / Swallowed, smoked	
Psilocybin	Magic mushroom, purple passion, shrooms	I / Swallowed	*For psilocybin:* nervousness, paranoia
Opioids and Morphine Derivatives			
Codeine	Empirin with Codeine, Fiorinal with Codeine, Robitussin A-C, Tylenol with Codeine; Captain Cody, Cody, schoolboy; (with glutethimide) doors & fours, loads, pancakes and syrup	I, II, IV / Injected, swallowed	Pain relief, euphoria, drowsiness Nausea, constipation, confusion, sedation, respiratory depression and arrest, tolerance, addiction, unconsciousness, coma, death *Also, for codeine*: less analgesia, sedation, and respiratory depression than morphine
Fentanyl and fentanyl analogs	Actiq, Duragesic, Sublimaze; Apache, China girl, China white, dance fever, friend, goodfella, jackpot, murder 8, TNT, Tango and Cash	I, II / Injected, smoked, snorted	

/ continues

TABLE 9–1 **Commonly Abused Drugs** / continued

Substance: Category and Name	Commercial and Street Names	DEA Schedule* / How Administered†	Intoxication Effects and Potential Health Consequences
Opioids and Morphine Derivatives			
Heroin	Diacetylmorphine; brown sugar, dope, H, horse, junk, skag, skunk, smack, white horse	I / Injected, smoked, snorted	*For heroin:* staggering gait
Morphine	Roxanol, Duramorph; M, Miss Emma, monkey, white stuff	II, III / Injected, swallowed, smoked	
Opium	Laudanum, paregoric; big O, black stuff, block, gum, hop	II, III, V / Swallowed, smoked	
Oxycodone HCL	Oxycontin; Oxy, O.C., killer	II / Swallowed, snorted, injected	
Hydrocodone bitartrate, acetaminophen	Vicodin; vike, Watson-387	II / Swallowed	
Stimulants			
Amphetamine	Biphetamine, Dexedrine; bennies, black beauties, crosses, hearts, LA turnaround, speed, truck drivers, uppers	II / Injected, swallowed, smoked, snorted	Increased heart rate, blood pressure, metabolism; feelings of exhilaration, energy, increased mental alertness Rapid or irregular heart beat; reduced appetite, weight loss, heart failure, nervousness, insomnia *Also, for amphetamine*: rapid breathing
Cocaine	Cocaine hydrochloride; blow, bump, C, candy, Charlie, coke, crack, flake, rock, snow, toot	II / Injected, smoked, snorted	Tremor, loss of coordination; irritability, anxiousness, restlessness, delirium, panic, paranoia, impulsive behavior, aggressiveness, tolerance, addiction, psychosis *For cocaine:* increased temperature Chest pain, respiratory failure, nausea, abdominal pain, strokes, seizures, headaches, malnutrition, panic attacks *For MDMA:* mild hallucinogenic effects, increased tactile sensitivity, empathic feelings Impaired memory and learning, hyperthermia, cardiac toxicity, renal failure, liver toxicity
MDMA (methylenedi-oxymethamphetamine) (club drug)	Adam, clarity, ecstasy, Eve, lover's speed, peace, STP, X, XTC	I / Swallowed	

/ continues

TABLE 9–1 **Commonly Abused Drugs** / continued

Substance: Category and Name	Commercial and Street Names	DEA Schedule* / How Administered†	Intoxication Effects and Potential Health Consequences
Stimulants			
Methamphetamine (club drug)	Desoxyn; chalk, crank, crystal, fire, glass, go fast, ice, meth, speed	II / Injected, swallowed, smoked, snorted	
Methylphenidate (safe and effective for treatment of ADHD)	Ritalin; JIF, MPH, R-ball, Skippy, the smart drug, vitamin R	II / Injected, swallowed, snorted	
Inhalants	Solvents (paint thinners, gasoline, glues), gases (butane, propane, aerosol propellants, nitrous oxide), nitrites (isoamyl, isobutyl, cyclohexyl); laughing gas, poppers, snappers, whippets	Not scheduled / Inhaled through nose or mouth	

ADHD, attention deficit hyperactivity disorder.

*Schedule I and II drugs have a high potential for abuse. They require greater storage security and have a quota on manufacturing, among other restrictions. Schedule I drugs are available for research only and have no approved medical use; Schedule II drugs are available only by prescription (unrefillable) and require a form for ordering. Schedule III and IV drugs are available by prescription, may have five refills in 6 months, and may be ordered orally. Most Schedule V drugs are available over the counter.

†Taking drugs by injection can increase the risk of infection through needle contamination with staphylococci, HIV, hepatitis, and other organisms.

‡*Associated with sexual assaults.

Source: National Institute on Drug Abuse, Commonly Abused Drugs. Web available at http://www.nida.nih.gov/DrugPages/DrugsofAbuse.html

SSRN

Gibson, F. (January 2010). Drugs, discrimination, and disability. La Trobe Law School Legal Studies Research Paper No. 2010/1. http://ssrn.com/abstract=1540602

SSRN

Carneiro, L. P. (August 2009). The political economy of illicit drugs in Latin America: Magnitude, concepts and public policies. http://ssrn.com/abstract=1472428

Illicit Drug Use Around the World

Information about illicit drug use across the globe is subject to interpretation. Much of what is known is extrapolated from a wide variety of sources. The United Nations Office on Drugs and Crime, however, has led the way to an increasingly accurate picture of drug production, trafficking, and use across the globe. It is estimated that there are between 155 and 250 million illicit drug users worldwide, or between 3.5% and 5.7% of all persons between the ages of 15 and 64 (United Nations, 2010). Cannabis or marijuana is clearly the most frequently used drug across the globe. The estimated minimum number of cannabis users is 128.9 million; other drug use is as follows: cocaine, 15.1 million; amphetamines, 13.7 million; opiates, 12.8 million; and ecstasy, 10.4 million (United Nations, 2010) (**Figure 9–1**). Nonetheless, active drug users represent a relatively small percentage of the world's population (**Figure 9–2**).

	Cannabis users in the past year		Opiate users in the past year		Cocaine users in the past year		Amphetamines-group users in the past year		Ecstasy users in the past year	
Region/subregion	**Number (lower)**	**Number (upper)**	**Number (lower)**	**Number (upper)**	**Number (lower)**	**Number (upper)**	**Number (lower)**	**Number (upper)**	**Number (lower)**	**Number (upper)**
Africa	**27,680,000**	**52,790,000**	**680,000**	**2,930,000**	**1,020,000**	**2,670,000**	**1,550,000**	**5,200,000**	**350,000**	**1,930,000**
North Africa	4,680,000	10,390,000	130,000	540,000	30,000	50,000	260,000	540,000	*estimate cannot be calculated*	
West and Central Africa	14,050,000	22,040,000	160,000	340,000	640,000	830,000	*estimate cannot be calculated*		*estimate cannot be calculated*	
Eastern Africa	4,490,000	9,190,000	150,000	1,730,000	*estimate cannot be calculated*		*estimate cannot be calculated*		*estimate cannot be calculated*	
Southern Africa	4,450,000	11,170,000	240,000	320,000	290,000	900,000	310,000	1,090,000	220,000	420,000
Americas	**38,210,000**	**40,030,000**	**2,290,000**	**2,440,000**	**8,720,000**	**9,080,000**	**4,760,000**	**5,890,000**	**3,040,000**	**3,280,000**
North America	29,950,000	29,950,000	1,290,000	1,380,000	6,170,000	6,170,000	3,090,000	3,200,000	2,490,000	2,490,000
Central America	580,000	600,000	100,000	110,000	120,000	140,000	320,000	320,000	20,000	30,000
The Caribbean	430,000	-1,730,000	60,000	90,000	110,000	320,000	30,000	510,000	10,000	240,000
South America	7,300,000	7,530,000	840,000	870,000	2,330,000	2,450,000	1,320,000	1,860,000	510,000	530,000
Asia	**31,510,000**	**64,580,000**	**6,460,000**	**12,540,000**	**430,000**	**2,270,000**	**4,430,000**	**37,990,000**	**2,370,000**	**15,620,000**
East/South-East Asia	5,370,000	23,940,000	2,830,000	5,060,000	390,000	1,070,000	3,430,000	20,680,000	1,460,000	6,850,000
South Asia	16,490,000	27,550,000	1,390,000	3,310,000	*estimate cannot be calculated*		*estimate cannot be calculated*		*estimate cannot be calculated*	
Central Asia	1,890,000	2,140,000	340,000	340,000	*estimate cannot be calculated*		*estimate cannot be calculated*		*estimate cannot be calculated*	
Near and Middle East	7,790,000	10,950,000	1,890,000	3,820,000	*estimate cannot be calculated*		*estimate cannot be calculated*		*estimate cannot be calculated*	
Europe	**29,370,000**	**29,990,000**	**3,290,000**	**3,820,000**	**4,570,000**	**4,970,000**	**2,500,000**	**3,190,000**	**3,850,000**	**4,080,000**
West/Central Europe	20,850,000	20,990,000	1,090,000	1,370,000	4,110,000	4,130,000	1,600,000	1,710,000	2,180,000	2,190,000
East/South-East Europe	8,520,000	9,010,000	2,210,000	2,460,000	470,000	840,000	900,000	1,480,000	1,680,000	2,890,000
Oceania	**2,140,000**	**3,410,000**	**120,000**	**150,000**	**300,000**	**390,000**	**470,000**	**630,000**	**840,000**	**910,000**
GLOBAL ESTIMATE	**128,910,000**	**190,750,000**	**12,840,000**	**21,880,000**	**15,070,000**	**19,380,000**	**13,710,000**	**52,900,000**	**10,450,000**	**25,820,000**

FIGURE 9–1 Estimated number of illicit drug users in the past year aged 15–64 years, by region and subregion, 2008.

Source: United Nations Office on Drugs and Crime.

Number of people who inject drugs aged 15–64 years: 11–21 million persons

Number of "problem drug users" aged 15–64 years: 16–38 million persons

Number of people who have used drugs atleast once in the past year aged 15–64 years: 155–250 million persons

Total number of people aged 15–64 years in 2008: 4,396 million persons

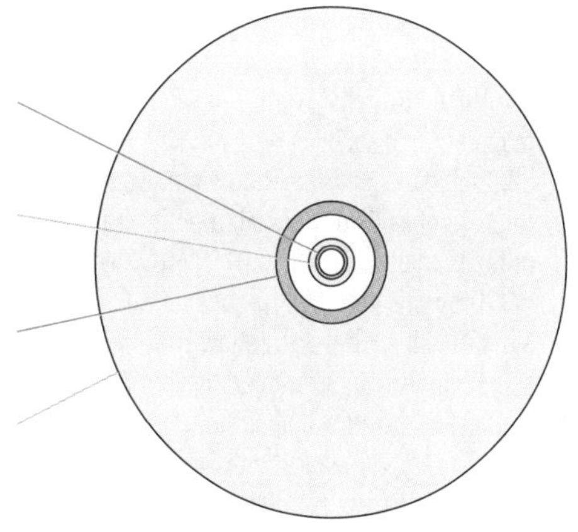

FIGURE 9–2 Illicit drug use at the global level, 2008.

Source: Adapted from United Nations, Office on Drugs and Crime, World Drug Report. Vienna, Austria, 2005; 2010.

SSRN

Tauchmann, H. (August 2008). West-east convergence in the prevalence of illicit drugs: Socioeconomics or culture? Ruhr Economic Paper No. 61. http://ssrn.com/abstract=1280175

SSRN

Feijen, E. H.B. (January 2007). Estimating the impact of illicit drugs use on gambling behavior: Evidence from the U.S. Casino Industry and Drugs Arrests. http://ssrn.com/abstract=951843

Illicit Drug Use in the United States

About 20 million people in the United States (6.5% of the population) use illicit drugs. The most common drug is marijuana, used by three of every four illicit drug users. About 57% of illicit drug users limit their consumption to marijuana, 18.4% combine marijuana with another drug, and about 24% use drugs other than marijuana. Far less commonly used drugs are cocaine (1.9 million), including about 265,000 crack users; hallucinogens (1.1 million); and heroin (200,000) (Substance Abuse and Mental Health Services Administration [SAMHSA], 2010).

Poppies growing in Afghanistan. Following the fall of the Taliban, poppy growing became the primary means of livelihood for a significant segment of the Afghanistan population. What drug is derived from poppies?

Global Illcit Drug Markets

The United Nations' World Drug Reports (2005, 2010) provide detailed estimates of the monetary value of illicit drug markets around the world. Illicit drug market revenues exceed $322 billion each year. The annual worldwide illicit drug market revenues are more than the GDP of 88% of the countries in the world. Cannabis accounts for the largest share of the market ($113 billion), followed by cocaine ($88 billion) and opiates ($65 billion).

Drug markets may be considered on three levels: producer, wholesaler, and retailer. Most recent global data show that in the equivalent of U.S. dollars:

- Illicit drug producers netted $12.8 billion annually.
- Illicit drug wholesalers realized $94 billion—more than seven times the monetary value of illicit drug production.
- Illicit drug retailers gained $214 billion—or more than 2.3 times illicit drug wholesalers and 16.7 times more than the producers of illicit drugs.

For example, consider that cannabis is the most profitable drug marketed worldwide. On the retail market, the sale of cannabis accounts for more than $113 billion, that is, about 1 of every 3 dollars spent by illicit drug users around the world. However,

- Cannabis growers (other than "home grown" dealers) gain only 1/13th of the profit from its retail sale, and
- Cannabis wholesalers make slightly more than 26 cents for every retail sales dollar.

Cocaine is the second most profitable illicit drug worldwide with annual retail sales of $88 billion. As with cannabis, the illicit drug retailers realize an inordinate percentage of the profits. For example,

- Cocaine producers make about $500 million annually, or $1 for every $176 realized by the cocaine retailers.
- Cocaine wholesalers make $18.8 billion annually, or $1 dollar for every $468 made by retailers, but about 38 times more than cocaine producers.

Source: Adapted from United Nations, Office on Drugs and Crime, World Drug Report. Vienna, Austria, 2005; 2010.

Age, Gender, and Race

Figure 9–3 shows current drug use for persons 12 years of age and older.

AGE. Illicit drug use is most common between the ages of 16 and 25, declining rapidly after the age of 29. Persons between the ages of 18 and 20 are most likely to use illicit drugs (21.5 %), followed by those between the ages of 21 and 25 and 16 and 17. As might be expected, persons over the age of 65 are decidedly unlikely to use illicit drugs of any kind. Among 12- to 13-year-olds, nonmedical use of prescription drugs was the most common form of illicit drug offending, followed by marijuana and inhalants. After the age of 14, the use of marijuana far exceeds the use of any other drug (SAMHSA, 2010).

AT A GLANCE

Global Patterns and Trends

- The use of illicit drugs is increasing in many developed countries.
- It is estimated that there are between 155 and 250 million illicit drug users worldwide, or between 3.5% and 5.7% percent of all persons between the ages of 15 and 64.
- Cannabis or marijuana is clearly the most frequently used drug across the globe. The estimated minimum number of cannabis users is 128.9 million; other drug use is as follows: cocaine, 15.1 million; amphetamines, 13.7 million; opiates, 12.8 million; and ecstasy, 10.4 million.
- Illicit drug market revenues exceed $322 billion each year. The annual worldwide illicit drug market revenues are more than the GDP of 88% of the countries in the world.

U.S. Patterns and Trends

- About 20 million people in the United States (6.5% of the population) use illicit drugs.
- The most common drug is marijuana, used by three of every four illicit drug users.
- About 57% of illicit drug users limit their consumption to marijuana, 18.4% combine marijuana with another drug, and about 24% use drugs other than marijuana.
- Far less commonly used drugs are cocaine (1.9 million), including about 265,000 crack users; hallucinogens (1.1 million); and heroin (200,000).

Sources: United Nations. Office of Drugs and Crime (*World drug report*; 2010, Vienna, Austria; SAMHSA. (2010). *Overview of findings from the 2010 National Survey on Drug Use and Health.* Rockville, MD: U.S. Department of Health and Human Services.

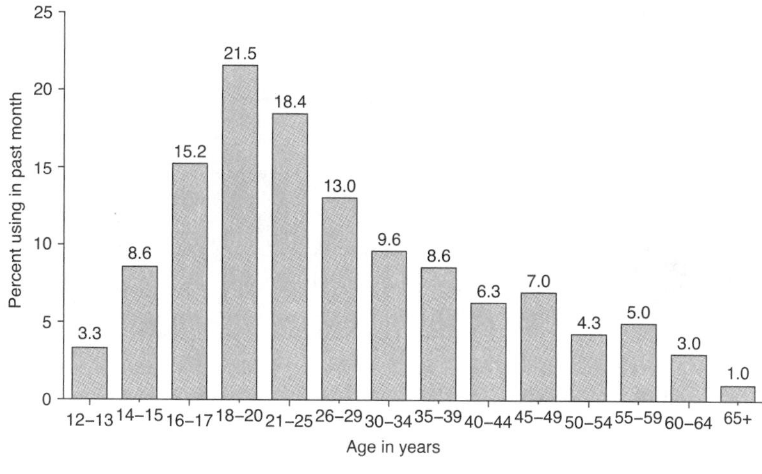

FIGURE 9–3 Past month illicit drug use among persons aged 12 or older, by age, 2008.
Source: SAMHSA 2010: 10.

GENDER. Overall, illicit drug use tends to be more common among men than women. In the United States about 9.9% of men and 6.3% of women use drugs illegally. Men are far more likely to use marijuana (7.9%) than women (4.4%). Men and women are, however, approximately equally likely to use psychotherapeutic drugs without prescription: pain relievers, tranquilizers, stimulants, methamphetamine, and sedatives (SAMHSA, 2010).

RACE AND ETHNICITY. **Figure 9–4** shows that in the United States, drug use is most common among persons of mixed race (14.7%), African Americans (10.1%), Native Americans/Alaska Natives (9.5%), Whites (8.2%), Native Hawaiians or other Pacific Islanders (7.3%), Hispanics or Latinos (6.2%), and Asians (3.6%) (SAMHSA, 2010).

Employment Status and Regional Variations

Persons who are not employed full-time are far more likely to use illicit drugs (19.6%) compared with persons employed full-time (8.0%) and part-time (10.2%). However, about three of every four illicit drug users (73%) in the United States are employed (SAMHSA, 2010).

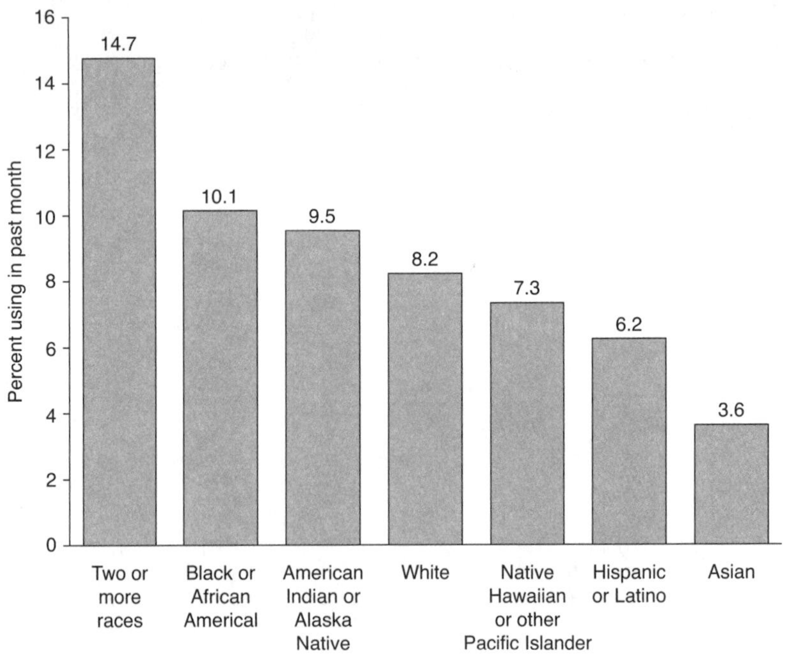

FIGURE 9–4 Past month illicit drug use among persons aged 12 or older, by race/ethnicity, 2008.
Source: SAMHSA 2010: 12–13.

Men smoke hookahs in Jerusalem's Old City. Drug use has a long tradition in the Middle East and in other parts of the world. Do we have similar traditions in the West?

Variations in illicit drug use are evident across the United States. The Western region has the highest rate of illicit drug use (9.8%), followed by the Northeast (8.2%), the Midwest (7.6%), and the South (7.1%) (SAMHSA, 2010).

College Students

The use of multiple substances is common among undergraduate students. Typically, binge drinking accompanies marijuana smoking or the use of other drugs. About 9 of every 10 college students who smoke marijuana also binge drink or use other illicit drugs. Similarly, 87% of undergraduates who use illicit drugs other than marijuana also binge drink or use multiple illicit drugs (National Center on Addiction and Substance Abuse, 2007; Gledhill-Hoyt et al., 2000). Put another way, the more frequently an undergraduate binge drinks, the more likely the student will also be to smoke marijuana, use cocaine, or other illicit drugs (National Center on Addiction and Substance Abuse, 2007; Jones et al., 2001). The physiological and mind-altering effects of alcohol and most psychotropic drugs are affected by several factors, including an individual's physical health, level of fatigue, emotional state, and social circumstances surrounding the use of the drug (Hanson & Venturelli, 2001).

More than one in three college students (36.6%) are occasional drug users, most of whom are marijuana users (33.3%). The next most commonly used drugs by college students are cocaine (5.7%), hallucinogens

(5.0%), and ecstasy (2.9%). About one in five college students are current drug users (19.5%), with a strong preference for marijuana (17.5%). Only 1 in 12 college students use illicit drugs other than marijuana.

College men are more likely to use illicit drugs occasionally and to use them in the past month. Slightly more than 4 in 10 college men have used illicit drugs in the past year, compared with 34.2% of college women. And, almost 23% of college men are current illicit drug users while 17.5% of college women do so.

Explanations for Illicit Drug Dependence

Although numerous theories have been offered to explain drug dependence, particular attention is given here to sociological and social psychological formulations (**Table 9–2**). We begin with those that fall under the sociological heading.

Opportunity Structures

Richard Cloward and Lloyd Ohlin (1960) identify three subcultural opportunity structures: criminal, violent, and retreatist. The retreatist subculture emerges when the opportunities for financial gain from criminal activities are not available and social status cannot be achieved by violent means. The retreatist subculture may provide access to illicit drugs and a supportive environment for their use. The participants in a retreatist subculture are socialized into the use of illicit drugs, taught various justifications for their use, and given a safe haven from detection by legal authorities.

Social Integration

To Robert Merton (1968), retreatism is an adaptation to anomie, a disjunction between institutionalized means and culturally approved goals in society. When the institutionalized means do not lead to culturally approved goals, both means and goals may be rejected. Individuals may seek to retreat to the illicit drug use to blunt the effects of the emotional turmoil of an anomic life.

Social Conflict

Alex Thio (1983), an influential power-control theorist, contends that members of the more powerful strata of society foster the stereotype of an illicit drug user as a lower-class person who would rather use drugs than work and one who is largely a burden on society. This view deflects attention from drug use among the members of the upper socioeconomic groups. There is then in Thio's terms "high consensus" about who will be

TABLE 9–2 Explanations of Rates of Alcohol and Illicit Drug Dependence

Theory and Theorists	Sociological Predictors	Hypotheses
Social Integration		
Merton	Anomie	The greater the disjunction between institutionalized means and culturally approved goals, the higher the rate of illicit drug use.
	Retreatism	The greater the rejection of institutionalized means and culturally approved goals, the greater the retreatist behavior in society. The greater the retreatist behavior in society, the higher the rate of illicit drug use.
Subcultural Opportunities		
Cloward and Ohlin	Retreatism subcultures	The fewer the subcultural opportunities—either legitimate or illegitimate—for success, the more likely retreatist subcultures will emerge. The more retreatist subcultures in a given society, the higher the rate of illicit drug use.
Social Class/Power		
Thio	High consensus/low consensus deviance	The higher the consensus about the social characteristics of illicit drug users, the higher the publicly defined rates among the lower socioeconomic groups in society.

Explanation of Individual Illicit Drug Use

Theory and Theorists	Sociological Predictors	Hypotheses
Social Strain		
Agnew	Stress/tension	As stress and tension increases, negative emotions increase. As negative emotions increase, the likelihood of illicit drug use increases.
Self-Derogation		
Kaplan	Self-derogation	The greater the self-derogation, the greater the likelihood of illicit drug use.
Euphoria, Cognitive Association, and Seduction		
McAuliffe and Gordon	Euphoria	The greater the desire to experience euphoria associated with illicit drug use and the greater the desire to avoid prolonged periods without euphoria, the greater the likelihood of illicit drug use.

/ continues

TABLE 9–2 **Explanations of Rates of Alcohol and Illicit Drug Dependence** / continued

Explanation of Individual Illicit Drug Use		
Theory and Theorists	**Sociological Predictors**	**Hypotheses**
Euphoria, Cognitive Association, and Seduction		
Lindesmith	Cognitive association	The greater the association between the severe distress of drug withdrawal, the more likely illicit drug use will continue.
Katz	Seduction	The greater the feeling of excitement, thrill, or adrenaline "rush" associated with illicit drug use, the more likely illicit drug use will occur.
Social Learning		
Akers	Differential association	The greater the primary association with persons who define illicit drug use as justifiable and pleasurable, the more likely those definitions will be reinforced and illicit drug use will be imitated. The more involvement in the illicit drug use learning process, the more likely illicit drug will occur.
	Definitions Differential reinforcement Imitation	
Becker	Learning process	If the substance abuse learning process involves effective socialization techniques for its use and the ability to associate pleasure from its use, then substance dependence becomes more likely.
Self-Control		
Gottfredson and Hirschi	Self-control	The lower the individual's self-control, the greater the likelihood of illicit drug use.

publicly labeled a "drug addict" and relatively low consensus about illicit drug use among the corporate and professional elite.

Self-Derogation

The first of the psychological explanations is self-derogation. Howard Kaplan (1995) argues that self-derogating individuals are particularly prone to deviate from the norms of conventional society. Self-derogation—or negative self-attitudes—result from the perception of social devaluation. As such, they are a persistent source of stress for the individual. The use of mind-altering substances provides an escape from the pains of perceived rejection by others and the accompanying derogation of one's self.

Social Strain

Robert Agnew (1992) argues that negative social relations commonly result in emotional distress. Feelings of anxiety, depression, anger, and futility are typical among persons mired in adverse interpersonal relationships. Mood-altering drugs may provide a respite from their negative emotional state. Illicit drug use is viewed as an immediate, albeit short-term, solution to an intractable interpersonal problem.

Cognitive Association, Euphoria, and the Seduction of Substance Use

Key to Alfred Lindesmith's (1947, 1968) view of substance dependency is the association of severe distress with the cessation of drug use. If an individual believes that a physical or emotional disorder can only be averted if he or she continues to engage in substance use, then dependency is more likely to ensue.

Two additional theoretical formulations can be applied to the onset and continuation of alcohol and other drug use. William McAuliffe and Robert Gordon (1974) contend that the euphoria associated with drug use, particularly heroin, is the key factor that sustains its use. Withdrawal resulting from the interruption of substance use, they contend, is a consequence of the absence of euphoria, more so than the fear of experiencing distress from the discontinuation of its use. Similarly, sociologist Jack Katz's (1988) attention to the seduction of crime is consistent with McAuliffe and Gordon's view. Katz argues that individuals are attracted to criminal and deviant behavior simply because it is inherently exciting. Risk-taking behaviors, such as underage drinking and illicit drug use, provide an adrenaline "rush" or "high" apart from the effects of the substance itself. Engaging in illicit substance use or drinking to excess is tantamount to a flagrant disregard for conventional social behavior.

Social Learning

Learning theorists in the sociological tradition, principally Ronald Akers (1985, 1992) and Howard Becker (1963), point out that drug and alcohol use involves a process of learning appropriate methods of substance use and learning to associate its effects with a sense of pleasure.

Central to Ronald Akers's (1985) social learning formulation are four interrelated concepts: *differential association, definitions, differential reinforcement,* and *imitation.* These concepts provide a framework for the process of learning to engage in deviant forms of substance use. The concept of differential association, drawn from Edwin Sutherland's (1947) theory by the same name, refers to the extent of interaction with members of groups that advocate deviant substance use. Primary drug-using groups provide a social milieu that facilitates learning to use various drugs. Definitions of substance use as justifiable, desirable, and pleasurable are learned in the context of primary group interaction. Differential reinforcement refers to the anticipation that the rewards of drug use markedly exceed any possible negative sanctions. Deviant substance use is differentially reinforced when the expected pleasure overshadows any adverse social or legal response. Imitation is simply modeling one's behavior after that of others. Novel forms of acting, use of language and dress, and music and entertainment are readily imitated by the young.

In his classic study, *Becoming a Marijuana User* (1953), Howard Becker provides an analysis of the process of learning to use marijuana and learning to associate its effects with a sense of pleasure. Rather than assuming that drug users are suffering from a psychological disorder, Becker argues that the introduction into marijuana use, for example, occurs largely by chance. Friends make marijuana available, encourage the newcomer to try it, and provide instruction in its use.

Given certain conditions, experimental drug use may escalate into more routine involvement with drugs. To Becker there are three stages in the process of becoming a regular marijuana user. The first stage, *learning the technique,* assumes that a novice marijuana smoker must be taught the techniques necessary to achieve a "high" and to associate that feeling with pleasure. The second stage, *learning to perceive the effects,* follows from mastering the techniques necessary to use marijuana effectively. Once the novice user is able to experience the effects of marijuana, he or she must then recognize the effects and associate them with the use of the drug. It is possible to be "high" on marijuana without being aware of it. The novice user must learn to recognize the symptoms of being "high" and to associate those symptoms with use of marijuana. The continued use of marijuana depends on achieving the third stage in the process, *learning to enjoy the effects.* The effects of marijuana tend to involve a mix of sensations, some pleasurable, others not. The user must be able to differentiate the ill effects of the drug's use from desirable experiences. One novice marijuana user observed the following (Becker, 1963, p. 53):

> It started taking effect, and I didn't know what was happening, you know what it was, and I was very sick. I walked around the room, walking around the room trying to get off, you know; it just scared me at first, you know. I wasn't use to that kind of feeling.

As experience with marijuana use increases, so too does the ability to control its deleterious effects. Fellow users are able to interpret the sensations that accompany a marijuana "high" as pleasurable and desirable rather than frightening and repugnant.

Self-Control

Gottfredson and Hirschi's *General Theory of Crime* (1990) posits that low self-control is the central precipitant of criminal behavior. Several elements of low self-control—impulsivity, risk-taking, and short-sightedness—place an individual at particularly high risk for illicit drug use. The inability to defer immediate gratification tends to accompany low self-control. Given the opportunity to engage in illicit drug use, a person with hedonistic tendencies and low self-control is vulnerable to experimenting with mind-altering substances.

Chapter Summary

Definitional issues related to substance dependence involve the following concepts:

- A drug is defined as a physical substance that causes recognizable physical or psychological effects.
- Addiction refers to a physiological dependence on a substance, that, in its absence, involves pronounced distress, known as withdrawal or abstinence syndrome. Addiction may also involve psychological dependence or a strong emotional need for the substance in the absence of a physical dependence on it.
- Tolerance refers to either the need for increased amounts of the substance to achieve intoxication (or the desired effect) or a marked diminished effect with continued use of the same amount.

Wide variations in the use of illicit drugs and excessive drinking practices are found around the world. Substance abuse is particularly prevalent among the young worldwide. The processes of globalization tend to increase the availability of mind-altering substances.

About 20 million people in the United States use illicit drugs. The most common drug is marijuana, used by three of every four illicit drug users.

This chapter considers both sociological and psychological explanations for individual involvement in illicit drug use. Opportunity structures, social integration, social conflict, social learning, strain theory, and other possible explanations are discussed.

Key Concepts

Drug: A physical substance may be classified as a drug if it causes recognizable physical or psychological effects.

Addiction: A physiological or psychological dependence on a substance and accompanying withdrawal symptoms when its use is discontinued.

Tolerance: Either a need for increased amounts of the substance to achieve the desired effect or marked diminished effect with continued use of the same amount.

Withdrawal: Physical and emotional distress that accompanies the cessation of alcohol and other drug use.

Critical Thinking Questions

1. Are illicit drug users markedly different across the socioeconomic class spectrum? Does the social class of illicit drug users affect their motivations and rationalizations for using controlled substances?
2. How does the sociopolitical structuring of society influence the definition of illicit drug use and attempts to control it?
3. How would you differentiate between experimental or recreational drug users and persons who are addicted to illicit drugs?
4. To what extent does the availability of illicit drugs account for the prevalence of their use? Put another way, does the availability of certain illicit drugs determine the number of people in a given population who use illicit drugs or simply the kinds of drugs that are used?

Web Extra

Web-based media materials from high-quality sources such as CNN, Time, and National Public Radio are available in support of this textbook. Visit go.jblearning.com/deviance to access them.

Check out these websites for additional information on drug abuse:

http://www.nida.nih.gov

http://www.samhsa.gov

http://www.whitehousedrugpolicy.gov

http://www.drugpolicy.org

Sexual Offending

CHAPTER 10

Learning Objectives

After reading this chapter you should know

- Definitions, prevalence, and victim and offender characteristics of rape, sexual assault, and child sexual abuse.
- What constitutes sexual trafficking.
- Rates of criminal sexual offending around the world and in the United States.
- The characteristics of sexual offenders and their victims.
- What factors influence the reporting of sex crimes to the authorities.
- The types of rapists that can be identified.
- The characteristics of juvenile sex offenders.
- Definitions, prevalence, and types of prostitutes.
- Nature of online sexual victimization.
- The consequences of childhood sexual abuse.
- Theoretical understanding of criminal sexual deviance.

Recently, the tune for a song called "Date Rape," performed by a Long Beach California band named Sublime, was made available via the Internet for use as a cell phone ring tone. The song is on the band's "Greatest Hits" album, and a former member of Sublime, Bradley Nowell, now deceased, is credited with writing its lyrics.

Nowell once explained why he wrote the song by saying, "We were at a party a long time ago and we were all talking about how much date rape sucked. This guy was like, 'Date rape isn't so bad; if it wasn't for date rape I'd never get laid.' Everyone at the party was laughing about it, and I was cracking up so I wrote a funny song about it." A triple-X music video was made based on the song's lyrics, and pornographic actor Ron Jeremy played the leading role. The song is also featured on the 2006 album, *Still Stuck in Your Throat*, by the group Fishbone, and a milder video version of the song was available on YouTube as this book went to press.

Not everyone, however, sees the humor in Nowell's lyrics. Jen Nedeau, for example, writing for the Women's Rights section of Change.org, says that "Rape and date rape are serious matters. No one should make rape a joke or try to get laughs at the expense of rape victims" (Nedeau, 2009).

Most countries around the world define some forms of sexual behavior as deviant. There is, nonetheless, considerable variation in the kinds of sexual acts that are considered criminal. Sexual behaviors considered criminal in some societies are accepted forms of cultural ritual in others. This chapter focuses on criminal sexual offending—rape, child sex abuse, and prostitution—from a global perspective. Variations in prevalence, victim and offender characteristics, and issues related to each form of criminal sexual offending are examined. Theoretical explanations of the incidence and prevalence of criminal sexual offending and victimization are discussed.

In reference to sexual trafficking of women and children, a UN spokesperson states as follows: "There is less law enforcement… The earnings are incredible. The overhead is low—you do not have to buy cars or guns. Drugs you sell once and they are gone. Women can earn money for a long time."
—Bertone (2000, p. 4)

Definitions of Criminal Sexual Offending

Various sources of data on criminal sexual offending and victimization—principally the United States' National Crime Victimization Survey (NCVS), Uniform Crime Reports (UCR), and National Incident-Based Reporting System (NIBRS)—differ somewhat in their definitions of rape, sexual assault, and sex offenses. The age of the victim may determine whether a sexual act is considered a crime. Forcible rape, statutory rape, a variety of sexual assaults, and other sexual offenses of lewd acts, sodomy, fondling, and molestation are examples. Other "hands-off" or nonviolent sexual offenses include exhibitionism and voyeurism. Prostitution and related forms of sexual deviance, discussed later in the chapter, are also examples of criminal sexual offending.

Rape

As defined by the UCR, "**forcible rape** is the carnal knowledge of a female forcibly and against her will" (Federal Bureau of Investigation [FBI], 2009).

Assaults and attempts to commit rape are also included in this definition. Rape, as defined by the NCVS, is defined as "forced sexual intercourse in which the victims may be either male or female and the offender may be of a different sex or the same sex as the victim" (Greenfeld, 1997, p. 30). This definition also includes attempts and threats to commit rape; however, victims must be at least 12 years old. The NIBRS definition of forcible rape includes both male and female victims and rapes committed without the use of force where the victim is incapable of giving consent (i.e., temporary or permanent mental or physical capacity).

"My life was like an animal's. I was sold three times. I begged my boss to let me go home, but she said I owed much money and must pay it back. Every day I had to sleep with men. I was not allowed to leave even during menstruation. I was told if I escaped, they would track me, kill me—and my parents, too."

—A former Thai prostitute (Leuchtag, 1995, p. 12)

Date rape is forcible rape that involves romantic partners or acquaintances in a dating relationship. Sexual assault and rape in the context of a date typically involve the various forms of verbal or physical coercion, the inebriation of the victim, or the use of a date rape drug to subdue the victim. The ability of the victim to give consent to her dating partner is a key issue in the determination of the criminality of the act (Koss & Cleveland, 1997).

Sexual Assault

Sexual assault "includes a wide range of victimizations involving attacks in which unwanted sexual contact occurs between the victim and offender" (Greenfeld, 1997, p. 31). The FBI broadly defines **sex offenses** as acts "against chastity, decency, morals, and the like" (Greenfeld 1997, p. 31). Victimizations may include sodomy, sexual assault with an object, fondling, molestation and indecent liberties, and **incest**. The NIBRS provides the following definitions of sexual assault (Greenfeld, 1997):

- *Forcible sodomy:* Oral or anal sexual intercourse with another person, forcibly and/or against that person's will.
- *Sexual assault with an object:* Use of an instrument or object to unlawfully penetrate the genital or anal opening of the body of another person, forcibly and/or against that person's will.
- *Forcible fondling:* The touching of the private body parts of another person for the purpose of sexual gratification, forcibly and/or against that person's will, including indecent liberties and molestation.
- *Incest:* Nonforcible sexual intercourse between persons who are related to each other within the degree wherein marriage is prohibited by law.

Nonviolent Sexual Offenses

Voyeurs or "peeping toms" achieve sexual gratification by spying on others, usually strangers. They particularly enjoy watching other people have sex.

Exhibitionists repeatedly expose their genitals to unsuspecting people, usually women and children, in public places as a way of experiencing sexual arousal. Nonviolent sexual offenses such as voyeurism and exhibitionism are typically not physically harmful to victims. Victims, however, may experience psychological or emotional trauma or, at the least, become disturbed by such events (Greenfeld, 1997; Sarason & Sarason, 1996).

Sexual offenders often engage in fondling, caressing, and other nonviolent behaviors. **Frottage** describes the touching or rubbing against a nonconsenting person for sexual arousal (Righthand & Welch, 2001). For example, an offender may brush against the breasts of a passing woman. In crowded settings, as may be the case on a tightly packed elevator, the victim is often unaware that frottage has occurred.

Stalking refers to "a course of conduct directed at a specific person that involves repeated visual or physical proximity, nonconsensual communication, or verbal, written or implied threats, or a combination thereof, that would cause a reasonable person fear" (Violence Against Women Grants Office, 1998, p. 6). Specifically, stalking victims may be followed, receive unwanted phone calls or letters, or be threatened. Stalkers may vandalize property or simply watch the victims without their consent.

Sexual Offenses Against Children

Statutory rape is defined as "the carnal knowledge of a person without force or the threat of force when that person is below the statutory age of consent" (Greenfeld, 1997, p. 31). The age of consent varies by jurisdiction across the United States. The NIBRS designates statutory rape as a separate sexual offense category. The UCR includes statutory rape as a sex offense, whereas the NCVS does not include reports on victims under the age of 12.

Sexual assaults of children, excluding forcible or statutory rape, are described as "lewd acts with children." These acts are similar to sexual assaults of adults, but apply specifically to children. Fondling, indecent liberties, immoral practices, molestation, and other indecent behaviors with children are included.

Pedophilia, sexual abuse, and child molestation are terms used interchangeably to describe sexual offenses against children. No generally accepted definition exists to describe each term. As a result, much confusion exists surrounding the understanding of pedophiles and the prevalence of child sexual abuse. According to the American Psychiatric Association's *Diagnostic and Statistical Manual of Mental Disorders* (2000), **pedophilia** includes intense and recurrent sexual urges and sexually arousing fantasies involving some form of sexual activity with a prepubescent child. Definitions of **child molestation** and sexual abuse may include, but are not limited to, the definition of pedophilia. The American Medical Association recommends that the definition of sexual abuse of children include "exploitation of a child for gratification or profit of an adult" (Murray, 2000, p. 211). Pedophilia, child molestation, and child sexual abuse may take a variety of forms, ranging from exhibition, fondling, sexual intercourse, or use of a child in pornographic material. Pedophiles and child molesters are often defined by their use of manipulation, persuasion, and friendship to sexually assault children.

Offenders groom their victims rather than use force. **Grooming** refers to attempts to manipulate or coerce someone into performing sexual acts for a proposed reward (Office for Victims of Crime, 2001). The offender tries to build the trust of a child to get what he or she ultimately wants from the child. For example, an offender may give or let a victim borrow an item such as candy, a book, a magazine, or a toy in return for engagement in sexual acts.

Prostitution

Prostitution refers to any sexual exchange for money or other reward (Meier & Geis, 1997). Varying sexual acts may be exchanged, including oral and anal sex; sadistic, masochistic, and exhibitionist acts; as well as traditional forms of sexual relations. Male or female prostitutes may perform these acts.

Although legal in certain parts of the world, prostitution, the solicitation of prostitutes, and commercial vice are often considered criminal, dehumanizing, and immoral. Consequently, efforts are made to socially control and legally respond to prostitution and related behaviors. In places where prostitution is permitted, there are certain restrictions as to where prostitutes may solicit customers. For example, Nevada allows licensed brothels to operate under strict legal arrangements. In Great Britain prostitution is permitted, but prostitutes are not allowed to solicit customers on the streets.

Kingsley Davis (1976), a noted social theorist, views prostitution as functional for society. He argues that prostitution contributes to the preservation of the moral order, the integration of society, the purity of marriage, and feminine virtue among nonprostitutes. Immoral, stigmatized females are given work while men away from home or those who desire deviant sexual activity can buy the services of prostitutes.

Prostitutes, Pimps, and Violence

Many prostitutes enter the business with dreams of making good money. A closer analysis of what actually results in this illegal business is that pimps are the ones who benefit the most from prostitution. After paying the pimps, many prostitutes receive only 10% to 20% of a night's earnings. "It is estimated that over 90% of street prostitutes are controlled by pimps." Pimps can be fathers, mothers, brothers, establishment owners, drug dealers, men, or women. All lure, kidnap, or sell young girls—particularly homeless runaways—into prostitution. Recently, 14 alleged pimps were arrested in Atlanta, Georgia, for luring girls as young as age 10 into prostitution.

Coyotes, people who bring others illegally across the U.S.–Mexican border, also act as pimps or sexual traffickers. For example, Maria, a Honduran woman looking for work in the United States, was approached by a Honduran coyote who befriended her and promised good jobs and safe passage into the United States. Once in the United States the coyote demanded $450 from her. When she couldn't pay, she was sold to a cantina owner and forced to work as a cantina girl, sitting and dancing with male customers, until she could pay off her debt.

In addition, many are forced into prostitution by their families, sold to pimps for a price of $1,000. In some third-world countries, young girls are sold for only $17. Once bought, a prostitute becomes indebted to the pimps and finds it extremely difficult to escape. Pimps, through violence and fear, physically, emotionally, and financially control prostitutes. Prostitutes are raped, beaten, and tortured. One prostitute states, "He had a six-foot bullwhip and he hit me in the head with it. . . . We got home and he beat me with that bullwhip and told me to go to sleep."

The government acts as an international pimp for the sex tourism industry in Thailand. Tour agencies recruit customers from Germany, the Netherlands, Japan, Saudi Arabia, Australia, and the United States with brochures advertising Thai women as "slim, sunburnt, and sweet . . . masters of the art of making love by nature" and as "little slaves who give real Thai warmth." Banks, airlines, hotels, and bar and brothel owners form a network of agents who extract profits from the $4 billion-a-year multinational sex tour industry.

Sources: M. Hornblower, "The Skin Trade," Time, 141 (25) (June 21, 1993), p. 44(8); A. Leuchtag, "Merchants of Flesh," The Humanist, 55(2) (March-April 1995), p. 11(6); H. Jei, "The Flesh Trade's Empty Promises," Connexions, 46. (Summer 1994), p. 11(1); N. Katyal, "Men Who Own Women: A Thirteenth Amendment Critique of Forced Prostitution," Yale Law Journal, 103 (3). (December 1993), pp. 791–826; and "Pinch on the Pimps," Time, 157 (11) (March 19, 2001), p. 63.

Sexual Trafficking of Women and Children

In many countries prostitution is associated with large-scale operations of **sexual trafficking**. Trafficking occurs when women or children are (Bertone, 2000, p. 4)

> [I]llicitly engaged (recruited, kidnapped, sold, etc.) and/or moved, either within national or across international borders; [or when] intermediaries (traffickers) during any part of this process obtain economic or other profit by means of deception, coercion and/or other forms of exploitation under conditions that violate the fundamental human rights.

In essence, women and children are traded, exchanged, or sold often against their will into sexual slavery and prostitution services. Countries such as India, Thailand, Brazil, and the Philippines are especially well known for the illicit trafficking of women and children. Many women in these countries hold attitudes favorable toward prostitution and see it as an opportunity to make money for their families. The relatives of young girls and women encourage a permissive view of prostitution and

There are more than 1 million children held as sex slaves and prostitutes in Asia, principally in Vietnam, China, Cambodia, Thailand, and the Philippines. Who are the customers?

Pimps, Mexican Women, and Prostitution in the United States

The scenario is typical—played out around the world. Desperate poverty, men aspiring to "pimp" unsuspecting women for imagined riches, and an insatiable market for their sexual services. When boys in Tenancingo, Mexico, were asked "What do you want to do when you grow up?", they reply "I want to have lots of sisters and a lot of daughters to make lots of money."

As a prosecutor observes, "The way they fish for their victims is very cruel, very Machiavellian, but very effective. When someone is isolated, or unprotected, they are the perfect victim."

"Mostly, the pimps concentrate on isolating women, lying to them, and breaking down their self-esteem." Promises of a better life, money for themselves and their families, and even marriage are ploys to gain the trust of young women.

One victim reported she was told she would be sent to the United States where she would be helped to find work. If she refused, then she would never see her young daughter again. Following her arrival, she was provided clothing—"mostly short, tight skirts and tops"—and shelter—"a small, sparely furnished apartment." She quickly learned her new "job." She would be picked up around 4 P.M. and taken to work—providing sexual services to as many as 40 to 50 men each night in her new "home"—inner city Atlanta, Georgia.

Source: Kate Brumback and Mark Stevenson, Pimps force Mexican Women into Prostitution in U.S., posted at: www. msnbc. com/cleanprint/CleanPrinProxy.aspx?1282496877263

often sell female family members into the sex industry for payment and future profits.

Rates of Criminal Sexual Offending

Around the World

Conflicting views of sexual offending make it difficult to estimate its prevalence around the world. The United Nations' survey of crime trends provides data on rape rates for 65 countries. The countries with the highest rape rates (the number per 1,000 people in the general population) are South Africa (1.19), Seychelles (0.79), Australia (0.78), Montserrat (0.75), Canada (0.73), Jamaica (0.48), Dominica (0.35), United States (0.30), Iceland (0.25), and Papua New Guinea (0.23). The countries with the lowest per capita rates of rape are Saudi Arabia (0.003), Azerbaijan and Yemen (0.004), Indonesia (0.006), Armenia (0.009), Georgia (0.010), Greece (0.011), Macedonia (0.013), Qatar and India (0.014), and Hong Kong (0.015) (United Nations Office on Drugs and Crime, 2000).

Variations in the prevalence of sexual assaults of women across the globe have also been considered. The findings of Jan van Dijk, John van Kesteren, and Paul Smit's study, "Criminal Victimisation in International Perspective," show wide disparities in the sexual victimization of women across 30 countries. Overall, 0.6% of the total population of the countries studied report being sexually victimized in a 1-year period. The United States and Iceland were found to have the highest 1-year prevalence rate (1.4%), followed by Sweden (1.3%) and Northern Ireland (1.2%); Norway, England and Wales, and Switzerland were tied (0.9%). Rates of 0.1% or less are reported in Spain, Bulgaria, Hungary, and Mexico.

Cities with the highest prevalence rates include Maputo (Mozambique) (1.8%), New York (1.5%), Copenhagen and Helsinki (1.4%), Reykjavik (1.3%), and Istanbul (1.1%). The cities with the lowest rate (0.1%) are Madrid, Dublin, Budapest, Brussels, Vienna, and Lisbon (van Dijk et al., 2008).

In about half of the incidents of sexual assault the victim knew the offender; in about one in three cases the victim knew the offender by name. In those instances in which the victim knew the offender's name, the assailant was most likely to be a colleague or boss (17%), close friend (16%), spouse or boyfriend (11%), or current partner (8%) (van Dijk et al., 2008).

In the United States

Most recently, the NCVS finds that in a given year, there are over 203,000 rape and sexual assault victims in the United States (U.S. Department of

Justice, 2009). The NCVS defines rape as "forced sexual intercourse including both psychological coercion as well as physical force. Forced sexual intercourse means penetration by the offender(s). Includes attempted rapes, male as well as female victims, and both heterosexual and homosexual rape. Attempted rape includes verbal threats of rape" (U.S. Department of Justice, 2009). In the same year, 89,000 cases of forcible rape across the United States were recorded in Crime in the United States. Crime in the United States defines forcible rape as "the carnal knowledge of a female, forcibly and against her will. "Rapes by force and attempts or assaults to rape regardless of the age of the victim are included" (Crime in the United States, 2009). The NCVS includes the victimization of females and males 12 years of age and over. However, the FBI's Crime in the United States only records offenses committed against women.

Figure 10–1 shows a significant decline in rape victimization in the United States since 1973. However, there has been a slight increase in more recent years.

Characteristics of Criminal Sexual Offending

Victim Characteristics

Although most victims of violent crime are male, females predominate among victims of rape and sexual assault. For adults, over 90% of rape

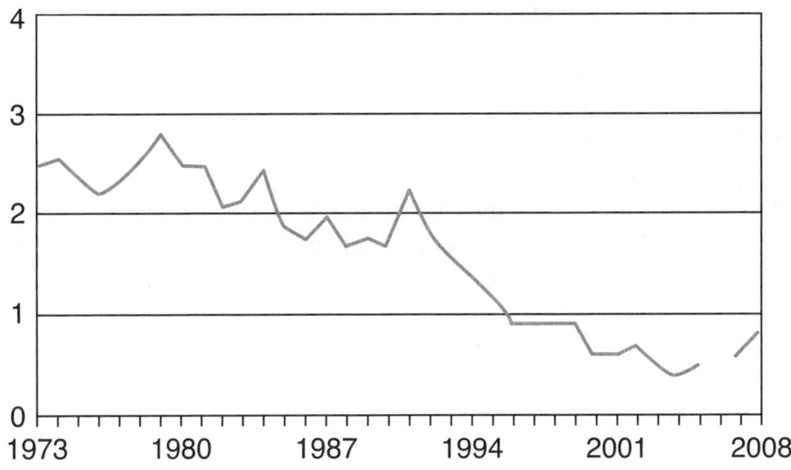

FIGURE 10–1 Rape victimization in the United States, per 1,000 persons ages 12 and older, 1973–2008.
Source: Bureau of Justice Statistics.

or sexual assault victims are female, approximately 10 female victims for every 1 male victim (Greenfeld, 1997). In the United States 1.3 females are raped or sexually assaulted per every 1,000 adults age 12 and older (U.S. Department of Justice, 2009).

A greater number of rape and sexual assault victims vary widely by race of the victim. The highest rates of rape and sexual assault are reported by Black women (1.9 per 1,000), followed by women of other races (including Native American, Alaska Natives, Asians, Native Hawaiians, and other Pacific Islanders) (0.9). White and Hispanic women have the lowest victimization rates of rape and sexual assault (0.6).

Rape and sexual assault victimization is concentrated among the young. The highest rates are among persons between ages 16 and 24 (2.2), followed by 12- to 15-year-olds (1.6). After the age of 25, rape and sexual assault rates drop sharply to 0.7 until the age of 50 and 0.2 thereafter.

Juvenile victims of violent crime are most likely to be sexually assaulted (52%) than victims of aggravated assault (39%), robbery (8%), or murder (less than one-half of 1%) (Snyder, 2006). An estimated 68,500 substantiated cases of sexual abuse of children occur across the United States each year (Finkelhor, Jones, & Shattuck, 2008). Distinct gender and age differences are evident in the violent victimization of the young. Young girls are most likely to be sexually assaulted, whereas young boys are more likely to be victims of aggravated assault. Three of every four female juvenile victims of violent crime are sexually assaulted, and about 6 in 10 male juvenile victims experience an aggravated assault. In addition, victims under the age of 12 accounted for almost half (47%) of all juvenile sexual assault victims (Snyder, 2006).

Offender Characteristics

As expected, males commit nearly all officially recorded forcible rapes (99%). Females rarely rape and commit relatively few other sexual offenses (approximately 7.5%) (Greenfeld, 1997). A study of 115 sexually assaulted males shows that men assault 87% of men. Furthermore, a man and a woman together assault 6% of men, and a lone woman assaults 7% of the male victims. Females sexually assault other females in less than 1% of the cases (King & Woollett, 1997). Overall, 6% of offenders who sexually assault juveniles are female. Female offenders are most common in assaults of children under the age of 6 (Snyder, 2000).

Most rape and sexual assault offenders are aged 18 and over, with 4 of every 10 incidents involving offenders over age 30. About one-fourth of the incidents reported to a law enforcement agency involve offenders under age 21. Juvenile offenders assault only 4% of adult victims (Greenfeld, 1997; Snyder, 2006).

Social and Situational Characteristics of Sexual Offenses

VICTIM–OFFENDER RELATIONSHIP. Sexual offenders and their victims are likely to have a prior relationship, either as family members or acquaintances. Between 8% and 11% of adults are victimized by family members. Adults (those over 18) are seven times more likely to be victimized by an acquaintance than a family member. Victims over the age of 30 are more likely to be raped or sexually assaulted by a stranger than are children, by a ratio of 12 to 1 (Greenfeld, 1997).

The sexual victimization of children and adolescents is rarely carried out by strangers. Overall, 95% of sexual assaults of persons 17 years of age or younger are committed by either a family member (35%) or an acquaintance (60%). As children age, those who sexually assault them are less likely to be family members and more likely to be acquaintances (Snyder, 2006). As might be expected, younger children (those under the age of 11) are most likely to be sexually assaulted in a residence, whereas older children are more likely to be victimized outside a home. Almost 9 of 10 victims under the age of 6 and 3 of 4 of victims between 6 and 11 are sexually assaulted in a residence. Half the sexual assaults of victims between 15 and 17 years old occur in places other than a residence (Synder, 2006).

Reporting Rape, Sexual Assault, and Child Sexual Abuse

According to Greenfeld (1997), one-third of rape and sexual assault victims report their victimization to a law enforcement agency. A study of gender differences in rape reporting concludes the following (Pino & Meier, 1999):

- Male victims are less likely to report a rape or sexual assault to police than female victims.
- Sexual assaults are almost twice as likely to be reported when the offender is a stranger.
- Sexual assaults are nearly five times as likely to be reported if something was stolen during the assault.
- The odds of reporting increase if injuries are sustained or if the victim requires medical attention.
- The presence of a weapon also increases rape/sexual assault reporting.

- To a lesser extent, higher levels of education and lower levels of income were related to rape/sexual assault reporting.

AT A GLANCE

Global Patterns

- The highest rates of sexual assault are found in the United States, Sweden, Northern Ireland, Norway, and England and Wales.
- More than 1 million children annually are estimated to be victims of sexual abuse worldwide.
- Rape is most common in South Africa, Seychelles, Australia, Montserrat, and Canada.
- Rape is least likely to occur in Saudi Arabia, Azerbaijan, Yemen, and Indonesia.
- Industrialized countries such as the United States, Australia, the United Kingdom, and Canada report similar rates of rape, sexual assault, child victimization, and prostitution.
- Native Americans and Alaska Natives are rape victims more often than other ethnic and racial groups.

U.S. Trends and Patterns

- Nearly all cases of sexual assault involve male perpetrators and female victims.
- Black females are especially vulnerable to rape and sexual assault.
- Victims of rape and sexual assault are usually between the ages of 16 and 19.
- Most sex offenders are over the age of 18.
- Juvenile sexual offenders disproportionately victimize persons of a similar age.
- In most cases—especially those of young children—victims and offenders know each other.
- College students are at particularly high risk for involvement in sexually assaultive behavior, both as victims and offenders.
- Internet sexual solicitation of children and child pornography are among the more rapidly increasing forms of sexual offending.

Sources: Snyder, H. 2000. Sexual Assault of Young Children as Reported to Law Enforcement: Victim, Incident, and Offender Characteristics. Washington, DC: U.S. Department of Justice, Office of Justice Programs, and Bureau of Justice Statistics; Greenfeld, L. 1997. Sex Offenses and Offenders: An Analysis of Data on Rape and Sexual Assault. Washington, DC: U.S. Department of Justice, Office of Justice Programs, and Bureau of Justice Statistics); Fisher, B. et al. 2000. The Sexual Victimization of College Women. Washington, DC: National Institute of Justice; National Sexual Violence Resource Center. 2000. Sexual Assault in Indian Country: Confronting Sexual Violence. Enola, PA: Author; Office for Victims of Crime. 2001. Internet Crimes Against Children. Washington, DC: U.S. Department of Justice, Office of Justice Programs, and Office for Victims of Crime; Amanpour, C. 1997. "South Africa copes with skyrocketing rape, abuse rates," CNN. February 23. Web posted at http://www.cnn.com/WORLD/9702/23/safrica.rapes/; Bray, M. 2001. "Call for crackdown on child sex laws," CNN. November 22. Web posted at http://www.cnn.com/2001/WORLD/asiapcf/southeast/11/22/asia.childsex/index.html; CNN. 2002. "Dozens arrested in child porn probe: 50 more arrests expected by week's end." March 19. Web posted at http://www.cnn.com/2002/US/03/18/fbi.child/porn/?related.html; David Finkelhor, Childhood Victimization, New York; Oxford University Press, 2008.

Gender differences in likelihood of reporting rape are related the perceived seriousness by the victim. Female victims typically view personal injury, the presence of weapons, unknown perpetrators, and acts of theft as particularly serious. Victims who are assaulted under these circumstances are therefore more likely to report a rape to the police. Males, on the other hand, only perceive a rape as serious enough to report when bodily injury occurs (Pino & Meier, 1999).

Victims fail to report rapes to police in an effort to avoid the emotional and humiliating experience of being questioned by investigators and prosecutors. Many withhold reports because they fear the police will do nothing to help them. Rape victims are often accused of precipitating the assault with provocative actions, clothing, or circumstances (Pino & Meier, 1999).

The age of child sexual abuse victims often mitigates the reporting of the offense. Reports of childhood rape and assault, however, are frequently made later in life. One study of sexually assaulted males shows that victims who are assaulted before age 16 are likely to delay reporting the incident for more than 17 years (King & Woollett, 1997). Both children and adults are responsible for false allegations of childhood sexual abuse. For example, some cases of day care and teacher abuse often result in false allegations of sexual abuse of children. Elizabeth Loftus (1997), a psychologist who specializes in distortions of memory, finds that suggestion and imagination can create childhood memories of sexual abuse that never occurred.

> SSRN
> Mialon, H. M., & Mialon, S. H. (2004). An econometric study of rape victim silence: Competition, selection, and deterrence. http://ssrn.com/abstract=598881 or doi:10.2139/ssrn.598881

Typology of Rapists

Several typologies of rape offenders are offered, and many are based on the motivation of the offender and issues of power, anger, and aggression. Nicholas Groth (1983) identifies three motivations for rape: power, anger, and sadism. Murray Cohen and colleagues (1975) offer a similar typology, which describes rapists as sexual aim, aggressive aim, or sexual-aggression diffusion rapists. Each type of rapist reacts in such a way that sexuality becomes an expression of conquest, a hostile act, or an erotic expression of anger and power.

Another typology, formulated by Richard Rada (1978), identifies rapists according to (1) situation stress, (2) masculine identity conflict, (3) sadistic tendencies, (4) sociopathic personality, or (5) psychotic personality. A situational stress rapist responds to severe disruption in personal life, such as job conflicts, family dysfunction, and financial difficulty. Masculine identity conflict, sadistic, and sociopathic offenders rape because of sexual uncertainty, violent tendencies, and sexual desires. Robert Hazelwood and Ann Burgess (1995) offer an additional typology that includes four types of rapists: power-assertive rapists, power-reassurance rapists, anger-retaliatory rapists, and anger-excitation rapists.

Groth, Cohen et al., Rada, Hazelwood, and Burgess rely on strikingly similar theoretical concepts to construct their typologies of rapists. **Table 10–1** links types of rapists with patterns of assaultive behavior.

Dennis Stevens (1999) offers a typology of rapists based on premeditation factors, victim selection, style of the attack, and the degree of violence. To Stevens, there are three primary motives for rape: righteous rape, peer rape, and fantasy rape. Righteous rapists justify their actions and view their victims as responsible for the attacks. They contend that in

TABLE 10–1 **Types of Rapists**

Groth	Cohen et al.	Rada	Hazelwood & Burgess	Description of the Offender's Behavior
Power rape	Aggressive aim	Situational stress	Power-assertive	Seduce victims, plan their crimes, and use a great deal of force. Assert their masculine power through the act of rape.
Anger rape			Anger-retaliatory	Attack by surprise and subdue victims with direct or physical force. Act out of anger; rape becomes the expression of anger.
	Sexual aim	Masculine identity	Power-reassurance	Attack strangers, select victims in advance through stalking, and often contact victims after the rape. Act out of a sense of social or sexual inadequacy.
Sadistic rape	Sexual-aggression diffusion	Sadistic tendencies	Anger-excitation	Involve strangers, planning, and careful execution. Stimulated by the infliction of pain toward victim. Often record activities and keep a souvenir of the attack.
		Sociopathic/ psychotic personalities		Primarily motivated by sexual desires.
		Psychotic personalities		Severe psychiatric impairment associated with rape and sexual assaultive behavior.

Sources: Adapted from Groth, N., Rape: Behavioral Aspect, in Encyclopedia of Crime and Justice, vol. 4, S. Kadish (ed.), New York: Free Press (1983); Cohen, M. et al. The Psychology of Rapists, in Forcible Rape: The Crime, The Victim and the Offender, D. Chappell et al. (ed.), New York: Columbia University Press (1977). Rada, T., Clinical Aspects of the Rapist, New York: Grune and Stratton (1978), Hazelwood, R. and A. Burgess (eds.), Practical Aspects of Rape Investigation: A Multidisciplinary Approach, New York: CRC Press (1995).

some way their victims consented to sex. Peer rapists blame their attacks on current friendships, described as "bad company." Fantasy rapists are motivated to rape by "some imaginary goal that had been a part of their past" (Stevens, 1999, p. 50).

Diana Scully (1990) presents a similar broad typology of admitters and deniers. Similar in nature to righteous rape, deniers contend that sexual relations with victims are consensual. Scully's work with Joseph Marolla (1996) examines how deniers justify and admitters excuse rape accounts. Five themes are identified with regard to rape justifications: (1) women as seductresses, (2) women mean "yes" when they say "no," (3) most women eventually relax and enjoy it, (4) nice girls don't get raped, and (5) raping as being guilty of a minor wrongdoing. Each theme is an attempt to discredit and blame the victim while the rapist tries to present his actions as justified in the context. Three themes are found in the excuses of admitters: (1) the use of alcohol and drugs, (2) emotional problems, and (3) nice guy image. Each excuse tries to explain the rape in a way that allows the rapists a semblance of moral integrity.

Juvenile Sexual Offenders

A few research studies attempt to classify juvenile sex offenders based on the type of offense and the characteristics of the victims. These characteristics include the offenders' social competence, antisocial behavior and impulsivity, degree of sexual preoccupation, and extent of contact with victims (Righthand & Welch, 2001). Such typologies outline juvenile sexual offenders as pedophilic, child molesters, rapists, sexually reactive children, fondlers, and paraphilic offenders. Pedophilic juveniles, child molesters, and sexually reactive offenders victimize younger children (under the age of 12). There is typically a 3- to 5-year difference in age between offenders and victims. Juveniles described as a sexual assaulter, rapist, or fondler often assault somewhat older children. Groups of undifferentiated and unclassifiable offenders commit mostly "hands-off" assaults including exhibitionism and obscene phone calls.

SSRN

Smith, B. V. (2009). Fifty state survey of juvenile sex offender registration laws. http://ssrn.com/abstract=1517372

SSRN

Zimring, F. E., Piquero, A. R., Jennings, W., & Hays, S. A. (2007). The predictive power of juvenile sex offending: evidence from the second Philadelphia Birth Cohort Study. http://ssrn.com/abstract=995918

Prostitution

Extent of Prostitution

The extent of prostitution in the United States and around the world can only be estimated. Crime in the United States indicates that more than 61,000 prostitute-related arrests are made each year, for a rate of 34 arrests per 100,000 inhabitants. Women are almost twice as likely to be arrested for prostitution as are men. However, nearly 38% of the arrests for prostitution are of males. Patterns of arrests show that a substantial number of arrests are made starting at age 18 and then decreasing after the age of 40. The greatest number of arrests for prostitution is made in the 25 to 40 age range. Although the highest rate of arrests for prostitution is found in the Midwest, the Western region makes a greater number of arrests compared with all other regions. Nearly all arrests for prostitution are in large cities with populations over 250,000. The urban rate of arrest is 137 per 100,000 inhabitants, or four times the total prostitution arrest rate (FBI, 2000). Almost one-fourth of these arrests are of the "johns"—customers of prostitutes (Meier & Geis, 1997).

Arrest data provide notoriously poor indicators of the number of prostitutes actually operating and give no indication of other aspects of the sex trade industry. It is estimated that 500,000 prostitutes work in the United States each year. However, as many as 5 million women in the United States aged 18 to 64 may have prostituted themselves at some point in their life. Additionally, 16% to 20% of adult men report having had some experience with prostitutes (Clinard & Meier, 1998; Janus & Janus, 1993).

Prostitution, sex tourism, and sexual trafficking are extremely prevalent in many Asian countries, such as Thailand, Japan, and South Korea. Sexualized work developed during periods of wartime and is now common in South and Southeast Asia. Military and local police allow a variety of types of prostitution to continue, disregard evidence of sexual trafficking, and rarely punish lawbreakers. In addition to the Asian experience, women from Eastern Europe, the former Soviet Union, Israel, Turkey, Italy, and Germany work sexual trafficking routes around the world. In the former Soviet Union, abducted women are placed on auction blocks, partially naked, and sold for an average price of $1,000 (Bertone, 2000).

Estimates of underage prostitution indicate that 800,000 underage prostitutes work in Thailand, 400,000 in India, 250,000 in Brazil, and 60,000 in the Philippines. UNICEF reports estimate that nearly one-third of sex workers in these areas are child prostitutes. More than 90,000 underage prostitutes provide sexual services in the United States. The child sex industry brings in billions of dollars a year, making up about 15% of Thailand's gross national product (Bray, 2001).

Typology of Prostitution

Prostitutes are classified according to their methods of operation, their degree of privacy, and their income. Three major types of prostitutes include streetwalkers, bar girls, and call girls (Clinard & Meier, 1998). Most prostitutes are considered **streetwalkers** who solicit clients in relatively public places (e.g., on the street corner) in mainly large urban areas, generally within established territories. Streetwalkers provide the cheapest type of prostitution services available and often possess long arrest records for prostitution. **Call girls** are well-paid, high-status prostitutes who work largely away from public scrutiny, with little interference from the police. They serve wealthy clients who are referred by known and trusted sources. Call girls typically go to the hotel room or residence of their clients. **Bar girls** solicit clients in public bars, either working alone, in groups, or with pimps. The bar girl, or B-girl, is present in the bar in the guise of a patron. Prostitution is also commonly practiced in massage parlors, photographic studios, or commercial escort agencies (Cavan, 1970).

Street Life, Drugs, and Prostitution

Complex interrelationships exist among life on the street, drugs, and prostitution (Potterat et al., 1998). Homeless and runaway youth engage in prostitution as **survival sex**—exchanging sexual favors for food, shelter, and other basic necessities. Many of these youth are from middle-class backgrounds. Both girls and boys engage in heterosexual and homosexual survival sex (Arena, 2001).

Illicit drug use among prostitutes often occurs before entry into sexualized work. Studies show that most prostitutes are involved in illicit drug use; more than half began using drugs before becoming prostitutes. However, prostitutes are not always lured by drugs into their work and do not continue to work to support a drug addiction. Poverty and violent victimization often act as antecedents to drug use as well as prostitution (Goldstein, 1979; Gossop et al., 1994; Potterat et al., 1998; Silbert et al., 1982).

Prostitutes in upscale restaurants and bars discretely solicit customers, many of whom are in the city on business or for a convention. Street solicitation may well be detached, sophisticated, and highly selective.

Online Sexual Solicitation and Pornography of Youth

Recent reports and surveys of online sexual solicitation and pornography of youth note that because so many children are online today, predators can easily find and exploit them. To meet children and gain their trust, sexual predators may present themselves as someone of a different age, gender, or occupation. Online predators victimize children and teenagers by (Office for Victims of Crime, 2001)

- Enticing them through online contact for the purpose of engaging them in sexual acts
- Using the Internet for the production, manufacture, and distribution of child pornography
- Using the Internet to expose youth to child pornography and encourage them to exchange pornography
- Enticing and exploiting children for the purpose of sexual tourism (travel with the intent to engage in sexual behavior), for commercial gain, and/or personal gratification.

Internet Sex Offenders and Their Victims: Myths and Realities

Myth 1: Most Internet-initiated sex crimes involve adult men who use the Internet to meet and seduce underage adolescents into sexual encounters.
Reality: The great majority of victims are aware they are conversing with adults. Offenders rarely deceive victims about their sexual interests. Sex is usually broached online, and most victims who meet offenders face-to-face go to such meetings expecting to engage in sexual activity.

Myth 2: Naive and inexperienced young children are vulnerable to online child molesters.
Reality: Most victims have considerable experience with the Internet and are developmentally advanced enough to understand sexual behavior in a rudimentary way.

Myth 3: Youth who interact online with unknown people are at risk for sexual victimization.
Reality: Interacting with unknown persons does not place a young person at risk for sexual victimization. However, youth who send personal information (e.g., name, telephone number, pictures) to unknown people or talk online to such people about sex are more likely to receive aggressive sexual solicitations.

Patterns of risky online behavior make youth vulnerable to sexual victimization, for example, talking online to unknown people about sex, seeking pornography online, or being rude or nasty online. Also, youth with histories of sexual or physical abuse and other troubled youth may be particularly vulnerable.

Myth 4: Online sexual offenders are pedophiles who victimize young children indiscriminately.
Reality: Pedophiles typically target prepubescent children. However, online sexual offenders are more likely to be interested in adolescent girls, particularly those who are sexually active.

Source: Janis Wolak, David Finkelhor, Kimberly J. Mitchell, and Michele L. Ybarra. 2008. Online "Predators" and their Victims: Myths, Realities and Implications for Prevention and Treatment, American Psychologist, 63, 111–128.

Completed Internet seductions and **aggressive sexual solicitations** (actual offline contact, attempts for offline contact, and requests for offline contact between victim and offender through regular mail, telephone, or in person) are very serious types of victimization. A recent study of online victimization shows that 1 in 33 youth surveyed received an aggressive sexual solicitation. A special type of online victimization involves **traveler cases**, where adults or youth travel to physically meet and have sex with someone they first came to know on the Internet. These offenses are estimated to be less common than stranger sexual assaults or intrafamily sexual abuse. The National Center for Missing and Exploited Children estimates that nearly 800 traveler cases, confirmed or under investigation, have been identified by law enforcement sources (Finkelhor, Mitchell, & Wolak, 2001).

Physical contact between the child and the perpetrator does not have to occur for a crime to be committed. **Sexual solicitations** refer to "requests to engage in sexual activities or sexual talk or give personal sexual information that was unwanted or, whether wanted or not, were made by an adult" (Mitchell et al., 2001, p. 3011). The online victimization survey also shows that "approximately one in five youth surveyed received a sexual solicitation over the Internet in the last year" (Finkelhor et al., 2001, p. 1).

Demographic and other risk factors are associated with online sexual solicitation. Girls are more likely to be solicited online than boys of a similar age. Older youth (ages 14 to 17) tend to be at greater risk primarily because they spend more time on the Internet, are often unsupervised, or are at households other than their own. Because Internet use is related to computer ownership, many child victims are from middle-class homes. Additionally, participation in chat rooms, risky online behavior, and talking to strangers online put youth at greater risk for victimization. Risk is higher for troubled or rebellious teens and emotionally vulnerable youth who may be dealing with issues of sexual identity. Alienated or depressed youth are also more vulnerable to online solicitation by strangers (Mitchell et al., 2001).

With regard to online offenders, recent survey results show that other youth and females account for much of the offending behavior (Mitchell et al., 2001). For example, one survey finds that 48% of the offenders are youth, whereas one in four of the aggressive episodes is initiated by females (Office for Victims of Crime, 2001). Internet pedophiles and other online sexual predators who are arrested include law enforcement officers, nurses, teachers, and school bus drivers (CNN, 2002).

Law enforcement agencies including the FBI as well as legislators from around the world are currently responding to various forms of Internet victimization (CNN, 1997, 2002). Committees from the United Nations and UNICEF are calling for action against child sexual abuse and the 23,000 websites that have already been detected as advocating sex with children (CNN, 1999b). Local and national level special operations target child pornography rings and Internet pedophiles in efforts to expand the knowledge base about the types of crimes, the victims, and the offenders. A recent FBI investigation ("Operation Candyman"), which focused on an online child pornography web group, identified 7,000 e-mail addresses linked to the group, with 4,600 in the United States and 2,400 in other countries. This investigation led to the arrest of 40 individuals from 20 states. Previous arrests were made through similar investigations. "Operation Rip Cord" led to more than 120 arrests in the United States, Germany, and the United Kingdom for child pornography, trading pictures of minors, or soliciting child sex over the Internet. Other arrests have been widely publicized in South Korea and Japan (CNN, 1997, 2001, 2002; Reuters, 2000b).

Investigations, which involve officers who "decoy" themselves as youth to try to catch online offenders, offer great potential for capturing Internet pedophiles and child pornographers. In one such investigation an agent pretending to be a teenage girl entered a chat room limited to 23 children. All 22 other youths turned out to be adults seeking improper contact with other children (CNN, 1998).

SSRN

Williams, C. R., & Draganich, S. (2006). Admissibility of propensity evidence in paedophilia cases. Monash University Faculty of Law Legal Studies Research Paper No. 2006/65; *Deakin Law Review, 11*(1), 1–32. http://ssrn.com/abstract=1096419

Consequences of Childhood Sexual Victimization

There is considerable evidence that childhood sexual victimization has immediate traumatic effects and may well have pronounced negative consequences later in life. Consequences of victimization include behavioral and psychological problems such as acting out, running away, truancy, conduct disorder, delinquency, promiscuity, and inappropriate sexual behavior. Increased rates of psychiatric disorders—including depressive disorders, anxiety disorders, and alcohol and drug abuse, as well as sexual problems—are seen in adult life and are cited as some of the most common long-term effects of childhood sexual abuse (Mullen, 1991; Ryan et al., 1996; Widom, 1995).

Studies are now at odds as to whether childhood sexual abuse is linked to the development of criminal behavior later in life (Browne & Finkelhor, 1986). Longitudinal studies of abuse victims find that compared with nonvictims, victims are at higher risk of arrest for committing crimes as adults, including sex crimes (Widom, 1995). The most frequent type of crime associated with childhood victimization is prostitution. Studies of prostitutes, however, find that prostitute and nonprostitute samples do not differ significantly in prior experience with childhood sexual abuse (Nadon et al., 1998).

Sex offenders have often been sexually victimized as children. Nearly 35% of sexual assault offenders and over 20% of rapists report childhood sexual victimization (Greenfeld, 1997). Among juvenile sexual offenders, nearly 40% are victims of sexual abuse (Ryan et al., 1996). Similarly, a self-report study of pedophiles finds that 42% of these offenders were sexually abused during childhood (Murray, 2000). Pedophiles report choosing victims who are the same age as they were at the time of their childhood sexual abuse. It remains, however, that two-thirds of convicted sex offenders are not victims of childhood sexual abuse (Greenfeld, 1997). Furthermore, the vast majority of child sex abuse victims are not arrested for sex crimes or any other crimes as adults (Widom, 1995).

Finkelhor, Ormrod, and Turner (2007) investigated the extent and consequences of poly-victimization—the experience of several forms of child victimization by the same person. In a nationally representative sample of children between the ages of 2 and 17, they found that 22% of the children surveyed experienced four or more different forms of victimization. Traumatic symptoms that followed poly-victimization were more severe than the experience of repeated victimization by the same kind of abusive behavior. Children who experienced poly-victimization suffered significantly more anxiety and depression and exhibited more anger and aggressive behavior.

Explanations for Criminal Sexual Offending

Theoretical Explanations

Several sociological and social psychological theories of deviant behavior explain the prevalence or incidence of sexually violent and exploitive behavior, including prostitution (**Tables 10–2** and **10–3**). The psychological perspective, however, has dominated the understanding of child sexual offenders. Therefore, pedophilia and child molestation are viewed as a mental health problem as well as a criminal offense. Two conflicting views of sexual crimes against women are evident. The first holds that forcible rape and sexual assault are motivated by the offender's need to exert power, control, and dominance over the victim; the second considers rape to be driven by innate, sexual desires.

TABLE 10–2 Explanations of Rates of Criminal Sexual Deviance

Theories and Theorists	Sociological Predictors	Hypotheses
Sociobiological Perspectives		
Thornhill and Palmer	Sexual motivation	The greater the sexual motivation in a given population, the higher the rate of rape and sexual assault.
Feminist Perspective		
Straus et al.	Power and dominance	The more prevalent the belief that men should exert power and dominance over women, the higher the rates of rape and sexual assault.
Yllö; Dobash and Dobash	Patriarchy	The greater the belief in patriarchy, the higher the rates of rape and sexual assault.
Brownmiller	Power, control, dominance	The greater the need of men to maintain power, control, and dominance over women, the higher rates of rape and sexual assault.
Integration		
Merton	Anomie	The greater the level of anomie, the higher the rates of sexual offending.
Subcultural		
Wolfgang and Ferracuti	Subcultures of violence	The more pervasive is a subculture of violence, the greater the probability that violent sexual offending will occur.
Miller	Focal concerns: trouble, toughness, smartness, fate, autonomy	The greater the acceptance of focal concerns of the lower class, the greater the rates of rape and sexual assault.
Conflict		
Sellin	Cultural conflict Primary Secondary	The greater the ratio of primary to secondary culture conflict, the higher the rates of criminal sexual offending.
Thio	Power, status groups	The lower the social status and power of members of a group, the greater the probability of criminal sexual offending.
Integrated Theories		
Barron and Straus	Gender inequality, social disorganization, subcultural support	The greater the gender inequality, social disorganization, and support for legitimate violence, the higher the rates of rape and sexual assault.

TABLE 10–3 Individual Level Explanations of Sexual Offending

Theories and Theorists	Sociological Predictors	Hypotheses
Social Learning		
Sutherland	Differential association	The more an individual is exposed to definitions favorable toward acts of sexual offending, the more likely he or she will engage in sexually deviant behaviors.
Glaser	Differential identification	The more an individual identifies with another who views acts of sexual offending as acceptable, the more likely he or she is to engage in sexually deviant behaviors.
Philips	Imitations	The more often an individual observes or is victimized by childhood rape or sexual assault, the more likely he or she is to engage in sexually deviant behaviors.
Routine Activities		
Cohen and Felson	Motivated offender Suitable target Absence of guardian	The greater the probability that a suitable target, a motivated offender, and a lack of a capable guardian will co-occur, the greater the likelihood that an individual will engage in predatory sexual offending.
Control-Exchange		
Gelles	Inequality Privacy Social control	The greater the gender inequality, the less the costs of interpersonal violence, the more likely individual family members will engage in sexual assaultive behaviors. The greater the privacy of a family, the more likely individual family members will engage in sexual assaultive behaviors. The less effective social controls over family relations become, the less the costs of interpersonal violence, and the more likely individual family members will engage in sexual assaultive behaviors.
Rational Choice		
Cornish and Clarke	Cost-to-benefit analysis	The greater the benefit anticipated from sexual deviance, the more likely an individual is to engage in sexual offending.
Strain		
Agnew	Strain/stress	The greater the strain experienced by an individual, the greater the experience of negative emotions. The greater the experience of negative emotions, the more likely an individual will engage in sexual deviance.

/ continues

TABLE 10–3 Individual Level Explanations of Sexual Offending / continued

Theories and Theorists	Sociological Predictors	Hypotheses
Frustration-Aggression		
Dollard et al.	Frustration	The greater the frustration experienced by an individual, the greater the probability that the individual will engage in acts of aggression. The greater the number of acts of aggression, the greater the likelihood of involvement in rape and sexual assault.

Explaining Rates of Criminal Sexual Offending

Anomic conditions and areas characterized by social disorganization and conflict often produce high rates of criminal sexual offending. Robert Merton's (1968) theory holds that members of society react to anomie, the disjunction between cultural goals and structured means for achieving goals, either through conformity or deviance. Deviant reactions result in a rejection of culturally prescribed goals and/or means. Frustrated by blocked opportunities for legitimate cultural success, members may adopt a sexually deviant lifestyle as a means of achieving some form of success. Prostitutes may earn substantial amounts of money, whereas rapists and sexual offenders acquire a sense of power and control over victims.

Culture conflict theory as proposed by Thorsten Sellin (1938) suggests that crime is nothing more than a disagreement over what constitutes acceptable behavior. As a result, certain types of crime may occur in one society but not in another. Conduct norms, or definitions of what is and is not deviant, provide the basis for acceptable behavior in specific group settings. A clash of values, customs, and definitions of behavior may produce deviance. Rape and sexual assault can therefore occur because the conduct norms of one group clash with those of another. These behaviors, according to Sellin, are considered primary conflict, or a fundamental clash of cultures.

Sellin, however, considers prostitution as a form of secondary conflict, or conflicts between smaller groups within the larger culture (e.g., class conflicts). Prostitution is often viewed by lower-class groups as an acceptable way of life; members are not condemned for participating in prostitution. Middle-class values, however, form the basis for most criminal laws. Because the act of prostitution is opposed to middle-class standards, it becomes criminal.

Alex Thio (1978) further explains the conflict between higher-status, powerful groups and lower-status, less powerful groups. Power theory holds that the powerful condemn the lower-class offenders in an effort to maintain control and power. Lower-class sexual deviance becomes criminal, whereas the coercive sexual exploitations of the upper class are unrecognized as rape or sexual assault. Similarly, streetwalkers and common prostitutes experience more attention in the way of criminal punishment than call girls and prostitutes who work for upper-class clientele.

Subcultural theories of Walter Miller (1958) and Marvin Wolfgang and Franco Ferracuti (1967) help to explain how the acceptance of subcultural values results in violent behavior. Miller's subcultural formulation centers on the focal concerns of the lower class—trouble, toughness, smartness, excitement, fate, and autonomy. He proposes that lower-class focal concerns provide a path for subculturally recognized success. This path of trouble, toughness, and excitement may include involvement in criminal sexual deviance. Wolfgang and Ferracuti similarly argue that some subcultures see violence as a way of life and therefore support violent reactions and adaptations to life circumstances. The violent adaptations are learned within the context of the group and come to be an expected means for settling disputes and maintaining prestige within the group. The advantages of engaging in violent behavior are emphasized, legitimized, and accepted.

Feminist theorists argue that patriarchy, or male dominance, teaches men that violence is an acceptable means to socially control women and maintain power and control over them. Men are viewed as naturally aggressive and are socialized to believe that male aggression is normal, even in the context of rape and coerced sexual relations. Susan Brownmiller (1975) is one of the first feminist theorists to assert that rape is an act of power and violence. Similar theories provided by Kersti Yllö (1984), Yllö and Bograd (1988), and the Dobashes (1988), as well as Catherine MacKinnon (1989) and Andrea Dworkin (1981), view rape as an unnatural behavior that has nothing to do with sex. This view is now one of the most widely accepted explanations for why men rape. Feminist theorists also tend to consider prostitution a consequence of the power of men to sexually exploit women.

Similar types of theories focus on patriarchy, power, and dominance to explain rape, sexual assault, and other forms of violence in the family context. Murray Straus' (1983) power dominance theory explains violence within the family context, and why husbands and fathers use violence to socially control their wives and children. The acceptance of violence in the family is prescribed by the larger society and then translated into the family system. Stress and frustrations make violence more probable.

Straus also argues that violence within the family is more likely if the stress is coupled with violent childhood experiences of the parent.

Larry Barron and Murray Straus (1989) offer an integrated theory of rape, which combines elements from gender inequality, social disorganization, and subcultural theories. Areas with high levels of gender inequality and social disorganization are often characterized by support for legitimate violence. In contrast, areas where the status of women is higher and marked by economic parity between men and women, rape rates tend to be lower.

Individual Level Explanations of Criminal Sexual Offending

According to social learning theorists, all behavior, including crime, is learned. Edward Sutherland (1947) first introduced differential association, the process of learning criminal values. Learning crime occurs in interaction with others who hold definitions favorable to crime and who advocate involvement in criminal activity. Rapists, sexual offenders, and prostitutes may learn specialized techniques, motives, and rationalizations for committing crime during this process.

Victims of childhood sexual abuse may later imitate this behavior and victimize others (Phillips, 1974). Childhood victims of sexual abuse, however, do not always become sexual offenders or rapists. Glaser's (1960) theory of differential identification explains how an individual is more likely to commit rape or sexual assault if he or she identifies with another person who views such behavior as acceptable. If a person who has been a victim of sexual abuse does not identify with his or her assailant, then he or she is less likely to perpetuate the cycle of sexual offending.

Strain theory holds that individuals experience a negative emotional reaction to stress and strain. According to Robert Agnew (1992), strain may result from blocked opportunities for success, the loss of something positive in one's life, or the presence of negative events. As a result of this emotional reaction, individuals may engage in rape, sexual assault, or prostitution in an effort to cope with or adapt to a stressful life situation.

Dollard and his colleagues (1939) propose that crime, specifically aggressive types of behavior, is a response to frustration. The frustration-aggression thesis suggests that high levels of frustration increase levels of aggression. Direct aggression toward others is the most likely consequence. Aggression may also be displaced on someone who is not the source of aggression.

Rapists, sexual offenders, and prostitutes often rationally choose criminal sexual offending by weighing the costs and benefits of doing so (Cornish & Clarke, 1987). If the benefits outweigh the costs, then an individual is more likely to engage in that behavior. Prostitutes may find that the associated income is greater than the costs involved, or a sexual offender may believe the costs of being caught or reported to the police are extremely low.

Cohen and Felson's (1979) routine activity theory suggests that crime is most likely to occur when there is a (1) suitable target, (2) motivated offender, and (3) lack of a capable guardian. Incidents of rape and sexual assault often occur in secret, when no one is around to intervene. Offenders choose targets that are easy to physically control or manipulate. Children, women of small stature, and anyone with emotional or cognitive deficits are therefore suitable and attractive targets for some sexual predators.

Richard Gelles' (1983) control-exchange theory explains how sexual offending occurs within families. The costs and benefits of using violence, rape, or sexual assault are first assessed. Family members are more likely to rape or offend other members if the costs are less than the rewards. The lack of effective social controls decreases the costs associated with rape and sexual assault of another family member. Social control also decreases as the privacy within the family increases. Privacy allows for more opportunities to commit sexual offenses without being caught. Inequalities among family victims and offenders reduce the costs associated with offending. Powerful family members are then able to exert control over weaker members.

Chapter Summary

- Forms of sexual deviance are found around the world, although all are not considered criminal. Those that are may not be punished or legally controlled to any great extent.
- The prevalence of sexual deviance is largely unknown. Research shows, however, that certain types of victims and offenders are more likely to be involved in sex crimes.
- Women and girls are more likely than men to be victims.
- Men are almost always the offenders.
- Victims are usually between the ages of 16 and 19.
- Offenders are more likely to be over the age of 18.
- Juvenile sexual offenders victimize other youth most of the time.

- Most victims and offenders know one another.
- One-third of victims report a rape or sexual assault.
- Males are less likely to report rape than females.
- Differences in reporting are related to the perceived seriousness of the offense.
- Typologies of rapists are on motivations to rape. Rapists may
  - Exert power or masculinity over women
  - Act out of a sense of sexual inadequacy
  - Express anger through rape
  - Be stimulated by the infliction of pain
- Righteous rapist or deniers contend that sexual relations are consensual.
- Juvenile sexual offenders are classified according to characteristics of the offense, age of victim, and offender traits such as social competence, antisocial behavior and impulsivity, and degree of sexual preoccupation.
- Prostitution, sexual trafficking, and sex tourism are found across the globe but are considered extremely prevalent in many Asian countries such as Thailand, Japan, and South Korea.
- Prostitutes are classified according to methods of operation, degree of privacy in work, and incomes. Three types are offered:
  - Streetwalkers
  - Call girls
  - Bar girls
- Internet pedophiles, online solicitation of youth, and child pornography are of special interest to law enforcement and legislators.
- It is estimated that one in five children receives a sexual solicitation online. A few solicitations are considered aggressive.
- Risk factors for online sexual solicitation are identified. Girls, youth aged 14 to 17, youth who engage in risky online behavior, and troubled, rebellious, and emotionally disturbed youth are at greatest risk. Youth and females account for much of the online offending.
- Studies are at odds as to whether childhood sexual victimization is associated with later criminal deviance. Prostitution is commonly associated with childhood sex abuse.

Key Concepts

Forcible rape: Forced sexual intercourse in which the victim may be either male or female and the offender of a different sex or the same sex as the victim.

Date rape: A forcible rape that occurs in the context of a dating relationship.

Sexual assault: A variety of victimizations in which unwanted sexual contact occurs between the victim and offender as described in the National Crime Victimization Survey.

Sex offenses: Unwanted sexual contacts as described by the FBI Uniform Crime Report.

Incest: Nonforcible sexual intercourse between persons who are related to each other within the degree wherein marriage is prohibited by law.

Voyeurs: Those who achieve sexual gratification as they spy on others; also known as "peeping toms."

Exhibitionists: Those who repeatedly expose their genitals to unsuspecting people in public places as a way of experiencing sexual arousal.

Frottage: The touching or rubbing against nonconsenting persons for sexual arousal.

Stalking: Repeated visual or physical proximity, nonconsensual communication, or verbal, written, or implied threats that would cause fear in a reasonable person.

Statutory rape: Sexual intercourse with a person below the statutory age of consent.

Pedophilia: Intense and recurrent sexual urges and sexually arousing fantasies involving some form of sexual activity with a prepubescent child.

Child molestation: Any sexual abuse of a child where the child is exploited for the gratification or profit of an adult.

Grooming: Attempts to manipulate or coerce someone into performing sexual acts for a proposed reward.

Prostitution: Any sexual exchange for money or other reward.

Sexual trafficking: The trading, exchanging, or selling of persons against their will into sexual slavery and prostitution services.

Streetwalkers: Prostitutes who solicit clients on the street; provide the cheapest type of prostitution services.

Call girls: Well-paid, high-status prostitutes who serve wealthy clients.

Bar girls: Typically solicit clients in public bars, massage parlors, or photographic studios.

Survival sex: Exchanging sexual favors for food, shelter, and other basic necessities.

Aggressive sexual solicitation (online): Internet solicitations of children in which actual offline contact, attempts for offline contact, and requests for offline contact are made through regular mail, telephone, or in person.

Traveler cases: Cases where adults or youth travel to physically meet and have sex with someone they first came to know on the Internet.

Sexual solicitation (online): Requests to engage in sexual activities or sexual talk or give personal information that were unwanted or, whether wanted or not, were made by an adult.

Critical Thinking Questions

1. Write a script for a date between college students who have been dating for 2 months. Describe where they will meet and the places they will go. Consider the interaction between the two students, when they are with others and when they are alone. Give examples of their verbal and nonverbal communication that might lead to misunderstanding about their intentions. How might the interpretation of the situation differ between the male and female student? What are the possible consequences of this misinterpretation?
2. Imagine that two total strangers—a male and female—meet by chance at a party. Neither of them knows anything about the other. However, the male has engaged in forced sexual relations on several occasions with his "dates" and the female has been a victim of sexual assault. Describe the interaction between the two strangers. How would their interaction differ if the female had not been a victim of sexual assault?
3. What differentiates sexual predators who victimize adults from those who victimize children? What are the social situations, motivations, and rationalizations that give rise to the sexual victimization of adults compared with children?
4. How do the theoretical formulations of rates and the incidence of sexual offending compare? Are the explanations of the prevalence of sexual offending in a given group incompatible with the explanations of individual involvement in such behavior?

 Web Extra

Web-based media materials from high-quality sources such as CNN, Time, and National Public Radio are available in support of this textbook. Visit go.jblearning.com/deviance to access them.

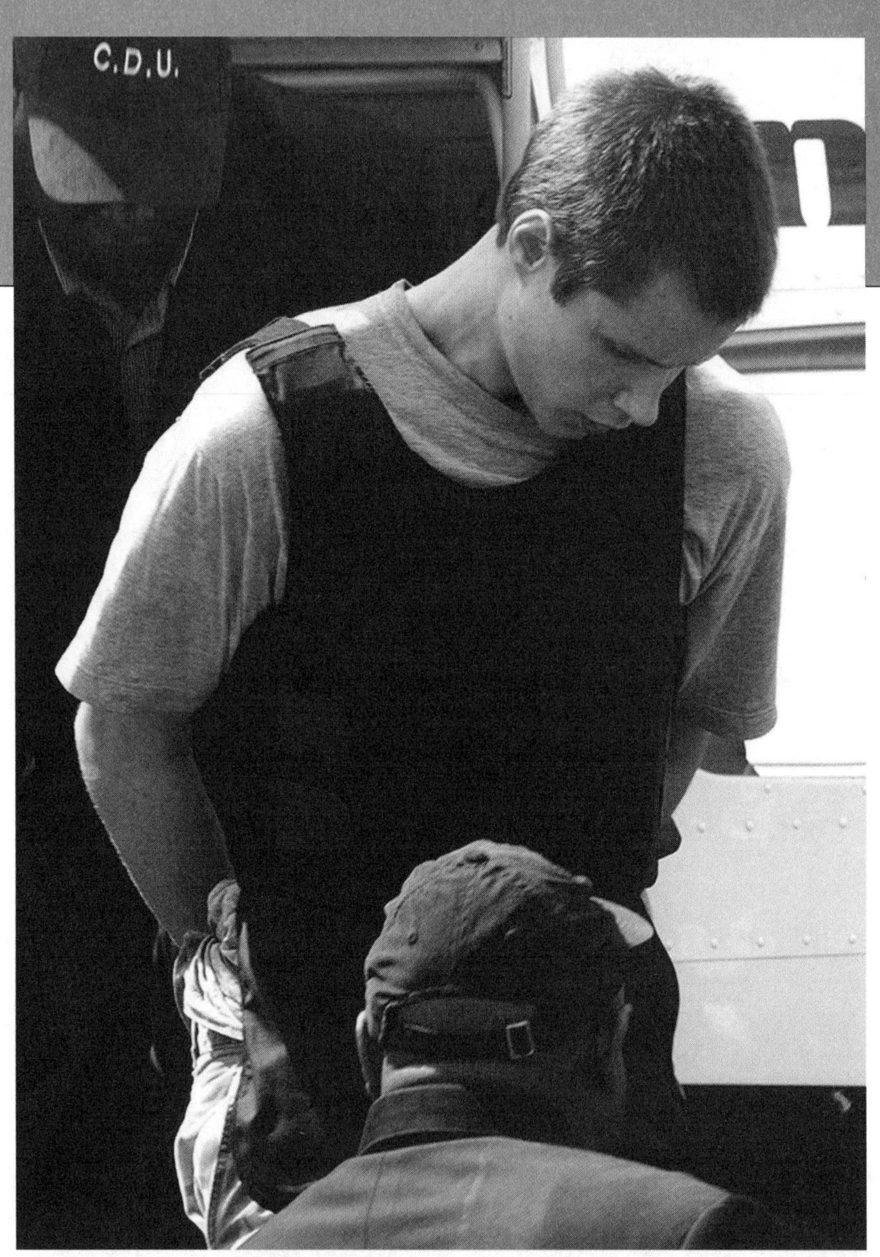
C.D.U.

Property Crimes

CHAPTER 11

Learning Objectives

After reading this chapter you should know

- The nature and statutory definitions of property crimes, including burglary, robbery, and larceny-theft.
- The prevalence of property crimes in the United States.
- The prevalence of property crimes in other countries.
- The costs of property crimes to their victims and to society as a whole.
- The characteristics of victims and offenders of property crimes.
- The nature and elements of criminal decisions involving property crimes.
- The types of thieves and the differences between professional, persistent, and occasional thieves.
- Reasons to explain the criminality of property offenders.

In 2010, 19-year-old Colton Harris-Moore, of Camano Island, Washington, became something of a folk hero, with an estimated following of 70,000 fans on Facebook and other online social networks. The 6-foot, 5-inch Harris-Moore, otherwise known as the Barefoot Bandit, is suspected of carrying out a crime spree lasting more than 2 years and covering at least eight states, Canada, and the Bahamas (Jabail-Nash,

2010). The crimes of which Harris-Moore is suspected include more than 100 burglaries, auto thefts, the theft of powerboats, and the stealing of at least five airplanes. He earned his nickname by committing some offenses while barefoot and leaving footprints behind. In one crime, the burglary of a grocery store, Harris-Moore is said to have traced his bare feet with chalk on the store's floor.

He was captured by police in the Bahamas after crashing an airplane there and fleeing in a stolen powerboat. The plane had been stolen in Indiana, and officers had to shoot out the boat's engines before they could apprehend the teen. Harris-Moore waived extradition to the United States and was soon taken back to his native Washington to face a number of charges. Shortly after his arrest, one of Harris-Moore's Facebook fans posted: "Dude bummer that u got caught, but u made history and no one will forget that" (ABC News, 2010).

Harris-Moore's first conviction, for stolen property, came when he was only 12 years old. His two-year crime spree began after he climbed out of a window at a juvenile detention facility in Washington state. As this book goes to press, CBS News is reporting that 20th Century Fox film studies is making a movie about the teenager's exploits. How can the popularity of property criminals like Harris-Moore be explained? "One of our national characteristics is rooting for the underdog," says Ralph Himmelsbach, a retired Portland-based FBI agent. "And when people learn that no one gets killed or injured, and the only losses were covered by a major corporation, they feel like, what the heck. Who cares?" (Carlin, 2010).

"... stickups have major elements in common. The first is a radical redefinition of the situation—of who has the power—for everyone concerned, especially if a gun is involved. The second is social exchange—'your money or your life'."
—Elijah Anderson (1999, p. 125)

Property crime is found to a greater or lesser extent across the globe. Larceny is the most common crime reported followed by burglary and then robbery. Strikingly similar rates of robbery are found in cities worldwide. This chapter considers the most prevalent forms of property crime, variations in rates of offending, and characteristics of the offenders and offenses. Attention is also given to the emergence of technologically sophisticated methods for the commission of property offenses and the precipitants of the prevalence and incidence of property crimes.

SSRN

Jakobs, G. (2008). Right deprivation as a crime against property. *InDret, 4*. http://ssrn.com/abstract=1396214

Statutory Definitions

Property crimes involve the "illegal taking or damaging of property, including cash and personal belongings" (Federal Bureau of Investigation [FBI], 2002a, n.p.) from individuals, motor vehicles, residences, and businesses. **Burglary**, **robbery**, and **larceny-theft** are examples of property crimes. **Fraud**, **vandalism**, and **arson** are also considered property crimes.

Rates in the United States

In the United States there are two sources of data on the prevalence of property crimes: the National Crime Victimization Survey (NCVS) and Crime in the United States (fbi.gov, 2008). The NCVS is conducted in 77,200 households across the United States each year. Approximately 134,000 persons over the age of 12 are asked about their criminal victimization. Crime in the United States, published annually by the FBI, is a compilation of data provided by police and sheriff's departments in the United States. Data included in Crime in the United States include the crimes reported to the local law enforcement agencies and found to be valid, arrest rates, and demographic information on persons arrested for major criminal activity. Although the methods of data collection differ, the NCVS and Crime in the United States allow researchers to compare reports of the incidence and prevalence of criminal victimization and offending across the United States.

Figure 11–1 shows a dramatic decline in the rate of property crimes in the United States over the past three decades. Since the turn of the century the property crime victimization rate has fallen about 32%. Nonetheless, the most recent findings of the NCVS indicate that in about 16.3 million households a property crime took place, for a rate of 135 per 1,000 households. However, only 4 in 10 property crimes are reported to the police (NCVS, 2009).

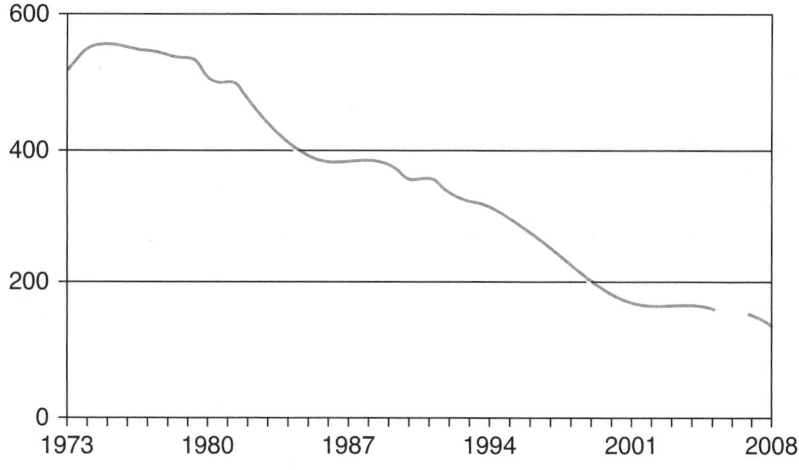

FIGURE 11–1 Property crime victimization rates per 1,000 households, 1973–2008.

Source: Bureau of Justice Statistics, Office of Justice Programs, National Crime Victimization Survey 2009, posted at www.ojp.usdoj.gov; Uniform Crime Report, 2008.

"Burglary is easy, man. I've done about 500 [burglaries] and only been convicted one time."
—Billy, a juvenile burglar, in Cromwell (2004, p. 297)

In 2008, Crime in the United States estimates that 9,767,915 property crimes took place across the country. That is, a property offense occurred every 3.2 seconds, larceny-thefts occur every 4.8 seconds, burglaries every 14.2 seconds, and motor vehicle thefts every 33 seconds. Larceny-theft is the most common form of property crime, accounting for about 68% of all property offenses, burglaries make up about 23%, and motor vehicle theft slightly less than 10% (Crime in the United States, 2008).

Larceny

The NCVS defines theft as a "completed or attempted theft of property or cash without personal contact. Incidents involving theft of property from within the sample household would be classified as theft if the offender has a legal right to be in the house (such as a maid, delivery person, or guest)." Similarly Crime in the United States defines larceny as the "unlawful taking, carrying, leading, or riding away of property from the possession or constructive possession of another" (Crime in the United States, 2008).

Figure 11–2 shows that larceny-theft victimization rates have steadily fallen over the past three decades. The larceny-theft victimization rate has declined by more than one-third in the past 10 years. However, Crime in the United States indicates that about 6.6 million larceny-thefts occurred in the United States in 2008. The largest single category of larceny-thefts

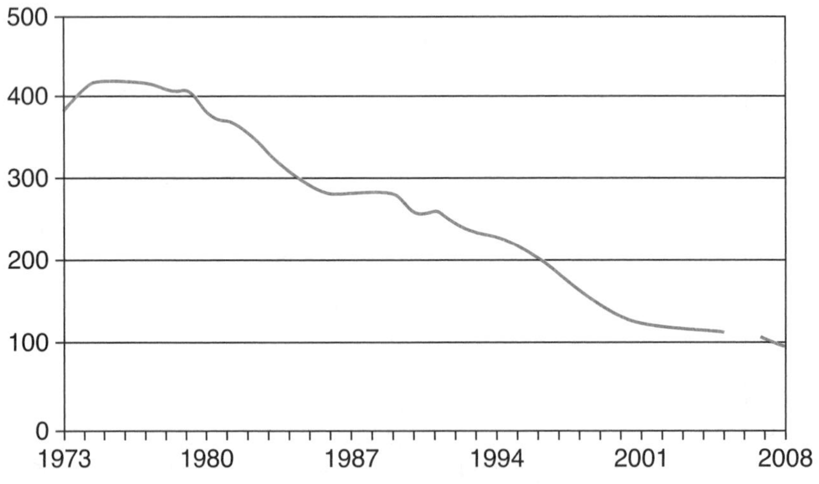

FIGURE 11–2 Theft victimization rates per 1,000 households, 1973–2008.

Source: Crime in the United States. Uniform Crime Report, 2008. Federal Bureau of Investigation. U.S. Department of Justice.

(about 36%) is the stealing of motor vehicle parts, accessories, or property found in the vehicles themselves (Crime in the United States, 2008).

Burglary

Figure 11–3 also shows a steady decline in the burglary victimization rate across the United States over the past three decades. In the past decade the burglary victimization rate has dropped about 23%. The NCVS defines household burglary as "the unlawful or forcible entry or attempted entry of a residence." A household burglary does not need to involve force, nor does it necessarily have to involve theft. In addition, the NCVS includes structures other than a place of residence (e.g., garage, shed, or other building) in its definition of household burglary. Crime in the United States also defines burglary as "the unlawful entry of a structure to commit a felony or theft" (Crime in the United States, 2008). Crime in the United States does not require force to be involved for an offense to be considered a burglary. Crime in the United States distinguishes three types of burglaries: (1) entrance gained by force, (2) unlawful entry without force, and (3) attempted entrance by force. Again, the structure is not limited to a residence but may be a variety of enclosures, including apartments, boats, barns, or offices.

The offense of burglary usually involves theft, whereas illegal entry without force is usually referred as criminal trespass. Most burglaries take place in a residence (slightly more than 7 of 10) and about 61%

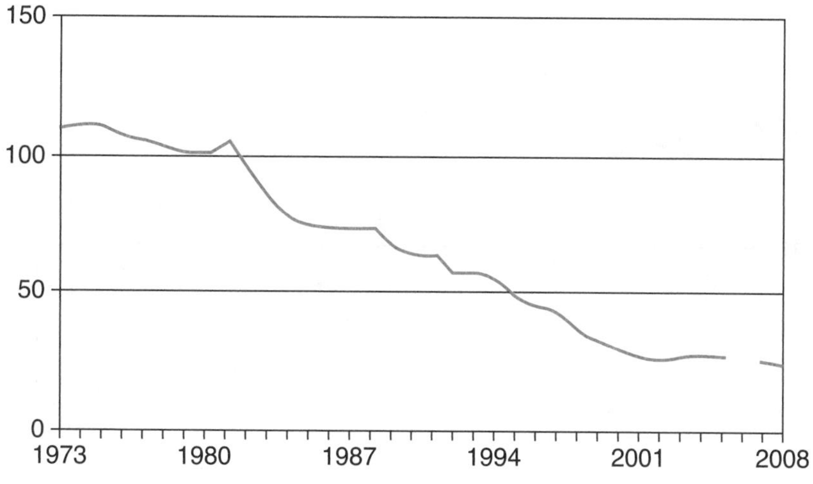

FIGURE 11–3 Burglary victimization rates per 1000 households, 1973–2008.

Source: Crime in the United States. Uniform Crime Report, 2008. Federal Bureau of Investigation. U.S. Department of Justice.

involve forcible entry. Unlawful entries without force make up about 33% of all burglaries and unsuccessful forcible entries about 6%. Burglaries are distinct from robberies, although the terms are often mistakenly interchanged. Homes or businesses are burglarized, whereas people are robbed. A burglary may become a robbery if the offender confronts the homeowners or residents at the time of the burglary. This is termed a **home invasion** or **household robbery.** Burglaries of residences that occur at night are considered more serious and are punished more severely than daytime burglaries because homeowners and residents are usually home during this time (Schmalleger, 2002).

The NCVS defines motor vehicle theft as the "stealing or unauthorized taking of a motor vehicle, an automobile, truck, motorcycle, or any other motorized vehicle legally allowed on public roads and highways. Includes attempted thefts" (NCVS, 2009). Crime in the United States defines motor vehicle theft as the "theft or attempted theft of a motor vehicle" (Crime in the United States, 2008). A motor vehicle is a self-propelled land vehicle that does not run on rails. Crime in the United States estimates that there are about 315 motor vehicle thefts for every 100,000 persons in the United States, or about 957,000 thefts annually. **Figure 11–4** shows that motor vehicle theft has been on the decline over the past decade, falling more than 34%.

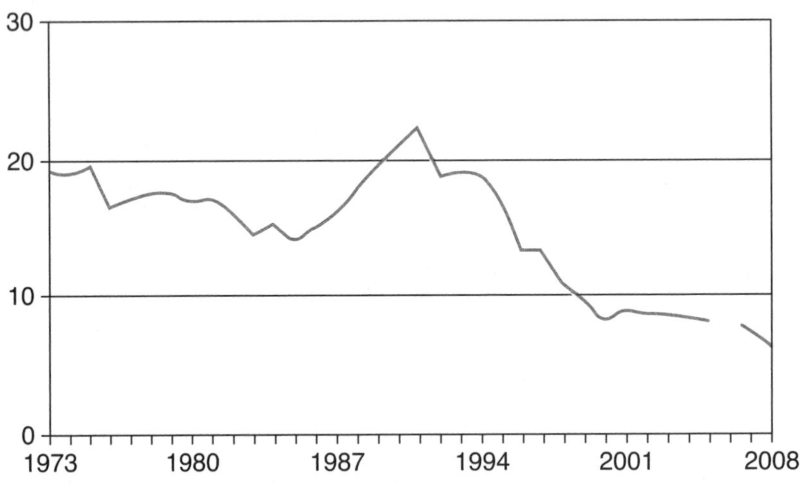

FIGURE 11–4 Motor vehicle theft rates per 1,000 households, 1973–2008.

Source: Crime in the United States. Uniform Crime Report, 2008. Federal Bureau of Investigation. U.S. Department of Justice.

Robbery

Robbery is defined by the NCVS as the "completed or attempted theft, directly from a person, of property or cash by force or threat of force, with or without a weapon, and with or without injury." Similarly, the FBI defines robbery as the "taking or attempting to take anything of value from the care, custody or control of a person or persons by force or the threat of force and/or by violence or by putting the victim in fear" (Crime in the United States, 2008).

The crime of robbery is both a property and violent crime in that it involves direct contact with the victim. Robbery can occur on the street or other outdoor location, take place in a private residence, or happen in a commercial establishment. **Personal crimes** or personal robberies involve specific individuals or occur in personal residences, whereas **institutional robberies** occur in commercial settings (e.g., banks and convenience stores). Robberies take several forms: **highway robbery**, **strong-arm robbery**, and **armed robbery**. Highway robbery, sometimes referred to as a "mugging," occurs in a public place. Strong-arm robbery does not involve the use of a weapon, whereas the brandishing of a weapon is an essential element in the commission of an armed robbery. Robberies and attempted robberies can occur with or without injury to the victim. Almost half of all felony murders, however, occur during the commission of a robbery (Crime in the United States, 2008).

Figure 11–5 shows the rapid fall (more than 39%) in the rate of robbery victimization in the United States over the past decade. However, the FBI's Crime in the United States indicates that in more recent years (2004–2008) the robbery rate has increased about 10% (Crime in the United States, 2008). Crime in the United States estimates that there are about 145 robberies for every 100,000 persons in the United States, or about 442,000 robberies annually.

Figure 11–6 shows that robbery is most common on a street or highway and least likely to occur in a bank, gas or service station, followed by a convenience store. Residences and commercial establishments are similarly likely to be the location of a robbery.

Figure 11–7 shows that the Southern region of the United States has the highest rates of property and violent crime, whereas the New England region has the lowest rates of criminal activity. The Western region has the second highest rates of property and violent crime, followed by the Midwest.

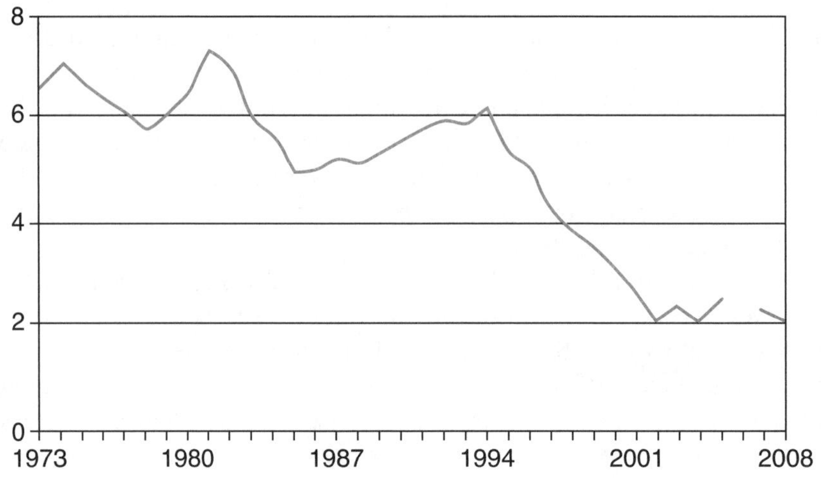

FIGURE 11–5 Robbery victimization rates per 1,000 persons ages 12 and older, 1973–2008.

Source: Crime in the United States. Uniform Crime Report, 2008. Federal Bureau of Investigation. U.S. Department of Justice.

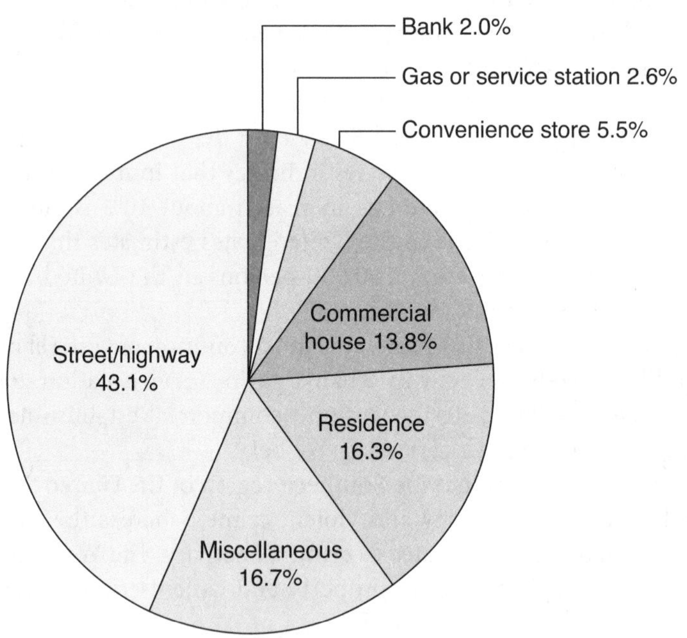

FIGURE 11–6 Robbery locations/distribution by percent, 2008.

Source: Crime in the United States. Uniform Crime Report, 2008. Federal Bureau of Investigation. U.S. Department of Justice.

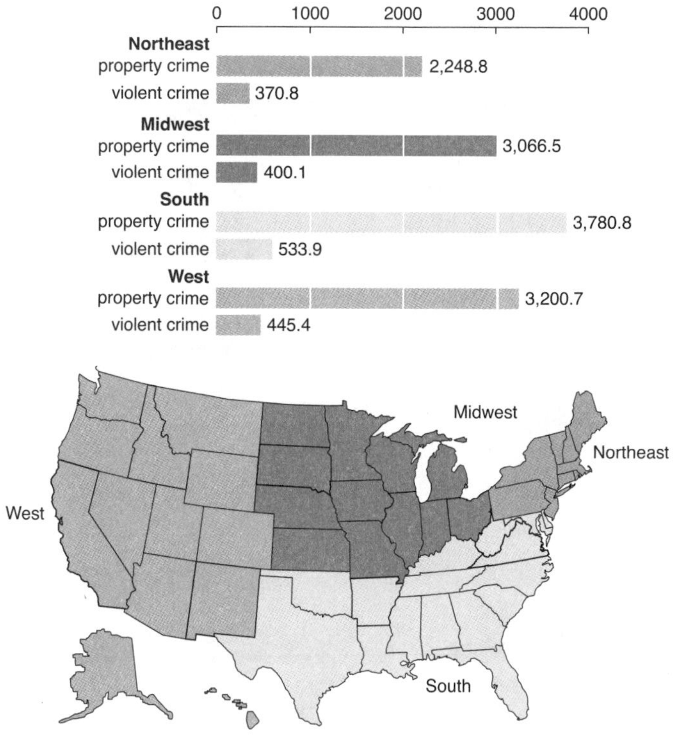

FIGURE 11–7 U.S. regional property and violent crime rates per 100,000, 2008.

Source: Crime in the United States. Uniform Crime Report, 2008. Federal Bureau of Investigation. U.S. Department of Justice.

Property Crimes Around the World

Table 11–1 shows the percentage of the total population victimized by property crime in each country. The property crimes considered in this table are limited to burglary and attempted burglary, car theft, and theft from a car. Although about the average for the countries shown, the United States ranks seventh highest in the percentage of the population victimized by property crime. Japan and Austria rank the lowest, whereas the inhabitants of New Zealand and Australia are particularly vulnerable to property crime.

Property crime, although on the decline in many countries, remains the most prevalent type of criminal activity in the world. Larceny-theft is the most common form of property crime. Theft from cars and bicycle theft are the most prevalent forms of property crime around the world. Rates of property crime are particularly high in Ireland, Iceland, and

TABLE 11–1 Property Crime Victims by Country

Rank	Countries	Population Victimized (%)
1	New Zealand	14.8%
2	Australia	13.9%
3	Italy	12.7%
4	United Kingdom	12.2%
5	Malta	10.9%
6	Canada	10.4%
7	United States	10.0%
8	Poland	9.0%
9	France	8.7%
10	Sweden	8.4%
11	Belgium	7.7%
11	Slovenia	7.7%
13	Denmark	7.6%
13	Saint Kitts and Nevis	7.6%
15	Portugal	7.5%
16	Netherlands	7.4%
17	Switzerland	4.5%
18	Finland	4.4%
19	Japan	3.4%
20	Austria	3.1%
	Weighted average	8.6%

Source: UNICRI (United Nations Interregional Crime and Justice Research Institute). 2002. Correspondence on data on crime victims. March. Turin via NationMaster. http://www.nationmaster.com/red/graph/cri_pro_cri_vic-crime-property-victims. Used with permission of NationMaster.

SSRN

Dalla Pellegrina, L. (April 2006). Crime deterrence and courts efficiency (an application to crimes against property in Italy). http://ssrn.com/abstract=921049

England and Wales and lowest in Japan. Burglary is the next most frequently occurring property offense. England and Wales, New Zealand, Mexico, and Denmark have the highest rates of burglary, whereas Sweden, Spain, Finland, Austria, and Germany have the lowest rates. Robbery is a less frequently occurring property offense but is most common in Mexico and least likely to occur in Japan and Hong Kong (van Dijk et al., 2007).

Victims of Property Crimes

Robbery is the property offense that involves direct contact between the victim and offender. The NCVS (U.S. Department of Justice, 2010) finds that men are victimized at higher rates than women for robbery. For every 1,000 males (aged 12 and older) 3.4 are victims of robbery, more than twice the robbery rate for females (1.4). Black males have the highest rate (7.6), and White females have the lowest rate (1.3). White males and black females are equally likely to be a victim of robbery, with a rate of (2.6) (U.S. Department of Justice, 2010).

Adolescents (persons 19 years of age or younger) have the highest rates of robbery victimization, and senior citizens (those 65 years of age or older) have the lowest rates. The highest rates are experienced by young persons aged 16 to 19 years (6.4 per 1,000) and next by adolescents aged 12 to 15 years (4.2). The risk of robbery victimization declines with age, with the lowest rate (0.6) found among seniors (U.S. Department of Justice, 2010).

Persons of mixed race, Hispanics, and Blacks are disproportionately victimized by property crime in general, larceny-theft, burglary, and motor vehicle theft. The overall rate of property crime among mixed race persons (296.7 per 1,000), Hispanics (190.5), and Blacks (170) is markedly higher than the rates for Whites (141.9) and other races (129.2). Persons of mixed race are also most likely to be the victim of larceny-theft and motor vehicle theft followed by Hispanics and Blacks. Again, persons of mixed race are most likely to experience a burglary, followed by Blacks, and then Hispanics. Whites are consistently the least likely to be the victim of a property crime (U.S. Department of Justice, 2010).

The lower the household income, the more likely the family will experience a property crime. Families with a household income of $7,500 or less have a property crime rate of 213.1, compared with the lowest rate (144.3) found in households with incomes from $50,000 to $74,999. Households with an income of $75,000 or more have a slightly higher rate (146.3) but considerably lower than households with an income of less than $50,000. Put another way, the more affluent the family becomes, the less likely the household will be victimized by a property offender. Not surprisingly, the older the head of household, the less likely the family is to be the victim of a property crime. The highest rate of property crime is found in households headed by persons under the age of 19 (343 per 1,000), compared with the rate for households headed by persons 65 years of age or older (75 per 1,000). There is a consistent decrease in the risk of property crime victimization as the age of the head of household increases (U.S. Department of Justice, 2010).

Costs of Property Crime

The economic cost of property crime in the United States is staggering. A loss of more than $17.2 billion is suffered each year by victims of property crime. Larceny-theft accounts for about two of every three property crimes, resulting in a loss of $6.1 billion, or $925 per offense. The total loss from burglary was $4.6 billion, or $2,079 per offense. Overall, motor vehicle theft represented a loss of $6.4 billion, or an average loss per vehicle of $6,751. It should be noted that 72% of vehicles stolen are automobiles. The monetary loss due to robbery each year is $581 million, and the average value of property taken is $1,315 (Crime in the United States, 2008).

Victim–Offender Relationship

Robbery tends to involve offenders and victims who are male and who are strangers to one another. Males account for 86.3% of offenders, and in about 8 in 10 of all robberies the offenders are strangers to their victims (U.S. Department of Justice, 2010). Males are more apt to be robbed by a stranger (89.2%), whereas 62.4% of females are victimized by someone unknown to them.

Robbery is the crime that is most likely to be interracial, but for the most part offenders victimize members of their own race. Robbery offenders are most apt to be Black (47.8%), followed by White (31.0%) and other races (8.0%) (13.2% are unknown). Intraracial robbery is most common. When a Black person becomes a robbery victim, about 86% of the time the offender is also Black. However, when a White person is robbed, slightly more than 43% of the time the offender is White and about a third of the time the offender is Black. The victimization of a Black person by a White offender is rare.

John Conklin's (1992, p. 37) research on robbery shows the following:

> Because thieves have access to the property of people they know well, they do not need to use force to steal from them. They can simply take the property by stealth in a larceny. In addition, a potential robber's need for cash can be explained to those with whom he or she is close, and so the would-be robber may be given or loaned the necessary money rather than having to steal it. Concern for people whom they know well may lead robbers to think that if they must use force to steal, they might as well use that force against strangers rather than against relatives or friends. Moreover, strangers are less likely to be able to identify them to the police.

When acquaintances are robbed, it is often because the victim is also involved in criminal activity. In an ethnographic study of armed street robbers, Richard T. Wright and Scott H. Decker (1997) find that 6 of 10 robbers target others who are involved in illegal activities. Because the robber's victims are also breaking the law, they are unlikely to report their victimization to the police. A recent study of acquaintance robbery finds that such robberies may be expressions of grievances or revenge, whereas others may involve inside information about what the victim is carrying. Further evidence suggests that although acquaintances can identify their robbers, they are reluctant to report incidents to the police (Felson et al., 2000).

The relationship between larceny victims and offenders usually depends on the nature of the offense. Personal larceny is typically not committed against a person whom the offender knows personally. Because larceny is often a crime of opportunity, offenders and victims are most likely to be strangers. One survey of larceny victims indicates that as many as 9 of 10 personal thefts are committed by strangers (Hindelang, 1976).

Unlike robbery or larceny, burglaries are most often committed by someone known to the victim. About half of all burglary offenders select residences familiar to them but rarely target homes of close friends or relatives (Wright & Decker, 1994). Burglars typically do not need to break in a friend or family member's home to steal property or cash. Would-be burglars, however, are able to familiarize themselves with the daily routines of acquaintances well enough to break and enter successfully.

Two scenarios are common when friends or family members' homes are targets of burglars. The first involves either an alleged wrongdoing on the part of the victim. Revenge, for example, motivates the burglar more than economic gain. The second scenario is played out when the burglar has a desperate need for money (Wright & Decker, 1994). Many burglary offenders repeatedly exploit family and friends by asking for personal loans. When these loans are not repaid, family and friends become less willing to offer assistance. Offenders may then see burglary as a viable option (Shover & Honaker, 1996).

Criminal Decision Making

The decision to commit a crime is influenced by the offender's assessment of risk and perception of available opportunities for its commission. The nature of the offense and its method of execution are also key considerations in the decision to commit a crime. Planning and target selection are essential elements of property crimes. Target selection depends on the type of crime along with attractiveness and opportunity to carry out the crime. The attractiveness of a particular target is influenced by the location of the target and the lifestyle of the victim.

Planning

Robbery is typically a crime of opportunity. As a result, most robberies are carried out with little planning (Feeney, 1986). One study shows that more than 40% of juveniles and 25% of adults who commit robberies do not intend to do so until the opportunity arises (Feeney & Weir, 1974). Robbery is usually committed when the offender has a desperate need for money or is motivated by revenge. Because many robbery offenders are not sure whether to commit a crime until the last minute, robbers use

AT A GLANCE

Global Patterns and Trends

- Rates of property crimes have followed a curvilinear trend over the past two decades worldwide.
- Theft from cars and bicycle theft are the most common forms of property crime, followed by burglary.
- Robbery accounts for a minority of all property crimes reported around the world.
- The prevalence of property crimes and robbery is markedly higher in cities around the world than in less densely populated areas.
- Rates of property crime are found to be particularly high in New Zealand, Australia, Ireland, Iceland, and England and Wales.
- Rates of property crime are reported to be lowest in Japan and Austria.

U.S. Patterns and Trends

- According to Crime in the United States, the rates of larceny, burglary, motor vehicle theft, and robbery continues to decline into the 21st century.
- Property crimes account for about 7 of 10 of all crimes reported to the police.
- Minority persons—mixed race, Hispanics, and Blacks—are disproportionately victimized by property crimes.
- Lower income households fall victim to property crime most frequently.
- Property crimes account for more than $17.2 billion lost annually in the United States.

Sources: Jan van Dijk, van Kesteren, J., and Smit, P. Criminal Victimization in International Perspective. Key Findings from the 2004-2005 The International Crime Victims Survey, The Hague: Ministry of Justice, 2007; Newman, G. (ed.), Global Report on Crime and Justice. New York: Oxford University Press, 1999; U.S. Department of Justice, The National Crime Victimization Survey (NCVS) 2007, Washington, DC: U.S. Department of Justice and Bureau of Justice Statistics, 2010; Federal Bureau of Investigation, Crime in the United States, 2008, Washington, DC: USGPO, 2009.

improvisation skills and communicative signals. Thus, conversations are short and criminal intent is left unspoken. When asked about any conversations before the robbery, one robber replied, "Well, there wasn't much of a conversation to it, really. . . . I asked him if he was ready to go, if he wanted to go do something, you know. And he knew what I meant. He wanted to go make some money somehow, any way it took" (Shover & Honaker, 1996, p. 91). Commercial robbery, however, does involve considerably more planning to be successful (Feeney, 1986).

Unlike robberies, burglaries are usually planned ahead of time, although most are not carefully or extensively planned (Wright & Decker, 1994). In planning, burglars examine building structure and layout for ease of entry and escape. Burglars also check out alarm systems, occupants, and any nearby witnesses, police, or security patrols. Most of the time planning for a burglary is spent in carefully selecting targets (Reppetto, 1974).

Larceny, like robbery, is a crime of opportunity. Amateur shoplifters rarely plan their crimes but decide to act on the spur of the moment. Access to attractive targets, temptations for theft, and the emergence of an opportunity are important considerations in the decision to commit a theft. Professional shoplifters, however, carefully plan their crimes; much thought is given to the goods to be stolen, methods of concealment, and strategies for avoiding apprehension (Cameron, 1964).

Target Selection

An attractive target most often sparks a spontaneous robbery, burglary, or larceny. Selected targets include those that are readily available and easily accessible, along with those that present themselves at ideal times and locations. Thus, situational factors and social circumstances influence the likelihood of becoming a victim of robbery, burglary, or larceny.

Robbers target victims who share common vulnerabilities. Many times robbers assume and accept notions about certain types of individuals based on characteristics and vulnerabilities. Selected targets of personal robberies often include those who carry large amounts of cash. This is the case for many illegal immigrants, Hispanics, and known drug dealers (Wright & Decker, 1997). Illegal immigrants may carry large amounts of cash because many do not have social security numbers and are unable to acquire bank accounts. Because drug dealers are involved in illegal activities, they are attractive targets for robbers. People who frequent automatic teller machines and people who count their money in public are also targeted in many robberies (Shover & Honaker, 1996). Other selected targets include individuals who are unlikely to report robberies to police (Felson et al., 2000). These may include anyone involved in illegal activities or those without the resources, knowledge, or contacts to make such reports. These individuals often live and work in areas with high population densities, high unemployment, and low social cohesion—social conditions that foster robbery (Felson, 1998).

Neighborhood and store characteristics are assessed before carrying out robberies in retail locations. Staffing, store hours, cash handling policy, customer activity, and the presence of security precautions are important considerations for commercial robbers. Commercial robbers most often target liquor stores, taverns, and pawnshops where large amounts of cash are readily available. Older, poor neighborhoods are often targeted repeatedly for robbery because stores in these areas cannot afford the necessary security precautions to deter crime (Hendricks et al., 1999).

Seasonal variations show that robbery is distinctly higher in the winter than in the summer. The number of dark hours during the day in winter and mass shopping during the holiday season provide greater opportunities for robbery and a greater need for money among potential robbers. For example, winter robberies are most frequent in the month of December (van Koppen & Jansen, 1999).

Attractive targets for burglary include homes with single-adult occupants and those that have younger heads of households (Sampson & Wooldredge, 1997). These residences often lack the necessary security systems and therefore make attractive targets. Areas characterized by low population density are also frequent targets for burglars. Houses located in low density areas have more space between them; more trees, bushes, gardens, and large yards; and numerous points of entry that make it easy for burglars to enter and escape a residence without detection (Felson, 1998).

Burglars select residences or retail locations based on their knowledge of the occupants and thorough observation of potential targets (Wright & Decker, 1994). Research on criminal decision making finds that occupancy and surveillance are the biggest deterrents against entering a property. Alarms and dogs are effective security deterrents for private homes (Association of British Insurers, 1999).

Because burglars want to avoid contact with household occupants, business owners, and witnesses, more residences are burglarized during the day when occupants are usually out of the home; retail locations, however, are more often burglarized at night. Burglaries are thought to be more frequent during the summer months and during good weather when most people are out of their homes. Vacations and outdoor activities result in homes left unguarded for extended periods of time (U.S. Department of Justice, 2000).

Victims of personal theft are less likely to be older, married men, whereas women and individuals with higher socioeconomic status are more often selected as potential targets (Sampson & Wooldredge, 1997). High levels of street activity and high population density along with high levels of family disruption and low social cohesion create higher victimization risks for personal and motor vehicle theft (Felson, 1998).

Shoplifters select targets based on a variety of factors, including the location of the store, security precautions, the ease of picking up merchandise, and their ability to exit the store (Weiner, 1970). For example, a study of middle-class shoplifters shows that these shoplifters select stores in areas where lower class people shop. One shoplifter explains that "store detectives and clerks pay little attention to clean, neat, well-mannered people downtown because they are so concerned with trouble from poorer, more suspicious-looking shoppers" (Weiner, 1970, p. 217).

A man steals a purse from a parked car. Why are thefts of items from automobiles so common?

Types of Thieves

Offenders vary by their level of professionalism, their specializations, and the frequency with which they commit crimes. Three broad categories of property crime offenders are widely accepted and are most often classified as professional, persistent, or occasional thieves.

Professional, Persistent, and Occasional Thieves

Edwin Sutherland's (1956) classic study of **professional thieves** defines this type of offender as one who makes a regular business of stealing. Professional thieves differ from other thieves in their careful planning and knowledge of technical skills and methods. These offenders move from locale to locale in their criminal pursuits to avoid capture and to select targets with large payoffs. Neil Shover (1996) adds that professional criminals spend long periods of their lives in criminal pursuits, although they spend little time incarcerated. **Persistent thieves**, on the other hand, commit a variety of property offenses without specializing to any significant degree. Unlike professionals, persistent thieves are less successful despite their persistence. John R. Hepburn (1984) and others (Wright & Decker, 1994) offer another category of property criminals—**occasional thieves**. These offenders are defined by the nature and character of their offenses rather than their frequency of offending. Occasional thieves commit crimes in favorable situations, that is, when the opportunity for theft, burglary, or robbery arises. The crimes "occur on those occasions in which there is an opportunity or situational inducement to commit the crime" (Hepburn, 1984, p. 76). Their crimes do not involve planning, do not involve prior experience or skills, and usually are committed by a lone offender.

Gibbons (1968) offers an additional typology of property crime offenders that ranges from the most professional to the unprofessional. Gibbons' status hierarchy of offenders includes (1) professional heavies, (2) professionals, (3) semiprofessionals, and (4) amateurs. Professional heavies are considered experts at large-scale burglary and robbery operations. Heavies usually work in groups, each member exhibiting specialized, technical skills of their trade. The group consists of highly successful professional criminals. One level down from the heavies is the professional. These offenders fall into property crime as a way of life but seldom obtain the large amounts of money from their crimes, as do the heavies. Semiprofessionals are persistent property offenders who possess few skills and rarely plan their crimes. These offenders may view themselves as professionals, but because they lack criminal knowledge and skills they are more often arrested and incarcerated. Amateur property offenders commit a variety of offenses but do not possess the same level of criminal skills as do other groups of offenders. These offenders usually hold conventional jobs, typically do not have a criminal record, and rarely define themselves as criminals.

SSRN

Bjerk, D. (2008). Thieves, thugs, and neighborhood poverty. Robert Day School of Economics and Finance Research Paper No. 2008-17. http://ssrn.com/abstract=1288896

Robbers

Based on interviews with 67 convicted robbers, Conklin (1972) offers a fourfold typology of robbery offenders: (1) professionals, (2) opportunists, (3) addicts, and (4) alcoholics. Professional robbers are committed to crime as a source of livelihood and obtain a major portion of their income from illegal activities. As a result, professional robbers select targets based on the likelihood of a high monetary return. Professional robbers usually plan and organize their crimes before committing them and often work in loosely organized groups. Members of the group maintain different roles for carrying out the robbery. The "wheel man" may steal a car, map out an escape route, or drive to and from the robbery site. The wheel man or another member of the group may act as the "lookout" or the "peek man." On occasion members of the group are hired to help with the robbery for a set percentage of the profits, usually 10%. These members, referred to as "10 percenters," often later become full-time members of the robbery group.

Opportunist, addict, and alcoholic robbers do not plan robberies and are not committed to a career of robbery. Rather, they prey on readily available targets usually when the need for money arises. Opportunists typically obtain less than $20 in each robbery. Addict robbers commit robberies to support a drug habit or while under the influence of drugs. Addicts would rather commit burglaries or thefts but resort to robbery when they become financially desperate. Alcoholic robbers typically commit robberies after an unrelated assault precipitated by excessive drinking. Intoxicated robbery offenders are motivated less by monetary gain than by their need to aggress against any available person, often with little or no provocation.

Burglars

Michael Maguire (1982) offers a basic typology of burglary types that includes (1) low-level burglars, (2) middle-range burglars, and (3) high-

An armed robbery in progress. What types of robbers does this book identify?

level burglars. Low-level burglars, typically juveniles, work in unsophisticated groups and commit burglaries based on opportunity and attractive targets. Security devices such as alarms and locks are often deterrents for these types of burglars. Typically, the property or monetary value of the items stolen is insignificant. Low-level burglars tend to grow out of their criminal pursuits as they get older and therefore do not depend on burglary for a livelihood. Middle-range burglars are generally older than low-level burglars and are often involved with alcohol and drugs. Quite often these offenders fluctuate between legitimate work and criminal pursuits. Because these offenders select targets based on their anticipation of a significant payoff, they are not as easily deterred by security precautions. In some cases middle-range burglars make out with substantial amounts of property and cash. These offenders, however, lack the necessary connections of the high-level, more professional burglars. High-level burglars work in professionally organized groups of thieves and possess sophisticated breaking and entering skills and knowledge about potential targets. As a result, these offenders are able to carefully select targets and plan their crimes. High-level burglary groups carry out well-researched, highly organized, large-scale thefts involving substantial profits.

Car Thieves

Cars are stolen for a variety of reasons—for joyriding, for parts and other types of profit, or during the commission of a crime. Car thieves specialize in stealing and stripping cars for parts and profit. The most common types of parts stolen are stereo equipment and external parts such as tires, wheels, antennas, windshield wipers, luggage racks, and mirrors (Sallybanks & Thomas, 2000). **Jockeys** steal cars regularly on a "steal to order basis" (Trembley et al., 1994). These professional car thieves work in groups, making up vast networks of stolen car dealers. Specific types of cars are targeted, and a great deal of planning goes into these thefts.

Professionals steal cars for parts and for profit, whereas amateur thieves are likely to be **joyriders.** Joyriders, typically teenagers, take cars without the owners' consent as the opportunity arises, but they do not intend to keep them. Rather, the need for excitement motivates the typical joyrider. Unlocked cars and easily accessible car keys present attractive targets. Often, juveniles steal cars for joyriding from someone they know (Clarke & Harris, 1992; Meithe & McCorkle, 1998).

Shoplifters

Shoplifters comprise a heterogeneous group of property offenders. Professionals and amateurs, the young and senior citizens, the poor and the well-to-do engage in shoplifting. Typologies categorize shoplifters based on motivations and demographic characteristics, prior offending, psychological factors, and measures of life purpose (Cameron, 1964; Kivivuouri, 1998; Klemke, 1992; McShane & Noonan, 1993; Moore, 1984).

Mary Owen Cameron (1964) offers the most well-known typology of shoplifters. She identifies professional and novice shoplifters as boosters and snitches. **Boosters,** a small percentage of all shoplifters, are professionals who steal store items and later sell them for profit. **Snitches,** or amateur shoplifters, make up a large percentage of all shoplifters. They steal primarily for personal reasons, most often because of a lack of money or simply for excitement. Many amateur shoplifters are adolescents who engage in shoplifting for a certain amount of time and then cease shoplifting all together (Kivivuouri, 1998).

Often, shoplifters are able to afford the items they steal, but the thrill and excitement of shoplifting motivates their behavior. Stolen items are typically of little monetary value: They are often discarded or never used by amateur shoplifters (Katz, 1988).

In a study of convicted shoplifters, Richard H. Moore (1984) identifies five types of offenders: impulsive, occasional, episodic, amateur, and semiprofessional. Impulsive shoplifters are inexperienced offenders who rarely plan their thefts. Occasional shoplifters offend more frequently than the impulsive group and usually do so for the approval of their peers. Episodic shoplifters, a small percentage of offenders, are typically beset by emotional distress. Amateur shoplifters offend on a fairly regular basis with a maximum profit and minimal risk. Semiprofessional shoplifters are highly skilled thieves who target expensive items, later to be sold to a fence—a buyer of stolen goods.

Theoretical Explanations

Various theoretical formulations are applicable to the understanding of the incidence and prevalence of property crime. Macro-level theories—social integration, social disorganization, culture, conflict, and economic inequalities—provide an explanation of the rates of various forms of property crime (**Table 11-2**). Micro-level theories—social learning, rational choice, routine activities, and others—focus on precipitants of an individual's involvement in property crime and why certain persons, places of residence, and business locations are more likely to become victims of robbery, burglary, larceny, and other types of property crimes (**Table 11–3**).

TABLE 11–2 **Explanations of Rates of Property Crime**

Theories and Theorists	Sociological Predictors	Hypotheses
Integration		
Merton	Anomie	The greater the anomie, the greater the likelihood of property crimes.
Social Disorganization		
Shaw and McKay	Social disorganization	The greater the social disorganization, the higher the rates of property crimes.
Opportunity and Subculture		
Miller	Focal concerns	The greater the acceptance of the focal concerns, the greater the probability of property crimes.
Cloward and Ohlin	Opportunity	The more a subculture advocates the commission of property crime and provides opportunities for its commission, the higher the rate of property crime.
Cohen	Status frustration and reaction formation	The greater the status frustration of lower-class youth, the greater the likelihood they will react against middle-class values. The greater the reaction of lower-class youth against middle-class values, the greater probability of involvement in property crime.
Conflict		
Thio	Status/power groups	Higher-status, more powerful groups are more likely to commit lower-consensus deviance (e.g., white-collar crimes), whereas lower-status, less powerful groups are more likely to commit higher-consensus crimes (e.g., robbery, burglary, and larceny).
Sellin	Primary culture conflict Secondary culture conflict	The higher the ratio of primary culture conflict to secondary culture conflict, the greater the rate of individual property offending (e.g., robbery, burglary, and larceny).
Quinney	Power groups	The more powerful groups define the behavior of the less powerful groups as criminal, the greater the perceived need to control the behavior of the powerless. The greater the perceived need by the powerful to control the behavior of the powerless, the higher the rate of property crime.

TABLE 11–3 Explanations of Individual Property Crime

Theories and Sociological Theorists	Predictors	Hypotheses
Social Bonding and Control		
Hirschi	Attachment	The weaker the attachment to conventional society, the more likely the individual will commit property crimes.
	Commitment	The weaker the commitment to conventional society, the more likely the individual will commit property crimes.
	Involvement	The greater the involvement in conventional activities, the less likely the individual will commit property crimes.
	Belief	The stronger the belief in conventional values and norms, the less likely the person will commit property crimes.
Social Learning		
Sutherland	Differential association	The greater the exposure to definitions favorable toward property crime, the greater the probability of engaging in property offending.
Rational Choice		
Clarke and Cornish	Cost-to-benefit analysis	The greater the benefit associated with property crime, the more likely the individual will commit the offense.
Techniques of Neutralization		
Sykes and Matza	Denial of responsibility, denial of injury, denial of a victim, condemnation of condemners, appeal to higher loyalties	Individuals are more likely to commit property crimes when they neutralize, rationalize, or provide excuses for having committed these offenses.
Routine Activities		
Cohen and Felson	Suitable targets Motivated offenders Guardians	The presence of a suitable target, a motivated offender, and the lack of capable guardians increases the probability of committing a property crime.
Seductions of Crime		
Katz	Sneaky thrills	The greater the need for excitement or sneaky thrills, the greater the likelihood of engaging in property offending.

Explanations of Rates of Property Crime

Robert Merton's (1968) macro-level formulation of social integration and anomie adds to the explanation of property crime rates among lower-class offenders. According to Merton, high levels of anomie and low social integration are a part of lower-class neighborhoods. Members of these neighborhoods internalize and accept culturally approved goals for success but lack the means to achieve such goals. As a result, some members reject the culturally defined goals and/or means and engage in a variety of forms of property crimes throughout their lives. Rates of property crime in these areas are therefore expected to be fairly high.

In studying crime and urban growth, Shaw and McKay (1969) find that rates of crime are higher in large urban areas; rates decline with movement away from inner city areas. Crime in urban areas is correlated with a number of economic characteristics and social conditions. To Shaw and McKay, social disorganization characterizes areas marked by group conflict, strain, and failure to achieve culturally defined success goals. Instabilities and social pathologies in neighborhoods and families foster conflicting moral and value systems, thus leading to criminal lifestyles that may be transmitted from one generation to another.

In a similar vein, the theorizing of Walter Miller (1958), Cloward and Ohlin (1960), and Albert Cohen (1955) supports and extends the social disorganization perspective. Specifically, Miller's lower-class subculture formulation examines everyday "focal concerns" of lower-class culture. To Miller, lower-class focal concerns—trouble, toughness, "street smarts," belief in fate, and the need for personal autonomy—give rise to involvement in property offending as well as other forms of criminal and deviant activity. Cohen's concepts of status frustration and reaction formation provide an understanding of lower-class property crime. Frustrated by their inability to perform well in school—a middle-class oriented institution—lower-class boys react by adopting values that are diametrically opposed to those espoused by conventional society. Theft and destruction of property are common acts of revenge engaged in by frustrated lower-class adolescents. Cloward and Ohlin's opportunity structure explains how criminal subcultures recruit and train select individuals for lives of theft.

While higher-status persons do steal, most everyday theft occurs in lower-class neighborhoods and subcultures. Conflict theories of Alex Thio (1978), Richard Quinney (1970), and Thorsten Sellin (1938) are therefore applicable in the explanation of property crime rates. Thio's power theory provides the framework for these types of theories. He asserts that higher-status, more powerful groups define, apprehend, try, and punish lower-class individuals for property violations. At the same time, higher-status groups commit white-collar, corporate, and government crimes without the social stigma or punishment. Sellin reasons that everyday theft is viewed differently across social classes. Although lower-class groups engage in property thefts for a variety of subcultural reasons, higher-class groups consider this behavior as deviant and in need of social control. Quinney adds that powerful groups, particularly those in capitalistic societies, cause the powerless to take on criminal roles and then punish them for their actions in an effort to maintain power and control in business, government, and other societal organizations. Crimes of higher-status groups are aimed at increasing and maintaining power.

Explanations of Individual Property Crime

Several micro-level theories explain why offenders commit property crimes. Offenders may hold values that are favorable to committing property crime or they may rationally choose if, when, and where they will commit an offense. Other theorists propose that offenders are seduced by crime and criminal lifestyles. A few theories also explain why certain individuals become victims of robbery, burglary, and theft.

Travis Hirschi's (1969) social bond theory holds that individuals who endorse the norms of conventional society are less likely to engage in property offenses. Individuals often engage in robbery, burglary, and theft because of weak attachments to conventional groups. Attachment to unconventional groups that support property crimes encourages individuals to engage in these activities as well. Edwin Sutherland's (1947) differential association explains how individuals who are exposed to behavioral definitions that favor involvement in property crime are likely to commit these types of offenses.

Property crime offenders may rationally choose to commit robbery, burglary, or theft (Cornish & Clarke, 1986). In doing so, the consequences of committing crime are weighed against the anticipated rewards gained from its commission. If the benefits associated with a particular property crime outweigh the costs or risks, an individual is more likely to carry out that crime. New avenues of research on property crime indicate that the cost-to-benefit analysis used by offenders is complicated by factors associated with self-indulged needs and wants, status, and "a party lifestyle" (Shover & Honaker, 1996).

Techniques of neutralization, identified by Sykes and Matza (1957), are ways in which property offenders rationalize their decision to commit robbery, burglary, or theft. Neutralizations also give insight as to why certain victims are targets of thieves. Burglars may rationalize their crime by convincing themselves that the victim's insurance will cover the cost of the stolen items. Robbers may claim that because they do not use a weapon no one is actually injured. Offenders may also blame forces beyond their control for their actions or adhere to a "quasi–Robin Hood" mentality to steal from the rich. Thieves rationalize thefts from large corporations or wealthy individuals by denying injury or victimization or by claiming that the corporations or individuals are engaging in illegal activities as well.

Cohen and Felson's (1979) formulation of routine activities is appropriate for the explanation of how offenders decide to commit property crimes and how individuals become victims of such crimes. Routine activities theory contends that crime is more likely when three conditions are present: a suitable target, a motivated offender, and a lack of guardianship (i.e., someone capable of preventing the crime). Unless all conditions are met, crime is less likely to occur.

In *Seductions of Crime,* Jack Katz (1988) argues that property crimes—shoplifting, vandalism, youthful burglaries, and joyriding—are committed because of a desire for excitement or a "sneaky thrill." His theory adds to the understanding of why members of the upper and middle classes commit property crimes. Many times these offenders can afford the items they steal and may not actually need the pilfered goods. Only occasionally are these items used. Rather, they act as souvenirs, reminders of the thrill of committing the crime. In the case of shoplifting, Katz argues that the desire for an object does not lead to the crime, but the crime itself makes the object desirable.

Chapter Summary

Property crimes involve the illegal taking of property, either cash or property, from individuals or places without the consent of the owner. Burglary, robbery, and larceny-theft are examples of property crimes. Robbery is also considered a crime against persons. The use of physical force or threat distinguishes robberies from larcenies and burglaries.

Larceny is the most common type of property crime. Burglary is the next most common type, and robbery accounts for a small percentage of all crime.

Burglars, robbers, and other thieves differ in their professionalism, sophistication, and criminal decision making. Burglars usually plan their crimes, whereas robbers and other thieves act spontaneously in response to opportunity and attractive targets. Professional thieves as opposed to persistent or occasional thieves make a living from crime. They often work in specialized groups whose members have technical skills and perform specific jobs.

Key Concepts

Property crimes: The illegal taking or damaging of property.

Burglary: The unlawful or forcible entry or attempted entry of a structure with the intent to commit an offense therein.

Robbery: Taking of property or cash directly from a person by force or theft of force.

Larceny-theft: Attempted theft of property or cash without using force or illegal entry.

Fraud: Theft or attempted theft of property or cash in which deception is a major component; does not involve the actual taking of property or money directly from the victim.

Vandalism: Unlawful destruction of property without the consent of the owner.

Arson: Any willful or malicious burning or attempt to burn, with or without intent to defraud the personal property of another.

Home invasion (household robbery): A burglary in which the offender confronts the homeowner or residents at the time of the burglary.

Personal crimes: Robberies that involve specific individuals or occur in personal residences.

Institutional robberies: Robberies that occur in commercial settings such as banks or convenience stores.

Highway robbery: A robbery that takes place in a public place.

Strong-arm robbery: A robbery in which a weapon is not used in the commission of the crime.

Armed robbery: A robbery in which a weapon is used in the commission of the crime.

Professional thieves: Offenders who make a regular business of stealing and who carefully plan and possess special knowledge, technical skills, and methods.

Persistent thieves: Offenders who commit a variety of property crime offenses without specializing to any significant degree.

Occasional thieves: Offenders who commit property crimes when the opportunity arises.

Jockeys: Offenders who steal cars on a steal-to-order basis and/or sell cars or car parts for profit.

Joyriders: Offenders who take cars without the owners' consent but do not intend to keep them; theft satisfies a need for excitement.

Boosters: Professional shoplifters who steal items to later sell for profit.

Snitches: Amateur shoplifters who steal primarily for personal reasons, because of a lack of money, or for excitement.

Critical Thinking Questions

1. Which sociocultural and social psychological factors differentiate the occasional, opportunistic property offender from the career or professional property offender who depends on criminal activity for his or her livelihood?
2. Are property crimes precipitated by the general level of poverty in a given society or the consequence of relative deprivation? Are there other explanations that account for property offending specifically?

3. How do the processes of globalization influence the incidence and rate of property offending across the world? How will globalization affect countries with historically low rates of property crime compared with those with consistently higher rates of property offending?
4. Which sociocultural and situational factors account for the incidence and prevalence of property crimes that involve the use of violence compared with those property offenses in which the offender does not confront the victim directly?

Web Extra

Web-based media materials from high-quality sources such as CNN, Time, and National Public Radio are available in support of this textbook. Visit go.jblearning.com/deviance to access them.

Check out these websites for additional information on property crime:

http://www.ojp.usdoj.gov/bjs

http://www.fbi.gov

http://www.ncjrs.org

White-Collar and Organized Crime

CHAPTER 12

Learning Objectives

After reading this chapter you should know

- The nature, definitions, and extent of white-collar, corporate, and government crime.
- Some theoretical explanations for white-collar and organized crime.

In 2009, 71-year-old Bernard (Bernie) Madoff, a formerly wealthy investment counselor, was convicted of multiple fraud and securities violations and sentenced to serve 150 years in prison. For 20 years preceding his conviction, Madoff had fooled thousands of investors into entrusting him with billions of their dollars. In typical Ponzi scheme fashion, Madoff used recently invested money to convince earlier investors that his business was solid. Among his victims were some very wealthy people from places as diverse as New York City and Palm Beach, Florida (*Time*, 2009). Some estimates put investor losses from Madoff's fraudulent activities as high as $65 billion. Madoff's scheme has been called "the largest investor fraud ever committed by a single person" (*New York Post*, 2009).

White-collar and organized criminal activities are special cases of offending largely for monetary gain. To the extent that both forms of deviance are similarly motivated, they may be considered

"Drug trafficking in the late twentieth century will be remembered as the primary catalyst for the internationalization of organized crime."
—Albanese et al. (2003, p. 439)

together. Both white-collar and organized crime may involve a network of offenders working in concert or, on occasion, an offender acting alone. White-collar offenses may be committed to enhance the interests of an organization—usually a corporation or government agency—but may also be motivated by the prospect of personal gain by the offender. Typically, organized crime is primarily intended to enhance the interests of the controlling members of the crime group or network but may directly benefit individual members of the organization.

This chapter considers the various forms that white-collar crime may take within legitimate organizations, most often corporations and government agencies. The operation of illegitimate criminal organizations in the United States and around the world is reviewed.

SSRN

Tomasic, R. A. (2005). From white collar to corporate crime and beyond: The limits of law and theory. In D. Chappell & P Wilson (Eds.), *Issues in Australian crime and criminal justice* (pp. 252–267). LexisNexis Butterworths. http://ssrn.com/abstract=1433437

White-Collar, Corporate, and Government Crime

The term "white-collar crime" originated in 1939 when Edwin Sutherland first defined it in his American Sociological Society presidential address. According to Sutherland (2002, p. 67) white-collar crimes are crimes "committed by a person of respectability and high social status in the course of his occupation." Sutherland's (2002, p. 67) definition specifically excludes "murder, intoxication, or adultery, since these are not a part of the occupational procedures" as well as similar types of crimes committed by those who lack respectability and high social status.

Because crime was largely seen as a phenomenon of the lower classes, Sutherland's concept of white-collar crime created considerable controversy. Since this time, however, new forms of crime have prompted researchers to reexamine the nature of white-collar crime. As a result, the definition of white-collar crime has evolved and expanded to include new forms of crime and a variety of offender types (Coleman, 2002).

SSRN

Moohr, G. S. (2009). An Enron lesson: The modest role of criminal law in preventing corporate crime. *Florida Law Review, 55*(4). University of Houston Law Center No. 2009-A-3. http://ssrn.com/abstract=1323917

Definitions and Forms of White-Collar Crime

A half century ago Herbert Edelhertz (1970, p. 3), a former prosecutor with the U.S. Department of Justice, proposed an alternative definition of white-collar crime as "an illegal act or series of illegal acts committed by nonphysical means and by concealment or guile to obtain money or property, to avoid the payment of loss of money or property, or to obtain business or personal advantage." The definition Edelhertz offered does not require a white-collar offender to be of high social status; instead, it focuses on the nature of the crime committed and on the way in which it is carried out.

SSRN

Russell, S. From the red core to the black sky: Corporate crime in the transnational matrix. http://ssrn.com/abstract=872326

Later, David Simon (1996) proposed another term—**elite deviance**—to further describe white-collar crime. According to Simon and others, forms of elite deviance share common characteristics. In defining elite deviance, Simon (1996, p. 11) offers the following common characteristics:

- The acts are committed by persons from the highest strata of society: members of the upper and upper-middle classes.
- Some of the acts are crimes in that they violate criminal statues and carry penalties such as fines and imprisonment. Other acts violate administrative or civil laws, which may also involve punishment. Other acts, although not illegal, are regarded by most Americans as unethical or immoral (i.e., deviant). Thus, elite deviance may be either criminal or noncriminal in nature.
- Some of the actions are committed by elites themselves for personal gain, or they were committed by the elites or their employees for purposes of enhancing the power, profitability, or influence of the organizations involved.
- The acts are committed with relatively little risk. When and if the elites are apprehended, the punishments inflicted were in general quite lenient, compared with those given common criminals.
- Some of the incidents pose great danger to the public's safety, health, and financial well-being.
- In many cases the elites in charge of the organization are able to conceal their illegal or unethical actions for years before they become public knowledge.

Former Enron Corp. Chairman Kenneth Lay being sworn in before a congressional hearing in 2002. Lay refused to answer questions from lawmakers about his role in the collapse of the former energy giant, but was eventually found guilty on six counts of conspiracy and securities fraud in 2006. He died suddenly before sentencing. What are the most significant differences between white collar and street crime?

Marshall Clinard and Richard Quinney (1980) suggested several other ideas (referred to by others as subtypes of white-collar crime) to describe the complex nature and forms of white-collar crime. **Table 12–1** presents definitions of white-collar crime and some specific examples of these offenses. **Organizational** or **business crimes** generally are "committed by an organization in the course of its regular business" (Clinard & Meier, 1998, p. 198).

TABLE 12–1 **White-Collar Crime**

	Definition	Offenses
Occupational	A violation of trust by an employee, usually for personal financial gain.	Employee theft Embezzlement Insider trading Fraud
Corporate	Offenses committed primarily to enhance the financial and competitive interests of the corporation.	False advertising Consumer fraud Anti-trust violations Price fixing Environmental crimes
Government	Illegal activities engaged in by agents of the government to protect or advance the political position of an administration, regime, or ruling party.	Abuse of power Bribery/corruption Concealing illegal activity

A similar form of white-collar crime is corporate crime. **Corporate crime** involves any illicit activity by members of the organization to advance its interests. In short, the business rather than the individual benefits when corporate crime occurs. The term "**occupational crime**" is applied only to crimes committed by individuals in the context of the offenders' job duties. These offenders act solely in their own personal interest and typically do not benefit their employers.

Law professor J. Kelly Strader (2002) distinguishes white-collar crime from other forms of criminal activity, or what he calls "street" crime. To Strader, white-collar crime is different from street crime because it does **not**

- Necessarily involve force against a person or property
- Directly relate to the possession, sale, or distribution of narcotics
- Directly relate to organized crime activities
- Directly relate to such national policies as immigration, civil rights, and national security
- Directly involve "vice crimes" or the common theft of property.

Government crimes are not unlike the types of white-collar offenses previously described. Public officials and other government employees, however, carry out these offenses. Alex Thio (1978) cites three motives for governmental criminal activity: (1) monetary gain, (2) the acquisition of power, or (3) condescending attitudes of government officials toward the public. Public officials and political candidates may accept illegal campaign contributions, embezzle government money, misuse taxpayer money, or further abuse power through criminal actions or discrimination.

Gary S. Green (1990) expands the idea of occupational crime by identifying four emergent categories. His typology of occupational offenses and offenders is as follows:

- **Organizational occupational crime**: Crimes committed for the benefit of an employing organization. In such instances only the organization or the employer benefits, not individual employees.
- **State authority occupational crime**: Crimes by officials through the exercise of their state-based authority. Such crime is occupation specific and can only be committed by officials in public office or by those working for them.
- **Professional occupational crime**: Crimes by professionals in their capacity as professionals. The crimes of physicians, attorneys, psychologists, and the like are included here.
- **Individual occupational crime**: Crimes by individuals as individuals. This is a kind of catchall category that includes personal income tax evasion, the theft of goods and services by employees, the filing of false expense reports, and the like.

Engaging in fraudulent activities is one of the major types of white-collar crime. Defrauding banks, insurance companies, and investment/securities schemes are examples of fraudulent crimes. False information is presented to gain a financial profit from the target (e.g., a bank, insurance company) or to dupe a potential investor by misrepresenting the risks involved and the profits to be gained from the investment. Computer fraud and credit card fraud are also common forms of fraudulent criminal activity. Computer hackers steal identifying information to gain access typically to bank or credit card accounts and pose as its rightful owner.

Ponzi schemes, like the one described at the start of this chapter, rank among the most lucrative fraudulent crimes. Ponzi schemes involve an investor who is convinced that in a short time his or her investment will yield a very high return. Funds are given to the organizer of the Ponzi but are never invested. Rather, the unusually high dividends paid to the new investor come from funds received from other investors. The new investor recommends that others quickly invest their money with the same broker. Large dividends are a sure thing. The Ponzi scheme crashes when there are not enough "new" investors to generate the funds needed to keep the scheme going or when the organizer of the Ponzi leaves with all the funds.

Extent of White-Collar Crime

The extent of white-collar crime around the world and in the United States can only be estimated. The Federal Bureau of Investigation recently released *The Measurement of White Collar Crime* (2002b). Using the Uniform Crime Reporting Data, the Federal Bureau of Investigation estimates that white-collar crimes—that is, five types of fraud, bribery, counterfeiting/forgery, embezzlement, and other offenses—account for 4% of crime reported. Corporate, government, and other types of white-collar crime are largely undetected. Furthermore, such crimes are often unknown to the public. According to James William Coleman (2002, p. 7), "One of the most basic difficulties in measuring white-collar crime is that the victims often do not realize they have been victimized."

Of the crimes that are known, the consequences are devastating, with financial costs in the hundreds of billions of dollars. The estimated annual loss from fraud is $994 billion, or 7% of the revenues of U.S. organizations (Association of Certified Fraud Examiners, *Report to the Nation*, 2008). One in four organizations incurs a loss of $1 million due to occupational fraud. The offenders typically are college-educated White men, with the criminal activity of managers costing about four times more than that of employees. Three main forms of fraud and abuse

Common Characteristics of Organized Crime Around the World

Jay S. Albanese and Dilip K. Das outline five commonalities of organized crime around the world:

1. Criminal activities are conducted in a *planned* manner for the purpose of profit.
2. There is a *continuing enterprise* or conspiracy that is based on a preexisting social, ethical, or business relationship or around a particular illegitimate product or opportunity.
3. *Intimidation, threats, and sometimes violence* are used to obtain access to the illicit opportunity and to maintain it from competing criminal groups.
4. *Corruption* (bribery and extortion) is often used to maintain a degree of immunity from government interference (law enforcement and prosecution).
5. Organized crime groups show tremendous *adaptability* in responding to changes in supply, demand, law enforcement, and competition. They sometimes move geographically, shift to another illicit product, find new partners, or take other measures to ensure profitability and degree of success in evading law enforcement.

Source: Albanese, Jay S., Dilip K. Das, and Arvind Verma. 2003. Organized Crime: World Perspectives. Upper Saddle River, NJ: Prentice Hall, p. 6.

are asset misappropriation, corruption, and fraudulent statements (Association of Certified Fraud Examiners, *Report to the Nation*, 2008).

Several studies of victims and offenders have attempted to estimate the extent of white-collar crime. A study of 477 U.S. corporations extends these findings. Marshall Clinard and Peter Yeager (2002, p. 88) find that "approximately three-fifths of the 477 manufacturing corporations had at least one action initiated against them" and that "200 corporations, or 42 percent of the total, had multiple cases charged against them." Clinard and Yeager (2002, p. 91) also find that "the oil, pharmaceutical, and motor vehicle industries were the most likely to violate the law."

The extent of white-collar crime is frequently measured by public attitudes toward large corporations and government entities. Surveys show that public confidence in many elite organizations is declining with

AT A GLANCE

- The estimated annual loss from fraud is $994 billion, or 7% of the revenues of U.S. organizations.
- One in four organizations incurs a loss of $1 million due to occupational fraud.
- The offenders typically are college-educated White men, with the criminal activity of managers costing about four times more than that of employees.
- Three main forms of fraud are asset misappropriation, corruption, and fraudulent statements.
- It is estimated that a total of $125 billion is generated from the global illicit crime markets, 85% of which is accounted for by illicit drug markets.
- The cocaine market in the United States alone generates $38 billion, with the European cocaine market contributing an additional $34 billion in revenue.
- Heroin sales in Europe and Russia tally $20 billion and $13 billion, respectively.
- The financial worth of the drug cartels in Colombia is greater than the total expenditures of the Peruvian and Colombian governments.

Sources: Mayhew, P. and J. J. M. van Dijk. 1997. Criminal Victimization in Eleven Industrialized Countries: Key Findings from the 1996 The International Crime Victims Survey (ICVS). The Hague: Ministry of Justice, WODC; Newman, G. (ed.) 1999. Global Report on Crime and Justice. New York: Oxford University Press; U.S. Department of Justice. 2000. Criminal Victimization, 2000: Changes 1999–2000 with Trends 1993–2000. Washington, DC: U.S. Department of Justice, Bureau of Justice Statistics; Federal Bureau of Investigation, 2000. Crime in the United States, 2002. Washington, DC: USGPO; Office for Victims of Crime. 2000. Victims of Fraud and Economic Crime: Results and Recommendations From an OVC Focus Group Metting. Web posted at http://www.ojp.usdoj.gov/ovc/publications/infores/fraud/victfraud.txt. Ryan, P. J. 2003. Organized Crime, Santa Barbara: ABC-CLIO. Schweitzer, H.O. "Organized Crime: An American Perspective," in Jay S. Albanese, Dilip K. Das, and Arvind Verma. 2003. Organized Crime: World Perspectives, Upper Saddle River, NJ: Prentice Hall; Ruiz de Olano, R. "Organized Crime: A South American Perspective," paper presented at Organized Crime Symposium, Yokohama, Japan, cited in Jay S. Albanese, Dilip K. Das, and Arvind Verma. 2003. Organized Crime: World Perspectives. Upper Saddle River, NJ: Prentice Hall; United Nations, The Globalization of Crime, 2010; Association of Certified Fraud Examiners, Report to the Nation 2008).

the increase in public awareness of large-scale corporate deviance. Simon (1996) notes that deviance by elites provides motivation and rationalization for nonelites to commit profit-oriented crimes. White-collar or elite criminals are rarely arrested or punished for their offenses (Coleman, 2002; Sutherland, 2002). The federal U.S. Sentencing Commission finds that for white-collar crimes prosecuted by federal courts, sentences tend to be extremely light; nearly half entail a fine of $5,000 or less, 80% are fined $25,000 or less, and even probation against executives is imposed less than one-fifth of the time. Jail and prison time tends to be almost nonexistent. As a result the stigma associated with many conventional crimes does not apply to white-collar criminals; many are not considered "real" criminals (Goode, 2005).

For the most part corporate elites have reaped considerable financial profit from their wrongdoing; and most have avoided criminal prosecution. In recent years, for example, the Securities and Exchange Commission referred 609 cases to U.S. attorneys for prosecution. About 31% were tried, but only 14% resulted in a jail sentence (*Fortune,* 2002).

Rising incidence of new forms of white-collar crimes, specifically high-tech crimes, gives a grim picture of the extent of these forms of white-collar crime. Until recently these types of offenses were rarely reported. The Federal Trade Commission's Bureau of Consumer Protection estimates that reports of identity theft may increase to 200,000 incidents annually. The misuse of Social Security numbers is closely linked to identity theft. Social Security numbers provide the basis for more than 8 in 10 cases of identity theft (Noack, 2000; Werrell, 2002).

Extent of Organized Crime

Efforts to assess the extent of **organized crime** worldwide are underway. The United Nations report, *The Globalization of Crime* (2010, p. 19), defines organized crime simply as "a serious offence committed by a group of three of more people with the aim of making money." A criminal group is defined as follows (United Nations, 2010, p. 25):

- A group of three or more persons that are not randomly formed;
- Existing for a period of time;
- Acting in concert with the aim of committing at least one crime punishable by at least 4 years imprisonment;
- In order to obtain, directly or indirectly, a financial or other monetary benefit.

The UN report argues, however, that the focus should be on the types of criminal activity and the criminal market of illicit goods rather than on organized criminal groups (e.g., the mafia). Markets for illicit goods tend to increase over time, whereas individual criminal groups may cease to exist.

Figure 12–1 shows the sources and directions of the major organized crime flows around the world. The flow of illicit drug trafficking from Afghanistan into central Asia and Russia, and southeastern Europe and West, and from the Andean region of South America through Central America and Mexico into the United States and West and Central America and Central Europe accounts for a significant volume of organized criminal activity (United Nations, 2010).

Figure 12–2 shows the dollar values of the major illicit organized crime markets worldwide. It is estimated that a total of $125 billion is gen-

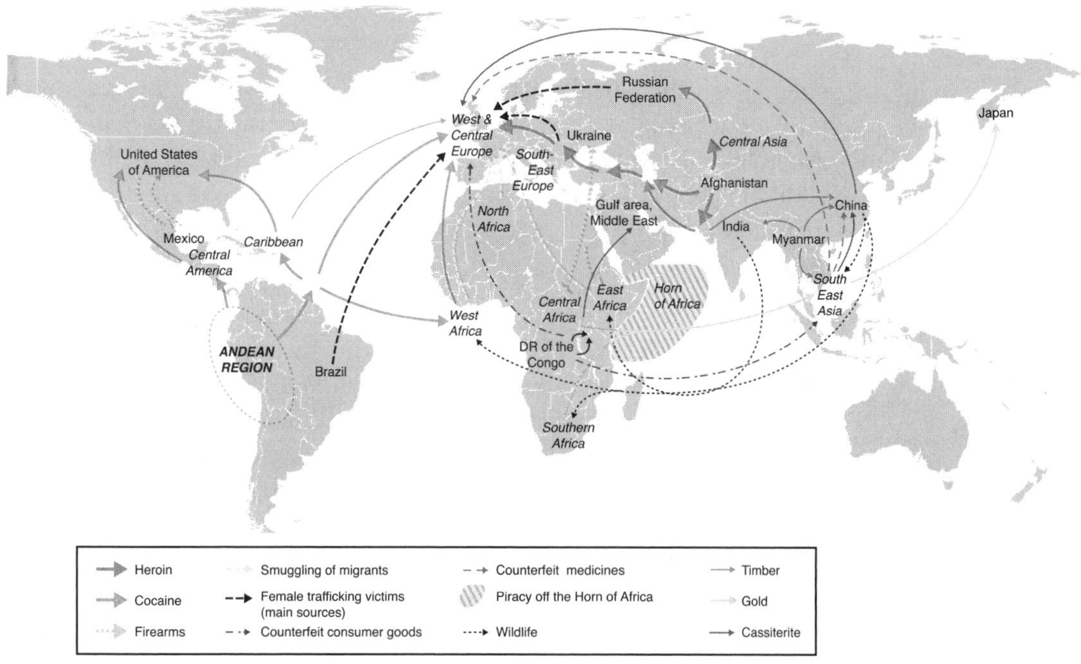

FIGURE 12–1 Global transitional organized crime flow chart.
Source: United Nations, 2010.

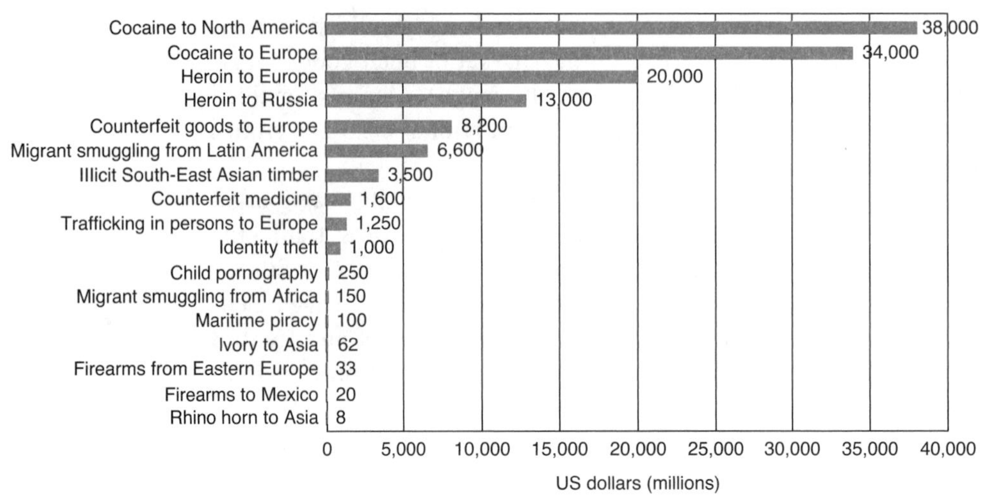

FIGURE 12–2 Monetary values of the major original crime markets worldwide, in U.S. dollars.
Source: United Nations, 2010.

erated from the global illicit crime markets, 85% of which is accounted for by illicit drug markets. The cocaine market in the United States alone generates $38 billion, with the European cocaine market contributing an additional $34 billion in revenue. Heroin sales in Europe and Russia tally $20 billion and $13 billion, respectively (United Nations, 2010).

ORGANIZED CRIME GROUPS. Organized crime groups often operate across the globe in concert, creating vast networks for enhanced profit and market control (Lungren, 1996). Organized criminal groups and international terrorist organizations routinely collaborate on drug trafficking, money laundering, and the marketing and transportation of munitions. The Italian Mafia, the Russian Mafia, the Mexican and Colombian cartels, and Asian crime families are among the most prominent transnational organized crime groups.

The Italian Mafia is among the most influential of the globally organized crime groups. La Cosa Nostra is the largest and most important of the Italian mafias. It is estimated that there are 1,100 "made" or full members of La Costa Nostra across the United States and about 10,000 associate members, with 80% of the active members in the New York metropolitan area. There are five crime families in New York City: the Bonanno, the Colombo, the Genovese, the Gambino, and the Lucchese families. Other cites with a mafia presence are Boston, Chicago, Philadelphia, and Miami/

south Florida area. Other families across the United States are organized in a similar way. The head of each family, known as the "boss," is that family's ultimate decision maker. Assisting the boss is an underboss and a consigliere, or advisor to the boss. Next are the capo-regimes who oversee "made members" or soldiers and associate members. Although the Italian Mafia is well known for gambling, racketeering, and extortion, the establishment also shares in a portion of the illicit U.S. drug market, in particular cocaine and heroin trafficking (Finckenauer, 2007).

Napster, Inc. founder Sean Fanning leaves a federal courthouse in San Francisco on July 26, 2000. The case against Napster gave the record industry a major win in the battle over copyrights and music sharing on the Internet. What other types of deviance does the Internet facilitate?

Russian organized crime is rapidly growing around the world. Between 5,000 and 6,000 multiethnic Mafiya groups operate within Russia, with a total of approximately 100,000 members (Lindberg & Markovic, 2002). These groups control an estimated 80% of all private business and a large portion of the nation's wealth through real estate and bank ownership (Finckenauer & Voronin, 2001). Bribery of government officials ensures political influence. Russian Mafiya groups are believed to be operating in 29 countries. Twelve to 15 organized groups with approximately 4,000 core members operate in 17 U.S. cities and 14 states (Finckenauer & Voronin, 2001). Illegal activities include many types of fraud—bank, health insurance, credit card, and telecommunications—extortion, and illegal trafficking along with various forms of larceny and violent criminal activity.

Colombian and Mexican cartels focus their activities on the drug business. Approximately 35 crime families in Medellin and Cali control the manufacture, marketing, and distribution of cocaine and other drugs through vast agricultural enterprises, laboratories, and production facilities. Between 50% and 70% of the South American cocaine and 80% of the marijuana is sold in the United States. South American organized crime groups also produce 20% to 30% of the heroin consumed in the United States (www.ojp.usdoj.nij/internationaltrafficking.html; Finckenauer, Fuentes, & Ward, 2001).

Asian crime groups, or Triads, participate in Hong Kong, Taiwan, Japan, and mainland China. Hong Kong–based groups support over 160,000 members in 50 different organizations, including the Sun Yee On, the 14K, and the Woo Group. Taiwan's major Triads include the Sung Lian, Tian Dao Man, Four Seas, and the United Bamboo. Membership ranges from several hundred to approximately 10,000 members in the United Bamboo group. Their activities revolve around legitimate businesses such as massage parlors, restaurants, and construction projects as well as a broad range of illegal enterprises. Japanese crime groups, or yakuza, maintain strong historical crime roots in Japan. Legislation that prohibits yakuza membership, however, has resulted in decreased membership and organized criminal activities throughout Japan. It is estimated, though, that yakuza expansions in Europe and the United States generate nearly $10 billion for legitimate businesses. Chinese "tongs," or gangs, are found throughout the United States as well and provide for much of the heroin importation from Southeast Asia (Finckenauer, Fuentes, & Ward, 2001).

Table 12–2 summarizes key explanations of the rates of white-collar and organized crime.

TABLE 12–2 **Explanations of Rates of White-Collar and Organized Crime**

Theories and Theorists	Sociological Predictors	Hypotheses
Opportunity		
Cloward and Ohlin	Opportunity	The more a subculture or organization provides opportunities for the commission of organized or white-collar crime, the higher the rate of those kinds of offenses.
Conflict		
Thio	Status/power groups	The higher the status, and the more power the sociopolitical group holds, the greater the likely of lower-consensus deviance (e.g., white-collar crimes).
Sellin	Primary culture conflict Secondary culture conflict	The greater the primary culture conflict, the greater the rate of organized criminal activity.
Quinney	Power groups	The more the powerful segments of society attempt to control the behavior of the powerless, the higher the rate of organized criminal activity.

Theoretical Explanations

Explanations of white-collar and organized crime may be considered on two levels of analysis. Macro-level theories—opportunity structures, culture conflict, power relations, and economic inequalities—may explain variations in the rates of white-collar and organized crime. Macro-level explanations for white-collar and organized crime are summarized in **Table 12–2**. Micro-level theories—social learning, rational choice, techniques of neutralization, and the seduction of crime—consider why certain individuals may become involved in white-collar or organized crime. Micro-level explanations are summarized in **Table 12–3**.

TABLE 12–3 **Explanations of Individual Involvement in White-Collar and/or Organized Crime**

Theories and Theorists	Sociological Predictors	Hypotheses
Social Learning		
Sutherland	Differential association	The greater the association with persons who advocate involvement in white-collar or organized criminal activity, the greater the probability of those forms of offending.
Rational choice		
Clarke and Cornish	Cost-to-benefit analysis	The greater the benefits anticipated from white-collar or organized crime, the more likely an individual will become involved in those forms of offending.
Techniques of neutralization		
Sykes and Matza	Denial of responsibility Denial of injury Denial of a victim Condemnation of condemners Appeal to higher loyalties	The greater the ability of an individual to neutralize any guilt involved in the commission of a white-collar or organized crime, the greater the likelihood of engaging in those forms of offending.
Seductions of crime		
Jack Katz	Sneaky thrills	The greater the need for excitement or sneaky thrills, the greater the likelihood of engaging in white-collar and/or organized offending.

Explanations of Rates of White-Collar and Organized Crime

Cloward and Ohlin's concept of opportunity structure explains how criminal subcultures provide their members with the means, motivations, and support for the commission of property offenses. The criminal subcultures are largely networks of offenders who socialize recruits about criminal possibilities and ensure them that the risk of apprehension is extremely low. Criminal subcultures thrive on the belief that the larger network of offenders can be trusted to act in the interests of its constituent members. A code of secrecy and honor is central to the workings of white-collar offending committed to enhance the organization as a whole and of organized crime groups.

Power relations, economic inequality, and culture conflict are threaded through the theories of Alex Thio (1978), Richard Quinney (1970), and Thorsten Sellin (1938). Each theoretical formulation is applicable to white-collar and organized crime. Thio argues that higher-status, more powerful groups define the elements of "high-consensus" crimes, largely committed by members of lower-status, less powerful groups in society. The higher-status members then prosecute and often incarcerate the lower-status members of the commission of the high-consensus offenses. However, higher-status persons are more apt to engage in "lower-consensus" crimes—white-collar, corporate, and government crimes—often with impunity.

Quinney contends that the more powerful groups in society seek to maintain their advantaged position by defining the behaviors of the less powerful as criminal and taking steps to legally control them. The disproportionate involvement of racial minorities and the poorer members of society in the criminal justice system is striking. Quinney points out those corporate and governmental criminal activities committed largely by higher-status individuals are intended to enhance their influence and power.

Sellin contends that often the interests of a minority culture conflict with those of the dominant culture. When this clash of cultures occurs, representatives of the dominant culture may seek revenge by actively retaliating against the minority culture by criminalizing their behaviors or by making access very difficult to needed opportunities and resources—housing, jobs, medical care, and educational opportunities. Certain members of the minority culture may respond by involvement in organized criminal activity.

Explanations of an Individual's Involvement in White-Collar and Organized Crime

Edwin Sutherland's (1947) differential association combines subcultural and learning formulations to explain criminal behavior. The motivations, rationalizations, and techniques for engaging in white-collar and organized crime are learned by interacting with other persons who advocate committing either form of offending. The greater the association with others who foster criminal activity, the more likely an individual will engage in the commission of a crime. Much of white-collar and organized criminal behavior is learned directly from active offenders.

White-collar and organized criminal offenders typically rationally choose to engage in criminal activity. Cornish and Clarke (1986) argue that the benefits of committing a crime are weighed against the rewards that are anticipated. When the anticipated benefits markedly outweigh the possible risks involved, the decision to carry out the crime is typically made. White-collar and organized crimes are, for the most part, committed for a financial reward. Careful planning is essential to successfully commit a technically complicated white-collar offense or in sustaining a lucrative drug trafficking and money laundering operation. Cost and benefit analyses are commonly undertaken before engaging either in white-collar or organized criminal offending.

Sykes and Matza's (1957) techniques of neutralization are readily applicable to white-collar and organized criminal offenders. Both types of offenders engage in a process of neutralizing any guilt that may be associated with the violation of the law. The techniques of neutralization—denial of responsibility, denial of injury, denial of a victim, the condemnation of those who might condemn them, and appeal to higher loyalties—serve to justify a wide range of white-collar and organized criminal activities, from insider trading to marketing drugs. The decision to commit the offense may not have been theirs alone; the harm that results may be to anonymous persons who are devalued by the offender. Agents of the criminal justice system—police, prosecutors, judges—are themselves corrupt and not worthy of respect, and the allegiance to one's corporation, government agency, or organized crime group or family supersedes any loyalty to society as a whole.

Jack Katz's (1988) conception of the *seduction of crime* provides intriguing possibilities for the understanding of white-collar and organized criminal offenders. The instrumental nature of white-collar and organized criminal activity suggests that the offenders are always and exclusively driven to realize some monetary gain. However, financial profit underlies both legitimate and illegitimate business practices. Trading stocks legally or illegally are intended for the same purpose—to make money. Yet, involvement in all criminal activities carries the risk of apprehension, prosecution, and possibly incarceration. The "thrill" of engaging in a high-risk venture, the surge of adrenaline that accompanies involvement in criminal activity, can become seductive. For some offenders the prospect of monetary rewards may be less important than the emotional payoff derived from committing the crime.

Chapter Summary

White-collar crimes are defined as criminal violations committed by people of high respectability and high social status in the course of their occupations. Individuals, businesses, and governments may engage in white-collar crimes. Advanced technology and the widespread availability of computers facilitate several forms of white-collar crimes, including identity theft, fraud, forgery, and counterfeiting.

Organized crimes are committed by formally structured criminal organizations that strive to monopolize markets and undermine the legal institutions of society. Organized crime is usually equated with ethnically homogeneous groups.

Organized crime, like most other crimes, is becoming global. Vast criminal networks exist in the United States, Russia, South America, Asia, Africa, and Middle Eastern countries. These groups are involved in illegal profiting from drug production, marketing, and distribution; theft; fraud; and violent crime.

Key Concepts

White-collar crime: Crimes committed by persons of respectability and high social status in the course of their occupations.

Elite deviance: Term introduced by David Simon that describes the variety of white-collar crimes.

Organizational (business) crime: Offenses committed by entire firms or industries in the course of regular business.

Corporate crime: Any criminal violation by a corporation or its executives, employees, or agents, who act on behalf of or for the benefit of the corporation.

Occupational crime: Crimes committed by individuals in the context of the offender's job duties for personal gain.

Government crime: White-collar crimes committed by public officials and other government employees.

Organizational occupational crime: Crimes committed for the benefit of an employing organization.

State authority occupational crime: Crimes by officials through the exercise of their state-based authority.

Professional occupational crime: Crimes by professionals in their capacity as professionals.

Individual occupational crime: Crimes by individuals as individuals.

Organized crime: Criminal activity by an enduring structure or organization developed and devoted primarily to the pursuit of profits through illegal means.

Critical Thinking Questions

1. How are the explanations of white-collar offending similar to and different from other forms of property crime? What are the unique features of white-collar crime that distinguish it from other property offenses?
2. How are white-collar offenses committed within corporations and government agencies similar to and different from organized criminal activities? Provide examples to illustrate your answer.
3. What characteristics of an organization increase the likelihood of systematic criminal activity? How do individual members of the organization who are legally sanctioned for their involvement in white-collar crime neutralize their guilt?
4. How do the processes of globalization affect organized criminal activity within particular countries and across the world? How does globalization facilitate the forms that organized crime may take and its ability to persist through time?

Web Extra

Web-based media materials from high-quality sources such as CNN, Time, and National Public Radio are available in support of this textbook. Visit go.jblearning.com/deviance to access them.

Check out these websites for additional information on white-collar crime:

http://www.fbi.gov

http://www.nw3c.org

http://www.ojp.usdoj.gov/nij/international

Inside 'What's wrong with being a misogynist?' Bret Easton Ellis, cover story, G2 9
theguardian
Massive leak of secret files exposes true Afghan war
White House condemns Pakistan over aid for Taliban
theguardian

Cyberdeviance

CHAPTER 13

Learning Objectives

After reading this chapter you should know

- The various forms of cyberdeviance and the different definitions of computer crime.
- The extent and nature of cybercrimes in the United States.
- Methods used in committing cybercrimes.
- Types of cyberdeviants and cybercriminals.
- The nature and characteristics of cyberdeviant subculture.
- Ethics, values, and norms of the cyberdeviant subculture.
- Motivations behind cyberdeviance.
- Explanations for cyberdeviance.

A spark of recognition clicked in the mind of Temple Grandin, a professor at Colorado State University, as she watched famed computer hacker Kevin Mitnick being interviewed on CBS's *60 Minutes* in 2001 (Zuckerman, 2002). Mitnick's traits, which she later identified as "a twitchy lack of poise, inability to look people in the eye, stunted formality in diction and obsessive interest in technology," are characteristic symptoms of Asperger syndrome. Asperger syndrome is closely related to autism, and Grandin theorizes that it may underlie the personalities of a large number of computer hackers. Grandin, 53, should know. As a child she was diagnosed as an autistic savant, but later psychological inventories showed that she suffered from Asperger syndrome.

Mitnick himself has considered the possibility of an Asperger-hacking link. After his 1995 arrest by the FBI, Mitnick said, "I met this hacker from the U.K. who told me he was diagnosed with this Asperger syndrome: people who are not good in social relationships, but they are very good with numbers, very good at focusing on a problem for a very long period of time." Mitnick went on: "As he described it, I realized, 'Wow, that sounds like me.' The more I thought about it, it seemed to describe people I know who are into hacking."

Security expert Donn Parker agrees. Parker, who has conducted sit-down interviews with various kinds of offenders, including hackers, says he has found "significant similarities" between Asperger syndrome and many hackers—"particularly," he says, "social traits of speaking too loudly, not waiting for a break in conversation to join in and seemingly not caring if the other person is comprehending what they are being told."

SSRN

Wall, D. S. (2008). Cybercrime and the culture of fear: Social science fiction(s) and the production of knowledge about cybercrime (revised May 2010). *Information, Communication & Society, 11*(6), 861–884. http://ssrn.com/abstract=1155155.

Personal computers are increasingly a part of everyday life. Global participation in the information age is largely a result of the expanding opportunities provided by the Internet. Access to information from sources around the world and the ability to communicate and interact directly with fellow computer users unencumbered by time, distance, or expense provide a global perspective unknown in previous times. Opportunities to engage in the process of discovery and innovation abound. The adventure of exploring the contributions of diverse cultures and interacting with others in nonphysical space intrigues many computer users. However, the opportunities for the creative use of cyberspace are not limited to legitimate pursuits. Various forms of cyberdeviance have emerged with the potential for worldwide consequences.

"... the reason that I was involved in hacking was the intellectual challenge, the quest for knowledge, the thrill and escape."

—Kevin Mitnick (http://www.mmorpg.com/gamelist.cfm/game/11/view/forums/post/77910#77910)

Cyberdeviance ranges from relatively benign invasive acts directed at particular computer systems to intentionally destructive attacks against unknown Internet users. Acts of cyberdeviance result in enormous financial losses, disrupt the operations of the military and key governmental agencies, compromise the security of corporations and businesses, and victimize untold numbers of individual computer users.

Cyberdeviance has revolutionized our concepts of crime and deviance in the 21st century. The sudden, clandestine acts of a lone computer programmer can wreak unprecedented havoc around the world. The sociocultural underpinnings of cyberdeviance, its scope and consequences, and theoretical understanding of cyberdeviance are considered in this chapter.

Definition

"The more things that you can do online, the more things we can do to you."
—Taltos, a cracker (http://www.wired.com/science/discoveries/news/2001/02/41625)

Computer crime and deviance may take various forms with targets ranging from individual victims, either known or unknown to the perpetrator, to identifiable social groups, governmental agencies, large-scale corporations, or masses of anonymous persons (**Table 13–1**). Efforts to legally define each form of computer offending and to draft legislation at the federal and state levels that is both constitutionally defensible and legally enforceable have been a challenge. For example, in 1984 the U.S. Congress passed the first Computer Fraud and Abuse Act. This legislation was amended in 1986, 1994, 1996, and 2001, a reflection of the increasing complexity of computer-related offenses.

In addition to the federal statute, 33 states have passed legislation related to computer crime. Each of these state statutes prohibits unauthorized access to computers and databases, using the computer to commit fraud, and using the computer to destroy the contents of computers and their software. The successful enforcement of these statutes, however, has been difficult. Corporations and financial institutions are

TABLE 13–1 **Definitions of Cybercrimes Most Frequently Reported**

1. **FBI scams:** Scams in which it appears the FBI is trying to get something from the complainant (e.g., money, identity, etc.).
2. **Advance free fraud:** An incident involving communications that would have people believe that to receive something they must first pay money to cover some sort of incidental cost or expense.
3. **Identification theft:** An incident in which someone steals or tries to steal an identity (or identity information), but only when there is no other discernible crime involved (e.g., credit card theft).
4. **Nondelivery of merchandise (nonauction):** An incident in which the complainant bought something but it never arrived.
5. **Overpayment fraud:** An incident in which the complainant receives an invalid monetary instrument, with instructions to deposit it in a bank account and to send excess funds or a percentage of the deposited money back to the sender.
6. **Miscellaneous funds:** Incidents involving a fraudulent attempt to get the complainant to send money and where nothing is bought or sold.
7. **SPAM:** Unsolicited and unwelcome e-mail, usually mass distributed.
8. **Credit card fraud:** An incident in which someone is attempting to charge goods and services to the complainant's credit card account.
9. **Auction fraud:** A fraudulent transaction or exchange that occurs in the context of an online auction site.
10. **Computer damage (destruction/damage/vandalism of property):** This category is used to classify complaints involving crimes that target and cause damage to computers, or "true computer crimes."

Source: Bureau of Justice Statistics, Internet Crime Report, 2009.

reluctant to admit that an intruder has breached the security of their computer systems. Consumer confidence may erode, liability claims may arise, and investors may be less willing to risk buying stock in a company that is particularly vulnerable to computer criminals (Conley & Bryan, 1999).

Extent and Patterns

The extent of computer-related offending is largely a matter of speculation. What is certain is that anyone with a personal computer and access to the Internet has the opportunity to commit a computer crime. Opportunities for offending far exceed the motives and technical ability to carry out cyberdeviance.

The Bureau of Justice Statistics reports that two of every three businesses are the victim of some form of cybercrime—about 22 million incidents each year. The monetary loss to businesses that results from cybercrime exceeds $867 million. Cyberthefts make up more than half the losses ($450 million), and cyberattacks account for about $314 million. About 1.5 million computer virus infections were suffered by businesses and nearly 126,000 incidents of cyberfrauds occur each year (Bureau of Justice Statistics, 2008).

Cybercrime Around the World

Figure 13–1 depicts the distribution of cybercrime across the globe. The highest number of incidents of cybercrime is found in the United States. The United States accounts for more than 92% of cybercriminal activity; Canada ranks second with 1.8%, and the United Kingdom ranks third with less than 1%. Other countries ranked in order of cybercrime victimization are Australia, India, Puerto Rico, Germany, Mexico, South Africa, and Philippines (Bureau of Justice Statistics, 2009).

Cybercrime in the United States

Figure 13–2 shows the states in the United States that report the highest incidents of cybercrime. California accounts for almost 14% of all cybercriminal activity, followed by Florida (7.5%), Texas (7.3%), New York (5.2%), and New Jersey (5.0%). States with less than 4% of the incidents of cybercrime include Illinois, Pennsylvania, Ohio, Virginia, and Washington. The rates of cybercriminal activity, however, differ from its prevalence. Alaska has the highest rate of cybercrime (485.9 per 100,000 people), followed by New Jersey (166.7), Colorado (143.2), Nevada (135.7), and the District of Columbia (Bureau of Justice Statistics, 2009).

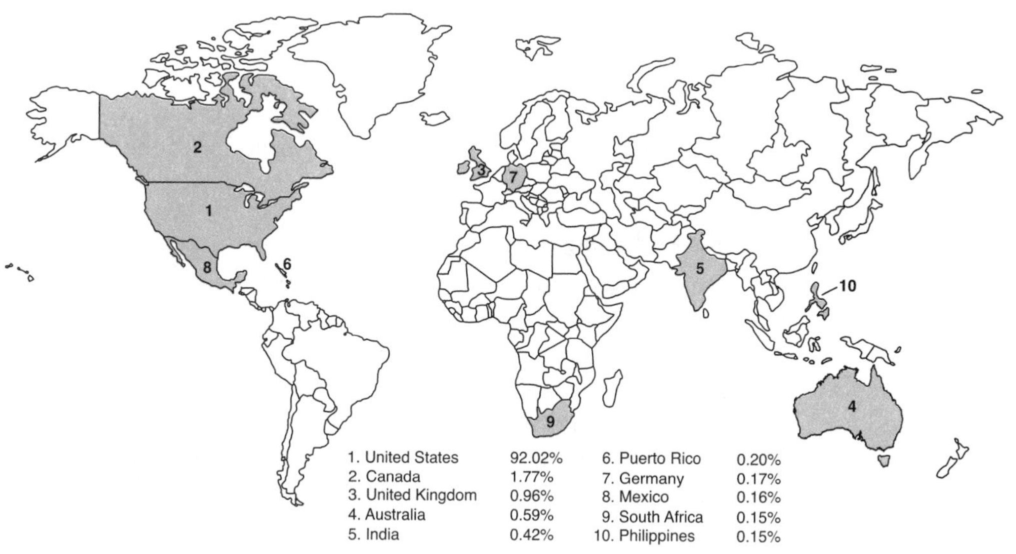

FIGURE 13–1 Top 10 countries by count: Individual complainants (numbered by rank).
Source: Bureau of Justice Statistics, Internet Crime Report, 2009.

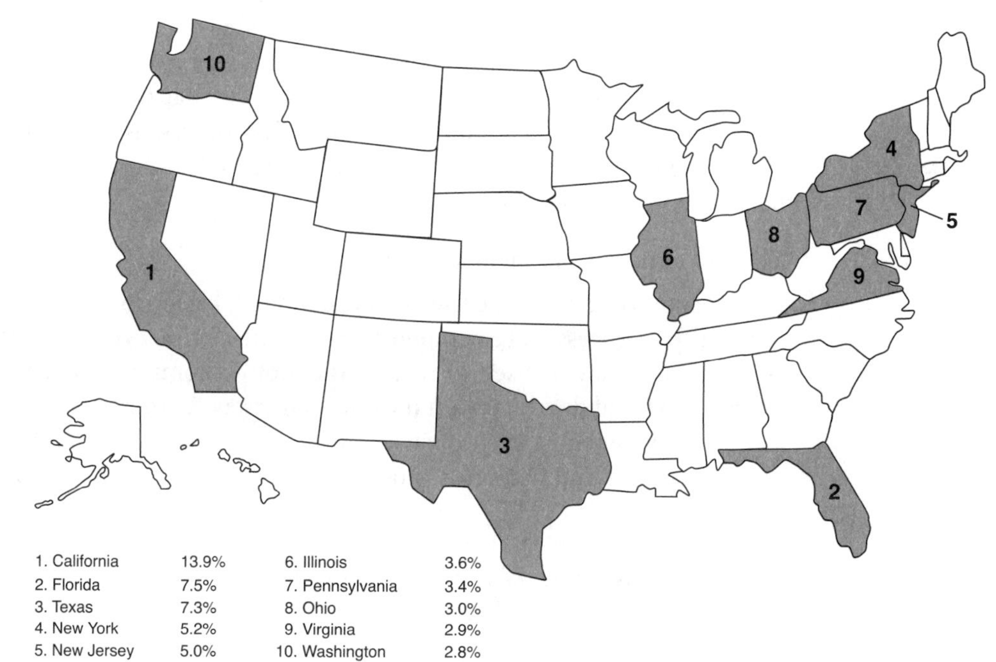

FIGURE 13–2 Top 10 states by count: Individual complainants (numbered by rank).
Source: Bureau of Justice Statistics, Internet Crime Report, 2009.

Types of Computer Crimes

David Carter (1995) has identified four types of computer crimes: computer as the target, computer as the instrument of the crime, computer as incidental to other crimes, and crimes associated with the prevalence of computers.

Computer as the Target

The computer is the target when a cyberdeviant makes use of a computer to obtain information or damage operating programs (Carter, 1995). An offender may pretend that he or she is the system's manager and gain access to the system's files. Typical of such offenses are the altering, theft, or sabotage of intellectual property; theft of marketing information (e.g., consumer lists, pricing data, or marketing plans); or blackmail based on information gained from computerized files (e.g., medical information, personal history, or sexual preference). Computers containing criminal justice and other government records (e.g., arrest and criminal history data, outstanding warrants, driver's license information, passports, and tax records) are common targets of computer criminals.

Technovandalism and **technotrespass** are two related forms of computer as target offenses (Carter, 1995). Both offenses involve unlawful access to a computer. Technovandalism may involve malicious intent but is often motivated by the offender's need to show that the challenge of unlawful access to a computer can be met. Technotrespass refers to an unlawful exploration of computer files simply to look at the contents, not to damage, alter, or steal any information.

Computer as the Instrument of the Crime

Instrumentality refers to the use of an instrument, legally in one's possession (e.g., the processes of a computer), to commit a crime. The operations of a computer may be used to reprogram another computer's analytical processes to fraudulently convert the financial assets of others to one's own purposes. Examples of such offenses include theft from bank accounts, credit card fraud, and fraudulent stock market transactions (Carter, 1995).

Computer as Incidental to Other Crimes

The computer is incidental to other crimes when it is not necessary to commit the crime but does facilitate its commission. Computers may accelerate the commission of certain offenses, allowing the offender to process a great deal of information very rapidly and make the detection of the offense and the apprehension of the offender less likely. Examples of these offenses are bookmaking, money laundering, altering crime records, and unlawful bank transactions. Offenders may encrypt incriminating evidence stored in computers that are programmed to destroy the data if the computer is not accessed properly (Carter, 1995).

Computers have been used to distribute child pornography, solicit clients for prostitutes, and provide instruction on methods of criminal offending. An extreme example of the use of a computer to facilitate the commission of a crime involved the altering of a hospital patient's medication records that resulted in the administration of a fatal overdose. The offender was subsequently charged with criminal homicide (Carter, 1995).

Crimes Associated with the Prevalence of Computers

The global demand for computers and related products has led to the proliferation of black markets for counterfeit equipment and software. Common offenses are the violation of copyright restrictions of commercial software and the duplication of word processing, spreadsheet, and database programs.

Computers can also be used as a tool to commit traditional forms of criminal activity (e.g., counterfeiting, fraud, larceny, embezzlement, and sexual solicitation). Ronald Standler has outlined three ways computers may be used to commit "new" forms of criminal activity: (1) unauthorized use of the computer, (2) releasing a malicious computer program, and (3) harassment and stalking in cyberspace (see www.rbs2.com/ccrime.htm).

UNAUTHORIZED COMPUTER USE. Unauthorized use of the computer typically involves the following:

- Computer voyeurism: The offender simply reads confidential documents without altering them in any way.
- Changing data: Records and financial accounts are changed, usually to the advantage of the offender.
- Deleting data: Entire computer files are deleted or are sabotaged.

MALICIOUS COMPUTER PROGRAMS. The Internet has made it possible to transmit malicious computer programs across the globe in fractions of a second. Malicious computer programs, as the name implies, are intended to destroy or wreak havoc on the computer capabilities of an unknown number of anonymous victims. These programs include viruses, worms, Trojan horses, and logic bombs.

HARASSMENT AND STALKING. Computers also provide a means to harass or stalk a computer user. The intent of the perpetrator is to create emotional distress, malign, or compromise the victim's reputation. Threats of injury,

SSRN

Lastowka, G., & Hunter, D. Virtual crime. *New York Law School Law Review*, Forthcoming. http://ssrn.com/abstract=564801

sexual innuendo, or hate messages are common forms of harassment and stalking. Forged e-mail sent in the name of the victim, which conveys racist or malicious messages, is used by the harasser to harm the victim socially and psychologically.

Methods of Cyberdeviance

Trap Doors

Trap doors are installed in computer software to allow programmers to make changes without going through complicated access procedures. Often, these trap doors are eliminated when the program has been installed in a computer. However, when a trap door is left in place, a cybercriminal may readily gain access to system programs and files (see http://legal.practitioner.com/computer-crime/computercrime_3_2_4.htm).

Timing Attacks

Timing attacks refer to the destruction or alteration of data in a computer before being processed. A timing attack may also occur by placing one's own name in someone else's data file before it is processed or altering the order of jobs in the computer's processing or printing queue (see http://oreilly.com/catalog/crime/chapter/cri_02.html).

Trojan Horses

Trojan horses are used to infiltrate a computer system with the intention of disabling the system. A Trojan horse carries instructions into a computer program that are disguised as authorized and useful. Hidden in the Trojan horse are various destructive devices for rendering a computer system ineffective, such as viruses, worms, logic bombs, or salamis (see http://legal.practitioner.com/computer-crime/computercrime_3_2_3.htm).

Viruses

Viruses are computer programs that have the ability to reproduce themselves. Similar to their biological counterparts, computer viruses need a host or program to continue to multiply. The virus alters a computer program by adding commands that will activate the virus (Power, 2000). When the computer is activated, the virus begins to affect its operation. A computer virus may alter and destroy data or render disk space or memory unusable. Viruses may infect a computer in two ways. First, the virus may be transmitted in an e-mail message that, when opened, permeates the victim's computer. Second, the victim may unwittingly download an infected file (Icove et al., 1995).

SSRN

Wall, D. S. (2010). The Internet as a conduit for criminal activity. In A. Pattavina (Ed.), *Information technology and the criminal justice system* (pp. 77–98). Sage. http://ssrn.com/abstract=740626

How a Computer Virus Works

A computer virus is a program that secretly invades another computer.

- It typically gains access to a computer as an e-mail attachment or less often by an infected disk.
- Activation of the virus occurs when the e-mail attachment is opened or the infected disk is loaded into the computer.
- When activated, the programmed virus begins its destructive mission.
- The virus spreads to other computers by reading the user's e-mail address book and sending itself to all persons found.
- Viruses may alter or delete files, cause damage to a computer's hardware, or render existing programs unusable.

Adapted from Schaefer, M. (2001). Computer viruses take turn for the worst. *Foster's Daily Democrat,* December 9.

Worms

Unlike viruses, **worms** are computer programs that exist independently of other programs. With the ability to replicate itself, a worm is considered to be more powerful than a virus. A worm invades a computer by means of the Internet and begins to search for other computers attached to its original victim. Similar to viruses, worms may attack computer software, destroying data and operating procedures (Icove et al., 1995).

Logic Bombs

Trojan horses may be used to plant **logic bombs** in a computer system. A logic bomb instructs the computer to execute a certain function under certain conditions, usually on a given date and time. Logic bombs may work in concert with a virus and are potentially as destructive (Icove et al., 1995).

Salamis

A **salami** attack may also be launched by means of a Trojan horse. The salami attack alters financial data by slicing small amounts of money from large accounts, as a serving of salami is cut from a larger piece. The victim, who rarely misses the financial loss, is not likely to report the offense. A typical salami attack may involve the reallocation of funds that remain in an account after a rounding procedure, say, from $100.003 to an even $100. Multiplied by thousands of accounts, the fraction of a cent diverted to the offender's personal account may in time become a substantial amount (Icove et al., 1995).

Typology of Cyberdeviants

Hackers

Hackers are computer aficionados who are driven to explore the intricacies of computer programming and to extend the boundaries of their expertise. The intent of the hacker is typically not to do harm but rather to explore uncharted computer applications. This quest may lead them to attempt to gain access to unauthorized computer systems housing confidential governmental, military, or personal information. The hacker is motivated by the challenge that inaccessible computer systems present. The thrill of accessing secured computer systems inspires the hacker to devise increasingly more intricate computer software. In a sense, computer hackers are intensely curious, creative, yet meddlesome, individuals (Raymond, 1997).

Crackers

Unlike hackers, crackers intend to damage, manipulate, or destroy the computer operations of others. They are motivated to disrupt or destroy vital computer systems of governmental and military agencies, corporations, and financial institutions. Crackers are not simply interested in proving they can infiltrate highly secure computer systems and networks, but they are bent on demonstrating the kinds of confusion and disorder they can create. Planting viruses, worms, logic bombs, and salamis are routine activities of crackers (Raymond, 1997).

AT A GLANCE

- Two of every three businesses are the victims of some form of cybercrime—about 22 million incidents each year.
- The monetary loss to businesses that results from cybercrime exceeds $867 million.
- Cyberthefts make up more than half the losses ($450 million), and cyberattacks account for about $314 million. About 1.5 million computer virus infections were suffered by businesses, and nearly 126,000 incidents of cyberfrauds occur each year.
- The United States accounts for more than 92% of cybercriminal activity. Canada ranks second with 1.8%, and the United Kingdom ranks third with less than 1%.
- California accounts for almost 14% of all cybercriminal activity, followed by Florida (7.5%), Texas (7.3%), New York (5.2%), and New Jersey (5.0%).
- The rates of cybercriminal activity, however, differ from its prevalence. Alaska has the highest rate of cybercrime (485.9 per 100,000 people), followed by New Jersey (166.7), Colorado (143.2), Nevada (135.7), and the District of Columbia (116.25).

Source: Internet Crime Complaint Center, 2009 Internet Crime Report (Bureau of Justice Assistance, 2010.

Crackers typically band together in clandestine groups to plan and carry out their criminal missions. Similar to other relatively small-scale criminal "gangs," crackers provide themselves with ominous names—Toxic Shock Group, Computer Chaos Club, AcidMaster, or Exploiter (Taylor, 1999).

Marc Rogers, a Canadian behavioral scientist and cyberdetective, provides four types of computer hackers:

1. *Old school hackers:* Before the advent of the Internet, the old school hackers were driven to know and crack the codes of computer systems and to explore their contents. They did not intend to steal anything or to damage the operation of the computer they hacked. Old school hackers were motivated by personal curiosity and the desire to learn more about the workings of computer systems.
2. *Script kiddies or cyberpunks:* Script kiddies or cyberpunks are typically young (teenagers and young adults), White, and male. Their interest in the computer supersedes anything else. As a consequence, they often are high school dropouts who are consumed by hacking into computer systems with the intent to do harm.
3. *Professional criminals or crackers:* Professional criminals or crackers derive their livelihood from their illicit activities on the Internet. They may work independently or may be employed by organized criminal groups, governments, or corporations.
4. *Coders and virus writers:* Coders and virus writers devise codes and viruses that are then used by hackers bent on destruction of computer systems, often around the world. The network of coders and virus writers, or "zoo," provides them with an opportunity to experiment with their destructive codes and viruses before they are released into the "wild" or Internet (see http://atlas.kennesaw.edu/~kmp7062/Hackers.html).

Donn Parker (1998) has identified seven different types of cybercriminals: (1) pranksters, (2) hacksters, (3) malicious hackers, (4) personal problem solvers, (5) career criminals, (6) extreme advocates, and (7) malcontents, addicts, irrational, and incompetent people. Pranksters simply engage in playing tricks on others without intending significant harm to them. Typically, pranksters leave messages or embed jokes or strange characters into computer systems. Malicious hackers, however, intend to disrupt the work of others or to cause them significant loss. For example, they may generate computer viruses or destroy computer files and records. A common type of computer criminal is the personal problem solver. Often, these offenders have experienced considerable frustration in resolving their personal problems (e.g., financial, emotional, or psychological) and have resorted to computer crime to meet their needs. Career criminals earn most of their income from the illicit use of the computer. Various schemes, including fraud, the misrepresentation of goods or services for sale, and false investment opportunities, may result in considerable profit for the career computer criminal. Terrorists and political, social, or religious zealots are classified as extreme advocates. Their unwavering commitment to their cause provides them with a justification for engaging in cybercrime and deviance. Persons who are malcontent, addicted, irrational, or generally incompetent comprise the last group of cyberdeviants. Their internal discord and need to strike out against others underlie much of their deviant activity in cyberspace, where they can remain anonymous.

Cyberdeviant Subculture

A computer hacker at work. What types of cybercriminals can be identified?

Sociologist Paul Taylor (1999) provides a general outline of some key elements of the hacker subculture. These elements include technology content, secrecy and fluidity, and the generation gap and seeds of antipathy.

Technology Content

Technology content refers to the wide familiarity among the young with the computer and its various applications. Computers have been incorporated into classroom instruction beginning in the primary grades and have become vital to educational success. The Internet has provided the vehicle for the dissemination of information among cyberdeviants around the world. The sharing of advances on common computer-related problems and the recognition of individual discoveries provides the foundation for the development of a unique subculture of computer aficionados. This subculture is based on common interests and goals that are not related to typical sociological dimensions of subcultural affiliation—race or ethnicity, religious or traditional background, geographic location, and the proximity of interaction (Taylor, 1999).

Russia's Hacking Culture

Many of their peers in the Western world say Eastern Europe's computer crackers and hackers are the most skillful in the world—far superior to the so-called script kiddies who have gained a fair amount of notoriety.

"We call Russia the Hackzone because there are so many of us here, and we are so good at what we do," said Igor Kovalyev, a self-described cracker living in Moscow. "Here hacking is a good job, one of the few good jobs left."

Kovalyev said that stealing credit card numbers is the "best résumé" for a Russian cracker. But other popular activities are studying the ways to "get into networks of foreign businesses, plus virus writing, and password discovery," said Kovalyev, who believes that Russian websites such as *Hackzone* and "launched in Russia" *Drink or Die* are the most sophisticated of all hacking sites.

"Russian crackers do amazing things with very limited computing power. They are smart and they cover their tracks very well," said Frank Voden, a consultant with U.K. firm TechSolutions.

"And they have excellent programming skills, which many of the so-called crackers in the United States do not possess. These Russian guys aren't just downloading tools and running them without knowing what they are doing. They know exactly what they are doing."

Source: Michelle Delio, Russia's Hacking Culture, Web posted at: http://www.wired.com/news/culture/0,1284,42346,00.html.

Secrecy and Fluidity

The cyberdeviant subculture depends in large measure on its members maintaining their own anonymity and keeping secret the activities of the subculture members. Because cyberdeviants are engaged in varying degrees of illicit activity, they must be assured that their fellow members will hold in confidence the information that is shared as well as its source. Not only do cyberdeviants operate in secrecy, but also the structure of their subculture is characterized by a fluidity of organization that, in turn, protects them.

There is no organized structure in the computer underworld, no mysterious chairman of the board to run things. The underground is anarchic, a confederation of phreakers/hackers and virus writers from all over the world whose common interests transcend culture or language. Most hackers have two or three handles and operate on a number of boards. They change identifications, aliases, sites, their methods, targets, and gang membership as rapidly as the authorities track them. Stamping out hacking is like trying to pin down mercury (Clough & Mungo, 1992).

To Paul Taylor (1999), a cyberdeviant subculture is made possible by a process of "disembodied anonymity." The organization of the cyberdeviant subculture differs in many ways from that of other common interest groups. The trappings of status and power are missing. Physical appearance, socioeconomic status, age, race, and gender do not influence the ranking of a cyberdeviant within his or her subculture. Communication among the members of the subculture is carried out in an impersonal way, largely by e-mail, bulletin boards, and newsgroups. Without the kinds of social clues that typically accompany other forms of interpersonal communication, correspondence within the cyberdeviant subculture focuses more on the content of the message and less on the social characteristics of the sender. This method of communication serves to preserve the anonymity of the cyberdeviant and provides for a more equalitarian subcultural structure (Clough & Mungo, 1992).

Gender Gap and Antipathy

Around the world the young dominate the cyberdeviant subculture. Hackers and other cyberdeviants tend to either age out of their nefarious pursuits as they approach the age of 30 or to be replaced by more accomplished cyberdeviants who are still teenagers. As technical sophistication increases among elementary and middle school computer users, a desire to know more and a drive to explore the potential of the computer increase. Often, young computer users become more advanced than their teachers. Their frustration with the limits of the educational opportunities provided by their teachers may lead to their seeking answers on their own. Electronic bulletin boards, chat rooms, and newsgroups provide opportunities for the young to connect with the cyberdeviant subculture (Clough & Mungo, 1992).

Ethics and the Cyberdeviant

A distinct ethos permeates the cyberdeviant subculture. Levy (1984) has identified five ethical standards that are commonly held by members of the computer underground:

- All information should be free.
- Mistrust authority and promote decentralization.
- Hackers should be judged by their hacking, not by bogus criteria such as degrees, age, race, or position.
- You can create art and beauty on a computer.
- Computers can change life for the better.

Adherence to these ethical principles varies within the hacking community. Elite hackers tend to hold themselves to a higher standard of behavior than more deviant members of the computer underground. The "inner circle" epitomizes the ethos of the hacker elites.

No inner circle member ever deletes or damages information that belongs to a legitimate user of the system in any way that the member cannot easily correct him- or herself. No member leaves another hacker's name or phone number on any computer system. Members leave their own on a system only at their own risk. All members are expected to obtain and contribute their own account information rather than use only information given to them by other members (Landreth, 1985).

In short, an elite hacker seeks to protect the property of others against harm or destruction. Elite hackers view themselves as "explorers, not spies, and . . . damaging computer files was not only clumsy and inelegant—it was wrong" (Landreth, 1985, p. 25).

Motives

Often, computer hackers want to demonstrate that their technical expertise far exceeds any system's capability to prevent an invasion. Their primary intention is to flaunt their computer prowess, to succeed against all odds to crack an allegedly impenetrable computer fortress. The harm that is created is secondary to their own sense of accomplishment and possible increase in status among their peers. Other computer criminals, however, do intend harm to specific targets (e.g., military installations, corporate headquarters, or a financial institution) or nonspecific targets—unknown victims of a computer virus.

To Donn Parker (1998), "intense personal problems" underlie most cyberdeviance. In his study of 80 young computer hackers in the United States and Europe, he identifies the following psychological and behavioral traits that are commonly held by cyberdeviants:

- Precociousness, curiosity, and persistence
- Habitual lying, cheating, stealing, and exaggerating
- Juvenile idealism (e.g., "power to the people," "if it feels good, do it")
- Hyperactivity
- Drug and alcohol abuse

These psychological and behavioral traits are manifest, according to Parker (1998), in one of two syndromes, either differential association or "Robin Hood." The differential association syndrome refers to the involvement of the cyberdeviant with other cyberdeviants who provide a justification for their actions. If everyone around the cyberdeviant appears to be committing some form of computer-related offense, then there is the opportunity to learn more about its commission and the rationale for doing so. Parker (1998) also notes that cyberdeviants rationalize their actions by asserting that persons themselves are not harmed, only computers (Parker, 1998, p. 141):

> Cybercriminals often distinguish between the unacceptable practice of doing harm to people and the impersonal acts of doing harm to or through computers. Yet, many receive a measure of satisfaction in their crimes by personifying the computers they attack, viewing them as adversaries and deriving some enjoyment from ripping them off.

The "Robin Hood" syndrome refers to the justification that cybercriminals use to steal from corporations or large-scale organizations. However, Parker (1998) points out that unlike the Robin Hood of legend, cybercriminals tend to keep what is stolen rather than give it to the poor.

Canadian behavioral scientist Marc Rogers and psychiatrist Jerrold M. Post also note that common traits distinguish hackers who engage in criminal activities from those who do not. Rogers observes that criminal hackers may minimize the consequences of their computer crimes by rationalizing they are actually benefiting others by their actions. Computer systems, they may argue, are not human, so there really is not a "true" victim. Post agrees that criminal hackers use an "ethical flexibility" to neutralize any feelings of guilt associated with their behavior. The hacker is just playing a game, the consequences of which they rarely take seriously (see http://atlas.kennesaw.edu/~kmp7062/Hackers.html).

British sociologist Paul Taylor (1999, p. 47) has identified six motivations for involvement in computer hacking:

- Feeling of addiction
- The urge of curiosity
- Boredom with educational system
- Enjoyment of feelings of power
- Peer recognition
- Political mission

Computer hacking requires total absorption—a single-minded dedication to the task at hand. Hackers easily become obsessed with the problem of the moment. The thrill of discovery, of "cracking the code" is seductive—in many ways tantamount to an adrenaline rush that accompanies completing a dangerous physical feat or the use of certain drugs.

In Their Own Words...

Raphael Gray, a hacker from rural Wales, talked about the thrill of cyberdeviance.

> *After the first 10 minutes, when I was waiting for the five and a half thousand credit cards I was to download from the first site. . . . certainly there was a great rush from doing it, definitely, There was a lot of adrenaline, if nothing else, while you're trying to track it down. I sometimes spend 2 days without sleep, without anything, just constantly trying to do it.*

An anonymous hacker explained his obsession with the Internet in this way:

> *Well, it's power at your fingertips. You can control all the computers from the government, from the military, from large corporations. And if you know what you are doing, you can travel through the Internet, at your will, with no restrictions. That's power, it's a power trip.*
>
> *. . . Everybody likes to feel in control. . . . it's intellectual. It stimulates my mind. It's a challenge.*

Source: Public Broadcasting System, Frontline, Hackers Interviews: posted at: www. pbs.org/wgbh/pages/frontline/shows/hackers/interviews

The seductiveness of hacking may be addictive. A member of the Toxic Shock Group observes the following (Taylor, 1999, p. 47):

> We are addicted to information and knowledge, and our drugs are withheld from us. We are forced to seek our precious information and knowledge elsewhere. We have to find challenge somewhere, somehow, or it tears our very souls apart. And we are, eventually, forced to enter someone's system.

Hackers are intensely curious people. They have an incessant need to expand their knowledge of the computer and its potential uses. Problems that are resolved lead to further problems that capture their attention. As Sherlock Holmes abhorred boredom and lack of mental stimulation, so, too, do computer hackers. They typically find the standard curriculum in high schools and colleges to be stiflingly oppressive to their quest for knowledge about the only thing that matters to them—the mysteries of the computer.

Status, power, and prestige are closely linked social phenomena. Hackers rarely receive positive recognition from persons other than those in the hacking community. A hacker's status, power, and prestige are almost exclusively provided by the hacker subculture. The "outside" world is unable to understand the social milieu of the hacker.

Hackers who desire status, power, and prestige may be driven to engage in acts of cyberdeviance that have political implications. Freedom of information and rebellion against the right to own intellectual property rights are issues that propel much of the politically motivated cyberdeviance. Many hackers and other computer aficionados want to make available to all computer users all computer-related information and technology. Their political mission is to break the bureaucratic and legal shackles that limit access to useful information, software, and technology.

Theories of Cyberdeviance

Although little theoretical work has been done on the various forms of cybercrime and deviance discussed in this chapter, existing theoretical formulations can help us understand these behaviors (**Table 13–2**). Information about the incidence and prevalence of cybercrime and deviance is

TABLE 13–2 **Explanations of Cyberdeviance**

Theories and Theorists	Sociological Predictors	Hypotheses
Integration		
Merton	Anomie	The greater the level of anomie, the more likely that an individual is to engage in cyberdeviance.
Social Bonding and Control		
Hirschi	Attachment	The weaker the attachment to conventional society, the more likely the individual is to engage in cyberdeviance.
	Commitment	The weaker the commitment to conventional society, the more likely the individual is to engage in cyberdeviance.
	Involvement	The greater the involvement in conventional activities, the less likely the individual is to engage in cyberdeviance.
	Belief	The stronger the belief in conventional values and norms, the less likely the individual is to engage in cyberdeviance.
Social Learning		
Sutherland	Differential association	Individuals who are exposed to definitions favorable toward cyberdeviance are more likely to engage in cyberdeviance.
Akers	Differential reinforcement	The greater the punishment for cyberdeviance, the less likely an individual is to engage in cyberdeviance.

/ continues

nonsystematic, incomplete, and largely anecdotal. Therefore, our discussion of the theoretical understanding of cybercrime and deviance does not attempt to distinguish between explanations and predictions of individual and rates of computer-related offending.

Seduction of Crime

Sociologist Jack Katz (1988) offers an explanation of crime and deviance that differs from traditional theoretical formulations that focus on the offender's psychological background or social environment. Rather, Katz is concerned with the experience of committing a crime, the "distinctive sensual dynamics" involved in deviant activity. To Katz (1988, p. 9), the central question in investigating the etiology of deviance and crime is this: "What are people trying to do when they commit a crime?" In the present instance, "What does a cybercriminal hope to achieve by engaging in an illicit use of the computer?"

TABLE 13–2 **Explanations of Cyberdeviance** / continued

Theories and Theorists	Sociological Predictors	Hypotheses
Seductions of Crime		
Katz	Sneaky thrills	The greater the thrill of the experience, the more likely an individual is to engage in cyberdeviance.
Neutralization Theory		
Sykes and Matza	Denial of responsibility	If an individual fails to accept responsibility for his or her own actions, then he or she is more likely to engage in cyberdeviance.
	Denial of injury	If an individual maintains that no one is hurt by his or her behavior, then he or she is more likely to engage in cyberdeviance.
	Denial of a victim	If an individual feels that his or her victim deserves to be victimized, then he or she is more likely to engage in cyberdeviance.
	Condemnation of condemners	If an individual views others as hypocrites or hidden deviants, then he or she is more likely to engage in cyberdeviance.
	Appeal to higher loyalties	If an individual feels that the demands of his or her group affiliation take precedence over societal values and rules, then he or she is more likely to engage in cyberdeviance.
Rational Choice		
Cornish and Clarke	Cost-to-benefit analysis	The greater the benefit associated with cyberdeviance, the more likely an individual is to engage in cyberdeviance.

Katz sets forth three processes that provide individual offenders with the necessary conditions to engage in criminal or deviant behavior. First, there must be a *path of action*—"distinctive practical requirement for successfully committing the crime" (Katz, 1988, p. 9). Second, the offender must engage in a *line of interpretation*—"unique ways of understanding how one is and will be seen by others" (Katz, 1988, p. 9). And, third, there is an *emotional process*—seductions and compulsions that have special dynamics. The process, then, that results in any criminal behavior, including cybercrime, involves the engagement of the offender in a plan for the illicit activity, a "definition of the situation" that makes sense of the crime and an anticipation of sensual pleasure from its commission.

Underlying the process of engaging in criminal activity is a series of "moral emotions"—humiliation, righteousness, arrogance, ridicule, cynicism, defilement, and vengeance—that compel the offender to act. Cybercriminals may be motivated to demonstrate their computer expertise in an arrogant manner. Hackers, for example, may seek to gain access to an unauthorized, highly secure computer system simply to show they can do it. Crackers may be driven by a need to defile the property of others, whereas righteousness or vengeance may compel others to commit computer theft.

A public library building in New York City. How has digital content changed perceptions of deviance?

Social Learning, Differential Reinforcement, and Differential Association

Social learning, differential reinforcement, and differential association formulations are particularly relevant to the understanding of cyberdeviance (Akers & Burgess, 1966; Sutherland & Cressey, 1978). In many ways cyberdeviants are computer virtuosos—masters of the intricacies of the Internet, software design, and manipulation. They are driven to continually learn more about the possibilities that global computer systems offer. Largely through trial and error, cyberdeviants have the ability to learn many of the mysteries of computer technology. However, considerable sharing of information and technique takes place within the computer underworld—a loose confederation of cyberdeviants who exchange news of their discoveries and claim recognition for them.

Central to differential association theory is the contention that deviant behaviors are learned from others through personal interaction. Sutherland and Cressey (1978) further hold that differential associations

Sexting: Internet Crime, Deviance, or Neither?

Sexting has been defined as "the act of sending, receiving, or forwarding sexually explicit messages, photos, or images via cell phone, computer, or other digital device" (Berkshire District Attorney's Office, mhtml:file://E:\Sexting.mnt). The extent of sexting is beginning to be documented cross the United States. The Pew Research Center conducted a nationally representative survey of persons between the ages of 12 and 17 about their use of cell phones to engage in sexting activities. Their findings were as follows:

- Four percent of cell-owning teens ages 12 to 17 say they have sent sexually suggestive nude or nearly nude images of themselves to someone else via text messaging.
- Fifteen percent of cell-owning teens ages 12 to 17 say they have received sexually suggestive nude or nearly nude images of someone they know via text messaging on their cell phone.
- Older teens are much more likely to send and receive these images; 8% of 17-year-olds with cell phones have sent a sexually provocative image by text and 30% have received a nude image on their phone.

Focus group discussions revealed three sexting scenarios:

1. Images are shared between two romantic partners in lieu of, as a prelude to, or as a part of sexual activity.
   I've heard of people getting these types of pictures and usually it's someone's girlfriend, but the people who receive them aren't even the person that they are dating—they are sent to like 10 other guys.
2. Images are sent between friends or between two people where at least one of the pair is hoping to become romantically involved.
   Almost all the time it's a single girl sending to a single guy. Sometimes people trade pictures like "Hey you sent me a pic I'll send you one."
3. Sexually suggestive images sent to the privacy of the phone have become a form of relationship currency.
   When I was about 14 or 15 years old, I received/sent these types of pictures. Boys usually asked for them to start that type of conversation. My boyfriend, or someone I really liked, asked for them. And I felt like if I didn't do it, they wouldn't continue to talk to me. At the time, it was no big deal. But now looking back it was definitely inappropriate and over the line.

Source: Pew Research Center, Teens and Sexting, December 15, 2009.

vary in "frequency, duration, priority, and intensity." Although cyberdeviants engage in virtual interaction with their counterparts across the globe, they typically value these associations more so than most of the personal contacts they have with others. By differentially associating with members of the computer underworld, would-be cyberdeviants learn the "motives, drives, rationalization, and attitudes" necessary to engage in computer-related illicit activity. They also learn the techniques that may be used to commit various computer-related offenses.

Related to Sutherland and Cressey's differential association is Akers and Burgess' concept of differential reinforcement. When a cyberdeviant is sufficiently socialized into the computer underworld, acts of illicit computer ingenuity become widely known and admired. The cyberdeviant is granted considerable recognition and respect within the cyberdeviant subculture. Acts of computer mayhem may well be "differentially reinforced"—and as a result motivate the offender to engage increasingly more daring computer-related deviance.

Rational Choice

To Derek Cornish and Ronald Clarke (1986), rational choice theory holds that the decision to commit a deviant or criminal act is primarily influenced by the need to maximize pleasure while minimizing pain. The decision to engage in computer-related criminal activity tends to involve a deliberate, rational process. The offender must first acquire the highly sophisticated computer expertise to access secured computer property. They decide that their expertise can be markedly improved by invading the computer space of others. Cyberdeviants weigh the pleasure and possible recognition that may attend the commission of a computer crime against the costs involved in being apprehended for such an offense. Cyberdeviants engage in a process of rationally deciding to carry out a computer-related crime. The anticipation of the thrill of discovery or of personally conquering a seemingly insurmountable obstacle—for example, breaking into the computer system of the Pentagon—may override any perceived risk involved in their criminal activity. In short, cyberdeviants make a "rational choice" to commit a computer-related offense.

Techniques of Neutralization

Cyberdeviance may well lend itself to techniques that have been used to neutralize guilt associated with the commission of deviant or criminal acts. Nondestructive computer hackers or cyberdeviants who access the intellectual property or software of others or pirate long-distance phone service may employ one or several of Greshman Sykes and David Matza's (1957) techniques of neutralization. Sykes and Matza identify five techniques of neutralization that may be invoked by persons who engage in deviant acts: *denial of responsibility, denial of injury, denial of the victim, condemnation of the condemners,* and *appeal to higher loyalties.* Cyberdeviants who engage in what they view to be innocuous cyber exploration may well deny that an injury has occurred or that there is a real victim involved in their foray into cyberspace. Even when there is intentional theft, say, of software or computer games, the cyberdeviant may contend that their loyalties to their fellow computer users supersede any concern they may have for the losses that may be incurred by the owners of the pirated software. The cyberdeviant may argue that if computer technology or software can potentially benefit the world at large, then no one person or corporate entity can have exclusive rights to it (see Ethics and the Cyberdeviant, above).

Social Control

Central to Travis Hirschi's (1969) bonding theory of social control is the contention that individuals who are integrated into conventional society are less apt to engage in acts of crime or deviance. The bonds to conventional society include attachment, commitment, involvement, and belief. Cyberdeviants tend to be less interested in the everyday activities of conventional life and more absorbed in the intricacies of cyberspace. As a group, they are less attached to the norms of conventional society and less interested in observing the social customs and mores that are important to others. Although they may not deliberately choose to violate rules of social conduct, they simply are disinterested in them. They commit little time or energy to everyday affairs—having lunch with friends, recreation and leisure activities, or community projects. Their lack of involvement in everyday life signals their rejection of a common set of beliefs and values that may guide their behavior.

Anomie

Robert Merton's (1968) specification of Emile Durkheim's (1951) original conceptualization of anomie further helps to explain involvement in cyberdeviance. To Merton, anomie occurs when there is a disjunction between the institutionalized means and culturally approved goals in society. Individuals experience anomie as stress, strain, or tension that must be adapted to in their everyday lives. Merton identifies five adaptations to the stressful consequences of anomie: conformity, innovation, ritualism, retreat, and rebellion. Two of these adaptations are particularly applicable to cyberdeviance: innovation and retreatism. Innovation refers to the acceptance of culturally approved goals while rejecting the institutionalized means to those goals.

Cyberdeviants may aspire to status and recognition, financial gain and power, or autonomy and self-determination. Rather than engaging in conventional means to these ends, the cyberdeviant uses innovative strategies to gain illicit access to computer systems or cyber-related intellectual property.

Cyberdeviants may also use their computer expertise to devise intricate underground networks of fellow computer aficionados. These underground networks provide the opportunity to retreat into cult-like areas of cyberspace. In cyberworld, a cyberdeviant, in Merton's terms, can reject both institutionalized means and culturally approved goals found in conventional society.

Chapter Summary

Cyberdeviance encompasses a wide spectrum of computer-related offenses. The federal government and individual states have only recently passed legislation that legally defines forms of computer-related offending. The successful enforcement of the legislation is difficult, and numerous amendments to such legislation are necessary to keep up with the evolving and complex nature of computer crime.

The extent of computer-related offending is largely unknown. However, most U.S. corporations surveyed report being victims of cybercrime. Cyberdeviants use a variety of cyberdeviant methods including

- Trap doors
- Timing attacks
- Trojan horses
- Viruses
- Worms
- Logic bombs
- Salamis

Parker identifies seven types of cybercriminals:

- Pranksters
- Hacksters
- Malicious hackers
- Personal problem solvers
- Career criminals
- Extreme advocates
- Malcontents, addicts, irrational, and incompetent people

Cyberdeviants, especially hackers, are a part of a subculture of cyberdeviance who hold common beliefs, share knowledge, and abide by ethical standards, norms, and values. Taylor provides three key elements of the hacker subculture: technology content, secrecy and fluidity, and generation gap and antipathy.

Parker identifies two syndromes that characterize cyberdeviants: differential association and Robin Hood. Differential association refers to the involvement of the cyberdeviant with other cyberdeviants and the learning process by which cyberdeviants rationalize and justify their computer-related offenses. The Robin Hood syndrome is one justification cyberdeviants use to steal from corporations or large-scale organizations.

British sociologist Paul Taylor has identified six motivations for involvement in computer hacking as follows:

- Feeling of addiction
- Urge of curiosity
- Boredom with educational system
- Enjoyment of feelings of power
- Peer recognition
- Political mission

Theoretical explanations of cyberdeviance have yet to be formulated; however, traditional sociological theories can be applied.

Key Concepts

Cyberdeviance: The use of the computer or Internet to victimize computer systems; ranges from relatively benign invasive acts directed at particular computer systems to intentionally destructive attacks against unknown Internet users.

Computer Fraud and Abuse Act: Legislation passed by Congress to address various forms of computer offending.

Technovandalism: A form of computer crime where unlawful access to a computer is gained; the offender may have malicious intent but most often tries to meet the challenge of the unlawful entry.

Technotrespass: A form of computer crime where unlawful access to a computer is gained; refers to an unlawful exploration of computer files simply to look at the contents, not to damage, alter, or steal information.

Trap doors: Device installed in computer software that allows programmers to make changes without going through complicated access protocols.

Timing attacks: Destruction or alteration of data in a computer before being processed, placing one's own name on someone else's data file before it is processed, or altering the order of jobs in the computer's processing or printing queue.

Trojan horse: Device that carries instructions into a computer program that is disguised as authorized and useful but has hidden within it viruses, worms, or logic bombs used to disable a system. Trojan horses are commonly used in computer frauds and sabotage.

Viruses: Programs that are sent through e-mail or downloaded from the Internet that have the ability to reproduce themselves, alter computer programs, alter and destroy data, or render disk space or memory unusable.

Worms: Computer programs that invade a computer by means of the Internet and attack computer software, destroying data and operating procedures; they exist independently of other programs and possess the ability to replicate themselves and attack other computers attached to the original victim.

Logic bombs: Computer programs that work in concert with a virus to instruct the computer to execute a certain function under certain conditions, usually on a given date and time.

Salami: Computer attack that alters financial data by slicing small amounts of money from a much larger account; the victim rarely misses the financial loss.

Hackers: Cyberdeviants who are driven to explore the intricacies of computer programming and uncharted computer applications and to extend the boundaries of their expertise; typically their intent is not to do harm.

Crackers: Cyberdeviants who intend to damage, manipulate, or destroy the computer operations or computer systems of others.

Critical Thinking Questions

1. What sociocultural characteristics distinguish cyberdeviants from other forms of deviant actors? What social psychological factors may account for the motives for and continued involvement in cyberdeviance?
2. What factors may distinguish between occasional or episodic involvement in cyberdeviance and long-term involvement in cyberdeviance?

3. How are cyberdeviant subcultures formed and sustained through time? How are members recruited, selected, and socialized by a cybercrime subculture?
4. What are the differences between cyberdeviants who do not intend harm to other computer users or their computer systems and those who intend malicious damage and theft?

Web Extra

Web-based media materials from high-quality sources such as CNN, Time, and National Public Radio are available in support of this textbook. Visit go.jblearning.com/deviance to access them.

Check out this website for additional information on cybercrime:

http://www.cybercrime.gov

FOOD & DRUG

Positive Deviance

CHAPTER 14

Learning Objectives

After reading this chapter you should know

- The nature, definition, and types of positive deviance.
- The characteristics of positive deviants.
- Explanations of positive deviance.

Not all forms of deviance are bad. Some, although they may be surprising, provide examples of human altruism, bravery, and exceptional honesty. On Christmas Day in 2009, for example, two Safeway stores in Roseville, California, were mistakenly left unlocked and unattended (*Salt Lake City Headlines Examiner*, 2009). Because both stores are normally open for business 24 hours a day, arriving customers expected them to be open. Once customers arrived and gained entry to the stores, however, not a single employee could be found. At that point store video surveillance cameras began recording an unusual occurrence. Customers were recorded pushing shopping carts up and down the isles and then leaving small piles of cash at the checkout registers to pay for the items they had taken. No looting occurred, and personal honesty became the rule for anyone who "shopped" at the store that day.

This story provides an example of positive deviance, but most of what we know about deviant behavior is derived from analyses

> "Problems cannot be solved at the same level of awareness that created them."
> —Albert Einstein (www.therightside.demon.co.uk/quotes/einstein/ae5.htm)

of its negative forms. Positive deviance, however, receives scant attention. Yet, positive deviance in the form of innovation, creativity, and acts of extreme altruism has the potential to energize the social media and cultural environment. To thrive, societies must foster positive deviance in the form of creative problem solving or risk decline and possible extinction.

Positive Deviance Defined

> "We can do no great things; only small things with great love."
> —Mother Teresa (http://home.comcast.net/~motherteresasite/quotes.html)

Typically, when we think about deviant behavior, visions of negative behaviors (e.g., crime and destruction, harm and disorder, aberrations and pathologies) come to mind. The deviant behavior of others evokes fear, disgust, and avoidance but rarely admiration and the desire to emulate it. We do not consciously try to socialize our children to harm others, to be mentally ill or self-destructive, to be addicted, or to be sexually perverse. Nor do we intentionally encourage others to engage in deviant behaviors. All in all, there seems little reason to recommend involvement in behaviors that are violations of commonly held social norms.

Positive deviance is often viewed as an oxymoron, a contradiction in terms (Best & Luckenbill, 1994; Goode, 1991; Sagarin, 1985). Yet some sociologists contend that the concept of positive deviance helps to clarify theorizing about the nature and consequences of deviant behavior (Ben-Yehuda, 1990). For our purposes, **positive deviance** refers to behaviors that exceed normative standards in a positive way—that is innovative, virtuous, or altruistic behaviors (Winslow, 1970).

Behaviors that are judged to contribute significantly to highly prized cultural values (e.g., patriotism, entrepreneurism, athletic prowess in the extreme) may be deviant in the sense of being abnormal or very unusual (Norland et al., 1976; Scarpitti & McFarlance, 1975). The discovery of the North Pole, the climbing of a previously unscaled mountain, or sailing across the Atlantic in an open boat are all positive acts of daring and accomplishment that may qualify as acts of positive deviance.

Five types of positive deviance have been identified: **altruism**, **charisma**, **innovation**, **supraconformity**, and **innate characteristics** (Heckert, 2000). Altruism refers to acts of self-sacrifice that are intended to benefit others without the expectation of extrinsic reward. Charisma is a characteristic of persons with extraordinary ability to inspire others to follow their lead. Charismatic leadership is premised on the intention of the leader to draw others to his or her teachings and example (e.g., Gandhi and Jesus Christ) and the desire of others to place their faith and trust in the charismatic leader. Charismatic leadership need not be positive, of course, as in the case of Adolph Hitler or David Koresh of the Branch Davidian compound near Waco, Texas; Jim Jones, leader of the Jonestown mass suicide; or Marshall Applewhite, the leader of the Heaven's Gate movement and associated mass suicide in California.

Highly innovative persons also engage in positive deviance. Persons who are able to put existing things or ideas together in new and imaginative ways that have the potential to benefit others are rare in society. Scientific discoverers, literary and artistic masters, and inventors are examples of persons whose innovative abilities set them apart from the mainstream in a positive way. Supraconformity results from the adherence to certain societal norms to the extreme. Norms may function on two levels: (1) the ideal, which may be preferred but is exceedingly difficult to accomplish, and (2) the real—or something that is well within the ability of most people to achieve. The behavior of the supraconforming positive deviant complies in an ideal way with the requirements of particular social norms. For example, ideally we should be honest in our dealings with others and tell the truth. However, to always be honest and truthful may be harmful to others, as in the case when a person is asked his or her opinion about someone's new clothes or choice of boyfriend or girlfriend. A more realistic interpretation of the norm of honesty may be less deviant than its strict adherence.

Finally, although it does not refer to immediate forms of behavior, we should recognize the fact that persons who possess innate characteristics that are culturally valued, such as exceptional good looks, intelligence, athletic or musical ability, may be viewed as positive deviants. Certainly, there are subcultural variations as to what constitutes beauty or intelligence or useful talents. It may be, for example, that physical prowess or seductiveness, being streetwise, and having the ability to make a living from a variety of criminal enterprises are more positively valued by members of an oppositional subculture.

Heckert and Heckert (2002, 2004) advanced a "new" typology of deviance that includes both positive and negative forms of deviant behavior. Their typology integrates two perspectives on the definition of deviance: normative expectations and societal evaluations (**Figure 14–1**).

A normative approach to the definition of deviance defines negative forms of deviance as either nonconformity or underconformity or overconformity to expectations. Examples of nonconformity or underconformity to normative expectations include criminal activity or less conventional political views (e.g., White supremacists groups). Overconformity to normative expectations may be negatively evaluated if it is not realistically attainable by the average person. For example, "rate busters"

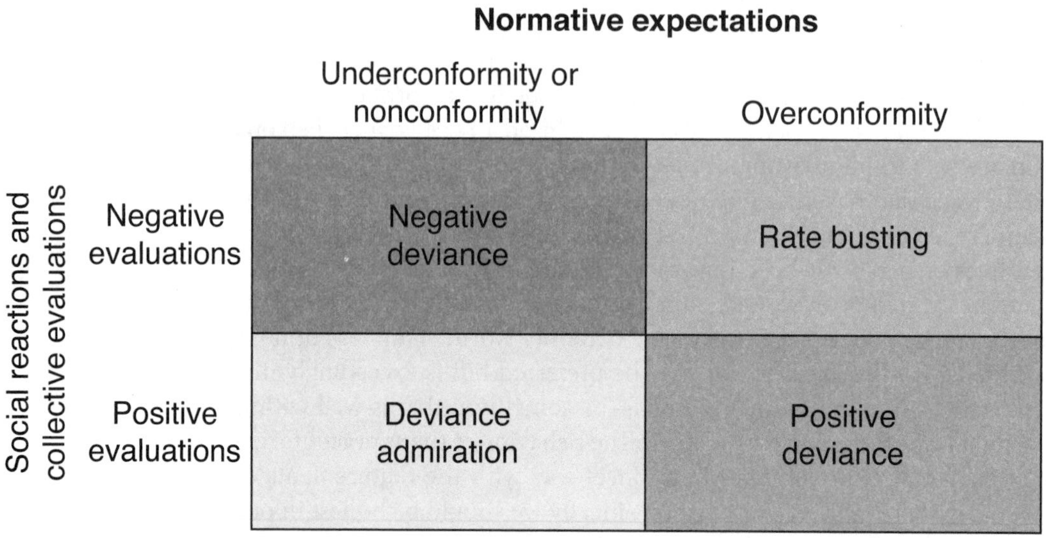

		Normative expectations	
		Underconformity or nonconformity	Overconformity
Social reactions and collective evaluations	Negative evaluations	Negative deviance	Rate busting
	Positive evaluations	Deviance admiration	Positive deviance

FIGURE 14–1 Deviance typology.

Source: Adapted from Alex Heckert and Druann Maria Heckert, Using an integrated Typology of Deviance to Analyze Ten Common Norms of the U.S, Middle Class, The Sociological Quarterly, vol. 45, no. 2, p. 212.

are persons whose performance in school or on the job far exceeds what is possible for most people.

Deviance admiration involves underconformity or nonconformity that is positively evaluated, for example, a notorious person whose behavior is considered exemplary (e.g., Robin Hood or Bonnie and Clyde) and, although illegal, was praised by those who benefited from their transgressions. To Heckert and Heckert (2002, 2004) truly positive deviant behavior involves overconformity to normative expectations that are positively viewed by society at large. Extreme forms of altruism are examples of positive deviance. Mother Teresa is an apt example of a life dedicated to the "poorest of the poor," as are those who risk their lives to rescue other in danger.

Heckert and Heckert (2004) advanced their understanding of positive deviance by integrating their typology of deviance with the Tittle and Paternoster (2000) schema of the normative system of the middle class. **Table 14–1** links the middle-class norms identified by Tittle and Paternoster with forms of positive deviance and provides examples of each form.

TABLE 14–1 Classification of U.S. Middle-Class Deviance, Positive Deviance

Norm	Positive Deviance	Examples
Group loyalty	Altruism	Kamikaze pilots; martyrs; sharing food or other resources; daring rescues (e.g., at sea, mountains); patriot
Privacy	Circumspection	CIA operatives; FBI/Justice Department agents; loyal company employees (e.g., Oliver North)
Prudence	Discretion	The good friend who practices discretion; a person who denies themselves pleasures to achieve a goal (e.g., Olympians & other athletes)
Conventionality	Properness	Junior League members; Martha Stewart's followers; Boy Scouts, Girl Scouts, and similar groups
Responsibility	Hyperresponsibility	Overachiever; straight-A student (as viewed by parents and teachers); workaholic (as viewed by management); overzealous athlete (e.g., Tiger Woods, Michael Jordan)
Participation	Cooperation	Athletic team where individual talents are deemphasized so the team can win; employees who are positively viewed as team players
Moderation	Temperance	Monks; nuns; Women's Temperance Movement; Mothers Against Drunk Driving
Honesty	Forthrightness	Honest Abe Lincoln; George Washington cutting down the cherry tree
Peacefulness	Pacifism	Gandhi; Martin Luther King Jr.; Jimmy Carter
Courtesy	Gentility	Miss Manners; the old-fashioned practitioners of southern hospitality who are admired; the gentleman; the "southern belle"

Source: Alex Heckert and Druann Maria Heckert, Using an integrated Typology of Deviance to Analyze Ten Common Norms of the U.S, Middle Class, The Sociological Quarterly, vol. 45, no. 2, p. 221.

Altruism refers to an extreme form of loyalty to interests of a group. Religious martyrs or political figures who have made extraordinary sacrifices for their beliefs are examples of altruism. Circumspection is practiced by those in positions that require adherence to the norm of privacy, such as the confidentiality required by persons who have access to sensitive information (e.g., military personnel, doctors, lawyers, and clergy members). Discretion is practiced by those who forgo self-indulgence to achieve a high goal (e.g., students committed to their academic pursuits, athletes, and artists). Properness involves extreme participation in civic or voluntary activities.

Hyperresponsibility refers to an unwavering commitment to following through on all promises to complete a task. Cooperation underpins the value of team or group success versus individual honors. Temperance emphases the moderation of pleasure-seeking to further a high interest or more spiritual direction. Forthrightness recognizes that honesty is always preferred over a less truthful response to a situation. Pacifism is the preference for peace in all affairs—interpersonal as well as international. And, gentility is recognized as the practice of courtesy and an open, hospitable manner in dealing with others.

Functions

Beyond its obvious contributions, positive deviance serves important social functions. First, the many forms of positive deviance provide for cultural change. Unless societies actively seek solutions to the problems posed by their physical and cultural environment, they will soon regress and face extinction.

Second, positive deviance ensures that cultural change proceeds in a beneficial way. Cultural change may be either adaptive or maladaptive. That is, it may generate solutions to societal problems or it may exacerbate those problems. By providing innovative and creative solutions to urgent as well as everyday problems, positive deviance enhances social well-being.

Third, widely recognized positive deviance provides a basis for defining other behaviors as less positive or negatively deviant. It is only when we define exceptionally positive behavior that we can define behaviors that are not in the interest of society, those that threaten the functioning of the society as a whole and the well-being of its individual members.

Fourth, the acclaim that society provides for its exemplary members encourages others to engage in positive deviance, which in turn increases the problem-solving ability of that society. In short, positive deviance serves the function of perpetuating itself (Heckert, 2000; Norland et al., 1976; Scarpitti & MacFarlane, 1975).

Creative Process

Robert Sternberg and Todd Lubart (1995) argue that creativity is not innate but can be developed. They propose a process by which individuals can enhance their creativity:

1. *Redefine problems.* Don't accept what you've been told about how to think or act. This step involves the questioning of basic assumptions about the nature of a problem or the possibilities for its solution.
2. *Look for what others don't see.* Put things together in ways that others don't and think about how past experiences, even ones that may

initially seem irrelevant, can play a part in your creative endeavors. To be creative it is necessary to interpret environmental clues in ways that others have not. Creative people are not only able to see what others see but to perceive what could be there.

3. *Learn to distinguish your good from your poor ideas and pay attention to their potential contribution.* The ability to separate ideas that have a potential for making a meaningful scientific or artistic contribution from those that are trivial or marginally important significantly relates to the creative process. Time and energy is not wasted going down paths that lead nowhere.
4. *Don't feel that you have to know everything about the domain in which you work before you are able to make a creative contribution.* Often, innovative ideas come from persons who are not "the" expert in a given field but from a younger member of a research team or someone from another discipline who has recently changed a field of study.
5. *Cultivate a legislative, global style.* Creativity depends, in part, on the desire to explore alternatives to the ways things are traditionally done. The creative process is also enhanced by the ability to think on a global level, beyond the mundane problems faced locally.
6. *Persevere in the face of obstacles, take sensible risks, and be willing to grow.* Obstacles to the creative enterprise are inevitable, so too is failure. Creative persons are able to pursue their goal despite the obstacles that come along.
7. *Discover and tap into your intrinsic motivations.* Creative persons are far more apt to be driven by internal rather than external rewards. That is, involvement in the creative process is its own reward. The possible benefits granted by others are of less concern to a creative person.
8. *Find or create environments that reward you for what you like to do.* The working conditions of a creative person may either enhance or impede the creative process. When imaginative thinking is discouraged or penalized, innovation and creativity are most unusual.
9. *Resources needed for creativity are interactive, not additive.* Individual resources (e.g., intelligence, internal motivation, persistence, and so on) must be present for the creative process to be successful. In addition, an environment that is conducive to creativity is an important element in the process.
10. *Make a decision about a way of life that fosters creativity.* The willingness to redefine a problem or discard assumptions about its solvability is essential to creativity. Creativity involves a conscious decision to look at ideas and things differently.

Discovery Processes

Robert Root-Bernstein (1999, p. 559) defines **discovery** as "the finding of something unexpected" and says that "discoveries change not only the extent of what is known but also how we think about it. Discoveries, in short cause us to rethink and restructure knowledge and the actions we derive from it." To Root-Bernstein (1999) discovery is not the consequence of a single act of inspiration but the result of a process—a series of interlinked steps: (1) the recognition of a problem, (2) the collection of relevant information, (3) the formulation of hypotheses to explain and predict outcomes, (4) the testing of hypotheses, and (5) the verification of the findings. Most often, the findings either do not support the hypotheses as stated or provide little or no support. Therefore, the hypotheses must be reformulated and the process begun again. In the event that the findings support the hypotheses, the next step is to convince the scientific community and larger society of the merits of the findings and that they are to be trusted and acted upon.

Root-Bernstein (1999) provides analyses of six key issues about the processes of discovery: who discovers, what is discovered, when discoveries are made, where discoveries are made, why discoveries are made, and how discoveries are made.

WHO DISCOVERS. Discoveries tend to be made by single persons rather than groups of researchers, "think-tanks," or corporations. The distinguishing characteristics of persons who make significant discoveries are (1) mentoring by an accomplished scientist or scholar (e.g., Nobel Prize winner or highly innovative researcher), (2) intense involvement in creative hobbies or leisure pursuits (e.g., poetry, painting, music, sculpture), and (3) age (younger persons are more apt to make significant discoveries than are older researchers or scholars). The peak age for mathematicians is 25; for physicists, 30; for chemists, 35; and for biologists, the early 40s. Notable discoveries are made by two groups of researchers: those that make a single discovery only (e.g., Jonas Salk, the polio vaccine, and James Crick and Francis Watson, the structure of DNA [deoxyribonucleic acid]) and those who are extremely productive throughout their lifetimes (e.g., Thomas Edison, who was granted 1,093 patents, and Linus Pauling, who contributed significantly to our understanding of chemical bonding, protein structure, and the effects of vitamin C). Amateur scientists (e.g., Charles Darwin, Jane Goodall) also provide discoveries far greater than their academically trained peers.

WHAT IS DISCOVERED. We tend to believe what is discovered is a solution to a problem. Certainly, James Watson and Francis Crick worked on an existing problem—the structure of DNA—that stumped their fellow scientists.

Albert Einstein

"With just a pen and paper, he peeked further behind Nature's curtain than any one had since Newton—then spent the rest of his years living it down. Now when we think of genius we see his face."

"Everything's relative. Speed, mass, space, and time are all subjective. Nor are age, motion, or the wanderings of the planets measures that humans can agree on any more; they can be judged only by the whim of the observer. Light has weight. Space has curves. And coiled within a pound of matter, any matter, is the explosive power of 14 tons of TNT. We know all this ... because of Albert Einstein."

In 1905 Einstein, a 26-year-old Swiss patent clerk, submitted three papers to *Annalen der Physik*, a leading journal in physics. His three papers on theoretical physics, published in the same issue of the journal, immediately revolutionized the way physicists viewed the world—everything became relative. He refined his ideas over the next 11 years and in 1916 proposed his general theory of relativity, verified some 3 years later. To Einstein, "Light had mass, and space and time were simply space-time." The profundity of his thought is sometimes lost in the simplicity of its expression. $E = mc^2$ is widely known, but few understand the depth of the mystery it unravels.

Einstein won the 1922 Nobel Prize in Physics, and by 1935 he joined the faculty at Princeton University. His requirements were simply: "A desk, some pads and a pencil, and a large wastebasket—to hold all of my mistakes." Einstein was to live out his life on the campus thinking about theories of quantum physics, helping children with their homework, and more than occasionally forgetting his address.

Source: "The Time 100: Albert Einstein," *Time*, March 29, 1999. Retrieved November 1, 2010 from http://205.188.238.109/time/time100/scientist/profile/einstein.html

Their discovery was, in large part, made possible by the efforts of other geneticists and technicians who provided the groundwork and analytical equipment necessary to solve the problem. However, much of discovery involves the finding of a new problem or a redefinition of an existing one. Not posing the "right" question can never result in a significant discovery.

Discoverers then are able to perceive dimensions of an existing problem that others do not and thereby recast the research question that will lead to a previously unanticipated solution. Or, discoverers may pose a previously unrecognized question resulting in an equally surprising solution.

WHEN DISCOVERIES ARE MADE. Significant discoveries are usually made within the first 5 to 10 years of a scientist's career. For the most part, an individual will make a single discovery but will be unable to make a second discovery without changing scientific fields. For most discoverers the creative process must begin again for any one person to arrive at a recognized "breakthrough" in science. Changing one's field of inquiry is one way to rejuvenate creative energy.

Curiously enough, only about a third of discoveries are the result of the dogged determination of the scientist. The image of the "mad scientist" working day and night until the problem is solved does not accurately reflect the process of discovery used by most acclaimed scientists. Rather, about a third of the time the scientific breakthroughs occur when the discoverer has stopped working on the problem and has focused attention on other questions. And, the final third of the discoveries are made when the scientist is not working at all but relaxing, playing, or even sleeping.

The prevailing social and cultural climate also influences the creative processes and prevalence of discoveries. Discoveries are more common during times of economic prosperity and the confluence of cultural and intellectual resources. Growing economies provide the assets and time necessary to engage in scientific inquiry. The coming together of culturally diverse perspectives and intellectual traditions extends the boundaries of scientific inquiry. By looking at problems from unfamiliar vantage points, the creative person is energized, the creative process is reshaped, and the chance of making a discovery is enhanced.

WHERE DISCOVERIES ARE MADE. To Thomas Kuhn (cited in Root-Bernstein, 1999), science may be divided into normal and revolutionary. Normal science is conducted within the parameters of carefully constructed theoretical formulations, well-defined conceptualized problems, and standard methods of empirical analysis. Normal science constitutes much of the work that is conducted in our major research universities and laboratories. Revolutionary science, however, seeks to redefine the problems that science is intended to address, questions the theoretical paradigms that guide "normal" scientific inquiry, and proposes alternative strategies for analysis. An additional form of science—"new science"—has been added to Kuhn's typology. New science refers to the development of entirely new fields of study. For example, radiology, immunology, and genetic engineering emerged in the latter part of the 20th century.

Scientific discoveries tend to emanate from the nontraditional centers of research. Ironically, creativity is enhanced in settings that do not carry out large mainstream research projects that typically depend on federal funding. Rather, many important breakthroughs are made in less prestigious institutions where more innovative researchers are free to carry out "revolutionary" science. New science also emerges in institutional settings at the periphery of the mainstream scientific community.

AT A GLANCE

- The United States has won 231 Nobel Prizes, outright or shared, including the most for Physiology or Medicine (74), Physics (62), Chemistry (43), Peace (18), and Economics (23). France has won the most for Literature, with 12.
- There are over 6 million patents in the United States alone and tens of millions in other countries. Almost 3 million U.S. patents have been issued since 1975.
- The Library of Congress is the largest library in the world, with nearly 119 million items on approximately 530 miles of bookshelves. The collections include some 18 million books, 2 million recordings, 12 million photographs, 4 million maps, and 53 million manuscripts. The Library receives some 22,000 items each working day and adds approximately 10,000 items to the collections daily. Most collections are received through the copyright registration process, as the Library is home to the U.S. Copyright Office.

Source: Guiness Book of Records, 1998. http://www.britannica.com/eb/article?eu=60174. Library of Congress http://www.loc.gov/about

WHY DISCOVERIES ARE MADE. Root-Bernstein (1999, p. 567) notes that discoverers are motivated by "control, curiosity, necessity, serendipity, or aesthetics." Creative people, for the most part, want to be in control of their lives, free to exercise their curiosity and pursue their own goals. Dreaded diseases, for example, polio or smallpox, have motivated scientists to discover vaccines to eradicate them. Serendipity—making a discovery when looking for something else—accounts for about half of all scientific breakthroughs. Surprising discoveries, although not rare in science, are nonetheless a consequence of a process of orderly inquiry. Finally, discoverers are often driven to search for the aesthetic in science or in the arts and literature.

HOW DISCOVERIES ARE MADE. Although simple "how to" recommendations for making a discovery are not realistic, certain strategies tend to increase its possibility. First, focus on fundamental questions within a field of inquiry. Incongruities between theories and observations, gaps in our basic knowledge about a given scientific field, or inconsistencies in research findings may point to the kinds of basic issues that lead to important discoveries.

The discoverers' attention to basic issues within a field of inquiry is related to their willingness to repeatedly fail. Discovery often comes unexpectedly after a series of failures, mistakes in judgment and focus, or simply asking the wrong questions. Building on the errors of others and extrapolating from discoveries in related areas are also important strategies for making a significant discovery. An awareness and understanding of failures as well as the successes of others greatly enhance the creative process.

Characteristics of Positive Deviants

Robert Sternberg and Todd Lubart (1995) note six individual resources that are essential for creative activity: intelligence, knowledge, thinking styles, personality, motivation, and environmental context. Related to intelligence is the ability to be synthetic, analytic, and practical. Synthetic refers to the ability to view the problem or recast it in a wholly different way. This synthesis of information allows the person to view problems and challenges from a unique perspective. Analytic ability is key in making information understandable and in assessing the relative merits of the findings. Practical intelligence is the ability to present the idea or innovation to others in an understandable and appealing manner.

Knowledge refers to the awareness of the state of one's field of endeavor—what are the assumptions, the generally accepted information, and parameters for the advancement of the field? With this base of knowledge the creative person can begin to improvise alternative strategies for assessing key problems and their solutions. Thinking styles refers to the ways in which individuals use their intelligence and knowledge. Unconventional thinking styles—questioning the prevailing order and understandings—are characteristic of creative persons.

Typically, the total personality of the person is involved in the creative process. Much of the self is invested in the attempt to innovate or discover something new. "Durus epidermis"—a thick skin—is extremely helpful for creative persons to be able to withstand attempts to discredit them and the fruits of their innovative work. Motivation is intrinsic, highly charged, and persistent. Creative people are undaunted in their pursuit of their goal, undeterred by obstacles and personal affronts. Environmental context may foster the creative process or impede it. The expression of ideas and the desire to engage in exploratory projects may be either encouraged or condemned. Creativity in stifling environments is most unusual (Sternberg & Lubart, 1995).

In Kenneth Hardy's (1974) study of the social origins of U.S. scientists and scholars, he isolates seven basic values espoused by highly productive scientists and scholars that distinguish them from their unproductive peers: (1) naturalism, (2) intrinsic valuation of learning and knowledge, (3) dignity of man, (4) personal dedication, (5) egalitarianism, (6) antitraditional orientation, and (7) being centered on near future. **Table 14–2** provides a comparison of the basic values of productive and unproductive scientists and scholars.

As Table 14-2 shows, the worldview of highly productive scholars differs markedly from that of their less accomplished colleagues. Highly

TABLE 14–2 Cultural Values Associated with High or Low Production of Scholars and Scientists

High Productivity	Low Productivity
Naturalism. Belief in a world of order, law, pattern, meaning.	*World is unknowable, incomprehensible.* Events are capricious, mysterious, whimsical.
Intrinsic valuation of learning, knowledge. To be learned, wise, is highly valued. Broad conception of valued learning.	*Suspicion of learning, education.* Constricted view of valued learning. Anti-intellectual.
Dignity of man. Optimism concerning man's ability to discover truth, accomplish things, change the world.	*Disparagement of man.* Man is powerless, at the mercy of fate, destiny, luck, chance. He is evil, incompetent.
Personal dedication. Seriousness of purpose, sense of mission, positive mysticism. Long-range striving. Responsibility beyond family.	*Sense of indirection.* Must take, enjoy what is available now. Loyalty to family, kin.
Egalitarianism. Active promotion of causes to improve status of disadvantaged. High status for women, children. Pacifism.	*Authoritarianism.* Reliance on authority. Power relations important. Patriarchal order; male dominance. Aggressiveness, militarism.
Antitraditional orientation. Not satisfied with established ways of doing things. Restless, inquiring spirit.	*Traditional.* Past is respected, romanticized. Filial piety valued.
Being centered on near future. Concerned with this world. Orientation toward the foreseeable future.	*Centered on present and distant future.* Hope for a better break in the distant future, the next life.

Source: Reprinted with permission from Hardy, K.R., Science 185: 497–506 (1974). Copyright 1974 AAAS.

productive scholars tend to believe in naturalism—the view that the world is orderly and that empirical events form discernible patterns. This belief leads to an intrinsic valuation of learning and knowledge. Learning what is known and engaging in the discovery of what is not known stands among the most honorable of human pursuits. The value attached to learning and discovery is closely aligned with the belief in the dignity of man. The intrinsic worth of human beings prompts the desire to change things in the world that diminish the human condition. Highly productive scholars are driven by personal dedication to accomplish as much as possible in their lifetimes. Typically, other goals—leisure, material, power—are set aside to pursue their life's passion. It is by advancing our understanding of the world and the ways in which things work that a more just society can be realized. Egalitarianism—the value of providing all persons with the advantages gained by scientific advances—is highly valued among accomplished scholars. The willingness to disrupt the status quo, or antitraditionalism, is also commonly valued among elite scholars. They want to change the world in which they live. Being centered on the near future rather than distancing themselves from their social environment ensures that the results of their labors benefit their world. Taken together, these values focus the attention of scientists and scholars on the natural order of the world, the intrinsic worth of human beings, and the significance of creativity in the pursuit of knowledge that benefits others in the here and now (Hardy, 1974).

Social Characteristics of Discoverers and Creative Persons

Certain social characteristics set persons who make significant scientific discoveries or who are recognized for their creativity apart from others. Harriet Zuckerman's (1997) in-depth investigation of 93 Nobel laureates in science shows that much of the success experienced by the Nobel laureates is the result of the "accumulation of the advantage in science." Advantage in science "accumulates when certain individuals or groups repeatedly receive resources and rewards that enrich the recipients at an accelerating rate and conversely impoverish (relatively) the nonrecipients" (Zuckerman, 1997, pp. 59–60).

There are certain prerequisites for acquiring an "advantage in science." Zuckerman notes that the socioeconomic status of the person's family of origin, religious background, and prestige colleges and universities attended combine to provide social advantages that facilitate entrance into the community of scientific elites.

With regard to the Nobel laureates' families of origin, Zuckerman finds that 82% of their fathers are professionals, managers, or proprietors, compared with 11% in the U.S. population; persons from a Jewish background are disproportionately found among Nobel laureates. This is true for prizewinners from the United States and the world at large. That is, although Jews comprise about 3% of the U.S. population, they account for 27% of the U.S. Nobel prizewinners. This compares with 72% of U.S. Nobel laureates who come from 66% of the overall population with Protestant backgrounds, and 1% of the prizewinners are drawn from 25% of the Catholic families across the United States.

Worldwide, 19% of the 286 Nobel laureates in Zuckerman's study are awarded to Jews—a distinctly disproportionate number compared with their percentage of the general population across the globe. In other words, Jews are vastly overrepresented and Catholics greatly underrepresented. In addition, Zuckerman observes that one in four Nobel laureates graduated from one of five Ivy League institutions: Columbia, Harvard, Yale, Cornell, and Dartmouth. Berkeley, MIT, Cal Tech, the University of Chicago, and the University of Illinois account for an additional 24% of the Nobel Prize winners. That is, Zuckerman finds that 10 U.S. colleges and universities produce about half of the Nobel laureates in science in the United States (Zuckerman, 1997).

The advantages of social origin set in motion two processes—self-selection and social selection—that facilitate the "accumulation of the advantage in science." Self-selection refers to a process by which a student decides to seek admission to an elite university or college to study with a particularly eminent professor (preferably a Nobel laureate) in his or her chosen field. The desire to participate in the research of a Nobel prizewinner must be coupled with the willingness of the laureate to mentor the student. If the master-apprentice relationship is established, then the process of accumulating the advantages in science begins. Older Nobel laureates mentor over half of Nobel laureates in science from the United States. This mentoring relationship is even more common in Nobel laureates in Europe. This intense working relationship with an eminent scientist provides access to resources and the opportunity to become involved in an important and typically highly funded research project (Zuckerman, 1997).

Equally important, the student is socialized into the scientifically elite community. The Nobel prizewinners in Zuckerman's study consistently report that the process of socialization into the scientific community is more important than the substantive information that their mentors pass on to them. The confidence they gain in their own abilities to creatively assess problems in science and to devise alternative approaches to their solution far surpass any technical knowledge gained from their mentors. Being effectively socialized into the scientific culture, being able to understand and accept the value of scientific inquiry with its uncompromising standards, and being able to immerse themselves in the scientific enterprise flow from being socialized by a member of the scientific elite (Zuckerman, 1997).

The advantage of being mentored by an eminent scientist significantly affects the student's initial job placement. Almost all the Nobel laureates in Zuckerman's study (93%) are university faculty members, and 7 in 10 begin their careers in an elite university, compared with 41% of their peers who are not mentored by as prominent scientists (Zuckerman, 1997).

Explanations of Positive Deviance

A number of explanations can be offered as to why positive deviance occurs (**Table 14–3**). The sections that follow explore four such explanations.

TABLE 14–3 Explanations of Positive Deviance

Theories and Theorists	Sociological Predictors	Hypotheses
Social Integration and Control		
Durkheim	Social integration	The greater the social integration, the less the involvement in positive forms of deviance (e.g., innovation and creativity).
Merton	Anomie	The more anomic social life becomes, the greater the involvement in positive forms of deviance (e.g., innovation and creativity).
Hirschi	Attachment	The weaker the attachment to conventional society, the more likely positive forms of deviance (e.g., innovation and creativity) will occur.
	Commitment	The weaker the commitment to conventional society, the more likely positive forms of deviance (e.g., innovation and creativity) will occur.
	Involvement	The greater the involvement in conventional activities, the less likely positive forms of deviance (e.g., innovation and creativity) will occur.
	Belief	The stronger the belief in conventional values and norms, the less likely positive forms of deviance (e.g., innovation and creativity) will occur.
Agnew	Strain	The more strained social relationships become, the more likely positive forms of deviance (e.g., innovation and creativity) will occur.
Societal Reaction		
Becker	Societal reaction	The more affirmative the societal reaction to positive forms of deviance, the more likely those forms of behavior will continue.
Social Conflict		
Coser	Conflict	The greater the conflict in society, the greater the need for social change. The greater the need for social change, the greater the likelihood of positive deviance (e.g., innovation and creativity).
Opportunity and Cultural Supports		
Cloward and Ohlin	Opportunity	The greater the access to opportunities for positive forms of deviance, the more likely innovation and creativity will occur.

Opportunity Theory

A disproportionate number of elite scientists and highly creative persons acquire considerable advantages from the status of their families and the opportunity to be educated in elite institutions. Families that socialize their children to value learning and encourage creativity and critical thinking immeasurably increase their potential for excellence.

Richard Cloward and Lloyd Ohlin's (1960) delinquent opportunity structure theory of negative deviance may be applied to innovative and creative forms of positive deviance. Opportunity structures (e.g., familial, educational, and associational) facilitate innovation and creativity.

James Watson and Francis Crick

"On February 28, 1953, Francis Crick walked into the Eagle Pub in Cambridge, England, and, as James Watson later recalled, announced that 'we had found the secret of life.' Actually, they had. That morning, Watson and Crick had figured out the structure of deoxyribonucleic acid, DNA. And that structure—'a double helix' can 'unzip' to make copies of itself—confirming suspicions that DNA carries life's hereditary information."

This profound discovery was the result of Watson and Crick's unwillingness to accept many of the prevailing ideas of the scientific community. To the American Watson, "A goodly number of scientists are not only narrow-minded and dull but also just stupid." The precocious Watson graduated from the University of Chicago at the age of 19 and earned a doctorate 3 years later. Although 12 years older than Watson, Francis Crick, an Englishman, was less academically accomplished and far less driven to compete with his fellow scientists. Nonetheless, their harmonious working relationship allowed them to exchange ideas freely with one another and to maximize their unique strengths.

Other scientists, notably Rosalind Franklin and her colleague Maurice Wilkins, were also trying to discover the structure of DNA. However, friction between Franklin and Wilkins led to Wilkins' providing Watson and Crick with Franklin's best X-ray diffraction pictures of DNA. This information was key to Watson and Crick's ability to "crack the code" of DNA. Although the work of Franklin was instrumental to Watson and Crick's discovery, she received little public recognition. Four years after the death of Rosalind Franklin, the Nobel Prize was awarded to Watson, Crick, and Wilkins.

Writing about Watson and Crick's monumental scientific breakthrough, psychologist Robert Wright notes, "... one truth seems likely to endure, universal and immutable. It emerges with equal clarity whether you examine the DNA molecule or the way in which it was revealed. The secret of life is complementarity."

Source: "The Time 100: James Watson and Francis Crick," Time, March 29, 1999; http://205.188.238.109/time/time100/scientist/profile/watsoncrick.html

Opportunity structures include a selection and recruitment process, socialization strategies for instilling essential values and norms of conduct, and an organizational structure that provides for increased access to resources and opportunities.

As mentioned earlier, being educated in elite colleges and universities by eminent scientists and scholars significantly enhances the students' opportunities to excel later in life. Although it is possible to be innovative and creative apart from exceptional educational and socialization advantages, it is far less common. Many artists and writers, however, do develop their talents through personal experience, self-education, and dogged determination. They take advantage of informal opportunity structures (i.e., association with other artists and writers) that provide a testing ground for ideas and a source of encouragement and reward.

Both formal and informal opportunity structures enhance individual innovation and creativity. In a sense these opportunity structures serve to maximize the potential of individuals to deviate positively from their peers in science, literature, or the arts. Just as the opportunity to become a car thief does not guarantee a successful career, positive opportunity structures can only provide the conditions that are more apt to lead to high achievement.

Social Integration

Innovation, creativity, and exceptional altruism are unusual under conditions of high social integration. When individuals are tightly bound into conventional society, when they accept without question the cultural scripts for living—what is important, what to do, and how to do it—there is little need or motivation to innovate, create, or deviate from what is considered "right." Change is viewed as threatening to the social order; the individual who advocates change is either punished or ostracized.

However, under conditions of low integration—when values are less commonly held or individuals challenge the existing social and cultural order—innovation, creativity, and unconventional positive behaviors are more likely. Positive deviance is also more probable when anomic conditions are prevalent. When societies are undergoing rapid change, when the social order is threatened by economic turmoil or cultural upheaval, innovative and creative solutions to problems are more necessary and become more highly valued. When the stock market plummets or soars to unprecedented heights, when urban rioting and racial strife abound, when standards for sexual conduct or drug use are questioned, social creativity and innovation are more common.

To Robert Merton (1968), individuals resort to innovation when institutionalized means for achieving culturally approved goals are not available or are unworkable for them. When institutionalized means typically do not lead to culturally approved goals, when graduating from college does not result in a job with considerable opportunity for advancement, society is said to be in a state of anomie. Considerable stress and tension is experienced as members of society struggle to realize those goals particularly valued in their culture. Alternative strategies for achieving the goals of money, material goods, status, or power are sought. Innovative means are developed, tested, refined, and put into practice. As innovative strategies become more effective and are socially accepted, they may become institutionalized, and a new conventional order is created.

Similarly, Robert Agnew (1992) argues that when an individual's social interactions do not benefit him or her or when others block that person's attempts to gain certain goals, negative emotions, anger, rage, self-deprecation, and loss of self-esteem may follow. These negative emotions create considerable strain for the individual that must be alleviated. Often, attempts to lessen strain—"to blow off stream"—involve negative behaviors, verbal or physical aggression, or self-inflicted harm. However, strain may also trigger more creative ways to resolve the problem. The person is forced to alter the existing conflicted situation by developing new ways to deal with it or by exploring alternative ways to achieve desired goals.

High social integration tends to lessen creative and innovative thinking. Conventional ways of conducting everyday life are widely accepted and stringently defended. Travis Hirschi (1969) contends that when the bonds that tie an individual to society are very strong, that person is less likely to engage in negatively defined deviance. The greater the involvement in conventional society and acceptance of the prevailing value structure, the less the desire to deviate from deeply held norms and beliefs. Similarly, individuals who are tightly bound into conventional society are considerably less prone to engage in positive deviance, less likely to find the need for innovation and creativity. Why disrupt things that seem to be working just fine for them? There is little room for social or cultural change. Under conditions of tightly meshed values and behavior, innovation and creativity are deemed unnecessary, more often threatening to the social order, and subject to control and eradication. When positive forms of deviance are widely condemned, social stagnation ensues.

Conflict

Conflict at both the micro and macro levels of sociological analysis is recognized as a source of cultural and interpersonal change. Where there is widespread discontent and violence, when urban areas erupt in riots, when citizens take to the streets to protest governmental policy or threatening social conditions, a signal for change is made publicly manifest. Likewise, when relations between two or more persons become so contentious they are no longer able to resolve their conflicts peacefully, when communication deteriorates into verbal abuse and accusation, when physical violence is either threatened or actually carried out, change is necessary to avoid irreversible destruction. Rolf Dahrendorf (1959) and Lewis Coser (1967) argue that social conflict does function to bring about cultural change. Conflict between social groups and between large segments of society and national and local governments generates strain on the existing social order.

Similarly, at the individual level, interpersonal relations marked by chronic conflict are stressful for all parties involved—wives and husbands, their children, and friends—and often threaten the health of the combatants and others near them, their relations with others outside the conflictual relationship (e.g., coworkers, neighbors, and so on), and their social and legal status in the community.

Unless conflict leads to change either at the societal or individual level that positively resolves the dispute, negative outcomes may well follow. Violence and destruction are common. Strife becomes institutionalized and is transmitted from one generation to the next, as in the case of Protestants and Catholics in Northern Ireland or the legendary Hatfields and McCoys. This cultural transmission of fundamental conflict between nations or social and cultural groups is acquired through the socialization process of children as they learn about their heritage and what is right and wrong, good and bad, prized and condemned and is mindlessly played out in everyday life.

Responses to conflict may be negative or positive. That is, conflict at the societal, group, or individual level may generate violent or other destructive outcomes, or it may spark innovation or creativity. Innovative ways of resolving complex sociopolitical conflicts may be devised. Technological or medical advances may result from the demand to protect oneself from harm at the hand of an enemy or outbreak of disease or other threats to physical or mental health. Such innovations may find widespread support and encouragement.

Alex Thio's (1978) power theory, although intended to account for negative deviance, may be applied to positive deviance as well. Thio argues that the powerless, those with few economic or political advantages, do not have access to professional organizations, governmental agencies or representatives, or other influential groups. As a consequence, outlets for their innovative or creative ideas are limited. Departure from normative behavior, positive as well as negative, by the powerless tends to be discouraged. Deviations from acceptable modes of conduct may be viewed by the powerful as threatening and therefore negatively defined. To Thio, then, the powerless are more apt to engage in high-consensus deviant behavior. Innovations and creativity among the powerless tend to be ignored or deliberately blocked from public expression.

However, the powerful tend to be economically, politically, and socially in a position to have their creative or innovative ideas and products recognized positively. The powerful have the educational and professional opportunities to develop their potential for creativity. As we have seen, prominent scientific, literary, and artistic persons typically have access to social institutions (e.g., universities, "think tanks," and professional organizations) that provide the facilities and financial resources necessary to carry out creative and innovative work. Perhaps more of the creative capital of the powerful concerns their contribution to economic gain. Product development and innovation, marketing and advertising, investment and management of financial resources are paramount concerns of corporations and smaller scale business enterprises. To survive in an expanding free market economy, businesses must continually be ahead of their competition. Innovation and creativity is highly valued, rewarded, and compensated, particularly in the United States.

Societal Reaction

A central tenet of societal reaction or labeling formulations of deviant behavior is an individual's behavior will tend to be consistent with the reaction of others or the "label" that is attached to it. Becker (1963) notes that the deviant is one to whom the label has been successfully applied. By successful application, he means that the person has accepted the label in that he or she has defined himself or herself in the same way that others do.

The dynamics of societal reaction or labeling are the same whether they are applied to negative or positive behaviors. For example, if a child is defined by a schoolteacher as bright and creative, then that child is more likely to be inquisitive, to want to explore new things, to be confident in expressing ideas and perceptions. Societal reaction or labeling plays a large part in socializing persons to be innovative and creative. Montessori schools are intentionally designed to encourage discovery and creative expression in children. The rigid curricula of traditional

SSRN

Hoffman, A. J., & Haigh, N. (2010). Positive deviance for a sustainable world: Linking sustainability and positive organizational scholarship. Ross School of Business Paper No. 1139. http://ssrn.com/abstract=1586363

schools are replaced by a flexible method of instruction that maximizes the student's control over the educational process.

However, institutional arrangements for the socialization of children (e.g., familial, day care, after-school programs) tend to value conforming behavior. The more compliant children are, the easier it is for their guardians to care for them, their teachers to teach them, and their neighbors to accept them. In time they fit well into organized work settings and carry out functions in an orderly and predictable manner. Their contribution is not to deviate, either negatively or positively, but to ritualistically perform those tasks that have been assigned to them. In a sense they hold society together, but they do not advance it. The innovators, whose ideas and actions deviate from mainstream thought, are permitted to engage in unconventional activities early in life, defined positively for doing so, and consistently rewarded for their efforts.

Chapter Summary

Positive deviance refers to those behaviors that exceed normative standards in a way that benefits society and its members. These behaviors include

- Innovation—the ability to put existing things or ideas together in a new or imaginative way that has the potential to benefit society
- Altruism—acts of self-sacrifice
- Charisma—extraordinary leadership
- Supraconformity—adherence to certain societal norms to the extreme

Intelligence, knowledge, thinking styles, personality, motivation, and environmental context are six individual resources essential for creative activity. In addition, naturalism, intrinsic valuation of learning and knowledge, dignity of man, personal dedication, egalitarianism, antitraditional orientation, and centeredness on the near future are seven basic values held by highly productive scientists and scholars.

Explanations of positive deviance include social integration theories, theories of societal reaction, social conflict theory, and opportunity theory. Each of these theories was discussed in this chapter.

Key Concepts

Positive deviance: Behaviors that exceed normative standards in a way that benefits society and its members; behaviors that are judged to contribute significantly to a highly prized cultural value.

Altruism: Acts of self-sacrifice that are intended to benefit others without the expectation of extrinsic reward.

Charisma: A characteristic of persons with an extraordinary ability to inspire others to follow their lead.

Innovation: The ability to put existing things or ideas together in new and imaginative ways that have the potential to benefit others.

Supraconformity: Adherence to certain societal norms to the extreme.

Innate characteristics: Acquired characteristics such as exceptional good looks, intelligence, athletic, or musical ability.

Discovery: The finding of something unexpected.

Critical Thinking Questions

1. Imagine that you want to socialize a child to become a positive deviant. You may want her or him to become remarkably altruistic or to be a renowned writer, artist, or scientist. What would you consciously need to do to maximize the chances of your child's becoming a truly positive deviant? What would you do to minimize the likelihood of her or his becoming a positive deviant?
2. What sociocultural conditions must be present to ensure that a sufficient number of positive deviants—altruistic and creative persons—are generated to serve the interests of the larger society?
3. Can involvement in positive deviance be scientifically predicted? If so, what are the key macro- and micro-level variables that increase the likelihood of positively deviant behavior?
4. Consider a society in which positive deviance is not present. Altruism is unknown, innovation and creativity are shunned. How would you describe the everyday lives of members of this society, their emotional and psychological well-being, and the ways that they commonly interact with one another?

Web Extra

Web-based media materials from high-quality sources such as CNN, Time, and National Public Radio are available in support of this textbook. Visit go.jblearning.com/deviance to access them.

Check out this website for additional information on positive deviance:

http://www.positivedeviance.org

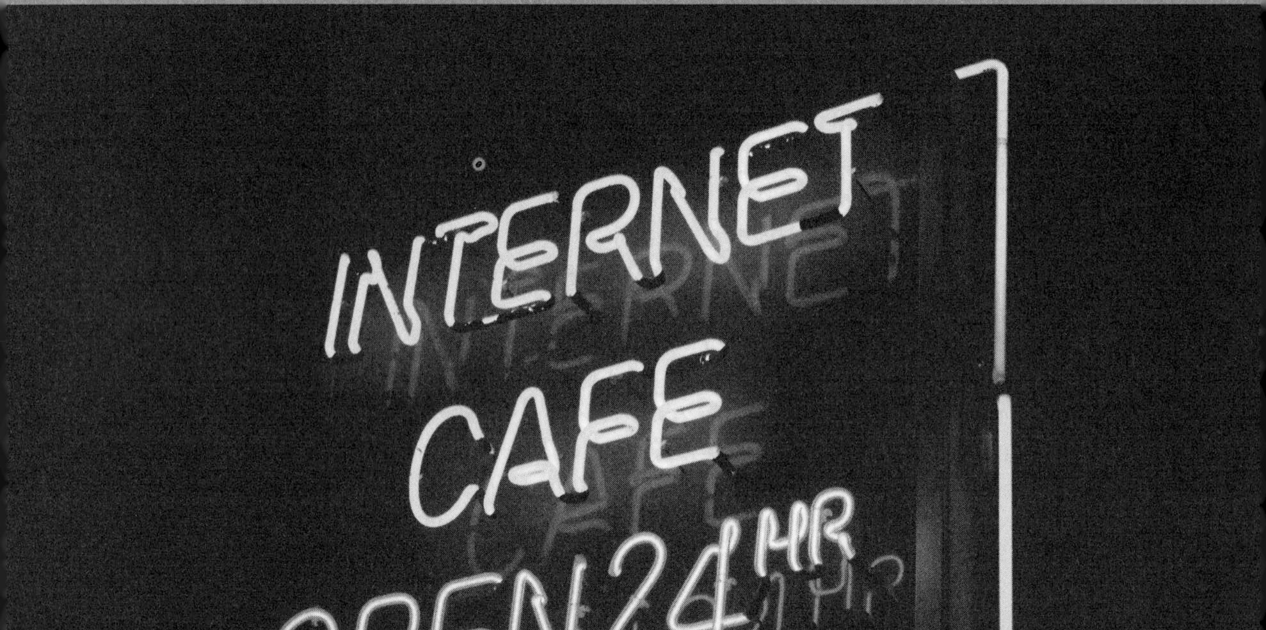
INTERNET
CAFE
OPEN 24 HR

Extreme Forms of Everyday Behaviors: Exercising, Working, and Web Surfing

CHAPTER 15

Learning Objectives

After reading this chapter you should know

- The nature, characteristics, and consequences of extreme forms of everyday behaviors.
- The nature and characteristics of overworking and of the overworked.
- The nature and characteristics of computer and Internet addiction.
- The nature and characteristics of extreme sports.
- Some theoretical explanations of workaholism, computer addiction, and extreme sports participation.

In a sad 2010 story, a 3-month-old little girl was neglected and starved to death while her parents spent their time at a Korean Internet cafe raising a virtual baby girl called Anima in a role-playing game (Tran, 2010). The game, similar to the web-based simulation "Second Life" or to the computer-based game "Sims," allows for intense and ongoing virtual interaction with other players. After one 12-hour gaming session, the couple came home to find their baby daughter dead. An autopsy later showed she died from neglect. The couple had occasionally fed her dried milk, but not often enough to provide the nourishment her growing body needed. According to police investigators, "they indulged themselves in the online game of raising a virtual character so as to escape from reality, which led to the death of their real baby" (*Huffington Post*, 2010).

This was not the first time South Koreans were shocked by obsessive behavior related to the Internet. Only a month earlier a 22-year-old Korean man was arrested and charged with killing his mother because she had nagged him for spending too much time playing Internet-based games. After the killing, the suspect allegedly sat down in a nearby Internet cafe to continue his game.

Recent research by British psychologists has found that "over-engaging in websites that serve to replace normal social function might be linked to psychological disorders like depression and addiction" (Morrison, 2010). "We now need to consider the wider societal implications of this relationship and establish clearly the effects of excessive Internet use on mental health," says Catriona Morrison, the study's lead researcher.

Almost everyone today uses computers, the Internet, and web-based services. Many people play computer games, and multiplayer Internet-supported games are commonplace. Still, most people are able to separate virtual worlds from real ones.

Extreme Forms of Everyday Behavior

"Workaholism masquerades as a positive trait in the cultural lore of our nation."
—Fassel (1992)

Everyday behaviors—working, exercising, surfing the Internet—are not typically viewed as deviant. They are things we do routinely; we seldom take particular notice of them. Although we are rarely conscious of the social norms that shape our everyday behaviors, they nonetheless guide even our routine actions. When we work incessantly, exercise or engage in extreme forms of athletic competition, or hack away on the computer day and night, our everyday behaviors take on deviant forms. In some instances these everyday behaviors practiced in the extreme may be viewed as positive. Persons who work far beyond what is required of them are often considered an asset to an organization; others who engage in extreme forms of competitive games or contests may be viewed as heroic, providing evidence of extraordinary human endurance and potential; and computer hackers may be perceived as able to develop innovative computer strategies that benefit others. Conversely, these same behaviors may have negative consequences not only for the actors but also for those closest to them and the society at large.

"I have been a computer addict since I was 11 .... I'm afraid that I will run away if my parents take my computer away ... it is almost like the computer owns me."
—14-year-old boy's e-mail (Cromie, 1999)

In this chapter we consider three extreme forms of everyday behavior: workaholism, computer addiction or "webaholism," and ultracompetitions. Although these behaviors are not typically considered in deviant behavior textbooks, it is important to understand how everyday behaviors are guided by social norms and supported by cultural values. Social norms provide a framework, albeit subtly, for our everyday behaviors. Cultural values reinforce social norms by defining the accepted meaning of our actions. When these boundaries are breached, our everyday behaviors take on a form of deviance that lies outside the realms of law, medicine, or religion. They are not crimes, illnesses, or sins, yet as extreme forms of everyday behavior they are of concern to us here.

"People may think we are mad. We think they are insane to endure such humdrum lives."

—David Kirke, world's first bungee jumper (Soden, 2003, p.1)

Nature of Overwork

In our increasingly fast-paced society, time is measured in nanoseconds. Time-deepening—doing multiple things simultaneously (e.g., driving while eating and drinking, listening to music, and talking on a cell phone)—is commonly practiced (Robinson & Geoffrey, 2008). The Internet allows us to communicate instantly day and night anywhere across the globe, and "24/7" has become the prevailing way to describe the working lives of a significant segment of U.S. society. Yet working to excess is a relatively recent phenomenon. Workers in the United States now spend more hours on the job than any other advanced industrial nation (Lardner, 1999). Judith Schor, a Harvard economist, in her book, *The Overworked American* (1991), provides considerable evidence that Americans have added a month of work a year in the latter part of the 20th century. In comparative terms, Americans on average work 2 months a year longer than the average western European. For example, in Norway and Sweden workers typically receive 4 to 6 weeks of vacation each year and as much as 1 year of parental leave from their jobs (Lardner, 1999). In France it is illegal to work more than 35 hours in any given week (United Press International, 1999).

Workaholics and Workaholism

Americans pride themselves on working hard. Hard work, thrift, and self-reliance are core values of U.S. culture, derived in large part from the Protestant work ethic. Yet in the latter third of the 20th century, Americans have increasingly compressed more work into less time, worked more hours, or taken on second jobs, ironically to pay for leisure time activities. The virtue of work is being raised to an unprecedented level. Economist Juliet B. Schor (1991) reports that overall Americans work the equivalent of about a month more each year than they did in 1970. American workers are also permitted fewer vacation days and actually take the fewest vacation days compared with their counterparts in other Western industrialized nations. For example, Americans on the average are allowed 14 days vacation but leave 3 days unused; the French are allowed 36 days and leave only 3 days unused; Spaniards, 30 days and take all but 2; Germans are given 26 days and leave 1 day unused; and the British, 24 days and leave 3 days unused (*Shadi*, 2007). Workaholism then has become commonplace in the American workplace.

The term "**workaholism**" was introduced in 1971 by Wayne Oates, a Protestant clergyman, who described it as an addiction, a compulsive need to work as long and as often as possible (Oates, 1971). To Oates, the workaholic has ". . . the compulsion or the uncontrollable need to work incessantly" (Oates, 1971, p. 11). The workaholic then is one who is over-committed, inflexible, and driven relentlessly to achieve.

Various definitions of a workaholic have been proposed to capture its essential characteristics. Psychologist Bryan Robinson notes that "workaholics are out of balance." To Robinson, "They do not have many friends. They don't take care of themselves. They don't have many hobbies outside of the office. A hard worker will be at his desk thinking about the ski slopes. A workaholic will be on the ski slopes thinking about his desk" (Robinson, 2007, p. 18). In short, Robinson points out that workaholism is synonymous with work addiction, which he defines as an "obsessive-compulsive disorder that manifests itself through self-imposed demands, an inability to regulate work habits, and an overindulgence in work to the exclusion of most other life activities" (Robinson, 2007, p. 7).

Spence and Robbins (1992) define a "workaholic triad" as work involvement, a feeling of being driven to work, and work enjoyment. Workaholics tend to be invested in their work, driven to work longer and harder to succeed, but derive little enjoyment from their efforts. Although various combinations of the elements of the workaholic triad are possible, to Spence and Robbins the "real workaholic" is high in work involvement, highly driven to work, but low in work enjoyment. Similarly, Snir and Zohar (2000) define workaholism as the inordinate devotion of time and thought to work-related activities far beyond what is necessary for a successful outcome. Workaholics then are often driven to reduce stress and anxiety associated with their job performance. They work incessantly to increase their self-esteem and sense of control over their lives.

Marilyn Machlowitz's (1980) in-depth investigation of the behavior of workaholics provides the basis for types of workaholics:

- *Dedicated* workaholics, single-minded and one-dimensional, are so involved in their work that any other activity is viewed as an intrusion and is consciously avoided.

- *Integrated* workaholics occupy jobs that require nonworking activities. Product representatives must travel to call on their potential customers, for example, and corporate executives must entertain politicians and community leaders. Travel and entertainment are viewed as essential to the performance of their jobs.
- *Diffused* workaholics are typically involved in several projects at the same time. They are able to juggle unrelenting demands on their time, retain the details of their various job-related commitments, and appear to be in control of their daily lives.
- *Intense* workaholics pursue leisure with the same passion, purposefulness, and pace as work. If told to relax and rest, they will do so with dogged intensity and on schedule. Leisure activities, golf or tennis, for example, are pursued with vengeance.

Common among workaholics, then, is their sense of "time urgency"—that is, the desire to accomplish something every minute of every day. They often attempt to do several things at the same time (time-deepening) to maximize their time and effort. Time spent away from the job is viewed as wasted. Eating, sleeping, and non–work-related family activities are seen as unfortunate necessities and impingements on their harried schedule and should be kept to a minimum.

Three behavioral patterns of workaholics are compulsive-dependent, perfectionist, and achievement-oriented. The compulsive-dependent workaholics are driven to work; they are unable to control their need to work incessantly. Although they may understand that their work habits are excessive, threats to their health and social well-being, and unnecessary, they are unable to stop themselves from continuing to work longer and longer hours. Not to work would be anxiety producing; working serves to reduce their symptoms of withdrawal and emotional upheaval. Perfectionist workaholics are characterized by their need to be in control of their work situation as well as all other aspects of their lives. To maintain control over their work environment, the perfectionist workaholic tends to be inflexible and rigid, focusing on details, rules, and lists. They often resort to aggressive and domineering tactics to control the work of their colleagues. Achievement-oriented workaholics have a strong desire for upward occupational mobility. They are strongly committed to their careers, are highly competitive, and are driven by the need to be a success. They devote far more time to work than is required. Even when not on the job, the achievement-oriented workaholics are thinking about solutions to work-related problems. They strive for excellence and recognition as leaders in their fields (Scott, Moore, & Miceli, 1997).

Types of Workaholics

Psychologist Bryan Robinson identified four types of workaholics:

1. *Relentless workaholic*
   A full-blown charge into any project prohibits devising an effective plan for its completion. Work is typically not delegated to others; gross inefficiency is often the result.
2. *Bulimic workaholic*
   They delve into projects at the last minute and panic when time is running out. These adrenaline rushes are followed by periods of inertia. Unrealistic expectations for performance lead to incessant worry about not meeting them.
3. *Attention-deficit workaholic*
   They move rapidly from one task to another, driven by the need for an adrenaline "high." Their inability to focus on the job at hand leads to chaos in the workplace.
4. *Savoring workaholic*
   The obsession over the details of a project repeatedly stalls its completion. Work never seems to be done quite "right"; more can always be done.

Source: Bryan E. Robinson, Chained to the Desk, New York: New York University Press, 2007: 54.

Extreme Jobs

The increasing complexity and unrelenting pressures of the global economy have led to an increasingly longer work week. The top 6% of all employees in the United States are persons between ages 25 and 34 who earn $75,000 or more and those 35 and over who earn $100,000 or more. Research on high earners finds that 62% work 50 hours a week or more, 35% more than 60 hours a week, and 10% more than 80 hours a week. Extreme jobs are held by those persons whose responsibilities and job expectations are not necessarily reflected in their pay. Most extreme job holders (56%) work 70 hours a week or more, and 9% are on the job 100 hours a week or more. Almost half of the extreme job holders (48%) report working an average of more than 16 hours each week than 5 years before the survey. About 45% of large corporate managers are in extreme jobs, working an average of 73 hours each week (Hewlett & Luce, 2006).

A survey of Canadian residents found that almost one in three (31%) considers themselves workaholics. Unlike nonworkaholic Canadians, the workaholics considered their work and home lives to be "out of kilter," which causes them a good deal of stress. Yet, the workaholics report they cannot control the use of their time. Their harried lives leave them little freedom to do all they would like. "Too much to do and too little time to do it" is a common theme of the lives of the workaholics (Keown, 2006).

Characteristics of Workaholics

Machlowitz (1980) characterizes workaholics as intense, energetic, competitive, and driven. Workaholics literally take the 24/7 view of work. They pursue their work goals in a relentless, untiringly way. They pride themselves on their capacity for work—7 days a week, 52 weeks a year. Their passion is to work, to constantly achieve new goals, and to set increasingly higher standards for themselves. Life is a zero-sum game, and they either win or lose; there is no middle ground.

Workaholics have strong self-doubts. Ironically, workaholics who appear to be the epitome of self-confidence, to always be in control of the situation, are often gripped by a fear that they are not up to the task they have set for themselves. Machlowitz (1980, p. 28) notes, "Working hard can be a way of concealing or compensating for such suspected shortcomings."

Manfred F. R. de Vries notes that many workaholics consider themselves frauds—imposters whose true identity will be found out by those around them. The *neurotic imposter* is a workaholic who does not believe his or her success is the result of ability but is simply "bluffing" his or her way through life. His or her accomplishments mean nothing; they are a curse. Their exposure is inevitable: It is simply a matter of time (de Vries, 2005).

Workaholics prefer labor to leisure. Workaholics derive their greatest pleasure from the work they do. All other activities—family activities, recreation, socializing—diminish their sense of well-being. Days off, typically Sundays and holidays, are stressful, depressing, or otherwise emotionally disconcerting to the workaholic. Withdrawal from their addiction to work is painful and to be avoided.

Time-Deepening: Acceleration of Life

Robinson and Godbey outline four ways in which time-deepening may occur:

1. *Attempting to speed up a given activity:* Eating only microwavable food, using an electric toothbrush
2. *Substituting a leisure activity that can be done more quickly for one that takes longer:* Playing computer golf rather than actually going to the golf course, walking on a treadmill rather than in the park
3. *Doing more than one activity at once:* Eating while talking on the phone, watching television, and doing Tai Chi
4. *Undertaking a leisure activity with more precise regard to time:* Scheduling work and leisure activities with little time in between.

Source: Robinson, John and Geoffrey Godbey. Time for Life: The Surprising Ways Americans Use Their Time.(Second Edition). University Park: The Pennsylvania State University Press, 1999: 39.

Workaholism: When More Is Less

Atlantan Carey Sipp was so consumed with work at one time that each time she was in the delivery room in labor with her two children she was on the phone with clients. At the time she was working 16-hour days, 6 days a week, and earning a six-figure salary creating fund-raising packages for nonprofit groups.

"I still read bedtime stories to my children and I breast-fed my children and they were in the house with me. But my big rush was to get downstairs and come up with a headline that worked and nail a deadline."

To Carey Sipp, working incessantly: "...beat the heck out of dealing with the financial and emotional side of my marriage." Work addiction, she argues, "like food addiction and alcoholism, is about escaping reality. But in our society, work addiction is the one addiction that is truly applauded."

After her divorce and bouts with ill health, she decided to forego her workaholic lifestyle, move into a much smaller home, and devote herself to raising her two children.

Source: Joyner, T. "All Work is American Way of Life." Atlanta Journal Constitution. November 14, 1999:R1.

Workaholics can—and do—work anytime and anywhere. The addiction to work must be satisfied at all times. Workaholics are very creative about finding times to indulge themselves in work. Weekends, late at night, and very early in the morning are times they are not distracted by phone calls or coworkers who want to socialize on the job. During these off-times the workaholic is able to concentrate more fully on the task at hand. The psychic rewards are great.

Workaholics make the most of their time. Time is to be treasured, hoarded, and protected from the constant threat of theft. There is a need to maximize every moment; time is not to be wasted—something must be accomplished. Workaholics are vigilant about their use of time, always striving to devise time-saving strategies and ways to do more things simultaneously.

Workaholics blur the distinctions between business and pleasure. Business is pleasure: There is no distinction. Workaholics typically derive their greatest, if not their only, pleasure from work. Misery is experienced away from the job; pleasure is found while working. Machlowitz (1980) quotes a workaholic as saying, "I don't think of work as any different from play. I mean I do enjoy it—I'd rather do that than anything else. I don't know why one has to draw the distinction" (p. 32).

Socialization and Psychological Factors in Overwork

Machlowitz (1980) notes that workaholics tend to be socialized by parents who encourage and reward profit-making activities (e.g., selling lemonade or magazines, shoveling snow, or raking leaves). Children who are involved in several extracurricular projects learn to manage their time to accomplish as much as possible. The more they do, the more their caretakers approve of them. However, the more children accomplish, the more they are expected to accomplish. They soon become trapped in a no-win situation. This endless cycle of increasing accomplishment and progressive expectations, Machlowitz argues, generates self-doubt in workaholics.

Self-doubt leads to a need to control all aspects of their lives, to maximize their own time as well as their associates'. Machlowitz (1980, p. 45) observes that "control—or the illusion thereof—is vitally important to workaholics." Accompanying this obsession with control is the haunting fear that things are spinning out of control, a fear that precipitates increasing self-doubt.

Based on his extensive psychotherapeutic experience with workaholics, Robinson (1998, 2007) finds they tend to come from two types of

A Portrait of Work Addiction

- Work addiction is a compulsive disorder that workaholics carry into the workplace. It is not created by the workplace.
- Work addiction is a mental health problem, not a virtue, and it can create more problems than it can solve for the workplace.
- The superhero facade masks deeper emotional and adjustment problems workaholics shield with their accomplishments.
- Workaholics do not sacrifice free time and families for their work; they do it for ego gratification.
- Although most workaholics say they enjoy their jobs, work satisfaction is not a prerequisite to work addiction.
- Workaholics become chemically addicted to their own adrenaline because of the stress they put themselves under, and they crave additional crises to maintain the work highs.
- Work addiction can be a primary or a secondary addiction that blends with other addictions.
- Workaholics do not have to be gainfully employed to become addicted; it can happen with any compulsive activity.
- Recovering one's balance after work addiction improves work quality and productivity and helps workaholics be happier and more effective at what they do.
- Achieving balance from reduced work addiction requires more than cutting back on work hours; it involves deep personal introspection and insights as well as attention to the parts of life that have been neglected.

Source: Robinson 2007:54.

families: the perfect family or the chaotic family. The perfect family is characterized by rigid rules and the maintenance of a "happy" facade. Robinson finds that the "message is clear: Say and do the right thing, pretend that everything is okay even when it isn't, don't talk about your feelings, and don't let people know what you are like on the inside." In chaotic families parents tend to be unpredictable, inconsistent, and very disconcerting to the children. Parents are unable to protect their children from social or psychological disruptions that emanate from outside the home. As a consequence children have an urgent need to control their immediate social environment and later their families and conditions of their job.

Consequences of Overwork

ON THE JOB. Workaholism is either viewed as a positive or a negative form of addiction. Some organizational theorists consider the passion for work that the workaholic exudes is an asset to be encouraged among employees (Korn, Pratt, & Lambrou, 1987; Sprankle & Ebel, 1987). It is in the organization's interest to encourage its workers to dedicate themselves wholly to the task at hand and to expect the same from their coworkers. Other researchers consider workaholism to be extremely dangerous to its victims and disruptive to their working associates (Naughton, 1987; Porter, 1996, 2001). Being driven by their need to work and their expectation that others keep pace, workaholics may well create conflicts and dissension within an organization. Anthony Brody (1979) finds that the behavior of workaholics is counterproductive—workaholics are inefficient, disruptive to their fellow workers, and the cause of high rates of absenteeism and loss of employees. In addition, the self-doubt and low self-esteem of the workaholic—the need for approval from others coupled with the relentless need to control the work environment—combine to undermine organizational functioning.

However unproductive they become, workaholics continue to work with increasing tenacity. Work may not result in any tangible rewards—recognition, economic gain, and self-worth—yet it is not abandoned. Only when working does the workaholic feel emotionally stable. Work is a necessity; its own reward (Machlowitz, 1980).

FAMILY. As expected, the demands of family life—time spent with a spouse and children—are often seen by the workaholic as an interference with his or her primary concern in life, to work. Workaholics are "role-bound" individuals. Activities other than work are disdained; every effort is made to keep them to a minimum.

AT A GLANCE

Extreme Forms of Everyday Activity

Exercising

- Extreme sports and competitive tests of endurance are now institutionalized forms of athletic events that rival traditional professional sports (e.g., baseball, basketball, and football) for media attention.

Working

- One in four American workers report they are "often" or "very often" burned out by their work and consider their jobs to be the worst stressor in their lives.
- Three in four Americans believe workers today suffer more on-the-job stress than workers a generation ago.
- Work-related problems result in more illness than any other source of stress, more than financial or family problems.
- The average American works the equivalent of an astonishing 8 weeks a year longer than the average western European. In Norway and Sweden, ordinary workers get 4 to 6 weeks of vacation and up to a year of paid parental leave.
- The average Japanese businessperson takes only half his or her paid holidays.

Computer Addiction

- About 7 in 10 office workers use the Internet for personal reasons during work hours (e.g., playing games, shopping, gambling, and visiting pornographic sites).
- Internet addiction is particularly high among persons who suffer from depression, anxiety disorders, social phobias, and other compulsive disorders.
- Cybersex addiction, online affairs, and online gaming are the most common forms of Internet addiction.
- Children who are addicted to the Internet also are more likely to suffer from depression, have school-related problems, and are more apt to develop physical illness and obesity.
- ReStart, the first residential Internet addiction treatment center in the United States, opened in 2009 near the headquarters of Microsoft.

Sources: www. netaddiction.com, Raymond, J. "Going to Extremes." American Demographics, June 1, 2002 http://www.netaddiction.com; Greene, R. 1998. "Internet Addiction." Computer World, September 21; U.S. News and World Report Editors. June 26, 2000. "No Time to slow down: Can we keep working harder and harder indefinitely?" http://www.cdc.gov/niosh/docs99-101

As a consequence, the workaholic's relationship with a spouse, children, or other family members tends to be forced, stressful, and emotionally draining for both the workaholic and his or her relatives and friends. Workaholics reluctantly schedule time with their family members. Often, these "appointments" to attend a child's music recital or athletic event are arranged by the parent's secretary. Known euphemistically as "quality time," there is very little time and possibly less quality involved in these arranged meetings with children and spouses (Machlowitz, 1980).

Divorce is common among workaholics. Spouses who choose not to divorce their workaholic partner may focus their attention on their children, creative outlets, or community activities. They may alternately engage in forms of addictive behaviors—alcohol, drugs, or sex—or become anxious, depressed, or develop other emotional or physical disorders (Coles, 1977).

HEALTH. Workaholism is termed a "progressively fatal disease" (Fassel, 1992, p. 13). The compulsion of workaholics to work well beyond their physical and mental capacity jeopardizes their health and emotional well-being. Cardiologists Friedman and Roseman (1974) contend that type A behavior patterns significantly increase the risk of a heart attack. Type A behavior patterns include the following:

- Conducting routine activities—walking, eating, talking—in a rapid manner
- Impatience with others who do things at a slower pace
- "Polyphasic thought or action"—trying to think about or do more than one thing at a time
- Persistent time urgency—the sense that time will run out before everything gets done

Workaholics, then, fit well the profile of the type A individual, placing them at greater risk for heart disease.

It has long been recognized that chronic stress may have deadly consequences (Rabin, 1999). Job-related stress is endemic and increasing in postindustrial societies. A U.S. survey shows that 40% of workers consider their jobs to be very or extremely stressful (http://www.cdc.gov/niosh/topics/stress/). The Second European Survey on Working Conditions (http://www.eurofound.europa.eu/publications/htmlfiles/ef9726.htm) indicates that 28% of workers report experiencing stress on the job. Job-related stress is even more pronounced in Japan where 63% of workers suffer from anxiety or worry about their job performance or conditions of employment. The Japanese also work significantly more hours than do their counterparts in Europe and the United States. The Management and Coordination Agency in Japan reports that full-time male workers between the ages of 25 and 49 work more than 2,500 hours a year, more than 4 months longer than their peers in France and Germany (Kato, 1995).

The consequences of excessive overworking in Japan are often fatal. **Karoshi** is the recently coined Japanese word for "death from overwork." It is estimated that *Karoshi* accounts for 10% of all male deaths in the Japanese work force (Yates, 1988). A survey conducted by the *Yomiuri Shimbun* newspaper posed the question, "Are you concerned that *Karoshi* might hit you or a family member?" Forty-eight percent of the Japanese public surveyed answered "yes." Survivors of *Karoshi* victims are now appealing to the courts in Japan for the loss of their family members. These petitions have taken two forms: death as the direct result of overwork and suicide precipitated by overwork.

Karoshi victims commonly experience exhaustion, insomnia, and fear of disappointing their employers and coworkers. The impact of chronic work-related stress may be so debilitating that sudden death ensues. Alternatively, chronic stress may lead to clinical depression, a sense of hopeless entrapment in an unrelenting work schedule that permits little time away from the job. The Japanese National Police Agency reports that "work-related problems" are the central etiological factor in suicides of persons 50 to 59 years of age (Robinson, 1996). Because suicide as a consequence of overwork is so common in Japan, a special term, *karo-jisatsu*, has emerged to distinguish it from other suicides.

Death by Overwork

In Japan, it's called *Karoshi*—"death by overwork"—and it is estimated to cause 1,000 deaths per year, nearly 5% of that country's stroke and heart attack deaths in employees under the age of 60. About one of every three work-related suicides is the result of overwork.

In the Netherlands overwork has resulted in a new condition known as "leisure illness," estimated to affect 3% of its entire population, according to one study. Workers actually get physically sick on weekends and vacations as they stop working and try, in vain, to relax.

In the United States workaholism remains what it's always been: the so-called respectable addiction that's as dangerous as any other and could affect millions of Americans—regardless of whether they hold jobs.

Source: WebMD Feature, "Workaholism: The 'Respectable'; Addiction" posted at: http://aolsvc.health.wemd.aol.com/content/Article/36/1728_57274.htm?printing=true

SSRN

Frangos, C. C. & Kiohos, A. (2010). Internet addiction among Greek university students: Demographic associations with the phenomenon, using the Greek version of Young's Internet addiction test. *International Journal of Economic Sciences and Applied Research, 3*(1). http://ssrn.com/abstract=1591822

The Nagano District Court ruled that the suicide of a Japanese man was the direct result of his routinely working 80-hour weeks. His survivors were awarded $17,000 a year compensation for his death. In a similar case the court awarded 168 million yen ($1.6 million) to the family of a 24-year-old advertising employee who worked for 17 months before his suicide without a day off, averaging between 30 minutes and 2 hours sleep a night (Kageyama, 1999). Overall, *Karoshi* victims appear to be getting younger. The father of a 24-year-old was awarded 126 million yen ($1.1 million) by the court when his son simply worked himself to death in an attempt to placate his employer.

Computer and Internet Addiction

Considerable controversy surrounds the recently emerging phenomenon of protracted use of the computer. Alternately known as computer addicts, Internet addicts, net addicts, or webaholics, persons who use their computers to excess have come to the attention of clinical psychologists, psychiatrists, academic researchers, and the media.

The term "**Internet addiction disorder**" was first recognized in 1995, and then only half seriously, by psychiatrist Ivan Goldberg (Yang, 2000). Since that time various definitions of computer and Internet addiction have been offered. Peter Mitchell, writing in *The Lancet*, defines Internet addiction as the "compulsive use of the Internet with disturbed and irritated behavior when access is denied, including withdrawal symptoms and the loss of emotional control" (2000, p. 632). Psychologist Kimberly Young defines Internet addiction as "any online compulsive behavior which interferes with normal living and causes severe stress on family, friends, loved ones, and one's work environment. It is compulsive behavior that dominates the addict's life" (http://www.netaddiction.com). Psychiatrist Jerald Block argues that Internet addiction should be included in the forthcoming revision of the American Psychiatric Association's *Diagnostic and Statistical Manual of Mental Disorders*. He considers Internet addiction to be a "compulsive-impulsive spectrum disorder that involves online and/or offline computer usage and consists of three subtypes: excessive gaming, sexual preoccupations, and e-mail/text messaging." Four components of the three forms of Internet addiction are identified by Block (2008, p. 6–7):

- *Excessive use,* often associated with a loss of sense of time or a neglect of basic drives
- *Withdrawal,* including feeling of anger, tension, and/or depression when the computer is inaccessible

- *Tolerance,* including the need for better computer equipment, more software, and more hours of use
- *Negative repercussions*, including arguments, lying, poor achievement, social isolation, and fatigue

To Harvard clinical psychologist Meressa Hecht Orzack (Cromie, 1999), computer addiction is "an emerging disorder suffered by people who find the virtual reality on computer screens more attractive than everyday reality." Although Orzack (Cromie, 1999) contends that normal and pathological computer use is difficult to define, there are symptoms of computer addiction:

- Using the computer for pleasure, gratification, or relief from stress.
- Feeling irritable and out of control or depressed when not using it.
- Spending increased amounts of time and money on hardware, software, magazines, and computer-related activities.
- Neglecting work, school, or family obligations.
- Lying about the amount of time spent on computer activities.
- Risking loss of career goals, educational objectives, and personal relationships.
- Failing at repeated efforts to control computer use.

Based on the American Psychiatric Association's *Diagnostic and Statistical Manual of Mental Disorders* (1994) definition of pathological gambling, Kimberly Young developed an eight-item Diagnostic Questionnaire to determine addictive Internet use. **Table 15–1** presents Young's questions.

TABLE 15–1 **Diagnostic Criteria for Internet Addiction Disorder**

Individuals are Internet dependent if they answer "yes" to four or more of following questions:

1. Do you feel preoccupied with the Internet (think about previous online activity or anticipate the next online session)?
2. Do you feel a need to use the Internet with increasing amounts of time to achieve satisfaction?
3. Have you repeatedly made unsuccessful efforts to control, cut back, or stop Internet use?
4. Do you feel restless, moody, depressed, or irritable when attempting to cut down or stop Internet use?
5. Do you stay online longer than originally intended?
6. Do you use the Internet as a way of escaping problems or relieving a dysphoric mood (e.g., feelings of helplessness, guilt, anxiety, or depression)?
7. Have you lied to family members, therapists, or others to conceal the extent of involvement with the Internet?
8. Have you jeopardized or risked the loss of a significant relationship, job, or educational or career opportunity because of the Internet?

Source: Dr. Kimberly S. Young, Executive Director of the Center for Online Addiction. Web posted at www.netaddiction.com/articles/symptoms.pdf

Internet Addiction: A Korean Response

MOKCHEON, South Korea.—The compound—part boot camp, part rehab center—resembles programs around the world for troubled youths. Drill instructors drive young men through military-style obstacle courses, counselors lead group sessions, and there are even therapeutic workshops on pottery and drumming.

But these young people are not battling alcohol or drugs. Rather, they have severe cases of what many in this country believe is a new and potentially deadly addiction: cyberspace.

South Korea boasts of being the most wired nation on Earth. In fact, perhaps no other country has so fully embraced the Internet. Ninety percent of homes connect to cheap, high-speed broadband, online gaming is a professional sport, and social life for the young revolves around the "PC bang," dim Internet parlors that sit on practically every street corner.

It has become a national issue here in recent years, as users started dropping dead from exhaustion after playing online games for days on end. A growing number of students have skipped school to stay online, shockingly self-destructive behavior in this intensely competitive society.

Up to 30% of South Koreans under 18, or about 2.4 million people, are at risk of Internet addiction, said Ahn Dong-hyun, a child psychiatrist at Hanyang University in Seoul, who just completed a 3-year government-financed survey of the problem.

Doctors in China and Taiwan have begun reporting similar disorders in their youth. In the United States Dr. Jerald J. Block, a psychiatrist at Oregon Health and Science University, estimates that up to 9 million Americans may be at risk for the disorder, which he calls pathological computer use.

Source: New York Times, Nov. 18, 2007.

Types of Internet Addiction

The Center for On-Line Addiction (www.netaddiction.com) has identified four specific types of Internet addiction:

1. **Cybersexual addiction**: The preoccupation with online pornography and involvement in the playing out of sexual fantasies in chat rooms.
2. **Cyberaffair/relational addiction**: The establishment of excessive virtual relationships in chat rooms or through e-mail. These relationships typically involve males and females who may engage in forms of virtual adultery.
3. **Net compulsions**: Obsessions involving gambling, gaming, shopping, or stock trading. Examples include virtual casinos, interactive games, e-Bay, and e-brokerage houses.
4. **Information overload**: The undue fascination with the availability of increasing amounts of information and data from around the world.

Prevalence of Computer Addiction

Few studies are available on the prevalence of computer addiction or dependency. Studies conducted in South Korea and China provide the best estimates of the prevalence of Internet/computer addiction. In South Korea Internet addiction is a grave public health problem. The most recent survey of Internet addiction conducted by the South Korean government finds that about 210,000 children between the ages of 6 and 19 require treatment for their addiction: 8 in 10 of those are in need of psychotropic drugs, and for 20% to 24% hospitalization is recommended (Ahn, 2007). It is estimated that the average high school student in South Korea plays computer games 23 hours each week, placing 1.2 million students at risk for addiction (Kim, 2007).

China is also deeply concerned about the prevalence of Internet addiction among the young. It is estimated that 10 million Chinese adolescents (13.7% of the adolescent population) are suffering from Internet addiction. In 2007 the Chinese government started restricting computer gaming to 3 hours a day (*People's Daily Online*, 2007).

In Asia use of the computer in public places—mostly in Internet cafes—is more common than in the United States. The privacy of commuter use in the United States makes it difficult to estimate the prevalence of Internet addiction. Issues related to comorbidity—the presence of more than one diagnosable psychiatric disorder—compound the problem of estimating the prevalence of Internet addiction. In South Korea about 86% of the Internet addicted are also suffering from another psychiatric disorder (Ahn, 2007). However, in Asia therapists are sensitive to issues of comorbidity, whereas in the United States patients tend to be treated for more typical psychiatric disorders (e.g., depression, social phobias, or anxiety) and not for Internet addiction.

Similar findings are reported in a survey of 162,000 school-aged and young people in 30 countries across the world. Particularly high rates of computer use were found in Estonia, Sweden, Norway, and Denmark. In Estonia, for example, 13-year-old boys reported using the computer more than 3 hours each day. One in five Finish boys between the ages of 13 and 15 also use the computer more than 3 hours each day, mostly to play games. Far fewer Finish girls (2% to 3%) spend as much time on the computer, typically to e-mail their friends and to participate in chat rooms. Recognizing the cultural differences inherent in Internet addiction, Block concludes that Internet addiction in the United States and around the world is "remarkably similar" (Block, 2008, p. 306). As access to personal computers expands and ease and attractiveness of their use becomes increasingly recognized by more diverse segments of the population, extreme computer use, addiction, and dependency are likely to escalate.

Stanford University psychiatry professor Elias Aboujaoude and his colleagues conducted a nationwide study of 2,513 randomly selected adults to gauge their computer use and found the following:

- 13.7% found it hard to stay away from the Internet for several days at a time.
- 12.4% stayed online longer than intended very often or often.
- 12.3% had seen a need to cut back on Internet use at some point.
- 8.7% attempted to conceal nonessential Internet use from family, friends, and employers.
- 8.2% used the Internet to escape problems or relieve negative moods.
- 5.9% believed their relationships suffered as a result of excessive Internet use.

The researchers concluded that the typical Internet addict is a "single, college-educated, white male in his 30's who spends approximately 30 hours a week on non-essential computer use" (http://news.stanford.edu/news/2006/october18/med-internet-101806.html).

GENDER DIFFERENCES. Recent research on gender differences in the use of the computer shows that the varying interests of women and men are played out in their use of the Internet. Kimberly Young (http:/ /www.netaddiction.com), a psychologist who specializes in Internet addiction, reports that men are attracted to online competitive games where power and dominance are at stake. Games that involve the establishment of status in the group based on the player's ability to destroy other participants and thereby to gain recognition and respect are particularly intriguing to men. Cybersex is another male-dominated online activity. Cybersex is carried out in chat rooms in which men and women converse in sexually explicit, uninhibited ways. This free exchange of sexual desires and fantasies allows the participants to engage in behaviors in a virtual way that they could not experience in real time and space. Cyberporn also provides men with vicarious sexual encounters unavailable to them in their everyday lives.

Women are drawn to chat rooms but for far different reasons. For the most part women use the Internet to establish warm, supportive relationships. Online friendships are sought to share common problems and explore various ways of handling their "real life" relationships. Help-seeking interactions are facilitated by the relative anonymity provided by e-mail and chat rooms.

Women also enjoy anonymous interaction with men with whom a relationship may develop. Personal appearance and social background are masked by online communication. The lack of physical attractiveness does not impede the process of developing a personal relationship. The advantages of not being judged on superficial visual characteristics attract and sustain women's interest in cybercommunication (http://www.netaddiction.com).

What Makes the Internet Addictive?

Kimberly Young (1997) also explores the issue of what makes computer-mediated communication addictive. She finds that the use of the Internet to gather information is far less addictive than virtual interaction provided in chat rooms and multiuser dungeons. Both chat rooms and multiuser dungeons allow simultaneous communication to occur among as many as 1,000 persons. Chat rooms typically involve multiple conversations among persons who are interested in a common topic or who have common characteristics that draw them together. Multiuser dungeons differ from chat rooms in that they involve the establishment of a game in which the players take on various character roles. For example, the game may involve a medieval battle with dragons and maidens, knights in armor, and villains hiding in the woods. By assuming a role in the drama, Internet players are provided opportunities for recognition and power typically not available to them in their everyday lives. Because the user's anonymity is ensured, they are able to experiment with new identities, personality characteristics, and social backgrounds. In addition, changes in gender—a male may become female, or vice versa—may greatly enhance identity transformation.

Anonymity also facilitates the process of seeking social support and involvement in sexually explicit online interactions. Users who otherwise may not be able to ask for help with an embarrassing or potentially socially stigmatizing problem may well seek counsel and support as an anonymous Internet patron. Similarly, persons who are interested in deviant sexual practices and who would not pursue them in everyday life may take advantage of their virtual availability on the Internet.

Extreme Sports

The wide variety of extreme sports makes arriving at a definition exceedingly difficult. However, Kelly Boyer Sagert in her *Encyclopedia of Extreme Sports* offers the following definition (2009):

> Extreme sports contain an element of danger; are generally individualistic attempts to master an activity, often through unexpected or

creative ways, with these individuals oftentimes interested in breaking records or exceeding previous limitations of human endeavor; and are closely connected to a young and alternative subculture.

In the 1990s **extreme sports** and athletic events gained considerable popularity. These forms of competitive and recreational activities range from high-risk, potentially life-threatening events (e.g., BASE jumping, rock climbing, street-luge racing, and sky surfing) to sports that test the endurance of the participants (e.g., ultraman marathons and the Ironman Triathlon events, Race Across America [bicycle race], and the Eco-challenge). BASE is an acronym for building, antenna, span (bridge), and earth (cliffs) jumping. The time between the start of the jump and the landing is so limited that a second chance to open the parachute is impossible. BASE jump-

A rope jumper in action. Rope jumping is akin to bungee jumping, but without the added elasticity of a bungee cord. Why do some people engage in extreme sports?

Types of Extreme Sports

Joe Tomlinson (2004) classifies extreme sports into three categories: those that take place (1) in the air, (2) on land, and (3) in the water. Examples derived from Tomlinson's typology are:

- Extreme air sports: rope and bungee jumping, hang gliding, high wire walking, and activities like freestyle sky diving and sky flying;
- Extreme water sports: barefoot water skiing, cliff diving, free diving, powerboat racing, round-the-world yacht racing, speed sailing, and whitewater kayaking; and
- Extreme land sports: adventure racing, caving in dangerous locales, extreme motocross, extreme skiing, ice yachting, sheer cliff climbing, and street luge.

One additional contemporary type of extreme land sport is street racing. Street racing is illegal motor racing that takes place on public roads. Street racing is sometimes spontaneous, but it can be planned and well coordinated.

Source: Adapted from Joe Tomlinson and Ed Leigh, Extreme Sports: In Search of the Ultimate Thrill. Bufflao, NY: Firefly Books, 2004.

ing is described as "a human leaving safety behind to leap into the void" (Greenfield et al., 1999, p. 9). In the first 18 years BASE-jumping claimed the lives of 46 participants, making it the sport with the highest fatality rate in the world.

Ultraman marathons and Ironman Triathlon events involve testing the limits of human endurance. Since 1983 ultramarathons have been organized around the world, with events in 2010 being held in Africa, Asia, Europe, North and South America, Oceania, and the Polar region. An ultramarathon is a 3-day event that includes a 6.2-mile open ocean swim followed by a 90-mile bike ride the first day, a 171.4-mile bike ride on day 2, and a 52.4-mile ride on the final day. Far more common are Ironman Triathlon events that require the participants to swim 2.4 miles, cycle 112 miles, and complete a marathon (26 miles, 385 yards) on the same day (http://www.ultramarathonrunning.com/; Greenfield et al., 1999).

The Eco-challenge involves four-person teams (men and women combined) who race 24 hours a day for 7 days over 300 miles of very hazardous, remote terrain. Each team, equipped with only a map and compass, must finish the race together. Only nonmotorized means of transportation—canoes, kayaks, mountain bikes, whitewater rafts, horses, and climbing ropes—are permitted. If any member of the team is injured, becomes ill, or cannot complete the course, the team is disqualified. A recent challenge "began with a marathon-length horse-back segment, in which team members took turns riding and running alongside for 26 miles. The teams then slogged through narrow, water-filled canyons, sometimes swimming with backpacks through 50-degree water; hiked more than 100 miles across stretches of waterless desert; negotiated 1,200-foot cliff faces on ropes; rafted class IV (advanced) rapids on the Colorado River; and capped it off with a 12-hour, 50-mile canoe paddle across Lake Powell" (Hamilton, 1995, p. 78).

The Race Across America (RAAM) is the longest nonstop bicycle race in the world, from the West to East coasts of the United States. The 2001 RAAM began in Portland, Oregon, and ended in Gulf Breeze, Florida, a distance of 2,980 miles. Rob Kish, a 37-year-old land surveyor, set a record time for the RAAM of 8 days, 3 hours, and 11 minutes (Pavelka, 1992). Kish openly admits that RAAM is his life: "It is all I do." When he arrived in New York City he "climbed off his bike looking like a man from a lifeboat after a month adrift: burned, peeling skin; thick, crusty lips; ratty beard and hair; a streak of dried blood in his nose" (Pavelka, 1992, p. 57).

SSRN

Saxena, K., & Dey, A. K. (2009). Treks'n rapids: identifying motivational factors for adventure sports. http://ssrn.com/abstract=1482565

A BASE jumper flings himself off of a cliff. What are four subscales of the Sensation Seeking Scale Form V (SSSV), and how do they apply to BASE jumping?

Extreme sports and athletic events, while involving varying degrees of risk, are all sensation-seeking activities. Psychologist Marvin Zuckerman (1994, p. 27) defines sensation as the "*seeking* of varied, novel, complex and *intense* sensations and experiences, and the willingness to take physical, social, and *legal*, and *financial* risks for the sake of such experience." Zuckerman's Sensation Seeking Scale Form V (SSSV) is widely used to assess the willingness to participate in nonconventional or high-risk behaviors, including substance use, experimenting with alcohol and other drugs, sexual behaviors, smoking, speeding, and risky sports. The SSSV includes four subscales: Thrill and Adventure Seeking, Experience Seeking, Disinhibition, and Boredom Susceptibility. The Thrill and Adventure Seeking subscale measures the individual's propensity to act in risky, impulsive, and adventurous activities (Malkin & Rabinowitz, 1998).

Overall, persons who engage in high-risk sports and athletic events typically score very high on Zuckerman's SSSV, and in particular on the Thrill and Adventure Seeking subscale (Wagner & Houlihan, 1994). Mountain climbers are found to have higher total SSSV scores as well as higher Experience Seeking and Thrill and Adventure Seeking subscale scores (Cronin, 1991). Persons who participate in high-risk sports are also likely to be high sensation seekers. Mountain athletes (free climbers, ski jumpers, and speleogists) score high on the total SSSV and each of its subscales except Boredom Susceptibility (Rossi & Cereatti, 1993). A study of elite mountain climbers—all members of the Norwegian Everest expedition—shows that they score higher overall and on all subscales of the SSSV, except Disinhibition (Breivik, 1996). The rush of adrenalin and the sense of accomplishment against all odds motivate persons to seek out extreme, sometimes life-threatening challenges.

Psychologist Frank Farley recognizes three personality types: type A, persons who are driven to perform in all areas of life; type B, persons who take a relaxed view toward life; and type T, persons who seek thrills and excitement. The type T personalities are either type T positive or type T negative. The type T positives tend to be creative or driven to the adventure of discovery. By contrast, type T negative personalities tend to be involved in criminal activities, illicit drug use, or compulsive gambling (Sagert, 2009).

Alain Robert is a particularly noteworthy example of a type T–positive personality. He is a unique "urban climber" who has scaled the four tallest buildings in the world bare-handed and without ropes. After climbing the tallest building in the world located in Kuala Lumpur in Malaysia (1,483 feet) in 1997, ten years later (2007) he put on a Spiderman suit and climbed and descended from the Jim Mao Tower (1,380 feet of iron and glass) in Shanghai, China. To Alain Robert (2010) extreme sports began to gain popularity as social policies concerning

Extreme Sports: In Search of Myself

> "Our society is so surgically sterile. It is almost like our socialization desensitizes us. Every time I'm out doing this I'm searching my soul. It's the Lewis and Clark gene, to venture out, to find what your limitations are."
>
> —Greenfield et al. (1999, p. 10)

Journalist Rob Schultheis, an inexperienced rock climber, recounts his attempt to scale a Colorado peak without ropes or hardware. On his descent he lost his grip on an overhang and landed on a ledge, very near a sheer drop of 200 feet. Seriously injured, he writes of his quest for survival:

> Something happened on that descent, something I have tried to figure out ever since, so inexplicable and powerful it was. I found myself very simply doing impossible things: dozens, scores of them, as I down-climbed Neva's lethal slopes. Shattered, in shock, I climbed with the impossible sureness of a snow leopard, a mountain goat. I crossed disintegrating chutes of rock holds vanishing from under my hands and feet as I moved, a dance in which a single missed beat would have been fatal. I used bits of rime clinging to the granite as fingerholds. They rattled away into space but I was already gone, away.... *What I am doing is absolutely impossible,* I thought. *I can't be doing this. But I have the grace, the radiant mojo, and here I am!...* Looking back on it, I really cannot explain or describe properly that strange person I found inhabiting my body that afternoon.... The person I became on Neva was the best version of myself, the person I should have been throughout my life.

Source: Schultheis, R. 1996. Bone Games: Extreme Sports, Shamanism, Zen, and the Search for Transcendence. New York: Breakaway Books, pp. 10–12.

public safety increased (e.g., seat belt laws, warning labels on medications, and so on). As life presumably became safer, ironically the need to create opportunities for risk-taking behavior grew stronger.

Theoretical Understandings of Extreme Forms of Everyday Behavior

Specific theoretical formulations have not been set forth to account for extreme forms of everyday behavior (**Table 15–2**). However, it is possible to draw on theories of negative deviant behaviors to better understand the workaholic, computer addict, and the extreme sports competitor.

Social Integration

As with positive forms of deviance, the extent of social integration—or the sharing of common values—affects involvement in extreme forms of everyday behavior (Durkheim, 1951). Persons who are highly integrated into conventional society, who structure their lives in a balanced and predictable way, tend not to be bothered by their daily routine behavior. Nine-to-five jobs, 2 weeks vacation, and a balance between family life, job, and civic responsibility are not seen as burdens but as a preferred way to live. In Robert Merton's (1968) terms, the conformists and ritualizers—persons who accept the conventional goals of society and the means for achieving them—are not likely to engage in extreme forms of behavior. To both conformists and ritualizers, culturally approved goals and the institutionalized means for attaining them are linked. Excessive working, computer obsession, or involvement in dangerous or extreme sports or games holds no interest for them. Persons who adopt an innovative strategy for achieving culturally approved goals, however, may work to excess, develop an addiction to the Internet, or seek out virtual alternatives to achieve their personal rewards and social acceptance unavailable to them in everyday life.

Reciprocity

Widespread thrill-seeking and risk-taking behaviors seem to depend on the societal conditions marked by economic prosperity and lack of external or internal conflict. Ironically, the general sense of economic well-being and minimal conflict or the sense that society is becoming a safer, healthier, more humane place may well precipitate the feeling of suffocating reciprocity in everyday life. Excessive reciprocity occurs when the playing out of our social roles—employee, student, spouse, parent, and friend—becomes too easy. That is, our actual role behavior—the ways in which we carry out our roles—and the expectations that we have for our performance for these roles closely match. Motivation is reduced and we go about daily lives in a disengaged, dispassionate way. As a consequence, involvement in risky, highly challenging sports and athletic events is on the rise.

TABLE 15–2 **Explanations of Extreme Forms of Everyday Behavior**

Theories and Theorists	Sociological Predictors	Hypotheses
Social Integration and Control		
Durkheim	Social integration	The greater the social integration, the less the involvement in extreme forms of everyday behavior.
Merton	Anomie	The more anomic social life is, the greater the involvement in extreme forms of everyday behavior.
Agnew	Strain	The more strained social relationships become, the more likely that extreme forms of everyday behavior will occur.
Societal Reaction		
Becker	Societal reaction	The more positive the societal reaction to extreme forms of everyday behavior, the more likely those forms of behavior will continue.
Social Conflict		
Coser	Conflict	The greater the conflict between the personal rewards of everyday behavior and the anticipated rewards of alternative behaviors, the greater the likelihood of extreme forms of everyday behavior.
Palmer	Role reciprocity	The greater the degree of role reciprocity, the greater the likelihood of extreme forms of everyday behavior.
Differential Association and Social Learning		
Sutherland	Differential association	The greater the interaction with others who advocate involvement in extreme forms of everyday behavior, the greater the likelihood that an individual will engage in those behaviors.
Akers	Social learning	The greater the personal rewards for engaging in extreme forms of everyday behavior, the more likely those behaviors will continue.
Rational Choice		
Clarke and Cornish	Rational choice	The more anticipated pleasure exceeds expected pain from extreme forms of everyday behavior, the more likely an individual will choose to engage in those behaviors.

Stuart Palmer (1970) sets forth a status-role reciprocity formulation of deviant and conforming behavior. Role reciprocity refers to "the extent to which performances of the status-roles mutually and simultaneously expedite one another" (Palmer, 1970, p. 42). The greater the status-role reciprocity, the less the tension both within social situations and the individuals involved. Conversely, the less the role reciprocity, the greater the tension both within social situations and the person involved. Palmer argues that extremes of tension, either too high or too low, lead to aberrant behavior. Too little tension may well result in an effort by the individual to increase it; too much tension signals a need for its reduction.

When excessive status-role reciprocity is obtained, persons are able to function quite well with a limited degree of effort. Those around them facilitate the playing out of their status roles. Employers, friends, wives, children, and so on are supportive and appreciative of the ways in which the person enacts complementary status roles. Under conditions of excessive status-role reciprocity, tension falls to dangerously low levels. To reintroduce a degree of tension into their lives, persons who are experiencing excessive status-role reciprocity may engage in high-risk or extreme forms of behavior. The rush of adrenaline for conquering an extraordinary physical and mental challenge provides the level of tension necessary to sustain an otherwise monotonous everyday life. Virtual life made possible by the Internet and devotion to working far beyond expectations are additional ways to ease a deadening routine.

Strain

Robert Agnew's (1992) strain theory may also be applied to extreme forms of everyday behavior. Strain is a consequence of the variation between individuals' actual goal attainment and what they would like to achieve. When relations with others are so contentious that role performance is greatly impeded, negative emotions may ensue. Alternative forms of social relations may be sought. Chat room and virtual relationships may be found to be far less stressful, more emotionally gratifying, and beneficial to other goal attainment. Excessive working may also provide a respite from negative social relationships—with spouse, children, or other family members or friends. Becoming immersed in work-related activities may provide the kinds of emotional benefits and status rewards not available in an individual's other spheres of life. Strain may also lead to involvement in extreme sports or unusually demanding physical contests.

Differential Association and Learning Theory

Differential association theory combines concepts found in social learning and subcultural conceptualizations. A central hypothesis of differential association theory is that the more interaction with others who advocate certain behaviors, the greater the likelihood that the motives, rationalizations, and techniques for engaging in those behaviors will be learned. In formulation differential association theory, Edwin Sutherland (1978) is primarily interested in explaining delinquent and criminal behavior. However, the principles of differential association theory may be applied to extreme forms of everyday behavior as well. Workaholics, computer and Internet addicts, and participants in extreme sports and games who interact with others of similar interests are more likely to continue their excessive behavior.

Ronald Akers (1998) extends differential association theory by introducing the concept of differential reinforcement. Differential reinforcement refers to the process by which individuals receive rewards and benefits for some behaviors but not others. Those behaviors that are rewarded tend to be repeated; those that do not benefit the individual are in time discarded. Extreme forms of everyday behavior tend to result in personal rewards, less so in social recognition. However, increasing media attention given to extreme sports has generated athletic identities and increasing economic benefit for those who excel.

Rational Choice

Rational choice theory—based on the hedonistic principle of human behavior—posits that the decision to act is governed by the desire to maximize anticipated pleasure and minimize expected pain. From this perspective, actor involvement in extreme forms of everyday behavior may be a rational expression of free will, an anticipation that pleasure will flow from atypical involvement in work, computer use, and athletic events and competitions. From the perspective of outsiders, persons who engage in extreme forms of everyday behavior may be irrational, disordered psychologically and emotionally, and destructive to themselves and to those close to them (Clarke & Cornish, 1985).

Societal Reaction

Manifestations of excessive behavior are met with mixed reactions (Becker, 1963). Workaholics may be viewed positively within certain organizations, whereas they are seen as disruptive in others. Junior members of large law firms, for example, are expected to work to excess to generate "billable hours" to demonstrate their organizational worth. Medical students and interns are expected to be available in the hospital and its laboratories sometimes around the clock to take advantage of unexpected opportunities to advance their medical education. In other organizational settings, however, overly zealous work habits are less expected and accepted by fellow workers.

Computer aficionados are valued members of many complex organizations. Their willingness to provide computer "troubleshooting" for their coworkers is most welcome. Those who are addicted to computer games or Internet interactions, however, devote an inordinate amount of their working day to the pursuit of their own interests. Organizational conflicts may arise that may threaten the continued employment of the computer addict.

Media attention has recently focused on extreme sports and games. Major television and cable networks have televised a wide variety of extreme athletic competitions and eco-challenges from around the globe. Accomplished extreme sport athletes are becoming widely known, more daring feats of physical agility and strength are being attempted, and corporate sponsors are increasingly becoming involved. New products—sporting equipment, nutritional and strength-enhancing aids, and apparel—are being introduced. Outstanding competitors in a variety of extreme sports and games are being recognized not only as exceptional athletes but also as media personalities and corporate representatives. As children and adolescents identify and attempt to emulate the abilities of extreme athletes, the recruitment into these forms of competition will increase. Traditional sports (e.g., baseball, football, and basketball) may be seen as passé—reserved for the less adventurous.

Chapter Summary

When we work incessantly, exercise or engage in extreme forms of athletic competition, or hack away on the computer day and night, our everyday behaviors may take on deviant forms. Workaholism—being highly committed to work, spending a disproportionate amount of time working, but showing little enjoyment in doing it—is common in the workplace. Workaholics tend to be intense, energetic, competitive, and driven; have strong self-doubts; prefer labor to leisure; work anytime and anywhere; and blur the distinctions between business and pleasure.

Four types of Internet addiction have been identified: cybersexual addiction, cyberrelational addiction, net gaming, and information overload. Adverse consequences have been documented for persons who use the computer to excess, including marital difficulties, school failures, job loss, financial problems, and health issues.

Extreme sports, a relatively new aspect of athletic endeavor, have led to the institutionalization of high-risk and potentially life-threatening forms of athletic competition. Extreme sports and athletic events, while involving varying degrees of risk, are all sensation-seeking activities.

Theoretical explanations for extreme forms of everyday behaviors are similar to those for other types of deviance, and involve social integration, the notion of reciprocity, and concepts taken from strain theory.

Key Concepts

Time-deepening: Doing several things at the same time to maximize time and effort.

Workaholism: An addiction to work, the compulsion or the uncontrollable need to work incessantly.

Karoshi: Death from overwork.

Internet addiction disorder: Compulsive use of the Internet with evidence of disturbed and irritated behavior when access is denied, including withdrawal symptoms and the loss of emotional control; an emerging disorder suffered by people who find the virtual reality on computer screens more attractive than everyday reality.

Cybersexual addiction: The preoccupation with online pornography and involvement in the playing out of sexual fantasies in chat rooms.

Cyberaffair/relational addiction: The establishment of excessive virtual relationships in chat rooms or through e-mail.

Net compulsion: Excessive gambling, gaming, shopping, or stock trading on the Internet.

Information overload: The undue fascination with the availability of increasing amounts of information and data from around the world.

Extreme sports: Forms of competitive and recreational activities that range from high-risk, potentially life-threatening events to sports that test the endurance of the participants.

Critical Thinking Questions

1. What are the nature, characteristics, and consequences of extreme forms of everyday behaviors?
2. What key sociocultural conditions give rise to workaholism? Why do these conditions motivate some individuals to engage in workaholism and not others?
3. Are workaholics, computer addicts, and participants in extreme sports affected by similar sociocultural conditions? If so, what might account for the behavioral differences that result from these conditions?
4. Can involvement in extreme forms of everyday behavior be predicted or are they forms of idiosyncratic behavior that fall outside the scope of scientific prediction?
5. Is it possible to engage in forms of extreme everyday behavior but otherwise have a conformist lifestyle?

Web Extra

Web-based media materials from high-quality sources such as CNN, Time, and National Public Radio are available in support of this textbook. Visit go.jblearning.com/deviance to access them.

Check out these websites for additional information on extreme forms of deviant behavior:

http://www.netaddiction.com

http://www.computeraddiction.com

http://www.basejumper.org

FBI

CHAPTER 16

Terrorism

Learning Objectives

After reading this chapter you should know

- What terrorism is, and what kinds of actions should be considered acts of terrorism.
- The differences and similarities between terrorism and other forms of crime.
- Some of the official definitions of terrorism.
- The extent and patterns of terrorism and hate crime.
- Types of terrorism—international and domestic.
- Terrorist organizational structure.
- The dynamics of terrorist organizations, including recruitment strategies.
- The various motivations behind terrorism.
- The definition and extent of cyberterrorism.
- Explanations for terrorism.

In what turned out to be a surprise to members of the local community, Paul Rockwood, the 35-year-old weatherman of King Salmon, Alaska, was arrested in 2010 and charged along with his wife of domestic terrorism–related conspiracy (Murphy, 2010). As part of a plea deal, Paul and Nadia Rockwood pleaded guilty in U.S. District Court in Anchorage of willfully making false statements to

"While nothing is easier than to denounce the evil doer, nothing is more difficult than to understand him."

—Fyodor Mikhailovich Dostoevsky (Hudson, 1999, p. 16)

the Federal Bureau of Investigation (FBI). Under the terms of the agreement, Rockwood agreed to serve 8 years in prison followed by 3 years of supervised release; his wife accepted a sentence of 5 years on probation (FBI, 2010).

Nadia, a stay-at-home mom, sang in the local choir and picked berries with her neighbors. Paul spent his days preparing short-term weather forecasts for fisherman and sending weather balloons soaring above the small community of 450 residents.

As details of the case emerged, it became known that Paul had converted to Islam in early 2002 while living in Virginia. Shortly thereafter, he became a follower of Anwar Awlaki, the radical Muslim cleric now thought to be in Yemen, and admitted to prosecutors that he considered it his personal duty to avenge Islam against anyone who disparaged it. That belief led to the creation of a list of assassination targets that Paul maintained, and also led him to research methods of killing efficiently. The FBI's Joint Terrorism Task Force subsequently obtained the target list and learned of Paul's plans.

Although the Rockwoods told neighbors they were Muslim, both of them attended plays and activities at local churches and seemed like any other family living in King Salmon. As one of the local residents explained, the case seemed strange. "We've known them since [their son] was a tiny little tyke," she said. "Then when this came out, we were all completely shocked. It's just impossible for me to imagine the friend that I knew being involved in anything like this."

This chapter considers key issues related to international terrorism that continually define life in the 21st century. Throughout the chapter attention is focused on the terrorist activities of Islamic extremist organizations—currently the most prevalent form of international terrorism. The chapter is structured as follows. First, various official definitions of terrorism are assessed. Second, the characteristics of three broad forms of terrorism—international, domestic, and hate crimes—are discussed. Third, a detailed typology of terrorism is presented. Two forms of terrorism are highlighted: suicide bombing and cyberterrorism. Fourth, the motivations that drive individuals to commit acts of terrorism and the processes of recruiting, selecting, and training potential members of terrorist organizations are explored. The structure and the clandestine nature of their organizations, methods of communication, and decision-making processes are also considered. Last, sociological and social psychological theories of deviant behavior that help us to understand the commission of terrorist acts are reviewed.

What Is Terrorism?

From the Reign of Terror in France (1793–1794) to the present, attempts to instill terror in the minds of one's adversaries have taken many forms. Alex P. Schmidt and Albert I. Jongman's (1988) survey of terrorist scholars revealed 109 different definitions of terrorism. The following elements were most commonly found in this array of definitions: violence, force (83.5%), political motivation (65%), intent to instilling fear or terror (51%), prior threats (47%), anticipated psychological effects (41.5%), victims distinguished from targets (37.5%), and intentional, planned action (32%). Schmidt (1984) considers three elements central to an understanding of terrorism: (1) the use of victims as symbolic target, (2) instilling fear as a result of an exceptional use of violence, and (3) the creation of an audience beyond the victims of the terrorist attack. Walter Laqueur (1987) opts for a simple definition of terrorism—the illegitimate use of force to achieve a political objective by targeting innocent people.

To Paul Pillar (2004), former deputy chief of the Central Intelligence Agency's Counterterrorism Center, terrorism is marked by four basic elements:

1. Premeditation—planned in advance, rather than an impulsive act of rage
2. Political motivation—not criminal, like the violence that groups such as the mafia use to get money, but designed to change the existing political order
3. Directed at civilian populations—not at military targets or combat-ready troops
4. Carried out by subnational groups rather than by a county's regular army

Harvard professor and terrorism expert Jessica Stern (1999, p. 11) defines terrorism as an "act or threat of violence against noncombatants with the objective of exacting revenge, intimidating, or otherwise influencing an audience." To Stern, terrorism differs from war in that noncombatants are victims, and from crime in that it elicits dread and creates fear in the larger society. Certainly, the events of September 11, 2001, the bombing of the federal building in Oklahoma, the burning of black churches in the South, and the killing of 10 persons by an unknown sniper in and around the nation's capital are acts committed against noncombatants, driven by revenge, with the intention of creating fear and dread among persons in the larger population.

Sociologist Donald Black (2002) argues that terrorism in its purest form must be viewed as a form of self-help. Black (2002) defines pure terrorism as "unilateral self-help by organized civilians who covertly inflict mass violence on other civilians." Black (1983, 1998) identifies nine characteristics of pure terrorism:

1. A form of self-help, that is, it is a way to address grievances by means of aggression
2. Highly violent
3. A punitive response to a moral wrong—a form of private capital punishment
4. Identifies a collective liability—persons located in social space characterized by nationality, race, religion, ethnicity, or political party
5. Recurrent, that is, a series of attacks that occur over time
6. Involves unilateral mass violence—terrorists are typically aggressors rather than victims
7. Well-organized, covert activity
8. A form of quasi-warfare, directed toward an outside ethnic group or nation
9. Typically done in small groups in which the missions may well involve terrorists' own destruction

Terrorism and Crime

Donald Black (2002) notes that criminal behavior often is a form of social control. Crime is committed to exert a form of control over persons whom the offender(s) views as immoral or threatening. Although unlike crime activity in many ways, terrorism is also a form of social control, a way to redress perceived wrongs committed against one's nationality, race, religion, ethnicity, or political party.

D. Douglas Bodrero (2000) draws distinctions between criminals and terrorists. He notes that politically disinterested persons often commit crimes for personal reasons. Crimes are committed as opportunities arise, and the perpetrator makes considerable effort to avoid detection and apprehension. Acts of terrorism, however, are typically ideologically or religiously motivated and involve a specific political purpose. The collective interests of terrorists supersede the self-interests of any member of a terrorist organization.

Official Definitions of Terrorism

Various official definitions of **terrorism** and **terrorists** have been formulated to guide the actions of national representatives or governmental agencies.

The United Nations defines terrorism as "the act of destroying or injuring civilian lives or the act of destroying or injuring civilian property without the expressly chartered permission of a specific government, thus, by individuals or groups acting independently or governments on their own accord and belief, in the attempt to affect some political goal" (United Nations, 2010). A terrorist is defined as "any person who, acting independently of the specific recognition of a country, or as a single person, or as a part of a group not recognized as an official part or division of a nation, acts to destroy or injure civilians or destroy or damage property belonging to civilians or governments in order to effect some political goal" (www.un.org/terrorism).

Title 22 of the U.S. Code, Section 2656f (d) defines terrorism as "premeditated, politically motivated violence, perpetrated against noncombatant targets by sub-national groups or clandestine agents, usually intended to influence an audience." International terrorism involves terrorist acts between "citizens or the territory of more than one country." And "terrorist group" refers to "any group practicing or that has significant subgroups that practice, international terrorism." The U.S. government has used this definition of terrorism to analyze terrorism since 1983.

The FBI defines terrorism as "the unlawful use of force and violence against persons or property to intimidate or coerce a government, the civilian population, or any segment thereof, in furtherance of political or social objectives" (*Code of Federal Regulations,* 28 C.F.R. Section 0.85).

Depending on the *origin, base,* and *objectives* of the terrorist organization, terrorism is considered by the FBI as either domestic or international (FBI, 2006):

- **Domestic terrorism** is the unlawful use, or threatened use, of force or violence by a group or individual based and operating entirely within the United States or Puerto Rico without foreign direction committed against persons or property to intimidate or coerce a government, the civilian population, or any segment thereof in furtherance of political or social objectives.
- **International terrorism** involves violent acts or acts dangerous to human life that are a violation of the criminal laws of the United States or any state, or that would be a criminal violation if committed within the jurisdiction of the United States or any state. These acts appear to be intended to intimidate or coerce a civilian population, influence the policy of a government by intimidation or coercion, or affect the conduct of a government by assassination or kidnapping. International terrorist acts occur outside the United States

or transcend national boundaries in terms of the means by which they are accomplished, the persons they appear intended to coerce or intimidate, or the locale in which their perpetrators operate or seek asylum.

Related to acts of terrorism are **hate and bias crimes**. The FBI defines hate and bias crimes as "a criminal act or attempted act against a person, institution, or property that is motivated in whole or in part by the offender's bias against a race, color, religion, gender, ethnic/national origin group, disability status, or sexual orientation group" (FBI, 2002a).

The FBI further distinguishes between types of terrorism and hate crimes. Characteristics of the offenders, victims, and the offense itself are considered in the classification of crimes of terrorism or hate. **Table 16–1** summarizes the FBI's classification schema.

TABLE 16–1 **Classification of Terrorist Acts and Hate Crimes**

	International Terror	Domestic Terror	Hate Crime
Offender			
Who/origin	Citizens, states, or territories of more than one country or person or group with connection to a foreign power	U.S. citizens—either groups or individuals—who are based and operate entirely within the United States without foreign direction or influence	Individuals or groups (e.g., hate groups)
Motive	Intimidate or coerce in furtherance of political and/or social objectives	Intimidate or coerce in furtherance of political and/or social objectives	In whole or in part by bias against a person's race, religion, sexual orientation, disability, or national origin
Victims/targets	Government, the civilian population, or any segment thereof—persons or property	Elements of the U.S. government or population	Person, group, institution, or property
Offense			
Where	Transcends national boundaries	United States	Any location
Examples	Suicide bombers; weapons of mass destruction	Pipe bombs; abortion clinic bombings; animal rights activists; skinheads	Church arsons; cross burnings; dragging

Source: Federal Bureau of Investigation, 1996b; 2002a.

Suicide Bomber's Letter

The following are excepts from a translation of a handwritten Arabic letter of instruction to the 9/11 hijackers found by FBI agents.

The Last Night

- Pledge of allegiance for death and renewal of intent.
- To be perfect with the plan very well of all its aspects and expecting the reaction or resistance from the enemy.
- Reading and understanding well . . . what Allah has prepared for the believers or the permanent bliss for the martyrs.
- Reminding one's self of listening well and obeying that night for you are going to face critical situations, which require strict abiding and obeying.
- Pray for your soul, the bag, the clothes, the knife, the stuff, whatever that stuff is, your ID, your passport, and all your papers.
- Check your weapons, before departure and before you leave . . . sharpen his knife.
- Tighten up your clothes and this is the medal of the righteous predecessors may God be content with them all.

The Second Stage

- When the taxi takes you to the airport . . . remember God much in the car (supplication of riding—supplication of the town—supplication of place . . .)
- When you arrive and get off the taxi then say the supplication of the place and every place you go say in it the supplication of the place and smile and be comforted for God is with the believers and the angels guard you and you do not feel them.
- And also do not let perplexing and confusion and nervous tension appear upon you. Be cheerful, happy, serene, and comforted because you are doing a job which God loves and accepts hence it will be day with God's permission you will spend it with the most beautiful women in paradise.
- Smile in the face of death, oh young man! For you are on your way to the everlasting paradise!
- Any place you go or any action you do you should supplicate and God is with his slaves the believers with support and guard with facilitation and success and conquest and victory and everything.

The Third Stage

- In combat hit firmly and strongly as the heroes do who do not wish to come back to the worldly life and say aloud God is Great for saying that (causes) horror and terror to enter the hearts of the disbelievers.
- Then apply the tradition of captivity and capture among them and kill them as God the Almighty said, "No Prophet must have prisoners of war until he weakens (the enemy) on the land. Do you want to have the best of the worldly life and God wants the hereafter and God is the most Mighty and the Most Wise."
- The zero hour came open up your jacket and open up your chest welcoming death for the way of God and . . . . and end with praying if it is possible start it before the target in a few seconds or the last of your speech is—There is no God except Allah and Muhammad is His Messenger.

Source: Paz, Reuven. 2001. Programmed Terrorists: An Analysis of the Letter Left Behind by the September 11 Hijackers. International Policy Institute for Counter Terrorism, December. Web posted at http://www.ict.org.il/articles/articledet.cfm?articleid=419

International Terrorism

Small bands of persons of common ancestry and common purpose find homes in various countries, integrate themselves into the daily life of the community, and become known simply as friendly, law-abiding, and hard-working. Their success depends in part on their anonymity, their ability to simply blend into the fabric of a foreign culture. These small groups of immigrants, also known as cells, are part of a larger network whose sole purpose is to engage in acts of international terrorism. Each cell stands ready to carry out a specific terrorist mission, usually against the citizens of their adopted country, when called on to do so.

Domestic Terrorism

Antigovernment activists also typically form into small groups to carry out their mission—to disrupt significantly the operation of the political order. By attacking agencies of the federal government, for example, domestic terrorists hope to focus attention on acts of political injustice and elicit public sympathy for their acts of retaliation.

The 1995 bombing of the Alfred P. Murrah Federal Building in Oklahoma City was carried out by two anti-government activists—Timothy McVeigh and Terry Nichols. On April 19th around 9:00 in the morning, as children were being escorted into the daycare center in the federal building, a bomb made from fertilizer and fuel oil was delivered in a rented truck. The explosion that ensued caused the deaths of 169 persons. The bombing of the federal building was in response to the FBI's assault on the Branch Davidian compound in Mount Carmel, Texas, on the same date 2 years before. The Branch Davidians, a religious sect, were suspected of storing a large number of weapons in their compound. An initial attempt by the Bureau of Alcohol, Tobacco, and Firearms to seize the weapons in a surprise attack resulted in the deaths of four agents and six Branch Davidian members. After a 51-day siege, the FBI launched an all-out assault that resulted in the burning of several buildings in the compound and the deaths of 80 Branch Davidian members, including men, women, and children (PBS, 1995).

Hate Crimes

Extreme acts of violence tend to be committed by small groups or individuals motivated by an intense hatred of a particular sociocultural group. Neither political or ideological issues nor the prospect of material gain are involved in the commission of the typical hate crime. Rather, the primary motive is to seriously injure or cause the death of persons of a hated racial, ethnic, or religious group.

Consider, for example, the circumstances that surrounded the death of James Byrd in the small East Texas town of Jasper. On June 7, 1998, James Byrd, a 49-year-old black man, was kidnapped by three white supremacists—John William King, 24, Lawrence Brewer, 32, and Shawn Berry, 24. They beat James Byrd senseless, pulled down his pants, chained his ankles to the bumper of their pick-up truck, and dragged him more than 3 miles over a rough dirt road. His head and one shoulder were torn from his body. The remains of James Byrd were dumped at the entrance of a black cemetery for former slaves.

James Byrd, Jr., the victim of a vicious hate crime that took place in Texas more than a decade ago. Are hate crimes a form of terrorism?

John William King and Lawrence Brewer were members of the Confederate Knights of America—a racist group formed by inmates at Beto prison unit in Texas. When King and Brewer were released from prison, they tried to start a chapter of the Confederate Knights of America in Jasper. They befriended Shawn Berry with the hope of recruiting him into their newly formed racist organization. As part of Shawn Berry's initiation into the Confederate Knights of America, he was expected to participate in the kidnapping and murder of James Byrd (CNN, 1999a).

Extent of Worldwide Terrorism

Table 16–2 shows the extent of terrorism across the globe from 2005 through 2009. Beginning in 2008 terrorist attacks have been on the decline, reaching a 5-year low in 2009. Terrorist attacks in Iraq were the highest during the 2-year period 2006–2007 but dropped precipitously in 2009. Over the same time period, however, terrorist attacks in Afghanistan increased more than 400% from 494 to 2,126 attacks.

AT A GLANCE

- In 2009 there were 10,999 international terrorists attacks, a slight decrease from the 11,725 incidents recorded in 2008.
- In 2009, 58,142 were killed, wounded, or kidnapped as a consequence of terrorist attacks.
- About 44% of the terrorist attacks in 2009 occurred in South Asia, accounting for more than 4 in 10 terrorist-related deaths.
- Two of every three terrorist attacks that killed 10 or more people occurred in South Asia or the Near East in 2009.
- The U.S. Department of State designates four governments as state sponsors of international terrorism: Iran, Syria, Cuba, and Sudan.
- The U.S. Department of State designates 44 groups as Foreign Terrorist Organizations.

Source: U.S. Department of State. (2010). *Country Reports on Terrorism 2009.* National Counterterrorism Center, 2010. Retrieved 10/30/10 from http://www.state.gov/s/crt/2009/index.htm

TABLE 16–2 **Incidents of Terrorism Worldwide, 2005–2009**

	2005	2006	2007	2008	2009
Attacks worldwide	11,023	14,443	14,435	11,725	10,999
Attacks resulting in at least 1 death, injury, or kidnapping	7,963	11,278	11,097	8.411	7,875
Attacks resulting in the death of at least 1 individual	5,083	7,412	7,235	5,045	4,764
Attacks resulting in the death of 0 individuals	5,940	7,031	7,200	6,680	6,235
Attacks resulting in the death of only 1 individual	2,853	4,127	3,984	2,870	2,694
Attacks resulting in the death of at least 10 individuals	226	295	353	234	234
Attacks resulting in the injury of at least 1 individual	3,805	5,774	6,243	4,869	4,536
Attacks resulting in the kidnapping of at least 1 individual	1,156	1,343	1,156	961	877
People killed, injured, or kidnapped as a result of terrorism	74,327	74,616	71,856	54,653	58,142
People worldwide killed as a result of terrorism	14,482	20,515	22,736	15,727	14,971
People worldwide injured as a result of terrorism	24,795	38,314	44,139	34,057	34,057
People worldwide kidnapped as a result of terrorism	35,050	15,787	4,981	4,869	4,869
Incidents of Terrorism in Iraq and Afghanistan					
Terrorist attacks in Iraq	3,438	6,631	6,210	3,256	2,458
Attacks resulting in at least 1 death, injury, or kidnapping	2,648	5,910	5,507	2,878	2,167
People killed, injured, or kidnapped as a result of terrorism	20,629	38,878	44,012	19,077	16,869
Terrorist attacks in Afghanistan	494	962	1,124	1,222	2,126
Attacks resulting in at least 1 death, injury, or kidnapping	357	667	898	982	1,480
People killed, injured, or kidnapped as a result of terrorism	1,557	3,532	4,657	5,430	7,584

Source: U.S. Department of State, Country Reports on Terrorism 2009 (National Counterterrorism Center, 2010).

Typology of Terrorism

Various typologies of terrorism have been proposed. However, it is generally conceded that six forms of terrorism are most commonly practiced: nationalist, religious, state-sponsored, left-wing, right-wing, and anarchist (Hudson, 1999). The aim of **nationalist terrorism** is to create a self-governing nation that exists apart from its current political domination. Examples include the Irish Republican Army, the Palestinian Liberation Organization, the Basque Fatherland and Liberty, and the Kurdistan Workers' Party. Each of these organizations uses terrorist tactics to call attention to oppressive social conditions and to garner widespread support for its intention to establish an independent nation-state.

Religious terrorism is carried out to defend religious doctrines or sacred lands from assaults by nonbelievers. Bruce Hoffman (1995, 1999), a noted terrorism expert at RAND (Research and Development), notes that religious terrorists comprise about half of the 56 active international terrorist groups. Unlike nationalist terrorists, religious terrorists are not limited by considerations of nationalism or ideologies. Rather, as Bruce Hoffman (1995, 1999) points out, religious terrorists may victimize any member of a religious group that is not their own and engage in unrestrained violence against persons considered a religious "outsider." Extreme religious terrorists include al-Qaeda, Osama bin Laden's international network of terrorists; Hamas, the Palestinian Sunni Muslin organization; Hezbollah, the radical Israeli group; and Aum Shinrikyo, the fatalistic Japanese extremists.

State-sponsored terrorism refers to contracting the services of mercenary terrorists to carry out acts of destruction that serve the interests of the state or nation. Although the state provides financial support for acts of terrorism, it does not overtly engage in them. In 2004 the U.S. State Department identified four countries as sponsors of terrorist activities: Iran, Sudan, Syria, and Cuba.

At opposite ends of a political continuum are left- and right-wing terrorism. On the one hand, **left-wing terrorists** seek to overthrow capitalism and create a communistic or socialistic form of economic system. The German Baader-Meinhof group, the Japanese Red Army, and the Italian Red Brigades all sought to remedy what they considered the exploitation of capitalism. In addition, the Workers' World Party, Reclaim the Streets, and Carnival Capitalism operate on an international scale to disrupt the spread of the capitalistic economic system. On the other hand, the objective of **right-wing terrorists** is to replace liberal democratic governments with neo-Nazi or fascist states that establish Aryan supremacy. Examples of right-wing terrorists are the Skinheads in Europe and World Church of the Creator and the Aryan Nations in the United States—antigovernment organizations marked by distinct racial hatred. Last, **anarchist terrorism** simply wants to destroy any form of government and live unencumbered by the restrictions of political control. Groups that protest the creation of a world bank, the emergence of economic globalization, and the resultant blending of cultures around the world are examples of terrorists in pursuit of anarchy (U.S. State Department, 2004).

SSRN

Khan, A. (1987). A theory of international terrorism. *Connecticut Law Review, 19,* 945. http://ssrn.com/abstract=935347

Terrorist Organizational Structure

James Fraser and Ian Fulton (1984) contend that the hierarchical structure of a terrorist organization resembles a pyramid. There are four hierarchical levels: command, active cadre, active supporters, and passive supporters. At the top of the pyramid is the command, the smallest unit in the structure, responsible for setting policy and devising a strategic plan for the terrorist organization. Because secrecy is vital to the survival of the terrorist group, the commanders do not freely communicate with the other members of the organization. The active cadre is entrusted with carrying out specific acts of terrorism. Active supporters provide the assistance necessary for the active cadre to carry out its missions. Intelligence gathering, establishing means of communication, and providing places to hide from oppositional forces are responsibilities of the active supporters. The passive supporters, the largest segment of the terrorist organization, create conditions that are generally favorable to terrorist activities by fostering public acceptance and goodwill.

Terrorist organizations are composed of cells, each with a unique task. Each cell, typically made up of four to six persons, is responsible for carrying out a specific function—intelligence, technical assistance, training, supplies, and so on. Cells may be actively engaged in planning and carrying out a particular mission, or they may be "sleeper" cells whose members stand ready to respond to a call to participate in a terrorist activity at some future but unspecified time.

Central to the success of a terrorist organization is its ability to operate in complete secrecy. To ensure the secrecy of its activities, terrorist organizations must carefully control the flow of information within and between cells. Often, members of the organizations do not know what others are doing. The planning of missions is reserved for few terrorist leaders and divulged to the members only when the mission is to be carried out. The necessity to maintain utmost secrecy is also enhanced by a decentralized form of organization (White, 2002). Jonathan White (2002, p. 38) also notes that "the larger the (terrorist) group, the greater the degree of decentralization." Decentralized organizations enhance security—cell members, largely unknown to one another, can operate independently without fear of detection. The organizations' leaders coordinate the efforts of the various cells by demanding strict adherence to their directives. White (2002, pp. 36–37) notes, "In essence, what the commanders continually threaten to do is to terrorize the terrorist organization. Factionalism and autonomy are controlled through fear of retribution."

Terrorist Organizational Dynamics

Many of the recruits in terrorist organizations are marginal persons—young, uneducated, and powerless—with few prospects for a meaningful life. Acceptance into a terrorist organization offers a sense of belonging, self-worth, and purpose in life. To Eric Shaw (1986, pp. 38–39) the membership in terrorist organizations solves many life problems:

> The terrorist identity offers the individual a role in society, albeit a negative one, which is commensurate with his or her prior expectations and sufficient to compensate for past losses. Group membership provides a sense of potency, an intense and close interpersonal environment, social status, potential access to wealth and a share in what may be a grandiose but noble social design. The powerful psychological forces of conversion in the group are sufficient to offset traditional social sanctions against violence. . . . To the terrorists their acts may have the moral status of religious warfare or political liberation.

The identity of the "new recruit" is fused with that of the terrorist organization. In exchange for a meaningful identity, the new recruit abandons individual freedom of thought or action. The terrorist organization frames its mission, determines the extent of involvement of its individual members, and provides a justification for engagement in lethal violence (Post, 1986).

Albert Bandura (1990) outlines four strategies for moral disengagement that may be used by terrorist organizations. First, terrorism is viewed as necessary to combat an "evil" force and therefore morally justified. Second, individual members of the terrorist organization are simply carrying out the directives of their leaders and cannot be held responsible for their individual actions. Third, terrorists reject the notion that the pain and suffering of their victims is any greater than their own. In this way they insulate themselves from any guilt that may ensue from their acts of violence. Fourth, victims of terrorists' attacks tend to be depersonalized and dehumanized—a faceless, oppressive enemy that deserves to be destroyed. Bonnie Cordes (1987, p. 43) notes that "renaming themselves, their actions, their victims and their enemies accords the terrorist respectability."

Suicide Bombers

Yoran Schweitzer defines a **suicide attack** as "a violent, politically motivated attack, carried out in a deliberate state of awareness by a person who blows himself up together with his chosen target. The pre-meditated certain death of the perpetrator is the pre-condition for the success of the attack" (Schweitzer, 2001).

Noted terrorism expert Jerrold Post (2001), who has interviewed 35 failed suicide bombers imprisoned in Israel, reports that they did not exhibit any symptoms of uncontrolled rage or mental disorder, but were simply on a mission—a Jihad—to deliberately destroy the enemy. There are no moral constraints and no guilt associated with mass destruction.

Recruitment

Potential terrorists, particularly suicide bombers, are often identified in places of public prayer and religious teaching. The British Broadcasting Company reports that suicide bombers "are likely to be motivated by religious fervor" and typically are "picked out from mosques, schools and religious institutions" (Shuman, 2001). Al-Qassam, the military arm of Hamas, and the Palestinian Islamic Jihad both recruit suicide bombers. Members of these highly integrated terrorist cells frequently visit schools and mosques in the West Bank and Gaza Strip. Typically, they talk with students, usually between the ages of 12 and 17, about the prospect of dying for Allah. Those who express interest in the possibility of religious martyrdom are identified as having "special merit." With rare exception, the students who qualify for special merit are closely tied to a person who has been imprisoned, killed, or seriously hurt by the Israelis. Their personal suffering and sense of humiliation prepare them for the socialization process necessary to form a successful suicide bomber (Hudson, 1999).

Hamas, the radical Islamic group, reports that an intense period of indoctrination is provided to potential suicide bombers (Shuman, 2001):

Final Thoughts of a Suicide Bomber

One day soon Marwan Abu Ubeida plans to offer up a final prayer and then blow himself up along with as many U.S. or Iraqi soldiers as he can reach. Marwan says he has been training for months to carry out a suicide mission. . . . While he waits, he spends much of his time rehearsing that last prayer. "First I will ask Allah to bless my mission with a high rate of causalities among Americans. Then I will ask him to purify by soul so I am fit to see him, and I will ask to see my mujahedin brothers who are already with him." When Marwan Abu Ubeida agreed to become a suicide bomber, he remembers "it was the happiest day of my life."

Compared with his family and friends he says the jihadis are more religious people. "You ask them anything—anything—and they can instantly quote a relevant section of the Koran." The goal is one global Islamic state . . . "no alcohol, no music, and no Western influence." He fights first for Islam, second to become a "martyr" and win acceptance into heaven, and only third for control of his country.

Source: Excerpted from Aparisim Ghosh, "Inside the Mind of an Iraqi Suicide Bomber," Time, Vol. 166, Issue 1 (July 4, 2005).

> The bombers believe that they are sent on their missions from God, and by the time that they're ready to be strapped with explosives . . . they have reached a hypnotic state. Their rationale: that by blowing themselves up in a crowd of Israelis, they are forging their own gateway to heaven.

Intensive instruction in the Koran and the Hadith, the teachings of Prophet Mohammed, are provided to the potential suicide bomber. The extreme honor of dying for Allah, the promises of an afterlife with unimaginable sensuous pleasures, and the opportunity to strike a blow directly at the Israelis who, they argue, are responsible for stealing the homeland of the Muslims are key elements of the process of indoctrination. In addition, Hamas provides the poverty-ridden families of the suicide bomber with a monthly stipend of about $1,000, food and household supplies, resettlement funds for families who are targets of Israeli retaliation, and scholarships for the remaining children (Hudson, 1999).

During the final days before the suicide attack, the recruit prepares himself by repeating scriptural verses that ensure his immediate entrance into heaven and neutralize any guilt that he may have for taking the lives of persons unknown to him. Among the more common verses is this: "Think not of those who are slain in Allah's way as dead. No, they live on and find their sustenance in the presence of their Lord" (Hudson, 1999, p. 118). Comforted by this belief, the suicide bomber is able to mingle among his victims in a relaxed and causal manner. An additional safeguard against the detection of the mission and the recruit's last-minute change of heart is the practice of reserving instruction in the use of explosives for the end of his training, just before the mission is to be carried out (Hudson, 1999).

New Suicide Bomber

A new suicide bomber is emerging, working alongside those traditionally recruited by Hamas and Islamic Jihad. Young Palestinians driven by the desire to avenge the ravages of perceived political oppression volunteer to become suicide bombers. They do not receive the kinds of intense indoctrination that is typically provided young recruits whose public demonstrations of devotion set them apart from their peers and whose view of their chances of a worthwhile life are particularly bleak. Rather, young, secular, college-educated Palestinians are offering to serve as suicide bombers. Often less than a week elapses before they are provided with an explosive device, directed toward a suitable target, and given instructions as to how to carry out the suicide attack.

A transformation in Palestinian culture is occurring, which according to Dr. Iyad Sarraj (Bennet, 2002), a Palestinian psychiatrist, shapes the meanings that children attach to life and death. In a culture marked by powerlessness and humiliation, where suicidal attacks are commonplace, personal power is achieved only in a death that involves the killing of the enemy. Martyrdom is an expression of righteous rage. *New York Times* reporter James Bennet (2002) observes, "But as much as any manipulative militant leader, it appears to be the very culture of a ravaged and disoriented Palestinian society that now feeds the recruitment of suicide bombers."

Terrorism: Psychopathology Versus Rational Behavior

On the surface it may appear that acts of terrorism—the killing of innocent civilians unknown to the assailants—provide evidence of insanity. Viewed from the outside, suicide bombers are easily understood as individuals driven by a psychotic rage. Yet, considered within a sociopolitical and cultural context, terrorist behaviors may be interpreted as the reactions of psychologically normal individuals to extraordinary circumstances and processes.

The aftermath of the 9/11 terrorist attacks on the Pentagon. What are the principle motivations of terrorists?

Psychologist Clark R. McCauley (2001) notes that terrorists' behavior is shaped by their single-minded dedication to a cause and their intense involvement with a terrorist group. Potential members of a terrorist organization are identified and recruited based on their demonstration of an inordinate public commitment to a cause. Once they have been accepted into a terrorist group, they are effectively isolated from the influence of competing values from the outside. The process of separation and isolation are commonly practiced by a wide range of groups interested in molding the mentality and behaviors of its members. The merging of the individual's identity and sense of purpose with that of the terrorist group results in the creation of a person capable of carrying out self-sacrificing acts of terrorism.

To Brookings Institute Fellow Shibley Telhami (2002), the "most pervasive psychology in the Arab world today is collective rage and feelings of helplessness." Governments are no longer able to resolve international conflicts. Individual action is needed to counter the humiliation of the chronic political ineptness. Telhami (2002) argues that "suicide bombings thrive in anarchy." They "take root because they free the desperate from the need to rely on governments altogether." Suicide bombers are not limited, Telhami (2002) observes, to radical Islamic groups such as Hamas but are also found among secular Palestinians who find it an effective political strategy. Mouin Rabbani, director of the Palestinian American Research Center in Ramallah, also contends that intractable political oppression creates the willingness to engage in suicide bombing attacks.

Without exception, suicide bombers have lived their lives on the receiving end of a system designed to trample their rights and crush every hope of a brighter future. Confronted by a seemingly endless combination of death, destruction, restriction, harassment and humiliation, they conclude that ending life as a bomb—rather than having it end by a bullet—endows them, even if only in their final moments, with a semblance of purpose and control previously considered out of reach (Telhami, 2002).

SSRN

Seto, T. P. (2002). The morality of terrorism. *Loyola of Los Angeles Law Review, 35*, 1227. http://ssrn.com/abstract=341600 or doi:10.2139/ssrn.341600.

Motivations

The motivations for involvement in terrorist activities may be classified into three categories: rational motivation, psychological motivation, and cultural motivation (http://www.timeenoughforlove.org/saved/TerrorismResearchCenterBasics.htm).

SSRN

Neumayer, E., & Pluemper, T. (2009). International terrorism and the clash of civilizations. *British Journal of Political Science, 39*(4), 711–734. http://ssrn.com/abstract=952208

RATIONAL MOTIVATION. A rational decision-making process may well precede the commission of a terrorist act. Terrorist organizations set goals and objectives to advance their causes. The costs and benefits of engaging in a specific terrorist act are weighed. A critical question is can the proposed terrorist act achieve its goals without causing a reaction that will jeopardize the cause?

PSYCHOLOGICAL MOTIVATION. Dissatisfaction with life and a dismal view of one's future tend to characterize persons engaged in terrorist activities. Potential terrorists are often described as "true believers" who perceive the world in dichotomous terms—their cause is sacred and righteous, those who oppose them are evil and inhuman. There is a strong need to belong to a group that will advance their beliefs and provide them with a sense of purpose in life.

CULTURAL MOTIVATION. Terrorist behaviors must be understood within a sociocultural framework. The view that the life of every individual must be protected and preserved is commonly held in Europe and North America. Other societies, particularly in the Middle East and Asia, consider identification with a group—nation, family, or tribe—to take precedence over individual life. Threats to the survival of a culture—its ethnic identity, religion, language, or territory—often result in uncompromising retaliatory acts of violence. Terrorism in the defense of religious belief is, arguably, carried out with the most intense fervor. The sacrifice of one's life for the good of cultural preservation is uniformly valued and highly rewarded.

Doctrine of Necessity

H. H. A. Cooper (1977) contends that terrorists justify the commission of violent acts against innocent persons, including women, children, and the elderly, by concluding that peaceful means for conflict resolution are not viable and must be rejected. The use of violence is viewed as the most reasonable way to achieve their goals. Cooper (1977) argues that terrorists adopt a "doctrine of necessity" to justify their acts of destruction. Violence becomes a moral imperative.

For example, al-Qaeda and other Islamic extremists seek to preserve their Islamic cultural heritage, including their interpretation of *Sharia* or Islamic law. To do so they must engage in a *Jihad* or holy war against the enemies of Islam. The United States and Israel are among the principal opponents of Islam as, they believe, Allah intended it to be practiced.

SSRN

Saul, B. (2006). Defending "terrorism": Justifications and excuses for terrorism in international criminal law. *Australian Yearbook of International Law, 25,* 177–226. Sydney Law School Research Paper No. 08/122. http://ssrn.com/abstract=1291584

Cyberterrorism

In a report commissioned by the National Academy of Sciences, the potential destructive force of **cyberterrorism** is highlighted. The report begins as follows (National Research Council, 1991):

> We are at risk. America depends on computers. They control delivery, communications, aviation, and financial services. They are used to store vital information, from medical records to business plans to criminal records. Although we trust them, they are vulnerable—to the effects of poor design and insufficient quality control, to accident and perhaps most alarmingly, to deliberate attack. The modern thief can steal more with a computer than with a gun. Tomorrow's terrorist may be able to do more damage with a keyboard than with a bomb.

Definition

To Mark M. Pollitt cyberterrorism involves two elements: cyberspace and terrorism (http://www.cs.georgetown.edu/~denning/infosec/pollitt.html). Pollitt adopts the U.S. State Department definition of terrorism—the "premeditated, politically motivated violence perpetrated against noncombatant targets by subnational groups or clandestine agents" (Pollitt, 2010, n.p.). Combining the two definitions, Pollitt defines cyberterrorism as "the premeditated, politically motivated attack against information, computer systems, computer programs, and data which results in violence against noncombatant targets by subnational groups or clandestine agents" (Pollitt, 2010, n.p.)

Computers may be used in the furtherance of terrorist activities. Increasing global dependence on computer technology has resulted in an unprecedented vulnerability to attack. Rod Stark (1999) defines cyberterrorism as follows:

> The purposeful or threatened use of politically, socially, economically or religiously motivated cyber warfare or cyber-targeted violence, conducted by a non-state or state-sponsored group for the purposes of creating fear, anxiety, and panic in the targeted population, and the disruption of military and civilian assets.

The development of the Internet has led to acceleration of the "information age," the global economy, and the increasing possibilities of cyberterrorism. Warfare is also becoming transformed. The dependence of civilian populations on the flow of information to conduct their everyday lives makes them particularly attractive targets for cyberterrorist attacks. Cyberterrorism may involve the destruction, alteration, and/or the acquisition and retransmission of information. Disruptions in the flow of information have the potential to confuse and demoralize civilian populations across the world simultaneously. Confidence in the viability of economic transactions, in the safety of public transportation, and in the ability to rely on the validity of medical records may well be undermined (Collin, 1996; Shahar, 1997).

Explanations for Terrorism

Sociological or social psychological theorizing about the precipitants of terrorism, its organization, and its perpetuation is relatively uncommon compared with other forms of violent behavior. However, it is possible to apply extant theories of violence to issues related to terrorist activities (**Table 16–3**).

Although they provide an incomplete understanding, the theoretical formulations considered here help us to think about the intricacies of terrorism and its social context.

Rational Choice

Derek B. Cornish and Ronald V. Clarke's (1986) rational choice formulation of criminal behavior is useful in understanding acts of terrorism.

TABLE 16–3 Explanations for Terrorism

Theories and Theorists	Sociological Predictors	Hypotheses
Social Integration/Anomie		
Durkheim	Social integration	The greater the social integration, the greater the possibility of altruistic suicide. The greater the possibility of altruistic suicide, the greater the possibility of terrorism.
Routine Activities		
Cohen and Felson	Motivated offender Suitable target Lack of a guardian	The convergence of an offender who is motivated to engage in terrorism with a suitable target and the lack of an adequate guardian for the target, the greater the probability that an act of terrorism will be carried out.
Social Learning		
Sutherland	Differential association	The greater the exposure to definitions favorable toward terrorism, the greater the probability of engaging in terrorist activities.
Akers	Differential association Definitions Differential reinforcement Imitation	The greater the interaction with members of terrorist organizations, the greater the value assigned to acts of terrorism, the greater the actual or anticipated rewards for engagement in terrorism, and the more terrorists are viewed as models for one's behavior, the greater the likelihood of involvement in terrorist behaviors.
Subcultural		
Cloward and Ohlin	Opportunity	The more a subculture advocates the commission of terrorism and provides opportunities for its commission, the higher the incidence of terrorism.
Wolfgang and Ferracuti	Subculture of violence	The greater the integration into a subculture of violence, the greater the probability of involvement in acts of terrorism.
Cultural Conflict		
Sellin	Culture conflict	The more intense the primary culture conflict, the greater the likelihood an act of terrorism will occur.

/ continues

TABLE 16–3 Explanations for Terrorism / continued

Theories and Theorists	Sociological Predictors	Hypotheses
Frustration Aggression/Strain		
Dollard et al.	Blocked goals	The greater important needs and goals are perceived to be blocked by others, the greater the experience of frustration. The greater the experience of frustration caused by others, the greater the probability of outwardly directed aggression. The greater the likelihood of outwardly directed aggression, the greater the probability of engagement in terrorist behaviors.
Agnew	Negative social interaction	The greater the experience of negative social relations, the greater the experience of negative emotions. The greater the experience of negative emotions, the greater the probability of engagement in terrorist behaviors.
Rational Choice		
Cornish	Cost-to-benefit analysis	The greater the benefit associated with terrorism, the more likely the individual will commit terrorist activities.
Techniques of Neutralization		
Sykes and Matza	Denial of responsibility Denial of injury Denial of the victim Condemnation of the condemners Appeal to higher loyalties	The greater the use of the techniques of neutralization, the less guilt associated with acts of terrorism. The less guilt associated with acts of terrorism, the greater the probability of involvement in terrorist behaviors.

They argue that before committing a crime, the offender rationally and deliberately assesses the cost and benefits involved in its commission. If the potential benefits substantially outweigh the possible costs that may be incurred, then the offender may well carry out the crime. Terrorists tend to be driven by an overwhelming desire to advance an extremely highly valued cause—one that is inextricably tied to personal identity and provides an elemental meaning to life. Involvement in acts of terrorism provides an opportunity to contribute to the larger social good—to redress political oppression and humiliation at the hand of the enemy. The cost of the terrorist life is considered minimal compared to the immediate and everlasting rewards of martyrdom.

Social Integration

To Emile Durkheim (1951), the degree of social integration—or the adherence to a set of strongly held common values—provides an explanation for deviant behaviors. His seminal study of rates of suicide links the extent of social integration of a society with three distinct types of suicide. Under conditions of low integration, marked by the absence of commonly held values, egoistic suicide tends to occur. In societies marked by high integration, where important social values are held in common, altruistic suicide is more usual. And, in societies undergoing rapid and unpredictable social change, normlessness more typically characterizes everyday life. Under these conditions, anomic suicide is more likely to occur. Terrorism is more common when social integration is high and individuals are willing to sacrifice themselves for the good of a recognized social entity. Suicide bombers and other forms of self-destructive terrorist acts are typically carried out to advance well-defined political or religious objectives.

Routine Activities

Lawrence Cohen and Marcus Felson (1979) advance a routine activities explanation of criminal behavior. Their theoretical formulation includes three components: a motivated offender, suitable target, and the absence of an effective guardian. The commitment of terrorists to the success of their mission is essential. Ambivalence on the part of a would-be terrorist may well result in failure of the mission and compromise the security of the organization. Further, terrorists take into account the attractiveness of their intended target, assessing the potential for instilling widespread and lasting "terror" in the minds of the members of the larger public. The likelihood that a guardian of the target will thwart the terrorist's mission is also carefully considered. In brief, the routine activities theory identifies the three criteria for a successful terrorist attack.

Culture Conflict

Thorsten Sellin (1938) argues that clash of conduct norms may give rise to the occurrence of various forms of deviant behavior. Conflict in norms may occur when distinct sociocultural groups are in close proximity with one another, when the laws of a dominant sociocultural group are imposed on a less powerful group, or when one sociocultural group moves into the lands occupied by another group. Recent terrorist activities, particularly emanating from the Israeli-Palestinian conflict, are consistent with Sellin's cultural conflict formulation. Disputes arising from the right to occupy certain lands, most notably the West Bank and the Gaza Strip, and the resultant sense of cultural degradation have led to the proliferation of suicide bombings of Israeli targets by young Palestinians.

Frustration–Aggression

John Dollard and his colleagues (1939) contend that frustration, usually thought to involve the blockage of important needs and goals, inevitably leads to some form of aggression. The more critical the personal needs and the more vital the cultural goals that are blocked, the more intense the experience of frustration and the more violent the resultant aggression.

Aggression may either be directed outwardly—a violent act committed against an external target—or directed inwardly toward the self. Frustration may also result in an individual acting in such a way as to harm or destroy an external target as well as him- or herself. The experience of long-term frustration (e.g., over self-governance) at the hands of a dominant political force (e.g., the conflict between the Irish Republican Army and the British Government or the clash between the Palestinians and the Israelis) has led to repeated acts of terrorism over several years.

Strain

Closely related to the frustration-aggression hypothesis is Robert Agnew's (1992) strain theory of deviant behavior. Agnew argues that negative social interaction, typically involving blockage of important needs and goals, is particularly stressful for an individual. Sustained negative social interaction results in the chronic experience of negative emotions such as anger, rage, depression, and anxiety. An unalleviated negative emotional state often drives an individual to seek immediate and permanent relief. Terrorists often consider the experience of long-term humiliation at the hand of a dominant political foe to cause them to resort to extreme acts of terrorism, often resulting in their own death.

Social Learning

Edwin Sutherland (1939) and Ronald Akers (1998) argue that deviant behavior is, for the most part, learned in the process of interacting with others who serve as role models. Both Sutherland's theory of differential association and Akers' social structure and social learning formulation articulated the processes involved in becoming a deviant. To Sutherland, the more an individual interacts directly with others who advocate the violation of the law, the more likely that individual will learn the motives, drives, rationalization, and techniques that are essential in the commission of deviant acts. Potential terrorists are carefully selected, rigorously trained to carry out terrorist missions, and indoctrinated by terrorist organizers.

Intense and exclusive interaction with members of terrorist cells over an extended period of time results in the molding of a reliable and unwavering member of a terrorist organization.

Ronald Akers's social structure and social learning formulation provides a context for understanding the learning process involved in becoming a terrorist. To Akers there are four social structural conditions that facilitate learning to engage in deviant acts. The first condition is *differential social organization*—the conditions of the community that give rise to criminal acts (e.g., social inequality, economic deprivation, and illicit opportunities). The second condition is the individual's *differential location in the social structure*, or the sociodemographic characteristics that position them in the larger socioeconomic structure of society. The third condition is the presence within the community of *theoretically defined structural variables*, or a critical mass of known precipitants of criminal involvement (e.g., strain, deprivation, exclusion, and degradation). The fourth condition, *differential social location*, refers to the placement in the larger social structure of an individual's most important membership groups, family, social organizations, and religious affiliations.

Persons who engage in acts of terrorism are often drawn from communities that are marginal to the mainstream of society. Their opportunities for economic success are limited, as are their chances for other forms of positive social recognition. They are members of devalued ethnic and religious groups who have suffered long-standing humiliations and political disenfranchisement. Their social structural positioning has rendered them personally powerless to combat the forces of oppression. As a consequence, they become highly motivated to seek revenge through acts of terrorism.

Techniques of Neutralization

Gresham Sykes and David Matza (1957) consider the issue of guilt that may attend the commission of a deviant or criminal act. Given that intense guilt may impede engagement in acts of terrorism, it must be "neutralized" to ensure the success of a terrorist mission. Sykes and Matza identify five techniques that may effectively neutralize any guilt associated with terrorist activities: denial of responsibility, denial of injury, denial of the victim, condemnation of the condemners, and appeal to higher loyalties.

Terrorists often invoke a *denial of responsibility*, arguing that they were forced to engage in extreme forms of violence because of their demeaning living conditions and the humiliations that they suffered at the hands of their oppressors. Although *denial of injury* is less usual, some Islamic terrorists believe God will provide well for their victims in the afterlife. More often, terrorists engage in a process of *denial of the victim*—the belief that the victim is really the offender and acts of terrorism are necessary to remedy a protracted state of domination and humiliation. *Condemnation of the condemner* is a common practice among members of terrorist organizations. Those who condemn the acts of terrorism are themselves often considered morally corrupt, demonized, and unworthy to render judgment. Finally, a related strategy used by terrorists to neutralize guilt is an *appeal to higher loyalties*. Terrorist missions are viewed mandated by the will of God—divinely inspired and justified. The terrorist is acting as an instrument of the God they envision. No secular government or sociocultural group of "nonbelievers" can legitimately question their actions, however violent or self-destructive they may be.

Chapter Summary

Terrorism has emerged as a specific and extreme form of deviant behavior with global implications. Most definitions of terrorism include the unlawful use of force against civilians/noncombatant targets by subnational groups/clandestine agents in furtherance of a political or social objective. Depending on the origin, base, and objectives of the terrorist organization, terrorism is considered either domestic or international.

Domestic terrorism includes acts of terrorism by U.S. citizens without foreign influence and directed at elements of the U.S. government or population. International terrorism involves citizens of more than one country and transcends national boundaries.

Terrorist motivations may be understood from three perspectives: rational, psychological, and cultural.

Cyberterrorism refers to any terrorist attack against information, computer systems, computer programs, or data that may result in violence or disruption and create fear, anxiety, or panic in the target population.

Explanations for terrorism fall into many of the same categories used throughout this book: rational choice theories, concepts involving social integration, and the routine activities approach.

Key Concepts

Terrorism: The act of destroying or injuring civilian lives or property without governmental permission in the attempt to affect some political goal.

Terrorist: Any person acting without governmental permission to destroy or injure civilian or government property to bring about some political goal.

Domestic terrorism: The commission of acts of terrorism by U.S. citizens, either groups or individuals, who are based and operate entirely within the United States without foreign direction or influence and whose acts are directed at elements of the U.S. government or population.

International terrorism: Terrorism involving citizens or the territory of more than one country; terrorism committed by a group or individual who has some connection to a foreign power or whose activities transcend national boundaries.

Hate crime (bias crime): A criminal act or attempted act against a person, institution, or property that is motivated in whole or in part by the offender's bias against a race, color, religion, gender, ethic/national origin group, disability status, or sexual orientation.

Nationalist terrorism: Terrorism aimed at the creation of a self-governing nation that exists apart from its current political domination; a response to oppressive social conditions.

Religious terrorism: Terrorism carried out to defend religious doctrines or sacred lands from assaults by nonbelievers.

State-sponsored terrorism: Terrorism contracted out to mercenary terrorist groups to serve the interests of the state or nation.

Left-wing terrorism: Terrorism aimed at overthrowing capitalism to create a communistic or socialistic form of economic system.

Right-wing terrorism: Terrorism aimed at replacing liberal democratic governments with neo-Nazi or fascist states that establish Aryan supremacy.

Anarchist terrorism: Terrorism aimed at destroying any form of government in order to end political control and restrictions.

Suicide attack (bombing): A violent, politically motivated attack carried out by a person who blows him- or herself up with the chosen target.

Cyberterrorism: Any terrorist attack against information, computer systems, computer programs, or data that may result in violence or disruption and create fear, anxiety, or panic in the target population.

Critical Thinking Questions

1. What distinguishes acts of terrorism from other forms of violent behavior? Are there unique sociocultural conditions that generate terrorist behavior? Or, are the underlying causes of terrorism and violence similar?
2. Do the processes of globalization (e.g., worldwide communication, transnational commerce and trade, and borderless political and cultural exchange) precipitate terrorist activities? If so, how do the processes of globalization give rise to transnational terrorism and/or domestic terrorism?
3. In what ways are suicide bombers and "homicide followed by suicide offenders" similar to and different from each other? Compare the societal and individual dynamics that lead to each form of violent behavior.
4. Compare cyberterrorism with more traditional forms of terrorism. Consider the similarities and differences in the processes of recruitment, socialization, and organization of each form of terrorism. Other than sophisticated technological skills, what distinguishes cyberterrorists from terrorists who commit more direct acts of violence?

Web Extra

Web-based media materials from high-quality sources such as CNN, Time, and National Public Radio are available in support of this textbook. Visit go.jblearning.com/deviance to access them.

Check out these websites for additional information on terrorism:

http://www.state.gov

http://www.dhs.gov

http://www.defenselink.mil

http://www.fbi.gov

http://www.ict.org/il

http://www.terrorism.com

http://www.ojp.usdoj.gov/nij/international

References

Abadinsky, H. (1989). *Drug abuse: An introduction.* Chicago, IL: Nelson-Hall.

ABC News. (2010, July 14). *"Barefoot Bandit" Colton Harris-Moore back on U.S. soil, vows to turn life around.* Retrieved March 7, 2011, from http://abcnews.go.com/GMA/TheLaw/barefoot-bandit-colton-harris-moore-vowed-turn-life/story?id=11159980&page=2

Acharya, K. (2001). Poverty and mental health in the developing world. *Contemporary Review, 279,* 136–137.

Agnew, R. (1992). Foundation for a general strain theory of crime and delinquency. *Criminology, 30,* 47–88.

Ahn, D. H. (2007). Korean policy on treatment and rehabilitation for adolescents' Internet addiction, in the International Symposium on the Counseling and Treatment of Youth Internet Addiction. Seoul, Korea: National Youth Commission.

Akers, R. (1985). *Deviant behavior: A social learning approach* (3rd ed.). Belmont, CA: Wadsworth Publishing Company.

Akers, R. (1991). Addiction: The troublesome concept. *Journal of Drug Issues, 21,* 777–793.

Akers, R. L. (1992). *Drugs, alcohol, and society: Social structure, process, and policy.* Belmont, CA: Wadsworth.

Akers, R. (1994). *Criminological theories: Introduction and evaluation.* Los Angeles, CA: Roxbury.

Akers, R. (1998). *Social learning and social structure.* Boston, MA: Northeastern University Press.

Akers & Burgess. (1966). A differential association-reinforcement theory of criminal behavior. *Social Problems, 14,* 128–147.

Albanese, J. S., Das, D. K., & Verma, A. (2003). *Organized crime: World perspectives.* Upper Saddle River, NJ: Prentice Hall.

Alcoholics Anonymous. (2001). *Alcoholics Anonymous* (4th ed.). New York, NY: Alcoholics Anonymous World Services, Inc..

Alcoholics Anonymous World Services. (1970). *Alcoholics Anonymous comes of age: A brief history of A.A.* New York, NY: Alcoholics Anonymous World Services, Inc.

Alexander, L., & LaRosa, J. (1994). *New dimensions in women's health.* Boston, MA: Jones and Bartlett Publishers.

American Psychiatric Association. (1994). *Diagnostic and statistical manual of mental disorders (DSM-IV)* (4th ed.). Washington, DC: American Psychiatric Association

American Psychiatric Association. (2000). *Diagnostic and statistical manual of mental disorders (DSM-IV-TR)* (4th ed.). Washington, DC: American Psychiatric Association.

Anderson, E. (1994). The code of the streets. *The Atlantic Monthly, 273(5),* 80–94.

Anderson, E. (1999). *Code of the street: Decency, violence, and the moral life of the inner city.* New York, NY: W.W. Norton.

Arena, K. (2001, September 10). *Child sex abuse study debunks myths.* Retrieved from http://www.cnn.com/2001/LAW/09/10/arena.child.abuse.otsc/index.html

Associated Press. (2006). *Afghan Christian convert flees to Italy.* Retrieved March 7, 2011, from http://www.foxnews.com/story/0,2933,189440,00.html

Association of British Insurers. (1999, October 11). *News release: Most property crime premeditated according to new research.* Retrieved from http://www.abi.org.uk/

Association of Certified Fraud Examiners. (2008). *Report to the nation on occupational fraud and abuse.* Retrieved from http://www.acfe.com/rttn/2008-rttn.asp

Atkinson, R. L., & Hilgard, E. R. (1996). *Hilgard's introduction to psychology.* Fort Worth, TX: Harcourt Brace College Publishers.

Bachman, R. (1991). An analysis of American Indian homicide: A test of social disorganization and economic deprivation at the reservation county level. *Journal of Research in Crime and Delinquency, 28,* 456–471.

Bachman, R. (1992). *Death and violence on the reservation—homicide, family violence, and suicide in American Indian populations.* Westport, CT: Auburn House.

Bachman, R., & Saltzman, L. (1995). *Violence against women: Estimates from the redesigned survey.* Washington, DC: U.S. Department of Justice, Office of Justice Programs, Bureau of Justice Statistics.

Bales, R. A. (1946). Cultural differences in rates of alcoholism. *Quarterly Journal of Studies on Alcohol, 6,* 480–500.

Bandura, A. (1990). Mechanisms of moral disengagement. In W. Reich (Ed.), *Origins of terrorism: Psychologies, ideologies, theologies, states of mind* (pp. 161–191). Cambridge, MA: Cambridge University Press.

Barnett, C. (2004). *The measurement of white-collar crime using uniform crime reporting (UCR) data.* Washington, D.C.: U.S. Department of Justice, Federal Bureau of Investigation, Criminal Justice Information Services (CJIS) Division.

Barron, L., & Straus, M. (1989). *Four theories of rape in American society: A state-level analysis.* New Haven, CT: Yale University Press.

Beals, J., Piasecki, J., Nelson, S., Jones, M., Keane, E., Dauphinais, P., Shirt, R., Sack, W. H., & Manson, S. M. (1997). Psychiatric disorder among American Indian adolescents: Prevalence in northern plains youth. *Journal of the American Academy of Child and Adolescent Psychiatry, 36,* 1252–1259.

Beccaria, C. (1963). *On crimes and punishment.* Indianapolis, IN: Bobbs-Merrill.

Becker, H. S. (1953). Becoming a marijuana user. *American Journal of Sociology, 59*(3), 235–242.

Becker, H. (1963). *Outsiders: Studies in the sociology of deviance.* New York, NY: Free Press.

Bennet, J. (2002, June 21). Mideast turmoil: The bombers; rash of new suicide bombers exhibit no patterns or ties. *The New York Times*, p. 1A.

Bentham, J. (1948). *The principles of morals and legislation.* New York, NY: Hefner.

Ben-Yehuda, N. (1990). Positive and negative deviance: More fuel for a controversy. *Deviant Behavior, 11,* 221–243.

Berg, B., & Glassner, B. (1980). How to avoid alcohol problems. *American Sociological Review, 45,* 647–664.

Bernard, J. (1982). *The future of marriage* (2nd ed.). New York, NY: Bantam.

Bertone, A. (2000). Sexual trafficking women: International political economy and the politics of sex. *Gender Issues, 18,* 4.

Best, J., & Luckenbill, D. (1994). *Organizing deviance.* Englewood Cliffs, NJ: Prentice-Hall.

Best, J., & Luckenbill, D. (1982). *Organizing deviance.* Englewood Cliffs, NJ: Prentice-Hall.

Black, D. (1976). *The behavior of law.* New York, NY: Academic Press.

Black, D. (1983). Crime as social control. *American Sociological Review, 48,* 34–45.

Black, D. (1998). *The social structure of right and wrong.* San Diego, CA: Academic Press.

Black, D. (2002, Spring). Terrorism as social control (Parts I and II). *American Sociological Association's Crime Law and Deviance Newsletter, Spring,* 3–5 and *Summer,* 3–5.

Blankstein, A., & and Rubin, J. (2010, June 18). LAPD officers questioned in gunshots outside restaurant. *Los Angeles Times.* Retrieved March 7, 2011, from http://www.latimes.com/features/food/la-me-0618-officers-drinking-2-20100618,0,6203998.story

Block, J. J. (2008). Issues for DSM-V: Internet addiction. *American Journal of Psychiatry, 65,* 306–307.

Blum, R. H., & Blum, E. M. (1969). A cultural case study. In R. H. Blum & Associates (Eds.), *Drugs I: Society and drugs* (pp. 188–227). San Francisco, CA: Jossey-Bass.

Bodrero, D. D. (2000). *State Roles: community assessment, and personality profiles.* Tallahassee, FL: Institute for Intergovernment Research.

Bowers, P. (2009, March 2). Final exit: Compassion or assisted suicide? *Time.* Retrieved March 7, 2011, from http://www.time.com/time/nation/article/0,8599,1882418,00.html

Braithwaite, J. (1989). *Crime, shame, and reintegration.* New York, NY: Cambridge University Press.

Bray, M. (2001, November 22). *Call for crackdown on child sex laws.* Retrieved from http://www.cnn.com/2001/WORLD/asiapcf/southeast/11/22/asia.childsex/index.html

Brians, P. (2000, May 18). *The enlightenment.* Retrieved from www.wsu.edu/~brians/hum_303/enlightenment.html

Breivik, G. (1996). Personality, sensation seeking, and risk taking among Everest climbers. *International Journal of Sport Psychology, 27,* 308–320.

Brent, D. A., Johnson, B.A., Perper, J., Connolly, J., Bridge, J., Bartle, S., & Rather, C. A. (1994). Personality disorder, personality traits, impulsive violence, and completed suicide in adolescents. *Journal of American Academy of Child and Adolescence Psychiatry, 33,* 1080–1086.

Brezina, T. (1999). Teenage violence toward parents as an adaptation to family strain: Evidence from a national survey of male adolescents. *Youth and Society, 30,* 416–444.

Brians, P. (2000, May 18). *The enlightenment.* Retrieved from www.wsu.edu/~brians/hum_303/enlightenment.html

Brody, A. (1979, December 19). The work-obsessed. *The New York Times.*

Browne, A. (1987). *When battered women kill.* New York, NY: Macmillan Free Press.

Browne, A., & Finkelhor, D. (1986). Impact of sexual abuse: A review of the research. *Psychological Bulletin, 99,* 66–77.

Brownmiller, S. (1975). *Against our will: Men, women, and rape.* New York: Simon and Schuster.

Bureau of Justice Statistics (BJS). (1994). *Violence between intimates.* Washington, DC: U.S. Department of Justice, Office of Justice Programs, Bureau of Justice Statistics.

Bureau of Justice Statistics (BJS). (2008). *Cybercrimes against businesses.* Washington, DC: U.S. Department of Justice, Office of Justice Programs, Bureau of Justice Statistics.

Bureau of Justice Statistics (BJS). Internet Crime Report (2009). Washington, DC: U.S. Department of Justice, Office of Justice Programs, Bureau of Justice Statistics. Retrieved March 7, 2011, from http://www.ic3.gov/media/annualreport/2009_ic3report.pdf

Cameron, M. (1964). *The booster and the snitch: Department store shoplifting.* New York, NY: Free Press.

Carlin, P.A. (2010, July 17). Colton Harris-Moore: 'Barefoot Bandit' is latest all-American outlaw to capture public eye. *Oregon Live.* Retrieved March 7, 2011, from http://www.oregonlive.com/opinion/index.ssf/2010/07/colton_harris-moore_barefoot_b.html

Carter, C. J. (1998, April 17). U.S. leads riches nations in gun deaths. *Associated Press.* Retrieved March 7, 2011, from http://www.guncite.com/cnngunde.html

Carter, D. L. (1995). Computer crime categories. *FBI Law Enforcement Bulletin, 64,* 21.

Castells, M. (1996). *The rise of the network society, The information age: economy, society, and culture, vol. II.* Oxford: Blackwell.

Cavan, S. (1970). B-girls and prostitutes. In J. Douglas (Ed.), *Observations of deviance* (pp. 55–63). New York, NY: Random House.

Child Abuse Prevention and Treatment Act (CAPTA). (2003). 42 USC 510g Sec. 111. Washington, DC: U.S. Department of Health and Human Services.

Clarke, R., & Cornish, D. (Eds.). (1985). *Crime control in Britain: A review of police and research.* Albany, NY: State University of New York Press.

Clarke, R., & Harris, P. (1992). Auto theft and its prevention. In M. Tonry (Ed.), *Crime and justice: A review of research.* Chicago, IL: University of Chicago Press.

Clifton, K., & Lee, D. (1995). Gender socialization and women's suicidal behaviors. In S. S. Canetto & D. Lester (Eds.), *Women and suicidal behavior.* New York, NY: Springer.

Clinard, M., & Meier, R. (1998). *Sociology of deviant behavior* (10th ed.). Fort Worth, TX: Harcourt Brace Publishers.

Clinard, M., & Quinney, R. (1980). *Criminal behavior systems.* New York, NY: Free Press.

Clinard, M., & Yeager, P. (2002). Corporate crime: Clarifying the concept and extending the data. In M. Ermann & R. Lundman (Eds.), *Corporate and governmental deviance: Problems of organizational behavior in contemporary society* (6th ed.) (pp. 82–94). New York, NY: Oxford University Press.

Clough, B., & Mungo, P. (1992). *Approaching zero: Data crime and the computer underworld.* London, England: Faber and Faber.

Cloward, R., & Ohlin, L. (1960). *Delinquency and opportunity*. Glencoe, IL: Free Press.

CNN. (1997, September 30). *Internet sting identifies 1,500 suspected child pornographers.* Retrieved from http://www.cnn.com/US/9709/30.old/cybersting/index.html

CNN. (1998, March 11). *FBI to parents: Internet pedophiles a serious threat.* Retrieved from http://www.cnn.com/TECH/computing/9803/11/cyber.stalking/index.html

CNN. (1999a, October 26). *Racism to be key issue in third dragging-death trial: Accused to blame co-defendants.* Retrieved from http://www.nytimes.com/1999/11/19/us/third-defendant-is-convicted-in-dragging-death-in-texas.html?ref=jamesjrbyrd

CNN. (1999b, June 15). *UNESCO launches campaign to fight Internet pedophilia.* Retrieved from http://articles.cnn.com/keyword/pedophilia

CNN. (2001, August 28). *Sex offenders put online in S. Korea.* Retrieved from http://edition.cnn.com/2001/WORLD/asiapcf/east/08/28/korea.sexoffenders/index.html

CNN. (2002, March 19). *Dozens arrested in child porn probe: 50 more arrests expected by week's end.* Retrieved from http://www.cnn.com/2002/US/03/18/fbi.child.porn/index.html

CNN International. (2010, June 23). *Alleged drug kingpin arrested in Jamaica.* Retrieved from http://edition.cnn.com/2010/WORLD/americas/06/22/jamaica.dudus.captured/index.html

Code of Federal Regulations. 28 C.F.R. Section 0.85. Retrieved February 16, 2011, from http://www.gpoaccess.gov/cfr/retrieve.html

Cohen, A. (1955). *Delinquent boys.* New York, NY: Free Press.

Cohen, L., & Felson, M. (1979). Social change and crime rate trends: A routine activity approach. *American Sociological Review, 44,* 588–608.

Cohen, M. L., Garofalo, R., Boucher, R., Seghorn, T. (1975). The psychology of rapists. In S. A. Pasternack (Ed.), *Violence and Victims* (pp. 113–140). New York: Spectrum Publications.

Coleman, J. W. (2002). *The criminal elite, understanding white-collar crime* (5th ed.). New York, NY: Worth Publishers.

Coles. (1977). *The privileged ones.* Vol. 5 of Children in Crisis. Boston: Little, Brown.

Collin, B.C. (1996). *The future of cyber terrorism: Where the physical and virtual worlds converge.* Paper presented at the 11th annual International Symposium on Criminal Justice Issues. Chicago, IL: The University of Illinois at Chicago.

Conklin, J. (1972). *Robbery and the criminal justice system.* Philadelphia: Lippincott.

Conklin, J. (1992). *Criminology* (4th ed.). New York, NY: Macmillan Publishing Company.

Conley, J. M., & Bryan, R. M. (1999). A survey of computer crime legislation in the United States. *Information and Technology Law, 8,* 35–57.

Cooley, C. H. (1902). *Human nature and the social order.* New York, NY: Scribner.

Cooney, D. (2006, March 20). Christian convert face death penalty in Afghanistan. *The Guardian.* Retrieved from http://www.guardian.co.uk/world/2006/mar/20/afghanistan.islam

Cooper, H. H. A. (1977). What is a terrorist? A psychological perspective. *Legal Medical Quarterly, 1,* 8–18.

Cordes, B. (1987). *When terrorists do the talking: Reflections on terrorist literature.* Santa Monica, CA: Rand.

Cornelius, J. R., Salloum, I. M., Mezzich, J., Cornelius, M. D., Fabrega Jr., H., Ehler, J. G., Ulrich, R. F., Thase, M. E., & Mann J. J. (1995). Disproportionate suicidality in patients with comorbid major depression and alcoholism. *American Journal of Psychiatry, 152,* 358–364.

Cornish, D. B., & Clarke, R. V. (Eds.). (1986). *The reasoning criminal.* New York, NY: Springer-Verlag.

Cornish, D. B., & Clarke, R. V. (1987). Understanding crime displacement: An application of rational choice theory. *Criminology, 25,* 936–947.

Coser, L. (1967). *Continuities in the study of social conflict.* New York, NY: Macmillan.

Cromie, W. (1999, January 21). Computer addiction is coming on-line. *The Harvard University Gazette.* Retrieved from http://www.news.harvard.edu/gazette/1999/01.21/computer.html

Cromwell, P. (2004). Burglary: The offender's perspective. In A. Thio & T. C. Calhoun (Eds.), *Reading in deviant behavior,* (6th ed., pp. 302–307). Boston, MA: Pearson Education, Inc.

Cronin, C. (1991). Sensation seeking among mountain climbers. *Journal of Personality and Individual Differences, 12,* 653–654.

Cross National Collaborative Group. (1992). The changing rate of major depression: Cross-national comparisons. *The Journal of the American Medical Association, 268,* 3098–3105.

Dahrendorf, R. (1959). *Class and class conflict in industrial society.* Stanford, CA: Stanford University Press.

Daly, K., & Chesney-Lind, M. (1988). Feminism and criminology. *Justice Quarterly, 5,* 497–538.

Danner, M. (1989). Socialist feminism: A brief introduction. *Critical Criminologist, 1,* 1–2.

Daro, D., & Cohn, A. (2000, February 15). *Child abuse prevention: Accomplishments and challenges.* Paper presented at the meeting of the Collaborative Violence Prevention Initiative. San Francisco, CA.

Davis, K. (1976). Sexual behavior. In R. Merton and R. Nisbet (Eds.), *Contemporary Social Problems* (pp. 245–252). New York: Harcourt Brace Jovanovich.

deVries, M. F. R. (2005, September). The dangers of feeling like a fake. *Harvard Business Review.* Retrieved from http://hbr.org/2005/09/the-dangers-of-feeling-like-a-fake/es

Dobash, R., & Dobash, R. (1988). Research as social action: The struggle for battered women. In K. Yllö & M. Bograd (Eds.), *Feminist perspectives on wife abuse* (pp. 51–74). Newbury Park, CA: Sage.

Dodds, P. (2007, June 11). Father found guilty in honor killing in U.K. *Associated Press.* Retrieved from http://www.usatoday.com/news/world/2007-06-11-honorkilling_N.htm

Dohrenwend, B., & Dohrenwend, B. (1975). Socio-cultural and socio-psychological factors in the genesis of mental disorders. *Journal of Health and Social Behavior, 16,* 365–392.

Dohrenwend, B., Dohrenwend, B. P. Levav, I., Shrout, P. E. Schwartz, S., Naveh, G., Link, B. G., Skodol, A. E., & Stueve, A. (1992). Socioeconomic status and psychiatric disorders: The causation-selection issue. *Science, 255,* 946–952.

Dollard, J., Dood, L., Miller, N., Mower, O., & Sears, R. (1939). *Frustration and aggression.* New Haven, CT: Yale University Press.

Dorell, O. (2009, November 29). Honor killings in USA raise concerns. *USA Today.* http://www.usatoday.com/news/nation/2009-11-29-honor-killings-in-the-US_N.htm

Douglas, J. (1967). *The social meanings of suicide.* Princeton, NJ: Princeton University Press.

Durkheim, E. (1938). *The rules of the sociological method.* New York, NY: Free Press.

Durkheim, E. (1951). *Suicide: A study in sociology.* Glencoe, NY: Free Press.

Dutton, M. (1993). Understanding women's responses to domestic violence: A redefinition of battered women syndrome. *Hofstra Law Review, 21,* 1191–1242.

Dworkin, A. (1981). *Pornography: Men possessing women.* New York, NY: Plenum.

EchoHawk, M. (1997). Suicide: The scourge of Native American people. *Suicide and Life-Threatening Behavior, 27,* 60.

Edelhertz, H. (1970). *The nature, impact, and prosecution of white collar crime.* Washington, DC: U.S. Government Printing Office.

Edelson, J. (2000). *Primary prevention and adult domestic violence.* Paper presented at the meeting of the Collaborative Violence Prevention Initiative. San Francisco, CA.

Egbert, A. M. (1993). The older alcoholic: Recognizing the subtle clinical clues. *Geriatrics, 48,* 63–69.

Erickson, K. (2005). *Wayward puritans.* New York, NY: John Wiley and Sons.

ERRI Counter-Terrorism Archive Page. (2001). *World-wide/CIA assessment: DCI Tenet says Usama Bin Laden biggest threat to U.S.* Retrieved from http://www.360doc.com/content/06/0525/17/7349_121890.shtml

Fadel, L. (2010, June 18). Iraq ill-equipped to cope with an epidemic of mental illness. *The Washington Post.* Retrieved from http://www.washingtonpost.com/wp-dyn/content/article/2010/06/17/AR2010061706034_pf.html

Farber, M. (1968). *Theory of suicide.* New York, NY: Funk and Wagnalls.

Farberow, N., & Schniedman, E. (Eds.). (1961). *The cry for help.* New York, NY: McGraw-Hill.

Farrington, D. (1986). Age and crime. In M. Tonry & N. Morris (Eds.), *Crime and justice: An annual review of research* (pp. 189–250). Chicago, IL: University of Chicago Press.

Fassel, D. (1992). *Working ourselves to death.* San Francisco, CA: Harper Collins Publisher.

Federal Bureau of Investigation (FBI). (1999a). *Crime in the United States, 1999.* Washington, DC: USGPO.

Federal Bureau of Investigation (FBI). (1999b). *Terrorism in the United States, 1999.* Washington, DC: USGPO. Retrieved from http://www.fbi.gov/stats-services/publications/terror_99.pdf

Federal Bureau of Investigation (FBI). (2000). *Crime in the United States.* Washington, DC: USGPO. Retrieved from http://www.fbi.gov/about-us/cjis/ucr/crime-in-the-u.s/2002/crime2003.

Federal Bureau of Investigation (FBI). (2002a). *Crime in the United States, 2002.* Washington, DC: USGPO. Retrieved from http://www.fbi.gov/ucr/ucr.htm

Federal Bureau of Investigation (FBI). (2002b). *White collar crime study.* Washington, DC: USGPO.

Federal Bureau of Investigation (FBI). (2006). National Counterterrorism Center, Report on Terrorism Incidents—2006. Retrieved from http://www.fbi.gov/stats-services/publications/terror_06.pdf

Federal Bureau of Investigation (FBI). (2008). *Crime in the United States.* Washington, DC: USGPO. Retrieved from http://www.fbi.gov/about-us/cjis/ucr/crime-in-the-u.s/2009/crime2009

Federal Bureau of Investigation (FBI). (2009). *Crime in the United States.* Washington, DC: USGPO. Retrieved from http://www.fbi.gov/about-us/cjis/ucr/crime-in-the-u.s/2009/crime2010

Federal Bureau of Investigation (FBI). (2010). *Crime in the United States.* Washington, DC: USGPO. Retrieved from http://www2.fbi.gov/ucr/cius2009/index.html

Feeney, F. (1986). Robbers as decision makers. In D. Cornish & R. Clarke (Eds.), *The reasoning criminal* (pp. 53–71). New York, NY: Springer-Verlag.

Feeney, F., & Weir, A. (Eds.). (1974). *The prevention and control of robbery.* Davis, CA: Center on Administration of Criminal Justice, University of California at Davis.

Felson, M. (1998). *Crime and everyday life* (2nd ed). Thousand Oaks, CA: Pine Forge Press.

Felson, R., Baumer, E. P., & Messner, S. F. (2000). Acquaintance robbery. *Journal of Research in Crime and Delinquency, 37,* 284–305.

Finckenauer, J. O. (2007). *Mafia and organized crime.* Oxford, England: Oneworld Publications.

Finckenauer, J. O., Fuentes, J. R., & Ward, G. L. (2001). *Mexico and the United States: Neighbors confronting drug trafficking.* Retrieved from http://www.unodc.org/pdf/crime/publications/forum1vol2.pdf

Finckenauer, J., & Voronin, U. (2001). *The threat of Russian organized crime.* Washington, DC: National Institute of Justice. Retrieved from http://www.ncjrs.gov/pdffiles1/nij/187085.pdf

Finkelhor, D. (1997). The homicides of children and youth: A developmental perspective. In G. Kaufman Kantor & J. Jasinski (Eds.), *Out of darkness: Contemporary perspectives on family violence* (pp. 17–34). Thousand Oaks, CA: Sage.

Finkelhor, D. (2008). *Childhood victimization: Violence, crime, and abuse in the lives of young people.* New York: Oxford University Press.

Finkelhor, D., Jones, L., & Shattuck, A. (2008). *Up-dated trends in child maltreatment.* Durham, NH: University of New Hampshire, Crimes Against Children Research Center.

Finkelhor, D., Mitchell, K., & Wolak, J. (2001). *Online victimization: A report on the nation's youth.* Arlington, VA: National Center for Missing and Exploited Children.

Finkelhor, D., & Ormrod, R. (2000). *Juvenile victims of property crimes* (NCJ# 184740). Washington, DC: U.S. Department of Justice and Office of Juvenile Justice and Delinquency Prevention.

Finkelhor, D., & Ormrod, R. (2001a). *Homicides of youth and children* (NCJ# 187239). Washington, DC: U.S. Department of Justice, Office of Justice Programs, and Office of Juvenile Justice and Delinquency Prevention.

Finkelhor, D., & Ormrod, R. (2001b). *Child abuse reported to the police*. Washington, DC: U.S. Department of Justice and Office of Juvenile Justice and Delinquency Prevention.

Finkelhor, D., Ormrod, R., & Turner, H. (2007). Poly-victimization: A neglected component in child victimization trauma. *Child Abuse & Neglect, 31*, 7–26.

Finkelhor, D., & Yllö, K. (1985). *License to rape: Sexual assault of wives.* New York, NY: Holt, Rinehart, and Winston.

Fisher, B., Cullen, F. T., & Turner, M. G. (2002). Being pursued: Stalking victimization in a national study of college women. *Criminology and Public Policy, 1*, 257–308.

Flavin, D. K., & Morse, R. M. (1991). What is alcoholism. *Alcohol Health and Research World, 15*, 266–271.

Fortune. (2002, March 18). *The odds against doing time.* New York, NY: Time, Inc.

Fox, J., & Zawitz, M. (2010). *Bureau of Justice statistics crime data brief: Homicide trends in the United States.* Washington, DC: U.S. Department of Justice, Office of Justice Programs, and Bureau of Justice Statistics.

Fox News. (2010, June 18). *Crowd protests Murfreesboro mosque plans.* Retrieved from http://www.myfoxmemphis.com/dpp/news/local/061810-crowd-protests-murfreesboro-mosque-plans

Fraser, J., & Fulton, I. (1984). *Terrorism counteraction.* Fort Leavenworth, KS: U.S. Army Command and General Staff College.

Friedman, M., & Roseman, R. H. (1974). *Type A behavior and your heart.* New York, NY: Knopf.

Friedman, M., & Friedman, R. (1984). *Tyranny of the status quo.* San Diego, CA: Harcourt Brace Javonovich.

Gelles, R. (1983). An exchange/social control theory. In D. Finkelhor, R. J. Gelles, G. T. Hotaling, & M. A. Straus. (Eds.), *The dark side of families: Current family violence research* (pp. 268–284). Beverly Hills, CA: Sage.

Gelles, R. (1987). *Family violence.* Newbury Park, CA: Sage.

Gelles. (1994). An exchange/social control theory. In S. H. Traub and C. B. Little (Eds.), *Theories of Deviance,* (4th ed., pp. 268–284). Itasca, Illinois: F.E. Peacock Publishers.

Gelles, R., & Harrop, J. (1989). Violence, battering, and psychological distress among women. *Journal of Interpersonal Violence, 4*, 400–420.

Gelles, R., & Straus, M. (1979). Determinants of violence in the family: Towards a theoretical integration. In W. Burr, R. Hill, I. Nye, & I. Reiss (Eds.), *Contemporary theories about the Family.* New York, NY: Free Press.

Gibbons, D. (1968). *Changing the lawbreaker.* Englewood Cliffs, NJ: Prentice-Hall.

Gibbs, J. (1968). *Suicide.* New York, NY: Harper and Row.

Gibbs, J. (1989). *Norms, deviance, and social control.* New York, NY: Elsevier.

Gibbs, J., & Martin, W. (1964). *Status integration and suicide.* Eugene, OR: University of Oregon Press.

Giddens, A. (2000). *Runaway world: How globalization is reshaping our lives.* New York, NY: Routledge.

Giles-Sims, J. (1998). The aftermath of partner violence. In J. Jasinski & L. Williams (Eds.), *Partner violence: A comprehensive review of 20 years of research* (pp. 44–72). Thousand Oaks, CA: Sage.

Glaser, D. (1956). Criminality theories and behavioral images. *American Journal of Sociology, 61,* 433–444.

Glaser, D. (1960). Differential association and criminological prediction. *Social Problems, 8,* 6–14.

Glass, A. J. (1998, February 26). U.S. Military face potential cyberattack. *Atlanta Journal Constitution,* p. 8A.

Gledhill-Hoyt, J., Hang, L., Strote, J., & Wechsler, H. (2000). Increased use of marijuana and other illicit drugs at U.S. colleges in the 1990s: Results of three national surveys. *Addiction, 95,* 1655–1667.

Goffman, E. (1961). *Asylums.* Garden City, NY: Doubleday-Anchor.

Goldstein, P. (1979). *Prostitution and drugs.* Lexington, MA: Lexington Books.

Gomberg, E. S. (1995). Older women and alcohol use and abuse. In M. Galanter (Ed.), *Development in Alcoholism* (Vol. 12) (pp. 61–79). New York, NY: Plenum Press.

Goode, E. (1991). Positive deviance: A viable concept. *Deviant Behavior, 12,* 289–308.

Goode, E. (2005). *Deviant behavior* (7th ed). Upper Saddle River, NJ: Prentice-Hall.

Goode, E. (2008). *Deviant behavior* (8th ed). Upper Saddle River, NJ: Prentice-Hall.

Goode, W. J., & Hatt, P. K. (1952). *Methods in social research.* New York, NY: McGraw Hill.

Gossop, M., Powis B., & Griffiths P, (1994). Sexual behavior and its relationship to drug-taking among prostitutes in South London. *Addiction, 89,* 961–970.

Gottfredson, M., & Hirschi, T. (1983). Age and the explanation of crime. *American Journal of Sociology, 89,* 552–584.

Gottfredson, M., & Hirschi, T. (1990). *A general theory of crime.* Palo Alto, CA: Stanford University Press.

Gove, W.R, Hughes, M., & Style, C. B. (1983). Does marriage have positive effects on the psychological well-being of the individual? *Journal of Health and Social Behavior, 24,* 122–131.

Granfield, R., & Cloud, W. (1996). The elephant that no one sees: Natural recovery among middle-class addicts. *Journal of Drug Issues, 26,* 45–61.

Green, G. (1990). *Occupational crime.* Chicago, IL: Nelson-Hall.

Greenfeld, L. (1997). *Sex offenses and offenders: An analysis of data on rape and sexual assault* (NCJ #163392). Washington, DC: U.S. Department of Justice, Office of Justice Programs and Bureau of Justice Statistics.

Greenfield, K., Dowell, W., Rawe, J., Fulton, G. , Krantz, M., Maloney, J., Marshall, E., Roche, T., & Woodbury, R. (1999, September 6). Life on the edge. *Time,* p. 9.

Groenewoud J. H., et al. (2000, February 24). Clinical problems with the performance of euthanasia and physician-assisted suicide in the Netherlands. *New England Journal of Medicine, 342,* 551–556.

Groth, N. (1983). Rape: Behavioral aspect. In S. Kadish (Ed.), *Encyclopedia of crime and justice* (Vol. 4). New York, NY: Free Press.

Gulezian, L.A. (2010, June 16). *Right to die billboard causes a big stir.* Retrieved from http://abclocal.go.com/kgo/story?section=news/local/san_francisco&id=7502970

Gunroe, M., & Mariner, C. (1997). Toward a developmental-contextual model of the effects of parental spanking on children's aggression. *Archives of Pediatric and Adolescent Medicine, 151,* 768–775.

Gupta, K. (1993). Alcoholism in the elderly: Uncovering a hidden problem. *Postgraduate Medicine, 93,* 203–206.

Guthmann, E. (2005, October 30). Lethal beauty--The allure: Beauty and an easy route to death have long made the Golden Gate Bridge a magnet for suicides. *SFGate.* Retrieved from http://www.sfgate.com/cgi-bin/article.cgi?f=/c/a/2005/10/30/MNG-2NFF7KI1.DTL

Haddock, D. (2001). *Granny D: Walking across America in my 90th year.* New York, NY: Villard Books.

Hagan, J. (1989a). *Structural criminology.* New Brunswick, NJ: Rutgers University Press.

Hagan, J. (1989b). Micro and macro-structures of delinquent causation and a power-control theory of gender and delinquency. In F. S. Messner, M. D. Krohn, & A.E. Liska (Eds.), *Theoretical Integration in the Study of Deviance and Crime: Problems and Prospects* (pp. 213–237). Albany: State University of New York Press.

Hamilton, K. (1995, June 19). Outer limits. *Newsweek.* Retrieved from http://www.highbeam.com/doc/1G1-17028974.html

Hanson, G., & Venturelli, P. (2001). *Drugs and society.* Sudbury, MA: Jones and Bartlett Publishers.

Hardy, K. R. (1974). Social origins of American scientists and scholars. *Science, 185,* 497–506.

Harris, C., & Barraclough, J. (1997). Suicide as an outcome for mental disorders: A meta-analysis. *British Journal of Psychiatry, 170,* 205–228.

Hazelwood, R., & Burgess, A. (Eds.). (1995). *Practical aspects of Rae investigation: A multidisciplinary approach.* New York, NY: CRC Press.

Heath, D. B. (1982). Sociocultural variants in alcoholism. In E. M. Pattison & E. Kaufman (Eds.), *Encyclopedic handbook of alcoholism* (pp. 426–440). New York, NY: Gardner Press.

Heath, D. B. (1995). *International Handbook on Alcohol and Culture.* Westport, CT.: Greenwood Press.

Heckert, A., & Heckert, D. (2002). A new typology of deviance: Integrating normative and reactivist definitions of deviance. *Deviant Behavior, 23,* 449–479.

Heckert, A., & Heckert, D. M. (2004). Using an integrated typology of deviance to analyze ten common norms of the U.S. middle class. *Sociological Quarterly, 45*(2), 209–228.

Heckert, D. M. (2000). Positive deviance. In P. Adler & P. Adler (Eds.), *Constructions of deviance: Social power, context, interaction* (pp. 30–42). Belmont, CA: Wadsworth.

Hendricks, S., Landsittel D. P., Amandus H. E., Malcan J., & Bell J. (1999). A matched case-control study of convenience store robbery risk factors. *Journal of Occupational and Environmental Medicine, 41,* 995–1004.

Henriksson, M., Aro, M. J., Marttunen, M. E., Heikkinen, E. T., Isometsa, K. I., & Lonnqvist, J. K. (1993). Mental disorders and comorbidity in suicide. *American Journal of Psychiatry, 150,* 935–940.

Henry, A., & Short, J. (1954). *Suicide and homicide.* New York, NY: Free Press.

Hepburn, J. R. (1984). Occasional property crime. In R. Meier (Ed.), *Major Forms of Crime*. Beverly Hills, CA: Sage.

Hewlett, S. A., & Luce, C. B. (2006). Extreme jobs: The dangerous allure of the 70-hour workweek. *Harvard Business Review*. Retrieved from http://hbr.org/2006/12/extreme-jobs/es#

Hindelang, M. (1976). *Criminal victimization of eight American cities: A descriptive analysis of common theft and assault*. Cambridge, MA: Ballinger.

Hirschi, T. (1969). *Causes of delinquency*. Berkeley, CA: University of California.

Hoffman, B. (1999). *Inside terrorism*. New York, NY: Columbia University Press.

Hollingshead, A., & Redlich, F. (1958). *Social class and mental illness*. New York, NY: Wiley.

Holmes, M. D., & Antell, J. A. (2001). The social construction of American Indian drinking: Perceptions of American Indian and white officials. *The Sociological Quarterly, 42*,151–174.

Hotaling, G., & Sugarman, D. (1986). *Long term effects of domestic violence*. Retrieved from http://www.aardvarc.org/dv/p-effects.html

Hotaling, G., & Sugarman, D. (1990). A risk marker analysis of assaulted wives. *Journal of Family Violence, 5*, 1–13.

Hudson, R. A. (1999). *The sociology and psychology of terrorism: Who becomes a terrorist and why?* Washington, DC: Library of Congress.

Huff, C. R. (1978). Historical explanations of crime: From demons to politics. In J. Inciardi & K. Hass (Eds.), *Crime and Criminal Justice Process* (pp. 208–220). Dubueque, Iowa: Kendall Hunt Publishing.

Huffington Post. (2010, March 5). Couple let baby starve to death while raising virtual baby online. http://www.huffingtonpost.com/2010/03/05/couple-let-baby-starve-to_n_487287.html

Hui, S. (2010, May 28). Criminology student in curt in prostitute deaths. *The Associated Press*.

Icove, D. J., Seger, K. A., & VonStorch, W. R. (1995). *Computer crime: A crimefighter's handbook*. Cambridge, MA: O'Reilly & Associates.

Increasing signs of stress (1983, August 1). (Japan). *Time*, p. 67. Retrieved from http://www.time.com/time/magazine/article/0,9171,921332-2,00.html

Insel, T. R. (2008). Assessing the economic costs of serious mental illness. *American Journal of Psychiatry, 165*, 663–665.

Ishii, K. (1991). Measuring mutual causation: Effects of suicide news on suicides in Japan. *Social Science Research, 20*, 188–195.

Jabail-Nash, N. (2010, July 16). *Barefoot Bandit to be extradited to Seattle where he will face charges*. Retrieved from http://www.cbsnews.com/8301-504083_162-20010796-504083.html

Jacobs, J. (1967). A phenomenological study of suicide notes. *Social Problems, 15*, 60–73.

Jaffe, P., Wolfe, D. A., & Wilson, S. K. (1990). *Children of battered women*. Newbury Park, CA: Sage.

Jamison, K. (1999). *Nights falls fast: Understanding suicide*. New York, NY: Alfred A. Knopf.

Janinski, J., & Williams, L. (Eds.). (1998). *Partner violence: A comprehensive review of 20 years of research.* Thousand Oaks, CA: Sage.

Janus, S. S., & Janus, C. L. (1993). *The Janus report on sexual behavior.* New York, NY: John Wiley and Sons.

Jellinek, E. M. (1960). *The disease concept of alcoholism.* New Haven, CT: College and University Press.

Jessor, R., Graves, T. D., Hanson, R. C. and Jessor, S. L. (1968). *Society, personality and deviant behavior: A study of a tri-ethnic community.* New York: Holt, Rinehart, and Winston.

Jonas, K. (1992). Modeling and suicide: A test of the Werther effect. *British Journal of Social Psychology, 31,* 295–306.

Jones, L., & Finklehor, D. (2001). *The decline in child sexual abuse cases* (NCJ # 184741). Washington, DC: U.S. Department of Justice and Office of Juvenile Justice and Delinquency Prevention.

Jones, S. E., Oeltmann, J., Wilson, T. W., Brener, N. D., & Hill, C. V. (2001). Binge drinking among undergraduate college students in the United States: Implications for other substance abuse. *Journal of American College Health, 50,* 33–38.

Joyner, T. (1999, November 14). Job addict. *Atlanta Journal Constitution.* Retrieved from http://www.accessatlanta.com/partners/ajc/read/workholics/

Kageyama, Y. (1999, March 13). Court orders Japanese government to pay for suicide from overwork. *The Detroit News.* Retrieved from
http://chronicle.augusta.com/stories/1999/03/13/bus_256007.shtml

Kaplan, H. (1980). *Deviant behavior in defense of self.* New York, NY: Academic Press.

Kaplan, H. B. (1995). Drugs, crime, and other deviant adaptations. In H. B. Kaplan (Ed.), *Drugs, crime, and other deviant adaptations: Longitudinal studies.* New York, NY: Plenum.

Kato, T. (1995, February). Workaholism: It's not in the blood. *Look Japan,* p. 1. Retrieved from http://members.jcom.home.ne.jp/katori/WORKAHOLISM.html

Katz, J. (1988). *Seductions of crime: Moral and sensual attractions in doing evil.* New York, NY: Basic Books.

Keller, M., & Doria, J. (1991). On defining alcoholism. *Alcohol Health and Research World, 15,* 253–259.

Keown, L. A. (2006). *Time escapes me: Workaholics and time perception.* Retrieved from
http://www.statcan.gc.ca/pub/11-008-x/2007001/9629-eng.htm

Kessler, R., & Cleary, P. (1980). Social class and psychological distress. *American Sociological Review, 45,* 463–478.

Kessler, R. C. Heeringa, S., Lakoma, M. D., Petukhova, M., Rupp, A. E. Schoenbaum, M., Wang, P. H., & Zaslavsky, A. M. (2008). *American Journal of Psychiatry, 165,* 703–711.

Kim, B. N. (2007). From Internet to "family-net": Internet addict vs. digital leader. in 2007 International Symposium on the Counseling and Treatment of Youth Internet Addiction. Seoul, Korea, National Youth Commission, p 196.

King, M., & Woollett, E. (1997). Sexually assaulted males: 115 men consulting a counseling service. *Archives of Sexual Behavior, 26,* 579–588.

Kivivuouri, J. (1998). The case of temporally intensified shoplifting. *British Journal of Criminology, 38,* 663.

Klaus, P. (2000). *Crimes against persons age 65 or older*. Washington, D.C.: U. S. Department of Justice, Office of Justice Program, and Bureau of justice Statistics. (NCJ 176352).

Klemke, L. (1992). *The sociology of shoplifting: Boosters and snitches today*. Westport, CT: Praeger.

Knickerbocker, B. (1998, December 3). Sanctioned euthanasia: Lessons from abroad. *Christian Science Monitor*. Retrieved from http://www.religioustolerance.org/euth_wld.htm

Korn, E., Pratt, G., & Lambrou. P. (1987). *Hyper-performance: The AIM strategy for releasing your business potential*. New York, NY: John Wiley & Sons.

Koss, M., Gidycz, C.A., & Winiewski, N. (1987). The scope of rape: Incidence and prevalence of sexual aggression and victimization in a national sample of higher education students. *Journal of Consulting and Clinical Psychology, 55,*162–170.

Koss, M. P., & Cleveland, H. H. (1997). Stepping stones: Social roots of date rape lead to intractability and politicalization. In M. D. Schwartz (Ed.), *Researching sexual violence against women: Methodological and personal perspective* (pp. 4–21). Thousand Oaks, CA: Sage.

Kreager, D. A. & Staff, J. (2009). The sexual double standard and adolescent peer acceptance. *Social Psychology Quarterly.*

Krug, E. G., Powell, K. E., & Dahlberg, L. L. (1998). Firearm-related deaths in the United States and 35 other high- and upper-middle-income countries. *International Journal of Epidemiology, 27,* 214–221.

Landau, S. (1975). Pathologies among homicide offenders: Some cultural profiles. *British Journal of Criminology, 15,*157–168.

Landreth, B. (1985). *Out of the inner circle.* Washington, DC: Microsoft Press.

Langan, P., & Farrington, D. (1998). *Crime and justice in the United States and England and Wales, 1981–96* (NCJ # 169284). Washington, DC: U. S. Department of Justice, Office of Justice Programs, and the Bureau of Justice Statistics. Retrieved from http://bjs.ojp.usdoj.gov/content/pub/html/cjusew96/contents.cfm

Laquer, W. (1987). *The age of terrorism.* Boston, MA: Little, Brown.

Lardner, J. (1999, December 20). World-class workaholics: Are crazy hours and takeout dinners the elixir of America's success? *U.S. News and World Report, 127,* 42–53.

Lash, L., & Urry, J. (1994). *Economies of signs and space.* London, England: Sage.

Leenarrs, A. (Ed.). (1999). *Lives and deaths: Selections from the works of Edwin S. Schneidman.* Philadelphia, PA: Brunner/Mazel.

Lemelson, R., & Winters, J. (2001, December). Strange maladies. *Psychology Today, Nov./Dec.*, 60–64.

Lemert, E. (1967). *Human deviance, social problems, and social control.* Englewood Cliffs, NJ: Prentice Hall.

Leuchtag, A. (1995). Merchants of flesh. *The Humanist, 55,* 11–16.

Levy, S. (1984). *Hackers: Heroes of the computer revolution.* New York, NY: Bantam, Doubleday, Dell.

Lidz, T., & Fleck, S. (1965). *Schizophrenia and the family.* New York, NY: International Universities Press.

Lindberg, R., & Markovic, V. (2002). *Organized crime outlook in the new Russia. Paying the Price of a Market Economy in Blood.* Search International 23 April.

Lindesmith, A. R. (1947). *Opiate addiction.* Bloomington, IN: Principia Press.

Lindesmith, A. R. (1968). *Addiction and opiates.* Chicago, IL: Aldine.

Linton, R. (1955). *The tree of culture.* New York, NY: Knopf.

Liptak, K. (2010, June 18). Good read: Mental illness goes untreated across Iraq. *The Huffington Post.* http://huffpostfund.org/blog/2010/06/18/good-read-mental-illness-goes-untreated-across-iraq

Loftus, E. (1997). Creating false memories. In M. Acker (Ed.), *Perspectives: Social psychology* (pp. 12–17). Boulder, CO: Coursewise Publishing, Inc.

Luckenbill, D. (1977). Homicide as a situated transaction. *Social Problems, 25,* 176–186.

Lungren, D. (1996). *California attorney general, Russian organized crime.* Sacramento, CA: California Department of Justice. Retrieved from http://www.fas.org/irp/world/para/docs/rusorg1.htm

Machlowitz, M. (1980). *Workaholics: Living with them, working with them.* Reading, MA: Addison-Wesley.

MacKinnon, C. (1989). *Toward a feminist theory of the state.* Cambridge, MA: Harvard University Press.

Maguire, M. (1982). *Burglary in a dwelling.* London, England: Heinemann.

Malkin, M., & Rabinowtiz, E. (1988). Sensation seeking and high-risk recreation. *Parks & Recreation, 33,* 6.

Maris, R. (1981). *Pathways to suicide—A survey of self-destructive behaviors.* Baltimore, MD: The Johns Hopkins University Press.

Mark T. L., Levit K. R., Coffey R. M., McKusick D. R., Harwood H. J., King E. C., Bouchery, E., Genuardi J. S., Vandivort-Warren, R., Buck, J. A., & Ryan K. (2007). National expenditures for mental health services and substance abuse treatment, 1993–2003. SAMHSA Publication SMA 07-4227. Rockville, MD: Substance Abuse and Mental Health Services Administration.

Marx, K. (1956). *Selected writings in sociology and social philosophy.* New York, NY: McGraw Hill.

Matsumoto, D. (1997). *Culture and modern life.* Pacific Grove, CA: Brooks/Cole Publishing Company.

May, P. A. (1996). Overview of alcohol abuse epidemiology for American Indian populations. In G. Sandefur, R. Rindfuss, & B. Cohen (Eds.), *Changing numbers, changing needs: American Indian demography and public health* (pp. 235–261). Washington, DC: National Academy Press.

McAuliffe, W. E., & Gordon, R. A. (1974). A test of Lindesmith's theory of addiction: The frequency of euphoria among long-term addicts. *American Journal of Sociology, 79,* 795–840.

McCauley, C. R. (2001). *The psychology of terrorism.* New York, NY: The Social Science Research Council. Retrieved from http://www.ssrc.org/sept11/essays/mccauley.htm

McGrew, A. (1992). A global society? In S. Hall, D. Held, & A. McGrew (Eds.), *Modernity and its futures.* Cambridge, MA: Polity Press.

McIntosh, J. L. (1980–1981). Suicide among Native American: A compilation of finding. *Omega, 11,* 303–316.

McLeer, S., & Anwar, R. (1989). A study of battered women presenting in an emergency department. *American Journal of Public Health, 79,* 65–66.

McShane, F., & Noonan, B. (1993). Classification of shoplifters by cluster analysis. *International Journal of Offender Therapy and Comparative Criminology, 37,* 29–40.

Mead, G. H. (1934). *Mind, self, and society*. Chicago, IL: University of Chicago Press.

Mechanic, D. (1968). *Medical sociology.* New York, NY: Free Press.

Meier, R., & Geis, G. (1997). *Victimless crime: Prostitution, drugs, homosexuality, and abortion.* Los Angeles, CA: Roxbury.

Meithe, T., & McCorkle, R. (1998). *Crime profiles: The anatomy of dangerous persons, places, and situations.* Los Angeles, CA: Roxbury.

Merton, R. K. (1957). *Social theory and social structure.* Glencoe, IL: Free Press.

Merton, R. (1968). *Social theory and* social *structure.* New York, NY: Free Press.

Metro. (2010, May 28). *Stephen Griffiths 'is a lizard-loving loner who studied crime on the web.* Retrieved from http://www.metro.co.uk/news/828225-stephen-griffiths-is-a-lizard-loving-loner-who-studied-crime-on-the-web

Meuer, T., Seymour, A., & Wallace, H. (2002). Domestic violence. In A. Seymour, M. Murray, J. Sigmon, M. Hook, C. Edmunds, M. Gaboury, & G. Coleman (Eds.), *National victim assistance academy textbook* Washington, DC: Office for Victims of Crime.

Miech, R., Caspi, A., Moffitt, T. E., Wright, B. R. E., & Silva, P. A. (1999). Low socioeconomic status and mental disorders: A longitudinal study of selection and causation during young adulthood. *The American Journal of Sociology, 104,*1096–1131.

Miller, W. (1958). Lower class culture as a generating milieu of gang delinquency. *Journal of Social Issues, 14*(3), 5–19.

Mitchell, K., Finkelhor, D., & Wolak, J. (2001). Risk factors for and impact of online sexual solicitation of youth. *Journal of the American Medical Association, 285,* 3011–3014.

Mitchell, P. (2000). Risk factors for and impact of online sexual solicitation of youth. *Journal of the American Medical Association, 285,* 3011–3014.

Mitchell, P., & Meloy, J. R. (2000). Clinical and forensic indicators of suicide by cop. *Journal of Forensic Science, 45,* 384–389.

Mohandie, K., Meloy, J. R., & Collins, P. I. (2009). Suicide by cop among officer involved shooting cases. *Journal of Forensic Sciences, 54*(2), 456–462.

Moore, C. (1790). *A full inquiry into the subject of suicide* (Vol. 1). London, England: Rivington.

Moore, R. (1984). Shoplifting in middle America: Patterns and motivational correlates. *International Journal of Offender Therapy and Comparative Criminology, 23,* 55–64.

Moore, M. The 2009 Time 100. Bernie Madoff. Retrieved July 20, 2009, from http://www.time.com/time/specials/packages/article/0,28804,1894410_1893837_1894189,00.html

Moran, P. A., & Moran, J. R. (1995). Prevention of alcohol misuse: A review of health promotion among American Indians. *American Journal of Health Promotion, 9,* 288–299.

More Women Serve As College Presidents, ACE Survey Shows, *Higher Education and National Affairs*, v. 49, no. 16 (Sept. 11, 2000), from the American Council on Education.

Morrison, C. M., & Gore, H. (2010). The relationship between excessive Internet use and depression: A questionnaire-based study of 1,319 young people and adults. *Psychopathology, 43,* 121–126.

Mosiciki, E. (1996). Epidemiology of suicidal behavior. *Suicide and Life-Threatening Behavior, 25,* 22–35.

Mulford, H. A., & Fitzgerald, J. L. (1992). Elderly versus younger drinker profiles: Do they indicate a need for special programs for the elderly? *Journal of Studies on Alcohol, 53,* 601–610.

Mullen, P. (1991). The consequences of child sexual abuse: Psychosocial disorders are common in adults abused as children. *British Medical Journal, 303,* 144–145.

Mumford, E. (1983). *Medical Sociology: Patients, providers, and policies.* New York, NY: Random House.

Murphy, J. M. (1976). Psychiatric labeling in cross-cultural perspective. *Science, 191,* 1019–1028.

Murphy, K. (2010, July 23). Terrorism case baffles remote Alaska town. *The Los Angeles Times.* Retrieved from http://www.latimes.com/news/nationworld/nation/la-na-adv-alaska-terrorists-20100723-1,0,255098,full.story

Murray, C. (1996). *Summary: The global burden of disease: A comprehensive assessment of mortality and disability from diseases, injuries, and risk factors in 1990 and projected to 2020.* Cambridge, MA: Harvard School of Public Health on behalf of the World Health Organization and the World Bank, Harvard University Press. Retrieved from www.who.int/mip/2003/other_documents/en/globalburdenofdisease.pdf

Murray, C. J., & Lopez, A. D. (1996). The global burden of disease: A comprehensive assessment of mortality and disability from diseases, injuries and risk factors in 1990 and projected to 2020. Cambridge, MA:

Harvard School of Public Health, (Global Burden of Disease and Injury Series, vol. I).

Murray, J. (2000). Psychological profile of pedophiles and child molesters. *The Journal of Psychology, 134,* 211–224.

Nadon, S., Koverola, C., & Schludermann, E. H. (1998). Antecedents to prostitution: Childhood victimization. *Journal of Interpersonal Violence, 13,* 206–221.

National Center on Addiction and Substance Abuse at Columbia University. (2001). *So help me god: Substance abuse, religion and spirituality.* New York: Author.

National Center on Addiction and Substance Abuse at Columbia University (2007). *Wasting the best and the brightest: Substance abuse at America's colleges and* universities. New York: Author

National Crime Victimization Survey (NCVS). (2009). *Property crime.* Retrieved from http://bjs.ojp.usdoj.gov/content/glance/house2.cfm

National Elder Abuse Incidence Study. (1998). The Administration for Children and Families and The Administration on Aging in The U.S. Department of Health and Human Service.

National Institute of Mental Health (NIMH). (1999a). Mental Health: Report of the Surgeon General. *Chapter 7: Sociocultural and environmental processes.* Bethesda, MD: National Institute of Mental Health and National Institutes of Health. Retrieved from http://www.ncbi.nlm.nih.gov/books/NBK44250/

National Institute of Mental Health (NIMH). (1999b). *Brief notes on the mental health of children and adolescents.* Bethesda, MD: National Institute of Mental Health and National Institutes of Health.

National Institute of Mental Health (NIMH). (2001a). *The numbers count: Mental disorders in America.* Bethesda, MD: National Institute of Mental Health and National Institutes of Health. Retrieved from http://www.nimh.nih.gov/health/publications/the-numbers-count-mental-disorders-in-america/index.shtml

National Institute of Mental Health (NIMH). (2001b). *The impact of mental illness on society.* Bethesda, MD: National Institute of Mental Health and National Institutes of Health.

National Institute of Mental Health (NIMH). (2001c). *Women hold up half the sky: Women and mental health research: A brief overview of research into mental illness in women.* Bethesda, MD: National Institute of Mental Health and National Institutes of Health.

National Institute of Mental Health (NIMH). (2003). *In harm's way: Suicide in America.* Bethesda, MD: National Institute of Mental Health and National Institutes of Health. Retrieved from http://www.sprc.org/library/event_kit/nimh_harmsway.pdf

National Research Council. (1991). *Computers at risk.* Washington, D.C.: National Academy Press.

Naughton, T. (1987). A conceptual view of workaholism and implications for career counseling and research. *The Career Development Quarterly, 35,* 180–187.

Nedeau, J. (2009, November 23). Dear Sofia Vergara, rape is no laughing matter. *Women's Rights.* Retrieved from http://womensrights.change.org/blog/view/dear_sofia_vergara_rape_is_no_laughing_matter

Neuman, G. (Ed.). (1999). Global report on crime and justice. New York, NY: Oxford University Press.

New York Post. (2009). Topic: Bernard Madoff. Retrieved August 12, 2009, from http://www.nypost.com/topics/topic.php?t=Bernard_Madoff

Noack, D. (2000, March 8). Identity theft thrives in cyberspace. APBNews.com

Nordenmark, M., & Strandh, M. (1999). Towards a sociological understanding of mental well-being among the unemployed: The role of economic and psychosocial factors. *Sociology, 33,* 577–597.

Norland, S., & Hepburn, J. R. (1976). The effects of labeling and consistent differentiation in the construction of positive deviance. *Sociology and Social Research, 61,* 83–95.

Oates, W. (1971). *Confessions of a workaholic: The facts about work addiction.* New York, NY: World Publishing.

Office for Victims of Crime. (2001, December). *Internet crimes against children.* Washington, DC: U.S. Department of Justice, Office of Justice Programs, and Office for Victims of Crime. Retrieved from http://www.ojp.usdoj.gov/ovc/publications/bulletins/internet_2_2001/NCJ184931.pdf

O'Leary, K. D., Barling, J., Arias, I., Rosenbaum, A., Malone, J. & Tyree, A. (1989). Prevalence and stability of marital aggression between spouses: A longitudinal analysis. *Journal of Consulting and Clinical Psychology, 57,* 263–268.

Orava, T. (1996). Perceptions of control, depressive symptomatology, and self-esteem of women in transition from abusive relationships. *Journal of Family Violence, 11,* 167–186.

Oregon Revised Statutes. (1997). *Oregon Death with Dignity Act.* Retrieved from http://www.oregon.gov/DHS/ph/pas/docs/statute.pdf?ga=t

Palmer, S. (1970). *Deviance and conformity.* New Haven, CT: College and University Press.

Palmer, S. (1972). *The violent society.* New Haven, CT: College and University Press.

Palmer, S., & Humphrey, J. A. (1990). *Deviant behavior: Patterns, sources, and control.* New York, NY: Plenum Press.

Park, R., Burgess, E., & McKenzie, R. (Eds.). (1928). *The city.* Chicago, IL: The University of Chicago Press.

Parker, D. (1998). *Fighting computer crime: A new framework for protecting information.* New York, NY: John Wiley & Sons, Inc.

Pavelka, E. (1992). RAAM slam: Kish dethrones Forney in record time to win the closest-ever race across America. *Bicycling, 57*(3).

Paykel, E. S. (1974). Life stress and psychiatric disorder: Applications of the clinical approach. In B. Dohrenwend & B. Dohrenwend (Eds.), *Stressful life events: Their nature and effects* (pp. 135–149). New York, NY: John Wiley & Sons.

PBS. (1995). *Waco: The inside story.* Retrieved from http://www.pbs.org/wbgh/pages/frontline/waco

Pearson, J. L., [AU: Pls list all authors]. (1997). Elder suicide: A multinational view. *Aging and Mental Health, 1*(2), 107–111.

Peck, D. (1984). Lethality of method of suicide among a youthful sample of committers: An examination of the intent hypothesis. *Psychological Reports, 55, 861–862.*

Peck, D. (1985–1986). Complete suicides: Correlates of choice of method. *Omega, 16,* 309–323.

Peoples Daily Online. (2007). Retrieved from http://english.peopledaily.com.cn/

Philips, D. (1974). The influence of suggestion on suicide: Substantive and theoretical implications of the Werther effect. *American Sociological Review, 39,* 340–354.

Pillar, P. (2004). *Terrorism: An introduction.* Council on Foreign Relations. Retrieved from http://www.cfr.org/

Pino, N., & Meier, R. (1999). Gender differences in rape reporting. *Sex Roles: A Journal of Research, 40,* 979–990.

Pollard, N. (2004). Terrorism and transnational organized crime: Implications of convergence. Washington, D.C. Terrorism Research Center. Retrieved from http://www.powerbase.info/index.php/Terrorism_Research_Center

Pollitt, M. (2010, n.p.). *Cyberterrorism—fact or fancy?* Retrieved from http://www.cs.georgetown.edu/~denning/infosec/pollitt.html

Porter, G. (1996). The organizational impact of workaholism: Suggestions for researching the negative outcomes of excessive work. *Journal of Occupational Health Psychology, 1,* 70–84.

Porter, G. (2001). Workaholic tendencies and the high potential for stress among co-workers. *International Journal of Stress Management. 8,* 147–164.

Post, J. M. (1986). Hostilite, conformite, franternite: The group dynamics of terrorist behavior. *International Journal of Group Psychology, 36,* 211–224.

Post, J. M. (2001). *Killing in the name of God: Osama Bin Laden and radical Islam.* Retrieved from http://theapm.org/cont/posttext.html

Potterat, J., Rothenberg, R. B., Muth, S. Q., Darrow, & Phillips-Plummer, L. (1998). Pathways to prostitution: The chronology of sexual and drug abuse milestones. *The Journal of Sex Research, 35*(4), 333–340.

Power, R. (2000). *Tangled web.* Indianapolis, IN: Que.

Pynoos, R., & Nader, K. (1988). Children who witness the sexual assaults of mothers. *Journal of the American Academy of Child and Adolescent Psychiatry,* 27: p. 567–572.

Quinney, R. (1970). *The social reality of crime.* Boston, MA: Little Brown.

Quinney, R. (1977). *Class, state, crime.* New York, NY: Longman.

Rabin, B. (1999). *Stress, immune function, and health: The connection.* New York: Wiley-Liss.

Rada, T. (1978). *Clinical aspects of the rapist.* New York, NY: Grune and Stratton.

Radomsky, E., Haas, G. L., Mann, J. J., & Sweeney, J. A. (1999). Suicidal behavior in patients with schizophrenia and other psychotic disorders. *American Journal of Psychiatry, 156,* 1590–1595.

Rand, M. (1997). *Violence-related injuries treated in hospital emergency departments.* Washington, DC: U.S. Department of Justice, Office of Justice Programs, and Bureau of Justice Statistics. Retrieved from http://bjs.ojp.usdoj.gov/content/pub/pdf/VRITHED.PDF

Raymond, E. S. (1997). *The hacker's dictionary* (3rd ed.). Cambridge, MA: MIT Press.

Reppetto, T. (1974). *Residential crime.* Cambridge, MA: Ballinger.

Reuters. (2000) June 20). *Japanese man charged for child porn in Cambodia.* Retrieved from http://www.ageofconsent.com/cambodia.htm

Righthand, S., & Welch, C. (2001). *Juveniles who have sexually offended: A review of the professional literature.* Washington, DC: U.S. Department of Justice, Office of Justice Programs, and Office of Juvenile Justice and Delinquency Prevention.

Rigler, S. K. (2000). Alcoholism in the elderly. *American Family Physician, 61,* 1710–1716.

Robert, A. (2010). *With bare hands: The true story of Alain Robert, the real-life spiderman.* Hong Kong: Blacksmith Books.

Robins, L., & Reiger, D. (Eds.). (1991). *Psychiatric disorders in America: The epidemiologic catchment area study.* New York, NY: The Free Press.

Robinson, B. E. (2007). *Chained to the desk.* New York, NY: New York University Press.

Robinson, G. (1996, November 27). *Death-by-overwork suits on the rise in Japan.* Institute for Global Communications. Retrieved from www.hartford-hwp.com/archives/55a/021.html

Robinson, B. E. (1998). *Chained to the desk.* New York, NY: New York University Press.

Robinson, J., & Godbey, G. (2008). *Time for life: The surprising ways Americans use their time.* University Park, PA: The Pennsylvania State University Press.

Robinson, J., & Godbey, G. (1999). *Time for life: The surprising ways Americans use their time.* University Park, PA: The Pennsylvania State University Press.

Root-Bernstein, R. (1999). Discovery. In M. A. Runco & S. R. Pritzker (Eds.), *Encyclopedia Creativity.* San Diego, CA: Academic Press.

Rosenbaum, M. (1990). The role of depression in couples involved in murder-suicide and homicide. *American Journal of Psychiatry, 147,* 1036–1039.

Rosenhan, D. L. (1973). On being sane in insane places. *Science, 179,* 250–258.

Rossi, B., & Cereatti, L. (1993). The sensation seeking in mountain athletes as assessed by Zuckerman's sensation seeking scale. *International Journal of Sport Psychology, 24,* 417–443.

Rowan, R. (1986, November 10). The biggest mafia bosses. *Fortune*, pp. 24–38.

Roy, M. (1988). *Children in the crossfire: Violence in the home—how does it affect our children?* Deerfield Beach, FL: Health Communications.

Ruiz de Olano, R. (2003). Organized crime: A South American perspective. In J. S. Albanese, D. K. Das, & A. Verma (Eds.), *Organized crime: World perspectives.* Upper Saddle River, NJ: Prentice Hall.

Ryan, G., Miyoshi, T., Metzner, J., Krugman, R., & Fryer, G. (1996). Trends in a national sample of sexually abusive youths. *Journal of the American Academy of Child and Adolescent Psychiatry, 35,* 17–25.

Sagarin, E. (1985). Positive deviance: An oxymoron. *Deviant Behavior, 6,* 169–181.

Sagert, K. B. (2009). *Encyclopedia of sports.* Westport, CT: Greenwood Press.

Sahadi, J. (2007). *Who gets the most (and least) vacation.* Retrieved from http://money.cnn.com/2007/06/12/pf/vacation_days_worldwide/

Sallybanks, J., & Thomas, N. (2000). Thefts of external vehicle parts: An emerging problem. *Crime Prevention and Community Safety: An International Journal, 2,*17–22.

Salt Lake City Headlines Examiner (2009, December 27). California Safeway store doors unlocked curing Christmas … People leave cash. Retrieved from http://www.examiner.com/examiner/x-19632-Salt-Lake-City-Headlines-Examiner~y2009m12d27-California-Safeway-store-doors-unlocked-during-Christmaspeople-leave-cash

Sampson, R., & Laub, J. (1993). *Crime in the making: Pathways and turning points through life.* Cambridge, MA: Harvard University Press.

Sampson, R., & Wilson, W. (1995). Toward a theory of race, crime, and urban inequality. In J. Hagan & R. Peterson (Eds.), *Crime and inequality* (pp. 37–54). Stanford, CT: Stanford University Press.

Sampson, R., & Wooldredge, J. (1997). Linking the micro- and macro-level dimensions of lifestyle—routine activity and opportunity models of predatory victimization. *Journal of Quantitative Criminology, 3,* 371–393.

Sarason, I., & Sarason, B. (1996). *Abnormal psychology: The problem of maladaptive behavior* (8th ed.). Upper Saddle River, NJ: Prentice Hall.

Saxena, J. (2010, April 2). Stop the Sag' Billboards are Up. *The Gothamist.* Retrieved July 14, 2010, from http://gothamist.com/2010/04/02/stop_the_sag_billboards_are_up.php

Scarpitti, F. R., & McFarlance, P. T. (1975). *Deviance: Action, reaction, interaction.* Reading, MA: Addison-Wesley.

Schaer, M. (1996). *The EXIT program: The practice of assisted suicide in Switzerland.* Retrieved from http://www.finalexit.org/dr_schaer_switzerland_1996-97_report.html

Scheff, T. J. (1966). *Being mentally ill: A sociological theory (rev. ed.)* New York: Aldine de Gruyter.

Schmalleger. F. (1999). *Criminal law today: An introduction with capstone cases.* Upper Saddle River, NJ: Prentice Hall.

Schmalleger, F. (2002). *Criminal law today: An introduction with capstone cases.* Upper Saddle River, NJ: Prentice Hall.

Schmidt, A. P. (1984). *Political terrorism: A research guide to concepts, theories, data bases, and literature.* New Brunswick, NJ: Transaction.

Schmidt, A. P., & Jongman, A. I. (1988). *Political terrorism.* SWIDOC: Amsterdam and Transaction Books.

Schneidman, E., Farberow, N. L, & Litman, R. (1994). *Psychology of suicide.* Northvale, NJ: Jason Aronson.

Schneidman, E. (1996). *The suicidal mind.* New York, NY: Oxford University Press.

Schnittker, J., Freese, J., & Powell, B. (2000). Nature, nurture, neither, nor: Black-white beliefs about the causes and appropriate treatment of mental illness. *Social Forces, 78,* 1101–1130.

Schor, J. (1991). *The overworked American.* New York, NY: Basic Books.

Schur, E. M. (1971). *Labeling deviant behavior: Its sociological implications.* New York, NY: Harper and Row.

Schweitzer, H. O. (2003). Organized crime: An American perspective. In J. S. Albanese, D. K. Das, & A. Verma (Eds.), *Organized crime: World perspectives.* Upper Saddle River, NJ: Prentice Hall.

Schweitzer, Y. (2000, August 21). *Suicide terrorism: Development and characteristics.* International Policy Institute for Counter-Terrorism. Retrieved from http://www.ict.org.il

Schweitzer, Y. (2001). Suicide bombings: The ultimate weapon. Retrieved from http://www.ict.org.il/Articles/tabid/66/Articlsid/68/Default.aspx

Scott, K., Moore, K., & Miceli, M. (1997). An exploration of the meaning and consequences of workaholism. *Human Relations, 50*(3), 287–314.

Scully, D. (1990). *Understanding sexual violence: A study of convicted rapists.* New York, NY: Routledge.

Scully, D., & Marolla, J. (1996). Convicted rapists' vocabulary of motive: Excuses and justifications. In D. Kelly (Ed.), *Deviant behavior* (5th ed.) (pp. 103–116). New York, NY: St. Martin's Press.

Sellin, T. (1938). *Culture, conflict, and crime.* New York: Social Science Research Council.

Shadi, J. (2007, June 14). Who gets the most (and least) vacation. *CNN Money.* Retrieved from http://money.cnn.com/2007/06/12/pf/vacation_days_worldwide/

Shaffer, D., Fisher, P., Dulcan, M. K., & Davies, M. (1996). The NIMH diagnostic interview schedule for children version 2.3 (DISC-2.3): Description, acceptability, prevalence rates, and performance in the MECA study. Methods for the epidemiology of child and adolescent mental disorders study. *Journal of the American Academy of Child and Adolescent Psychiatry, 35,* 865–877.

Shahar, Y. (1997, February 26). *Information warfare: The perfect terrorist weapon.* International Policy Institute for Counter-Terrorism. Retrieved from http://www.iwar.org.uk/cyberterror/resources/CIT.htm

Shaw, C., & McKay, H. (1969). *Juvenile delinquency and urban areas.* Chicago, IL: The University of Chicago Press.

Shaw, E. D. (1986). Political terrorists: Dangers of diagnosis and an alternative to the psychopathology model. *International Journal of Law and Psychiatry, 8,* 359–368.

Shover, N. & Honaker, D. (1996). The Socially Bounded Decision Making of Persistent Property Offenders In D. Kelly (Ed.), *Deviant behavior: A text reader in the sociology of deviance* (5th ed.). New York, NY: St. Martin's Press.

Shover, N. (1996). *Great pretenders: Pursuits and careers of persistent thieves.* Boulder, CO: Westview Press.

Shuman, E. (2001, June 4). What makes suicide bombers tick? *Israel Insider.* Retrieved from: http://www.israelinsider.com/channels/security/articles/sec_0049.htm

Silbert, M., Pines, A. M., & Lynch, T. (1982). Substance abuse and prostitution. *Journal of Psychoactive Drugs, 14,* 193–197.

Silverman, R., & Mukherjee, S. K. (1987). Intimate homicide: An analysis of violent social relations. *Behavioral Science and the Law, 5,* 37–47.

Simon, D. (1996). *Elite deviance.* Boston, MA: Allyn and Bacon.

Simons, R. L., Lin, K., & Gordon, L. (1998). Socialization in the family of origin and male dating violence: A prospective study. *Journal of Marriage and the Family, 60,* 467–478.

Snir, R., & Zohar, D. (2000). *Workaholism: Work-addiction or workphilia?* Paper presented at the International Conference on Psychology—Psychology after the Year 2000. Haifa, Israel: University of Haifa.

Snyder, H. (2000). *Sexual assault of young children as reported to law enforcement: Victim, incident, and offender characteristics.* Bureau of Justice Statistics, U.S. Department of Justice.

Snyder, H. & Sickmund, M. (2006). *Juvenile Offenders and Victims: 2006 National Report.* Washington, DC: U.S. Department of Justice, Office of Justice Programs, Office of Juvenile Justice and Delinquency Prevention. Retrieved from http://www.ojjdp.gov/ojstatbb/nr2006/downloads/chapter3.pdf

Soden, G. (2003). *Falling.* New York, NY: W.W. Norton and Company.

Spence, J. T., & Robbins, A. S. (1992). Workaholism: Definition, measurement, and preliminary results. *Journal of Personality Assessment, 58,* 160–178.

Sprankle, J., & Ebel, H. (1987). *The workaholic syndrome.* New York, NY: Walker Publishing.

Srole, L., & Fischer, A. (Eds.). (1978). *Mental health in the metropolis: The midtown Manhattan study.* New York, NY: New York University Press.

Stack, S. (1996). The effect of the media on suicide: Evidence from Japan 1955–1985. *Suicide and Life-Threatening Behavior, 26,* 132–142

Stack, S. (1997). Homicide followed by suicide. *Criminology, 35,* 436–454.

Stares, P. (1996). *Global habit: The drug problem in a borderless world.* Washington, DC: The Brookings Institution.

Stark, R. (1999). *Cyber terrorism: Rethinking new technology.* Washington, DC: Department of Defense and Strategic Studies.

Stephens, J. (1987). Cheap thrills and humble pie: The adolescence of female suicide attempters. *Suicide and Life-Threatening Behavior, 17,* 107–118.

Stephens, R. C. (1987). *Mind-altering drugs: Use, abuse, and treatment.* Beverly Hills, CA: Sage.

Stern, J. (1999). *The ultimate terrorist.* Cambridge, MA: Harvard University Press.

Sternberg, R., & Lubart, L. (1995). *Defying the crowd.* New York, NY: Free Press.

Stets, J., & Straus, M. (1990). Gender differences in reporting of marital violence and its medical and psychological consequences. In M. Straus & R. Gelles (Eds.), *Physical violence in American families: Risk factors and adaptations to violence in 8,145 families.* New Brunswick, NJ: Transaction Publishers.

Stevens, D. (1999). *Inside the mind of a serial rapist.* San Francisco, CA: Austin and Winfield.

Strader, J. K. (2002). *Understanding white collar crime.* Newark, NJ: LexisNexis.

Straus, M. (1980). *Behind closed doors: Violence in the American family.* Garden City, NJ: Anchor.

Straus, M. (1983). Ordinary violence, child abuse, and wife-beating: What do they have in common? In D. Finkelhor, R. Gelles, G. Hotaling, & M. Straus (Eds.), *The dark side of families.* Beverly Hills, CA: Sage.

Straus, M. (1992). *Children as witnesses to marital violence: A risk factor for lifelong problems among a nationally representative sample of American men and women.* Paper presented at the Twenty-third Ross Roundtable on Critical Approaches to Common Pediatric Problems.

Straus, M. (1997). Spanking by parents and subsequent antisocial behavior of children. *Archive of Pediatric and Adolescent Medicine, 151,* 761–767.

Straus, M., & Donnelly, D. (2006). *Beating the devil out of them: Corporal punishment by American families and its effects on children* (2nd ed.). New Brunswick, NJ: Transaction Publications.

Straus, M. (2000). The benefits of never spanking: New and more definitive evidence and a possible backlash. In M. Straus & D. Donnelly (Eds.), *Beating the devil out of them: Corporal punishment by American families and its effects on children* (2nd ed.). New Brunswick, NJ: Transaction Publications.

Straus, M., & Kantor, G. (1994). Corporal punishment of adolescents by parents: A risk factor in the epidemiology of depression, suicide, alcohol abuse, child abuse, and wife beating. *Adolescence, 29,* 543–562.

Straus, M., & Paschall, M. (1998). *Corporal punishment by mothers and child's cognitive development: A longitudinal study.* Paper presented at the 14th World Congress of Sociology, Montreal, Quebec, Canada. Durham, NH: Family Research Laboratory, University of New Hampshire.

Straus, M., & Gelles, R. (1995). *Physical violence in American families: Risk factors and adaptations to violence in 8,145 families.* New Brunswick, NJ: Transaction Publishers.

Straus, M., Sugarman, D., & Giles-Sims, J. (1997). Corporal punishment by parents and subsequent anti-social behavior of children. *Archives of Pediatrics & Adolescent Medicine, 155,* 761–767.

Substance Abuse and Mental Health Services Administration. (2009). *Results from the 2008 National Survey on Drug Use and Health: National Findings* (Office of Applied Studies, NSDUH Series H-36, HHS Publication No. SMA 09-4434). Rockville, MD.

Substance Abuse and Mental Health Services Administration (SAMHSA). (2010). *Results from the 2009 national survey on drug use and health: Vol.1. Summary of national findings.* Rockville, MD: U.S. Department of Health and Human Services.

Sugarman, D., & Hotaling, G. (1989). Dating violence: Prevalence, context, and risk markers. In A. A. Pirog-Good & J. E. Stets (Eds.), *Violence in dating relationships: Emerging social issues* (pp. 3–31). New York, NY: Praeger.

Sumner, W. G. (1906). *Folkways*. Boston, MA: Ginn.

Sutherland, E. (1940). White-collar criminality. *American Sociological Review, 5*, 2–10.

Sutherland, E. (1956). *The professional thief*. Chicago, IL: University of Chicago Press.

Sutherland, E. (2002). White collar crime: Formulating the concept and providing corporate crime baseline data. In M. Ermann & R. Lundman (Eds.), *Corporate and governmental deviance: Problems of organizational behavior in contemporary society* (6th ed.) (pp. 67–81). New York, NY: Oxford University Press.

Sutherland, E., & Cressey, D. (1978). *Criminology* (10th ed.). Philadelphia, PA: Lippincott.

Sutherland, E. (1947). *Criminology*. Philadelphia, PA: Lippincott.

Sykes, G., & Matza, D. (1957). Techniques of neutralization: A theory of delinquency. *American Sociological Review, 22*, 664–670.

Schweitzer, H. O. (2003). Organized crime: An American perspective. In J. S. Albanese, D. K. Das, & A. Verma (Eds.), *Organized crime: World perspectives*. Upper Saddle River, NJ: Prentice Hall.

Szasz, T. (1974). *The myth of mental illness* (Rev. ed.). New York, NY: Harper and Row.

Tannenbaum, F. (1938). *Crime and the community*. Boston, MA: Ginn.

Tansella, M. (1998). Gender differences in mental health. *World Health, 51*(5), 26–27.

Taylor, P. A. (1999). *Hackers*. London, England: Routledge.

Telhami, S. (2002, April 4). Why suicide terrorism takes root. *The New York Times*, p. 23A.

The National Center on Addiction and Substance Abuse at Columbia University. (2001). *So help me God: Substance abuse, religion and spirituality*. New York, NY: Author.

The National Center on Addiction and Substance Abuse at Columbia University. (2007). *Wasting the best and the brightest: Substance abuse at American colleges and universities*. New York, NY: Author.

Thio, A. (1983). *Deviant behavior*. Boston, MA: Houghton Mifflin.

Thio, A. (1978). *Deviant behavior*. Boston, MA: Houghton Mifflin.

Thomas, W. I., & Znaniecki, F. (1918). *The Polish peasant in Europe and America*. Chicago, IL: University of Chicago Press.

Tittle, C.R. & Paternoster, R. (2000). Social *deviance and crime: An organizational and theoretical approach*. New York: Oxford University Press.

Tittle, C. R., & Paternoster, R. (1993). *Social deviance and crime*. Los Angeles, CA: Roxbury Publishing Co.

Tittle, C. (1995). *Control balance: Toward a general theory of deviance*. Boulder, CO: Westview Press.

Tolan, P. (2000). *Youth violence prevention*. Paper presented at the meeting of the Collaborative Violence Prevention Initiative. San Francisco, CA:

Tomlinson, J. (1999). *Globalization and culture*. Chicago, IL: University of Chicago Press.

Tomlinson, J., & Leigh, E. (2004). *Extreme sports: In search of the ultimate thrill*. Buffalo, NY: Firefly Books.

Tondonato, P., & Crew, B. (1992). Dating violence, social learning theory, and gender: A multivariate analysis. *Violence and Victims, 7*, 3–14.

Tran, M. (2010, March 5). Girl starved to death while parents raised virtual child in online game. *The Guardian*. Retrieved from http://www.guardian.co.uk/world/2010/mar/05/korean-girl-starved-online-game

Tremblay, P., Clermont, Y., & Cusson, M. (1994). Jockeys and joyriders: Changing patterns in car theft opportunity structures. *British Journal of Criminology, 34,* 307–321.

Tsushima, M. (1996). Economic structure and crime: The case of Japan. *The Journal of Socio-Economics, 25,* 497–515.

Tullis, L. (1991). *Handbook of research on illicit drug traffic: Socioeconomic and political consequences.* Westport, CT: Greenwood Press.

Turk, A. (1969). *Criminality and legal order*. Chicago, IL: Rand-McNally.

United Nations, United Nations Office on Drugs and Crime. (2010). *The globalization of crime*: Transnational organized crime threat assessment. Retrieved from http://www.unodc.org/documents/data-and analysis/tocta/TOCTA_Report_2010_low_res.pdf

United Nations Office on Drugs and Crime. (2000). *United Nations world drug report.* New York, NY: United Nations Publications.

United Nations Office on Drugs and Crime. (2005). *United Nations world drug report.* New York, NY: United Nations Publications.

United Nations Office on Drugs and Crime. (2010). *United Nations world drug report.* New York, NY: United Nations Publications.

United Press International. (1999, January 15). *French workaholics told to stop.* United Press International.

U.S. Department of Health and Human Services. (1999a). *Mental health: A report of the surgeon general.* Rockville, MD: U.S. Department of Health and Human Services, Substance Abuse and Mental Health Services Administration, Center for Mental Health Services, National Institutes of Health, National Institute of Mental Health. Retrieved from http://www.surgeongeneral.gov/library/mentalhealth/home.html

U.S. Department of Health and Human Services. (2001). Mental Health: Culture, Race, and Ethnicity—A Supplement to Mental Health: A Report of the Surgeon General. Rockville, MD: U.S. Department of Health and Human Services, Substance Abuse and Mental Health Services Administration, Center for Mental Health Services. Retrieved from http://www.ncbi.nlm.nih.gov/books/NBK44243/

U.S. Department of Health and Social Services. Child Maltreatment (2009). Retrieved from http://www.acf.hhs.gov/programs/cb/pubs/cm09/cm09.pdf

U.S. Department of Homeland Security. (2008). *One team, one mission, securing our homeland: U.S. Department of Homeland Security strategic plan fiscal years 2008–2013.* Washington, DC: Author. Retrieved from http://www.dhs.gov/xlibrary/assets/DHS_StratPlan_FINAL_spread.pdf

U.S. Department of Justice (USDOJ). (2000). *National crime victimization survey.* Washington, DC: U.S. Department of Justice and Bureau of Justice Statistics.

U.S. Department of Justice (USDOJ). (2009). *National crime victimization survey.* Washington, DC: U.S. Department of Justice and Bureau of Justice Statistics.

U.S. Department of Justice (USDOJ). (2010). *National crime victimization survey.* Washington, DC: U.S. Department of Justice and Bureau of Justice Statistics.

U.S. State Department. (2002). *Patterns of global terrorism 2001.* Washington, DC: author. Retrieved from http://www.state.gov/documents/organization/10319.pdf

U.S. State Department. (2004). *Patterns of global terrorism 2003.* Washington, DC: author.

van Dijk, J. (1994). Understanding crime rates: On the interactions between the rational choices of victims and offenders. *British Journal of Criminology, 34,* 105–121.

van Dijk, J. J. M., Manchin, R., van Kesteren, J. N., & Hideg, G. (2007). *The burden of crime in the EU, a comparative analysis of the European survey of crime and safety (EU ICS) 2005.* Brussels, Belgium: Gallup Europe.

van Dijk, J. J. M., van Kesteren, J. N., & Smit, P. (2008). *Criminal victimisation in international perspective, key findings from the 2004–2005 ICVS and EU ICS.* The Hague, The Netherlands: Boom Legal Publishers.

van Koppen, P., & Jansen, R. (1999). The time to rob: Variations in time of number of commercial robberies. *Journal of Research in Crime and Delinquency, 36*(1), 7–29.

Violence Against Women Grants Office. (1998, July). *Stalking and domestic violence: The third annual report to Congress under the Violence Against Women Act* (NCJ# 172204). Washington, DC: Violence Against Women Grants Office. Retrieved from http://www.ncjrs.gov/pdffiles1/ovw/172204.pdf

Wagner, A., & Houlihan, D. (1994). Sensation seeking trait anxiety in hang-glider pilots and golfers. *Journal of Personality and Individual Differences, 16,* 975–977.

Walker, L. (1979). *The battered woman.* New York, NY: Harper Row.

Walker, L. (2000). *The battered woman syndrome.* New York, NY: Springer.

Wasserman, I. (1984). Imitation and suicide: A re-examination of the Werther effect. *American Sociological Review, 49,* 427–436.

Wechsler, H., Lee, J. E., Kuo, M. Seibring, M., Nelson, T. F., & Lee, H. (2002). Trends in college binge drinking during a period of increased prevention efforts: Findings from 4 Harvard School of Public Health college alcohol study surveys: 1993–2001. *Journal of American College Health, 50*(5), 203–217.

Wechsler, H., G W Dowdall, A Davenport and S Castillo (1995). Correlates of college binge drinking. *American Journal of Public Health, 85,* 921–926.

Weich, S., & Lewis, G. (1998). Poverty, unemployment, and common mental disorders: Population based cohort study. *British Medical Journal, 317,* 115–119.

Weiner, N. (1970). The teen-age shoplifter: A microcosmic view of middle-class delinquency. In J. Douglas (Ed.), *Observations of deviance* (pp. 213–217). New York, NY: Random House.

Weitzer, R. (Ed.). (2002). *Deviance and social control: A reader.* New York, NY: McGraw Hill.

Weiss, M. & Sanderson, B. (2010, May 28). Kingpin's NYC turf. *Post Wire Services.* Retrieved from http://www.nypost.com/p/news/local/bronx/kingpin_nyc_turf_Kopql42iOt7Jrz3ZXAHdIO

Werrell, J. (2002, March 3). Identity theft. *The Herald,* pp. 1E, 3E.

West, D. (1966). *Homicide followed by suicide.* Cambridge, MA: Harvard University Press.

West, D. J., & Farrington, D. (1977). *The delinquent way of life, third report of the Cambridge study of delinquent development.* London, England: Heinmann Educational Books, Ltd.

Wheaton, B. (1980). The sociogenesis of psychological disorder: An attributional theory. *Journal of Health and Social Behavior, 21,* 100–124.

White, J. R. (2002). *Terrorism: An introduction* (3rd ed.). Belmont, CA: Wadsworth Group.

Widom, C. (1992). *The cycle of violence.* Washington, DC: National Institute of Justice.

Widom, C. (1995). *Victims of childhood sexual abuse—later criminal consequences* (NCJ# 151525). Washington, DC: U.S. Department of Justice, Office of Justice Programs, and National Institute of Justice.

Wilson, W. (1987). *The truly disadvantaged: The inner city, the underclass, and public policy.* Chicago, IL: University of Chicago Press.

Winslow, R. W. (1970). *Society in transition: A social approach to deviance.* New York, NY: Free Press.

Wolak, J., & Finkelhor, D. (1998). Children exposed to partner violence. In J. Janinski & L. Williams (Eds.), *Partner violence: A comprehensive review of 20 years of research* (pp. 73–111). Thousand Oaks, CA: Sage.

Wolfe, D., Wekerle, C., Reitzel, D. & Gough, R. (1995). Strategies to address violence in the lives of high risk youth. In P. Jaffe & J. Edelson (Eds.), *Ending the cycle of violence: Community responses to children of battered women* New York, NY: Sage.

Wolfgang, M. (1958). An analysis of homicide-suicide. *Journal of Clinical and Experimental Psychopathology and Quarterly Review of Psychiatry and Neurology, 19,* 208–221.

Wolfgang, M., & Ferracuti, F. (1967). *The subculture of violence.* London, England: Tavistock.

Wolfgang, M., Figlio, R., & Sellin, T. (1972). *Delinquency in a birth cohort.* Chicago, IL: University of Chicago Press.

Wolfgang, M., Thornberry, T., & Figlio, R. (1987). *From boy to man, from delinquency to crime.* Chicago, IL: University of Chicago Press.

World Health Organization (WHO). (1991). *World health statistics quarterly.* Geneva, Switzerland: WHO.

World Health Organization (WHO). (1995). *World health report.* Geneva, Switzerland: WHO.

World Health Organization (WHO). (2004). *Global status report on alcohol.* Geneva, Switzerland: WHO.

World Health Organization (WHO). (2009). *Suicide prevention (SUPRE).* Geneva, Switzerland: WHO. Retrieved from http://www.who.int/mental_health/prevention/suicide/suicideprevent/en/

World Health Organization (WHO). (2010). *Global status report on alcohol.* Geneva, Switzerland: WHO.

Wright, R., & Decker, S. (1994). *Burglars on the job: Streetlife and residential break-ins.* Boston, MA: Northeastern University Press.

Wright, R., & Decker, S. (1997). *Armed robbers in action: Stickups and street culture.* Boston, MA: Northeastern University Press.

Yang, D. (2000, January 15). Craving your next web fix. *U.S. News and World Report,* p. 41.

Yates, R. (1988, November 13). Japanese live and die for their work. *Chicago Tribune.* p. 531.

Yllö, K. (1984). The status of women, marital equality, and violence against wives. *Journal of Family Issues, 5,* 307–320.

Yllö, K., & Bograd, M. (Eds.). (1988). *Feminist perspectives on wife abuse.* Newbury Park, CA: Sage.

Young, K. S. (1997). *What makes the Internet so addictive: Potential explanations for pathological Internet use?* Paper presented at the Annual Meeting of the American Psychological Association. Chicago, IL.

Zinberg, N. E. (1981). Alcohol addiction: Toward a more comprehensive definition. In M. H. Bean & N. E. Zinberg (Eds.), *Dynamic approaches to the understanding and treatment of alcoholism* (pp. 97–227). New York, NY: Free Press.

Zuckerman, M. J. (2002, February 6). What fuels the mind of a hacker? *USA Today.* Retrieved from http://www.usatoday.com/tech/news/2001-03-29-hacker.htm

Zuckerman, H. (1997). *Scientific elite.* New York, Free Press.

Zuckerman, H. (1994). *Expressions and biosocial bases of sensation seeking.* New York, NY: Cambridge University Press.

Zuckerman, M. (1983). Sensation seeking and sports. *Journal of Personality and Individual Differences, 4,* 285–293.

Glossary

Addiction: A physiological or psychological dependence on a substance and accompanying withdrawal symptoms when its use is discontinued.

Aggravated assault: An assault that is committed with the intention of committing an additional crime.

Aggressive sexual solicitation (online): Internet solicitations of children in which actual offline contact, attempts for offline contact, and requests for offline contact are made through regular mail, telephone, or in person.

Alcohol dependence syndrome: As noted by the National Institute on Alcoholism and Alcohol Abuse, a syndrome characterized by craving, loss of control, physical dependence, and tolerance as each relates to the use of alcohol.

Alcoholics Anonymous: Founded by Bill Wilson and Dr. Bob Smith as a spiritually based recovery program and support group for alcoholics.

Alcoholism: A primary, chronic disease with genetic, psychosocial, and environmental factors that influence its development and manifestations; often progressive and fatal.

Altruism: Acts of self-sacrifice that are intended to benefit others without the expectation of extrinsic reward.

Anarchist terrorism: Terrorism aimed at destroying any form of government in order to end political control and restrictions.

Anomie: Normlessness; the dissociation between cultural goals and available means for attaining goals.

Anxiety disorders: Anxiety that is disproportionate to the circumstance, that is difficult for the individual to control, or that interferes with normal functioning.

Armed robbery: A robbery in which a weapon is used in the commission of the crime.

Arson: Any willful or malicious burning or attempt to burn, with or without intent to defraud the personal property of another.

Assault: An attempt to commit bodily injury to another human being; putting another in fear of imminent bodily injury.

Assisted suicide: Suicide act by which a physician can assist in the termination of life.

Bar girls: Typically solicit clients in public bars, massage parlors, or photographic studios.

Battery: The actual offensive touching or unwanted physical contact between the assailant and victim.

Behavioral norms: What persons "typically" do when occupying a particular social role or in a given social situation.

Bipolar (manic-depressive) disorder: Serious mood disorder classified in the DSM-IV; characterized by episodes of manic and depressive behavior.

Boosters: Professional shoplifters who steal items to later sell for profit.

Burglary: The unlawful or forcible entry or attempted entry of a structure with the intent to commit an offense therein.

Call girls: Well-paid, high-status prostitutes who serve wealthy clients.

Charisma: A characteristic of persons with an extraordinary ability to inspire others to follow their lead.

Child abuse and neglect: Any act or failure to act on the part of a parent or caretaker that results in death, serious physical or emotional harm, sexual abuse or exploitation; an act or failure to act that presents an imminent risk of serious harm.

Child maltreatment: Child abuse and neglect, sexual abuse, and emotional abuse.

Child molestation: Any sexual abuse of a child where the child is exploited for the gratification or profit of an adult.

Computer Fraud and Abuse Act: Legislation passed by Congress to address various forms of computer offending.

Control ratio: An individual's potential for control over circumstances relative to the potential those circumstances have to control her or him.

Corporal punishment: The use of physical force with the intention of causing a child to experience pain, but not injury, for the purpose of correction or control of the child's behavior.

Corporate crime: Any criminal violation by a corporation or its executives, employees, or agents, who act on behalf of or for the benefit of the corporation.

Crackers: Cyberdeviants who intend to damage, manipulate, or destroy the computer operations or computer systems of others.

Craving: A strong need or compulsion to drink.

Crime displacement: Changing the location of criminal and deviant behavior to a more conducive environment.

Criminal homicide: The intentional killing of one human being by another without justification or excuse.

Cultural relativism: Cross-cultural variation in the social construction of reality.

Cultural Transmission Theory: Process by which traditions of delinquency are transmitted through successive generations.

Culture-bound disorders: Mental disorders that are unique to the culture in which they are found.

Culture: A body of widely shared customs and values that provides general orientations toward life and specific ways of achieving common goals.

Culture: The norms, values, and beliefs of a given society or group.

Cyberaffair/relational addiction: The establishment of excessive virtual relationships in chat rooms or through e-mail.

Cyberdeviance: The use of the computer or Internet to victimize computer systems; ranges from relatively benign invasive acts directed at particular computer systems to intentionally destructive attacks against unknown Internet users.

Cybersexual addiction: The preoccupation with online pornography and involvement in the playing out of sexual fantasies in chat rooms.

Cyberterrorism: Any terrorist attack against information, computer systems, computer programs, or data that may result in violence or disruption and create fear, anxiety, or panic in the target population.

Cycle of violence: The term coined by Lenoir Walker to describe the process that characterizes intimate partner violence.

Date rape: A forcible rape that occurs in the context of a dating relationship.

Death with Dignity Act: Oregon statute that established certain criteria that must be met before a physician can assist in the termination of life.

Deterrence doctrine: A crime control perspective based on weighing the personal costs and benefits associated with committing a deviant or criminal act.

Developmental approach (life-course perspective): Attempts to understand the onset, persistence, and desistence of deviant activity across the life span.

Deviant behavior: Activity that violates the normative structure of society and is socially condemned.

***Diagnostic and Statistical Manual of Mental Disorders*, 4th edition (DSM-IV-TR):** Publication of the American Psychiatric Association used to diagnose mental disorders according to standardized criteria.

Differential association: Term proposed by Edwin Sutherland to describe how individuals socially learn to commit criminal and deviant behavior. Also used by Ronald Akers.

Discovery: The finding of something unexpected.

Domestic terrorism: The commission of acts of terrorism by U.S. citizens, either groups or individuals, who are based and operate entirely within the United States without foreign direction or influence and whose acts are directed at elements of the U.S. government or population.

Domestic violence: The involvement of any family member in the intentional physical injury of another; coercion through the use of intimidating, threatening, harmful, or harassing behavior.

Dramatization of evil: Process of labeling deviance and deviant actors to describe the arresting, adjudicating, and sentencing of offenders.

Drug: A physical substance may be classified as a drug if it causes recognizable physical or psychological effects.

Dysfunctions: Consequences of a social action that lessen the adaptation or adjustment of a given social system.

Elite deviance: Term introduced by David Simon that describes the variety of white-collar crimes.

Emotional abuse: Acts of omission to acts by the parents or other caregivers that have caused or could cause serious behavioral, cognitive, emotional, or mental disorders.

Excusable homicide: The accidental or non-negligent killing of another human being.

Exhibitionists: Those who repeatedly expose their genitals to unsuspecting people in public places as a way of experiencing sexual arousal.

Expectational norms: Behaviors that are "ideal" for individuals who are enacting a particular social role or who are in a given social situation.

Experience of a life crisis or trauma: The loss of an important status or social role.

Extreme sports: Forms of competitive and recreational activities that range from high-risk, potentially life-threatening events to sports that test the endurance of the participants.

Feminist perspective: Theoretical perspective on crime and deviance that calls attention to the gender bias in theorizing and research.

Forcible rape: Forced sexual intercourse in which the victim may be either male or female and the offender of a different sex or the same sex as the victim.

Fraud: Theft or attempted theft of property or cash in which deception is a major component; does not involve the actual taking of property or money directly from the victim.

Frottage: The touching or rubbing against nonconsenting persons for sexual arousal.

Frustrated personal relationships: The chaotic nature of the personal relationship found between the victim and offender in homicide–suicide cases.

Functional disorders: Group of related disorders whose causes are less well known.

Functional perspective: Sociological perspective that focuses on the purpose, usefulness, or contribution that a given social phenomenon makes to the social order.

General Theory of Crime: Focuses on self-control rather than on bonds to conventional social life.

Government crime: White-collar crimes committed by public officials and other government employees.

Grooming: Attempts to manipulate or coerce someone into performing sexual acts for a proposed reward.

Hackers: Cyberdeviants who are driven to explore the intricacies of computer programming and uncharted computer applications and to extend the boundaries of their expertise; typically their intent is not to do harm.

Hate crime (bias crime): A criminal act or attempted act against a person, institution, or property that is motivated in whole or in part by the offender's bias against a race, color, religion, gender, ethic/national origin group, disability status, or sexual orientation.

Hedonistic calculus: Links the appropriate penalty or pain to each criminal offense.

Hedonistic principle: Belief that persons are motivated to maximize their pleasure and minimize their pain.

Highway robbery: A robbery that takes place in a public place.

Home invasion (household robbery): A burglary in which the offender confronts the homeowner or residents at the time of the burglary.

Homicide–suicide: Suicide committed by a person who has just killed someone else.

Incest: Nonforcible sexual intercourse between persons who are related to each other within the degree wherein marriage is prohibited by law.

Individual occupational crime: Crimes by individuals as individuals.

Information overload: The undue fascination with the availability of increasing amounts of information and data from around the world.

Innate characteristics: Acquired characteristics such as exceptional good looks, intelligence, athletic, or musical ability.

Innovation: The ability to put existing things or ideas together in new and imaginative ways that have the potential to benefit others.

Institutional robberies: Robberies that occur in commercial settings such as banks or convenience stores.

International terrorism: Terrorism involving citizens or the territory of more than one country; terrorism committed by a group or individual who has some connection to a foreign power or whose activities transcend national boundaries.

Internet addiction disorder: Compulsive use of the Internet with evidence of disturbed and irritated behavior when access is denied, including withdrawal symptoms and the loss of emotional control; an emerging disorder suffered by people who find the virtual reality on computer screens more attractive than everyday reality.

Jockeys: Offenders who steal cars on a steal-to-order basis and/or sell cars or car parts for profit.

Joyriders: Offenders who take cars without the owners' consent but do not intend to keep them; theft satisfies a need for excitement.

Justifiable homicide: Court-ordered executions of convicted offenders or the killing of an enemy by a member of the military in the line of duty.

Karoshi: Death from overwork.

Larceny-theft: Attempted theft of property or cash without using force or illegal entry.

Latent functions: Consequences of a social action neither intended nor recognized by the participants in the social system but that benefit the system.

Learned helplessness: The inability to predict how an abuser will react to one's actions; a process that results in devising ways to adapt to an abusive relationship.

Left-wing terrorism: Terrorism aimed at overthrowing capitalism to create a communistic or socialistic form of economic system.

Logic bombs: Computer programs that work in concert with a virus to instruct the computer to execute a certain function under certain conditions, usually on a given date and time.

Loss of control: The frequent inability to stop drinking once a person has begun.

Macro-level analysis: Considers the ways in which structural and cultural characteristics of social collectivities—societies, subcultures, and social groupings—affect crime rates and acts of social deviance.

Malice aforethought: An unjustifiable, inexcusable, and unmitigated person-endangering state of mind.

Malice: The intentional doing of a wrongful act without just cause or legal excuse.

Manifest functions: Intended consequences of a social action that are recognized by participants in the social system and that benefit a given system.

Manslaughter: A form of homicide that involves less premeditation or malice aforethought on the part of the offender and greater victim provocation than other forms of homicide.

Medical model: Mental disorders are attributed to some genetic abnormality or other inherited vulnerability.

Micro-level analysis: Focuses on social processes and personal characteristics that may account for an individual's involvement in criminal or deviant behavior.

Mood swings: Rapid changes in personality.

Murder: A form of homicide that involves premeditation and malice aforethought on the part of the offender.

Nationalist terrorism: Terrorism aimed at the creation of a self-governing nation that exists apart from its current political domination; a response to oppressive social conditions.

Neoclassical School: School of thought developed during the time of the Enlightenment, based on the idea that human beings possess free will and rationally decide to act or refrain from certain activities.

Net compulsion: Excessive gambling, gaming, shopping, or stock trading on the Internet.

Neuroses: The less severe disorders such as depression and anxiety; often referred to as minor disorders.

Occasional thieves: Offenders who commit property crimes when the opportunity arises.

Occupational crime: Crimes committed by individuals in the context of the offender's job duties for personal gain.

Organic disorders: Mental disorders that originate from physiological or organic causes.

Organizational (business) crime: Offenses committed by entire firms or industries in the course of regular business.

Organizational occupational crime: Crimes committed for the benefit of an employing organization.

Organized crime: Criminal activity by an enduring structure or organization developed and devoted primarily to the pursuit of profits through illegal means.

Pedophilia: Intense and recurrent sexual urges and sexually arousing fantasies involving some form of sexual activity with a prepubescent child.

Persistent thieves: Offenders who commit a variety of property crime offenses without specializing to any significant degree.

Personal crimes: Robberies that involve specific individuals or occur in personal residences.

Personality disorders: Maladaptive, immature, and inappropriate ways of coping with stress or solving problems, manipulative behavior, disorganized and unstable mood or behavior, and thought disturbances.

Physical dependence: The occurrence of withdrawal symptoms such as nausea, sweating, and anxiety when a drug is no longer used.

Positive deviance: Behaviors that exceed normative standards in a way that benefits society and its members; behaviors that are judged to contribute significantly to a highly prized cultural value.

Premeditation: The act of deliberating or meditating upon, or planning, a course of action.

Processes of globalization: Complex set of processes that involve immediate worldwide communication, transnational commerce and trade, and borderless opportunities for political and cultural exchange.

Professional occupational crime: Crimes by professionals in their capacity as professionals.

Professional thieves: Offenders who make a regular business of stealing and who carefully plan and possess special knowledge, technical skills, and methods.

Property crimes: The illegal taking or damaging of property.

Prostitution: Any sexual exchange for money or other reward.

Provocation: The active involvement of the victim, either verbal or physical, in the lethal encounter.

Psychoses: The more severe forms of mental disorders; often require long-term treatment.

Rational Choice Theory: An individual makes a conscious, rational decision before acting.

Reintegrative shaming: Process by which the community conveys its disapproval of a deviant person's behavior but maintains respect for the individual.

Religious terrorism: Terrorism carried out to defend religious doctrines or sacred lands from assaults by nonbelievers.

Right-wing terrorism: Terrorism aimed at replacing liberal democratic governments with neo-Nazi or fascist states that establish Aryan supremacy.

Robbery: Taking of property or cash directly from a person by force or theft of force.

Routine Activities Theory: The likelihood of crime increases when there is a suitable target, a motivated offender, and the lack of a capable guardian.

Salami: Computer attack that alters financial data by slicing small amounts of money from a much larger account; the victim rarely misses the financial loss.

Schizophrenia: Severe and chronic mental disorder classified in the DSM-IV; characterized by alterations in thought, perception, and consciousness, for example, hallucinations or delusions.

Scientific method: Observation, hypothesis development, data collection and analysis, and hypothesis reformulation used in the quest for knowledge.

Scientific theory: A set of interrelated and interdependent propositions designed to predict a given phenomenon.

Seduction of crime: The exhilaration that accompanies the commission of a criminal or deviant act.

Self-control: A person's ability to alter responses and behavior in an effort to resist committing a crime or deviance.

Self-derogation: The process by which a person comes to accept the largely negative judgments of others.

Self-destructive behavior: Risk-taking behaviors and pronounced drug or alcohol use.

Sex offenses: Unwanted sexual contacts as described by the FBI Uniform Crime Report.

Sexual abuse: The employment, use, persuasion, inducement, or coercion of any child to engage in any sexual behavior, including rape, statutory rape, incest, molestation, prostitution, or other form of sexual exploitation of children.

Sexual assault: A variety of victimizations in which unwanted sexual contact occurs between the victim and offender as described in the National Crime Victimization Survey.

Sexual solicitation (online): Requests to engage in sexual activities or sexual talk or give personal information that were unwanted or, whether wanted or not, were made by an adult.

Sexual trafficking: The trading, exchanging, or selling of persons against their will into sexual slavery and prostitution services.

Snitches: Amateur shoplifters who steal primarily for personal reasons, because of a lack of money, or for excitement.

Social bonds: The integration of an individual with conventional society.

Social causation tradition: Idea asserting the role of social stressors in the etiology of mental illness.

Social control theory: A perspective that predicts that weakened or absent social controls lead to deviant behavior.

Social disorganization: Decrease of the influence of existing social rules of behavior on individual members of the group, or the inability of local communities to realize the common values of their residents or solve commonly experienced problems.

Social integration: The extent to which individuals accept common cultural values and societal norms to structure their behavior.

Social integration: The extent to which persons are bound into social life or alternatively isolated from it.

Social norms: Generally agreed on guides for behavior that provide boundaries for interpersonal relations.

Social organization: The means for carrying out the complex network of social interactions between individuals, social groups, and institutions.

Social roles: A set of social norms for the behavior of individuals who occupy given statuses within society.

Social selection tradition: Idea asserting that social stressors are a consequence of mental disorders.

Societal reaction or labeling perspective: Theoretical perspective that focuses on how society reacts to and labels deviance and deviant actors, and how these reactions and labels affect the deviant actor.

Stalking: Repeated visual or physical proximity, nonconsensual communication, or verbal, written, or implied threats that would cause fear in a reasonable person.

State authority occupational crime: Crimes by officials through the exercise of their state-based authority.

State-sponsored terrorism: Terrorism contracted out to mercenary terrorist groups to serve the interests of the state or nation.

Statutory rape: Sexual intercourse with a person below the statutory age of consent.

Stigmatization: Disrespectful shaming; the person as well as his or her behavior is labeled as criminal or deviant.

Strain: Stress experienced when aspirations and expectations are not consistently linked with fulfillment.

Streetwalkers: Prostitutes who solicit clients on the street; provide the cheapest type of prostitution services.

Strong-arm robbery: A robbery in which a weapon is not used in the commission of the crime.

Suicide attack (bombing): A violent, politically motivated attack carried out by a person who blows him- or herself up with the chosen target.

Suicide by cop: An event in which an individual's behavior constitutes an imminent danger of serious injury or death and is intended to cause a law enforcement officer to use fatal force to defend him- or herself.

Suicide: The willful, deliberate, and voluntary termination of one's life.

Supraconformity: Adherence to certain societal norms to the extreme.

Survival sex: Exchanging sexual favors for food, shelter, and other basic necessities.

Symbolic Interaction Theory: Theory that observes interpersonal interaction as primarily symbolic and meaningful.

Techniques of neutralization: Techniques used to justify a deviant act and absolve the offender's guilt.

Technotrespass: A form of computer crime where unlawful access to a computer is gained; refers to an unlawful exploration of computer files simply to look at the contents, not to damage, alter, or steal information.

Technovandalism: A form of computer crime where unlawful access to a computer is gained; the offender may have malicious intent but most often tries to meet the challenge of the unlawful entry.

Terrorism: The act of destroying or injuring civilian lives or property without governmental permission in the attempt to affect some political goal.

Terrorist: Any person acting without governmental permission to destroy or injure civilian or government property to bring about some political goal.

Time-deepening: Doing several things at the same time to maximize time and effort.

Timing attacks: Destruction or alteration of data in a computer before being processed, placing one's own name on someone else's data file before it is processed, or altering the order of jobs in the computer's processing or printing queue.

Tolerance: Either a need for increased amounts of the substance to achieve the desired effect, or marked diminished effect with continued use of the same amount.

Tolerance: Either a need for increased amounts of the substance to achieve the desired effect or marked diminished effect with continued use of the same amount.

Trap doors: Device installed in computer software that allows programmers to make changes without going through complicated access protocols.

Traveler cases: Cases where adults or youth travel to physically meet and have sex with someone they first came to know on the Internet.

Trojan horse: Device that carries instructions into a computer program that is disguised as authorized and useful but has hidden within it viruses, worms, or logic bombs used to disable a system. Trojan horses are commonly used in computer frauds and sabotage.

Unipolar (major) depression: Serious mood disorder classified in the DSM-IV; characterized by emotional, cognitive, motivational, and physical symptoms.

Vandalism: Unlawful destruction of property without the consent of the owner.

Victim-precipitated homicide: Concept introduced by Marvin Wolfgang to describe homicides where the victim was the first one to use physical force against the person who ultimately became the homicide offender.

Viruses: Programs that are sent through e-mail or downloaded from the Internet that have the ability to reproduce themselves, alter computer programs, alter and destroy data, or render disk space or memory unusable.

Voyeurs: Those who achieve sexual gratification as they spy on others; also known as "peeping toms."

White-collar crime: Crimes committed by persons of respectability and high social status in the course of their occupations.

Withdrawal: Physical and emotional distress that accompanies the cessation of alcohol and other drug use.

Withdrawal: The unwillingness to communicate or desire to be left alone.

Workaholism: An addiction to work, the compulsion or the uncontrollable need to work incessantly.

Worms: Computer programs that invade a computer by means of the Internet and attack computer software, destroying data and operating procedures; they exist independently of other programs and possess the ability to replicate themselves and attack other computers attached to the original victim.

Author Index

D

E

F

G

Subject Index

S

T

Y

Photo Credits

Title page © Martin Barraud/age fotostock

Chapter 1

Opener © Hill Street Studios/age fotostock; **page 6** © Darren Baker/ShutterStock, Inc.; **page 9** © artcphotos/ShutterStock, Inc.

Chapter 2

Opener © SW Productions/age fotostock; **page 34** © tci/age fotostock; **page 39** © The Plain Dealer/Landov

Chapter 3

Opener © AP Photo/ Ariana Television via AP Television News; **page 64** © Koscusko/Dreamstime.com; **page 66** © auremar/ShutterStock, Inc.; **page 69** © Blazej Maksym/ShutterStock, Inc.

Chapter 4

Opener © John Giles/Press Association via AP Images; **page 87 (body under sheet)** © Jack Dagley Photography/ShutterStock, Inc.; **(Mexican cartel)** © REUTERS/Mario Vazquez /Landov; **page 92** © Design Pics/age fotostock

Chapter 5

Opener © REUTERS/Wilson Chu/Landov; **page 120** © Gladskikh Tatiana/ShutterStock, Inc.

Chapter 6

Opener Courtesy of FinalExitNetwork.org; **page 144** © erics/ShutterStock, Inc.; **page 155** © Richard Sheinwald/AP Photos

Chapter 7

Opener © pavel/ShutterStock, Inc.; **page 175** © wavebreakmedia ltd/ShutterStock, Inc.

Chapter 8

Opener © The Washington Times/Landov; **page 209** © Photos.com

Chapter 9

Opener © Gary Paul Lewis/ShutterStock, Inc.; **page 231** © Anthony Hall/Dreamstime.com; **page 235** © Mikhail Levit/ShutterStock, Inc.

Chapter 10

Opener © Photos.com; **page 251** © Philip Date/ShutterStock, Inc.

Chapter 11

Opener © AP Photo/Felipe Major; **page 293** © Digital Vision/age fotostock; **page 295** © Digital Vision/age fotostock

Chapter 12

Opener © Landov; **page 309** © REUTERS/Win McNamee/Files /Landov; **page 317** © REUTERS/ Lou

Chapter 13

Opener © REUTERS/Andrew Winning /Landov; **page 336** © Andrew Buckin/ShutterStock, Inc.; **page 344** © Ritu Manoj Jethani/ShutterStock, Inc.

Chapter 14

Opener © AP Photo/Paul Sakuma

Chapter 15

Opener © photocritical/ShutterStock, Inc.; **page 396** © Vitalii Nesterchuk/ShutterStock, Inc.; **page 398** © Vitalii Nesterchuk/ShutterStock, Inc.

Chapter 16

Opener Courtesy of FEMA; **page 417** © Reuters/Landov; **page 424** © Photos.com